Ordinal/Ordinais

first		
seco		
thir		
four		
fifth		
sixtl		
seve		
eigh		
nint		
tentl		
eleve		primeiro
twelfth	12°	décimo segundo
twentieth	20°	vigésimo
twenty first	21°	vigésimo primeiro
thirtieth	30°	trigésimo
fortieth	40°	quadragésimo
fiftieth	50°	qüinquagésimo
sixtieth	60°	sexagésimo
seventieth	70°	septuagésimo
eightieth	80°	octogésimo
ninetieth	90°	nonagésimo
one hundredth	100°	centésimo
one thousandth	1.000°	milésimo
one millionth	1.000.000°	milionésimo

Weights and Measures/Pesos e Medidas

1 centímetro	=	.3937 inches
1 metro	=	39.37 inches
1 quilômetro	=	.621 mile
1 centigrama	=	.1543 grain
1 grama	=	15.432 grains
1 quilograma	=	2.2046 pounds
1 tonelada	=	2.204 pounds
1 centilitro	=	.338 ounces
1 litro	=	1.0567 quart (liquid);
		.908 quart (dry)
1 quilolitro	=	264.18 gallons
1 inch	=	2.54 centímetros
1 foot	=	0.305 metros
1 mile	=	1.61 quilômetros
1 grain	=	0.065 gramas
1 pound	=	0.455 quilogramas
1 ton	=	0.907 toneladas
1 ounce	=	2.96 centilitros
1 quart	=	1.13 litros
1 gallon	=	4.52 litros

D0819017

The
Random House
Portuguese
Dictionary

PORTUGUESE-ENGLISH
ENGLISH-PORTUGUESE

PORTUGUÊS-INGLÊS
INGLÊS-PORTUGUÊS

Edited by
Bobby J. Chamberlain
University of Pittsburgh

RANDOM HOUSE
NEW YORK

Library of Congress Cataloging-in-Publication Data

The Random House Portuguese dictionary: Portuguese-English, English-Portuguese = Português-Inglês, Inglês-Português / edited by Bobby J. Chamberlain.—1st ed.
    p.   cm.
  ISBN 0-679-40060-5
  1. Portuguese language—Dictionaries—English. 2. English language—Dictionaries—Portuguese. 3. Portuguese language—Brazil—Dictionaries—English. 4. English language—United States—Dictionaries—Portuguese. I. Chamberlain, Bobby J. PC5333.R36 1991   469.3'21—dc20   90-8886

Manufactured in the United States of America

First Edition

Note on Brazilian and Continental Portuguese

Unlike most previous Portuguese-English, English-Portuguese dictionaries, the present work stresses the Brazilian variety of Portuguese.

In the cases of most important lexical differences, the Continental equivalent, labeled with a "P.," is also provided. Where there are spelling or accentuation variances, I have usually given the Brazilian form. Notable examples include *ação/acção, ato/acto, fato/facto, direto/directo, irônico/irónico* and *Antônio/António, dezenove/dezanove* in which the second items represent the spelling and pronunciation variants of the Continental dialect.

Pronunciation guidelines too in the main reflect the predominant Brazilian patterns, though there is some attention given to Continental speech.

Concise Portuguese Pronunciation Guide

Stress

1. Words ending in a single vowel *a, e*, or *o*, or in one of these letters followed by *m, n* or *s* are normally stressed on the next-to-last syllable: *livro, cama, livros, camas, falam.*

2. Words ending in a consonant except *m, n* or *s*, in a single vowel *i* or *u* or *i* or *u* followed by *s* or *m*, or in a diphthong (oral or nasal) or a diphthong followed by *s* are normally stressed on the last syllable: *hotel, senhor, rapaz, aqui, tabu, tabus, cacau.*

Words that do not conform to these patterns generally indicate stressed syllables with accent marks.

Accent Marks

1. Acute accent (´) marks a stressed syllable and, in the case of *a, e* and *o*, indicates openness: *fácil, música, língua, Mário, café, avó.*

2. Circumflex accent (ˆ) indicates a stressed close *a, e* or *o: câmara, você, avô.*

3. Grave accent (`) is used over the letter *a* in certain words to indicate a contraction. It does not indicate stress: *à, às, àquela.*

4. The *til* (˜, Eng. "tilde") nasalizes certain vowels and diphthongs and indicates stress unless there is another written accent or unless the word has an ending that is normally stressed: *irmã, irmão, lições, pães, Joãozinho.*

Openness and closeness of vowels is not normally indicated in words unless accent marks are needed to indicate stress or for other reasons. Accent marks are occasionally used simply to differentiate homographs.

iii

Vowels

a
1. Open like *a* in English *father* in stressed and before stressed syllables unless nasal: *pá, cavalo, caro, Brasil.*
2. Like the *a* of English *sofa* in unstressed, particularly word-final, position unless nasal. This pronunciation often used also before stressed syllables in Portugal: *mesa, xícara.*
3. Nasal *a*, a nasalized version of no. 2, similar to the vowel of English *hunh?*, when written *ã*, in *-an-* or *-am-* (except in verb endings): *irmã, canta, cama.*

e
1. Close *e* like the vowel sound of English *pay*, but more clipped; found in stressed and before stressed syllables: *lê, medo, verde.*
2. Open *e* between vowel sounds of English *met* and *mat*, mostly in stressed syllables: *pé, completo, velho.*
3. Nasal *e*, a nasalized close *e* or *ei*, in *-en-* and *-em-*: *tem, bem, entendo, tempo.*
4. Like Portuguese *i*:
   a. In unstressed monosyllables: *de, me, se, lhe.*
   b. In unstressed word-final position: *treze, face, vale.*
   c. Unstressed before another vowel: *compreender, teatro.*
   d. In the syllable before stressed *i*: *menino, feliz.*
   e. In initial position, esp. in the prefixes *ex-* and *es-*: *enorme, exame.*
   f. In many other unstressed syllables: *pequeno, descanso.*

In Portugal, usually pronounced like *a* of English *sofa* in positions a and b.

i
1. Similar to the *i* in English *machine*: *vi, tido, livro.*
2. Like English *y* before another vowel: *iate, ianque.*
3. Often like no. 2 followed by no. 1 when unstressed between vowels: *sai, meio.*
4. Nasal *i*, a nasalized version of no. 1, in *-in-* and *-im-*: *sim, fim, lindo.*

Note: In Brazil, an intrusive *i* (no. 1) is often inserted in pronunciation (not in spelling) at the end of a word ending in a "hard" consonant, between consonant clusters or between a stressed vowel and a syllable-final *s* or *z* (especially when the latter is pronounced as *sh*): *sob, objeto, advogado, psique, pneu, gás, nós, dez, paz, luz.*

o
1. Close *o* like *o* of English *vote*, but more clipped; in stressed and some unstressed (except word-final) syllables: *olho, ovelha, pôr, avô.*
2. Open *o* similar to the vowel of English *saw, ball* or *taught* as pronounced in the northeast U.S., mostly in stressed syllables: *só, porta, olhos, avó.*
3. Like Portuguese *u*:
   a. In unstressed monosyllables: *o, os, do, nos.*
   b. In unstressed word-final position: *livro, carro, falo.*
   c. Unstressed before another vowel (except *o*) unless it combines into a diphthong: *João, mágoa.*
   d. In the syllable before stressed *i*: *cozinha, dormimos.*
   e. In many other unstressed syllables: *conhecer, fogão.*
4. Nasal *o*, a nasalized version of close *o*, in *-on-* and *-om-*: *bom, conto, onde.*

u **1.** Like the vowel sound of English *boot*, but more clipped: *tu, puro, mula*.

    2. Like English *w* before a vowel, but only before *a* or *o* after *g* or *q* unless a dieresis (umlaut) is written over it: *uísque, guarda, quatro, freqüente*.

    3. Nasal *u*, a nasalized version of no. 1, in *-un-* and *-um-*: *um, uns, fumo*.

Diphthongs

Oral

au Like *ow* in English *cow*: *mau, cacau, Paulo*.

ai Like the vowel sound of English *pie*: *pai, mais*.

ei Like the vowel sound of English *pay*, but often clipped in *-eira/o*: *sei, leite, brasileiro/a*.

eu Close *e* directly followed by an *u* (no. 1): *eu, meu, seu*.

éi Open *e* directly followed by an *i* (no. 1): *hotéis*.

éu Open *e* directly followed by an *u* (no. 1): *céu, chapéu*.

iu *i* directly followed by an *u* (no. 1): *viu, sentiu*.

oi Like the vowel sound of English *boy*: *coisa, noite, boi*.

ou Like close *o* in Brazil; the *u* off-glide is usually pronounced in Portugal: *ou, sou, outro, falou*.

ói Open *o* directly followed by *i* (no. 1): *dói, espanhóis*.

ui Similar to the vowel sounds in English *phooey*; nasalized only in the words *muito* and archaic *mui*: *fui, ruivo, flui*. In some words, pronounced separately, not as a diphthong: *ruim*.

Nasal

ão Nasalization of a sound intermediate between the *ow* of English *how* and close *o*. In verb endings, *-am* is also pronounced this way: *mão, pão, João*.

ãe Nasalization of unstressed *a* directly followed by *i* (no. 1): *mãe, pães*.

õe Nasalization of the *oi* diphthong; similar to the vowel sound of English *oink*: *põe, nações*.

ui Nasalized only in *muito, mui*.

Consonants

b As in English (not Spanish): *bebe, bomba, rabo*. In syllable-final position, usually followed by an intrusive *i* in pronunciation (not in spelling): *sob*.

c **1.** Like English *s* before *e* and *i*: *certo, cinza*.

    2. Like *k* elsewhere: *caro, coco, crer, claro*. Syllable-final, it is often followed in pronunciation (not in spelling) by an intrusive *i* sound: *acne, PUC*.

ç Like *s*; used only before *a, o* or *u*: *dançar, açúcar*.

ch Like English *sh*: *chá, acho, chique*.

d   1. Similar to English "hard" *d* (not Spanish) before *a, o, u* or stressed *e* (close, open or nasal). Similar to Spanish "soft" *d* in parts of Portugal: *dar, dedo, lado.*
2. Before *i* or weak *e* (sounding like *i*), like the *j* of English *joke* in most regions of Brazil: *dia, digo, pode.* Regionally and in Portugal, like no. 1. In syllable-final position, often replaced in pronunciation (not in spelling) by an intrusive *i* and thus pronounced as *j: admirar, advogado.*

f   As in English: *fé, falar, chefe.*

g   1. After *e* or *i,* like *zh,* or the second *g* of *garage: gente, geral, página.*
2. Elsewhere, like the "hard" *g* of English *go: gado, grande, pago.* Syllable-final, tends to be followed in speech (not in spelling) by an intrusive *i* sound: *digno.*

gu   1. Before *e* or *i,* like the *g* of English *go,* the *u* being silent: *guerra, guincho.* When the *u* is not silent, a dieresis (umlaut) is written over it to indicate a *w* sound: *agüentar.*
2. Before *a* or *o,* like *gw: água, igual, ambíguo.*

h   Silent except as part of digraphs *ch, lh* and *nh: homem, história.*

j   Like *zh,* or the second *g* in English *garage: já, jeito, anjo.*

k   As in English; used only in words and names of foreign origin.

l   1. At the beginning of a syllable, similar to English, but with tongue in front of mouth: *ler, lá, falar.*
2. Syllable-final, either like the vowel sound of English *moot* or similar to the "dark" *l* of English *ball: sol, alto, bulbo.* The latter pronunciation is preferred in Portugal.

lh   Similar to the *lli* of English *million* or the *gli* of Italian *figlio: lhama, filha, alho.*

m   1. At the beginning of a syllable, as in English: *mão, fome.*
2. At the end of a syllable, merely nasalizes the preceding vowel but is not pronounced itself: *um, tom, samba.*

n   1. At the beginning of a syllable, as in English: *não, dona.*
2. At the end of a syllable, merely nasalizes the preceding vowel, but is not pronounced itself: *canta, falando.*

nh   Like a nasalized consonantal *y;* similar to but much less precise than the Spanish *ñ,* the French-Italian *gn* or the *ny* of English *canyon: tenho, manhã, nhame.*

p   Similar to English; with more breath than the Spanish *p: pai, pera, papo.*

qu   1. Like English *k* before *e* or *i,* the *u* being silent: *quente, máquina.* When the *u* is not silent, a dieresis (umlaut) is written over it to indicate a *w* sound: *freqüente.*
2. Before *a* or *o,* always like English *kw: quatro, quórum.*

r   1. Like an aspirated (hard) *h* or a Spanish *j* at the beginning of a word, when doubled, or after *n, l* or *s* in most regions of Brazil. Replaced in Southern Brazil by multiple trill and parts of Portugal with a gargled *r: Rio, roupa, carro, genro, melro.*
2. A single trill when written singly between vowels: *para, caro.*
3. Before consonants (syllable-final), as no. 1 or no. 2, above: *porta, carne, barba.*
4. In word-final position, as no. 1 or no. 2, above, or, especially in rapid speech, silent: *cor, morar, senhor.*

s 1. Like English *s* at the beginning of a word, usually after a consonant, or when doubled: *senso, observar, passo*.
2. Like English *z* when written singly between vowels or in word-final position before a word beginning with a vowel or *h* plus vowel: *casa, mesa, belas artes, os homens*.
3. Like English *sh* or *s* in word-final position (when not followed by another word), before *c* /k/, *f, p, q, t, ch*, or *x* within a word or final before these letters or *s* initiating a following word: *nós, lápis, risco, isto, aspa, as camas*.
4. Like *zh* or *z* before *b, d, g, j, l, m, n, v,* or *w* within a word or final before these letters initiating a following word: *desde, as vacas, as belas damas*.

sc Like *s* (in Portugal often *sh*) before *e* or *i*: *nascer*; like *shk* or *sk* before *a, o* or *u*: *escola, rosca*.

t 1. Similar to English *t* before *a, o, u* or stressed *e* (close, open or nasal): *tomo, pata*.
2. Before *i* or weak *e* (sounding like *i*), like the *ch* of *cheese* in most regions of Brazil: *tive, latino, pote*. Regionally and in Portugal, like no. 1. In syllable-final position, often followed in pronunciation (not in spelling) by an intrusive *i* and thus pronounced as *ch: aritmética*.

v Similar to English but more vigorous; not softened or indistinguishable from *b* as in Spanish: *vivo, vou*.

w Used only in foreign words and names. Like English *w* or *v*, depending on supposed language of origin.

x 1. Like *sh* at the beginning of a syllable (including usually between vowels): *xícara, xale, baixo, luxo, vexame*.
2. Like *s* between vowels in a few words only: *próximo, auxílio, trouxe*.
3. Like *ks* at the end of words or between vowels in a few words only: *látex, sexo, fixo*.
4. Like *sh* or *s* before a voiceless consonant: *sexto, expirar; zh* or *z* before a voiced consonant: *ex-marido*.
5. Like *z* in the prefix *ex-* followed by a vowel: *exame, exato*.

y Used only in foreign words and names. Pronounced as in the language of origin.

z 1. Like English *z* at the beginning of a syllable or word-final before followed by a vowel or *h* plus vowel: *zero, zonzo, fuzil, fez um*.
2. Like the Portuguese letter *s* would be pronounced when syllable-final: like *s* or *sh* in *paz, luz, faz tudo* and *z* or *zh* in *diz bobagens*.

Note: Where there are homographs that differ in pronunciation from one another only in the openness/closeness of stressed *e* or *o* (e.g., *ele, esse, lobo*), I have listed them separately, the word with the open vowel coming first. This order is also followed with other minimal pairs (e.g., *avó*, followed by *avô*).

Portuguese Subject Pronouns

	Singular	**Plural**
First Person Verbs	eu (I)	nós (we)
Third Person Verbs	você (you, *inform.*)	vocês (you, *inform.*)
	o senhor (you, *form., m.*)	os senhores (you, *form.*)
	a senhora (you, *form., f.*)	as senhoras (you, *form., f.*)
	ele (he)	eles (they)
	ela (she)	elas (they, *f.*)

Note: *Tu* (thou) and *vós* (ye), technically the second-person 'you' pronouns, have only limited use in Brazil. While the plural *vós* is usually considered archaic or is relegated to liturgical use, the singular *tu* is widespread in a few regions, particularly in the South, where it is used with the corresponding second-person singular verb forms. In addition, *tu* and especially the object pronoun *te* and possessive *teu/tua*, etc., often alternate in much of Brazil with *você* and its objective and possessive pronouns, appearing with third-person singular verb forms. Only the first- and third-person forms of the verb are supplied here, the latter being used with both the third-person pronouns (ele, ela, eles, elas) and second-person, or 'you', pronouns (você, o senhor, a senhora, vocês, os senhores, as senhoras).

Regular Portuguese Verbs

Infin.	Present	Preterite	Imperfect	Past Part.
falar	falo|falamos	falei|falamos	falava|falávamos	falado
	fala|falam	falou|falaram	falava|falavam	
comer	como|comemos	comi|comemos	comia|comíamos	comido
	come|comem	comeu|comeram	comia|comiam	
partir	parto|partimos	parti|partimos	partia|partíamos	partido
	parte|partem	partiu|partiram	partia|partiam	

Future	Conditional	Pluperfect
falarei|falaremos	falaria|falaríamos	tinha falado, etc.
falará|falarão	falaria|falariam	
comerei|comeremos	comeria|comeríamos	tinha comido, etc.
comerá|comerão	comeria|comeriam	
partirei|partiremos	partiria|partiríamos	tinha partido, etc.
partirá|partirão	partiria|partiriam	

Pres. Perfect	Present Participle	Present Subjunctive	
tenho falado, etc.	falando	fale	falemos
		fale	falem
tenho comido, etc.	comendo	coma	comamos
		coma	comam
tenho partido, etc.	partindo	parta	partamos
		parta	partam

Past Subjunctive		Future Subjunctive		Personal Infinitive	
falasse	falássemos	falar	falarmos	falar	falarmos
falasse	falassem	falar	falarem	falar	falarem
comesse	comêssemos	comer	comermos	comer	comermos
comesse	comessem	comer	comerem	comer	comerem
partisse	partíssemos	partir	partirmos	partir	partirmos
partisse	partissem	partir	partirem	partir	partirem

Irregular Portuguese Verbs

Infinitive	Present	Preterite	Infinitive	Present	Preterite
caber	caibo|	coube|	poder	posso|	pude|
	cabemos	coubemos		podemos	pudemos
	cabe|	coube|		pode|	pôde|
	cabem	couberam		podem	puderam
crer	creio|	———	pôr	ponho|	pus|
(ler)	cremos			pomos	pusemos
	crê|crêem			põe|	pôs|
dar	dou|	dei|		põem	puseram
	damos	demos	querer	quero|	quis|
	dá|	deu|		queremos	quisemos
	dão	deram		quer|	quis|
dizer	digo|	disse|		querem	quiseram
	dizemos	dissemos	rir	rio|	———
	diz|	disse|		rimos	
	dizem	disseram		ri|	
estar	estou|	estive|		riem	
	estamos	estivemos	saber	sei|	soube|
	está|	esteve|		sabemos	soubemos
	estão	estiveram		sabe|	soube|
fazer	faço|	fiz|		sabem	souberam
	fazemos	fizemos	ser	sou|	fui|
	faz|	fez|		somos	fomos
	fazem	fizeram		é|	foi|
haver	hei|	houve|		são	foram
	havemos	houvemos	ter	tenho|	tive|
	há|	houve|		temos	tivemos
	hão	houveram		tem|	teve|
ir	vou|	fui|		têm	tiveram
	vamos	fomos	trazer	trago|	trouxe|
	vai|	foi|		trazemos	trouxemos
	vão	foram		traz|	trouxe|
ouvir	ouço|	———		trazem	trouxeram
	ouvimos		valer	valho|	———
	ouve|			valemos	
	ouvem			vale|	
pedir	peço|	———		valem	
	pedimos		ver	vejo|	vi|
	pede|			vemos	vimos
	pedem			vê|	viu|
perder	perco|	———		vêem	viram
	perdemos		vir	venho|	vim|
	perde|			vimos	viemos
	perdem			vem|	veio|
				vêm	vieram

Irregular Portuguese Past Participles

	regular	irregular
abrir	---	aberto
aceitar	(aceitado)	aceito
acender	acendido	aceso
cobrir	---	coberto
dizer	---	dito
entregar	entregado	entregue
escrever	---	escrito
fazer	---	feito
ganhar	(ganhado)	ganho
gastar	(gastado)	gasto
matar	matado	morto
morrer	morrido	morto
pagar	---	pago
pegar	pegado	(pego)
pôr	---	posto
prender	prendido	preso
surpreender	surpreendido	surpreso
ver	---	visto
vir	---	vindo

Note: There are other, less common past participles.

1. In general, where there are two forms of a past participle, the *regular* form is used with the auxiliary *ter* (or *haver*) to form compound tenses, while the *irregular* form, treated as an adjective, is used with *ser, estar* and *ficar*.

2. Verbs derivative of those in the list form their past participles similarly:

e.g., compor   → composto
       descobrir   → descoberto
       descrever   → descrito
       satisfazer → satisfeito
       prever   → previsto

A Pronúncia do Inglês Americano

Devido à falta de uniformidade ortográfica da língua inglesa, a pronúncia das vogais, dos ditongos e de muitas consoantes tem uma variação enorme. As correspondências fonológicas, portanto, não são sistemáticas. Em geral, a sílaba tônica é a primeira. Há, porém, também muita diversidade nesse particular.

Vogais e Ditongos

a   Como o som *ei* (pronúncia longa) em português *(made, famous)* um *é* exageradamente aberto *(cat)* ou um *a* tônico *(art, ball)* ou átono *(sofa)*.

ai   Como o *ê (fail)*, o *é (said)* ou um *é* exageradamente aberto *(plaid)* em português.

au Como o *a* tônico ou o *ó* do português *(taut)*; às vezes como o *au* em português *(saw)*.

aw Como o *a* tônico ou o *ó* do português *(saw)*.

ay Como o som *ei* em português *(pay)*.

e   Como um *i* (pronúncia longa; *mete*) ou um *é (met)* em português; em posição final (ou seguido de *s* ou, às vezes, *d* final) depois de uma consoante, normalmente é mudo, transformando a vogal tônica em vogal longa *(like, likes, liked)*.

ea Como o *é (weather)*, o *i (eat)* ou o *a (heart)* do português.

ee Como um *i* em português *(feet)*.

ei Como o *ê (their)*, o *ê (vein)* ou o *i* tônico *(receive)* ou átono *(weird)* em português.

ew Como *iú (few)*.

ey Como o som *ei* em português *(they)*.

i   Como o som *ai* (pronúncia longa; *while*) em português ou um *i* tônico *(machine)* ou átono *(hit)*.

ie Como o *ai (tie)* ou o *i (yield)* do português.

o   Como o *ô* (pronúncia longa; *go)* em português, o *u (to)*, o *a* ou o *ó (on)*.

oa Como o *ô* do português *(coat)*.

oe Como o *ô* do português *(toe)*.

oi Como o *ói* em português *(boil)*.

oo Como o *u* tônico *(boot)* ou átono *(foot)* do português.

ou Como o som *au (house)*, um *a* tônico ou um *ó (fought)*, um *ô (though)*, um *u (through)* ou um *a* átono *(famous)* em português.

ow Como o som *au* em português *(how)*.

oy Como o som *oi* acima *(boy)*.

u   Como o som *iú (use)* ou o *u* tônico (pronúncias longas; *rude*) em português, o *u* átono *(put)* ou o *a* átono *(nut)*; às vezes tem o valor consonântico do *u* de *uísque*.

ue Como o som *iú* ou o *u* tônico *(due)* em português; às vezes como *ué* ou *uê (suede)*.

ui Como um *u* tônico em português *(fruit)*; às vezes como *uí (quit)*.

y   Como o *i* acima; às vezes tem o valor consonântico do *i* de *iate*.
     Obs.: É comum pronunciar as vogais *a, e, i, o* e *u* como o *a* átono de *nora* em posições átonas: *responsible, consonant*

Consoantes

b   Como em português *(baby)*.

bb Igual a *b (jabber)*.

c   Em geral, como *s* antes de *e, i* ou *y (cent, cinch, fancy);* como *k* antes de *a, o* ou *u (car, cog, cut)*.

ch Como a combinação *tch* em português ou o *t* palatalizado quando seguido de *i (chew, much);* às vezes como *k (chemical)*.

ci Freqüentemente como o som *ch* do português quando seguidos por outra vogal *(precious, precocious)*.

ck Como *k (tack, luck);* em geral, transforma a vogal tônica em som curto.

d   Como o *d* de *comida* no Brasil *(dead, do)*.

dd Igual a *d (daddy, hidden)*.

dg Como *dj (dodge)*.

f   Como o *f* em português *(fat, field)*.

ff Igual ao *f (coffee)*.

g   Como o *g (get, gill), dj (general, stranger)* ou, às vezes, *j (beige)* antes de *e, i* ou *y;* como o *g* de *gado* antes de *a, o, u,* em posição final ou seguido por uma outra consoante *(gas, go, bag, great, glow)*.

gg Igual ao *g* de *gado (bigger)*.

gh Como *f (laugh)* ou, freqüentemente, mudo *(though, through)*.

gu Em geral, como o *g* de *gado (guard, guide)* quando vem seguido de outra vogal; há exceções, como *argue,* nas quais se pronuncia o *u*.

h   Como o *h* aspirado de *hã* ou de *hall,* palavra inglesa.

j   Como o som *dj (jelly, jam)*.

k   Como o *c* de *cão (kid, ankle);* mudo na combinação *kn*.

l   Semelhante ao *l* em português, especialmente o de Portugal *(lad, black, tall)*.

ll Igual ao *l (sell, ball)*.

m   Como o *m* de *meu* em português *(man, time)*.

mm Igual ao *m (summer)*.

n   Como o *n* de *navio* em português *(nut, sun)*.

nn Igual ao *n (sunny)*.

p   Como o *p* em português *(paper, cap)*.

ph Como o *f (philosophy)*.

pp Igual ao *p (happen)*.

ps Como o *ss* em português *(psalm, psychology)*.

qu Em geral, como o *qu* de *quarto* em português *(quit, quart)*.

r   Em geral, como o *r* caipira no Brasil *(real, war, guard)*.

rr Igual ao *r (marry)*.

s   Como o *ss* em português *(sat, spit, mouse, pass);* às vezes como o *z* entre vogais *(house)* ou em posição final *(houses)*.

sc Como o *ss (science)* ou, às vezes, como o *ch* do português *(luscious)*.

sch Como *sk (school, schedule)*.

sh Como o *ch* do português *(shall, shred, push)*.

si Em geral, como o *j* em português antes de outra vogal *(fusion, Asian)*.

su Às vezes, como *j* em português antes ou de um *r (pleasure, measure)*.

t   Como o *t* de *todo* em português *(tar, bat)*.

th Como um *t* mas com a ponta da língua entre os dentes *(this, throw, with)* ou esse mesmo som mas com a voz *(the, rather)*.

xiii

ti	Freqüentemente como o *ch* do português quando seguido de outra vogal *(nation, partial).*
tt	Em geral, igual ao *t (tattle, matter).*
tu	Às vezes como *tch (adventure, virtue, Portuguese).*
v	Como em português *(vest, gave).*
w	Como o *w* de *Wilson.*
wh	Como *hw* ou *w (what, when).*
x	Normalmente como o *x* de *fixo* em português *(fix, boxes);* como *z* em posição inicial *(xylophone).*
y	Como o *i* de *iate.*
z	Como o *z* de *zero (zone, haze).*
zz	Igual ao *z (dizzy).*

O Plural do Substantivo Inglês

1. Acrescenta-se, normalmente, um *-s* à forma singular:

book	→ books	house	→ houses
bed	→ beds	page	→ pages

2. Se a forma singular termina em *-s, -sh, -x, -z* ou *-ch* (pronunciado /tch/), acrescenta-se a terminação *-es:*

glass	→ glasses	waltz	→ waltzes
rash	→ rashes	watch	→ watches
tax	→ taxes		

3. Um *-y* final precedido por qualquer consonante converte-se em *-ie* antes de se acrescentar o *-s* do plural:

lady	→ ladies	city	→ cities

4. Se o substantivo termina em *-o,* acrescenta-se um *-s* se o *-o* é precedido por uma vogal e *-s* ou *-es* se o *-o* é precedido por uma consoante:

radio → radios	piano → pianos	tomato → tomatoes
zoo → zoos	hero → heroes	

5. Alguns substantivos terminados em *-f* ou *-fe* pluralizam-se em *-s* ao passo que outros formam o plural em *-ves:*

roof	→ roofs	leaf	→ leaves	half	→ halves
safe	→ safes	life	→ lives		

6. Alguns substantivos têm plural irregular:

mouse	→ mice	woman → women	tooth	→ teeth
child	→ children	man → men	die	→ dice
foot	→ feet	goose → geese		

O Verbo em Inglês

1. A terceira pessoa singular do tempo presente é formada de acordo com as mesmas regras que governam o acréscimo de -*s*, -*es* e -*ies* na pluralização dos substantivos:

look	→ looks	fall	→ falls	kiss	→ kisses
feed	→ feeds	buy	→ buys	mix	→ mixes
judge	→ judges	laugh	→ laughs	carry	→ carries
place	→ places	pass	→ passes	cry	→ cries

2. Alguns verbos comuns formam a terceira pessoa singular do presente irregularmente:

do	→ does	go	→ goes
have	→ has	be	→ is

No caso de *be*, as outras pessoas do presente também são irregulares (I am, you are, she is, we are, they are), assim como o passado (I was, you were, he was, we were, they were) e o particípio *been*.

3. Em geral, o tempo passado e o particípio são formados de maneira idêntica, acrescentando-se a terminação -*ed* ou -*d*, conforme as seguintes regras:

a. Se o verbo termina em consoante, acrescenta-se -*ed*, constituindo este sílaba à parte só no caso de a consoante ser -*d* ou -*t*:

work	→ worked	toss	→ tossed	wait	→ waited
help	→ helped	kill	→ killed	need	→ needed
turn	→ turned	match	→ matched	want	→ wanted

b. Se o verbo termina em -*e*, acrescenta-se apenas -*d*:

face	→ faced	side	→ sided
dare	→ dared	free	→ freed

c. Se o verbo termina em -*y* precedido por uma consoante, o -*y* converte-se em -*ie* antes de se acrescentar o -*d*:

try	→ tried	deny	→ denied
carry	→ carried		

4. Alguns verbos comuns têm passado e particípio irregulares:

Verbo	Passado	Particípio
be	was/were	been
beat	beat	beaten
become	became	become
begin	began	begun
bend	bent	bent
bet	bet	bet
bite	bit	bitten
bleed	bled	bled
blow	blew	blown
break	broke	broken
bring	brought	brought
build	built	built
burst	burst	burst
buy	bought	bought
cast	cast	cast
catch	caught	caught
choose	chose	chosen

come	came	come
cost	cost	cost
creep	crept	crept
cut	cut	cut
deal	dealt	dealt
dig	dug	dug
do	did	done
draw	drew	drawn
drink	drank	drunk
drive	drove	driven
eat	ate	eaten
fall	fell	fallen
feed	fed	fed
feel	felt	felt
fight	fought	fought
find	found	found
flee	fled	fled
fly	flew	flown
forget	forgot	forgotten
freeze	froze	frozen
get	got	got/gotten
give	gave	given
go	went	gone
grow	grew	grown
hang	hung	hung
have	had	had
hear	heard	heard
hide	hid	hidden/hid
hit	hit	hit
hold	held	held
hurt	hurt	hurt
keep	kept	kept
know	knew	known
lead	led	led
leave	left	left
lend	lent	lent
let	let	let
lose	lost	lost
make	made	made
mean	meant	meant
meet	met	met
put	put	put
quit	quit	quit
read /i/	read /é/	read /é/
ride	rode	ridden
ring	rang	rung
rise	rose	risen
run	ran	run
say	said	said
see	saw	seen
seek	sought	sought
sell	sold	sold
send	sent	sent
set	set	set
shake	shook	shaken

shed	shed	shed
shine	shone/shined	shone
shoot	shot	shot
shrink	shrank/shrunk	shrunk/shrunken
shut	shut	shut
sing	sang	sung
sink	sank	sunk
sit	sat	sat
sleep	slept	slept
slit	slit	slit
speak	spoke	spoken
spend	spent	spent
spit	spit/spat	spit/spat
split	split	split
spread	spread	spread
stand	stood	stood
steal	stole	stolen
strike	struck	struck/stricken
swear	swore	sworn
sweep	swept	swept
swim	swam	swum
teach	taught	taught
tear	tore	torn
throw	threw	thrown
thrust	thrust	thrust
wear	wore	worn
wet	wet	wet
write	wrote	written

English Abbreviations/Abreviaturas Inglesas

abbr.	abbreviation; abreviatura
acad.	academic; acadêmico
adj.	adjective; adjetivo
adv.	adverb; advérbio
aer.	aeronautical; aeronáutico
agr.	agriculture; agricultura
anat.	anatomy; anatomia
arch.	architecture; arquitetura
art.	article; artigo
auto.	automotive; automobilístico
B.	Brazil; Brasil
biol.	biology; biologia
bot.	botany; botânica
cap.	capital; maiúscula
chem.	chemistry; química
coll.	colloquial; coloquial
com.	commercial; comercial
comput.	computer; computador
conj.	conjunction; conjunção
contr.	contraction; contração
cul.	culinary; culinária
def. art.	definite article; artigo definido
dem.	demonstrative; demonstrativo
dent.	dentistry; odontologia
dir. obj. pron.	direct object pronoun; pronome oblíquo (direto)
eccles.	ecclesiastical; eclesiástico
econ.	economics; economia
elec.	electricity; eletrônica
Eng.	English; inglês
entom.	entomology; entomologia
esp.	especially; especialmente
f.	feminine; feminino
fam.	familiar
fig.	figurative; figurado
fin.	finance; finanças
geog.	geography; geografia
govt.	government; governo
gram.	grammar; gramática
hist.	historical; histórico
ichth.	ichthyology; ictiologia
indef. art.	indefinite article; artigo indefinido
indir. obj. pron.	indirect object pronoun; pronome oblíquo (indir.)
interj.	interjection; interjeição
interrog.	interrogative; interrogativo
journ.	journalism; jornalismo
jur.	juridical; jurídico
m.	masculine; masculino
mech.	mechanics; mecânica
med.	medical; médico
mil.	military; militar

mus.	music; música
n.	noun; substantivo
nas.	nasal
naut.	nautical; náutico
neut.	neuter; neutro
obj.	object; oblíquo
ornith.	ornithology; ornitologia
P.	Portugal
pert.	pertaining
opt.	optics; óptica
phot.	photography; fotografia
pl.	plural
pol.	politics; política
poss.	possessive; possessivo
prep.	preposition; preposição/preposicional
pron.	pronoun; pronome
rel.	relative; relativo
s.	singular
sl.	slang; gíria
sport.	sports; esporte
subj.	subject; de sujeito, reto
theat.	theater; teatro
usu.	usually; usualmente
vb.	verb; verbo
vulg.	vulgar; chulo
zool.	zoology; zoologia

The
Random House
Portuguese
Dictionary

A

a, 1. *prep.* to, at. **2.** *f.s. def. art.*
the. **3.** *dir. obj. pron.* her, it,
you. **4.** *rel. pron.* the one (that).
5. *n.m.* the letter a.

à, *contr. of* **a** + **a.** to the, at the;
to the one (that); a la, in the
. . . way.

aba, *n.f.* rim, brim.

abacate, *n.m.* avocado.

abacaxi, *n.m.* pineapple; *(sl.)*
problem.

abade, *n.m.* abbot.

abadessa, *n.f.* abbess.

abadia, *n.f.* abbey.

abafado, *adj.* stuffy; hushed;
swamped.

abafar, *vb.* smother; hush; *(sl.)*
swipe; *(sl.)* control.

abaixar, *vb.* lower.

abaixo, *adv.* below. **abaixo de,**
under.

abaixo-assinado, *n.m.* petition.

abajur, *n.m.* lampshade.

abalar, *vb.* shake; stir; flee.

abalo, *n.m.* shaking; shock.

abalroar, *vb.* crash into.

abanar, *vb.* fan. **a. a cabeça,**
shake one's head.

abancar-se, *vb.* sit down.

abandonar, *vb.* abandon; leave.

abandono, *n.m.* abandon, abandonment.

abarcar, *vb.* embrace, contain.
**querer a. o mundo com as per-
nas,** bite off more than one can
chew.

abarrotar, *vb.* fill up, cram.

abastado, *adj.* affluent.

abastecer, *vb.* supply.

abater, *vb.* lower; knock down;
depress; slaughter.

abatimento, *n.m.* depression;
discount.

abdicar, *vb.* abdicate.

abdome, *n.m.* abdomen.

abelha, *n.f.* bee.

abelhudo, *adj. (coll.)* nosy.

abençoar, *vb.* bless.

aberração, *n.f.* aberration.

aberto, *adj.* open; frank; outgoing.

abertura, *n.f.* opening; overture.

abestalhado, *adj.* stupid.

abismar, *vb.* astound.

abismo, *n.m.* abyss.

abjeto, *adj.* abject.

abóbada, *n.f.* arch.

abóbora, *n.f.* pumpkin, squash.

abolição, *n.f.* abolition.

abolir, *vb.* abolish.

abominar, *vb.* abominate.

abonado, *adj. (coll.)* well-to-do.

abonar, *vb.* guarantee; attest to.

abonecado, *adj.* dolled up.

abono, *n.m.* security; bonus.

abordagem, *n.f.* approach.

abordar, *vb.* approach; deal
with.

aborígine, *n.m.f.* aborigine.

aborrecer, *vb.* abhor; bore;
bother. **a.-se,** get upset.

aborrecimento, *n.m.* abhorrence; boredom; annoyance.

abortar, *vb.* abort.

aborto, *n.m.* abortion.

abotoadura, *n.f.* cuff link.

abotoar, *vb.* button.

abraçar, *vb.* embrace, hug.

abraço, *n.m.* hug, embrace. **um
abraço!,** so long!

abrandar, *vb.* soften.

abranger, *vb.* encompass.

abrasileirar, *vb.* Brazilianize.

abrasivo, *adj.* abrasive.

abreviar, *vb.* abbreviate,
shorten.

abreviatura, *n.f.* abbreviation.

abricó, *n.m.* apricot.

abrideira, *n.f.* apéritif.

abridor, *n.m.* opener. **a. de lata,**
can opener.

abrigar, *vb.* shelter; harbor.
a.-se, take refuge.

abrigo, *n.m.* shelter, refuge. **a.
antiaéreo,** air-raid shelter.

abril, *n.m.* April.

abrir, *vb.* open; turn on (faucet); turn green (traffic light);

clear up (weather). **num a. e fechar de olhos,** in a flash; **a.-se,** open up; speak frankly; (sl.) smile.

ab-rogar, vb. abrogate.

abrolho, n.m. thistle; (pl.) obstacles.

abrupto, adj. abrupt.

abscesso, n.m. abscess.

absoluto, adj. absolute. **absolutamente!,** (coll.) absolutely not!

absolver, vb. absolve; pardon.

absolvição, n.f. absolution; pardon.

absorção, n.f. absorption.

absorto, adj. absorbed; ecstatic.

absorver, vb. absorb; engross.

absorvido, adj. absorbed.

abstêmio, 1. adj. abstinent. **2.** n.m. abstainer.

abstenção, n.f. abstention.

abster-se, vb. abstain; refrain.

abstinência, n.f. abstention; abstinence.

abstração, n.f. abstraction; daydreaming.

abstraído, adj. abstracted; absent-minded.

abstrair, vb. abstract.

abstrato, adj. abstract; absorbed.

absurdo, 1. adj. absurd. **2.** n.m. absurdity.

abundância, n.f. abundance.

abundante, adj. abundant.

abundar, vb. abound.

abusado, adj. bold; impertinent.

abusar, vb. abuse; deflower. **a. de,** abuse.

abusivo, adj. abusive.

abuso, n.m. abuse.

abutre, n.m. vulture.

acabado, adj. finished; worn out.

acabamento, n.m. finish.

acabar, vb. finish; end up. **a. com,** put an end to. **a. de . . ,** have just; **a. por,** end up by; **que não acaba mais,** galore; **a.-se,** run out; **acabou-se,** that's that.

acabrunhar, vb. crush; torment. embarrass.

acaçapar, vb. squash; humiliate.

academia, n.f. academy.

acadêmico, 1. adj. academic. **2.**

n.m. academician; college student.

açafrão, n.m. saffron.

acalanto, n.m. lulling; lullaby.

acalentar, vb. lull; cuddle.

acalento, n.m. lulling; lullaby.

acalmar, vb. calm.

acalorar, vb. heat up. **a.-se,** get excited.

acamado, adj. bedridden.

acampamento, n.m. camping; camp.

acampar(-se), vb. camp.

acanalar, vb. groove.

acanhado, adj. shy.

acanhar-se, vb. become shy.

acantonar, vb. billet.

ação, n.f. action, act; (com.) share. **a. de graças,** thanksgiving.

acarajé, n.m. beans, pepper, and palm oil in a banana leaf.

acariciar, vb. caress; harbor.

acarretar, vb. cart; bring on.

acaso, n.m. 1. chance. **ao a.,** at random; **por a.,** by chance. **2.** adv. perhaps.

acatar, vb. respect.

acautelar, vb. caution. **a.-se,** be cautious.

aceder, vb. accede.

aceitação, n.f. acceptance.

aceitar, vb. accept.

aceito, adj. accepted.

acelerador, n.m. accelerator.

acelerar, vb. accelerate.

acenar, vb. beckon; wave; provoke.

acender, vb. light, set fire to; turn on (light); provoke. **a.-se,** vb. light up; get irritated.

acendrar, vb. purify.

aceno, n.m. gesture, wave.

acento, n.m. accent mark; stress. **a. agudo,** acute accent; **a. circunflexo,** circumflex accent; **a. grave,** grave accent; **a. tônico,** stress.

acentuação, n.f. accentuation.

acentuar, vb. accentuate; stress.

acepção, n.f. meaning.

acepipe, n.m. delicacy.

acéquia, n.f. aqueduct; dam.

acerbo, adj. bitter; harsh.

acerca de, prep. about.

acercar-se, vb. approach.

acertado, adj. correct; wise.

acertar, *vb.* get/do right; hit the mark; set. **a. em,** hit (target); happen, chance.

acerto, *n.m.* correctness; wisdom; pact.

acervar, *vb.* amass.

acervo, *n.m.* heap; holdings.

aceso, *adj.* lit; excited; alert.

acessível, *adj.* accessible.

acesso, *n.m.* access; fit.

acessório, *adj., n.m.* accessory.

achacado, *adj.* sickly.

achado, 1. *n.m.* find; godsend. **2.** *adj.* found. **não se dar por a.,** play dumb.

achaque, *n.m.* chronic illness; vice.

achar, *vb.* find; think. **a. que sim/não,** think so/not; **a.-se,** be found; deem oneself.

achatar, *vb.* flatten; crush.

achega, *n.f.* addition; assistance.

acicatar, *vb.* prod. —**acicate,** *n.m.*

acidentado, 1. *adj.* uneven; eventful. **2.** *n.m.* accident victim.

acidental, *adj.* accidental.

acidentar-se, *vb.* have an accident.

acidente, *n.m.* accident.

acidez, *n.f.* acidity.

ácido, *adj., n.m.* acid; *(sl.)* LSD.

acima, 1. *adv.* above. **2. a. de,** *prep.* above; besides.

acionista, *n.m.f.* shareholder.

acirrar, *vb.* irritate; provoke. **a.-se,** get upset.

aclamação, *n.f.* acclamation.

aclamar, *vb.* acclaim, applaud.

aclarar, *vb.* clarify; clear up.

aclimar, *vb.* acclimate. **a.-se,** become acclimated.

aço, *n.m.* steel.

acocorar-se, *vb.* squat.

açodar, *vb.* hasten; incite.

acoitar, *vb.* harbor.

açoitar, *vb.* flog; devastate.

açoite, *n.m.* whip; beating; affliction.

acolá, *adv.* over there.

acolhedor, *adj.* welcoming, hospitable.

acolher, *vb.* welcome, receive. **a.-se,** take shelter.

acolhida, *n.f.* welcome, reception.

acólito, *n.m.* altar boy.

acometer, *vb.* assault. —**acometida,** *n.f.*

acomodado, *adj.* appropriate; comfortable; resigned.

acomodar, *vb.* accommodate; adapt. **a.-se,** lodge; adjust.

acomodatício, *adj.* accommodating.

acompanhamento, *n.m.* accompaniment.

acompanhar, *vb.* accompany; keep up with.

aconchegar, *vb.* cuddle; bundle up.

aconchego, *n.m.* coziness; protection.

acondicionar, *vb.* condition; wrap; arrange.

aconselhar, *vb.* advise.

acontecer, *vb.* happen; chance. **aconteça o que acontecer,** no matter what happens; **acontece que,** it so happens that.

acontecimento, *n.m.* happening, event.

acoplar, *vb.* couple, link.

acordado, *adj.* awake; alert.

acordar, *vb.* wake up; awaken.

acorde, 1. *adj.* in tune. **2.** *n.m. (mus.)* chord.

acordeão, *n.m.* accordion.

acordo, *n.m.* accord; consent; **de a.,** all right; **estar de a. (com),** agree (with).

Açores, *n.m.pl.* Azores.

açoriano -na, *adj., n.* Azorean.

acoroçoar, *vb.* encourage.

acorrer (a), *vb.* rush to.

acossar, *vb.* pursue, harass.

acostumado, *adj.* accustomed; usual.

acostumar, *vb.* accustom. **a.-se a,** get used to.

acotovelar, *vb.* elbow, nudge.

açougue, *n.m.* butcher's shop.

açougueiro, *n.m.* butcher.

acovardar, *vb.* intimidate. **a.-se,** cower.

acre, 1. *adj.* acrid. **2.** *n.m.* acre.

acreano -na, 1. *adj.* of/pert. to the state of Acre. **2.** *n.* native of Acre.

acreditar, *vb.* believe; credit; accredit. **a. em,** believe in.

acrescentar, *vb.* add; increase.

acrescer, *vb.* add; grow; happen too.

acréscimo, acrescimento, *n.m.* increase; growth.

acrílico, *adj., n.m.* acrylic.

acrimônia, *n.f.* acrimony.

acrobata, *n.m.f.* acrobat.

acrossemia, *n.f.* acronym.

açu, *adj.* big.

acuar, *vb.* corner, trap.

açúcar, *n.m.* sugar.

açucarado, *adj.* sugary.

açucareiro, 1. *adj.* of/pert. to sugar. **2.** *n.m.* sugar bowl; sugar refiner/dealer.

açucena, *n.f.* Easter lily.

açude, *n.m.* dam.

acudir (a), *vb.* rush to; respond to; obey; occur.

acuidade, *n.f.* acuity.

açular, *vb.* incite; sic.

aculturação, *n.f.* acculturation.

acume, *n.m.* acumen.

acumulação, *n.f.* accumulation.

acumulador, *n.m.* battery.

acumular, *vb.* accumulate; hold multiple (jobs).

acupuntura, *n.f.* acupuncture.

acurado, *adj.* accurate; painstaking.

acurralar, *vb.* corral.

acusação, *n.f.* accusation, charge.

acusado -da, *n.* accused.

acusar, *vb.* accuse, charge; show; acknowledge. **a. o recebimento de,** acknowledge receipt of.

acústico, *adj.* acoustic.

adaga, *n.f.* dagger.

adágio, *n.m.* adage; *(mus.)* adagio.

adamado, *adj.* effeminate.

Adão, *n.m.* Adam.

adaptação, *n.f.* adaptation.

adaptar, *vb.* adapt, adjust; **a.-se,** adapt.

adega, *n.f.* wine cellar.

adejar, *vb.* flutter. —**adejo,** *n.m.*

adelgaçar, *vb.* thin.

ademais, *adv.* besides.

ademanes, *n.m.pl.* affected gestures.

adentro, *adv.* inward.

adepto, *n.m.* follower; believer.

adequado, *adj.* adequate.

adequar, *vb.* adjust.

adereçar, *vb.* adorn.

adereço, *n.m.* decoration.

aderente, *n.m.f.* follower.

aderir (a), *vb.* adhere (to); espouse; join.

adesão, *n.f.* adherence.

adesivo, 1. *adj.* adhesive. **2.** *n.m.* sticker.

adestrar, *vb.* train.

adeus, *n.m., interj.* goodbye, farewell.

adiantado, 1. *adj.* advanced, early; fast (clock). **2.** *adv.* in advance.

adiantar, *vb.* advance; anticipate. **não adianta,** it won't do any good. **a.-se,** get ahead; *(coll.)* get fresh.

adiante, *adv.* ahead, forward.

adiar, *vb.* postpone.

adição, *n.f.* addition.

adicional, *adj.* additional.

adido, *n.m.* attaché.

aditamento, *n.m.* addition.

adivinha, *n.f.* riddle; fortuneteller *(f.)*

adivinhar, *vb.* guess.

adivinho, *n.m.* fortuneteller *(m.)*

adjacente, *adj.* adjacent.

adjetivo, *n.m.* adjective.

adjudicar, *vb.* adjudicate; award.

adjunto, *adj.* attached.

administração, *n.f.* administration.

administrador -ra, *n.* administrator.

administrar, *vb.* administer.

administrativo, *adj.* administrative.

admiração, *n.f.* admiration; wonder.

admirador -ra, *n.* admirer.

admirar, *vb.* admire; astonish. **não admira que,** it's no wonder that; **a.-se (de),** marvel (at).

admissão, *n.f.* admission.

admitir, *vb.* admit; allow.

admoestar, *vb.* admonish.

adoção, *n.f.* adoption.

adoçante, *n.m.* sweetener.

adoçar, *vb.* sweeten; soften.

adoecer, *vb.* get sick.

adoidado, *adj.* crazy.
adolescência, *n.f.* adolescence.
adolescente, *adj., n.m.f.* adolescent.
adoração, *n.f.* worship.
adorador -ra, *n.* worshiper.
adorar, *vb.* adore, worship; *(coll.)* be crazy about.
adormecer, *vb.* put to sleep; fall asleep.
adornar, *vb.* adorn.
adorno, *n.m.* decoration.
adotar, *vb.* adopt.
adotivo, *adj.* adopted.
adquirir, *vb.* acquire.
adrede, *adv.* deliberately.
adubar, *vb.* season; fertilize.
adubo, *n.m.* seasoning; fertilizer.
aduela, *n.f.* stave. **ter uma a. de mais/menos**, have a screw loose.
adulador -ra, *n.* adulator.
adular, *vb.* adulate, flatter.
adulterar, *vb.* adulterate.
adultério, *n.m.* adultery.
adúltero -ra, **1.** *adj.* adulterous. **2.** *n.* adulterer -ess.
adulto -ta, *adj., n.* adult.
adunco, *adj.* aquiline.
adusto, *adj.* scorched.
aduzir, *vb.* adduce.
adventício, **1.** *adj.* foreign; adventitious. **2.** *n.m.* foreigner.
advento, *n.m.* advent.
advérbio, *n.m.* adverb.
adversário -ria, *n.* adversary, opponent.
adversidade, *n.f.* adversity.
adverso, *adj.* adverse.
advertência, *n.f.* warning; advice.
advertir, *vb.* warn; note.
advir, *vb.* happen; befall.
advocacia, *n.f.* law practice; legal profession.
advogado -da, *n.* lawyer; advocate. **a. do diabo**, devil's advocate.
advogar, *vb.* advocate; practice law.
aéreo, *adj.* air, aerial; airy; in the clouds. **via aérea**, airmail.
aeromoça, *n.f.* flight attendant *(f.)*.
aeroporto, *n.m.* airport.
aerossol, *n.m.* aerosol.

afã, *n.m.* eagerness; effort; ado; anxiety.
afagar, *vb.* caress. **—afago**, *n.m.*
afamado, *adj.* famous.
afanar, *vb.* work hard (for); *(sl.)* swipe.
afastado, *adj.* distant, remote.
afastar, *vb.* drive away; separate. **a.-se**, withdraw.
afável, *adj.* affable.
afazer, **1.** *n.m.pl.* affairs, duties. **2.** *vb.* accustom. **a.-se**, get used (to).
afear, *vb.* make ugly; distort.
Afeganistão, *n.m.* Afghanistan.
afeição, *n.f.* affection.
afeiçoar, *vb.* fashion; adapt. **a.-se a**, take a liking to; get used to.
afeito, *adj.* accustomed.
aferir, *vb.* measure; compare.
aferrado, *adj.* stubborn.
aferrar, *vb.* clutch. **a.-se a**, cling to.
aferroar, *vb.* sting.
afetação, *n.f.* affectation.
afetado, *adj.* affected.
afetar, *vb.* affect; feign.
afeto, **1.** *adj.* fond. **2.** *n.m.* affection; affect.
afetuoso, *adj.* affectionate.
afiado, *adj.* sharp; prepared.
afiançar, *vb.* guarantee; stand bail.
afiar, *vb.* sharpen.
aficionado -da, **1.** *adj.* enthusiastic. **2.** *n.* fan.
afilhado -da, *n.* godchild; protégé(e).
afiliação, *n.f.* affiliation.
afiliar, *vb.* affiliate.
afim, *adj.* akin, similar.
afinal, *adv.* at last, finally. **a. de contas**, after all.
afinar, *vb.* tune; refine.
afinco, *n.m.* persistence.
afinidade, *n.f.* affinity.
afirmação, *n.f.* affirmation.
afirmar, *vb.* affirm; certify.
afirmativo, *adj., n.m.* affirmative.
afivelar, *vb.* buckle.
afixar, *vb.* affix, post.
aflição, *n.f.* affliction; sorrow; worry.

afligir, *vb.* afflict; trouble. **a.-se**, worry.

aflito, *adj.* afflicted; worried.

aflorar, *vb.* emerge.

afluência, *n.f.* abundance; influx; affluence.

afluente, **1.** *adj.* affluent. **2.** *n.m.* tributary.

afluir, *vb.* flow in; flock.

afobação, *n.f. (coll.)* · bustle; fluster.

afobar, *vb. (coll.)* hurry; fluster. **a.-se**, get flustered.

afogadilho, *n.m.* haste. **de a.**, hastily.

afogar, *vb.* drown; smother. **a. suas mágoas**, drown one's sorrows; **a.-se**, drown (oneself); **a.-se num copo d'água**, make a fuss about nothing.

afoito, *adj.* bold; eager.

afora, **1.** *adv.* outside. **pelo mundo a.**, throughout the world. **2.** *prep.* except; besides.

aforismo, *n.m.* aphorism.

aforrar, *vb.* free. **a.-se**, buy one's freedom.

afortunado, *adj.* fortunate.

africano -na *adj., n.* African.

afro-brasileiro -ra, *adj., n.* Afro-Brazilian.

afrodisíaco, *adj., n.m.* aphrodisiac.

afronta, *n.f.* affront; disgrace.

afrontar, *vb.* affront; confront.

afrouxar, *vb.* loosen; let up; weaken.

afugentar, *vb.* drive away.

afundar, *vb.* sink. **a.-se**, sink; flunk.

agá, *n.m.* the letter h.

agachar-se, *vb.* crouch; stoop.

agalinhar-se, *vb. (coll.)* chicken out; *(sl.)* be on an easy lay.

agarrar, *vb.* grab, clutch. **a.-se a/com**, cling to.

agasalhar, *vb.* shelter; bundle up.

agasalho, *n.m.* shelter; welcome; warm clothing.

agência, *n.f.* agency; branch office. **a. de viagens/turismo**, travel agency.

agenciar, *vb.* negotiate; represent; try to get.

agenda, *n.f.* agenda; appointment book.

agente, *n.m.f.* agent.

agigantar, *vb.* make large.

ágil, *adj.* agile.

agilidade, *n.f.* agility.

ágio, *n.m.* agio, premium.

agiota, *n.m.f.* usurer.

agir, *vb.* act; behave.

agitação, *n.f.* agitation.

agitador -ra, *n.* agitator.

agitar, *vb.* agitate, shake; stir.

aglomerar, *vb.* agglomerate.

aglutinar, *vb.* agglutinate.

agnóstico -ca, *adj., n.* agnostic.

agogô, *n.m. (mus.)* Afro-Brazilian bells.

agonia, *n.f.* agony.

agonizar, *vb.* agonize.

agora, *n.m., adv.* now; just now; right away. **a. mesmo**, right now.

agosto, *n.m.* August.

agoureiro, *adj.* ominous, foreboding.

agourento, *adj.* ominous.

agouro, *n.m.* omen. **mau a.**, ill omen.

agradar, *vb.* please; flatter.

agradável, *adj.* pleasant, agreeable.

agradecer, *vb.* thank.

agradecido, *adj.* grateful.

agradecimento, *n.m.* thanks, gratitude.

agrado, *n.m.* pleasure; flattery.

agrário -a, *adj.* agrarian. **reforma agrária**, agrarian reform.

agravar, *vb.* aggravate.

agravo, *n.m.* wrong.

agredir, *vb.* attack.

agregado -da, *n.* aggregate; boarder.

agregar, *vb.* aggregate; add.

agremiação, *n.f.* association.

agressão, *n.f.* aggression; attack.

agressivo, *adj.* aggressive.

agressor -ra, *n.* aggressor.

agreste, **1.** *adj.* rustic; wild. **2.** *n.m.* arid region of NE Brazil.

agrião, *n.m.* watercress.

agrícola, *adj.* agricultural.

agricultor -ra, *n.* farmer.

agricultura, *n.f.* agriculture.

agridoce, *adj.* bittersweet.

agrilhoar, *vb.* shackle.

agrimensor, *n.m.* surveyor.

agronomia, *n.f.* agronomy.

agropecuária, *n.f.* agriculture and cattle raising.

agrupamento, *n.m.* grouping.

agrupar, *vb.* group.

água, *n.f.* water; roof slope. **á. benta**, holy water; **á. mineral**, mineral water; **dar/fazer á. na boca**, make one's mouth water; **ficar/estar na á.**, *(sl.)* get/be drunk; **ir por á. abaixo**, *(sl.)* go down the drain.

aguar, *vb.* water; spoil.

aguardar, *vb.* await; expect.

aguardente, *n.f.* cane brandy.

açúcar, *vb.* sharpen; whet.

agudez, *adj.* sharpness.

agudo, *adj.* sharp; acute.

agüentar, *vb.* endure, stand, put up with. **a. a mão**, *(sl.)* hold on.

águia, *n.f.* eagle; sharpie.

aguilhão, *n.m.* cattle prod; stinger; stimulus.

aguilhoar, *vb.* goad; sting; spur.

agulha, *n.f.* needle. **procurar a. em palheiro**, look for a needle in a haystack.

ah, *interj.* ah! oh!

ai, *interj.* ouch! alas! **a. de mim!**, woe is me!

aí, *adv.* there; then. **a. está!**, that's it! exactly! **a. mesmo**, right there; **por a.**, around there; that way; more or less.

aia, *n.f.* governess.

aiatolá, *n.m.* ayatollah.

aidético -na, **1.** *adj.* pert. to AIDS. **2.** *n.m.* person with AIDS.

AIDS, *n.f.* AIDS.

ainda, *adv.* still. **a. assim**, even so; **a. bem**, luckily; **a. não**, not yet; **a. que**, although.

aipim, *n.m.* sweet manioc.

aipo, *n.m.* celery.

ajeitar, *vb.* fix, fix up; arrange.

ajoelhar-se, *vb.* kneel.

ajuda, *n.f.* help, aid. **dar uma a.**, give a hand.

ajudante, *n.m.f.* helper, assistant.

ajudar, *vb.* help, aid.

ajuntamento, *n.m.* assembly; collection.

ajuntar, *vb.* assemble; add.

ajustar, *vb.* adjust; settle.

ajuste, *n.m.* adjustment; agreement.

ala, *adj.* aisle; row; *(arch.)* wing; ward.

Alá, *n.m.* Allah.

álacre, *adj.* cheerful.

alagado, **1.** *adj.* flooded. **2.** *n.m.* flooded land.

alagar, *vb.* flood.

alagoano -na, **1.** *adj.* from/pert. to the state of Alagoas. **2.** *n.* Alagoan.

alambicado, *adj.* affected.

alambique, *n.m.* still.

alameda, *n.f.* tree-lined lane; park.

álamo, *n.m.* poplar.

alarde, *n.m.* ostentation; boasting.

alardear, *vb.* flaunt. **a.-se**, brag.

alargar, *vb.* widen; expand.

alarido, *n.m.* clamor.

alarma, *n.f.*, **alarme** *n.m.* alarm. —**alarmar**, *vb.*

alastrar(-se), *vb.* spread.

alaúde, *n.m.* lute.

alavanca, *n.f.* lever.

alazão -zã, *adj., n.* sorrel.

albarda, *n.f.* packsaddle.

albatroz, *n.m.* albatross.

albergar, *vb.* house; shelter.

albergue, *n.m.* inn, hostel; shelter.

álbum, *n.m.* album.

alça, *adj.* handle, strap.

alcácer, *n.m.* fortress.

alcachofra, *n.f.* artichoke.

alçada, *n.f.* jurisdiction; authority.

alcagüete, *n.m.* pimp.

alcaide, *n.m.* *(hist.)* governor; mayor.

alcançar, *vb.* reach; catch; be enough.

alcance, *n.m.* reach, range; grasp.

alçapão, *n.m.* trapdoor.

alçar, *vb.* lift, raise.

alcatéia, *n.f.* pack, gang.

alcatra, *n.f.* eye-round (beef).

alcatrão, *n.m.* tar.

alcatraz, *n.m.* albatross; pelican.

alce, *n.m.* moose.

álcool, *n.m.* alcohol.

alcoólatra, *n.m.f.* alcoholic.

Alcorão, *n.m.* Koran.

alcova, *n.f.* alcove.

alcoviteiro -ra, *n.* procurer, -ess.

alcunha, *n.f.* nickname.

aldeão -deã, *n.* villager, peasant.

aldeia, *n.f.* village; Indian village.

aldrava, aldraba, *n.f.* door knocker.

aleatório, *adj.* random.

alecrim, *n.m.* rosemary.

alegação, *n.f.* allegation.

alegar, *vb.* allege.

alegoria, *n.f.* allegory.

alegórico, *adj.* allegorical.

alegrar, *vb.* delight; enliven. a.-se, be glad.

alegre, *adj.* glad, cheerful; *(coll.)* fresh; *(sl.)* tipsy.

alegria, *n.f.* joy, cheer.

aleijado -da, 1. *adj.* crippled. 2. *n.* cripple.

aleijão, *n.m.* deformity.

aleijar, *vb.* cripple.

aleivosia, *n.f.* treachery.

aleivoso, *adj.* treacherous.

aleluia, *n.f., interj.* halleluia.

além, 1. *n.m.* distant place; hereafter. 2. *adv.* beyond, farther. a. de, beyond; besides; a. disso, besides; além do mais, moreover.

Alemanha, *adj.* Germany. A. Ocidental/Oriental, West/East Germany.

alemão -mã, *adj., n.* German.

além-mar, *n.m., adv.* overseas.

além-túmulo, *n.m.* beyond the grave.

alentar, *vb.* encourage.

alento, *n.m.* breath; vigor; courage; inspiration.

alergia, *n.f.* allergy.

alérgico, *adj.* allergic.

alerta, 1. *adj.* alert. 2. *n.m.* alert. 3. *interj.* attention!

alertar, *vb.* alert.

alfabético, *adj.* alphabetical.

alfabetizar, *vb.* make literate.

alfabeto, *n.m.* alphabet.

alface, *n.f.* lettuce.

alfaiate, *n.m.* tailor.

alfândega, *n.f.* customhouse; customs.

alfandegário, *adj.* customs.

alferes, *n.m. (hist.)* second lieutenant.

alfinetada, *n.f.* prick; barb.

alfinete, *n.m.* pin. a. de segurança, safety pin.

alfombra, *n.f.* carpet, rug.

alforje, *n.m.* saddlebag.

alforria, *n.f.* emancipation.

alforriar, *vb.* emancipate.

algaravia, *n.f.* gibberish.

algarismo, *n.m.* number, digit.

algazarra, *n.f.* uproar.

álgebra, *n.f.* algebra.

algemas, *n.f.pl.* handcuffs.

algemar, *vb.* handcuff.

algibeira, *n.f.* pocket.

algo, 1. *pron.* something, anything. 2. *adv.* somewhat.

algodão, *n.m.* cotton. a. doce, cotton candy.

algoz, *n.m.* executioner; torturer.

alguazil, *n.m.* bailiff.

alguém, *pron.* someone, anyone.

algum -ma, *adj., pron.* some, any; *(foll. noun)* no. a. coisa, something, anything; coisa a., nothing; not at all.

algures, *adv.* somewhere.

alheado, *adj.* engrossed; absent-minded; crazy.

alhear, *vb.* alienate; divert. a.-se, be enraptured; go mad.

alheio, 1. *adj.* someone else's; alien; irrelevant. 2. *n.m.* others' property. amigo do a., pickpocket.

alho, *n.m.* garlic.

alhures, *adv.* elsewhere.

ali, *adv.* there. por a., that way; around there.

aliado, *n.m.* ally. —aliar-se, *vb.* ally.

aliança, *n.f.* alliance; wedding ring.

aliás, *adv.* otherwise; that is; incidentally.

alicate, *n.m.* pliers.

alicerces, *n.m.pl.* foundation.

aliciar, *vb.* entice.

alienação, *n.f.* alienation; insanity.

alienado -da, 1. *adj.* enraptured; mad. 2. *n.* lunatic.

alienar, *vb.* alienate; enrapture.

alienígena, *n.m.f.* alien.

alienista, *n.m.f.* psychiatrist.

aligeirar, *vb.* hasten; lighten.

alimentação, *n.f.* nourishment.

alimentar, 1. adj. alimentary. **2.** vb. feed; hold (opinions, feelings, etc.).

alimentício, adj. food.

alimento, n.m. food; (pl.) allowance; alimony.

alinhado, adj. dressed up.

alinhar, vb. align.

alinhavar, vb. baste, tack.

alinho, n.m. alignment; neatness.

alisar, vb. smooth.

alistar(-se), vb. enlist.

aliviar, vb. relieve, ease.

alívio, n.m. relief.

aljava, n.f. quiver.

alma, n.f. soul, spirit; ghost.

almanaque, n.m. almanac.

almejar, vb. long for; covet.

almirante, n.m. admiral.

almíscar, n.m. musk.

almoçar, vb. lunch (on).

almoço, n.m. lunch.

almocreve, n.m. muleteer.

almofada, n.f. cushion, pillow.

almofadinha, n.m. dandy, fop.

almôndega, n.f. meatball.

almoxarife, n.m. stockroom steward.

alô, interj. hello! (telephone).

alojamento, n.m. lodging.

alojar, vb. lodge; shelter. **a.-se,** lodge.

alongar, vb. lengthen. **a.-se,** go away.

aloucado, adj. half-crazy.

alpendre, n.m. shed; porch.

alpercata, alpargata, n.f. sandal.

Alpes, n.m.pl. Alps.

alpinismo, n.m. mountain climbing.

alpinista, n.m.f. mountain climber.

alpiste, n.m., **-ta,** n.f. birdseed.

alquebrar, vb. weaken.

alquimia, n.f. alchemy.

alta, n.f. rise; release (hospital).

alta-fidelidade, n.f. high-fidelity.

altaneiro, adj. haughty.

altar, n.m. altar.

alta-roda, n.f. (coll.) high society.

altear, vb. raise.

alteração, n.f. alteration; unrest.

alterado, adj. upset; rebellious.

alterar, vb. alter; upset. **a.-se,** get mad.

altercação, n.f. altercation.

alternar, vb. alternate. —**alternado,** adj.

alternativa, n.f. alternative. —**alternativo,** adj.

alteza, n.f. height; (cap.) Highness.

altissonante, adj. high-sounding.

altitude, n.f. altitude, height.

altivo, adj. haughty.

alto, 1. adj. high, tall, upper; loud. **2.** n.m. height, top. **3.** adv. loudly. **4.** interj. halt!

alto-falante, n.m. loudspeaker.

alto mar, n.m. high seas.

altruísmo, n.m. altruism.

altura, n.f. height; occasion.

aluado, adj. moonstruck.

alucinação, n.f. hallucination.

alucinado, adj. hallucinating.

alucinar, vb. hallucinate.

alude, n.m. avalanche.

aludir, vb. allude.

alugar, vb. rent, lease, hire.

aluguel, n.m. rent; rental.

alumiar, vb. illuminate; inspire.

alumínio, n.m. aluminum.

alunissagem, n.f. moon landing.

aluno -na, n. pupil, student.

alusão, n.f. allusion.

alvará, n.m. permit; warrant.

alvarenga, n.f. barge.

alvenaria, n.f. masonry.

alvíssaras, 1. n.f.pl. reward. **2.** interj. good news!

alvissareiro, adj. auspicious.

alvo, 1. adj. white. **2.** n. target.

alvorada, n.f. dawn.

alvoroçar, vb. excite. **a.-se,** get excited.

alvoroço, n.m. excitement, commotion.

alvura, n.f. whiteness.

ama, n.f. nursemaid.

amabilidade, n.f. amiability.

amaciar, vb. soften, smooth.

amado -da, 1. adj. beloved. **2.** n. sweetheart.

amador -ra, adj., n. amateur.

amadurecer, vb. mature, ripen.

âmago, n.m. core; essence.

amainar, vb. calm; subside.

amaldiçoar, vb. curse.

amálgama, n.m./f. amalgam.

amalgamar, vb. amalgamate.

amalucado, adj. crazy.

amamentar, vb. breast-feed.

amancebar-se, vb. cohabit, take a lover.

amaneirado, adj. affected.

amanhã, n.m., adv. tomorrow. **depois de a.,** the day after tomorrow.

amanhecer, 1. n.m. dawn. **2.** vb. dawn; wake up.

amansar, vb. tame.

amante, n.m./f. lover; admirer.

amanuense, n.m./f. clerk.

amar, vb. love, like.

amarelinha, n.f. hopscotch.

amarelo, adj. yellow.

amargar, vb. make/be bitter. **ser de a.,** be rough.

amargo, adj. bitter.

amargura, n.f. bitterness.

amarra, n.f. line, rope.

amarrado, adj. tied; (coll.) married/engaged; (sl.) hooked (on).

amarrar, vb. tie. **a. a cara,** frown; **a.-se,** (coll.) get married/ engaged.

amarrotar, vb. crumple.

ama-seca, n.f. nursemaid.

amásia, n.f. concubine.

amasiar-se, vb. take a lover.

amassar, vb. crumple; knead.

amável, adj. kind, likeable.

Amazonas, n.m. Amazon (river).

amazonense, 1. adj. of/pert. to the state of Amazonas. **2.** n.m./f. native of Amazonas.

Amazônia, n.f. Amazon region.

amazônico, adj. Amazonian.

ambição, n.f. ambition.

ambicioso, adj. ambitious.

ambidestro, adj. ambidextrous.

ambiental, adj. environmental.

ambientar-se, vb. become acclimated.

ambiente, n.m. environment; atmosphere.

ambigüidade, n.f. ambiguity.

ambíguo, adj. ambiguous.

âmbito, n.m. field.

ambivalente, adj. ambivalent.

ambos, adj., pron. both.

ambulância, n.f. ambulance.

ambulante, adj. walking, traveling.

ameaça, n.f. threat, menace.

ameaçar, vb. threaten, menace.

amedrontar, vb. frighten.

amêijoa, n.f. clam.

ameixa, n.f. plum.

amém, interj. amen.

amêndoa, n.f. almond.

amendoim, n.m. peanut(s).

amenidade, n.f. pleasantness.

amenizar, vb. make pleasant.

ameno, adj. pleasant.

América, n.f. America. **A. Central,** Central America; **A. do Norte,** North America; **A. do Sul,** South America; **A. Latina,** Latin America.

americano -na, adj., n. American.

ameríndio -dia, 1. adj. Amerindian. **2.** n. Amerind.

amerissagem, n.f. water landing.

amestrar, vb. train.

amido, n.m. starch.

amiga, n.f. friend (f.); mistress.

amigação, n.f. illicit love affair.

amigar-se, vb. shack up.

amigável, adj. friendly.

amígdala, n.f. tonsil.

amigo -ga, n. friend.

amigo-da-onça, n.m. (coll.) false friend.

amimar, vb. fondle; pamper.

amistoso, adj. friendly.

amiudar, vb. repeat often.

amiúde, adv. often.

amizade, n.f. friendship.

amo, n.m. master.

amofinar, vb. annoy. **a.-se,** get upset.

amolação, n.f. (coll.) annoyance.

amolar, vb. (coll.) annoy; **vá á o boi!,** go jump in the lake!

amoldar, vb. mold. **a.-se,** adapt.

amolecer, vb. soften.

amoníaco, n.m. ammonia.

amontoar, vb. pile up.

amor, n.m. love. **fazer a.,** make love; **meu a.,** darling; **pelo a. de,** for the sake/love of.

amora, n.f. mulberry.

amordaçar, vb. muzzle.

amoroso, adj. amorous.

amor-próprio, *n.m.* self-esteem.

amortalhar, *vb.* shroud.

amortecedor, *n.m.* shock absorber.

amortecer, *vb.* deaden; diminish.

amortizar, *vb.* amortize.

amostra, *n.f.* sample. **a. acidental/randômica**, random sample.

amostragem, *n.f.* sampling.

amotinar-se, *vb.* mutiny, rebel.

amparar, *vb.* shelter; back.

amparo, *n.m.* protection; backing.

amplexo, *n.m.* embrace.

ampliação, *n.f.* amplification, enlargement.

ampliar, *vb.* amplify, enlarge.

amplificador, *n.m.* amplifier.

amplificar, *vb.* amplify, enlarge.

amplitude, amplidão, *n.f.* amplitude, vastness.

amplo, *adj.* ample, broad.

ampulheta, *n.f.* hourglass.

amputar, *vb.* amputate.

amuado, *adj.* sulky.

amuar, *vb.* sulk.

amuleto, *n.m.* amulet, charm.

amuo, *n.m.* sulkiness.

anacrônico, *adj.* anachronistic.

anacronismo, *n.m.* anachronism.

anágua, *n.f.* petticoat.

anais, *n.m.pl.* annals.

anal, *adj.* anal.

analfabetismo, *n.m.* illiteracy.

analfabeto, *adj., n.m.* illiterate.

analgésico, *adj., n.m.* painkiller.

analisar, *vb.* analyze.

análise, *n.f.* analysis.

analista, *n.m.f.* analyst.

analítico, *adj.* analytical.

analogia, *n.f.* analogy.

análogo, *adj.* analogous.

ananás, *n.m.* pineapple.

anão -nã, *n.* dwarf.

anarquia, *n.f.* anarchy.

anarquista, *n.m.f.* anarchist.

anarquizar, *vb.* confuse, mess up.

anatomia, *n.f.* anatomy.

anca, *n.f.* haunch, hip.

ancestral, **1.** *adj.* ancestral. **2.** *n.m.* ancestor.

ancho, *adj.* wide, broad.

ancião -ciã, 1. *adj.* ancient, elderly. **2.** *n.* elderly person.

ancinho, *n.m.* rake.

âncora, *n.f.* anchor. **—ancorar**, *vb.*

ancoradouro, *n.m.* anchorage.

andaime, *n.m.* scaffold.

andamento, *n.m.* walk; progress.

andar, 1. *n.m.* walk; story, floor. **a. térreo**, ground floor. **2.** *vb.* walk, go; move; run; be.

andarilho, *n.m.* walker.

andas, *n.f.pl.* stilts.

andino, *adj.* Andean.

andor, *n.m.* litter.

andorinha, *n.f. (ornith.)* swallow.

andrajos, *n.m.pl.* rags.

andrajoso, *adj.* ragged.

anedota, *n.f.* anecdote; joke.

anel, *n.m.* ring.

anelar, *vb.* desire, long for.

anelo, *n.m.* desire, longing.

anêmico, *adj.* anemic.

anestesia, *n.f.* anesthesia.

anexar, *vb.* attach.

anexim, *n.m.* proverb.

anexo, *adj.* attached. **em a.**, attached, enclosed.

anfíbio, *adj., n.m.* amphibian, amphibious.

anfiteatro, *n.m.* amphitheater.

anfitrião -trioa, *n.* host, -ess.

angariar, *vb.* attract; collect.

anglicismo, *n.m.* Anglicism.

anglo-saxão -xã, *adj., n.* Anglo-Saxon.

angolano -na, *adj., n.* Angolan.

angra, *n.f.* cove.

angu, *n.m.* cornmeal mush.

ângulo, *n.m.* angle.

angústia, *n.f.* anguish, anxiety.

angustiar, *vb.* anguish.

angusto, *adj.* narrow.

anhangá, *n.m.* (Indian) evil spirit.

aniagem, *n.f.* burlap.

anil, *n.m.* indigo.

animação, *n.f.* animation; liveliness.

animado, *adj.* animated; lively.

animal, *adj., n.m.* animal.

animar, *vb.* animate; enliven; cheer up; encourage.

ânimo, *n.m.* spirit; courage; disposition.

animosidade, *n.f.* animosity.
aninhar, *vb.* nestle.
aniquilar, *vb.* annihilate.
anistia, *n.f.* amnesty. —**anistiar,** *vb.*
aniversariante, *n.m.f.* birthday celebrant.
aniversário, *n.m.* birthday; anniversary.
anjo, *n.m.* angel.
ano, *n.m.* year. **a. bissexto,** leap year; **A. Bom,** New Year; **a. letivo,** school year; **fazer anos,** have a birthday.
anoitecer, 1. *n.m.* nightfall. **2.** *vb.* grow dark.
ano-luz, *n.m.* light-year.
anomalia, *n.f.* anomaly.
anômalo, *adj.* anomalous.
anonimato, *n.m.* anonymity.
anônimo, *adj.* anonymous.
anormal, *adj.* abnormal.
anotar, *vb.* jot down; annotate.
anseio, *n.m.* longing; anxiety.
ânsia, *n.f.* anguish; longing.
ansiar, *vb.* torment; long for.
ansiedade, *n.f.* anxiety, anguish; longing.
ansioso, *adj.* anxious; eager.
anta, *n.f.* tapir.
antagônico, *adj.* antagonistic.
antagonismo, *n.m.* antagonism.
antagonista, *n.m.f.* antagonist.
antanho, *adv.* in times past.
Antártica, *n.f.* Antarctica.
ante, *prep.* before, in front of.
antebraço, *n.m.* forearm.
antecedência, *n.f.* antecedence, advance. **com a.,** in advance.
antecedente, *n.m.* antecedent.
antecipação, *n.f.* anticipation; advance.
antecipado, *adj.* anticipated; in advance.
antecipar, *vb.* anticipate; do in advance.
antemão, *adv.* **de a.,** beforehand.
antena, *n.f.* antenna; feeler. **a. parabólica,** satellite dish.
anteontem, *adv.* the day before yesterday.
antepassado, *n.m.* ancestor.
anterior, *adj.* anterior, preceding.
antes, *adv.* before; rather. **a. de,** before.

anti-, *pref.* anti-.
antiaéreo, *adj.* antiaircraft.
antibiótico, *adj., n.m.* antibiotic.
anticoncepcional, *adj., n.m.* contraceptive.
anticorpo, *n.m.* antibody.
antídoto, *n.m.* antidote.
antigamente, *adv.* formerly.
antigo, *adj.* old, ancient, old-fashioned.
antiguidade, *n.f.* antiquity; (*pl.*) antiques.
Antilhas, *n.f.pl.* Antilles.
antipatia, *n.f.* antipathy.
antipático, *adj.* nasty, obnoxious.
antiquário -ria, *n.* antiquarian.
anti-séptico, *adj.* antiseptic.
antítese, *n.f.* antithesis.
antojo, *n.m.* whim.
antologia, *n.f.* anthology.
antro, *n.m.* cave; den; (*sl.*) dive.
antropofagia, *n.f.* cannibalism.
antropófago, *n.m.* cannibal.
antropologia, *n.f.* anthropology.
antropólogo -ga, *n.* anthropologist.
anual, *adj.* annual.
anuário, *n.m.* yearbook.
anuidade, *n.f.* annuity, fee.
anular, *vb.* annul.
anunciar, *vb.* announce; advertise.
anúncio, *n.m.* announcement; advertisement.
ânus, *n.m.* anus.
anzol, *n.m.* fishhook.
ao, *contr.* of **a** + **o.** to the, at the; to the one (that).
aonde, *adv.* whereto, where.
aos, *contr.* of **a** + **os.** to the, at the; to the ones (that).
apagar, *vb.* extinguish; turn off; erase; pass out; (*sl.*) kill; (*sl.*) die.
apaixonado, *adj.* in love; passionate, impassioned.
apaixonar-se (por), *vb.* fall in love (with).
apalavrar, *vb.* pledge.
apalpar, *vb.* touch, feel.
apanhado, *n.m.* summary; pleat.
apanhar, *vb.* pick up, grab.

aparador, *n.m.* sideboard, buffet.

aparar, *vb.* trim, pare.

aparato, *n.m.* pomp.

aparatoso, *adj.* showy.

aparecer, *vb.* appear, show up.

aparecimento, *n.m.* appearance.

aparelhar, *vb.* outfit, rig.

aparelho, *n.m.* apparatus, machine; telephone; toilet; *(dent.)* braces; *(anat.)* system.

aparência, *n.f.* appearance, air.

aparentar, *vb.* seem; feign.

aparente, *adj.* apparent.

aparição, *n.f.* appearance; apparition.

apartamento, *n.m.* apartment; hotel room.

apartar, *vb.* separate; seclude.

aparte, *n.m. (theat.)* aside.

apascentar, *vb.* graze.

apatia, *n.f.* apathy.

apático, *adj.* apathetic.

apavorar, *vb.* frighten.

apaziguar, *vb.* pacify.

apear-se, *vb.* dismount, alight.

apedrejar, *vb.* stone.

apegar-se, *vb.* adhere, stick.

apego, *n.m.* attachment; tenacity.

apelar, *vb.* appeal; resort; *(sl.)* **a. para a ignorância,** become rude.

apelido, *n.m.* nickname. **—apelidar,** *vb.*

apelo, *n.m.* appeal.

apenas, 1. *adv.* only; hardly. **2.** *conj.* as soon as.

apêndice, *n.m.* appendix.

apequenar, *vb.* make small.

aperfeiçoar, *vb.* perfect; improve.

aperitivo, *n.m.* apéritif.

apertado, *adj.* tight; miserly; in straits; *(coll.)* needing to go to the bathroom.

apertar, *vb.* tighten; squeeze; press; hasten; be pressing. **a. a mão,** shake hands.

aperto, *n.m.* tightening; squeeze; tight spot; urgency; crowd. **a. de mão,** handshake.

apesar de, *prep.* in spite of.

apetecer, *vb.* desire; appeal to.

apetecível, *adj.* appetizing.

apetrecho, *n.m.* equipment.

ápice, *n.m.* apex.

apiedar-se, *vb.* pity.

apimentado, *adj.* spicy, hot.

apinhar, *vb.* crowd, jam.

apitar, *vb.* blow a whistle.

apito, *n.m.* whistle. **que a. você toca?,** what's your line of work?

aplacar, *vb.* placate.

aplainar, *vb.* plane, level.

aplanar, *vb.* level, smooth.

aplaudir, *vb.* applaud.

aplauso, *n.m.* applause.

aplicação, *n.f.* application; use; diligence.

aplicar, *vb.* apply; inflict; invest.

apocalipse, *n.m.* apocalypse.

apodar, *vb.* mock; nickname.

apoderar-se, *vb.* take control.

apodo, *n.m.* nickname.

apodrecer, *vb.* rot.

apogeu, *n.m.* apogee.

apoiar, *vb.* support. **a.-se,** lean.

apoio, *n.m.* support; foundation.

apólice, *n.f.* policy, bond.

apologia, *n.f.* apology.

apontamento, *n.m.* note.

apontar, *n.m.* point (out); note; aim; appear.

apoplexia, *n.f.* apoplexy, stroke.

apoquentar, *vb.* annoy.

aportar, *vb.* arrive.

aportuguesado, *adj.* Portuguese-like.

após, *adv., prep.* after. **dia a. dia,** day after day.

aposentadoria, *n.f.* retirement; pension.

aposentar-se, *vb.* retire.

aposento, *n.m.* dwelling; room.

após-guerra, *n.m.* post-war period.

apossar-se, *vb.* seize.

aposta, *n.f.* bet. **—apostar,** *vb.*

apostila, *n.f.* class handout.

apóstolo, *n.m.* apostle.

apóstrofo, *n.m.* apostrophe.

apoucar, *vb.* diminish; belittle.

aprazar, *vb.* please.

apreçar, *vb.* appraise; price.

apreciar, *vb.* appreciate.

apreciável, *adj.* appreciable.

apreço, *n.m.* appreciation, regard.

apreender, *vb.* apprehend.

apreensão, *n.f.* apprehension.

apregoar, *vb.* announce.

aprender, *vb.* learn. **a. a,** learn how.

aprendiz, *n.m.f.* apprentice; learner.

aprendizado, *n.m.,* **aprendizagem,** *n.f.* apprenticeship.

apresentação, *n.f.* presentation; introduction.

apresentar, *vb.* present; introduce.

apressado, *adj.* hurried.

apressar, *vb.* hurry, rush.

aprimorar, *vb.* perfect.

aprisco, *n.m.* sheepfold.

aprisionar, *vb.* imprison.

aprofundar, *vb.* deepen; delve into.

aprontar, *vb.* prepare; *(sl.)* play (tricks).

apropriado, *adj.* appropriate. —**apropriar-se,** *vb.*

aprovação, *n.f.* approval.

aprovar, *vb.* approve; pass.

aproveitamento, *n.m.* utilization.

aproveitar, *vb.* take advantage of, use. **a.-se de,** exploit.

aproximação, *n.f.* approximation; close contact.

aproximar, *vb.* approximate. **a.-se de,** approach.

aprumar, *vb.* set upright. **a.-se,** straighten up.

aprumo, *n.m.* aplomb; uprightness.

aptidão, *n.f.* aptitude.

apto, *adj.* apt, able.

apunhalar, *vb.* stab.

apupar, *vb.* jeer.

apurado, *adj.* refined; in trouble.

apurar, *vb.* perfect; verify.

apuro, *n.m.* refinement; verification; jam. **em apuros,** in a fix.

aquarela, *n.f.* watercolor.

aquartelar, *vb.* billet.

aquático, *adj.* aquatic.

aquecer, *vb.* heat.

aquecimento, *n.m.* heating.

aqueduto, *n.m.* aqueduct.

aquele, aquela, *dem. adj., pron.* that; that one; the former.

àquele, àquela, *contr. of* a + aquele/a. to that (one).

aquém, *adv.* on this side; **a. de,** this side of; less than.

aquentar, *vb.* heat up.

aqui, *adv.* here. **por a.,** this way.

aquiescer, *vb.* acquiesce.

aquilatar, *vb.* appraise.

aquilo, *neut. dem. pron.* that; that thing.

àquilo, *contr. of* a + aquilo. to that, to that thing.

aquinhoar, *vb.* apportion.

aquisição, *n.f.* acquisition.

aquisitivo, *adj.* acquisitive.

ar, *n.m.* air; appearance. **a. condicionado,** air-conditioning; -conditioned; **dar-se ares,** put on airs.

árabe, 1. *adj.* Arab, Arabic. **2.** *n.m.* Arab; Arabic (language).

Arábia, *n.f.* Arabia. **A. Saudita,** Saudi Arabia.

arado, 1. *adj.* hungry. **2.** *n.m.* plow; plowed land.

aragem, *n.f.* breeze.

arame, *n.m.* wire; *(sl.)* money. **a. farpado,** barbed wire.

aranha, *n.f.* spider.

arapuca, *n.f.* trap.

arar, *vb.* plow.

arara, *n.f.* macaw, parrot.

arataca, *n.m.* Northerner.

arauto, *n.m.* herald.

arável, *adj.* arable.

arbitrar, *vb.* arbitrate.

arbitrário, *adj.* arbitrary.

arbítrio, *n.m.* discretion. **livre a.,** free will.

árbitro, *n.m.* arbiter, referee.

arbusto, *n.m.* bush.

arca, *n.f.* ark; chest. **a. de Noé,** Noah's ark.

arcabouço, *n.m.* framework.

arcada, *n.f.* arcade.

arcaico, *adj.* archaic.

arcanjo, *n.m.* archangel.

arcar, *vb.* bend; struggle. **a. com,** bear.

arcebispo, *n.m.* archbishop.

arco, *n.m.* arch; arc; bow.

arco-íris, *n.m.* rainbow.

ardente, *adj.* burning; ardent.

arder, *vb.* burn; sting.

ardil, *n.m.* trick, ruse.

ardor, *n.m.* ardor.

árduo, *adj.* arduous.

área, *n.f.* area; patio; work area.

areal, *n.m.* sandy stretch.

areia, *n.f.* sand. **a. movediça**, quicksand.

arejar, *vb.* air out; relax.

arena, *n.f.* arena.

arenga, *n.f.* harangue. —**arengar**, *vb.*

arenque, *n.m.* herring.

aresta, *n.f.* edge, corner.

arfar, *vb.* pant.

argamassa, *n.f.* mortar.

Argélia, *n.f.* Algeria; **Argel**, Algiers.

argentino -na, *adj.*, *n.* Argentine.

argila, *n.f.* clay.

argola, *n.f.* metal ring.

argúcia, *n.f.* subtlety, ingenuity.

argüir, *vb.* argue.

argumentar, *vb.* argue.

argumento, *n.m.* argument.

arguto, *adj.* subtle, ingenious.

aridez, *n.f.* aridity.

árido, *adj.* arid.

arisco, *adj.* shy; elusive.

aristocracia, *n.f.* aristocracy.

aristocrata, *n.m.f.* aristocrat.

aritmética, *n.f.* arithmetic.

arma, *n.f.* arm, weapon. **a. branca**, knife; **a. de fogo**, firearm.

armação, *n.f.* framework.

armada, *n.f.* armada, fleet.

armadilha, *n.f.* trap.

armador, *n.m.* shipowner.

armadura, *n.f.* armor.

armamento, *n.m.* armament.

armar, *vb.* arm; set up; cause.

armarinho, *n.m.* dry goods shop.

armário, *n.m.* wardrobe, closet.

armazém, *n.m.* warehouse; grocery store.

armazenar, *vb.* store.

arminho, *n.m.* ermine.

arnês, *n.m.* harness; armor; shelter.

aro, *n.m.* arc; hoop; rim.

aroma, *n.f.* aroma.

aromático, *adj.* aromatic.

arpão, *n.m.* harpoon. —**arpoar**, *vb.*

arquear, *vb.* arch.

arqueiro, *n.m.* archer; goalie.

arquejar, *vb.* pant.

arqueologia, *n.f.* archeology.

arqueólogo -ga, *n.* archeologist.

arquibancada, *n.f.* grandstand.

arquipélago, *n.m.* archipelago.

arquiteto -ta, *n.* architect.

arquitetônico, *adj.* architectural.

arquivar, *vb.* file; record; shelve; *(coll.)* forget.

arquivo, *n.m.* file; archive; file cabinet.

arrabalde, *n.m.* suburb.

arraia, *n.f.* (*ichth.*) ray.

arraial, *n.m.* small village.

arraia-miúda, *n.f.* riffraff.

arraigado, *adj.* deep-rooted.

arraigar-se, *vb.* take root.

arrancada, *n.f.* pull; start.

arrancar, *vb.* pull out; start up; leave.

arranha-céu, *n.m.* skyscraper.

arranhão, *n.m.* scratch, scrape.

arranhar, *vb.* scratch; scrape; scrape by in.

arranjar, *vb.* arrange, put in order; get. **a.-se**, get by, manage.

arranjo, *n.m.* arrangement; racket.

arranque, *n.m.* starter; sudden start.

arrasar, *vb.* demolish.

arrastão, *n.m.* drag; dragnet.

arrastar, *vb.* drag; drawl. **a.-se**, crawl.

arrasto, *n.m.* drag; crawl.

arrazoar, *vb.* justify.

arre, *interj.* darn it!

arrear, *vb.* saddle; array.

arrebanhar, *vb.* round up.

arrebatado, *adj.* rash; carried away.

arrebatamento, *vb.* anger; ecstasy.

arrebatar, *vb.* carry off/away; anger.

arrebentar, *vb.* burst, split.

arrebitado, *adj.* turned up.

arrecadar, *vb.* collect; levy.

arrecife, *n.m.* reef.

arredar(-se), *vb.* move away.

arredio, *adj.* withdrawn; stray.

arredondar, *vb.* round (off).

arredores, *n.m.pl.* surroundings.

arrefecer, *vb.* cool off.

arregaçar, *vb.* roll up.

arregalar, *vb.* open wide.

arreganhar, vb. grin; snarl.

arreio, n.m. harness; decoration.

arrelia, n.m. quarrel; anger.

arreliar, vb. annoy. **a.-se,** get mad.

arrematar, vb. finish; sell off.

arremedar, vb. imitate; mock.

arremedo, n.m. mimicry; mockery.

arremessar, vb. hurl. —**arremesso,** n.m.

arremeter, vb. assault. —**arremetida,** n.f.

arrendar, vb. lease.

arrenegar, vb. detest; curse.

arrepender-se, vb. repent; regret; change one's mind.

arrepiar, vb. horrify; bristle.

arrepio, n.m. chill, shiver.

arrestar, vb. (jur.) seize.

arrevesar, vb. reverse, turn around.

arriar, vb. weaken, collapse.

arribação, n.f. migration.

arribar, vb. migrate, leave.

arrimar, vb. prop. —**arrimo,** n.m.

arriscado, adj. risky.

arriscar, vb. risk. **a.-se,** run a risk.

arrochar, vb. squeeze. —**arrocho,** n.m.

arrogância, n.f. arrogance.

arrogante, adj. arrogant.

arrojado, adj. bold, daring.

arrojar, vb. fling.

arrojo, n.m. boldness.

arromba, n.f. **de a.,** (sl.) terrific.

arrombar, vb. break in/down.

arrotar, vb. belch. —**arroto,** n.m.

arroubar, vb. entrance.

arroz, n.m. rice.

arruaça, n.f. street fight.

arruela, n.f. washer.

arrufar, vb. annoy.

arruinar, vb. ruin, wreck.

arrumar, vb. arrange, straighten; get. **a.-se,** get by.

arsenal, n.m. arsenal.

arsênico, n.m. arsenic.

arte, n.f. art, craft; (coll.) mischief. **belas artes,** fine arts.

artefato, n.m. artifact.

artéria, n.f. artery.

artesanato, n.m. handicraft.

artesão -sã, n. artisan.

Ártico, adj. Arctic.

articulação, n.f. articulation; joint.

articular, vb. articulate.

articulista, n.m.f. article writer.

artífice, n.m.f. craftsman.

artificial, adj. artificial.

artifício, n.m. artifice.

artificioso, adj. skillful; sly.

artigo, n.m. article.

artilharia, n.f. artillery.

artimanha, n.f. trick.

artista, n.m.f. artist; (coll.) mischief-maker.

artístico, adj. artistic.

artrite, n.f. arthritis.

arvorar, vb. hoist.

árvore, n.f. tree.

as, f.pl. def. art. the.

às, contr. of **a** + **as** to the, at the; to the ones (that).

ás, n.m. ace.

asa, n.f. wing.

asa-delta, n.f. hang glider.

ascendência, n.f. ascendancy; ancestry.

ascendente, 1. adj. rising; **2.** n.m. ancestor.

ascender, vb. ascend.

ascensor, n.m. elevator.

ascensorista, n.m.f. elevator operator.

asco, n.m. nausea, disgust.

áscua, n.f. ember.

asfaltar, vb. asphalt, pave.

asfixiar, vb. asphyxiate.

asiático, adj. Asian, Asiatic.

asilo, n.m. asylum, shelter.

asma, n.f. asthma.

asneira, asnice, n.f. stupidity; stupid act/remark.

asno, n.m. donkey; idiot.

aspa, n.f. horn; (pl.) quotation marks.

aspecto, aspeto, n.m. aspect.

aspereza, n.f. roughness; harshness.

áspero, adj. rough; harsh.

aspiração, n.f. aspiration.

aspirador (de pó), n.m. vacuum cleaner.

aspirar, vb. aspire; aspirate.

aspirina, n.f. aspirin.

asqueroso, adj. disgusting.

assacar, vb. defame.

assado, adj. roasted. **assim ou**

a., in one way or another; **nem
assim nem a.**, in no way whatever.

assalariar, vb. salary.

assaltante, n.m.f. attacker; robber.

assaltar, vb. assault; hold up.

assalto, n.m. assault; hold-up.

assanhar, vb. excite; anger. **a.-se**, get excited.

assar, vb. roast.

assassinar, vb. kill, murder, assassinate.

assassínio, assassinato, n.m. murder, assassination.

assassino -na, n. murderer, assassin.

assaz, adv. enough; rather.

assear, vb. clean.

assediar, vb. siege. —**assédio**, n.m.

assegurar, vb. assure.

asseio, n.m. cleanliness, neatness.

assembléia, n.f. assembly.

assemelhar-se, vb. resemble.

assentar, vb. seat; set.

assentir, vb. assent, consent.

assento, n.m. seat; foundation.

asserção, n.f. assertion.

assessor -ra, n. adviser.

assessorar, vb. advise.

asseverar, vb. affirm.

assíduo, adj. assiduous.

assim, adv. thus, so, like this; therefore. **a. mesmo**, just so; even so; **a. que**, as soon as; **e a. por diante**, and so forth; **mesmo a.**, even so; **por a. dizer**, so to speak.

assimilação, n.f. assimilation.

assimilar, vb. assimilate.

assinalar, vb. mark, point out.

assinante, n.m.f. signer; subscriber.

assinar, vb. sign; subscribe (to).

assinatura, n.f. signature; subscription. **tomar a. com**, (coll.) pick on.

assistência, n.f. attendance; audience; assistance. **a. social**, social work.

assistente, 1. adj. assistant. 2. n.m.f. assistant; spectator.

assistir, vb. attend; watch (TV); assist.

assoalho, n.m. floor.

assoar(-se), vb. blow (one's nose).

assobiar, vb. whistle. —**assobio**, n.m.

associação, n.f. association.

associar, vb. associate. **a.-se**, associate; join up.

assolar, vb. devastate.

assomar, vb. rise; emerge. **a.-se**, get mad.

assombração, n.f. awe; fear; ghost.

assombrar, vb. astonish; frighten; haunt. **casa assombrada**, haunted house.

assombro, n.m. awe; fear.

assumido, adj. avowed.

assumir, vb. assume; avow.

assunção, n.f. assumption.

assunto, n.m. subject, topic, matter.

assustar, vb. frighten.

asterisco, n.m. asterisk.

astilha, n.f. chip, splinter.

astro, n.m. star.

astrologia, n.f. astrology.

astrólogo -ga, n. astrologer.

astronauta, n.m.f. astronaut.

astronomia, n.f. astronomy.

astronômico, adj. astronomical.

astrônomo -ma, n. astronomer.

astúcia, n.f. astuteness; trickery.

astucioso, adj. astute, tricky.

ata, n.f. minutes, records.

atabaque, n.m. large drum.

atacadista, n.m.f. wholesaler.

atacado, n.m. **por a.**, wholesale.

atacar, vb. attack.

atadura, n.f. bandage; band.

atalaia, n.m.f. sentry; n.f. watchtower.

atalho, n.m. short cut.

ataque, n.m. attack.

atar, vb. tie.

atarefado, adj. busy.

atarracado, adj. squat, stocky.

ataúde, n.m. coffin.

ataviar, vb. ornament. —**atavio**, n.m.

atazanar, vb. torment.

até, 1. prep. until. **a. amanhã**, until tomorrow; **a. logo**, so long. 2. adv. even.

atear, vb. light.

ateísmo, n.m. atheism.

ateliê, n.m. studio, workshop.

atemorizar, *vb.* frighten.

Atenas, *n.f.* Athens.

atenção, *n.f.* attention.

atencioso, *adj.* attentive; respectful.

atender, *vb.* tend, pay attention to; wait on; receive; answer.

atendimento, *n.m.* attention, reception.

atentar, *vb.* watch. **a. contra,** assault.

atento, *adj.* attentive; polite.

atenuar, *vb.* attenuate.

aterrar, *vb.* cover with dirt; terrify; land.

aterrissagem, -zagem, *n.f.* landing.

aterrissar, -zar, *vb.* land (a plane).

aterro, *n.m.* landfill.

aterrorizar, *vb.* terrify.

atestado, *n.m.* certificate. **a. de óbito,** death certificate; **a. de saúde,** health certificate.

atestar, *vb.* attest, certify.

ateu -téia, *n.* atheist.

atiçar, *vb.* stoke; incite.

atinar, *vb.* guess; discover.

atingir, *vb.* reach, attain.

atiradeira, *n.f.* slingshot.

atirador -ra, *n.* marksman -woman.

atirar, *vb.* throw; fire (gun).

atitude, *n.f.* attitude.

ativar, *vb.* activate.

atividade, *n.f.* activity.

ativista, *n.m.f.* activist.

ativo, 1. *adj.* active. **2.** *n.m.* assets.

Atlântico, *adj., n.m.* Atlantic.

atleta, *n.m.f.* athlete.

altlético, *adj.* athletic.

atletismo, *n.m.* track and field; athletics.

atmosfera, *n.f.* atmosphere.

ato, *n.m.* act.

à-toa, *adj.* careless; *(coll.)* useless.

atolar-se, *vb.* bog down; get in a jam.

atoleiro, *n.m.* mudhole; jam.

atômico, *adj.* atomic. **bomba atômica,** atomic bomb; **guerra atômica,** atomic war; **peso a.,** atomic weight; **reator a.,** atomic reactor.

átomo, *n.m.* atom.

atônito, *adj.* astonished.

átono, *adj. (gram.)* unstressed.

ator, *n.m.* actor.

atordoar, *vb.* daze, stun.

atormentar, *vb.* torment.

atração, *n.f.* attraction.

atracar, *vb.* dock.

atraente, *adj.* attractive.

atraiçoar, *vb.* betray.

atrair, *vb.* attract.

atrapalhar, *vb.* complicate, upset; get in the way.

atrás, 1. *adv.* back; behind; ago. **2.** *prep.* **a. de,** after, behind.

atrasado, *adj.* behind, late, slow (clock); backward; *(sl.)* sexually starved.

atrasar, *vb.* delay; arrive late.

atraso, *n.m.* delay; backwardness.

atrativo, 1. *adj.* attractive. **2.** *n.m.* attraction.

através, 1. *adv.* across. **2.** *prep.* **a. de,** across, through.

atravessar, *vb.* cross; place across.

atrelar, *vb.* harness; dominate.

atrever-se, *vb.* dare, risk.

atrevido, *adj.* daring; insolent.

atrevimento, *n.m.* daring; insolence.

atribuir, *vb.* attribute. —**atributo,** *n.m.*

atrito, *n.m.* friction; clash.

atriz, *n.f.* actress.

atrocidade, *n.f.* atrocity.

atrofiar(-se), *vb.* atrophy. —**atrofia,** *n.f.*

atropelar, *vb.* run over.

atropelo, *n.m.* running over; bustle; offense.

atroz, *adj.* atrocious.

atual, *adj.* present, current.

atualidade, *n.f.* the present; *(pl.)* news.

atualizar, *vb.* modernize, update.

atuar, *vb.* activate; act.

atulhar, *vb.* cram; block.

atum, *n.m.* tuna.

aturar, *vb.* endure.

aturdir, *vb.* daze, stun.

audácia, *n.f.* audacity.

audaz, *adj.* audacious.

audição, *n.f.* audition; hearing.

audiência, *n.f.* hearing; audience.

auditório, *n.m.* audience; auditorium.

auferir, *vb.* get, draw.

auge, *n.m.* peak, climax.

augúrio, *n.m.* augury, omen.

augusto, *adj.* august.

aula, *n.f.* class, lesson. **dar a.,** teach a class.

aumentar, *vb.* increase. **a. de peso,** gain weight.

aumentativo, *adj., n.m. (gram.)* augmentative.

aumento, *n.m.* increase; raise.

áureo, *adj.* golden.

auréola, *n.f.* halo.

aurora, *n.f.* aurora; dawn.

auscultar, *vb. (med.)* listen to.

ausência, *n.f.* absence.

ausentar-se, *vb.* absent oneself.

ausente, *adj.* absent.

auspício, *n.m.* auspice; omen.

auspicioso, *adj.* auspicious.

austeridade, *n.f.* austerity.

austero, *adj.* austere.

australiano -na, *adj., n.* Australian.

austríaco, *adj.* Austrian.

autenticidade, *n.f.* authenticity.

autêntico, *adj.* authentic.

auto, *n.m.* auto; *(jur.)* brief; edict; miracle play.

auto-, *pref.* self-.

autocrata, *n.m.f.* autocrat.

autóctone, *adj.* autochthonous.

auto-da-fé, *n.m.* auto-da-fé.

autodidata, 1. *adj.* self-taught. **2.** *n.m.f.* autodidact.

auto-estrada, *n.f.* freeway.

autógrafo, *n.m.* autograph. —**autografar,** *vb.*

automático, *adj.* automatic.

automobilismo, *n.m.* automobile racing.

automóvel, *n.m.* automobile. —**automobilístico,** *adj.*

autonomia, *n.f.* autonomy.

autônomo, *adj.* autonomous.

autópsia, *n.f.* autopsy.

autor -ra, *n.* author.

autoria, *n.f.* authorship.

autoridade, *n.f.* authority.

autoritário, *adj.* authoritarian.

autorizar, *vb.* authorize.

auxiliar, 1. *vb.* aid, help. **2.** *adj.* auxiliary.

auxílio, *n.m.* aid, help.

avacalhação, *n.f. (coll.)* mess.

avacalhar, *vb. (coll.)* mess up.

avalancha, *n.f.* avalanche.

avaliação, *n.f.* evaluation.

avaliar, *vb.* evaluate.

avançar, *vb.* advance. —**avanço,** *n.m.*

avantajar, *vb.* have/give an advantage over.

avante, *adv.* ahead, onward.

avarento, *adj.* greedy.

avareza, *n.f.* greed.

avaro, *adj.* greedy.

avaria, *n.f.* damage. —**avariar,** *vb.*

ave, 1. *n.f.* bird; poultry. **2.** *interj.* ave!, ave! hail!; **a. Maria!,** hail Mary! heavens!

aveia, *n.f.* oats.

avenida, *n.f.* avenue.

avental, *n.m.* apron.

aventura, *n.f.* adventure.

aventureiro -ra, *n.* adventurer -ess.

averiguar, *vb.* inquire; find out.

aversão, *n.f.* aversion.

avessas, *n.f.pl.* **às avessas,** upside down, inside out, backwards.

avesso, 1. *adj.* contrary, averse. **2.** *n.m.* reverse.

avestruz, *n.m.f.* ostrich.

aviação, *n.f.* aviation.

aviador -ra, *n.* aviator.

avião, *n.m.* airplane. **a. a jato,** jet plane.

aviar, *vb.* send off; carry out; fill (prescription).

avidez, *n.f.* avidness; greed.

ávido, *adj.* avid, eager, greedy.

aviltar, *vb.* degrade.

avisar, *vb.* notify, advise.

aviso, *n.m.* notice, warning.

avistar, *vb.* sight. **a.-se (com),** interview (with).

avivar, *vb.* enliven.

avo, *n.* fraction marker (eleven and up) e.g., **três doze avos** (3/12).

avó, *n.f.* grandmother.

avô, *n.m.* grandfather.

avós, *n.m.pl.* grandparents.

avoado, *adj.* dizzy, giddy.

avoengo, *n.m.* ancestor.

avulso, *adj.* separate, detached.

avultar, *vb.* enlarge; loom large.

axila, *n.f.* armpit.

axioma, *n.m.* axiom.

azáfama, *n.f.* bustle.

azar, 1. *n.m.* bad luck; chance. **2.** *interj.* **azar!,** tough luck!

azarado, azarento, *adj.* unlucky.

azedo, *adj.* sour.— **azedar,** *vb.*

azedume, *n.m.* sourness.

azeite, *n.m.* oil. **com/nos seus azeites,** in a bad mood.

azeitona, *n.f.* olive.

azeviche, *n.m.* jet; jet-black.

azia, *adj.* heartburn.

aziago, *adj.* ill-fated.

azo, *n.m.* opportunity.

azougue, *n.m.* quicksilver.

azucrinar, *vb.* annoy.

azul, *adj.* blue. **tudo a.?,** (coll.) everything OK?

azulão, *n.m.* bluebird.

azular, *vb.* make/turn blue; run away.

azulejo, *n.m.* decorative tile.

B

baba, *n.f.* saliva; slime.

babá, *n.f.* nursemaid.

babaçu, *n.m.* babassu palm.

babado, 1. *adj.* drooling; (coll.) infatuated. **2.** *n.m.* ruffle; (sl.) latest gossip.

babadouro, *n.m.* bib.

babalaô, *n.m.* Afro-Brazilian soothsayer.

babalorixá, *n.m.* Afro-Brazilian priest.

babão, 1. *adj.* drooling; foolish. **2.** *n.m.* drooler; idiot.

babaquara, 1. *adj.* stupid. **2.** *n.m.* dummy.

babar, *vb.* drool. **b.-se por,** (coll.) drool over.

baboseira, *n.f.* (coll.) stupid remark/action.

baboso, 1. *adj.* (coll.) drooling; infatuated. **2.** (coll.) idiot.

bacalhau, *n.m.* codfish; (coll.) skinny person; (coll.) Portuguese person.

bacalhoada, *n.f.* (P.) codfish stew, potatoes, and greens.

bacamarte, *n.m.* blunderbuss; (sl.) gun.

bacana, *adj.* (sl.) pretty; terrific.

bacanal, *n.m.* bacchanal, orgy.

bacharel, *n.m.f.* law school graduate, bachelor.

bacharelado, *n.m.* law degree; baccalaureate.

bacharelando -da, *n.* college senior.

bacharelar-se, *vb.* receive a law/bachelor's degree.

bacia, *n.f.* washbasin; basin.

baço, 1. *adj.* dull, dim; dark. **2.** *n.m.* spleen.

bacon, *n.m.* bacon.

bacorinho, *n.m.* suckling pig.

bactéria, *n.f.* bacterium.

báculo, *n.m.* shepherd's staff.

badalar, *vb.* toll, peal; (sl.) up, publicize; (sl.) flatter; (sl.) walk around; (sl.) frequent social events.

badalativo, *adj.* (sl.) flashy.

badalo, *n.m.* bell clapper.

badejo, *n.m.* fish similar to sea bass.

baderna, *n.f.* commotion.

bafafá, *n.m.* ruckus.

bafejar, *vb.* waft; caress; favor; inspire.

bafo, *n.m.* breath; breeze; odor; favor; inspiration; (sl.) hot air. **b. de onça,** (sl.) bad breath.

baforada, *n.f.* puff, whiff; breath; bad breath.

baga, *n.f.* berry; drop.

bagaceira, *n.f.* trash heap.

bagaço, *n.m.* bagasse; trash.

bagageiro, *n.m.* porter; baggage cart/rack.

bagagem, *n.f.* baggage; complete works.

bagana, *n.f.* (sl.) cigarette butt.

bagatela, *n.f.* trinket; trifle.

bago, *n.m.* grape; pellet; (sl.) money; (vulg.) testicle.

bagre, *n.m.* catfish.

bagulho, *n.m.* seed; (sl.) loot; (sl.) trash.

bagunça, *n.f.* (sl.) mess; (sl.) ruckus. **fazer uma b.,** (sl.) fool around.

bagunçado, *adj.* (sl.) messy, sloppy.

bagunçar, *vb.* (sl.) mess up.

bagunceiro -ra, *n.* (sl.) rowdy.

baia, *n.f.* stable stall.

baía, *n.f.* bay.

baiana, *n.f.* Bahian woman; female street vendor of Bahian food.

baianada, *n.f. (South. coll.)* stupid action; dirty trick; Bahians.

baiano -na, 1. *adj.* Bahian. **2.** *n.* Bahian; *(South. coll.)* Northeasterner; *(derog.)* black person; idiot.

baião, *n.m.* a Brazilian folk dance and music.

baila, *n.f.* **trazer/vir à b.,** bring/come up for discussion.

bailar, *vb.* dance.

bailarino -na, *n.* dancer; *n.f.* ballerina.

baile, *n.m.* dance, ball; *(sl.)* razzing; humiliation.

bailéu, *n.m.* scaffold, platform; shelf.

bainha, *n.f.* sheath; hem.

baio, *adj.* bay, chestnut; swarthy.

baioneta, *n.f.* bayonet.

bairrismo, *n.m.* parochialism.

bairro, *n.m.* neighborhood.

baiúca, *n.f.* dive, joint.

baixa, *n.f.* decrease; low, flat land; shoal; discharge; *(pl.)* casualties.

baixada, *n.f.* lowland.

baixa-mar, *n.f.* low tide.

baixar, *vb.* lower; humiliate; decree; go/come down.

baixela, *n.f.* tableware.

baixeza, *n.f.* lowness; indignity.

baixinho, 1. *adj.* short. **2.** *n.* short person. **3.** *adv.* quietly.

baixio, *n.m.* shoal.

baixo, 1. *adj.* low; short; lower; vile; *(mus.)* bass. **estar/andar por baixo,** (coll.) be in a bad way. **2.** *n.m.* bottom; *(mus.)* bass. **3.** *adv.* quietly.

bajulação, *n.f.* flattery.

bajulador -ra, 1. *adj.* flattering **2.** *n.* flatterer.

bajular, *vb.* flatter, grovel (to).

bala, *n.f.* bullet; bale; hard candy. **à prova de bala,** bulletproof.

balaço, *n.m.* gunshot.

balada, *n.f.* ballad.

balaio, *n.m.* basket.

balança, *n.f.* scale, balance; *(cap.)* Libra. **b. comercial,** balance of trade. **pesar na b.,** be important.

balançar, *vb.* sway; balance.

balancê, *n.m.* swing.

balanceio, *n.m.* swaying.

balancete, *n.m.* balance sheet.

balanço, *n.m.* swaying; *(com.)* balance, balance sheet; swing; inspection; *(sl.)* rehearsal.

balangandã, *n.m.* Afro-Brazilian amulet.

balão, *n.m.* balloon; *(sl.)* lie; *(sl.)* soccer ball. **b. de ensaio,** trial balloon; **dar um b.,** *(sl.)* stretch the truth; **fazer um b.,** turn around.

balar, balir, *vb.* bleat. —**balido,** *n.m.*

balaustrada, *n.f.* balustrade.

balaústre, *n.m.* stanchion.

balbuciar, *vb.* babble; stammer.

balbúrdia, *n.f.* commotion.

balcão, *n.m.* counter; balcony.

balconista, *n.m.f.* salesclerk.

balda, *n.f.* bad habit, flaw.

baldar, *vb.* foil; waste efforts.

balde, *n.m.* bucket, pail.

baldear, *vb.* bail; transfer.

baldio, 1. *adj.* useless; uncultivated. **terreno b.,** vacant lot. **2.** *n.m.* uncultivated land.

baldo, *adj.* useless, vain.

balear, *vb.* shoot.

baleeiro, 1. *adj.* whaling. **2.** *n.m.* whaler.

baleia, *n.f.* whale; baleen; *(coll.)* fatso.

balela, *n.f.* hearsay.

balístico, *adj.* ballistic.

baliza, *n.f.* marker; boundary; buoy; traffic signal; drum majorette; *n.* drum major -ette.

balizar, *vb.* demarcate; gauge; limit; distinguish.

balneário, *n.m.* spa, resort.

balofo, *adj.* puffy; vain, superficial.

balouçar, *vb.* sway; dangle.

balsa, *n.f.* raft; balsa.

bálsamo, *n.m.* balm.

baluarte, *n.m.* bulwark, bastion; support.

balzaquiana, *n.f. (coll.)* woman in her thirties.

bamba, 1. *n.m. (sl.)* tough guy; *(sl.)* expert.

bambear, *vb.* slacken; sag; waver.

bambo, *adj.* slack; indecisive.

bambolê, *n.m.* hula hoop.
bambolear, *vb.* wiggle. —**bamboleio**, *n.m.*
bambu, *n.m.* bamboo.
banal, *adj.* banal.
banana, *n.f.* banana; dynamite stick; (*sl.*) mess; vulgar gesture; *n.m.* (*coll.*) weakling.
bananeira, *n.f.* banana tree. **plantar b.**, do a handstand.
bananosa, *n.f.* **estar numa b.**, (*sl.*) be in a jam.
banca, *n.f.* stall; table; legal profession; examining board; bank (games). **b. de jornal/revista**, newsstand; **abafar a b.**, (*sl.*) dominate; **botar b.**, (*sl.*) act snobbish.
bancada, *n.f.* bench(es); legislative delegation.
bancar, *vb.* make like.
bancário -ria, 1. *adj.* bank. **2.** *n.m.* bank employee.
bancarrota, *n.f.* bankruptcy.
banco, *n.m.* bank; bench, stool; workbench; latrine. **b. de dados**, (*comput.*) data bank; **b. de sangue**, blood bank.
banda, *n.f.* band; strip; side; (*pl.*) region.
bandagem, *n.f.* bandage.
bandalheira, *n.f.* shamefulness; vile act.
bandear, *vb.* swing; shift. **b.-se**, change sides; band together.
bandeira, *n.f.* flag, banner; (*hist.*) exploratory expedition; **dar b.**, (*sl.*) give oneself away.
bandeirante, *n.m.* (*hist.*) colonial explorer; *n.m.f.* native of São Paulo state; *n.f.* Girl Scout.
bandeja, *n.f.* tray. **dar de b.**, (*coll.*) give for free.
bandido, *n.m.* bandit; villain.
banditismo, *n.m.* banditry.
bando, *n.m.* band; flock.
bandoleiro, *n.m.* outlaw.
bandolim, *n.m.* mandolin.
bandulho, *n.m.* (*coll.*) belly.
bangalô, *n.m.* bungalow.
bangüê, *n.m.* primitive sugar mill.
bangue-bangue, *n.m.* (*sl.*) cowboy movie; shooting.
banguela, *n.m.f.* person with

missing front tooth or speech defect.
banha, *n.f.* fat.
banhar, *vb.* bathe; **b.-se**, take a bath; go for a swim.
banheira, *n.f.* bathtub.
banheiro, *n.m.* bathroom.
banhista, *n.m.f.* bather; lifeguard.
banho, *n.m.* bath; swim; (*sl.*) defeat; (*pl.*) banns. **b. de chuveiro**, shower; **b. de mar**, dip in the ocean; **b. de sol**, sunbathing; **tomar um b.**, take a bath; **roupa de b.**, bathing suit; **vá tomar b.!**, go jump in the lake!
banho-maria, *n.m.* double boiler.
banir, *vb.* banish; outlaw.
banqueiro, *n.m.* banker.
banquete, *n.m.* banquet.
banquisa, *n.f.* ice floe.
banto, *adj.* Bantu.
banzé, *n.m.* (*coll.*) uproar.
baque, *n.m.* thud; instant.
bar, *n.m.* bar; café
barafunda, *n.f.* mess; commotion.
baralhar, *vb.* shuffle; mix up.
baralho, *n.m.* deck of cards.
barão, *n.m.* baron.
barata, *n.f.* cockroach.
baratear, *vb.* mark/go down (prices).
baratinar, *vb.* (*sl.*) confuse.
barato, 1. *adj.* cheap. **2.** *adv.* cheaply. **3.** *n.m.* (*sl.*) something terrific.
barba, *n.f.* beard. **fazer a b.**, shave; **nas barbas de**, under the nose of; **pôr as barbas de molho**, be on guard; **ter barbas**, be stale (joke).
barbada, *n.f.* (*sl.*) sure thing, hot tip.
barbado, *adj.* bearded.
barbante, *n.m.* string, twine.
barbaridade, *n.f.* barbarousness; absurdity.
barbarismo, *n.m.* barbarism.
bárbaro, 1. *adj.* barbarous; (*sl.*) terrific. **2.** *n.m.* barbarian.
barbatana, *n.f.* fin.
barbeador, *n.m.* shaver. **b. elétrico**, electric shaver.

barbear, *vb.* shave. **b.-se**, shave oneself.

barbearia, *n.f.* barber shop.

barbeiro, *n.m.* barber; (*coll.*) careless driver; bungler.

barbicha, *n.f.* goatee.

barbudo, **1.** *adj.* (heavily) bearded. **2.** *n.m.* heavily bearded man.

barca, *n.f.* barge, ferry.

barcaça, *n.f.* barge.

barco, *n.m.* boat. **b. a motor**, motorboat; **b. a vela**, sailboat; **b. de remos**, rowboat; **deixar o b. correr**, let things ride.

barda, *n.f.* hedge; railing.

bardo, *n.m.* bard.

barganha, *n.f.* trade; swindle. **—barganhar**, *vb.*

barítono, *adj., n.m.* baritone.

barlavento, *n.m.* windward.

barômetro, *n.m.* barometer.

baronesa, *n.f.* baroness.

barqueiro, *n.m.* boatman.

barra, *n.f.* bar; sandbar, narrow channel; daylight; (*sl.*) situation; **b. pesada**, (*sl.*) rough neighborhood; bad situation.

barraca, *n.f.* tent; booth; shack; beach umbrella.

barracão, *n.m.* shack.

barragem, *n.f.* barrier; (*mil.*) barrage; dam.

barranco, *n.m.* gully; cliff; (*sl.*) leftovers. **aos trancos e barrancos**, by fits and starts.

barra-pesada, *adj.* (*sl.*) dangerous; rough.

barrar, *vb.* bar.

barreira, *n.f.* barrier.

barricada, *n.f.* barricade.

barriga, *n.f.* belly. **b. da perna**, calf; **estar de b.**, (*coll.*) be pregnant; **tirar a b. da miséria**, have one's fill after a long privation.

barrigada, *n.f.* bellyful; litter.

barrigudo, *adj.* potbellied.

barril, *n.m.* barrel, keg.

barro, *n.m.* clay, mud; (*pl.*) pimples.

barroco, *adj., n.m.* baroque.

barulhento, *adj.* noisy; disorderly.

barulho, *n.m.* noise; disorder.

basbaque, *n.m.* (*coll.*) gawker; idiot.

basco, *adj., n.m.* Basque.

base, *n.f.* base; basis; foundation. **b. aérea/naval**, air/naval base.

basear-se, *vb.* be based.

básico, *adj.* basic.

basquete, basquetebol, *n.m.* basketball.

bastante, **1.** *adj.* enough. **2.** *adv.* quite.

bastão, *n.m.* cane; stick.

bastar, *vb.* be enough.

bastardo -da, **1.** *adj.* illegitimate. **2.** *n.* bastard.

bastidores, *n.m.pl.* backstage; behind-the-scenes gossip.

basto, *adj.* thick.

bata, *n.f.* smock.

batalha, *n.f.* battle; (*sl.*) job.

batalhão, *n.m.* battalion.

batalhar, *vb.* battle, fight; (*sl.*) work; (*sl.*) go after.

batata, *n.f.* potato. **b. frita**, French fry; **na b.**, on the button; certainly; **vá plantar batatas!**, go jump in the lake!

batata-doce, *n.f.* sweet potato.

bate-boca, *n.m.* (*coll.*) heated argument.

bate-bola, *n.m.* (*sl.*) soccer practice.

batedeira, *n.f.* mixer.

batedor, *n.m.* scout; minter; forerunner. **b. de carteiras**, (*sl.*) pickpocket.

bate-estaca, *n.m.* pile driver.

bate-fundo, *n.m.* (*coll.*) hubbub.

batel, *n.m.* small boat.

batelada, *n.f.* boatload; large quantity.

batente, *n.m.* doorjamb; (*sl.*) one's job.

bate-papo, *n.m.* (*coll.*) chat.

bater, *vb.* beat, hit, strike; knock; slam; stamp (foot); flap (wings); typewrite; roam; mint; (*sl.*) steal; (*sl.*) polish off; break (record); take (photo). **b.-se**, fight. **b. à máquina**, typewrite; **b. boca**, (*coll.*) have an argument; **b. em**, hit; knock on; end up in; **b. carteiras**, pick pockets; **b. palmas**, clap; **b. papo**, (*coll.*) chat; **b. para**, (*coll.*) head for; **b. um telefone**, (*sl.*) phone.

bateria, *n.f.* battery; drums.

n.m.f. drummer. **b. de cozinha,** kitchen utensils.

baterista, *n.m.f.* drummer.

batida, *n.f.* beating, blow; beat; crash; cocktail; exploration; *(coll.)* police raid.

batido, *adj.* trite.

batimento, *n.m.* impact; beat.

batina, *n.f.* cassock.

batismo, *n.m.* baptism.

batista, *adj., n.m.f.* Baptist.

batizado, *n.m.* baptism.

batizar, *vb.* baptize; water down.

batom, *n.m.* lipstick.

batota, *n.f.* cheating; trickery.

batucada, *n.f.* Afro-Brazilian percussion; rhythm; beat.

batucar, *vb.* beat; pound.

batuque, *n.m.* Afro-Brazilian percussion music and dance.

batuta, 1. *adj. (coll.)* clever. **2.** *n.f.* baton.

baú, *n.m.* trunk.

baunilha, *n.f.* vanilla.

bazar, *n.m.* bazaar.

bazófia, *n.f.* boasting.

bazuca, *n.f.* bazooka.

bê, *n.m.* the letter b.

bê-a-bá, *n.m.* ABCs; basics.

beataria, beatice, *n.f.* sanctimony.

beato, 1. *adj.* holy; sanctimonious. **2.** *n.m.* holy person; religious fanatic.

bêbado, -bedo, 1. *adj.* drunk. **2.** *n.m.* drunkard.

bebê, *n.m.f.* baby.

bebedeira, *n.f.* drunkenness.

bebedouro, *n.m.* drinking fountain; trough.

beber, *vb.* drink.

bebericar, *vb.* sip.

beberrão -rrona, *n.* drunkard.

bebida, *n.f.* beverage, drink.

beca, *n.f.* gown; *(sl.)* clothes.

beça, *n.f.* **à b.,** *(coll.)* galore; very.

beco, *n.m.* alley. **b. sem saída,** blind alley.

bedelho, *n.m.* door bolt. **meter o b.,** meddle.

beicinho, *n.m.* small lip. **fazer b.,** pout.

beiço, *n.m.* lip.

beiçudo, *adj.* thick-lipped.

beija-flor, *n.m.* hummingbird.

beijar, *vb.* kiss. —**beijo,** *n.m.*

beira, *n.f.* edge, bank.

beiral, *n.m.* eave.

beira-mar, *n.m.* seashore.

beirar, *vb.* border/verge on.

beisebol, *n.m.* baseball.

beldade, *n.f.* beauty.

beleza, *n.f.* beauty.

belga, *adj., n.m.f.* Belgian.

Bélgica, *n.f.* Belgium.

beliche, *n.m.* bunk, berth.

bélico, *adj.* war.

belicoso, *adj.* bellicose.

beligerante, *adj.* belligerent.

beliscar, *vb.* pinch; nibble. —**beliscão,** *n.m.*

belo, *adj.* beautiful, handsome; fine. **um b. dia,** one fine day.

belvedere, *n.m.* lookout point.

bem, 1. *n.m.* good; welfare; darling; *(pl.)* goods. **2.** *adv.* well; all right; very; certainly. **b. como,** as well as; **bem feito!,** it serves you (him, etc.) right! **passe bem!,** so long! **por b.,** willingly; **se bem que,** even though. **3.** *adj. (sl.)* high-class.

bem-amado -da, 1. *adj.* beloved. **2.** *n.* loved one.

bem-estar, *n.m.* well-being; comfort.

bemol, *n.m. (mus.)* flat.

bem-vindo, *adj.* welcome.

bênção, *n.f.* blessing.

bendito, *adj.* blessed.

bendizer, *vb.* praise; bless.

beneficência, *n.f.* beneficence; charity.

beneficiar, *vb.* benefit, improve; process.

beneficiário -ria, *n.* beneficiary.

benefício, *n.m.* benefit.

benéfico, *adj.* beneficial, favorable.

benemérito, *adj.* worthy, illustrious.

beneplácito, *n.m.* approval.

benesse, *n.f.* profit, gain.

benevolência, *n.f.* benevolence.

benévolo, *adj.* benevolent.

benfazejo, *adj.* beneficial.

benfeitor -ra, *n.* benefactor -ess.

benfeitoria, *n.f.* property improvement.

bengala, *n.f.* cane.

benigno, *adj.* benign; kind.

benjamim, *n.m.* favorite son (esp. youngest).

benquisto, *adj.* liked, respected.

bens, *n.m.pl.* goods; property. **b. comuns,** community property; **b. imóveis/de raiz,** real estate.

bento, *adj.* blessed, holy.

benzer, *vb.* bless.

berçário, *n.m.* nursery.

berço, *n.m.* cradle.

bergamota, *n.f.* tangerine.

berimbau, *n.* Afro-Brazilian bow-like percussion instrument.

berinjela, *n.f.* eggplant.

berlinda, *n.f.* brougham; litter. **estar na b.,** be in the limelight/on the spot.

berloque, *n.m.* trinket.

berrante, *adj.* gaudy, loud.

berrar, *vb.* yell; roar. —**berro,** *n.m.*

besouro, *n.m.* beetle.

bessa, *n.f.* **à b.,** *(coll.)* galore; very.

besta, 1. *adj.* silly; pretentious. **2.** *n.f.* beast; fool. **b. de carga,** beast of burden.

bestalhão -lhona, *n.* idiot.

besteira, *n.f.* *(coll.)* foolishness; foolish action/remark; trifle; profanity.

bestial, *adj.* beastly; stupid; *(P. sl.)* terrific.

bestificado, *adj.* dumbfounded.

besuntar, *vb.* *(coll.)* smear.

beterraba, *n.f.* beet.

betume, *n.m.* tar; putty.

bexiga, *n.f.* bladder; paint tube; smallpox, pockmarks.

bezerro -ra, *n.* calf.

bibe, *n.m.* child's smock.

bibelô, *n.m.* knickknack.

biberão, *n.m.* baby bottle.

Bíblia, *n.f.* Bible.

bíblico, *adj.* biblical.

bibliografia, *n.f.* bibliography.

biblioteca, *n.f.* library.

bibliotecário -ria, *n.* librarian.

biblioteconomia, *n.f.* library science.

biboca, *n.f.* hole; hut; *(coll.)* bar.

bica, *n.f.* faucet. **estar na b.,** be about (to), be in the offing; **suar em b.,** sweat bullets.

bicada, *n.f.* peck; *(sl.)* swallow.

bicar, *vb.* peck.

bicarbonato, *n.m.* bicarbonate. **b. de sódio,** bicarbonate of soda.

bicha, *n.f.* worm; *(sl.)* homosexual; *(P.)* queue.

bichano -na, *n.* kitty.

bichar, *vb.* get wormy.

bicharada, *n.f.* group of animals; *(sl.)* group of friends.

bicheiro, *n.m.* bookie.

bicho, *n.m.* animal; bug; *(coll.)* expert; *(sl.)* freshman; *(sl.)* guy. **matar o b.,** *(coll.)* take a drink of liquor; **virar b.,** *(coll.)* get mad.

bicho-papão, *n.m.* boogieman.

bicicleta, *n.f.* bicycle.

bico, *n.m.* beak; snout; *(coll.)* kisser; tip; nipple; *(coll.)* odd job; *(sl.)* fast-talk. **abrir o b.,** open one's mouth; **bom de b.,** smooth-talking; **calar o b.,** *(sl.)* shut up; pout; **molhar o b.,** wet one's whistle.

bicudo, *adj.* beaked; pointed.

bidê, *n.m.* bidet.

bienal, 1. *adj.* biennial. **2.** *n.f.* biennial art exhibition.

bife, *n.m.* steak; *(sl.)* punch in the face. **b. a cavalo,** *n.m.* steak topped with a fried egg.

bifurcar, *vb.* fork.

bigamia, *n.f.* bigamy.

bígamo -ma, 1. *adj.* bigamous. **2.** *n.* bigamist.

bigode, *n.m.* mustache.

bigorna, *n.f.* anvil.

bijuteria, *n.f.* costume jewelry.

bilhão, *n.m.* billion.

bilhar, *n.m.* billiards.

bilhete, *n.m.* ticket; note.

bilheteiro -ra, *n.* ticket seller.

bilheteria, *n.f.* ticket office.

bilíngue, *adj.* bilingual.

bílis, *n.f.* bile.

bilro, *n.m.* lace bobbin.

biltre, *n.m.* scoundrel.

binário, *adj.* binary.

binóculo, *n.m.* binoculars.

biodegradável, *adj.* biodegradable.

biografia, *n.f.* biography.

biográfico, *adj.* biographical.

biologia, *n.f.* biology.

biológico, *adj.* biological.

biombo, *n.m.* screen.
biônico, *adj.* bionic.
biopsia, *n.f.* biopsy.
biorritmo, *n.m.* biorhythm.
bipe, *n.m.* beeper.
biquíni, *n.m.* bikini.
birita, *n.f.* cane brandy; booze.
Birmânia, *n.f.* Burma.
birosca, *n. favela* grocery and bar.
birra, *n.f.* stubborn; dislike.
biruta, *adj. (sl.)* crazy.
bis, *interj.* encore!
bisagra, *n.f.* hinge.
bisavô, *n.f.* great-grandmother.
bisavô, *n.m.* great-grandfather.
bisavós, *n.m.pl.* great-grandparents.
bisbilhotar, *vb. (coll.)* gossip; snoop.
bisbilhoteiro -ra, *n. (coll.)* gossip; snoop.
bisbilhotice, *n.f.* gossip; nosiness.
biscate, *n.m.* odd job; *(sl.)* prostitute.
biscoito, *n.m.* cookie, cracker; *(sl.)* coaster.
bisnaga, *n.f.* tube (paint, etc.).
bisneto -ta, *n.* great-grandson -daughter.
bisonho, *adj.* inexperienced.
bispo, *n.m.* bishop.
bissexto, 1. *adj.* leap. **ano b.,** leap year. **2.** *n.m.* leap-year day.
bissexual, *adj.* bisexual.
bisturi, *n.m.* scalpel.
bitola, *n.f.* gauge; standard.
bitolado, *adj. (sl.)* narrow-minded.
bizarro, *adj.* extravagant; elegant; bizarre.
black-power, *n.m.* Afro hair style.
blague, *n.f. (F.)* joke.
blasfemar, *vb.* blaspheme.
blasfêmia, *n.f.* blasphemy.
blecaute, *n.m.* blackout.
blefar, *vb. (coll.)* bluff; deceive.
blefe, *n.m. (coll.)* bluff, -ing.
blindado, *adj.* armored.
blindagem, *n.f.* iron-plating.
bloco, *n.m.* block; bloc; writing tablet; Carnival dance group.
bloquear, *vb.* block.
bloqueio, *n.m.* blockade.

blusa, *n.f.* blouse; shirt; smock.
blusão, *n.m.* loose shirt/jacket.
boa, 1. *adj.f.s.* good. **2.** *n.f. (coll.)* fine mess; *(sl.)* attractive woman; *(sl.)* cane brandy. **numa b.,** *(sl.)* in a good way.
boa-praça, *n.m. (coll.)* nice person.
boas-vindas, *n.f.pl.* welcome.
boate, *n.f.* night club.
boato, *n.m.* rumor.
boa-vida, *n.m.f.* loafer.
bob, *n.m.* hair roller.
bobagem, *n.f.* foolish act/remark; nonsense; trifle.
bobalhão -ona, *n.* idiot.
bobear, *vb.* act foolishly.
bobina, *n.f.* bobbin, spool.
bobo -ba, 1. *adj.* foolish. **2.** *n.* fool; jester. **fazer-se de b.,** play dumb.
boboca, *adj. (coll.)* stupid, dumb.
boca, *n.f.* mouth; *(sl.)* place; *(sl.)* sinecure; *(sl.)* drug house. **b. de siri!,** mum's the word! **cala a b.!,** shut up!
bocado, *n.m.* bite; dab; quite a bit; little while; (bridle) bit.
boçal, *adj.* stupid.
bocejar, *vb.* yawn. —**bocejo,** *n.m.*
boceta, *n.f.* box; *(vulg.)* vagina.
bochecha, *n.f.* cheek.
boda, *n.f.* wedding anniversary.
bode, *n.m.* billy goat; *(sl.)* problem; *(sl.)* bad experience. **b. expiatório,** scapegoat.
bodega, *n.f.* bar; *(coll.)* junk.
bodoque, *n.m.* slingshot.
bodum, *n.m.* (body) odor.
boêmio -mia, *adj., n.* bohemian.
bofe, *n.m. (coll.)* lung; *(sl.)* ugly person. **ter maus bofes,** *(coll.)* be grouchy.
bofetada, *n.f.* slap (in the face); insult.
boi, *n.m.* steer, ox. **ter b. na linha,** *(coll.)* for there to be a snag.
bói, *n.m. (coll.)* errand boy.
bóia, *n.f.* buoy; chow.
bóia-fria, *n.m.f.* farm laborer; brown bagger.
boiar, *vb.* float; *(coll.)* not understand; eat.

boicotar, *vb.* boycott. **—boicote,** *n.m.*

boina, *n.f.* beret.

bojar, *vb.* bulge, puff out.

bojo, *n.m.* bulge; capacity.

bojudo, *adj.* bulging.

bola, *n.f.* ball; *(coll.)* head; fatso; *(coll.)* joke; *(sl.)* funny person; *(sl.)* bribe. **b. de gude,** marble; **b. de neve,** snowball; **bolas!,** shucks! **comer b.,** *(sl.)* take a bribe; **dar b. para,** *(coll.)* pay attention to; flirt with; **não dar b. para,** *(coll.)* not care about.

bola-ao-cesto, *n.m.* basketball.

bolacha, *n.f.* cracker, cookie; *(sl.)* slap; *(sl.)* coaster.

bolada, *n.f.* *(coll.)* pile of money.

bolar, *vb. (coll.)* plan, cook up.

bolear, *vb.* round; perfect; wiggle.

boléia, *n.f.* driver's seat. **pedir b.,** *(P.)* hitchhike.

boletim, *n.m.* bulletin; report card.

bolha, *n.f.* blister; bubble; *n.m.f. (sl.)* pest.

boliche, *n.m.* bowling.

bolinha, *n.f.* polka dot.

bolinho, *n.m.* little cake; cupcake.

boliviano -na, *adj., n.* Bolivian.

bolo, *n.m.* cake; (cards) pot; *(sl.)* fuss; **dar o b. em,** stand (someone) up.

bolor, *n.m.* mold, must.

bolota, *n.f.* acorn.

bolsa, *n.f.* purse; bag; scholarship; **b. de estudos,** scholarship; **b. (de valores),** stock market.

bolsista, *n.m.f.* scholarship holder.

bolso, *n.m.* pocket.

bom, 1. *adj.* good; kind; well. **2.** *n.m.* good person.

bomba, *n.f.* bomb; pump; firecracker; surprise; *(sl.)* dud. **levar b.,** *(sl.)* flunk.

bombardeado, *adj.* bombed; *(sl.)* bushed.

bombardear, *vb.* bomb, bombard.

bombardeio, *n.m.* bombing.

bombardeiro, *n.m.* bomber (plane); bombardier.

bomba-relógio, *n.f.* time bomb.

bombástico, *adj.* bombastic.

bombeiro, *n.m.* firefighter.

bombo, *n.m.* bass drum.

bombom, *n.m.* bonbon.

bombordo, *n.m. (naut.)* port.

bonachão -chona, 1. *adj.* very good/kind. **2.** *n.* very good/kind person.

bonança, *n.f.* calm, lull.

bondade, *n.f.* goodness, kindness.

bonde, *n.m.* trolley. *(sl.)* bill of goods.

bondinho, *n.m.* cable lift.

bondoso, *adj.* kind, good.

boné, *n.m.* cap (with visor).

boneca, *n.f.* doll (f.).

boneco, *n.m.* doll (m.); puppet; dandy. **b. de engonço,** marionette.

bonificação, *n.f.* reward; allowance.

bonificar, *vb.* give a reward/allowance.

bonitão -tona, 1. *adj.* very good-looking. **2.** *n.* good-looker.

bonito, *adj.* pretty, handsome.

bonomia, *n.f.* bonhomie.

bônus, *n.m.* bond.

bonzão, *adj. (coll.)* very good.

boqueirão, *n.m.* river mouth; water gap.

boquejar, *vb.* yawn; whisper. **—boquejo,** *n.m.*

boquiaberto, *adj.* astonished.

boquilha, *n.f.* cigarette holder; mouthpiece.

boquinha, *n.f. (coll.)* snack.

borboleta, *n.f.* butterfly; turnstile; bow tie.

borboletear, *vb.* flutter; daydream.

borbotão, *n.m.* spurt. **—borbotar,** *vb.*

borbulha, *n.f.* bubble; blister; blemish.

borbulhar, *vb.* bubble, gush.

borda, *n.f.* edge, rim, brim.

bordado, *n.m.* embroidery.

bordão, *n.m.* staff; support; speech crutch.

bordar, *vb.* embroider.

bordel, *n.m.* brothel.

bordo, *n.m. (naut.)* board; edge.

a bordo, aboard; **de alto b.,** first-rate.

bordo, *n.m.* maple.

boreste, *n.m.* starboard.

borla, *n.f.* tassel; mortarboard (hat).

borra, *n.f.* dregs.

borra-botas, *n.m.* dauber; nobody.

borracha, *n.f.* rubber; rubber eraser.

borralho, *n.m.* ashes.

borrar, *vb.* stain; daub. —**borrão,** *n.m.*

borrasca, *n.f.* storm.

borrego, *n.m.* lamb.

borrifar, *vb.* sprinkle. —**borrifo,** *n.m.*

borzeguim, *n.m.* high-laced boot.

bosque, *n.m.* woods.

bosquejo, *n.m.* outline. —**bosquejar,** *vb.*

bossa, *n.f.* hump; *(sl.)* talent; *(sl.)* style.

bossa nova, *n.f.* new style; bossa nova.

bosta, *n.f.* animal feces; *(coll.)* junk.

bota, *n.f.* boot. **bater as botas,** *(coll.)* die.

bota-fora, *n.m.* farewell party.

botaló, *n.m.* boom.

botânica, *n.f.* botany.

botânico -ca, 1. *adj.* botanical. **2.** *n.* botanist.

botão, *n.m.* button; knob; bud. **dizer/falar aos/com os seus botões,** *(coll.)* say/talk to oneself.

botar, *vb.* put, set; set up; put out; put on. **b. para quebrar,** *(sl.)* go all out.

bote, *n.m.* small boat; pounce; attack.

boteco, *n.m.* *(coll.)* bar.

botequim, *n.m.* bar.

botica, *n.f.* pharmacy.

boticário -ria, *n.* pharmacist.

botija, *n.f.* jug.

botina, *n.f.* high shoe.

boto, *n.m.* river dolphin.

botoeira, *n.f.* buttonhole.

bovino, *adj., n.m.* bovine.

boxe, *n.m.* boxing; brass knuckles; stall shower; *(journ.)* box.

boxeador, *n.m.* boxer.

boxear, *vb.* box.

brabeza, *n.f.* ferocity; fury.

brabo, *adj.* fierce; furious.

braçal, *adj.* manual.

bracejar, *vb.* move the arms; stretch.

bracelete, *n.m.* bracelet; handcuff.

braço, *n.m.* arm. **cruzar os braços,** do nothing; **dar o b. a torcer,** *(coll.)* give in; **de b. dado,** arm in arm; **meter o b. em,** *(coll.)* beat up; **nos braços de Morfeu,** asleep.

braço-de-ferro, *n.m.* ironhanded person.

braçudo, *adj.* strong-armed.

bradar, *vb.* shout, roar. —**brado,** *n.m.*

braguilha, *n.f.* fly (pants).

bramar, bramir, *vb.* roar, bellow. —**bramido,** *n.m.*

brancacento, *adj.* whitish.

brancarana, *n.f.* *(coll.)* lightskinned mulatta.

brancarrão -rona, 1. *adj.* lightskinned. **2.** *n.* light-skinned mulatto/a.

branco -ca, *adj., n.* white; blank; Caucasian.

brancura, *n.f.* whiteness.

brande, *n.m.* brandy.

brandir, *vb.* brandish.

brando, *adj.* soft, mild.

branquear, *vb.* whiten.

brânquia, *n.f.* gill.

brasa, *n.f.* ember, coal. **mandar b.,** *(sl.)* pour it on; **puxar a b. para a sua sardinha,** *(coll.)* look out for oneself.

brasão, *n.m.* coat of arms.

braseiro, *n.m.* brazier.

Brasil, *n.m.* Brazil.

brasileiro -ra, *adj., n.* Brazilian.

brasonar, *vb.* emblazon.

bravata, *n.f.* bravado.

braveza, *n.f.* ferocity.

bravio, *adj.* fierce, wild.

bravo, *adj.* brave; wild; furious.

bravura, *n.f.* bravery; wildness.

breca, *n.f.* cramp. **levado da b.,** naughty.

brecar, *vb.* brake.

brecha, *f.* opening, gap; *(sl.)* chance.

brejeiro, *adj.* mischievous.

brejo, *n.m.* swamp, marsh.

brenha, *n.f.* thick woods.

breque, *n.m.* brake.

breu, *n.m.* tar.

breve, **1.** *adj.* brief. **2.** *n.m.* scapular. **3.** *adv.* shortly.

brevê, *n.m.* pilot's license.

brevidade, *n.f.* brevity.

bricabraque, *n.m.* bric-a-brac.

brida, *n.f.* rein.

briga, *n.f.* fight; argument.

brigada, *n.f.* brigade.

brigadeiro, *n.m.* brigadier general; chocolate and condensed milk candy.

brigão -gona, **1.** *adj.* quarrelsome. **2.** *n.* troublemaker.

brigar, *vb.* fight; argue; break up.

brilhante, **1.** *adj.* brilliant, bright. **2.** *n.m.* diamond.

brilhantina, *n.f.* brilliantine.

brilhar, *vb.* shine; stand out.

brilho, *n.m.* shine; lip gloss; *(sl.)* cocaine.

brim, *n.m.* fine canvas, drill.

brincadeira, *n.f.* play, game, fun; joke; teasing; get-together.

brincalhão -ona, **1.** *adj.* playful. **2.** *n.* joker, cut-up; prankster.

brincar, *vb.* play; joke.

brinco, *n.m.* earring.

brindar, *vb.* toast; give a gift to.

brinde, *n.m.* toast; gift.

brinjela, *n.f.* eggplant.

brinquedo, *n.m.* toy. **companheiro/a de b.**, playmate.

brio, *n.m.* pride; spirit.

brioso, *adj.* proud; spirited.

brisa, *n.f.* breeze.

britânico -ca, **1.** *adj.* British. **2.** *n.* Britisher.

britar, *vb.* crush (rocks).

broca, *n.f.* drill.

brocado, *n.m.* brocade.

brocha, *n.f.* tack.

brochado, *adj.* paper-back.

broche, *n.m.* brooch, pin.

brochura, *n.f.* brochure; paperback.

brócolis, *n.m.pl.* broccoli.

bronca, *n.f. (sl.)* scolding; gripe; uproar.

bronco, *adj.* stupid; crude.

bronquear, *vb. (sl.)* gripe; get mad.

bronquite, *n.f.* bronchitis.

bronze, *n.m.* bronze.

bronzear, *vb.* bronze; tan.

brotar, *vb.* sprout; yield; gush.

brotinho, *n.m. (coll.)* young teenage girl.

broto, *n.m.* bud, sprout; sprouting; *(coll.)* young teenage girl.

broxa, *n.f.* paintbrush; *n.m. (vulg.)* impotent male.

broxar, *vb.* paint with a brush; *(vulg.)* become impotent.

bruaca, *n.f.* saddlebag, pouch; *(sl.)* hag.

bruços, *n.m.pl.* **de b.**, lying prone.

bruma, *n.f.* fog, mist.

brumoso, *adj.* foggy, misty.

brunir, *vb.* polish.

brusco, *adj.* brusque.

brutal, *adj.* brutal.

brutalidade, *n.f.* brutality.

brutalizar, *vb.* brutalize.

brutamontes, *n.m.* brute.

bruto -ta, **1.** *adj.* brute, stupid; coarse; raw; gross. **2.** *n.m.* brute, beast. **em b.**, in the rough.

bruxaria, *n.f.* witchcraft.

Bruxelas, *n.* Brussels.

bruxa, *n.f.* witch.

bruxo, *n.m.* sorcerer.

bruxulear, *vb.* flicker. —**bruxuleio**, *n.m.*

bucha, *n.f.* wad; plug.

bucho, *n.m. (coll.)* belly; *(sl.)* ugly person.

bucle, *n.m.* curl.

buço, *n.m.* fuzz (upper lip).

budista, *adj., n.m.f.* Buddhist.

bueiro, *n.m.* culvert; flue.

bufão, *n.m.* buffoon; braggart.

bufar, *vb.* puff; snort; boast; *(coll.)* gripe.

bufê, bufete, *n.m.* sideboard; buffet.

bufo, **1.** *adj.* comical. **2.** *n.m.* buffoon; miser.

bufonaria, *n.f.* buffoonery.

bugalho, *n.m. (coll.)* eyeball.

buginganga, *n.f.* trinket.

bugre, *n.m. (derog.)* Indian, savage.

bujão, *n.m.* stopper.

bula, *n.f.* medicine directions; papal bull.

bulbo, *n.m. (bot.)* bulb.

bule, *n.m.* teapot, coffeepot.

bulevar, *n.m.* boulevard.

búlgaro -ra, *adj., n.* Bulgarian.

bulha, *n.f.* noise, uproar.

bulício, *n.m.* murmur; commotion.

buliçoso, *adj.* restless.

bulir, *vb.* move, stir. **b. com**, tease; **b. em**, fool with.

bumba-meu-boi, *n.m.* folk pageant with ox as character.

bumbum, *n.m.* (coll.) fanny, rump.

bumerangue, *n.m.* boomerang.

bunda, **1.** *adj.* (coll.) crummy. **2.** *n.f.* (coll.) butt, rump.

buquê, *n.m.* bouquet.

buraco, *n.m.* hole; (coll.) jam. **b. negro**, black hole.

burburejar, *vb.* gurgle. —**burburejo**, *n.m.*

burburinho, *n.m.* murmur. —**burburinhar**, *vb.*

burguês -esa, **1.** *adj.* bourgeois. **2.** *n.* bourgeois(e).

burguesia, *n.f.* bourgeoisie, middle class.

burilar, *vb.* engrave; polish.

buriti, *n.m.* large palm tree.

burla, *n.f.* trick; swindle.

burlar, *vb.* cheat; mock.

burlesco, *adj.* burlesque; mocking.

burocracia, *n.f.* bureaucracy.

burocrata, *n.m.f.* bureaucrat.

burocrático, *adj.* bureaucratic.

burrice, **burrada**, *n.f.* stupid action/remark; stupidity.

burro, **1.** *adj.* stupid, dumb. **2.** *n.m.* donkey; dummy. **b. de carga**, pack animal; **pra burro**, galore; very.

busca, *n.f.* search.

buscar, *vb.* go and get, pick up; look for.

bússola, *n.f.* compass.

busto, *n.m.* bust.

buzina, *n.f.* horn.

buzinar, *vb.* honk.

búzio, *n.m.* conch; horn; diver.

C

cá, **1.** *n.m.* the letter k. **2.** *adv.* here.

caatinga, *n.f.* thorny, scrub vegetation.

cabaça, *n.f.* gourd.

cabaço, *n.m.* (vulg.) hymen; virginity.

cabal, *adj.* complete.

cabana, *n.f.* hut.

cabaré, *n.m.* cabaret.

cabeça, *n.f.* head; top; (n.m.) leader. **perder a c.**, go overboard.

cabeça-chata, *n.m.f.* Ceará native; northerner.

cabeçada, *n.f.* butt with the head; blunder.

cabeça-de-porco, *n.f.* slum tenement.

cabeçalho, *n.m.* headline; heading.

cabecear, *vb.* nod; butt with the head.

cabeceira, *n.f.* head (bed, table); bedside; headwaters.

cabeçudo, *adj.* big-headed; stubborn.

cabedal, *n.m.* capital; experience.

cabeleira, *n.f.* head of hair; wig; comet tail.

cabeleireiro, *n.m.* hairdresser.

cabelo, *n.m.* hair.

cabeludo, *adj.* hairy; obscene.

caber, *vb.* fit; suit; fall to.

cabide, *n.m.* clothes hanger. **c. de empregos**, person with many jobs.

cabimento, *n.m.* suitableness. **não ter c.**, be improper/ inconceivable.

cabina, **-ne**, *n.f.* cabin, compartment; booth. **c. telefônica**, phone booth.

cabisbaixo, *adj.* crestfallen.

cabível, *adj.* appropriate.

cabo, *n.m.* cape; end; handle; cable; corporal. **c. da Boa Esperança**, Cape of Good Hope; **c. eleitoral**, election canvasser; **ao c. de**, at the end of; **dar c. de**, do away with; **de c. a rabo**, from one end to the other; **levar a c.**, carry out.

caboclo -cla, *n.* mestizo; backwoodsman -woman.

cabograma, *n.m.* cablegram.

cabotagem, *n.f.* coastal navigation.

cabotino, *n.m.* traveling actor; ham actor.

Cabo Verde, *n.m.* Cape Verde.
cabo-verde, *n.m.f.* person of African and Amerindian ancestry.
cabo-verdiano -na, *adj., n.* Cape Verdean.
cabra, *n.f.* nanny goat; *n.m.* mulatto; *(coll.)* thug; *(sl.)* guy.
cabrão, *n.m. (coll.)* cuckold.
cabreiro -ra, 1. *adj. (coll.)* shrewd. **2.** *n.* goatherd.
cabresto, *n.m.* halter.
cabriolar, *vb.* caper. **—cabriola,** *n.f.*
cabrito, *n.m.* goat kid.
cabrocha, *n.f.* mulatto girl.
cábula, 1. *adj.* sly; truant. **2.** *n.m.f.* truant.
cabular, *vb.* cut classes.
caça, *n.f.* hunt; hunting; game; *(n.m.)* fighter plane.
caçada, *n.f.* hunt.
caçador -ra, *n.* hunter.
caçamba, *n.f.* bucket.
caça-minas, *n.m.* mine sweeper.
caça-níqueis, *n.m.* slot machine.
caçar, *vb.* hunt.
cacarecos, *n.m.pl. (coll.)* belongings.
cacarejar, *vb.* cackle.
caçarola, *n.f.* saucepan.
cacau, *n.m.* cacao, cocoa.
cacetada, *n.f.* beating; *(coll.)* bore.
cacete, 1. *adj. (coll.)* boring; annoying. **2.** *n.m.* club.
cacetear, *vb. (coll.)* annoy; bore.
cachaça, *n.f.* cane brandy; *(coll.)* hobby.
cachaceiro -ra, *n.* drunkard.
cachaço, *n.m.* nape.
cachê, *n.m.* entertainer's fee.
cachear, *vb.* curl.
cachecol, *n.m.* scarf.
cachenê, *n.m.* muffler.
cachimbar, *vb.* smoke a pipe.
cachimbo, *n.m.* tobacco pipe.
cacho, *n.m.* bunch; curl; *(sl.)* love affair; lover.
cachoeira, *n.f.* waterfall; rapids.
cachopa, *n.f. (P.)* lass.
cachopo, *n.m.* reef; *(P.)* lad.
cachorra, *n.f.* bitch.
cachorrice, *n.f. (coll.)* dirty trick.

cachorro, *n.m.* dog; *(coll.)* scoundrel.
cachorro-quente, *n.m.* hot dog.
cacife, *n.m.* ante.
cacimba, *n.f.* water hole.
cacique, *n.m.* Indian chief.
caco, *n.m.* shard.
caçoar, *vb.* tease, mock.
cacoete, *n.m.* nervous tic.
cacto, *n.m.* cactus.
caçula, *n.m.f.* youngest child.
cacunda, *n.f. (coll.)* shoulders, back.
cada, *adj.* each; strangest.
cadafalso, *n.m.* gallows.
cadastro, *n.m.* public land register.
cadáver, *n.m.* corpse; *(sl.)* creditor.
cadê, *interrog. (coll.)* where is/ are?
cadeado, *n.m.* padlock.
cadeia, *n.f.* chain; jail.
cadeira, *n.f.* chair; *(pl.)* hips. **c. de balanço,** rocking chair; **c. de rodas,** wheelchair.
cadela, *n.f.* bitch.
caderneta, *n.f.* small notebook; bank book.
caderno, *n.m.* notebook; newspaper section.
cadete, *n.m.* cadet.
cadinho, *n.m.* crucible.
caducar, *vb.* grow old; weaken; lapse.
caduco, *adj.* decrepit; senile; lapsed.
cafajeste, *n.m.* boor, cad.
café, *n.m.* coffee; breakfast; café. **c. da manhã,** breakfast.
cafeína, *n.f.* caffeine.
cafetão, *n.m.* pimp.
cafeteira, *n.f.* coffee pot.
cafetina, *n.f.* madam (brothel).
cafezal, *n.m.* coffee plantation.
cafezinho, *n.m.* demitasse coffee.
cafona, *adj. (sl.)* gaudy, tacky.
cafua, *n.f.* cave; hovel.
cafundó, *n.m.* gorge. **c. de judas,** *(coll.)* middle of nowhere.
cafuné, *n.m.* stroking of the head.
cafuzo -za, *n.* person of mixed African and Amerindian ancestry.

cágado, *n.m.* turtle.

caganeira, *n.f. (vulg.)* diarrhea.

cagão -gona, *n. (coll.)* coward.

cagar, *vb. (vulg.)* defecate.

caiar, *vb.* whitewash.

câibra, câimbra, *n.f.* cramp.

caibro, *n.m.* rafter.

caiçara, *n.m.* beachcomber, bum.

caído, 1. *adj.* fallen; *(coll.)* in love. **2.** *n.m.pl.* leftovers.

caimão, *n.m.* alligator.

caipira, *adj., n.m.f.* hillbilly.

caipora, 1. *adj.* unlucky. **2.** *n.m.* evil forest spirit; *n.m.f.* unlucky person.

cair, *vb.* fall; suit; happen; *(coll.)* be taken in.

cais, *n.m.* wharf.

caixa, *n.f.* box; cashbox; safe; *n.m.* cashier. **c. de som,** stereo speaker; **c. econômica,** federal savings bank; **c. postal,** p.o. box; **c. registradora,** cash register; **c. eletrônico,** automatic teller.

caixa-d'água, *n.f.* water tank.

caixa-forte, *n.f.* safe, vault.

caixão, *n.m.* box; coffin.

caixeiro -ra, *n.* salesperson. **c.-viajante,** traveling salesman.

caixilho, *n.m.* windowframe.

caixote, *n.m.* crate.

cajado, *n.m.* staff, crook.

caju, *n.m.* cashew fruit.

cal, *n.f.* lime, whitewash.

calabouço, *n.m.* dungeon.

calada, *n.f.* hush.

calado, 1. *adj.* silent. **2.** *n.m. (naut.)* draft.

calafetar, *vb.* calk.

calafrio, *n.m.* chill.

calamidade, *n.f.* calamity.

calão, *n.m.* slang. **baixo c.,** profanity.

calar, *vb.* silence; fix (bayonet); *(naut.)* draw. **c.-se.** keep quiet. **c. a boca,** *(coll.)* shut up.

calça, *n.f.* pants.

calçada, *n.f.* sidewalk; pavement.

calçado, *n.m.* shoe.

calçamento, *n.m.* paving.

calcanhar, *n.m.* heel. **c. de judas,** *(coll.)* middle of nowhere.

calção, *n.m.* shorts. **c. de banho,** swimming trunks.

calcar, *vb.* trample; crush.

calçar, *vb.* put on (shoes, socks, gloves); pave.

calças, *n.f.pl.* pants.

calcinhas, *n.f.pl.* panties.

calço, *n.m.* wedge, block.

calculadora, *n.f.* calculator.

calcular, *vb.* calculate; figure.

calculista, 1. *adj.* calculating. **2.** *n.m.f.* schemer.

cálculo, *n.m.* calculus; calculation; *(med.)* stone.

calda, *n.f.* syrup, sauce; *(pl.)* hot springs.

caldear, *vb.* weld; fuse; mix.

caldeira, *n.f.* caldron, boiler.

caldo, *n.m.* broth; soup; gravy; juice. **c. verde,** cabbage soup.

calefação, *n.f.* heating.

caleidoscópio, *n.m.* kaleidoscope.

caleira, *n.f.* roof gutter.

calejado, *adj.* callous(ed).

calembur, *n.m.* pun.

calendário, *n.m.* calendar.

calha, *n.f.* gutter.

calhamaço, *n.m.* large tome.

calhambeque, *n.m. (coll.)* jalopy.

calhar, *vb.* fit in; suit; happen.

calhau, *n.m.* pebble.

calhorda, 1. *adj.* low-down. **2.** *n.m.f.* scoundrel.

calibrar, *vb.* calibrate; fill (tires).

calibre, *n.m.* caliber.

cálice, *n.m.* chalice, wine glass.

cálido, *n.m.* warm, hot.

caligrafia, *n.f.* penmanship.

calistenia, *n.f.* calisthenics.

calma, *n.f.* calm; heat.

calmante, *adj., n.m.* sedative.

calmo, *adj.* calm.

calo, *n.m.* callus, corn.

calor, *n.m.* heat. **estar com c.,** be hot (person); **fazer/estar c.,** be hot (weather).

calorento, *adj.* hot; sensitive to heat.

caloria, *n.f.* calorie.

caloroso, *adj.* warm; enthusiastic.

calota, *n.f.* hub cap.

calote, *n.m. (coll.)* welshing.

calotear, *vb. (coll.)* welsh.

caloteiro -ra, n. (coll.) welsher.

calouro, n.m. freshman; novice.

calundu, n.m. ill-humor.

calúnia, n.f. slander.
—caluniar, vb.

calva, n.f. bald spot.

calvície, n.f. baldness.

calvo, adj. bald.

cama, n.f. bed. c. de casal/sol-
teiro, double/single bed; c. de
vento, cot.

camada, n.f. coat, layer; social
class.

camafeu, n.m. cameo.

camaleão, n.m. chameleon.

câmara, n.f. chamber; house;
council; camera. c. de ar, inner
tube; c. municipal/de vereadores, city council; C. dos
Deputados, Chamber of Deputies; c. lenta, slow motion.

camarada, n.m.f. comrade,
friend.

camaradagem, n.f. camaraderie.

camarão, n.m. shrimp.

camareiro -ra, n. chamberlain
-maid.

camarilha, n.f. clique.

Camarões, n.m.pl. Cameroun.

camarote, n.m. theater box;
(naut.) cabin.

cambada, n.f. bundle; gang.

cambaio, adj. bow-legged.

cambalacho, n.m. swindle.

cambalear, vb. stagger.

cambalhota, n.f. somersault.

cambar, vb. hobble; reel.

cambiar, vb. exchange (currency); change.

câmbio, n.m. currency ex-
change; exchange rate; gearshift. c. negro, black-market
currency exchange; casa de c.,
currency-exchange office; letra
de c., bill of exchange.

cambista, n.m.f. money-
changer; scalper.

cambito, n.m. leg of pork.

cambulhada, n.f. bunch.

camelo, n.m. camel.

camelô, n.m. street vendor.

caminhada, n.f. walk; hike.

caminhante, n.m.f. walker.

caminhão, n.m. truck.

caminhar, vb. walk; hike.

caminho, n.m. way; road.

camioneta, -nhonete, n.f. station wagon; pickup.

camisa, n.f. shirt.

camisa-de-força, n.f. strait
jacket.

camisa-de-meia, n.f. undershirt; T-shirt.

camisa-de-vênus, camisinha,
n.f. (coll.) condom.

camiseta, n.f. T-shirt; undershirt.

camisola, n.f. nightgown.

campa, n.f. tombstone; bell.

campainha, n.f. bell; doorbell.

campanário, n.m. bell tower.

campanha, n.f. fields; campaign.

campanudo, adj. bell-shaped;
pompous.

campar, vb. camp; brag; excel.

campeão -ã, n. champion.

campear, vb. camp; ride the
range; shine; show off.

campeonato, n.m. championship.

campestre, adj. country.

campina, n.f. meadow.

campismo, n.m. camping.

campista, n.m.f. camper.

campo, n.m. field, countryside;
camp; realm. c. de batalha,
battlefield; c. de concentração,
concentration camp.

camponês -nesa, 1. adj. rural. 2.
n. peasant.

campônio -nia, adj., n. rustic.

campo-santo, n.m. cemetery.

camuflar, vb. camouflage.
—camuflagem, n.f.

camundongo, n.m. mouse.

camurça, n.f. chamois; suede.

cana, n.f. cane; sugar cane; (sl.)
cane brandy; (sl.) jail.

Canadá, n.m. Canada.

cana-de-açúcar, n.f. sugar cane.

canadense, adj., n. Cana-
dian.

canal, n.m. canal; channel.

canalete, n.m. furrow, gutter.

canalha, n.f. rabble; n.m.f.
scoundrel.

canalizar, vb. channel.

canapé, n.m. settee; canapé.

canário, n.m. canary.

canastra, n.f. hamper; canasta.

canastrão, n.m. large hamper;
(sl.) ham actor.

canavial, *n.m.* canebrake.
canção, *n.f.* song. **c. de ninar,** lullaby.
cancela, *n.f.* gate.
cancelar, *vb.* cancel.
câncer, *n.m.* cancer; *(cap.)* Cancer.
cancha, *n.f.* field, track, court; experience.
cancioneiro, *n.m.* song/poem collection.
cancro, *n.m.* canker; chancre.
candango, *n.m.* builder/native of Brasília.
candeeiro, *n.m.* lamp.
candeia, *n.f.* oil lamp.
candelabro, *n.m.* candelabrum.
candente, *adj.* red-hot; fiery.
candidatar-se, *vb.* be a candidate.
candidato -ta, *n.* candidate.
candidatura, *n.f.* candidacy.
cândido, *adj.* innocent; white.
candomblé, *n.m.* an Afro-Brazilian religion.
candonga, *n.f.* flattery; gossip.
candura, *n.f.*, **-dor,** *n.m.* innocence; whiteness.
caneca, *n.f.*, **-co,** *n.m.* mug.
canela, *n.f.* cinnamon; shin. **esticar as canelas,** *(coll.)* die.
canelar, *vb.* groove.
caneta, *n.f.* (writing) pen.
canga, *n.f.* yoke.
cangaceiro, *n.m.* bandit.
cangaço, *n.m.* banditry.
cangote, *n.m.* nape.
canguru, *n.m.* kangaroo.
cânhamo, *n.m.* hemp.
canhão, *n.m.* cannon; canyon; *(sl.)* hag.
canhestro, *adj.* clumsy.
canhoneira, *n.f.* gunboat.
canhota, *n.f.* left hand.
canhoto -ta, 1. *adj.* left-handed; clumsy. **2.** *n.* lefty; *(coll.)* Devil.
canibal, *n.m.* cannibal.
caniço, *n.m.* reed.
canil, *n.m.* kennel.
canino, *adj.* canine.
canivete, *n.m.* pocketknife. **chover canivetes,** rain cats and dogs.
canja, *n.f.* chicken soup; *(sl.)* cinch.

canjica, *n.f.* sweetened hominy.
cano, *n.m.* pipe; gun barrel. **c. de descarga,** exhaust pipe; **entrar pelo c.,** *(sl.)* fall on one's face.
canoa, *n.f.* canoe.
cânon, -ne, *n.m.* canon.
cansaço, *n.m.* tiredness.
cansado, *adj.* tired.
cansar, *vb.* tire.
cansativo, *adj.* tiresome.
canseira, *n.f.* fatigue; toil.
cantada, *n.f.* *(sl.)* sweet talk.
cantador -ra, *n.* folk singer.
cantar, 1. *n.m.* song. **2.** *vb.* sing; *(sl.)* sweet-talk.
cântaro, *n.m.* jug. **chover a cântaros,** rain cats and dogs.
cantarolar, *vb.* hum.
canteira, *n.f.* stone quarry.
canteiro, *n.m.* flower bed; stone mason.
cantiga, *n.f.* song; *(sl.)* fast talk.
cantilena, *n.f.* ditty; *(coll.)* boring talk.
cantina, *n.f.* café; P.X.; canteen.
canto, *n.m.* corner; song, chant.
cantor -ra, *n.* singer.
canudinho, *n.m.* drinking straw.
canudo, *n.m.* tube; straw; *(coll.)* diploma.
cão, *n.m.* dog; *(coll.)* Devil.
caolho, *adj.* one-eyed; cross-eyed.
caos, *n.m.* chaos.
caótico, *adj.* chaotic.
capa, *n.f.* cape; book cover; layer; cover.
capacete, *n.m.* helmet.
capacho, *n.m.* doormat.
capacidade, *n.f.* capacity; ability.
capacitar, *vb.* qualify; convince. **c.-se,** convince oneself.
capadócio, *n.m.* rogue.
capanga, *n.m.* thug.
capar, *vb.* castrate.
capataz, *n.m.* foreman.
capaz, *adj.* capable; *(coll.)* likely.
capcioso, *adj.* crafty.
capela, *n.f.* chapel.
capelão, *n.m.* chaplain.
capelo, *n.m.* hood.
capenga, *adj.* lame.

capengar, *vb.* limp.

capeta, *n.m.* devil; *(coll.)* little devil.

capiau -oa, *n.* hick.

capim, *n.m.* grass.

capinar, *vb.* hoe, weed.

capital, 1. *adj.* principal. 2. *n.f.* capital city; *n.m.* capital (wealth).

capitalismo, *n.m.* capitalism.

capitalista, *adj.*, *n.m.f.* capitalist.

capitanear, *vb.* captain.

capitania, *n.f.* captaincy.

capitânia, *n.f.* flagship.

capitão, *n.m.* captain.

capitólio, *n.m.* capitol.

capitular, *vb.* capitulate; classify.

capítulo, *n.m.* chapter.

capivara, *n.f.* capybara.

capixaba, 1. *adj.* of/pert. to Espírito Santo state. 2. *n.m.f.* Espírito Santo native.

capô, *n.m.* hood (car).

capoeira, *n.f.* Afro-Brazilian leg-fighting; coop; undergrowth.

capota, *n.f.* car roof.

capotar, *vb.* capsize.

capote, *n.m.* coat, cloak.

caprichar, *vb.* do carefully; have a whim.

capricho, *n.m.* whim; care.

caprichoso, *adj.* capricious; meticulous.

Capricórnio, *n.m.* Capricorn.

cápsula, *n.f.* capsule.

captar, *vb.* capture; *(rad.)* pick up.

captor, *n.m.* captor.

capturar, *vb.* capture. —**captura**, *n.f.*

capuz, *n.m.* hood, cowl.

caqui, *n.m.* persimmon.

cáqui, *adj.*, *n.m.* khaki.

cara, *n.f.* face; look; gall; *(sl.)* dame; *n.m.* *(sl.)* guy. **c. ou coroa**, heads or tails; **dar a cara**, *(sl.)* show up; **meter a c**, *(sl.)* be obvious; **quebrar a c.**, *(sl.)* fall on one's face.

carabina, *n.f.* carbine.

caracol, *n.m.* snail; ringlet.

característica, *n.f.* characteristic. —**característico**, *adj.*

caracterizar, *vb.* characterize.

cara-de-pau, 1. *adj.* pokerfaced; brazen. 2. *n.f.* gall; *n.m.f.* pushy person.

caradura, 1. *adj.* brazen. 2. *n.m.f.* wise guy.

Caraíbas, mar das, *n.m.* Caribbean Sea.

caralho, 1. *n.m.* *(vulg.)* penis. 2. *interj.*, *(vulg.)* damn it!

caramanchão, *n.m.* arbor.

caramba, *interj.* gosh!

carambola, *n.f.* carom; gooseberry.

caramelo, *n.m.* caramel.

cara-metade, *n.f.* *(coll.)* better half, wife.

caraminguás, *n.m.pl.* *(coll.)* small change.

caraminhola, *n.f.* *(coll.)* nonsense.

caranguejo, *n.m.* crab; *(cap.)* Cancer.

carão, *n.m.* *(coll.)* scolding.

carapinha, *n.f.* tight curly hair.

carapuça, *n.f.* cap; hood; insinuation.

caráter *(pl.* **caracteres**), *n.m.* character.

caravana, *n.f.* caravan; student excursion group.

caravela, *n.f.* caravel.

carbono, *n.m.* carbon.

carburador, *n.m.* carburetor.

carcaça, *n.f.* carcass.

carcás, *n.m.* quiver.

cárcere, *n.m.* jail.

carcereiro, *n.m.* jailer.

carcinógeno, *n.m.* carcinogen.

carcomido, *adj.* worm-eaten, rotten.

cardápio, *n.m.* menu.

cardeal, 1. *adj.* cardinal. **pontos cardeais**, cardinal points. 2. *n.m.* *(eccles.*, *ornith.)* cardinal.

cardíaco, *adj.* cardiac.

cardinal, *adj.* cardinal; principal. **número c.**, cardinal number.

cardiologia, *n.f.* cardiology.

cardo, *n.m.* thistle.

cardume, *n.m.* school (fish).

careca, 1. *adj.* bald. 2. *n.f.* bald spot; *n.m.f.* bald person.

carecer, *vb.* need; lack.

careiro, *adj.* charging high prices.

carência, *n.f.* need, lack.

carente, *adj.* needy.

carestia, *n.f.* expensiveness.

careta, 1. *adj. (sl.)* square. 2. *n.f.* grimace; mask; *(sl.)* square.

carga, *n.f.* load, cargo; burden; charge. **c. útil**, payload.

cargo, *n.m.* duty, office. **a c. de**, in charge of.

cargueiro, *n.m.* freighter.

Caribe, *n.m.* Caribbean. —**caribenho**, *adj.*

caricatura, *n.f.* caricature.

carícia, *n.f.* caress.

caridade, *n.f.* charity.

caridoso, *adj.* charitable.

cárie, *n.f. (dent.)* cavity.

carijó, *adj.* speckled.

caril, *n.m.* curry.

carimbo, *n.m.* (rubber) stamp. —**carimbar**, *vb.*

carinho, *n.m.* affection.

carinhoso, *adj.* affectionate.

carioca, 1. *adj.* of/pert. to the city of Rio de Janeiro. 2. *n.m.f.* Rio native.

carisma, *n.m.* charisma.

caritativo, *adj.* charitable.

cariz, *n.m.* face; look.

carmesim, *adj.* crimson.

carnal, *adj.* carnal.

carnaúba, *n.f.* carnauba wax.

carnaval, *n.m.* Carnival.

carnavalesco, 1. *adj.* Carnival. 2. *n.m.* Carnival reveler.

carne, *n.f.* meat; flesh. **c. assada**, roast beef; **c. de boi/vaca**, beef; **c. de porco**, pork; **c. de sol**, sun-dried meat; **c. seca**, jerked beef; **c. verde**, fresh meat; **em c. e osso**, in the flesh; **nem c. nem peixe**, noncommittal.

carneiro, *n.m.* sheep, ram; *(cap.)* Aries.

carniça, *n.f.* carrion; carnage.

carniçaria, *n.f.* butchery.

carniceiro, 1. *adj.* carnivorous; bloodthirsty. 2. *n.m.* butcher.

carnificina, *n.f.* carnage.

carnívoro, *adj.* carnivorous

caro, 1. *adj.* dear; expensive. 2. *adv.* dearly.

carochinha, *n.f.* **história da c.**, fairy tale.

caroço, *n.m.* pit, seed; lump.

carola, 1. *adj.* very pious. 2. *n.m.f.* religious fanatic.

carona, *n.f.* ride, lift.

carpete, *n.m.* carpet.

carpintaria, *n.f.* carpentry.

carpinteiro, *n.m.* carpenter.

carpir, *vb.* mourn.

carraça, *n.f.* tick.

carranca, *n.f.* frown.

carrancudo, *adj.* frowning.

carrapato, *n.m.* tick; parasite.

carrapicho, *n.m.* bun (hair).

carrasco, *n.m.* hangman; tyrant.

carraspana, *n.f. (coll.)* drunken spree.

carrear, *vb.* cart; bring on.

carregado, *adj.* loaded; sad; dark.

carregador -ra, *n.* porter; loader.

carregamento, *n.m.* loading; load.

carregar, *vb.* load; carry (off); intensify.

carreira, *n.f.* career; race; route; major. **arrepiar c.**, turn back; **às carreiras**, hurriedly.

carreiro, *n.m.* trail; carter.

carreta, *n.f.* cart, wagon.

carreteiro, *n.m.* carter, driver.

carretel, *n.m.* spool.

carreto, *n.m.* cartage.

carril, *n.m.* furrow; rail.

carrilhão, *n.m.* carillon.

carrinho, *n.m.* small cart; spool. **c. de mão**, wheelbarrow.

carro, *n.m.* car; cart. **c. alegórico**, float.

carro-bomba, *n.m.* car-bomb.

carroça, *n.f.* cart, wagon.

carroçaria, *n.f.* auto body.

carroceiro, *n.m.* carter.

carro-chefe, *n.m. (sl.)* main attraction.

carrossel, *n.m.* carrousel.

carruagem, *n.f.* coach, carriage.

carta, *n.f.* letter; map; charter; card; menu. **c. branca**, carte blanche; **c. de crédito**, letter of credit; **c. registrada**, registered letter; **dar cartas**, deal cards.

cartão, *n.m.* card; cardboard. **c. de crédito**, credit card; **c. de embarque**, boarding pass; **c. de visitas**, business card.

cartapácio, *n.m.* large tome; scrapbook.

cartão-pedra, *n.m.* papier-mâché.

cartaz, *n.m.* poster; *(coll.)* fame.

cartear-se (com), *vb.* correspond (with).

carteira, *n.f.* wallet; notebook; desk; pack (cigarettes); I.D. card. **c. de motorista**, driver's license.

carteiro, *n.m.* mailman.

cartel, *n.m.* cartel.

cárter, *n.m.* crankcase.

cartilagem, *n.f.* cartilage, gristle.

cartilha, *n.f.* primer.

cartola, *n.f.* top hat.

cartolina, *n.f.* cardboard.

cartomante, *n.m.f.* fortune-teller.

cartório, *n.m.* registry.

cartucho, *n.m.* cartridge.

cartum, *n.m.* cartoon.

cartunista, *n.m.f.* cartoonist.

caruru, *n.m.* okra and seafood dish.

carvalho, *n.m.* oak.

carvão *n.m.* coal; charcoal.

cãs, *n.f.pl.* white hair.

casa, *n.f.* house; home; firm; advisors; buttonhole; square (chess); decimal place; *(coll.)* age bracket. **c. de cômodos**, rooming house; **c. de penhor**, pawnshop; **c. de tolerância**, bawdyhouse; **em c.**, at home.

casaca, *n.f.* tailcoat. **virar a c.**, be a turncoat.

casaco, *n.m.* coat, suit coat.

casadouro, *adj.* marriageable.

casa-forte, *n.f.* vault, safe.

casa-grande, *n.f.* manor house.

casal, *n.m.* married couple; couple; hamlet.

casamenteiro -ra, *n.* matchmaker.

casamento, *n.m.* marriage; wedding.

casar, *vb.* marry; match. **c.(-se)**, get married; **c.(-se) com**, marry.

casarão, *n.m.* mansion.

casario, *n.m.* **-ria**, *n.f.* row of houses.

casca, *n.f.* peel; shell; bark; scab.

cascalho, *n.m.* gravel.

cascata, *n.f.* cascade.

cascavel, *n.m.* jingle bell; *n.f.* rattlesnake.

casco, *n.m.* hoof; hull; helmet; empty bottle.

cascudo, *n.m.* rap on the head.

casebre, *n.m.* shack.

caseiro, **1.** *adj.* homemade; simple. **2.** *n.m.* caretaker.

caserna, *n.f.* barracks.

casinha, *n.f.* small house; outhouse.

casinhola, *n.f.* hovel.

casino, cassino, *n.m.* casino.

casmurro, *adj.* stubborn; morose.

caso, **1.** *n.m.* case; situation; event; story; *(sl.)* love affair; lover. **de c. pensado**, deliberately; **em todo c.**, in any event; **fazer c. de**, heed; **vir ao c.**, be relevant. **2.** *conj.* if.

casório, *n.m.* *(coll.)* wedding.

caspa, *n.f.* dandruff.

casquete, *n.m.* skullcap.

casquinha, 1. *adj.* *(coll.)* stingy, **2.** *n.f.* thin shell; advantage. **tirar c**, make the most of it.

cassação, *n.f.* revoking of rights.

cassar, *vb.* revoke the rights of.

cassete, *n.m.* cassette, cartridge.

cassetete, *n.m.* billy club.

casta, *n.f.* caste.

castanha, *n.f.* chestnut. **c. de caju**, cashew; **c. do pará**, Brazil nut.

castanho, *adj.* chestnut, brown.

Castela, *n.f.* Castile.

castelhano -na, *adj., n.* Castilian; *n.m.* Castilian (language).

castelo, *n.m.* castle.

castiçal, *n.m.* candlestick.

castiço, *adj.* high-born; thoroughbred; pure.

castidade, *n.f.* chastity.

castigar, *vb.* punish.

castigo, *n.m.* punishment.

casto, *adj.* chaste, pure.

castor, *n.m.* beaver.

castrar, *vb.* castrate.

casual, *adj.* casual, accidental.

casualidade, *n.f.* chance. **por c.,** by chance.

casulo, *n.m.* cocoon; pod.

cata, *n.f.* **à c. de,** in search of.

catacumba, *n.f.* catacomb.

catadupa, *n.f.* waterfall.

catadura, *n.f.* mien; look.

catalão -lã, 1. *adj.* Catalonian. **2.** *n.* Catalonian; Catalan (language).

catalisador, *n.m.* catalyst.

catalogar, *vb.* catalog.

catálogo, *n.m.* catalog. **c. telefônico,** phone directory.

Catalunha, *n.f.* Catalonia.

catapora, *n.f.* chicken pox.

catapulta, *n.f.* catapult.

catar, *vb.* hunt (for); scrutinize.

catarata, *n.f.* waterfall; cataract.

catarro, *n.m.* common cold.

catástrofe, *n.f.* catastrophe.

catatau, *n.m.* long talk; *(coll.)* lot; tome.

cata-vento, *n.m.* weather vane; windmill; pinwheel.

catecismo, *n.m.* catechism.

cátedra, *n.f.* professorship.

catedral, *n.f.* cathedral.

catedrático, *n.m.* full professor.

categoria, *n.f.* category.

catequese, *n.f.* catechism.

catequizar, *vb.* catechize.

caterva, *n.f.* gang; mob.

catimba, *n.f.* *(sl.)* tricks, nuisance tactics.

catimbar, *vb.* *(sl.)* use tricks/nuisance tactics.

catimbó, *n.m.* witchcraft.

catinga, *n.f.* body odor.

catita, *adj.* well-dressed.

cativar, *vb.* captivate.

cativeiro, *n.m.* captivity.

cativo -va, *adj., n.* captive.

catolicismo, *n.m.* Catholicism.

católico -ca, *adj., n.* Catholic.

catorze, *adj.* fourteen.

catre, *n.m.* cot.

caução, *n.f.* guarantee; bond.

caucho, *n.m.* gum tree.

caucionar, *vb.* guarantee; put up bond.

cauda, *n.f.* tail.

caudal, 1. *adj.* abundant. **2.** *n.m.* torrent.

caudaloso, *adj.* torrential; abundant.

caudilho, *n.m.* chief; political boss.

caule, *n.m.* stalk, stem.

causa, *n.f.* cause; lawsuit. **por c. de,** because of.

causar, *vb.* cause.

cáustico, *adj.* caustic.

cautela, *n.f.* caution; pawn ticket.

cauteloso, *adj.* cautious.

cauto, *adj.* cautious.

cavação, *n.f.* digging; *(coll.)* hustling; racket.

cavaco, *n.m.* splinter; chat. **c. do ofício,** occupational hazard.

cavador -ra, *n.* digger; *(coll.)* hustler; wheeler-dealer.

cavalaria, *n.f.* cavalry; knighthood, chivalry.

cavalariça, *n.f.* stable.

cavaleiro, *n.m.* horseman; knight.

cavalete, *n.m.* easel; sawhorse.

cavalgadura, *n.f.* mount; idiot.

cavalgar, *vb.* ride (horse); straddle.

cavalheiresco, *adj.* chivalrous.

cavalheiro, *n.m.* gentleman.

cavalo, *n.m.* horse; knight (chess); *(coll.)* boor; horsepower. **tirar o c. da chuva,** *(sl.)* call it quits.

cavalo-marinho, *n.m.* sea horse.

cavalo-vapor, *n.m.* horsepower.

cavanhaque, *n.m.* goatee.

cavaquear, *vb.* chat.

cavaquinho, *n.m.* small guitar, ukulele.

cavar, *vb.* dig; *(coll.)* hustle; *(coll.)* wheel and deal.

caveira, *n.f.* skull.

caverna, *n.f.* cavern, cave.

cavidade, *n.f.* cavity.

caviloso, *adj.* tricky.

cavo, *adj.* hollow.

caxemira, *n.f.* cashmere.

caxias, *n.m.* *(coll.)* disciplinarian; stickler.

caxumba, *n.f.* mumps.

cê, *n.m.* the letter c.

cear, *vb.* dine.

cearense, 1. *adj.* of/pert. to Ceará state. **2.** *n.m.f.* Ceará native.

cebola, *n.f.* onion.

cebolinha, *n.f.* green onion.

cecear, *vb.* lisp. **—ceceio,** *n.m.*

ceder, *vb.* cede; yield.

cediço, *adj.* stagnant; corrupt; old.

cedilha, *n.f.* cedilla.

cedo, *adv.* early.

cedro, *n.m.* cedar.

cédula, *n.f.* banknote; ballot; IOU.

cego, *adj.* blind. **—cegar,** *vb.*

cegonha, *n.f.* stork.

cegueira, *n.f.* blindness.

ceia, *n.f.* supper.

ceifa, *n.f.* harvest. **—ceifar,** *vb.*

cela, *n.f.* cell, cubicle.

celebração, *n.f.* celebration.

celebrar, *vb.* celebrate.

célebre, *adj.* celebrated.

celebridade, *n.f.* celebrity.

celeiro, *n.m.* granary, barn.

celeridade, *n.f.* speed.

celeste, *adj.* celestial.

celeuma, *n.f.* uproar.

celhas, *n.f.pl.* eyelashes.

celibatário, 1. *adj.* celibate. **2.** *n.m.* bachelor.

celibato, *n.m.* celibacy.

celofane, *n.m.* cellophane.

célula, *n.f.* (*biol.*) cell.

celulose, *n.f.* cellulose.

cem, *adj.* one hundred.

cemitério, *n.m.* cemetery.

cena, *n.f.* scene.

cenário, *n.m.* scenery.

cenho, *n.m.* frown.

cenoura, *n.f.* carrot.

censo, *n.m.* census.

censor, *n.m.* censor.

censura, *n.f.* censorship; censure.

censurar, *vb.* censor; censure.

centavo, *n.m.* cent.

centeio, *n.m.* rye.

centelha, *n.f.* spark, sparkle. **—centelhar,** *vb.*

centena, *n.f.* hundred.

centenário, 1. *adj.*, *n.m.* centenarian. **2.** *n.m.* centenary.

centésimo, *adj.*, *n.m.* hundredth.

centígrado, *adj.* centigrade.

centímetro, *n.m.* centimeter.

cento, *n.m.* hundred. **por c.,** percent.

central, 1. *adj.* central. **2.** *n.f.* central office.

centralizar, *vb.* centralize.

centrar, *vb.* center.

centrífuga, *n.f.* centrifuge.

centro, *n.m.* center; downtown; club.

centro-americano -na, *adj.*, *n.* Central American.

centúria, *n.f.* hundred; century.

CEP (código de endereçamento postal), *n.m.* zip code.

cepa, *n.f.* vine stock.

cepilho, *n.m.* plane.

cepo, *n.m.* stump, block.

cepticismo, *n.m.* skepticism.

céptico -ca, 1. *adj.* skeptical. **2.** *n.* skeptic.

cera, *n.f.* wax. **fazer c.,** stall.

cerâmica, *n.f.* ceramics.

cerca, 1. *n.f.* fence. **2.** *adv.* circa; about. **c. de,** nearly.

cercadinho, *n.m.* playpen.

cercado, *n.m.* enclosure.

cercanias, *n.f.pl.* outskirts, vicinity.

cercar, *vb.* fence; surround; besiege.

cercear, *vb.* cut close, clip; curb.

cerco, *n.m.* siege.

cerda, *n.f.* bristle.

cereal, *adj.*, *n.m.* cereal.

cérebro, *n.m.* brain.

cereja, *n.f.* cherry.

cerimônia, *n.f.* ceremony; formality.

cerimonial, *adj.* ceremonial.

cerimonioso, *adj.* ceremonious.

ceroulas, *n.f.pl.* long underwear.

cerração, *n.f.* fog; gloom.

cerrado, 1. *adj.* closed; cloudy; thick. **2.** *n.m.* enclosure; wooded pastureland.

cerrar, *vb.* close; tighten. **c.-se,** cloud up.

cerro, *n.m.* hillock.

certa, *n.f.* (*coll.*) **na c.,** surely.

certame, *n.m.* battle; contest.

certeiro, *adj.* well-aimed; precise.

certeza, *n.f.* certainty. **com c,** certainly. **ter c.,** be sure.

certidão, *n.f.* certificate. **c. de nascimento,** birth certificate.

certificado, *n.m.* certificate.

certificar, *vb.* certify; convince. **c.-se,** make sure.

certo, *adj.* certain; sure; right.

cerveja, *n.f.* beer.

cervejaria, *n.f.* brewery; beer hall.

cervejeiro, *n.m.* brewer; beer dealer.

cerviz, *n.f.* neck; (*fig.*) head.

cervo, *n.m.* buck, stag.

cerzir, *vb.* darn.

cesariana, *n.f.* caesarean section.

cessação, *n.f.* cessation.

cessão, *n.f.* cession, grant.

cessar, *vb.* cease.

cessar-fogo, *n.m.* cease-fire.

cesta, *n.f.* basket.

cesto, *n.m.* small basket.

cetim, *n.m.* satin.

cetro, *n.m.* scepter.

céu, *n.m.* sky; heaven; roof (mouth).

cevada, *n.f.* barley.

cevar, *vb.* fatten, feed.

chá, *n.m.* tea. **não ter tomado c. em pequeno,** be ill-mannered.

chã, *n.f.* plain; round (beef.)

chacal, *n.m.* jackal.

chácara, *n.f.* country place.

chacina, *n.f.* slaughter; carnage.

chacoalhar, *vb.* shake; (*sl.*) pester.

chacota, *n.f.* mock; jest.

chafariz, *n.m.* fountain.

chafurda, *n.f.* pigsty; mire.

chafurdar, *vb.* wallow in the mud.

chaga, *n.f.* wound, sore.

chalaça, *n.f.* joke, coarse jest.

chalé, *n.m.* chalet.

chaleira, *n.f.* kettle; *n.m.* (*coll.*) flatterer.

chaleirar, *vb.* (*coll.*) flatter, fawn.

chama, *n.f.* flame.

chamada, *n.f.* call; roll call. **fazer a c.,** call roll.

chamado, 1. *adj.* so-called. 2. *n.m.* call.

chamamento, *n.m.* call; convocation.

chamar, *vb.* call; attract. **c.-se,** be called.

chamariz, *n.m.* decoy; lure.

chamego, *n.m.* intimacy; courtship; necking.

chamejar, *vb.* flame.

chaminé, *n.f.* chimney; smokestack.

champanhe, -nha, *n.m.* champagne.

champinhon, *n.m.* mushroom.

chamuscar, *vb.* singe.

chance, *n.f.* chance, opportunity.

chancela, *n.f.* seal, stamp.

chanceler, *n.m.* chancellor.

chanchada, *n.f.* farce.

chantagem, *n.f.* blackmail. —**chantagear,** *vb.*

chantagista, *n.m.f.* blackmailer.

chão, chã, 1. *adj.* flat; simple; frank. 2. *n.m.* ground; floor.

chapa, *n.f.* plate, sheet; slate; snapshot; license plate. **de c.,** squarely; **meu c.,** (*sl.*) buddy.

chapada, *n.f.* plain; plateau.

chapado, *adj.* (*coll.*) downright.

chapéu, *n.m.* hat.

chapeuzinho, *n.m.* little hat; (*coll.*) circumflex accent.

chapinhar, *vb.* splash.

charada, *n.f.* charade.

charanga, *n.f.* brass band.

charco, *n.m.* bog, marsh.

charcutaria, *n.f.* pork shop.

charlar, *vb.* prattle. —**charla,** *n.f.*

charlatão, *n.m.* charlatan.

charneca, *n.f.* heath, moor.

charneira, *n.f.* hinge.

charque, *n.m.* jerky.

charrua, *n.f.* plow.

charutaria, *n.f.* tobacconist's.

charuto, *n.m.* cigar.

chasco, *n.m.* gibe. —**chasquear,** *vb.*

chassi, *n.m.* chassis.

chata, *n.f.* barge.

chateação, *n.f.* (*coll.*) annoyance; bore.

chateado, *adj.* (*coll.*) annoyed, bored.

chatear, *vb.* (*coll.*) annoy; bore.

chatice, *n.f.* (*coll.*) annoyance; bore.

chato, 1. *adj.* flat; (*coll.*) annoying; dull; obnoxious. 2. *n.m.* (*coll.*) pest, bore.

chauvinismo, *n.m.* chauvinism; male chauvinism.

chavão, *n.m.* mold; cliché.

chave, *n.f.* key; wrench; hold. **c. de fenda/parafuso,** screwdriver; **c. de ouro,** final flourish; **c. inglesa,** wrench.

chaveiro, *n.m.* key ring; turnkey.

chávena, *n.f.* cup.

chaveta, *n.f.* cotter pin.

checar, *vb.* check.

chefatura, *n.f.* headquarters.

chefe, *n.m.f.* chief, boss.

chefia, *n.f.* directorship.

chefiar, *vb.* head, direct.

chegada, *n.f.* arrival.

chegado, *adj.* close, intimate.

chegar, *vb.* arrive, come; reach; be enough. **chega!,** that's enough!

cheia, *n.f.* flood.

cheio, *adj.* full; crowded; *(coll.)* fed up. **c. de si,** conceited; **em c.,** fully.

cheirar, *vb.* smell. **c. a,** smell of.

cheiro, *n.m.* smell; aroma.

cheiroso, *adj.* fragrant.

cheque, *n.m.* check. **c. ao portador,** check made out to cash; **c. avulso,** counter check; **c. certificado,** postdated check; **c. nominal,** check made out to a specific person; **c. visado,** certified check; **descontar um c.,** cash a check.

chiada, *n.f.* squeak, screech.

chiado, *n.m.* creak; screech; wheeze.

chiar, *vb.* creak; screech; chirp; sizzle; wheeze; *(coll.)* get mad.

chibata, *n.f.* whip, switch.

chicana, *n.f.* chicanery.

chiclete, chicle, *n.m.* chewing gum.

chicote, *n.m.* whip.

chifrar, *vb.* butt, gore; *(coll.)* cuckold.

chifre, *n.m. (zool.)* horn. **botar os chifres em,** *(coll.)* cuckold.

chifrudo, 1. *adj.* horned; *(coll.)* cuckolded. **2.** *n.m. (coll.)* cuckold.

chileno -na, *adj., n.* Chilean.

chilique, *n.m. (coll.)* fainting spell.

chilrar, -rear, *vb.* chirp.

chimarrão, *n.m.* unsweetened maté.

chimpanzé, *n.m.* chimpanzee.

chinelo, *n.m.* , **-la,** *n.f.* slipper. **botar no c.,** *(coll.)* outshine.

chinês -nesa, *adj., n.* Chinese; *n.m.* Chinese (language).

chinfrim, 1. *adj. (coll.)* crummy. **2.** *n.m. (coll.)* uproar.

chinó, *n.m.* wig.

chio, *n.m.* screech; creak; chirp; hiss.

Chipre, *n.m.* Cyprus.

chique, *adj.* chic.

chiqueiro, *n.m.* pigpen.

chispa, *n.f.* spark. —**chispar,** *vb.*

chiste, *n.m.* wit; witticism.

chistoso, *adj.* witty.

chita, *n.f.* calico.

choça, *n.f.* hut.

chocadeira, *n.f.* incubator.

chocalhar, *vb.* rattle; guffaw; divulge.

chocalho, *n.m.* rattle.

chocante, *adj.* shocking.

chocar, *vb.* crash; shock; incubate, hatch.

chocarreiro -ra, 1. *adj.* joking. **2.** *n.* joker.

chocarrice, *n.f.* coarse joke.

chocho, *adj.* dry, insipid.

chocolate, *n.m.* chocolate.

chofer, *n.m.f.* driver.

chofre, *n.m.* sudden blow. **de c.,** suddenly.

chope, *n.m.* draft beer.

choque, *n.m.* crash; shock; clash.

choradeira,   *n.f.*   crying; mourner.

chorado, *adj.* lamented; mournful.

choramingar, *vb.* whimper.

choramingas,   *n.m.   (coll.)* crybaby.

chorão, -rona, 1. *adj.* crying. **2.** *n.* crybaby.

chorar, *vb.* weep, cry; lament. **c. o preço,** *(coll.)* haggle.

choro, *n.m.* crying; popular music type.

choupana, *n.f.* hut.

chouriço, *n.m.* sausage.

chove-não-molha, *n.m. (coll.)* wishy-washy person.

chover, *vb.* rain; abound. **c. no molhado,** carry coals to Newcastle.

chuchar, *vb. (coll.)* suck.

chuchu, *n.m.* chayote. **pra c.**, *(sl.)* galore; very.

chucrute, *n.m.* sauerkraut.

chulé, *n.m. (coll.)* foot odor.

chulo, *adj.* vulgar.

chumbado, *adj.* leaded; *(coll.)* drunk; *(sl.)* tired out.

chumbar, *vb.* lead; solder; *(coll.)* shoot.

chumbo, *n.m.* lead.

chupado, *adj. (coll.)* skinny.

chupão, *n.m. (sl.)* kiss; hickey.

chupar, *vb.* suck; guzzle; exploit.

chupa-sangue, *n.m.* bloodsucker.

chupeta, *n.f.* pacifier.

churrascaria, *n.f.* barbecue restaurant.

churrasco, *n.m.* barbecued meat; barbecue.

churrasqueira, *n.f.* barbecue grill.

churupitar, *vb. (coll.)* slurp.

chusma, *n.f.* crowd.

chutador -ra, *n.* kicker; *(sl.)* liar.

chutar, *vb.* kick; *(sl.)* throw out; *(sl.)* lie; *(sl.)* guess; *(sl.)* get rid of; *(sl.)* cheat.

chute, *n.m.* kick; *(sl.)* lies. **dar um c. em**, *(sl.)* swindle; jilt.

chuva, *n.f.* rain. **ficar na c.**, *(sl.)* get drunk.

chuvarada, *n.f.* heavy rain.

chuveiro, *n.m.* shower.

chuviscar, *vb.* drizzle. **—chuvisco**, *n.m.*

chuvoso, *adj.* rainy.

cianotipia, *n.f.* blueprint.

cibernética, *n.f.* cybernetics.

cicatriz, *n.f.* scar.

cicatrizar, *vb.* scar; heal.

cicerone, *n.m.f.* guide.

ciciar, *vb.* whisper; rustle; lisp. **—cicio**, *n.m.*

ciclismo, *n.m.* cycling.

ciclo, *n.m.* cycle.

ciclone, *n.m.* cyclone.

cíclotron, *n.m.* cyclotron.

cidadania, *n.f.* citizenship.

cidadão -dã, *n.* citizen.

cidade, *n.f.* city; downtown.

cidadela, *n.f.* citadel.

ciência, *n.f.* science; knowledge.

ciente, *adj.* aware.

científico, *adj.* scientific.

cientista, *n.m.f.* scientist.

cifra, *n.f.* cipher; number.

cifrar, *vb.* cipher; summarize.

cigano -na, *adj., n.* gypsy.

cigarra, *n.f.* cicada.

cigarreira, *n.f.* cigarette case.

cigarro, *n.m.* cigarette.

cilada, *n.f.* ambush.

cilha, *n.f.* cinch. **—cilhar**, *vb.*

cilindro, *n.m.* cylinder.

cílio, *n.m.* eyelash.

cima, *n.f.* top. **em c.**, above; **em c. de**, on top of; **por c.**, overhead.

címbalo, *n.m.* cymbal.

cimento, *n.m.* cement. **c. armado**, reinforced concrete.

cimentar, *vb.* cement.

cimo, *n.m.* top.

cincerro, *n.m.* cowbell.

cincha, *n.f.* cinch. **—cinchar**, *vb.*

cinco, *adj.* five.

cindir, *vb.* split.

cine, *n.m.* movie theater.

cineasta, *n.m.f.* film maker.

cinema, *n.m.* cinema, movies.

cinematografia, *n.f.* cinematography.

cinético, *adj.* kinetic.

cingir, *vb.* gird. **c.-se**, limit oneself.

cínico, 1. *adj.* cynical; shameless. **2.** *n.m.* cynic; shameless person.

cinismo, *n.m.* cynicism; shamelessness.

cinqüenta, *adj.* fifty.

cinqüentão -tona, *n.* person in his/her fifties.

cinqüentenário, *n.m.* fiftieth anniversary.

cinta, *n.f.* girdle; band.

cintilar, *vb.* scintillate.

cinto, *n.m.* belt. **c. de segurança**, safety belt.

cintura, *n.f.* waist.

cinza, 1. *adj.* gray. **2.** *n.f.* ash.

cinzeiro, *n.m.* ashtray.

cinzel, *n.m.* chisel. **—cinzelar**, *vb.*

cinzento, *adj.* gray, ashen.

cio, *n.m.* heat, estrus.

cioso, *adj.* jealous; zealous.

cipó, *n.m.* liana, vine.

cipreste, *n.m.* cypress.

ciranda, *n.f.* children's circle game.

circo, *n.m.* circus.

circuito, *n.m.* circuit.

circulação, *n.f.* circulation.

circular, 1. *adj.* circular. **2.** *vb.* circulate; circle.

círculo, *n.m.* circle.

circuncidar, *vb.* circumcise.

circuncisão, *n.f.* circumcision.

circundante, *adj.* surrounding.

circunferência, *n.f.* circumference.

circunflexo, *adj., n.m.* circumflex.

circunlóquio, *n.m.* circumlocution.

circunscrever, *vb.* circumscribe.

circunspeto, *adj.* circumspect.

circunstância, *n.f.* circumstance.

circunstante, 1. *adj.* surrounding. **2.** *n.* attender.

círio, *n.m.* large candle.

cirrose, *n.f.* cirrhosis.

cirurgia, *n.f.* surgery.

cirurgião -giã, *n.* surgeon.

cirúrgico, *adj.* surgical.

cisalha, *n.f.* shears.

cisão, *n.f.* split; fission.

ciscar, *vb.* rake; scratch; peck.

cisma, *n.m.* schism; *n.f.* preoccupation; obsession; suspicion.

cismar, *vb.* ponder; be preoccupied; be suspicious.

cisne, *n.m.* swan.

cisterna, *n.f.* cistern.

cisto, *n.m.* cyst.

citação, *n.f.* quotation; citation; subpoena.

citadino -na, 1. *adj.* city. **2.** *n.* city-dweller.

citar, *vb.* quote; cite; subpoena.

cítrico, *adj.* citrus.

ciumaria, -meira, *n.f.* jealous fit.

ciúme, *n.m.* jealousy; envy. **estar com ciúmes de,** be jealous of.

ciumento, *adj.* jealous.

cível, *adj. (jur.)* civil.

cívico, *adj.* civic.

civil, 1. *adj.* civil; civilian. **2.** *n.m.f.* civilian.

civilidade, *n.f.* civility.

civilização, *n.f.* civilization.

civilizar, *vb.* civilize.

cizânia, *n.f.* discord.

clã, *n.m.* clan.

clamar, *vb.* clamor; complain; call for.

clamor, *n.m.* clamor.

clamoroso, *adj.* noisy.

clandestino -na, 1. *adj.* clandestine. **2.** *n.* stowaway; illegal.

clara, *n.f.* egg white. **às claras,** openly.

clarabóia, *n.f.* skylight.

clarão, *n.m.* glare; clearing.

clarear, *vb.* clear up; grow light.

clareira, *n.f.* clearing.

clareza, *n.f.* clarity.

claridade, *n.f.* clarity; light; whiteness.

clarificar, *vb.* clarify.

clarim, *n.m.* bugle.

clarineta, *n.f.,* **-nete,** *n.m.* clarinet.

clarividente, *adj.* clairvoyant.

claro, 1. *adj.* clear; bright; light (color). **2.** *n.m.* space; clearing. **3.** *adv.* of course.

classe, *n.f.* class.

clássico, *adj., n.m.* classic.

classificação, *n.f.* classification.

classificar, *vb.* classify.

claudicar, *vb.* limp.

claustro, *n.m.* cloister; monastery; faculty.

claustrofobia, *n.f.* claustrophobia.

cláusula, *n.f.* clause.

clausura, *n.f.* enclosure; seclusion.

clava, *n.f.* club; cudgel.

clave, *n.f.* clef.

clavícula, *n.f.* collarbone.

clemência, *n.f.* clemency; mildness.

clemente, *adj.* merciful; mild.

cleptomania, *n.f.* kleptomania.

clerezia, *n.f.* clergy.

clerical, *adj.* clerical (clergy).

clérigo, *n.m.* clergyman.

clero, *n.m.* clergy.

clichê, *n.m.* cliché; printing plate; edition.

cliente, *n.m.f.* client, customer.

clientela, *n.f.* clientele.

clima, *n.m.* climate.

clímax, *n.m.* climax.

clínica, *n.f.* clinic; medical practice.

clínico, 1. *adj.* clinical. **2.** *n.m.* physician.

clipe, *n.m.* paper clip.

clister, *n.m.* enema.

cloaca, *n.f.* sewer.

cloro, *n.m.* chlorine.

clorofila, *n.f.* chlorophyll.

clorofórmio, *n.m.* chloroform.

clube, *n.m.* club.

coabitar, *vb.* cohabit.

coação, *n.f.* coercion.

coador, *n.m.* filter.

coagir, *vb.* coerce.

coagular, *vb.* coagulate.

coágulo, *n.m.* clot, curd.

coalescer, *vb.* coalesce.

coalhada, *n.f.* clabber.

coalhar, *vb.* curdle, clot.

coalho, *n.m.* clot, curd.

coalizão, *n.f.* coalition.

coar, *vb.* filter.

coaxar, *vb.* croak.

cobaia, *n.f.* guinea pig.

coberta, *n.f.* cover; deck.

coberto, *adj.* covered; overcast.

cobertor, *n.m.* blanket, cover.

cobertura, *n.f.* cover; coverage; topping; penthouse.

cobiça, *n.f.* greed.

cobiçar, *vb.* covet.

cobiçoso, *adj.* greedy.

cobra, *n.f.* snake; *n.m.* (*sl.*) expert.

cobrador -ra, *n.* ticket seller.

cobrança, *n.f.* collection.

cobrar, *vb.* charge, collect; demand.

cobre, *n.m.* copper.

cobrir, *vb.* cover. **c.-se,** don a hat; become cloudy.

cobro, *n.m.* end.

coca, *n.f.* coca; (*sl.*) cocaine; (*sl.*) coca-cola.

coça, *n.f.* (*coll.*) whipping.

cocada, *n.f.* coconut candy.

cocaína, *n.f.* cocaine.

cocar, 1. *n.m.* cockade. **2.** *vb.* peep.

coçar, *vb.* scratch; (*coll.*) beat; (*sl.*) dawdle.

cócegas, *n.f.pl.* tickle; (*fig.*) itch. **fazer c.,** tickle.

coceguento, *adj.* ticklish.

coceira, *n.f.* itch.

coche, *n.m.* coach.

cocheira, *n.f.* carriage house.

cocheiro, *n.m.* coachman.

cochichar, *vb.* whisper. **—cochicho,** *n.m.*

cochilar, *vb.* (*coll.*) nap. **—cochilo,** *n.m.*

cocho, *n.m.* trough.

coco, *n.m.* coconut; (*coll.*) head; folk dance.

cocô, *n.m.* bun (hair).

cocô, *n.m.* (*coll.*) excrement.

cócoras, *n.f.pl.* **de c.,** squatting.

cocorote, *n.m.* rap on the head.

côdea, *n.f.* bread crust; rind.

códice, *n.m.* codex.

código, *n.m.* code.

codorna, -niz, *n.f.* quail.

coelho, *n.m.* rabbit.

coentro, *n.m.* coriander, cilantro.

coerção, *n.f.* coercion.

coerente, *adj.* coherent.

coesão, *n.f.* cohesion.

coeso, -sivo, *adj.* cohesive.

coetâneo, *adj., n.m.* contemporary.

coexistir, *vb.* coexist.

cofre, *n.m.* safe, chest.

cogitar, *vb.* cogitate.

cognato, *adj., n.m.* cognate.

cognitivo, *adj.* cognitive.

cogumelo, *n.m.* mushroom.

coibir, *vb.* curb; prevent.

coice, *n.m.* kick; recoil.

coincidência, *n.f.* coincidence.

coincidente, *adj.* coincidental.

coincidir, *vb.* coincide.

coisa, *n.f.* thing; matter; *n.m.f.* so-and-so. **c. alguma/nenhuma,** nothing; **c. de,** approximately; **alguma c.,** something.

coitado -da, 1. *adj.* unfortunate. **2.** *n.* poor thing.

coito, *n.m.* coitus.

cola, *n.f.* glue; cheating; cheat sheet.

colaboração, *n.f.* collaboration.

colaborador -ra, *n.* collaborator; (*journ.*) contributor.

colaborar, *vb.* collaborate; (*journ.*) contribute.

colação, *n.f.* conferment. **c. de grau,** graduation ceremony.

colagem, *n.f.* collage.

colante, *adj.* tight, clinging.

colapso, *n.m.* collapse, breakdown.

colar, 1. *n.m.* necklace. **2.** *vb.*

glue; receive (degree); fit well; (coll.) cheat (exams).

colarinho, n.m. collar; (coll.) head (beer).

colateral, adj. collateral.

colcha, n.f. bedspread.

colchão, n.m. mattress.

colchete, n.m. hook; (pl.) brackets.

coldre, n.m. holster.

colear, vb. slither; meander.

coleção, n.f. collection.

colecionador -ra, n. collector.

colecionar, vb. collect.

colega, n.m.f. colleague; co-worker; schoolmate.

colegial, 1. adj. school; high-school. **2.** n.m.f. schoolboy, -girl.

colégio, n.m. (high) school; college.

coleira, n.f. animal collar.

cólera, n.f. wrath; n.f.m. cholera.

colérico, adj. irate.

colesterol, n.m. cholesterol.

coleta, n.f. collection.

coletânea, n.f. anthology.

colete, n.m. vest. **c. salva-vidas,** life jacket.

coletividade, n.f. collectivity.

coletivo, 1. adj. collective. **2.** n.m. bus.

coletor -ra, n. collector; n.m. sewer main.

coletoria, n.f. tax-collecting office.

colgadura, n.f. wall hanging.

colgar, vb. hang.

colheita, n.f. harvest, crop.

colher, n.f. spoon. **c. de chá,** teaspoon; **dar uma c. de chá,** (sl.) give a break; **meter a c.,** (coll.) meddle.

colher, vb. pick; gather; catch.

colibri, n.m. hummingbird.

cólica, n.f. colic.

colidir, vb. collide, clash.

coligação, n.f. coalition.

coligar, vb. unite.

coligir, vb. collect.

colina, n.f. hill.

colírio, n.m. eyedrops.

colisão, n.f. collision.

coliseu, n.m. coliseum.

collant, n.m. (F.) panty hose.

colmar, vb. pile; complete; thatch.

colmeia, n.f. beehive.

colmilho, n.m. tusk; fang; canine tooth.

colmo, n.m. thatch.

colo, n.m. lap; neck.

colocação, n.f. placement; job.

colocar, vb. place; employ.

colombiano -na, adj., n. Colombian.

colônia, n.f. colony; community.

colonial, adj. colonial.

colonialismo, n.m. colonialism.

colonizar, vb. colonize.

colono -na, n. colonist.

coloquial, adj. colloquial.

colóquio, n.m. colloquy; colloquium.

colorido, 1. adj. colored; colorful. **2.** n.m. coloring.

colorir, vb. color.

colossal, adj. colossal.

colosso, n.m. colossus.

coluna, n.f. column.

colunista, n.m.f. columnist.

colusão, n.f. collusion.

com, prep. with. **c. que então,** so.

coma, n.m.f. coma.

comadre, n.f. one's child's godmother or godchild's mother; (coll.) gossiper.

comandante, n.m.f. commander.

comandar, vb. command.

comando, n.m. command; commando.

comarca, n.f. district.

combalir, vb. weaken.

combate, n.m. combat. —**combater,** vb.

combatente, n.m.f. combatant.

combinação, n.f. combination; agreement; slip.

combinar, vb. combine; agree (on). **c. com,** go well with.

comboio, n.m. convoy; (P.) train.

combustão, n.f. combustion.

combustível, 1. adj. combustible. **2.** n.m. fuel.

começar, vb. begin, start. **c. a,** begin to.

começo, n.m. beginning.

comédia, n.f. comedy.

comediante, *n.m.f.* comedian -ena.

comedido, *adj.* moderate; reserved.

comedouro, *n.m.* feeder, trough.

comemoração, *n.f.* commemoration.

comemorar, *vb.* commemorate.

comemorativo, *adj.* commemorative.

comensal, *n.m.f.* fellow diner.

comentar, *vb.* comment (on); remark (about).

comentário, *n.m.* comment; commentary.

comentarista, *n.m.f.* commentator.

comer, *vb.* eat; omit; jump (checkers); *(vulg.)* have sex with.

comercial, *adj., n.m.* commercial.

comerciante, *n.m.f.* merchant.

comércio, *n.m.* commerce; business; business district.

comes, *n.m.pl.* c. e bebes, food and drink.

comestível, **1.** *adj.* edible. **2.** *n.m.pl.* food.

cometa, *n.m.* comet.

cometer, *vb.* commit; entrust.

comichão, *n.f.* itch.

comício, *n.m.* meeting, rally.

cômico, **1.** *adj.* comical. **2.** *n.m.* comedian.

comida, *n.f.* food.

comigo, *pron.* with me.

comilança, *n.f. (coll.)* overeating.

comilão **-lona**, **1.** *adj.* gluttonous. **2.** *n.* glutton.

cominho, *n.m.* cumin.

comiserar, *vb.* arouse pity. **c.-se**, commiserate.

comissão, *n.f.* commission; committee.

comissário **-ria**, *n.* commissioner; agent; inspector; purser. **c. de bordo**, flight attendant.

comitê, *n.m.* committee.

comitiva, *n.f.* entourage.

como, **1.** *adv.* how. **c.?**, what?; **c. vai?**, how are you? **2.** *conj.* as; like; since.

comoção, *n.f.* shock; emotion; upheaval.

cômoda, *n.f.* chest of drawers.

comodidade, *n.f.* comfort; convenience.

comodismo, *n.m.* self-indulgence.

cômodo, **1.** *adj.* comfortable; convenient. **2.** *n.m.* room.

comodoro, *n.m.* commodore.

comovente, **-vedor**, *adj.* moving.

comover, *vb.* move, touch.

compacto, *adj.* compact.

compadecer, *vb.* pity. **c.-se**, feel pity; harmonize.

compadre, *n.m.* one's child's godfather or godchild's father.

compaixão, *n.f.* compassion.

companheiro **-ra**, *n.* companion; mate; comrade.

companhia, *n.f.* company; firm.

comparação, *n.f.* comparison.

comparado, *adj.* compared; comparative.

comparar, *vb.* compare.

comparável, *adj.* comparable.

comparecer, *vb.* appear.

comparsa, *n.m.f. (theat.)* extra; take.

compartilhar, *vb.* share; partake.

compartimento, *n.m.* compartment; room.

compassado, *adj.* unhurried; steady.

compassivo, *adj.* compassionate.

compasso, *n.m. (mus.)* beat; time; drawing compass.

compatível, *adj.* compatible.

compatriota, *n.m.f.* compatriot.

compelir, *vb.* compel.

compêndio, *n.m.* compendium.

compenetração, *n.f.* conviction.

compenetrar, *vb.* convince.

compensação, *n.f.* compensation.

compensado, *n.m.* plywood.

compensar, *vb.* compensate; make up for.

competência, *n.f.* competence; jurisdiction.

competente, *adj.* competent; appropriate.

competição, *n.f.* competition; match.

competidor **-ra**, *n.* competitor.

competir, vb. compete; fall to.

compilar, vb. compile.

complacência, n.f. kindness.

compleição, n.f. constitution; temperament.

complemento, n.m. complement.

completo, adj. complete.
—completar, vb.

complexidade, n.f. complexity.

complexo, adj., n.m. complex.

complicação, n.f. complication.

complicar, vb. complicate.

componente, adj., n.m. component.

compor, vb. compose; arrange.

comporta, n.f. floodgate.

comportado, adj. behaved.

comportamento, n.m. behavior.

comportar, vb. contain. **c.-se,** behave.

composição, n.f. composition; arrangement.

compósito, adj. composite.

compositor -ra, n. composer.

composto, 1. adj. composed; composite; compound. **2.** n.m. compound.

compostura, n.f. composition; composure; arrangement; falsification.

compota, n.f. compote.

compra, n.f. purchase. **fazer compras,** shop.

comprador -ra, n. buyer.

comprar, vb. buy.

comprazer, vb. please. **c.-se,** be pleased.

compreender, vb. understand; include.

compreensão, n.f. comprehension, understanding.

compreensível, adj. understandable.

compreensivo, adj. understanding; comprehensive.

compressa, n.f. compress.

compressão, n.f. compression.

comprido, adj. long.

comprimento, n.m. length.

comprimido, n.m. tablet, pill.

comprimir, vb. compress, squeeze.

comprometer, vb. commit; pledge; risk; compromise. **c.-se,** commit oneself.

compromisso, n.m. commitment; compromise.

comprovante, n.m. voucher.

comprovar, vb. confirm, verify.

compulsivo, adj. compulsive.

compulsório, adj. compulsory.

compunção, n.f. compunction.

computador, n.m. computer.

computar, vb. compute.

comum, adj. common.

comungar, vb. give/receive Communion; commune.

comunhão, n.f. communion.

comunicação, n.f. communication; notice; paper.

comunicado, n.m. communication; communiqué.

comunicar, vb. communicate; convey. **c.-se (com),** communicate (with).

comunidade, n.f. community; commonwealth.

comunismo, n.m. communism.

comunista, adj. n.m.f. communist.

comutador, n.m. (elec.) switch.

comutar, vb. commute.

côncavo, adj. concave.

conceber, vb. conceive.

conceder, vb. concede.

conceito, n.m. concept; reputation; opinion.

conceituar, vb. conceive; evaluate; respect.

concelho, n.m. council.

concentração, n.f. concentration.

concentrar, vb. concentrate. **c.-se (em),** concentrate (on).

concepção, n.f. conception; opinion.

concernente a, prep. concerning.

concernir a, vb. have to do with.

concertar, vb. arrange; agree (on); harmonize.

concerto, n.m. concert.

concessão, n.f. concession.

concha, n.f. shell.

conchavo, n.m. agreement; collusion.

concidadão -dã, n. fellow citizen.

conciliar, vb. reconcile; attain.

concílio, n.m. church council.

concisão, n.f. conciseness.

conciso, adj. concise.

concitar, *vb.* incite.
concludente, *adj.* concluding; conclusive.
concluir, *vb.* conclude.
conclusão, *n.f.* conclusion.
concomitante, *adj.* concomitant.
concordância, *n.f.* agreement.
concordar, *vb.* agree.
concorde, *adj.* in agreement.
concórdia, *n.f.* concord.
concorrência, *n.f.* competition; attendance; crowd; agreement; bidding.
concorrente, *n.m.f.* competitor; contestant.
concorrer, *vb.* compete; run (for); flock (to); contribute.
concreto, *adj.*, *n.m.* concrete.
concubina, *n.f.* concubine.
concurso, *n.m.* contest; coincidence; cooperation; crowd; civil-service exam.
concussão, *n.f.* shock; embezzlement.
condão, *n.m.* magic power; gift.
conde, *n.m.* count, earl.
condecoração, *n.f.* decoration, medal.
condecorar, *vb.* give a medal to.
condenação, *n.f.* condemnation.
condenar, *vb.* condemn; sentence.
condensar, *vb.* condense.
condescendente, *adj.* compliant; obliging.
condescender, *vb.* acquiesce, accede.
condessa, *n.f.* countess.
condição, *n.f.* condition; situation; rank.
condicional, *adj.* conditional.
condicionar, *vb.* condition.
condigno, *adj.* deserved.
condimentar, *vb.* season.
condimento, *n.m.* condiment, seasoning.
condiscípulo -la, *n.* fellow student.
condizente, *adj.* appropriate.
condizer, *vb.* match, suit.
condoer, *vb.* arouse the pity of. **c.-se**, sympathize (with).
condolência, *n.f.* condolence.
condomínio, *n.m.* condominium.

condômino, *n.m.* joint owner.
condução, *n.f.* conduction; (*coll.*) transportation; bus.
conducente, *adj.* conducive.
conduta, *n.f.* conduct.
conduto, *n.m.* pipe, duct.
condutor -ra, *n.* conductor; guide; driver.
conduzir, *vb.* conduct; guide; drive; carry. **c.-se**, behave; **c. a**, lead to.
cone, *n.m.* cone.
cônego, *n.m.* (*eccles.*) canon (cleric).
conexão, *n.f.* connection.
confecção, *n.f.* making; ready-made suit.
confeccionar, *vb.* make, prepare.
confederação, *n.f.* confederation.
confederar, *vb.* confederate.
confeitaria, *n.f.* candy/pastry shop.
confeiteiro -ra, *n.* confectioner.
confeito, *n.m.* candy, sweets.
conferência, *n.f.* lecture; conference; comparison.
conferenciar, *vb.* confer; lecture.
conferencista, *n.m.f.* speaker.
conferir, *vb.* verify; compare; confer; agree.
confessar, *vb.* confess. **c.-se**, go to confession.
confessionário, *n.m.* confessional.
confesso, *adj.* confessed.
confessor, *n.m.* confessor.
confete, *n.m.* confetti.
confiado, *adj.* confident.
confiança, *n.f.* confidence, trust. **de c.**, trusted.
confiante, *adj.* confident.
confiar, *vb.* trust; entrust; confide. **c. em**, trust in.
confidência, *n.f.* secret.
confidencial, *adj.* confidential.
confidenciar, *vb.* confide (secret).
confidente, *n.m.f.* confidant(e).
configurar, *vb.* configure. **c.-se**, take shape.
confinar, *vb.* confine. **c. com**, border on.
confins, *n.m.pl.* borders, frontiers.

confirmação, *n.f.* confirmation.

confirmar, *vb.* confirm.

confiscar, *vb.* confiscate.

confissão, *n.f.* confession.

conflagração, *n.f.* conflagration.

conflito, *n.m.* conflict.

conformar, *vb.* form; reconcile; conform. **c.-se,** resign oneself.

conforme, 1. *adj.* alike; resigned; in accord. **2.** *adv.* accordingly. **3.** *prep.* according to. **4.** *conj.* as; depending (on).

conformidade, *n.f.* conformity; resignation.

conformista, *n.m.f.* conformist.

confortável, *adj.* comfortable.

conforto, *n.m.* comfort. —**confortar,** *vb.*

confraria, *n.f.* lay brotherhood.

confrontar, *vb.* confront; compare.

confundir, *vb.* confuse. **c.-se,** be confused; mingle.

confusão, *n.f.* confusion; uproar.

confuso, *adj.* confused.

confutar, *vb.* refute.

congelação, *n.f.* freezing, freeze.

congelador, *n.m.* freezer.

congelar, *vb.* freeze.

congênito, *adj.* congenital.

congestão, *n.f.* congestion.

congestionar, *vb.* congest.

conglomeração, *n.f.* conglomeration.

conglomerar, *vb.* conglomerate. —**conglomerado,** *n.m.*

congonha, *n.f.* maté; tea plant.

congraçar, *vb.* reconcile; harmonize.

congratulação, *n.f.* congratulation.

congratular, *vb.* congratulate. **c.-se,** rejoice; congratulate oneself.

congregação, *n.f.* congregation.

congregar, *vb.* assemble; combine. **c.-se,** congregate.

congressista, *n.m.f.* congressman -woman; conventioneer.

congresso, *n.m.* congress; conference. **c. sexual,** sexual intercourse.

conhaque, *n.m.* cognac.

conhecedor -ra, *n.* connoisseur.

conhecer, *vb.* know, be acquainted with; meet.

conhecido -da, 1. *adj.* known; well-known; versed. **2.** *n.* acquaintance.

conhecimento, *n.m.* knowledge; acquaintance; bill of lading.

conivência, *n.f.* complicity.

conivente, *adj.* complicit.

conjetura, *n.f.* conjecture. —**conjeturar,** *vb.*

conjugação, *n.f.* conjugation.

conjugal, *adj.* conjugal.

conjugar, *vb.* conjugate.

cônjuge, *n.m.f.* spouse.

conjunção, *n.f.* conjunction.

conjunto, 1. *adj.* conjoint. **2.** *n.m.* whole; set; combo.

conjuntura, *n.f.* juncture.

conjuração, *n.f.* conspiracy.

conjurar, *vb.* conjure; conspire.

conluio, *n.m.* collusion; plot.

conosco, *pron.* with us.

conotação, *n.f.* connotation.

conquanto, *conj.* although.

conquista, *n.f.* conquest.

conquistador, *n.m.* conqueror; ladies' man.

conquistar, *vb.* conquer; win over.

consagrar, *vb.* consecrate; dedicate; sanction.

consciência, *n.f.* conscience; consciousness. **ter c. de,** be aware of.

consciencioso, *adj.* conscientious.

consciente, 1. *adj.* conscious; conscientious. **2.** *n.m.* conscious.

consciente, *adj.* aware.

cônscio, *adj.* aware.

conscrição, *n.f.* conscription.

conscrito, *n.m.* conscript.

consecução, *n.f.* attainment.

consecutivo, *adj.* consecutive.

conseguinte, *adj.* consequent. **por c.,** consequently.

conseguir, *vb.* get; attain; manage to.

conselheiro -ra, *n.* advisor; counselor; council member.

conselho, *n.m.* advice, counsel; council.

consenso, *n.m.* consensus.

consentimento, *n.m.* consent.

consentir, *vb.* consent (to).

conseqüência, *n.f.* consequence.

conseqüente, *adj.* consequent; consequential.

consertar, *vb.* repair. **—conserto**, *n.m.*

conserva, *n.f.* canned food; preserves.

conservação, *n.f.* conservation.

conservador -ra, *adj., n.* conservative.

conservantismo, *n.m.* conservatism.

conservar, *vb.* conserve; preserve; keep.

conservatório, *n.m.* conservatory.

consideração, *n.f.* consideration; respect. **levar em c.**, take into consideration.

considerado, *adj.* respected.

considerar, *vb.* consider. **c.-se**, regard oneself.

considerável, *adj.* considerable.

consignação, *n.f.* consignment.

consignar, *vb.* consign; register.

consigo, *pron.* with him, her, you, them; to him-, her-, yourself; to them-, yourselves.

consistência, *n.f.* consistency.

consistente, *adj.* consistent; consisting.

consistir, *vb.* consist. **c. em**, consist of.

consoante, **1.** *n.f.* consonant. **2.** *prep.* according to.

consolação, *n.f.* consolation.

consolar, *vb.* console.

consolidar, *vb.* consolidate.

consolo, *n.m.* consolation.

consórcio, *n.m.* consortium; marriage.

consorte, *n.m.f.* consort.

conspícuo, *adj.* conspicuous; prominent.

conspiração, *n.f.* conspiracy.

conspirador -ra, *n.* conspirator.

conspirar, *vb.* conspire, plot.

conspurcar, *vb.* defile.

constância, *n.f.* constancy; perseverance.

constante, *adj.* constant; consisting.

constar, *vb.* consist; be evident; be said.

constatar, *vb.* verify; find out.

constelação, *n.f.* constellation.

consternação, *n.f.* consternation.

constipação, *n.f.* constipation; common cold.

constipado, *adj.* constipated; having a cold.

constipar-se, *vb.* become constipated; catch a cold.

constitucional, *adj.* constitutional.

constituição, *n.f.* constitution.

constituinte, **1.** *adj.* constituent. **2.** *n.m.f.* constituent; constitutional-convention delegate; *n.f.* constitutional convention.

constituir, *vb.* constitute.

constranger, *vb.* constrain; coerce; disturb.

constrangimento, *n.m.* constraint; discomfort.

constringir, *vb.* constrict.

construção, *n.f.* construction; structure.

construir, *vb.* construct, build.

construtivo, *adj.* constructive.

construtor -ra, *n.* builder.

construtora, *n.f.* construction company.

consuetudinário, *adj.* customary.

cônsul, *n.m.* consul.

consulado, *n.m.* consulate.

consular, *adj.* consular.

consulta, *n.f.* consultation. **livro de c.**, reference book; **horas de c.**, office hours.

consultar, *vb.* consult.

consultório, *n.m.* doctor's office.

consumação, *n.f.* cover charge.

consumar, *vb.* consummate. **—consumado**, *adj.*

consumidor -ra, *n.* consumer.

consumir, *vb.* consume. **c.-se**, fret.

consumo, *n.m.* consumption.

consumpção, -sunção, *n.f.* tuberculosis.

conta, *n.f.* count; account; bill; bead. **c. corrente**, charge/checking account; **fazer de c.**, make believe; **levar em c.**, take into account; **prestar contas**, give an account; **tomar c. de**, take care of.

contábil, *adj.* accounting.

contabilidade, *n.f.* accounting.

contabilista, *n.m.f.* accountant.

contacto, *n.m.* contact. —**contactar**, *vb.*

contador -ra, *n.* accountant; storyteller; meter.

contadoria, *n.f.* accounting department.

contagem, *n.f.* count; scoring. **c. regressiva**, countdown.

contagiar, *vb.* infect; contaminate.

contagioso, *adj.* contagious.

conta-gotas, *n.m.* eye dropper.

contaminação, *n.f.* contamination.

contaminar, *vb.* contaminate.

contanto que, *conj.* provided that.

contar, *vb.* count; tell. **c.-se**, regard oneself; **c. com**, count on.

contato, *n.m.* contact. —**contatar**, *vb.*

contemplar, *vb.* contemplate; behold.

contemporâneo -nea, *adj., n.* contemporary.

contenção, *n.f.* contention.

contenda, *n.f.* dispute.

contender, *vb.* contend.

contentamento, -tento, *n.m.* contentment.

contente, *adj.* content. —**contentar**, *vb.*

conter, *vb.* contain. **c.-se**, control oneself.

conterrâneo -nea, *n.* compatriot.

contestar, *vb.* contest.

conteúdo, *n.m.* contents.

contexto, *n.m.* context.

contigo, *pron.* with you (s.).

contíguo, *adj.* contiguous.

continência, *n.f.* continence; *(mil.)* salute.

continental, *adj.* continental.

continente, *n.m.* continent; mainland.

contingência, *n.f.* contingency.

contingente, *adj.: n.m.* contingent.

continuação, *n.f.* continuation.

continuar, *vb.* continue.

continuidade, *n.f.* continuity.

contínuo, 1. *adj.* continuous. **2.** *n.m.* office boy.

contista, *n.m.f.* short-story writer.

conto, *n.m.* story; short story; a thousand cruzados -zeiros; *(sl.)* con game. **passar um c.**, *(sl.)* pull a scam.

contorção, *n.f.* contortion.

contorcer, *vb.* contort. **c.-se**, writhe.

contornar, *vb.* circle; skirt.

contorno, *n.m.* contour.

contra, 1. *n.m.* con; opposition. **2.** *adv.* contrary. **3.** *prep.* against.

contra-, *pref.* counter-, contra-.

contrabaixo, *n.m. (mus.)* double bass.

contrabalançar, *vb.* counterbalance.

contrabandear, *vb.* smuggle.

contrabandista, *n.m.f.* smuggler.

contrabando, *n.m.* contraband; smuggling.

contração, *n.f.* contraction.

contradição, *n.f.* contradiction.

contraditório, *adj.* contradictory.

contradizer, *vb.* contradict.

contrafazer, *vb.* counterfeit. —**contrafeito**, *adj.*

contragosto, *n.m.* distaste. **a c.**, reluctantly.

contrair, *vb.* contract.

contramão, *n.f.* wrong way (street).

contrapartida, *n.f.* counterpart. **em c.**, on the other hand.

contrapelo, *n.m.* **a c.**, against the grain.

contrapeso, *n.m.* counterpoise.

contraponto, *n.m.* counterpoint.

contrapor, *vb.* place against; oppose.

contrariar, *vb.* contradict; displease.

contrariedade, *n.f.* contrariety; annoyance.

contrário, *adj.* contrary. **ao/pelo c.**, on the contrary; **do c.**, otherwise.

contra-senso, *n.m.* absurdity.

contraste, *n.m.* contrast. —**contrastar**, *vb.*

contratar, *vb.* contract, hire.

contratempo, *n.m.* contretemps.

contrato, *n.m.* contract.

contravir, *vb.* contravene; retort.

contribuição, *n.f.* contribution; tax.

contribuinte, **1.** *adj.* contributing. **2.** *n.m.f.* contributor; taxpayer.

contribuir, *vb.* contribute; pay taxes.

contrição, *n.f.* contrition.

contristar, *vb.* grieve; sadden.

contrito, *adj.* contrite.

controlar, *vb.* control.

controle, *n.m.* control. **c. de natalidade**, birth control.

controvérsia, *n.f.* controversy.

controverso, -vertido, *adj.* controversial.

controverter, *vb.* controvert.

contudo, *conj.* nevertheless.

contumácia, *n.f.* contumacy; contempt of court.

contundente, *adj.* bruising.

contundir, *n.f.* bruise.

conturbar, *vb.* perturb; stir up.

contusão, *n.f.* contusion, bruise.

convalescença, *n.f.* convalescence.

convalescente, *adj., n.m.f.* convalescent.

convalescer, *vb.* convalesce.

convenção, *n.f.* convention.

convencer, *vb.* convince.

convencido, *adj.* convinced; *(coll.)* conceited.

convencimento, *n.m.* conviction; *(coll.)* conceit.

convencional, *adj.* conventional.

conveniência, *n.f.* convenience; suitability.

conveniente, *adj.* convenient; suitable.

convênio, *n.m.* agreement.

convento, *n.m.* convent; monastery.

convergência, *n.f.* convergence.

convergir, *vb.* converge.

conversa, *n.f.* conversation; idle talk. **c. fiada/mole/para boi dormir**, *(coll.)* idle talk.

conversação, *n.f.* conversation.

conversão, *n.f.* conversion.

conversar, *vb.* converse; *(coll.)* fast-talk.

conversível, *adj., n.m.* convertible.

converter, *vb.* convert. **c.-se em**, become.

convertido -da, *n.* convert.

convés, *n.m. (naut.)* deck.

convexo, *adj.* convex.

convicção, *n.f.* conviction.

convicto, *adj.* convicted; convinced.

convidado -da, *n.* invited guest.

convidar, *vb.* invite.

convincente, *adj.* convincing.

convir, *vb.* agree; suit.

convite, *n.m.* invitation.

convivência, *n.f.* close contact.

conviver com, *vb.* live with; have close contact with.

convívio, *n.m.* familiarity; banquet.

convocar, *vb.* convoke; invite; draft.

convosco, *pron.* with you (pl.).

convulsão, *n.f.* convulsion.

cooper, *n.m. (sl.)* jogging. **fazer c.**, jog.

cooperação, *n.f.* cooperation.

cooperar, *vb.* cooperate.

cooperativa, *n.f.* cooperative.

cooperativo, *adj.* cooperative.

coordenação, *n.f.* coordination.

coordenada, *n.f.* coordinate.

coordenador -ra, *n.* coordinator.

coordenar, *vb.* coordinate.

copa, *n.f.* breakfast area; cup (trophy); treetop; *(pl.)* hearts (cards).

copeira, *n.f.* serving maid; china cupboard.

copeiro, *n.m.* butler.

cópia, *n.f.* copy; copiousness.

copiadora, *n.* copying machine.

copiar, **1.** *n.m.* veranda. **2.** *vb.* copy.

copioso, *adj.* copious.

copirraite, *n.m.* copyright.

copla, *n.f.* stanza; ballad.

copo, *n.m.* drinking glass.

copular, *vb.* copulate.

coque, *n.m.* rap on the head; chignon; coke (coal).

coqueiro, *n.m.* coconut palm.

coqueluche, *n.f.* whooping cough; *(coll.)* fad.

coquete, *n.f.* coquette.

coquetel, *n.m.* cocktail; cocktail party.

cor, *n.m.* **de c.**, by heart.

cor, n.f. color.

coração, n.m. heart; darling.

corado, adj. ruddy; blushing.

coragem, n.f. courage.

corajoso, adj. courageous.

coral, 1. adj. choral; coral. **2.** n.m. coral; chorale.

corante, 1. adj. coloring. **2.** n.m. dye.

corar, vb. color; paint; bleach; blush.

corcel, n.m. courser (horse).

corço, n.m. roebuck.

corcova, n.f. hump.

corcovado, adj. hunchbacked.

corcovar, -vear, vb. buck.

corcunda, 1. adj. hunchbacked. **2.** n.m.f. hunchback.

corda, n.f. rope; cord; (mus.) string. **dar c. a,** wind up.

cordão, n.m. cord; lace; cordon; Carnival dance group.

cordato, adj. sensible.

cordeiro, n.m. lamb.

cordel, n.m. twine. **literatura de c.,** popular poetry.

cor-de-rosa, adj. pink.

cordial, adj., n.m. cordial.

cordilheira, n.f. mountain range.

cordura, n.f. good sense.

coreano -na, adj., n. Korean; n.m. Korean (language).

Coréia, n.f. Korea.

coreografia, n.f. choreography.

coreto, n.m. bandstand.

coriscar, vb. flash. **—corisco,** n.m.

corista, n.m.f. chorister; chorine.

corja, n.f. gang; rabble.

corneta, n.f. bugle, cornet.

corno, n.m. horn, antler; (coll.) cuckold.

cornucópia, n.f. cornucopia.

cornudo, 1. adj. horned. **2.** n.m. cuckold.

coro, n.m. chorus, choir.

coroa, n.f. crown; tonsure; n.m.f. (sl.) oldster.

coroação, n.f. coronation.

coroar, vb. crown.

coroca, adj. old, decrepit.

coroinha, n.m. altar boy.

corolário, n.m. corollary.

coronário, adj. coronary.

coronel, n.m. colonel; rural political boss; sugar daddy.

coronha, n.f. rifle butt.

corpete, -pinho, n.m. bodice.

corpo, n.m. body; corps. **c. docente,** faculty.

corporação, n.f. corporation; body.

corpóreo, adj. bodily.

corpulento, adj. corpulent.

corpúsculo, n.m. corpuscle.

correção, n.f. correction; correctness.

corre-corre, n.m. dashing about.

corrediço, -dio, adj. running; sliding.

corredor, n.m. runner; corridor.

córrego, corgo, n.m. stream; gully.

correia, n.f. strap; belt; leash.

correio, n.m. post office; mail; courier.

correlação, n.f. correlation.

correlatar, -lacionar, vb. correlate.

corrente, 1. adj. running; current. **2.** n.f. current; chain.

correnteza, n.f. current.

correr, vb. run; go; hurry; run through; pull (curtains).

correria, n.f. hurrying; raid.

correspondência, n.f. correspondence; mail.

correspondente, 1. adj. corresponding. **2.** n.m. correspondent; letter-writer.

corresponder, vb. correspond. **c.-se com,** correspond with.

corretagem, n.f. brokerage.

correto, adj. correct.

corretor -ra, n. broker.

corrida, n.f. run; race.

corrigir, vb. correct.

corrimão, n.m. handrail.

corriola, n.f. (sl.) gang.

corriqueiro, adj. commonplace.

corroborar, vb. corroborate.

corroer, vb. corrode.

corromper, vb. corrupt.

corrosão, n.f. corrosion.

corrugar, vb. corrugate.

corrupção, n.f. corruption.

corrupto, adj. corrupt.

cortador -ra, n. cutter.

cortar, vb. cut; cut off.

corte, *n.m.* cut; cutting. **c. transversal,** cross section.

corte, *n.f.* court. **fazer a c. a,** court, woo.

cortejar, *vb.* court; flatter.

cortejo, *n.m.* cortege; procession.

cortês, *adj.* courteous.

cortesã, *n.f.* courtesan.

cortesão -sã, 1. *adj.* courtly. **2.** *n.m.* courtier.

cortesia, *n.f.* courtesy.

córtex, -tice, *n.m.* bark; cortex.

cortiça, *n.f.* cork.

cortiço, *n.m.* beehive; tenement.

cortina, *n.f.* curtain, drape.

coruja, *n.f.* owl. **pai/mãe c.,** *(coll.)* proud parent.

coruscar, *vb.* coruscate.

corvejar, *vb.* caw.

corveta, *n.f.* corvette.

corvo, *n.m.* crow; raven.

cós, *n.m.* waistband.

coser, *vb.* sew.

cosmético, *adj., n.m.* cosmetic.

cósmico, *adj.* cosmic.

cosmo, -mos, *n.m.* cosmos.

cosmopolita, *adj., n.m.f.* cosmopolitan.

costa, *n.f.* coast; *(pl.)* back.

costado, *n.m.* back. **dos quatro costados,** through and through.

costarriquenho -nha, -quense, *adj., n.* Costa Rican.

costeiro, *adj.* coastal.

costela, *n.f.* rib.

costeleta, *n.f.* chop (pork, etc.); *(pl.)* sideburns.

costumar, *vb.* be in the habit of. **c.-se a,** get used to.

costume, *n.m.* custom; habit; attire; woman's suit; *(pl.)* mores.

costumeiro, *adj.* customary.

costura, *n.f.* sewing; seam.

costurar, *vb.* sew.

costureira, *n.f.* seamstress.

cota, *n.f.* quota; dues; share; catalog number.

cotação, *n.f.* quotation; price list; rating; chances.

cotado, *adj.* respected.

cotão, *n.m.* fluff.

cotar, *vb.* quote (price); annotate; estimate.

cotejar, *vb.* compare.

cotidiano, *adj., n.m.* daily.

coto, *n.m.* stump.

cotonete, *n.m.* q-tip.

cotovelada, *n.f.* nudge.

cotovelo, *n.m.* elbow.

cotovia, *n.f.* skylark.

couraça, *n.f.* breastplate.

couraçado, 1. *adj.* armored. **2.** *n.m.* battleship.

couro, *n.m.* leather; hide. **c. cabeludo,** scalp.

cousa, *var. of* **coisa.**

couve, *n.f.* kale.

couve-de-bruxelas, *n.f.* Brussels sprouts.

couve-flor, *n.f.* cauliflower.

cova, *n.f.* grave; cave; hole; dimple.

covarde, 1. *adj.* cowardly. **2.** *n.m.f.* coward.

covardia, *n.f.* cowardice.

coveiro, *n.m.* gravedigger.

covil, *n.m.* den.

covinha, *n.f.* dimple.

coxa, *n.f.* thigh.

coxear, *vb.* limp.

coxim, *n.m.* cushion.

coxo, 1. *adj.* lame. **2.** *n.m.* cripple.

cozer, *vb.* cook.

cozido, *n.m.* stew.

cozinha, *n.f.* kitchen; cuisine; back (bus, train).

cozinhar, *vb.* cook. —**cozinheiro -ra,** *n.*

crachá, *n.m.* name tag; medal.

crânio, *n.m.* cranium; *(coll.)* smart person.

crápula, *n.m.f.* libertine; scoundrel.

craque, *n.m.* market crash; *(coll.)* expert.

crase, *n.f.* contraction, blending.

crasso, *adj.* crass.

cratera, *n.f.* crater.

cravar, *vb.* rivet; drive (nail).

cravo, *n.m.* nail; carnation; clove; harpsichord; blackhead.

creche, *n.f.* day-care center.

credenciais, *n.f.pl.* credentials.

credenciar, *vb.* accredit.

crediário, *n.m.* installment plan.

credibilidade, *n.f.* credibility.

creditar, *vb.* credit.

crédito, *n.m.* credit; faith.

credo, 1. *n.m.* credo. **2.** *interj.* goodness!

credor -ra, *n.* creditor.

crédulo, *adj.* credulous.

cremar, *vb.* cremate.

creme, 1. *adj.* cream-colored. **2.** *n.m.* cream; custard. **c. chantilly,** whipped cream; **c. de barbear,** shaving cream.

cremoso, *adj.* creamy.

crença, *n.f.* belief.

crendice, *n.f.* superstition.

crente, *n.m.f.* believer; *(coll.)* Protestant.

crepe, *n.m.* crepe; crape; mourning band.

crepitar, *vb.* crackle.

crepom, *n.m.* crepe fabric.

crepúsculo, *n.m.* twilight, dusk.

crer, *vb.* believe.

crescente, 1. *adj.* growing. **2.** *n.m.* crescent; *n.f.* high tide.

crescer, *vb.* grow; increase; rise up.

crescido, *adj.* full-grown.

crescimento, *n.m.* growth.

crespo, *adj.* rough; curly; threatening.

cretino -na, *n.* cretin.

cria, *n.f.* young animal; foster child.

criação, *n.f.* creation; rearing; breeding; livestock. **filho de c.,** foster child.

criada, *n.f.* maid.

criado, *n.m.* servant (m.).

criado-mudo, *n.m.* night stand.

criador -ra, 1. *adj.* creative. **2.** *n.* creator; breeder.

criança, *n.f.* child.

criançada, *n.f.* children; childishness.

criar, *vb.* create; bring up; breed; acquire. **c.-se,** be brought up.

criativo, *adj.* creative.

criatura, *n.f.* creature.

crime, *n.m.* crime.

criminal, *adj.* criminal.

criminoso -sa, *adj., n.* criminal.

crina, *n.f.* mane; horsehair.

crioulo -la, 1. *adj.* Creole; domestic; Negro. **2.** *n.* Creole; black.

cripta, *n.f.* crypt.

críptico, *adj.* cryptic.

crisálida, *n.f.* chrysalis.

crise, *n.f.* crisis.

crisol, *n.m.* crucible.

crispar, *vb.* crimp.

crista, *n.f.* crest; comb; *(fig.)* head.

cristal, *n.m.* crystal.

cristaleira, *n.f.* glass cupboard.

cristandade, *n.f.* Christianity.

cristão -tã, *adj., n.* Christian.

cristianismo, *n.m.* Christianity.

cristianizar, *vb.* Christianize.

Cristo, *n.m.* Christ.

critério, *n.m.* criterion; judgment.

crítica, *n.f.* criticism.

criticar, *vb.* criticize.

crítico -ca, 1. *adj.* critical. **2.** *n.* critic.

crivar, *vb.* pierce, riddle; grill.

crível, *adj.* credible.

crivo, *n.m.* sieve; *(sl.)* cigarette.

crochê, -ché, *n.m.* crochet.

crocitar, *vb.* caw.

crocodilo, *n.m.* crocodile.

cromo, *n.m.* chrome.

cromossomo, *n.m.* chromosome.

crônica, *n.f.* chronicle; newspaper column.

cronista, *n.m.f.* chronicler; columnist.

cronologia, *n.f.* chronology.

cronológico, *adj.* chronological.

cronômetro, *n.m.* chronometer; stop watch.

croquete, *n.m.* croquette.

crosta, *n.f.* crust; scab.

cru, crua, *adj.* raw; crude; cruel.

crucial, *adj.* crucial.

crucificação, -fixão, *n.f.* crucifixion.

crucificar, *vb.* crucify.

cruel, *adj.* cruel.

crueldade, *n.f.* cruelty.

cruento, *adj.* bloody; bloodthirsty.

crueza, *n.f.* rawness; crudeness; cruelty.

crustáceo, *n.m.* crustacean.

cruz, *n.f.* cross.

cruzada, *n.f.* crusade.

cruzado, *n.m.* cruzado (Brazilian monetary unit); crusader.

cruzamento, *n.m.* crossing; intersection.

cruzar, *vb.* cross; cruise. **c. com,** run across.

cruzeiro, *n.m.* large stone/wooden cross; cruise; cruiser; cruzeiro (Brazilian monetary unit).

cu, *n.m. (vulg.)* buttocks; anus.

cubano -na, *adj., n.* Cuban.

cúbico, *adj.* cubic.

cubículo, *n.m.* cubicle.

cubo, *n.m.* cube; hub.

cuca, *n.f. (sl.)* head.

cuco, *n.m.* cuckoo.

cuecas, *n.f.pl.* men's undershorts.

cueiro, *n.m.* diaper.

cuia, *n.f.* gourd.

cuíca, *n.f.* friction drum.

cuidado, 1. *n.m.* care. **2.** *interj.* look out!

cuidadoso, *adj.* careful.

cuidar, *vb.* take care of; think. **c.-se,** take care; **c. de,** take care of.

cujo, *pron.* whose.

culatra, *n.f.* breech (gun).

culinária, *n.f.* cuisine.

culinário, *adj.* culinary.

culminação, *n.f.* culmination.

culminar, *vb.* culminate.

culpa, *n.f.* blame; guilt; fault. **ter a c.,** be to blame.

culpabilidade, *n.f.* culpability.

culpado -da, 1. *adj.* guilty. **2.** *n.* guilty person.

culpar, *vb.* blame.

culpável, *adj.* culpable.

cultivação, *n.f.* cultivation.

cultivar, *vb.* cultivate, grow.

cultivo, *n.m.* cultivation.

culto, 1. *adj.* cultured. **2.** *n.m.* cult; religion.

cultuar, *vb.* idolize.

cultura, *n.f.* culture; cultivation.

cultural, *adj.* cultural.

cumbuca, *n.f.* calabash gourd.

cume, *n.m.* summit, top.

cumeada, *n.f.* mountain ridge.

cumeeira, *n.f.* roof ridge.

cúmplice, *n.m./f.* accomplice.

cumplicidade, *n.f.* complicity.

cumpridor, *adj.* reliable.

cumprimentar, *vb.* greet; compliment.

cumprimento, *n.m.* greeting; compliment; compliance.

cumprir, *vb.* comply; carry out; fulfill, accomplish.

cumular, *vb.* heap.

cumulativo, *adj.* cumulative.

cúmulo, *n.m.* culmination, height; heap; cumulus. **ser o c.,** be the limit.

cunha, *n.f.* wedge.

cunhada, *n.f.* sister-in-law.

cunhado, *n.m.* brother-in-law.

cunhar, *vb.* coin, mint.

cunho, *n.m.* stamp; nature.

cupê, *n.m.* coupe.

Cupido, *n.m.* Cupid.

cúpido, *adj.* greedy.

cupim, *n.m.* termite.

cupom, *n.m.* coupon.

cúpula, *n.f.* dome.

cura, *n.f.* cure; *n.m.* parish priest.

curador -ra, *n.* guardian, trustee.

curandeiro -ra, *n.* healer.

curar, *vb.* cure, heal. **c.-se,** get well. **c. de,** deal with.

curinga, *n.m.* joker (cards).

curiosidade, *n.f.* curiosity.

curioso, *adj.* curious.

curral, *n.m.* corral.

currículo, *n.m.* curriculum; curriculum vitae.

cursar, *vb.* traverse; frequent; travel; study.

curso, *n.m.* course. **em c.,** in progress; **ter c.,** be current.

curtição, *n.f. (sl.)* enjoyment.

curtir, *vb.* tan; pickle; inure; suffer; *(sl.)* enjoy.

curto, *adj.* short; stupid; laconic.

curto-circuito, *n.m.* short circuit.

curupira, *n.m.* forest monster.

curva, *n.f.* curve.

curvar, *vb.* curve, bend; subjugate. **c.-se,** humble oneself.

curveta, *n.f.* curvet. —**curvetear,** *vb.*

curvo, *adj.* curved.

cuscuz, *n.m.* cornmeal or coconut dish.

cúspide, *n.f.* cusp.

cuspir, *vb.* spit. —**cuspe, -po,** *n.m.*

custa, *n.f.* expense. **à c. de,** at the expense of.

custar, *vb.* cost; be difficult.

custear, vb. pay for, fund.

custo, n.m. cost.

custódia, n.f. custody.

custodiar, vb. take into custody; watch over.

custódio -dia, n. custodian.

custoso, adj. costly; troublesome.

cutelo, n.m. cutlass; cleaver.

cutia, n.f. agouti.

cutícula, n.f. cuticle.

cutilada, n.f. slash.

cútis, n.f. skin, complexion.

cutucar, vb. poke, nudge. —**cutucada**, n.f.

D

da, contr. of de + a.

dáblio, n.m. the letter w.

dádiva, n.f. gift.

dadivoso, adj. generous.

dado, 1. adj. given; affable. **d. a**, prone to; **d. que**, inasmuch as. 2. n.m.pl. dice; data.

daí, contr. of de + aí. adv. from there; thereafter; therefore. **d. a uma semana**, one week later; **d. em diante**, thenceforth; **e d.?**, (coll.) so what?

dali, contr. of de + ali. adv. from there; thenceforth; therefore.

daltonismo, n.m. color blindness.

dama, n.f. lady, dame; (pl.) checkers.

damasco, n.m. apricot; damask.

danação, n.f. damage; excitement; anger; damnation.

danado, adj. damned; furious; (coll.) heckuva. **d. de**, (sl.) very.

danar, vb. damage; damn; infuriate. **d.-se**, get mad; (sl.) rush off.

dança, n.f. dance; dancing.

dançar, vb. dance; (sl.) get fouled up.

dançarino -na, n. dancer.

dândi, n.m. dandy, fop.

danificar, vb. damage; spoil.

daninho, adj. harmful.

dano, n.m. damage.

danoso, adj. harmful.

dantes, adv. formerly.

daquela, contr. of de + aquela.

daquelas, contr. of de + aquelas.

daquele, contr. of de + aquele.

daqueles, contr. of de + aqueles.

daqui, contr. of de + aqui. adv. from here; hence. **d. a pouco**, soon; **d. em diante**, from now on.

daquilo, contr. of de + aquilo.

dar, vb. give; deal; strike (clock); (coll.) work out, be enough; (sl.) work out, be an easy lay. **d.-se**, happen; **d. certo**, (coll.) work out; **d. com**, run across; **d. em**, hit; come to; result in; **d. para**, face; be enough to; be suitable for; take to; **d. pé**, (coll.) work out; **d. por**, notice; **d. uma de**, (sl.) make like a.

dardo, n.m. dart; javelin; stinger.

das, contr. of de + as.

data, n.f. date. —**datar**, vb.

dátil, n.m. date (fruit).

datilografar, vb. type.

datilografia, n.f. typing.

datilógrafo -fa, n. typist.

DDD (discagem direta à distância), n.f. direct distance dialing.

de, prep. of; from; with; as.

dê, n.m. the letter d.

debaixo, adv. below. **d. de**, under.

debalde, adv. in vain.

debate, n.m. debate. —**debater**, vb.

debelar, vb. conquer.

debicar, vb. peck; nibble.

débil, adj. weak.

debilidade, n.f. weakness.

debilitar, vb. weaken.

débito, n.m. debit. —**debitar**, vb.

debochado, adj. debauched; mocking.

debochar, vb. debauch; mock. **d.-se**, become debauched.

deboche, n.m. debauchery; mockery.

debruçar(-se), vb. lean forward.

debulhar, vb. thresh; peel. **d.-se em lágrimas**, burst into tears.

debute, n.m. debut. —**debutar**, vb.

debuxar, vb. draw, sketch.
debuxo, n.m. drawing.
década, n.f. decade.
decadência, n.f. decadence.
decadente, adj. decadent.
decair, vb. decay, decline.
decalcomania, n.f., **decalque**, n.m. decal.
decálogo, n.m. decalogue.
decano -na, n. dean.
decantar, vb. decant; exalt.
decapitar, vb. decapitate.
decência, n.f. decency.
decênio, n.m. decade.
decente, adj. decent.
decepar, vb. sever; maim.
decepção, n.f. disappointment.
decepcionar, vb. disappoint.
decerto, adv. certainly.
decidir, vb. decide. **d.-se**, make up one's mind.
decifrar, vb. decipher.
décima, n.f. tenth.
decimal, adj.,n. decimal.
décimo, adj., n.m. tenth.
decisão, n.f. decision.
decisivo, adj. decisive.
declamação, n.f. declamation; speech.
declamar, vb. declaim.
declaração, n.f. declaration, statement.
declarar, vb. declare, state.
declinação, n.f. declination; declension.
declinar, vb. decline. —**declínio**, n.m.
declive, n.m. slope.
decodificar, vb. decode.
decolagem, n.f. take-off.
decolar, vb. take off.
de-comer, n.m. food.
decompor, vb. decompose.
decoração, n.f. decoration.
decorar, vb. decorate; memorize.
decorativo, adj. decorative.
decoro, n.m. decorum.
decoroso, adj. decorous.
decorrência, n.f. duration; consequence.
decorrente, adj. elapsing; deriving.
decorrer, vb. elapse; happen; derive.
decotado, adj. low-necked.
decote, n.m. low neckline.

decrépito, adj. decrepit.
decrescer, vb. decrease. —**decrescimento**, **decréscimo**, n.m.
decreto, n.m. decree. —**decretar**, vb.
decúbito, n.m. lying position.
decurso, n.m. duration, course.
dedal, n.m. thimble.
dedão, n.m. big toe.
dedicação, n.f. dedication.
dedicado, adj. dedicated, devoted.
dedicar, vb. dedicate, devote. **d.-se**, devote oneself.
dedicatória, n.f. dedication (book).
dedilhar, vb. strum.
dedo, n.m. finger; toe; talent.
dedo-duro, n.m.f. (sl.) informer.
dedução, n.f. deduction.
deduzir, vb. deduce; deduct.
defasado, adj. out of phase.
defecar, vb. defecate.
defectivo, adj. defective.
defeito, n.m. defect, flaw.
defeituoso, adj. defective.
defender, vb. defend.
defensivo, adj. defensive.
defensor -ra, n. defender.
deferência, n.f. deference.
deferir, vb. grant; approve; yield.
defesa, n.f. defense.
defeso, adj. prohibited.
deficiência, n.f. deficiency; handicap.
deficiente, adj. deficient; handicapped.
déficit, n.m. deficit.
definhar, vb. waste away.
definição, n.f. definition.
definido, adj. definite.
definir, vb. define.
definitivo, adj. definitive.
deflorar, vb. deflower.
deformar, vb. deform.
deformidade, n.f. deformity.
defraudar, vb. defraud.
defrontar, vb. face.
defronte, adv. facing. **d. de**, in front of.
defumar, vb. smoke, cure.
defunto, adj., n.m. deceased.
degelar, vb. defrost, thaw. —**degelo**, n.m.

degenerar, *vb.* degenerate. —**degenerado**, *adj.*

deglutir, *vb.* swallow.

degolar, *vb.* behead.

degradar, *vb.* degrade.

degrau, *n.m.* step.

degredado -da, *n.* exile (person).

degredar, *vb.* exile. —**degredo**, *n.m.*

degringolar, *vb.* fall apart.

degustar, *vb.* taste.

deidade, *n.f.* deity.

deitar, *vb.* put; lie down. **d.-se**, lie down, go to bed.

deixa, *n.f.* cue.

deixar, *vb.* leave; let. **d de**, stop; **não d. de**, not fail to.

dejeção, *n.f.* defecation.

dejetar, *vb.* defecate.

dela, *contr. of* **de + ela**. of her/ it; her; hers; its.

delamber-se, *vb.* (coll.) lick one's chops.

delas, *contr. of* **de + elas**. of them; their.

delatar, *vb.* denounce.

delator -ra, *n.* informer.

dele, *contr. of* **de + ele**. of him/ it; his; its.

delegação, *n.f.* delegation.

delegacia, *n.f.* police station.

delegado -da, *n.m.* delegate; precinct chief.

delegar, *vb.* delegate.

deleitar, *vb.* delight. —**deleite**, *n.m.*

delfim, *n.m.* dolphin; dauphin.

delgadeza, *n.f.* thinness.

delgado, *adj.* thin.

deliberar, *vb.* deliberate.

delicadeza, *n.f.* delicacy.

delicado, *adj.* delicate.

delícia, *n.f.* delight.

deliciar, *vb.* delight. **d.-se**, be delighted.

delicioso, *adj.* delightful; delicious.

delimitar, *vb.* delimit.

delineador, *n.m.* eye liner.

delinear, *vb.* delineate.

delinqüência, *n.f.* delinquency.

delinqüente, *adj., n.m.f.* delinquent.

delinqüir, *vb.* be delinquent.

delirar, *vb.* be delirious; rave.

delírio, *n.m.* delirium.

delito, *n.m.* crime.

delonga, *n.f.* postponement.

delta, *n.m.* delta.

demagogia, *n.f.* demagoguery.

demagogo -ga, *n.* demagogue.

demais, **1.** *adj.* too much/ many; other. **2.** *adv.* too much/many; a lot; moreover. **3.** *pron.* the others.

demanda, *n.f.* demand; fight; suit. **em d. de**, in search of.

demandar, *vb.* demand; seek; head for; sue.

demão, *n.f.* coating.

demarcar, *vb.* demarcate.

demasia, *n.f.* excess.

demasiado, *adj., adv.* too much.

demente, *adj.* demented.

demissão, *n.f.* dismissal.

demitir, *vb.* dismiss. **d.-se**, resign.

demo, *n.m.* (coll.) devil.

democracia, *n.f.* democracy.

democrata, *n.m.f.* democrat.

democrático, *adj.* democratic.

demolição, *n.f.* demolition.

demolir, *vb.* demolish.

demônio, *n.m.* demon, devil.

demonstração, *n.f.* demonstration.

demonstrar, *vb.* demonstrate.

demonstrativo, *adj., n.m.* demonstrative.

demora, *n.f.* delay. —**demorar**, *vb.*

dendê, *n.m.* African palm oil.

denegar, *vb.* deny.

denegrir, *vb.* denigrate.

dengoso, *adj.* affected; coy.

dengue -go, *n.m.*, **-guice**, *n.f.* affectation; coyness.

denodado, *adj.* bold.

denodo, *n.m.* boldness.

denominação, *n.f.* denomination.

denominador, *n.m.* denominator.

denominar, *vb.* denominate.

denotar, *vb.* denote.

densidade, *n.f.* density.

denso, *adj.* dense.

dentado, *adj.* toothed.

dentadura, *n.f.* set of teeth. **d. postiça**, false teeth.

dental -tário, *adj.* dental.

dente, *n.m.* tooth. **pasta de dentes**, toothpaste.

dentifrício, *n.m.* toothpaste.
dentista, *n.m.f.* dentist.
dentre, *prep.* from among; among.
dentro, *adv.* inside. **d. de/em,** within; **estar por d.,** *(sl.)* be in style; understand.
denúncia, *n.f.* denunciation.
denunciar, *vb.* denounce; disclose.
deparar, *vb.* make appear; meet. **d. com,** run across.
departamento, *n.m.* department.
depenar, *vb.* pluck; *(coll.)* fleece.
dependência, *n.f.* dependence; servants' quarters.
dependente, *adj.* dependent.
depender de, *vb.* depend on.
depilar, *vb.* depilate.
depilatório, *n.m.* depilatory.
deplorar, *vb.* deplore.
depoimento, *n.m.* deposition.
depois, *adv.* later. **d. de, d. que,** after; **d. de amanhã,** the day after tomorrow.
depor, *vb.* put down; testify.
deportar, *vb.* deport.
depositante, *n.m.f.* depositor.
depositar, *vb.* deposit. **—depósito,** *n.m.*
depravação, *n.f.* depravity.
depravar, *vb.* deprave.
deprecar, *vb.* beseech.
depreciar, *vb.* depreciate.
depredar, *vb.* depredate.
depressa, *adv.* fast.
depressão, *n.f.* depression.
deprimente, *adj.* depressing.
deprimir, *vb.* depress.
depurar, *vb.* purify.
deputado -da, *n.* congressman -woman, deputy.
deputar, *vb.* delegate; empower.
deriva, *n.f.* **à d.,** adrift.
derivação, *n.f.* derivation.
derivado, *n.m.* derivative.
derivar, *vb.* derive; divert. **d.-se,** originate.
derivativo, 1. *adj.* derivative. **2.** *n.m.* pastime.
dermatologia, *n.f.* dermatology.
derradeiro, *adj.* last, final.
derrama, *n.f.* spilling; tax.
derramamento, *n.m.* spilling.

derramar, *vb.* spill, shed; strew.
derrame, *n.m.* hemorrhage.
derrapar, *vb.* skid. **—derrapagem,** *n.f.*
derredor, *n.m.* around. **em d. de,** around.
derrelito, *adj.* abandoned.
derreter(-se), *vb.* melt.
derribar, *vb.* knock down; subdue; overthrow.
derrisão, *n.f.* derision.
derrocar, *vb.* tear down; overthrow.
derrotar, *vb.* defeat. **—derrota,** *n.f.*
derrubada, *n.f.* knocking down; mass dismissal.
derrubar, *vb.* knock down; destroy.
des-, *pref.* dis-, de-, un-.
desabafar, *vb.* uncover; release; unburden oneself.
desabafo, *n.m.* release, relief.
desabar, *vb.* cave in, slide.
desabitar, *vb.* evacuate.
desabonar, *vb.* discredit. **—desabono,** *n.m.*
desabotoar, *vb.* unbutton.
desabrido, *adj.* rude, harsh.
desabrigar, *vb.* deprive of shelter.
desabrochar, *vb.* blossom; develop.
desacatar, *vb.* disrespect; *(sl.)* dazzle.
desacato, *n.m.* disrespect; *(sl.)* wow.
desacerto, *n.m.* error.
desacompanhado, *adj.* unaccompanied.
desaconselhar, *vb.* advise against.
desacordado, *adj.* unconscious.
desacordo, *n.m.* disagreement.
desacoroçoar, *vb.* discourage.
desacostumado, *adj.* unaccustomed.
desacreditar, *vb.* discredit, disbelieve.
desafeito, *adj.* unaccustomed.
desafeto, 1. *adj.* disaffected. **2.** *n.m.* disaffection.
desafiar, *vb.* defy; challenge.
desafinado, *adj.* off key, out of tune.
desafinar, *vb.* play/sing out of tune; get mad.

desafio, n.m. defiance; challenge; duel.

desafogar, vb. relieve; let off steam. **d.-se,** unburden onself.

desafogo, n.m. relief.

desaforado, adj. impudent.

desaforo, n.m. insolence; insult.

desafortunado, adj. unfortunate.

desagradar, vb. be disagreeable.

desagradável, adj. disagreeable.

desagrado, n.m. displeasure; disfavor.

desagravar, vb. redress; avenge.

desagravo, n.m. redress.

desagregar, vb. separate; disintegrate.

desaguadouro, n.m. drain; drainage ditch.

desaguar, vb. drain; empty; (coll.) urinate.

desaire, n.m. gracelessness; impropriety.

desairoso, adj. graceless; improper.

desajeitado, adj. clumsy, awkward.

desajustado, adj. maladjusted.

desalentar, vb. discourage; lose heart.

desalento, n.m. discouragement; despair.

desalinhar, vb. disarrange; make slovenly.

desalinho, n.m. disorder; untidiness.

desalmado, adj. ruthless.

desalojar, vb. dislodge.

desamar, vb. stop loving; hate.

desamor, n.m. disaffection; contempt.

desamparar, vb. abandon.

desamparo, n.m. abandonment.

desancar, vb. beat; criticize.

desandar, vb. go back; unleash; result.

desanimar, vb. discourage; get discouraged.

desânimo, n.m. discouragment; depression.

desanuviar, vb. clear up; calm.

desaparecer, vb. disappear.

desapego, n.m. indifference; detachment.

desapiedar-se, vb. become merciless.

desapontar, vb. disappoint.

desapossar, vb. dispossess. **d.-se,** give up.

desapropriar, vb. dispossess. **d.-se,** deprive oneself.

desaprovar, vb. disapprove.

desaproveitar, vb. misuse; waste.

desarmamento, n.m. disarmament.

desarmar, vb. disarm; disassemble.

desarraigar, vb. uproot.

desarranjar, vb. disarrange; upset. **d.-se com,** argue with.

desarranjo, n.m. disarray.

desarrumar, vb. mess up.

desasseio, n.m. uncleanliness.

desassossego, n.m. disquiet.

desastrado, adj. disastrous; clumsy.

desastre, n.m. disaster.

desastroso, adj. disastrous.

desatar, vb. untie. **d. a,** begin to.

desatenção, n.f. disregard; discourtesy.

desatender, vb. disregard; be disrespectful to.

desatinar, vb. drive/go mad.

desatino, n.m. madness.

desavença, n.f. disagreement.

desavergonhado, adj. shameless, insolent.

desavir-se, vb. have a disagreement.

desbancar, vb. outclass.

desbaratar, vb. squander; destroy; defeat.

desbastar, vb. trim; polish.

desbocado, adj. foul-mouthed.

desbotar, vb. fade.

desbragado, adj. shameless.

desbravador -ra, n. trailblazer.

desbravar, vb. tame; open up (land).

desbravejar, vb. clear (land).

desbundar, vb. (sl.) overwhelm; lose control.

descabelado, adj. bald; disheveled; exaggerated.

descadeirado, adj. (coll.) tired.

descalabro, n.m. disaster.

descalço, adj. barefoot.

descambar, vb. fall; go down; degenerate.

descansar, vb. rest. **—descanso,** n.m.

descarado, adj. shameless.

descaramento, descaro, n.m., gall, nerve.

descarga, vb. discharge; unloading; flush.

descarnado, adj. fleshless; gaunt.

descarnar, vb. bone; peel; emaciate. **d.-se,** become thin.

descarregar, vb. unload.

descarrilar, vb. derail.

descartar, vb. discard.

descartável, adj. disposable.

descarte, n.m. discard; excuse.

descascar, vb. peel; berate.

descaso, n.m. disregard.

descendência, n.f. descent.

descendente, 1. adj. descending. **2.** n.m.f. descendant.

descender de, vb. be a descendant of.

descenso, n.m. descent.

descer, vb. go/come down; get off/out; lower.

descerrar, vb. open.

descida, n.f. descent.

desclassificado, adj. disreputable.

desclassificar, vb. disqualify; discredit.

descoberta, n.f. discovery, find.

descobridor -ra, n. discoverer.

descobrimento, n.m. discovery.

descobrir, vb. discover; uncover; reveal. **d.-se,** take off one's hat.

descolar, vb. unstick; (sl.) get.

descolorir, vb. discolor.

descomedido, adj. immoderate.

descompasso, n.m. lack of proportion; disharmony.

descompor, vb. insult; berate.

descompostura, n.f. reprimand.

descomunal, adj. extraordinary; colossal.

desconcertar, vb. disarrange; disconcert; disagree.

desconcerto, n.m. disorder.

desconexo, adj. disconnected.

desconfiado, adj. suspicious.

desconfiança, n.f. suspicion.

desconfiar, vb. suspect; suppose.

desconforto, n.m. discomfort.

descongelar, vb. thaw. —**descongelação,** n.f.

descongestionante, n.m. decongestant.

desconhecer, vb. not know; not recognize.

desconhecido, 1. adj. unknown. **2.** n.m. stranger.

desconsideração, n.f. inconsiderateness.

desconsiderar, vb. not consider; disrespect.

desconsolado, adj. disconsolate.

desconsolar, vb. grieve. **d.-se,** be disconsolate.

descontar, vb. discount; ignore; cash (check).

descontentamento, n.m. discontent.

descontentar, vb. dissatisfy.

descontente, adj. discontent.

descontinuar, vb. discontinue.

desconto, n.m. discount, deduction.

descontração, n.f. relaxation.

descontraído, adj. relaxed.

descontrair(-se), vb. relax.

descontrolado, adj. out of control.

descontrolar-se, vb. lose one's self-control.

descontrole, n.m. lack of control.

desconversar, vb. change the subject.

descorar, vb. discolor; pale.

descoroçoar, vb. dishearten; lose heart.

descortês, adj. discourteous.

descorticar, vb. peel.

descortinar, vb. reveal; discover.

descrédito, n.m. discredit.

descrença, n.f. disbelief.

descrente, adj. unbelieving.

descrer, vb. disbelieve.

descrever, vb. describe.

descrição, n.f. description.

descritivo, adj. descriptive.

descuidado, adj. careless; neglected; lazy.

descuidar, vb. neglect; be careless.

descuido, n.m. carelessness; error.

desculpa, n.f. excuse; apology. **pedir desculpas,** apologize.

desculpar, vb. excuse; absolve. **d.-se,** apologize. **desculpe!,** excuse me!

descurar, vb. neglect.

desde, prep. since, from. **d. que,** since; provided that.

desdém, n.m. disdain. **—desdenhar,** vb.

desdenhoso, adj. disdainful.

desdentado, adj. toothless.

desdita, n.f. unhappiness; misfortune.

desdizer, vb. contradict. **d.-se,** retract one's words.

desdobrar, vb. unfold; split. **d.-se,** unfold; develop; strive.

desdouro, n.m. tarnish. **—desdourar,** vb.

desejar, vb. desire, wish. **—desejo,** n.m.

desejável, adj. desirable.

desejoso, adj. desirous.

desembaraçado, adj. unobstructed; uninhibited.

desembaraçar, vb. free; untangle. **d.-se,** rid oneself.

desembaraço, n.m. disencumbrance; ease; poise.

desembarcar, vb. disembark.

desembargador -ra, n. appeals court judge.

desembarque, n.m. disembarkation.

desembocadura, n.f. mouth (river).

desembocar em, vb. flow/run into.

desembolsar, vb. disburse; spend.

desembolso, n.m. disbursement.

desembuchar, vb. unclog; (coll.) get off one's chest.

desempatar, vb. break a tie.

desempenhar, vb. redeem; perform.

desempenho, n.m. redemption; performance.

desempregado, adj. unemployed.

desempregar, vb. dismiss. **d.-se,** lose one's job.

desemprego, n.m. unemployment.

desencadear, vb. unchain; unleash.

desencalhar, vb. set afloat; free; sell off; (coll.) marry off.

desencaminhar, vb. lead astray.

desencantamento, desencanto, n.m. disillusionment.

desencantar, vb. disenchant.

desencarnar, vb. die.

desencontrar(-se), vb. fail to meet; disagree.

desencontro, n.m. failure to meet.

desencorajar, vb. discourage.

desenfadar, vb. amuse.

desenfado, n.m. amusement.

desenferrujar, vb. remove rust from; limber up. **d. as pernas,** stretch one's legs.

desenfrear, vb. unbridle; give free rein to.

desengano, n.m. disillusion. **—desenganar,** vb.

desengonçar, vb. unhinge; disjoint.

desenhar, vb. draw; design.

desenhista, n.m.f. designer; draftsman.

desenho, n.m. drawing; design.

desenlace, n.m. untying; outcome, dénouement.

desenredar, vb. untangle; solve.

desenredo, n.m. untangling; resolution.

desenrolar, vb. unroll; unwrap; explain.

desentender, vb. misunderstand. **d.-se,** have a misunderstanding.

desentendimento, n.m. misunderstanding; stupidity.

desenterrar, vb. unearth; exhume.

desentoar, vb. be out of tune.

desentranhar, vb. disembowel; unearth.

desenvolto, adj. forward; mischievous; shameless.

desenvoltura, n.f. impudence; shamelessness.

desenvolver, vb. develop. **d.-se,** develop, grow.

desenvolvimento, n.m. development.

desequilibrar, vb. unbalance. **d.-se,** become unbalanced.

desequilíbrio, n.m. imbalance.

deserção, n.f. desertion.

deserdar, vb. disinherit.

desertar, vb. desert.

deserto, 1. adj. deserted. **2.** n.m. desert.

desesperado, *adj.* desperate, hopeless.

desesperar, *vb.* despair.

desespero, *n.m.* despair.

desfalcar, *vb.* embezzle.

desfalecer, *vb.* weaken; faint.

desfalque, *n.m.* embezzlement.

desfavor, *n.m.* disfavor; contempt.

desfavorável, *adj.* unfavorable.

desfazer, *vb.* undo; destroy; annul. **d.-se,** come undone; give free rein; **d.-se de,** get rid of.

desfechar, *vb.* open; shoot; strike; cast; conclude.

desfecho, *n.m.* outcome, dénouement.

desfeita, *vb.* insult. —**desfeitear,** *vb.*

desferir, *vb.* strike; strum; fire; set sail.

desfiar, *vb.* ravel; shred; narrate.

desfigurar, *vb.* disfigure.

desfiladeiro, *n.m.* pass.

desfile, *n.m.* parade. —**desfilar,** *vb.*

desflorestamento, *n.m.* deforestation.

desfolhar, *vb.* defoliate. **d.-se,** shed leaves.

desforra, *n.f.* revenge.

desforrar, *vb.* avenge. **d.-se,** get even.

desfraldar, *vb.* unfurl.

desfrutar, *vb.* enjoy; live off of; mock.

desfrute, *n.m.* enjoyment; mockery.

desgarrar, *vb.* lead/go astray.

desgastar, *vb.* abrade.

desgaste, *n.m.* abrasion.

desgostar, *vb.* displease. **d. de,** not like; **d.-se,** be displeased.

desgosto, *n.m.* displeasure; grief; aversion.

desgostoso, *adj.* displeased; annoyed.

desgraça, *n.f.* misfortune.

desgraçado, *adj.* unfortunate; miserable; horrible.

desgraçar, *vb.* bring misfortune to; *(coll.)* deflower.

desgrenhado, *adj.* disheveled.

desidratar, *vb.* dehydrate.

designação, *n.f.* designation.

designar, *vb.* designate.

designio, *n.m.* plan, design.

desigual, *adj.* unequal; uneven.

desiludir, *vb.* disillusion; disappoint.

desilusão, *n.f.* disillusion; disappointment.

desimpedir, *vb.* disencumber; facilitate.

desinfetante, *n.m.* disinfectant.

desinfetar, *vb.* disinfect.

desintegrar, *vb.* disintegrate.

desinteressado, *adj.* disinterested.

desinteressar-se, *vb.* lose interest, not care.

desinteresse, *n.m.* disinterest.

desistir, *vb.* desist, give up.

desjejum, *n.m.* breakfast. —**desjejuar,** *vb.*

deslavado, *adj.* faded; shameless.

desleal, *adj.* disloyal; unfair.

desleixado, *adj.* careless; untidy.

desleixar, *vb.* neglect. **d.-se,** be negligent.

deslembrado, *adj.* forgetful; forgotten.

deslembrar, *vb.* forget.

desligado, *adj.* detached; off; *(coll.)* out of it.

desligar, *vb.* disconnect; hang up; turn off; release.

deslindar, *vb.* demarcate; untangle; investigate.

deslizar, *vb.* slip, slide; slip by; go astray.

deslize, *n.m.* slip, slide; lapse.

deslocar, *vb.* displace; dislocate.

deslumbrar, *vb.* dazzle.

deslustrar, *vb.* tarnish. —**deslustre,** *n.m.*

desmaiar, *vb.* faint. —**desmaio,** *n.m.*

desmamar, *vb.* wean.

desmancha-prazeres, *n.m.* killjoy.

desmanchar, *vb.* undo, break. **d.-se,** come undone.

desmandar, *vb.* countermand. **d.-se,** go overboard.

desmando, *n.m.* excess.

desmantelar, *vb.* dismantle.

desmarcar, *vb.* cancel.

desmascarar, *vb.* unmask.

desmazelado, *adj.* sloppy; *(coll.)* sickly.

desmazelo, *n.m.* sloppiness.

desmedido, *adj.* limitless; excessive.

desmembrar, *vb.* dismember.

desmemoriado, *adj.* forgetful.

desmentir, *vb.* deny, contradict.

desmerecer, *vb.* be unworthy of; fade.

desmesurado, *adj.* excessive.

desmilitarizar, *vb.* demilitarize.

desmiolado, *adj.* rattlebrained.

desmobilizar, *vb.* demobilize.

desmontar, *vb.* dismount; disassemble.

desmoralizar, *vb.* demoralize.

desmoronar, *vb.* destroy; knock down. **d.-se,** collapse.

desnatar, *vb.* skim (milk).

desnecessário, *adj.* unnecessary.

desnível, *n.m.* unevenness.

desnortear, *vb.* disorient.

desnudar, *vb.* undress; bare. **d.-se,** undress.

desnutrição, *n.f.* malnutrition.

desnutrir, *vb.* malnourish.

desobedecer, *vb.* disobey.

desobediente, *adj.* disobedient.

desobrigar, *vb.* exempt, relieve.

desocupado, *adj.* idle; unemployed; not busy; vacant.

desocupar, *vb.* vacate; free.

desodorante, *n.m.* deodorant.

desolação, *n.f.* desolation; sadness.

desolado, *adj.* desolate; sad.

desolar, *vb.* desolate; sadden.

desonesto, *adj.* dishonest; immoral.

desonra, *n.f.* dishonor. **—desonrar,** *vb.*

desonroso, *adj.* dishonorable.

desordeiro, *adj.* disorderly.

desordem, *n.f.* disorder.

desordenar, *vb.* disorganize.

desorganizar, *vb.* disorganize.

desorientar, *vb.* disorient.

desossar, *vb.* bone.

desova, *n.f.* spawning.

desovar, *vb.* spawn.

despachante, *n.m.f.* bureaucracy broker.

despachar, *vb.* settle; send off; dismiss; *(coll.)* kill.

despacho, *n.m.* dispatch; sending; settlement; Afro-Brazilian votive offering.

despautério, *n.m.* absurdity.

despedaçar, *vb.* tear up.

despedida, *n.f.* farewell; sendoff; dismissal.

despedir, *vb.* dismiss; see off; emit; shoot. **d.-se de,** say goodbye to.

despeitado, *adj.* spiteful; angry.

despeitar, *vb.* spite; anger. **d.-se,** get mad.

despeito, *n.m.* spite. **a d. de,** despite.

despejar, *vb.* clear; empty; evict.

despejo, *n.m.* garbage; eviction; impudence.

despencar, *vb.* plummet, fall.

despender, *vb.* expend.

despenhadeiro, *n.m.* precipice.

despenhar, *vb.* throw down. **d.-se,** jump/fall downward.

despensa, *n.f.* pantry.

despenteado, *adj.* disheveled.

despercebido, *adj.* unnoticed.

desperdiçar, *vb.* waste. **—desperdício,** *n.m.*

despertador, *n.m.* alarm clock.

despertar, *vb.* awaken, arouse.

despesa, *n.f.* expense.

despir, *vb.* undress; take off. **d.-se,** get undressed.

despistar, *vb.* mislead.

despojar, *vb.* despoil; strip.

despojos, *n.m.pl.* spoils; remains.

despontar, *vb.* dull; emerge.

desporto, *n.m.* sport.

desposar, *vb.* marry.

déspota, *n.m.f.* despot.

despotismo, *n.m.* despotism; whole lot.

despovoado, 1. *adj.* unpopulated. **2.** *n.m.* wasteland.

despovoar, *vb.* depopulate.

desprazer, *vb.* displease.

despregar, *vb.* unnail; avert (eyes); unfurl.

desprender, *vb.* untie; free; emit. **d.-se,** come/get loose.

despreocupado, *adj.* unworried, carefree.

despretensioso, *adj.* unpretentious.

desprevenido, *adj.* unprepared.

desprezar, vb. scorn. **—desprezo**, n.m.

desprezível, adj. contemptible.

desproporcionado, adj. disproportionate.

despropósito, n.m. nonsense, absurdity; whole lot.

desprovido de, adj. lacking.

despudorado, adj. shameless.

desqualificar, vb. disqualify; disable.

desquitado, adj. legally separated.

desquitar-se, vb. to legally separate.

desquite, n.m. legal separation.

desregrado, adj. unruly; profligate.

desrespeito, n.m. disrespect. **—desrespeitar**, vb.

desrespeitoso, adj. disrespectful.

dessa, contr. of de + essa.

dessas, contr. of de + essas.

desse, contr. of de + esse.

dessemelhante, adj. dissimilar.

desserviço, n.m. disservice, harm.

desses, contr. of de + esses.

desta, contr. of de + esta.

destabocado, adj. sassy.

destacado, adj. outstanding.

destacamento, n.m. (mil.) detachment.

destacar, vb. emphasize; (mil.) detail; separate; stand out.

destaque, n.m. distinction

destarte, adv. in this way.

destas, contr. of de + estas.

deste, contr. of de + este.

destemido, adj. fearless.

destemperar, vb. disorder; go mad.

desterrar, vb. exile. **—desterro**, n.m.

destes, contr. of de + estes.

destilar, vb. distill.

destilaria, n.f. distillery.

destinar, vb. destine. **d.-se**, devote oneself (to); be bound (for).

destinatário -ria, n. addressee.

destino, n.m. destiny; destination.

destituir, vb. dismiss; deprive.

destoar, vb. be out of tune; clash; disagree.

destreinado, adj. untrained; out of practice.

destreza, n.f. dexterity.

destripar, vb. eviscerate.

destro, adj. skillful; clever.

destroçar, vb. ruin; smash; defeat.

destroços, n.m.pl. debris.

destronar, vb. dethrone.

destruição, n.f. destruction.

destruir, vb. destroy.

destrutivo, adj. destructive.

desumano, adj. inhuman.

desunião, n.f. disunion.

desunir, vb. disunite.

desusado, adj. out of use.

desuso, n.m. disuse.

desvairado, adj. delirious.

desvairar, vb. be delirious.

desvalido, adj. helpless; destitute.

desvalorizar, vb. devalue.

desvanecer, vb. dispell. **d.-se**, vanish; fill with pride.

desvantagem, n.f. disadvantage.

desvantajoso, adj. disadvantageous.

desvão, n.m. attic.

desvario, n.m. delirium.

desvelar, vb. keep awake; unveil. **d.-se**, be diligent.

desvelo, n.m. diligence; fondness.

desvencilhar, vb. unfasten. **d.-se**, rid oneself.

desvendar, vb. unblindfold; reveal.

desventura, vb. misadventure.

desventurado, adj. unfortunate.

desviar, vb. divert; separate; save (from).

desvio, n.m. detour; diversion; error.

desvirginar, vb. deflower.

desvirtuar, vb. discredit; distort.

detalhe, n.m. detail. **—detalhar**, vb.

detectar, vb. detect.

detective, detetive, n.m. detective.

detector, n.m. detector. **d. de incêndio**, n.m. smoke detector.

detenção, n.f. detention.

detento, n.m. prisoner.

detentor -ra, n. holder.

deter, *vb.* detain; restrain; delay; retain. **d.-se**, linger; contain oneself.

detergente, *n.m.* detergent.

deteriorar(-se), *vb.* deteriorate; ruin.

determinação, *n.f.* determination.

determinar, *vb.* determine.

detestar, *vb.* detest, hate.

detonador, *n.m.* detonator.

detonar, *vb.* detonate.

detrair, *vb.* detract (from).

detrás, *adv.* behind. **d. de**, in back of.

detrator -ra, *n.* detractor.

detrimento, *n.m.* detriment.

detrito, *n.m.* debris.

deturpar, *vb.* pervert.

deus, -sa, *n.* god, -dess.

Deus, *n.m.* God. **D. me livre!**, God forbid!; **meu D. (do céu)!**, my gosh!; **graças a D.!**, thank God!; **pelo amor de D.!**, for God's sake!

deus-dará, *n.m.* **ao d.**, aimlessly; to fate.

deus-nos-acuda, *n.m.* commotion.

devagar, *adv.* slowly.

devanear, *vb.* daydream; be delirious.

devaneio, *n.m.* daydream.

devassar, *vb.* trespass; afford a view of; probe.

devassidão, *n.f.* debauchery.

devasso, *adj.* dissolute.

devastar, *vb.* devastate.

devedor -ra, *n.* debtor.

dever, 1. *n.m.* task; homework. **2.** *vb.* owe; ought to; should. **d.-se a**, be due to.

deveras, *adv.* indeed.

devir, *vb.* become.

devoção, *n.f.* devotion.

devolver, *vb.* return; refund. —**devolução**, *n.f.*

devorar, *vb.* devour.

devotar, *vb.* devote. **d.-se a**, devote oneself to.

devoto -ta, 1. *adj.* devoted. **2.** *n.* worshipper; devotee.

dez, *adj.* ten.

dezembro, *n.m.* December.

dezena, *n.f.* (group of) ten.

dezenove, *adj.* nineteen.

dezesseis, *adj.* sixteen.

dezessete, *adj.* seventeen.

dezoito, *adj.* eighteen.

dez-réis, *n.m.* old Portuguese coin; pittance.

dia, *n.m.* day. **bom d.**, good morning/day; **de d.**, by day; **em d.**, up to date; **mais d., menos d.**, sooner or later.

diabetes, *n.m.f.* diabetes.

diabo, *n.m.* devil. **pobre d.**, underdog.

diabólico, *adj.* diabolical.

diabrura, *n.f.* deviltry.

diácono, *n.m.* deacon.

diáfano, *adj.* transparent.

diafragma, *n.m.* diaphragm.

diagnose, *n.f.* diagnosis.

diagnosticar, *vb.* diagnose.

diagnóstico, 1. *adj.* diagnostic. **2.** *n.* diagnosis.

diagonal, *adj.* diagonal.

diagrama, *n.m.* diagram.

dial, *n.m.* dial.

dialética, *n.f.* dialectic.

dialeto, *n.m.* dialect.

diálogo, *n.m.* dialogue. —**dialogar**, *vb.*

diamante, *n.m.* diamond.

diante, *adv.* in front. **d. de**, in front of; **daqui em d.**, from now on; **e assim por d.**, and so forth; **para/em d.**, onward.

dianteira, *n.f.* lead. **estar na d.**, be in the lead.

dianteiro, *adj.* front; leading.

diapasão, *n.m.* pitch; tuning fork.

diapositivo, *n.m.* (*phot.*) slide.

diária, *n.f.* daily rate; per diem.

diário, 1. *adj.* daily. **2.** *n.* diary; daily paper.

diarréia, *n.f.* diarrhea.

diatribe, *n.f.* diatribe.

dica, *n.f.* (*sl.*) tip, pointer.

dicção, *n.f.* diction.

dicionário, *n.m.* dictionary.

dicotomia, *n.f.* dichotomy.

didático, *adj.* didactic.

diérese, *n.f.* dieresis, umlaut.

dieta, *n.f.* diet.

difamar, *vb.* defame.

diferença, *n.f.* difference.

diferençar, -ciar, *vb.* differentiate.

diferente, *adj.* different.

diferir, *vb.* defer; differ.

difícil, *adj.* difficult; hard.

dificuldade, n.f. difficulty.
dificultar, vb. make difficult.
difteria, n.f. diphtheria.
difundir, vb. diffuse, spread.
difusão, n.f. diffusion, spread.
difuso, adj. diffuse.
digerir, vb. digest.
digestão, n.f. digestion.
digesto, n.m. digest.
digital, adj. digital.
dígito, n.m. digit, number.
dignar-se, vb. deign.
dignidade, n.f. dignity.
dignificar, vb. dignify.
dignitário, n.m. dignitary.
digno, adj. worthy.
digressão, n.f. digression.
dilação, n.f. delay.
dilacerar, vb. lacerate.
dilapidar, vb. dilapidate; squander.
dilatar(-se), vb. dilate; spread; delay.
dilema, n.m. dilemma.
diligência, n.f. diligence; stage-coach.
diligente, adj. diligent.
diluir, vb. dilute.
dilúvio, n.m. flood, deluge.
dimensão, n.f. dimension.
diminuição, n.f. diminution.
diminuir, vb. diminish; subtract.
diminutivo, adj., n.m. diminutive.
diminuto, adj. minute.
Dinamarca, n.f. Denmark.
dinamarquês -quesa, 1. adj. Danish. **2.** n. Dane; n.m. Danish.
dinâmico, adj. dynamic.
dinamite, n.f. dynamite. **—dinamitar**, vb.
dínamo, n.m. dynamo.
dinastia, n.f. dynasty.
dinheirão, n.m., **-rada, -rama**, n.f. (coll.) lot of money.
dinheiro, n.m. money.
dinossauro, n.m. dinosaur.
diocese, n.f. diocese.
diploma, n.m. diploma.
diplomacia, n.f. diplomacy.
diplomado -da, n. graduate.
diplomando -da, n. degree candidate.
diplomar-se, vb. graduate.
diplomata, n.m.f. diplomat.

diplomático, adj. diplomatic.
dique, n.m. dike; dry dock.
direção, n.f. direction; directorate; steering.
direita, n.f. right.
direitista, n.m.f. rightist.
direito, 1. adj. right; straight. **2.** adv. right; straight. **3.** n.m. law (field); right; (com.) duty.
direta, n.f. direct election.
diretiva, n.f. directive.
direto, 1. adj. direct. **2.** adv. directly.
diretor -ra, n. director; manager; officer.
diretorado, n.m. directorship.
diretoria, n.f. directorship; directorate.
diretório, n.m. directorate; directory.
diretriz, n.f. directress; directive.
dirigente, n.m.f. director.
dirigir, vb. direct; drive (car); address. **d.-se a**, head for; tend towards; address.
dirigível, n.m. dirigible.
dirimir, vb. annul; settle.
discar, vb. dial (phone).
discernir, vb. discern.
disciplina, n.f. discipline. **—disciplinar**, vb.
discípulo -la, n. disciple, follower.
disco, n.m. disk; phonograph record. **d. rígido**, n.m. hard disk; **d. voador**, flying saucer; **unidade de d.**, disk drive.
discordar, vb. disagree.
discorde, adj. discordant.
discórdia, n.f. discord.
discorrer, vb. roam; discourse; think; elapse; go over.
discoteca, n.f. record library; disco.
discrepância, n.f. discrepancy; disagreement.
discrepar, vb. differ; disagree.
discreto, adj. discreet; discrete.
discrição, n.f. discretion.
discriminação, n.f. discrimination.
discriminar, vb. discriminate.
discursar, vb. discourse; make a speech.
discurso, n.m. speech; discourse.

discussão, *n.f.* discussion; argument.

discutir, *vb.* discuss; argue.

disenteria, *n.f.* dysentery.

disfarce, *n.m.* disguise. —**disfarçar,** *vb.*

disparada, *n.f.* dash, dart.

disparado, *adj.* daring; fast.

disparador, *n.m.* trigger.

disparar, *vb.* fire (gun); cast; dash.

disparatado, *adj.* nonsensical.

disparate, *n.m.* nonsense.

disparidade, *n.f.* disparity.

disparo, *n.m.* firing; shot.

dispêndio, *n.m.* expenditure.

dispendioso, *adj.* expensive.

dispensa, *n.f.* dispensation.

dispensar, *vb.* dispense; not need; bestow.

dispensário, *n.m.* soup kitchen.

dispersar(-se), *vb.* disperse.

displicência, *n.f.* bad humor; displeasure; negligence.

disponível, *adj.* available.

dispor, 1. *n.m.* disposal. **2.** *vb.* arrange; prepare; establish; dispose. **d.-se a,** get ready to/ for; **d. de,** have at one's disposal; dispose of; **disponha!,** you're welcome.

disposição, *n.f.* disposition; disposal.

dispositivo, *n.m.* device.

disposto, *adj.* disposed; willing.

disputa, *n.f.* dispute. —**disputar,** *vb.*

disquete, *n.m.* diskette.

dissabor, *n.m.* distaste; sorrow.

dissecar, *vb.* dissect.

disseminar, *vb.* disseminate.

dissentir, *vb.* dissent. —**dissenção,** *n.f.*

disse-que-disse,   disse-não-disse, *n.m.* rumor; gossip.

dissertação, *n.f.* dissertation.

dissertar, *vb.* discourse.

dissidente, *adj., n.m.f.* dissident.

dissídio, *n.m.* dissent. **d. coletivo,** collective bargaining.

dissimilar, 1. *adj.* dissimilar. **2.** *vb.* dissimilate.

dissimular, *vb.* dissimulate, dissemble.

dissipar, *vb.* dissipate.

disso, *contr.* of **de** + **isso.**

dissociar, *vb.* dissociate.

dissolução, *n.f.* dissolution.

dissoluto, *adj.* dissolute.

dissolver, *vb.* dissolve.

dissuadir, *vb.* dissuade.

distância, *n.f.* distance.

distanciar, *vb.* distance. **d.-se,** draw away.

distante, *adj.* distant.

distensão, *n.f.* détente.

dístico, *n.m.* couplet; label.

distinção, *n.f.* distinction.

distinguir, *vb.* distinguish.

distintivo, 1. *adj.* distinctive. **2.** *n.m.* badge.

distinto, *adj.* distinct; distinguished.

disto, *contr.* of **de** + **isto.**

distorção, *n.f.* distortion.

distorcer, *vb.* distort.

distração, *n.f.* distraction; amusement.

distraído, *adj.* distracted; absent-minded.

distrair, *vb.* distract; amuse.

distribuição, *n.f.* distribution.

distribuidor, *n.m.* distributor.

distribuir, *vb.* distribute.

distrito, *n.m.* district; police precinct.

distúrbio, *n.m.* disturbance.

dita, *n.f.* good fortune.

ditado, *n.m.* dictation; saying.

ditador -ra, *n.m.* dictator.

ditadura, *n.f.* dictatorship.

ditame, *n.m.* dictate; order.

ditar, *vb.* dictate.

ditatorial, *adj.* dictatorial.

dito, 1. *adj.* said. **2.** *n.m.* saying.

ditongo, *n.m.* diphthong.

ditoso, *adj.* happy, fortunate.

diurno, *adj.* diurnal.

divã, *n.m.* divan.

divagar, *vb.* wander; ramble; daydream.

divergente, *adj.* divergent.

divergir, *vb.* diverge.

diversão, *n.f.* diversion; amusement.

diversidade, *n.f.* diversity.

diversificar, *vb.* diversify.

diverso, *adj.* diverse, different; *(pl.)* several; various.

divertido, *adj.* amusing, funny.

divertimento, *n.m.* amusement, fun.

divertir, vb. divert; amuse. **d.-se,** have fun.

dívida, n.f. debt.

dividendo, n.m. dividend.

dividir, vb. divide.

divindade, n.f. divinity.

divino, adj. divine.

divisa, n.f. boundary; slogan; emblem; (pl.) foreign exhange credits.

divisão, n.f. division.

divisar, vb. sight; notice; demarcate.

divisor, n.m. divisor; divider.

divisória, n.f. dividing line.

divorciado -da, n. divorcé(e).

divorciar, vb. divorce. **d.-se,** get a divorce.

divórcio, n.m. divorce.

divulgar, vb. divulge. **d.-se,** be publicized.

dixe, n.m. trinket.

dizer, 1. n.m. say, expression. **2.** vb. say, tell. **d.-se,** call oneself; **como se diz?,** how do you say?; **não diga!,** you don't say!; **querer d.,** mean; **quer d.,** that is to say.

dízima, n.f. tithe; decimal fraction.

dizimar, vb. decimate.

dízimo, n.m. tenth; tithe.

diz-que-diz(-que), n.m. gossip.

do, contr. of **de** + **o.**

dó, n.m. pity.

doação, n.f. donation.

doador -ra, n. donor.

doar, vb. donate, give.

dobra, n.f. fold.

dobradiça, n.f. hinge.

dobradiço, adj. folding.

dobradinha, n.f. tripe stew; (sl.) bet; double feature.

dobrão, n.m. doubloon.

dobrar, vb. fold; bend; turn; double; toll. **d.-se,** bend.

dobre, n.m. toll, peal.

dobro, n.m. double.

doca, n.f. dock.

doce, adj.; n.m. sweet.

doceiro -ra, n. confectioner.

docente, adj. teaching; academic. **2.** n.m.f. professor.

dócil, adj. docile.

documentação, n.f. documentation.

documentário -tal, adj., n.m. documentary.

documento, n.m. document. —**documentar,** vb.

doçura, n.f. sweetness.

doença, n.f. illness.

doente, 1. adj. sick. **2.** n.m.f. sick person.

doentio, adj. sickly, sick.

doer, vb. ache, hurt.

dogma, n.m. dogma.

dogmático, adj. dogmatic.

doidice, n.f. craziness.

doidivanas, adj. scatterbrained.

doido, 1. adj. crazy. **d. por,** (coll.) crazy about. **2.** n.m. madman.

doído, adj. sore, achy.

dois, adj. two.

dólar, n.m. dollar.

dolorido, adj. painful, sore.

dolorosa, n.f. (sl.) bill, check.

doloroso, adj. painful; sorrowful.

dom, n.m. gift, talent.

Dom, title used before a king's or bishop's first name.

doma, domação, n.f. taming.

domador -ra, n. tamer.

domar, vb. tame. **d.-se,** control oneself.

domesticar, n.m. tame; civilize.

doméstico -ca, 1. adj. domestic. **2.** n. servant.

domiciliado, adj. residing.

domicílio, n.m. residence.

dominação, n.f. domination.

dominância, n.f. dominance.

dominante, adj. dominant.

dominar, vb. dominate.

domingo, n.m. Sunday.

dominicano -na, adj., n. Dominican.

domínio, n.m. dominion; domain; control.

dominó, n.m. domino(es).

dona, n.f. lady; woman; wife; owner; (cap.) title used before a lady's first name. **d. de casa,** housewife, lady of the house.

donaire, n.m. grace; decoration.

donatário -ria, n. grantee.

donde, adv. from where.

doninha, n.f. weasel.

dono -na, n. owner.

donzel, 1. *adj.* pure. **2.** *n.m.* squire.

donzela, *vb.* damsel; virgin.

dopar, *vb.* drug. **d.-se,** take drugs.

dor, *n.f.* pain, ache. **d. de cotovelo** or **de corno,** *(sl.)* jealousy.

doravante, *adv.* henceforth.

dormente, 1. *adj.* dormant. **2.** *n.m.* railroad tie; floor beam.

dormida, *n.f.* sleep.

dorminhoco -ca, *n.* *(coll.)* sleepyhead.

dormir, *vb.* sleep. **d. no ponto,** *(coll.)* be caught napping; **d. sobre os louros,** rest on one's laurels.

dormitar, *vb.* doze.

dormitório, *n.m.* dormitory; bedroom.

dorso, *n.m.* back.

dos, *contr. of* **de + os.**

dosagem, *n.f.* dosage.

dose, *n.f.* dose; shot (liquor). **ser d.** or **d. para elefante,** *(sl.)* be hard to take.

dossel, *n.m.* canopy; valance.

dossiê, *n.m.* dossier.

dotado, *adj.* endowed; talented.

dotar, *vb.* endow; give a dowry to.

dote, *n.m.* dowry; endowment.

doudo, *var. of* **doido.**

dourado, *adj.* golden.

dourar, *vb.* gild; brown. **d. a pílula,** gild the pill.

douto, 1. *adj.* learned. **2.** *n.m.* scholar.

doutor -ra, *n.* doctor *(acad.; med.; also used in addressing persons of position).*

doutorado, -ramento, *n.m.* doctorate.

doutoral, *adj.* doctoral.

doutorando -da, *n.* doctoral candidate.

doutorar-se, *vb.* receive a doctor's degree.

doutrina, *n.f.* doctrine.

doutrinal, *adj.* doctrinal.

doutrinar, *vb.* indoctrinate.

doutrinário -ria, *adj.* doctrinaire.

doze, *adj.* twelve.

draga, *n.f.* dredge.

dragão, *n.m.* dragon.

dragar, *vb.* drag, dredge.

dragona, *n.f.* epaulet.

drama, *n.m.* drama.

dramalhão, *n.m.* melodrama.

dramático, *adj.* dramatic.

dramatizar, *vb.* dramatize.

drmaturgo, *n.m.* dramatist, playwright.

drapear, -pejar, *vb.* drape; wave.

drástico, *adj.* drastic.

drenagem, *n.f.* drainage.

drenar, *vb.* drain. **—dreno,** *n.m.*

driblar, *vb.* *(sport.)* dribble around; *(sl.)* trick.

drinque, *n.m.* *(coll.)* (alcoholic) drink.

droga, 1. *n.f.* drug; junk; *(coll.)* bummer. **2.** *interj.* *(coll.)* darn it!

drogar, *vb.* drug. **d.-se,** take drugs.

drogaria, *n.f.* drugstore, pharmacy.

droguista, 1. *adj.* drug. **2.** *n.m.f.* druggist.

dual, *adj.* dual.

dualidade, *n.f.* duality.

duas, *adj. fem. of* **dois.**

dúbio, *adj.* dubious; hesitant.

dublagem, *n.f.* dubbing (film).

dublar, *vb.* dub (film).

ducha, *n.f.* shower; damper.

duelo, *n.m.* duel. **—duelar,** *vb.*

duende, *n.m.* sprite, elf.

dueto, *n.m.* duet.

dum, *contr. of* **de + um.**

duma, *contr. of* **de + uma.**

dumas, *contr. of* **de + umas.**

duna, *n.f.* dune.

duns, *contr. of* **de + uns.**

duo, *n.m.* duet; duo.

dupla, *n.f.* pair.

duplicar, *vb.* duplicate.

duplicata, *n.f.* duplicate; commercial paper.

dúplice, *adj.* double; duplicitous.

duplicidade, *n.f.* duplicity.

duplo, *adj.* double.

duque, *n.m.* duke.

duquesa, *n.f.* duchess.

duração, *n.f.* duration.

duradouro, *adj.* durable, lasting.

durão, *n.m.* *(coll.)* tough, bully.

dureza, *n.f.* hardness; *(sl.)* pennilessness.

duro, *adj.* hard; tough; difficult; stale; *(sl.)* broke. **dar (um) d.,** *(sl.)* work hard; **dar um d. em,** crack down on; **no d.,** *(sl.)* really.

dúvida, *n.f.* doubt. —**duvidar,** *vb.*

duvidoso, *adj.* doubtful.

duzentos, *adj.* two hundred.

dúzia, *n.f.* dozen.

E

e, *conj.* and.

é, 1. *n.m.* the letter e. **2.** *vb.* yes.

ébrio, *adj.* drunk.

eclesiástico, 1. *adj.* ecclesiastical. **2.** *n.m.* churchman.

eclético, *adj.* eclectic.

eclipse, *n.m.* eclipse. —**eclipsar,** *vb.*

eclodir, *vb.* emerge; bloom.

eclosão, *n.f.* emergence; blooming.

eclusa, *n.f.* canal lock.

eco, *n.m.* echo. —**ecoar,** *vb.*

ecologia, *n.f.* ecology.

economia, *n.f.* economy; thrift; economics.

econômico, *adj.* economical; thrifty.

economista, *n.m.f.* economist.

economizar, *vb.* economize, save.

Eden, *n.m.* Eden.

edição, *n.f.* edition.

edificar, *vb.* edify.

edifício, *n.m.* building.

edil, *n.m.* councilman.

edital, *n.m.* official notice.

editar, *vb.* publish.

edito, *n.m.* edict.

editor -ra, *n.* publisher.

editora, *n.f.* publishing house.

editoração, *n.f.* publishing.

editorial, 1. *adj.* editorial. **2.** *n.m.* editorial; *n.f.* publishing house.

educação, *n.f.* education; upbringing; manners.

educacional, *adj.* educational.

educado, *adj.* educated; polite.

educador -ra, *n.* educator.

educando -ra, *n.* pupil.

educar, *vb.* educate; bring up.

educativo, *adj.* educational.

efe, *n.m.* the letter f. **com todos os efes e erres,** in detail.

efeito, *n.m.* effect; purpose. **com e.,** in fact.

efêmero, *adj.* ephemeral.

efeminado, *adj.* effeminate.

efervescente, *adj.* effervescent.

efetivo, *adj.* actual, real.

efetuar, *vb.* effect. **e.-se,** take place.

eficácia, *n.f.* effectiveness.

eficaz, *adj.* effective.

eficiência, *n.f.* efficiency.

eficiente, *adj.* efficient.

efígie, *n.f.* effigy.

efusão, *n.f.* effusion; shedding (blood).

efusivo, *adj.* effusive.

égide, *n.f.* egis.

egípcio -cia, *adj., n.* Egyptian.

Egito, *n.m.* Egypt.

ego, *n.m.* ego.

egocêntrico, *adj.* egocentric.

egoísmo, *n.m.* selfishness.

egoísta, 1. *adj.* selfish. **2.** *n.f.* egoist.

egrégio, *n.m.* eminent.

égua, *n.f.* mare.

eira, *n.f.* threshing floor. **sem e. nem beira,** down and out.

eis, *adv.* here is/are.

eito, *n.m.* succession; hoeing; field.

eiva, *n.f.* crack; flaw.

eivar, *vb.* taint.

eixo, *n.m.* axle; axis; *(pl.)* right track.

ejacular, *vb.* ejaculate.

ejeção, *n.f.* ejection.

ejetar, *vb.* eject.

ela, *pron.* she; her; it.

elaborar, *vb.* elaborate.

elas, *pron.* they (f.). **e. por e.,** tit for tat.

elástico, 1. *adj.* elastic. **2.** *n.m.* rubber band.

ele, *n.m.* the letter l.

ele, *pron.* he; him; it.

elefante, *n.m.* elephant.

elegância, *n.f.* elegance.

elegante, *adj.* elegant.

eleger, *vb.* elect; choose.

elegível, *adj.* eligible.

eleição, *n.f.* election; choice.

eleito, 1. *adj.* elected; chosen. **2.** *n.m.* elected/chosen person.

eleitor -ra, *n.* elector.

eleitorado, *n.m.* electorate.

eleitoral, *adj.* electoral.

elementar, *adj.* elementary.

elemento, *n.m.* element.

elenco, *n.m.* (*theat.*) cast.

eles, *pron.* they (m.).

eletivo, *adj.* elective.

eletricidade, *n.f.* electricity.

eletricista, *n.m.f.* electrician.

elétrico, *adj.* electric.

eletrificar, -trizar, *vb.* electrify.

eletrocutar, *vb.* electrocute.

eletrodoméstico, *n.m.* appliance.

eletrônica, *n.f.* electronics.

eletrônico, *adj.* electronic.

elevação, *n.f.* elevation.

elevado, *adj.* elevated, high.

elevador, *n.m.* elevator.

elevar, *n.m.* elevate; exalt. **e.-se,** rise.

elidir, *n.f.* elide.

eliminar, *vb.* elimination.

elíptico, *adj.* elliptical.

elite, *n.f.* elite.

elmo, *n.m.* helmet.

elo, *n.m.* link.

elocução, *n.f.* elocution.

elogiar, *vb.* praise. **—elogio,** *n.m.*

eloqüência, *n.f.* eloquence.

eloqüente, *adj.* eloquence.

elucidar, *vb.* elucidate.

eludir, *vb.* elude.

em, *prep.* in; on; at; into; to.

ema, *n.f.* rhea.

emaciado, *adj.* emaciated.

emagrecer, *vb.* make/grow thin.

emanar, *vb.* emanate.

emancipação, *n.f.* emancipation.

emancipar, *vb.* emancipate.

emaranhar, *vb.* entangle. **e.-se,** get entangled.

emascular, *vb.* emasculate.

embaçar, *vb.* dull; daze; cheat.

embainhar, *vb.* sheathe; hem.

embair, *vb.* deceive.

embaixada, *n.f.* embassy.

embaixador -ra, *n.* ambassador.

embaixo, *adv.* below.

embalado, 1. *adj.* hurried; (*sl.*) terrific. **2.** *adv.* hurriedly.

embalagem, *n.f.* wrapper, package.

embalar, *vb.* rock; wrap; bale; trick; impel; load (gun).

embalo, *n.m.* swing; (*sl.*) party; (*sl.*) fad.

embalsamar, *vb.* embalm.

embandeirar, *vb.* adorn with banners.

embaraçar, *vb.* obstruct; entangle; upset; embarrass.

embaraço, *n.m.* obstacle; difficulty; embarrassment.

embaraçoso, *adj.* embarrassing; difficult.

embarafustar, *vb.* barge into.

embaralhar, *vb.* shuffle (cards); jumble.

embarcação, *n.f.* vessel, boat; embarkation.

embarcadiço, *n.m.* sailor.

embarcadouro, *n.m.* pier; harbor.

embarcar, *vb.* embark; load; (*sl.*) be taken in; (*sl.*) die.

embargar, *vb.* embargo; bar; (*jur.*) seize.

embargo, *n.m.* embargo; impediment; (*jur.*) seize. **sem e.,** nonetheless.

embarque, *n.m.* embarkation.

embasbacado, *adj.* amazed.

embate, *n.m.* shock; clash; resistance; (*pl.*) hard knocks.

embaucar, *vb.* trick.

embebedar, *vb.* inebriate. **e.-se,** get drunk.

embeber, *vb.* soak; instill; plunge. **e.-se,** get soaked; become absorbed.

embelecar, *vb.* deceive, lure.

embelezar, *vb.* embellish.

embestar, *vb.* be stubborn.

embevecer, *vb.* enrapture.

embirrar, *vb.* be stubborn. **e. com,** dislike.

emblema, *n.m.* emblem.

embocadura, *n.f.* mouth (river); bit; (*mus.*) mouthpiece; bent.

embolsar, *vb.* pocket.

embora, 1. *adv.* away. **2.** *conj.* although. **3.** *interj.* let's go!; scram!

emborcar, *vb.* overturn; drink down; spill; fall down.

embornal, *n.m.* feed bag.

emboscada, *n.f.* ambush. **—emboscar,** *vb.*

embotado, *adj.* dull, blunt.
—**embotar**, *vb.*

embrabecer, *vb.* rage.

embranquecer, *vb.* whiten.

embravecer, *vb.* enrage; harden; get mad.

embreagem, *n.f.* clutch (car).

embrenhar-se, *vb.* go into the woods; become absorbed.

embriagar, *vb.* inebriate. **e.-se**, get drunk.

embriaguez, *n.f.* intoxication.

embrião, *n.m.* embryo.

embrionário, *adj.* embryonic.

embromar, *vb.* deceive; dawdle.

embrulhada, *n.f.* imbroglio.

embrulhar, *vb.* wrap; upset; deceive.

embrulho, *n.m.* package; imbroglio; fraud.

embrutecer, *vb.* brutalize; stupefy.

embuço, *n.m.* hood.

emburrar, *vb. (coll.)* balk; pout.

embuste, *n.m.* trick, hoax.

embusteiro -ra, *n.* trickster.

embutido, **1.** *adj.* inlaid; built-in. **2.** *n.m.* mosaic.

embutir, *vb.* inlay; build in.

eme, *n.m.* the letter m.

emenda, *n.f.* amendment; correction.

emendar, *vb.* amend; correct.

ementa, *n.f.* menu; note; résumé.

emergência, *n.f.* emergency.

emergir, *vb.* emerge.

emigração, *n.f.* emigration.

emigrado -da, *n.* émigré(e).

emigrante, *n.m.f.* emigrant.

emigrar, *vb.* emigrate.

eminência, *n.f.* eminence.

eminente, *adj.* eminent.

emissão, *n.f.* emission; issuance.

emissário, *n.m.* emissary.

emissor, **1.** *adj.* issuing. **2.** *n.m.* sender; issuer.

emissora, *n.f.* radio station.

emitente, *n.m.f.* issuer.

emitir, *vb.* emit; issue; broadcast.

emoção, *n.f.* emotion.

emocional, *adj.* emotional.

emocionante, *adj.* exciting; moving.

emocionar, *vb.* excite. **e.-se**, be moved.

emoldurar, *vb.* frame.

emolumento, *n.m.* emolument.

emotivo, *adj.* emotional.

empacar, *vb.* balk.

empacotar, *vb.* pack.

empada, *n.f.* meat- or fish-filled patty.

empáfia, *n.f.* conceit.

empalhar, *vb.* bale; pack; stuff.

empalidecer, *vb.* pale.

empanada, *n.f.* meat pie.

empanar, *vb.* dull; tarnish.

empanturrar -zinar, *vb.* gorge.

empapar, *vb.* soak; absorb.

emparelhar, *vb.* pair; unite; rival.

empatar, *vb.* tie up (money); hinder; tie (game).

empate, *n.m.* tie, draw.

empecer, *vb.* impede.

empecilho, *n.m.* obstacle; hitch.

empedernido, *adj.* hardened; callous.

empenar, *vb.* warp.

empenhar, *vb.* pawn; risk; exert. **e.-se**, strive; go into debt; pledge.

empenho, *n.m.* pawn; pledge; diligence; influence.

emperrar, *vb.* be stubborn; jam. **e.-se**, get mad.

empertigado, *adj.* upright; haughty.

empilhadeira, *n.f.* fork lift.

empilhar, *vb.* pile up.

empinado, *adj.* steep; upright; bombastic.

empinar, *vb.* raise; fly (kite); drink. **e.-se**, rear; be proud.

empírico, *adj.* empirical.

emplacar, *vb.* license (car); *(sl.)* last another year.

emplastro, *n.m.* poultice.

empobrecer, *vb.* impoverish. **e.(-se)**, grow poor.

empoeirado, *adj.* dusty.

empola, *n.f.* blister.

empolado, *adj.* blistered; stilted.

empolgar, *vb.* grip; excite.

empombar, *vb. (coll.)* get mad.

emporcalhar, *vb.* dirty.

empório, *n.m.* emporium; grocery.

empossar, *vb.* swear in. **e.-se**, take office.

empreender, *vb.* undertake; endeavor.

empreendimento, *n.m.* undertaking.

empregada, *n.f.* employee; maid.

empregado, *n.m.* employee; servant.

empregador -ra, *n.* employer.

empregar, *vb.* employ.

emprego, *n.m.* employment, job; use.

empreitada, *n.f.* contract work; job.

empreiteiro, *n.m.* contractor.

emprenhar, *vb.* impregnate.

empresa, *n.f.* enterprise; company.

empresário -ria, *n.* entrepreneur.

emprestar, *vb.* lend, loan. **tomar emprestado**, borrow.

empréstimo, *n.m.* loan.

empunhar, *vb.* grasp, hold.

empurrar, *vb.* push, shove. **—empurrão**, *n.m.*

emudecer, *vb.* be silent.

emular, *vb.* emulate; rival.

êmulo -la, *n.* emulator; rival.

enaltecer, *vb.* exalt.

enamorado, *adj.* enamored.

enamorar, *vb.* enamor. **e.-se**, fall in love.

encabeçar, *vb.* head; start; persuade.

encabular, *vb.* embarrass.

encadear, *vb.* chain, link.

encadernação, *n.f.* binding.

encadernar, *vb.* bind (book).

encaixar, *vb.* pack, box; fit; insert. **e.-se**, fit (into).

encaixe, *n.m.* fitting; mortise.

encaixotar, *vb.* box, crate.

encalacrar-se, *vb.* get into debt.

encalço, *n.m.* trail; pursuit.

encalhar, *vb.* run aground; not sell.

encaminhar, *vb.* guide. **e-se**, set out.

encampar, *vb.* expropriate.

encanado, *adj.* piped; *(sl.)* in jail. **vento e.**, draft.

encanador, *vb.* plumber.

encanecido, *adj.* gray-haired; aged.

encantador -ra, **1.** *adj.* enchant-

ing; charming. **2.** *n.* sorcerer -ess; charmer.

encantar, *vb.* enchant; charm. **e.-se**, be charmed.

encanto, *n.m.* enchantment; charm.

encapotar, *vb.* cloak; hide.

encarar, *vb.* face; look at.

encarcerar, *vb.* incarcerate.

encardido, *adj.* grimy.

encarecer, *vb.* raise the price; extol; exaggerate.

encargo, *n.m.* duty; mission.

encarnação, *n.f.* incarnation.

encarnado, *adj.* incarnate; scarlet red.

encarnar, *vb.* incarnate; redden.

encarregado, **1.** *adj.* in charge (of). **2.** *n.m.* director; chargé.

encarregar, *vb.* put in charge. **e.-se**, take charge.

encenação, *n.f.* staging.

encenar, *vb.* stage; show.

enceradeira, *n.f.* floor polisher.

encerado, *n.m.* oilcloth; tarp.

encerar, *vb.* wax.

encerramento, *n.m.* closing.

encerrar, *vb.* end; encompass; enclose.

encetar, *vb.* begin.

encharcar, *vb.* soak. **e.-se**, get soaked.

enchente, *n.f.* flood.

encher, *vb.* fill; crowd; *(sl.)* pester; *(sl.)* make pregnant. **e.-se**, get filled; *(sl.)* get fed up. **e. a cuca/cara**, *(sl.)* get drunk; **e. as medidas**, fulfill expectations.

enchimento, *n.m.* filling; stuffing.

enchova, *n.f.* anchovy.

enciclopédia, *n.f.* encyclopedia.

encilhar, *vb.* saddle.

enciumado, *adj.* jealous.

enclausurar, *vb.* cloister; isolate.

encobrir, *vb.* conceal.

encolerizar-se, *vb.* get angry.

encolher, *vb.* shrink. **e.-se**, cringe. **e. os ombros**, shrug.

encomenda, *n.f.* order; commission.

encomendar, *vb.* order; commission; entrust.

encompridar, *vb.* lengthen.

encontrão, *n.m.* bump; shove.

encontrar, *vb.* find; encounter. **e.-se,** be found; meet.

encontro, *n.m.* encounter, meeting; collision.

encorajar, *vb.* encourage.

encosta, *n.f.* slope.

encostar, *vb.* lean (against); put together; lay down; outstrip; hit up (for). **e.-se,** lie down; lean (on).

encosto, *n.m.* backing; chair back.

encouraçado, 1. *adj.* ironclad. **2.** battleship.

encravado, *adj.* nailed; embedded; ingrown.

encrave, *n.m.* enclave.

encrenca, *n.f.* (coll.) problem; jam.

encrencar, *vb.* (coll.) mess up; get stuck; hit a snag.

encrenqueiro -ra, *n.* (coll.) troublemaker.

encrespar, *vb.* curl. **e.-se,** get upset.

encruzilhada, *n.f.* crossroads.

encurralar, *vb.* corral; confine.

encurtar, *vb.* shorten.

endecha, *n.f.* dirge.

endereço, *n.m.* address. **—endereçar,** *vb.*

endeusar, *vb.* deify.

endiabrado, *adj.* devilish; mischievous.

endinheirado, *adj.* wealthy.

endireitar, *vb.* straighten; correct; head (for). **e.-se,** straighten up.

endividar-se, *vb.* get into debt.

endoidecer, *vb.* drive/go mad.

endossar, *vb.* endorse.

endosso, *n.m.* endorsement.

endurecer, *vb.* harden.

ene, *n.m.* the letter n.

enegrecer, *vb.* blacken.

enema, *n.m.* enema.

energético, *adj.* pert. to energy (power).

energia, *n.f.* energy; electricity.

enérgico, *adj.* energetic.

enervar, *vb.* enervate.

enevoado, *adj.* foggy, cloudy.

enfadar, *vb.* tire; irk. **e.-se,** get bored/irked.

enfado, *n.m.* fatigue; annoyance.

enfadonho, *adj.* tiresome; annoying.

enfaixar, *vb.* band; bandage.

enfarte, -to, *n.m.* infarction, heart attack.

ênfase, *n.f.* emphasis.

enfastiar, *vb.* bore; irk. **e.-se,** grow bored/irked.

enfático, *adj.* emphatic.

enfatizar, *vb.* emphasize.

enfeitar, *vb.* adorn.

enfeite, *n.m.* decoration.

enfeitiçar, *vb.* bewitch.

enfermagem, *n.f.* nursing.

enfermar-se, *vb.* become ill.

enfermaria, *n.f.* infirmary.

enfermeiro -ra, *n.* nurse.

enfermidade, *n.f.* illness.

enfermo, *adj.* ill.

enferrujado, *adj.* rusty.

enferrujar, *vb.* rust.

enfezar, *vb.* stunt; annoy. **e-se,** get irked.

enfiada, *n.f.* series. **de e.,** in a row.

enfiar, *vb.* thread; stick in; put on. **e.-se,** enter.

enfileirar, *vb.* line up.

enfim, *adv.* finally; after all.

enfocar, *vb.* focus on.

enfoque., *n.m.* focus.

enforcar, *vb.* hang. **e.-se,** (coll.) get married.

enfraquecer, *vb.* weaken.

enfrentar, *vb.* confront.

enfurecer, *vb.* infuriate. **e.-se,** get furious.

engabelar, -gambelar, *vb.* (coll.) cheat, con.

engaiolar, *vb.* cage.

engajado, *adj.* engaged; engagé.

engajar, *vb.* engage.

enganado, *adj.* deceived; mistaken.

enganar, *vb.* deceive. **e.-se,** be mistaken.

engano, *n.m.* mistake.

enganoso, *adj.* deceptive; deceitful.

engarrafamento, *n.m.* traffic jam.

engarrafar, *vb.* bottle.

engasgar, *vb.* choke, gag.

engatar, *vb.* couple; hitch.

engatilhar, *vb.* cock; prepare.

engatinhar, *vb.* crawl; be a novice.

engendrar, vb. engender.

engenharia, n.f. engineering.

engenheiro -ra, n. engineer.

engenho, n.m. ingenuity; skill; wit; machine; sugar mill/plantation.

engenhoso, adj. ingenious.

engessar, vb. plaster; put in a cast.

englobar, vb. encompass; agglomerate.

engodo, n.m. bait; lure.

engolir, vb. swallow.

engomar, vb. starch and iron.

engonço, n.m. hinge.

engordar, vb. fatten; grow fat.

engraçadinho, adj. (coll.) cute.

engraçado, adj. funny.

engrandecer, vb. aggrandize; enlarge.

engravidar, vb. make/get pregnant.

engraxar, vb. shine; grease.

engraxate, n.m. shoeshiner.

engrenagem, n.f. gear; network.

engrenar, vb. put in gear, engage.

engrolar, vb. (coll.) mumble.

engrossar, vb. thicken; roughen; deepen (voice); increase; get rude.

engrupir, vb. (sl.) lie to, con.

enguia, n.f. eel.

enguiçar, vb. hex; (coll.) break down.

enguiço, n.m. hex; (coll.) breakdown; snag.

enigma, n.m. enigma.

enigmático, adj. enigmatic.

enjambrar, vb. warp; jam.

enjeitar, vb. reject; abandon.

enjoado, adj. nauseated; nauseating.

enjoar, vb. nauseate; sicken.

enjoativo, adj. nauseating.

enjôo, n.m. nausea.

enlaçar, vb. entwine; bind; embrace.

enlace, n.m. entwinement; marriage.

enlamear, vb. muddy; besmirch.

enlatar, vb. can (food).

enlear, vb. fasten; perplex.

enleio, n.m. entanglement; intrigue; perplexity.

enlevar, vb. enrapture.

enlevo, n.m. rapture.

enlouquecer, vb. drive/go mad.

enluarado, adj. moonlit.

enlutado, adj. in mourning.

enlutar-se, vb. go into mourning.

enobrecer, vb. ennoble.

enojar, vb. sicken; annoy; disgust.

enojo, n.m. nausea; disgust.

enorme, adj. enormous.

enormidade, n.f. enormousness; (sl.) great deal.

enquadrar, vb. frame; fit; (mil.) discipline. **e.-se,** adjust.

enquanto, conj. while; as long as. **e. isso,** meanwhile; **por e.,** for now.

enrabichar-se, vb. (coll.) fall in love.

enraivecer, vb. enrage. **e.-se,** get mad.

enraizar(-se), vb. take root.

enrascada, n.f. (coll.) jam.

enrascar-se, vb. (coll.) get into a jam.

enredar, vb. catch (net); entangle; weave; scheme.

enredo, n.m. plot; entanglement; intrigue.

enrijecer, vb. stiffen.

enriquecer, vb. enrich. **e.(-se),** get rich.

enrolar, vb. roll up; (coll.) mix up; (coll.) trick. **e.-se,** (coll.) get mixed up.

enroscar, vb. coil.

enrouquecer, vb. get hoarse.

enrugar, vb. wrinkle.

ensaboar, vb. soap, lather.

ensaiar, vb. rehearse; test; try.

ensaio, n.m. rehearsal; test; try; essay.

ensalmo, n.f. faith healing; witchcraft.

emsamblador -ra, n. joiner.

ensanchar, vb. widen.

ensandecer, vb. drive/go mad.

ensangüentar, vb. stain with blood.

enseada, n.f. cove.

ensejo, n.m. opportunity.

ensimesmado, adj. self-absorbed.

ensinamento, n.m. teaching.

ensinar, vb. teach.

ensino, n.m. teaching.

ensoberbecer-se, *vb.* get haughty.

ensolarado, *adj.* sunny.

ensopado, *n.m.* stew.

ensopar, *vb.* drench.

ensurdecer, *vb.* deafen; grow deaf.

entabular, *vb.* start, strike up.

entalar, *vb.* squeeze. **e.-se,** get in a jam.

entalhador -ra, *n.* woodcarver.

entalho, *n.m.* carving; groove.

entanto, *adv.* meanwhile. **no e.,** however.

então, *adv.* then.

entardecer, 1. *n.m.* nightfall. **2.** *vb.* grow late; near nightfall.

ente, *n.m.* being.

entead -dao, *n.* stepchild.

entediar, *vb.* weary.

entender, *vb.* understand; know; realize. **dar a v.,** imply; **no meu e.,** in my opinion.

entendido -da, *adj., n.* expert.

entendimento, *n.m.* understanding; knowledge.

enternecer, *vb.* move, touch. **e.-se,** be moved.

enterrar, *vb.* bury.

enterro, *n.m.* burial.

entesar, *vb.* stiffen.

entidade, *n.f.* entity.

entoação, *n.f.* intonation.

entoar, *vb.* intone, chant.

entomologia, *n.f.* entomology.

entontecer, *vb.* stun, dizzy.

entornar, *vb.* spill; upset; *(sl.)* guzzle. **e. o caldo,** *(coll.)* upset the applecart.

entorpecentes, *n.m.pl.* narcotics.

entorpecer, *vb.* numb; drug.

entortar, *vb.* twist.

entrada, *n.f.* entrance; entry; arrival; opportunity; admission ticket; appetizer; down payment; input. **dar e.,** file (application, etc.).

entrado, *adj.* **e. em anos,** elderly.

entrançar, *vb.* braid.

entranhar, *vb.* drive into. **e.-se,** penetrate.

entranhas, *n.f.pl.* entrails; *(fig.)* heart.

entrar, *vb.* enter, go in; *(coll.)*

fall for. **e. bem,** *(sl.)* get fouled up.

entravar, *vb.* obstruct.

entrave, *n.m.* obstruction.

entre, *prep.* between; among. **por. e.,** through.

entreaberto, *adj.* half-opened.

entrecho, *n.m. (lit.)* plot.

entrecortar, *vb.* interrupt periodically.

entrega, *n.f.* delivery; surrender; installment.

entregar, *vb.* deliver; hand in; surrender. **e.-se,** give oneself.

entregue, *adj.* delivered; given over.

entrelaçar, *vb.* interlace.

entrelinhas, *n.f.pl.* between the lines.

entreluzir, *vb.* glimmer.

entremear, *vb.* intersperse.

entrementes, *adv.* meanwhile.

entremeter, *vb.* insert. **e.-se,** meddle.

entreolhar-se, *vb.* eye one another.

entretanto, 1. *adv.* meanwhile. **2.** *conj.* however.

entretecer, *vb.* interweave.

entretenimento, *n.m.* entertainment.

entreter, *vb.* put off; entertain.

entrevar, *vb.* paralyze; consign to darkness.

entrever, *vb.* glimpse.

entrevero, *n.m.* confusion; skirmish.

entrevista, *n.f.* interview. **e. coletiva,** press conference.

entrevistar, *vb.* interview. **e.-se com,** interview with.

entristecer, *vb.* sadden.

entroncamento, *n.m.* junction.

entroncar, *vb.* connect.

entrosar, *vb.* mesh. **e.-se,** integrate oneself.

entrudo, *n.m.* Carnival.

entulho, *n.m.* rubble.

entupido, *adj.* clogged; *(coll.)* having a head cold; *(coll.)* constipated.

entupir, *vb.* stop up; choke.

entusiasmado, *adj.* enthusiastic.

entusiasmar, *vb.* make enthusiastic. **e.-se,** become enthusiastic.

entusiasmo, *n.m.* enthusiasm.

entusiasta, 1. *adj.* enthusiastic. **2.** *n.m.f.* enthusiast.

enumeração, *n.f.* enumeration.

enumerar, *vb.* enumerate.

enunciar, *n.f.* enunciate.

envaidecer, *vb.* grow vain.

envelhecer, *vb.* age; grow old.

envelope, *n.m.* envelope.

envenenar, *vb.* poison.

enverdecer, *vb.* make/grow green.

enveredar, *vb.* head for.

envergadura, *n.f.* wingspread; scope.

envergar, *vb.* bend.

envergonhado, *adj.* embarrassed.

envergonhar, *vb.* shame, embarrass. **e.-se,** get embarrassed.

envernizar, *vb.* varnish.

enviado, *n.m.* envoy.

enviar, *vb.* send.

envio, *n.m.* sending.

enviuvar, *vb.* become a widow -er.

envoltório, *n.m.* wrapper.

envolver, *vb.* wrap; embrace; involve. **e.-se,** get involved.

envolvimento, *n.m.* involvement.

enxada, *n.f.* hoe.

enxaguar, *vb.* rinse.

enxame, *n.m.* swarm of bees.

enxaqueca, *n.f.* migraine.

enxergar, *vb.* see, perceive.

enxerido, *adj.* meddlesome.

enxertar, *vb.* (*bot.*) graft. **—enxerto,** *n.m.*

enxó, *n.f.* adze.

enxofre, *n.m.* sulfur.

enxotar, *vb.* shoo away.

enxoval, *n.m.* trousseau.

enxovalhar, *vb.* crumple; soil; affront.

enxugar, *vb.* dry.

enxurrada, *n.f.* torrent.

enxuto, *adj.* dry; lean, trim.

épica, *n.f.* epic poetry.

épico, 1. *adj.* epic. **2.** *n.m.* epic poet.

epidemia, *n.f.* epidemic.

epidêmico, *adj.* epidemic.

Epifania, *n.f.* Epiphany.

epígrafe, *n.f.* epigraph.

epilepsia, *n.f.* epilepsy.

epílogo, *n.m.* epilogue.

episcopal, 1. *adj.* episcopal; Episcopalian. **2.** *n.m.f.* Episcopalian.

episódio, *n.m.* episode.

epístola, *n.f.* epistle.

epitáfio, *n.m.* epitaph.

epíteto, *n.m.* epithet.

epítome, *n.m.* epitome.

época, *n.f.* epoch, period.

epopéia, *n.f.* epic poem.

equação, *n.f.* equation.

equacionar, *vb.* equate.

equador, *n.m.* equator; (*cap.*) Ecuador.

equalizador, *n.m.* (*elec.*) equalizer.

equanimidade, *n.f.* equanimity.

equatoriano -na, *adj., n.* Ecuadorian.

eqüestre, *adj.* equestrian.

eqüidade, *n.f.* equity.

eqüídeo, *adj., n.m.* equine.

equilibrar, *vb.* balance.

equilíbrio, *n.m.* equilibrium, balance.

equilibrista, *n.m.f.* tightrope walker.

eqüino, *adj., n.m.* equine.

equipagem, *n.f.* crew; equipment.

equipamento, *n.m.* equipment.

equipar, *vb.* equip.

equiparar, *vb.* compare; accredit.

equipe, *n.f.* team; staff.

equitação, *n.f.* horsemanship.

eqüitativo, *adj.* equitable.

equivalente, *adj., n.m.* equivalent.

equivaler, *vb.* be equivalent.

equivocar-se, *vb.* make a mistake.

equívoco, 1. *adj.* equivocal. **2.** *n.m.* mistake; double meaning.

era, *n.f.* era.

ereção, *n.f.* erection.

eremita, *n.m.f.* hermit.

ereto, *adj.* erect.

erguer, *vb.* raise; erect. **e.-se,** rise.

eriçar, *vb.* bristle.

erigir, *vb.* erect.

ermida, *n.f.* chapel.

ermo, *adj.* desert, wilderness.

erosão, *n.f.* erosion.

erótico, *adj.* erotic.

erradicar, *vb.* eradicate.

errado, adj. wrong.

errante, adj. errant.

errar, vb. wander; err; miss.

errático, adj. erratic.

erre, n.m. the letter r.

erro, n.m. error, mistake.

errôneo, adj. erroneous.

eructar, vb. belch.

erudição, n.f. erudition.

erudito, 1. adj. learned. **2.** n.m. scholar.

erupção, n.f. eruption.

erva, n.f. grass; (sl.) money; (sl.) marijuana.

erva-mate, n.f. maté.

ervilha, n.f. pea.

esbaforido, adj. out of breath.

esbaldar-se, vb. (sl.) poop out.

esbanjar, vb. waste, squander.

esbarrar, vb. hurl; run into, hit.

esbelto, adj. svelte.

esboço, n.m. sketch; outline. —esboçar, vb.

esbofetear, vb. slap, hit.

esbórnia, n.f. orgy; binge.

esborrachar, vb. squash.

esbravejar, vb. shout.

esbregue, n.m. (coll.) chewing-out.

esbugalhar, vb. open wide (eyes).

esbulhar, vb. despoil.

esburacar, vb. fill with holes.

escabeche, n.m. pickling brine.

escabroso, adj. scabrous; coarse.

escada, n.f. stairs; ladder. **e. rolante,** escalator.

escadaria, n.f. stairway.

escafandrista, n.m.f. sea diver.

escafandro, n.m. diving suit.

escafeder-se, vb. (coll.) sneak away.

escala, n.f. scale; stopover. **em grande e.,** on a large scale.

escalão, n.m. step; echelon.

escalar, vb. scale; ravage; schedule (workers); select; stop over.

escaldado, adj. cautious.

escaldar, vb. scald.

escaler, n.m. small boat.

escalfar, vb. poach (eggs).

escalpelo, n.m. scalpel.

escama, n.f. fish scale.

escamoso, adj. scaly.

escamotear, vb. do magic tricks; palm.

escâncara, n.f. às escâncaras, openly.

escancarar, vb. open wide.

escandalizar, vb. scandalize, shock.

escândalo, n.m. scandal; scene.

escandaloso, adj. scandalous.

Escandinávia, n.f. Scandinavia.

escandinavo -va, adj., n. Scandinavian.

escangalhar, vb. wreck, break.

escanhoar-se, vb. shave closely.

escaninho, n.m. slot; nook.

escanteio, n.m. (sl.) chutar/botar para e., cast aside.

escapada, n.f. escape.

escapar, vb. escape, flee.

escapatória, n.f. (coll.) loophole; excuse.

escape, n.m. escape; (mech.) exhaust.

escapulir(-se), vb. (coll.) run away.

escarafunchar, vb. (coll.) delve in; pick.

escaramuça, n.f. skirmish. —escaramuçar, vb.

escaravelho, n.m. scarab, beetle.

escarcéu, n.m. surge of waves; uproar.

escarcha, n.f. hoarfrost.

escarlate, adj. scarlet.

escarlatina, n.f. scarlet fever.

escarmentar, vb. punish. **e.-se,** learn a lesson.

escarmento, n.m. punishment; warning.

escarnecer, vb. mock.

escárnio, n.m. mockery.

escarpado, adj. steep.

escarpamento, n.m. escarpment.

escarranchar, vb. straddle.

escarrar, vb. spit. —escarro, n.m.

escassear, vb. grow scarce.

escasso, adj. scarce; meager.

escavação, n.f. excavation.

escavar, vb. excavate.

escaveirado, adj. gaunt.

esclarecer, vb. clarify; light; enlighten. **e.-se,** dawn; be enlightened.

esclarecimento, *n.m.* clarification; enlightenment.

escoadouro, *n.m.* drain; sewer.

escoamento, *n.m.* drainage.

escoar-se, *vb.* drain; sneak off.

escocês -cesa, 1. *adj.* Scottish. **2.** *n.* Scotchman; *n.m.* Scottish.

Escócia, *n.f.* Scotland.

escol, *n.m.* finest; prime.

escolado, *adj. (coll.)* shrewd.

escolar, 1. *adj.* school. **2.** *n.m.f.* student.

escolaridade, *n.f.* schooling.

escolástico, *adj.* scholastic.

escolha, *n.f.* choice.

escolher, *vb.* choose, pick.

escolho, *n.m.* reef.

escolta, *n.f.* escort. **—escoltar,** *vb.*

escombros, *n.m.pl.* debris.

esconde-esconde, *n.m.* hide-and-seek.

esconder, *vb.* hide.

esconderijo, *n.m.* hiding place.

escondidas, *n.f.pl.* **às e.,** furtively.

esconjurar, *vb.* conjure; exorcise.

esconjuro, *n.m.* conjuration; exorcism.

escopo, *n.m.* aim.

escopro, *n.m.* chisel.

escora, *n.f.* prop. **—escorar,** *vb.*

escorbuto, *n.m.* scurvy.

escore, *n.m.* score.

escória, *n.f.* slag.

escorpião, *n.m.* scorpion; *(cap.)* Scorpio.

escorredouro, *n.m.* drain pipe.

escorregadio, -diço, *adj.* slippery.

escorregar, *vb.* slip.

escorreito, *adj. (coll.)* correct; well-groomed.

escorrer, *vb.* drain; trickle.

escoteiro, *n.m.* Boy Scout.

escotilha, *n.f. (naut.)* hatch.

escotismo, *n.m.* Scouting.

escova, *n.f.* brush. **e. de dentes,** toothbrush.

escovado, *adj. (coll.)* shrewd.

escovar, *vb.* brush.

escovinha, *n.f.* small brush. **cabelo à e.,** crew cut.

escrachar, *vb. (sl.)* unmask; chew out

escravatura, *n.f.* slavery.

escravidão, *n.f.* slavery.

escravizar, *vb.* enslave.

escravo, *n.m.* slave.

escrete, *n.m. (sport.)* all-star team.

escrever, *vb.* write. **e. à máquina,** typewrite.

escrevinhar, *vb.* scribble.

escrita, *n.f.* writing; bookkeeping.

escrito, 1. *adj.* written. **2.** *n.m.* writing; note.

escritor -ra, *n.* writer.

escritório, *n.m.* office; study.

escritura, *n.f.* deed, writ; writing. **E. Sagrada,** Holy Scripture.

escrituração, *n.f.* bookkeeping.

escriturar, *vb.* keep books.

escrivaninha, *n.f.* desk.

escrivão, *n.m.* scribe; clerk; registrar.

escroque, *n.m.* crook.

escroto, 1. *adj. (vulg.)* disgusting. **2.** *n.m.* scrotum.

escrúpulo, *n.m.* scruple.

escrupuloso, *adj.* scrupulous.

escrutar, *vb.* scrutinize.

esrutinar, *vb.* count votes.

escrutínio, *n.m.* balloting.

escudeiro, *n.m.* squire.

escudo, *n.m.* shield; escutcheon; escudo (Portuguese monetary unit).

esculachar, *vb. (sl.)* tell off; mess up.

esculacho, *n.m. (sl.)* scolding; mess.

esculhambação, *n.f. (sl.)* scolding; mess.

esculhambado, *adj. (sl.)* messy, sloppy.

esculhambar, *vb. (sl.)* scold; mess up.

esculpir, *vb.* sculpt.

escultor -ra, *n.* sculptor.

escultura, *n.f.* sculpture.

escuma, *n.f.* foam.

escuras, *n.f.pl.* **às e.,** secretly.

escurecer, *vb.* darken; grow dark.

escuridão *n.f.* darkness.

escuro, 1. *adj.* dark. **2.** *n.m.* dark; black or mulatto.

escusa, *n.f.* excuse.

escusado, *adj.* needless.

escusar, *vb.* excuse; exempt; have no need of. **e.-se**, excuse oneself.

escutar, *vb.* listen (to).

esfacelar, *vb.* smash; ruin.

esfaimado, *adj.* starved.

esfalfar, *vb.* tire. **e.-se**, get tired.

esfaquear, *vb.* stab.

esfarelar, *vb.* crumble.

esfarrapado, *adj.* ragged.

esfera, *n.f.* sphere.

esferográfica, *n.f.* ball-point pen.

esfinge, *n.f.* sphinx.

esfolar, *vb.* flay; rob.

esfolhar, *vb.* defoliate; shuck.

esfomeado, *adj.* starved.

esforçado, *adj.* diligent; strong; brave.

esforçar, *vb.* encourage. **e.-se**, strive.

esforço, *n.m.* effort.

esfregar, *vb.* rub; scrub.

esfriar, *vb.* cool; lose enthusiasm.

esfumar-se, *vb.* fade away.

esgalgado, *adj.* gangly.

esganar, *vb.* choke.

esgar, *n.m.* face; grimace.

esgaravatar, *vb.* scratch; probe.

esgotado, *adj.* exhausted; sold out.

esgotar, *vb.* exhaust, drain. **e.-se**, become exhausted.

esgoto, *n.m.* drain; sewer.

esgrima, *n.f.* fencing. —**esgrimir**, *vb.*

esguedelhado, *adj.* disheveled.

esgueirar-se, *vb.* slip away.

esguelha, *n.f.* slant. **olhar de e.**, look out of the corner of one's eye.

esguichar, *vb.* gush.

esguicho, *n.m.* jet; gush; nozzle.

esguio, *adj.* slim, lanky.

eslávico, *adj.* Slavic.

eslavo -va, **1.** *adj.* Slavic. **2.** *n.* Slav.

esmaecer-se, *vb.* fade; faint; weaken.

esmagador, *adj.* crushing; overwhelming.

esmagar, *vb.* crush.

esmalte, *n.m.* enamel; nail polish.

esmerado, *adj.* refined; painstaking.

esmeralda, *n.f.* emerald.

esmerar-se, *vb.* take great pains.

esmeril, *n.m.* emery.

esmero, *n.m.* refinement; care.

esmigalhar, *vb.* crumble.

esmiuçar, *vb.* crumble; scrutinize; detail.

esmo, *n.m.* rough estimate. **a e.**, at random.

esmola, *n.f.* alms, charity.

esmolambado, *adj.* tattered.

esmolar, *vb.* beg.

esmorecer, *vb.* discourage; be discouraged; weaken.

esmurrar, *vb.* sock, punch.

esnobe, **1.** *adj.* snobbish. **2.** *n.m.f.* snob.

esnobar, *vb.* act snobbish.

esotérico, *adj.* esoteric.

espacial, *adj.* spatial; space.

espaço, *n.m.* space. —**espaçar**, *vb.*

espaçoso, *adj.* spacious.

espada, *n.f.* sword; *(pl.)* spades (cards).

espadachim, *n.m.* swordsman.

espádua, *n.f.* shoulder blade; shoulder.

espaguete, *n.m.* spaghetti.

espairecer, *vb.* amuse; relax.

espaldar, *n.m.* chair back.

espalhafato, *n.m.* noise; fuss; commotion.

espalhafatoso, *adj.* noisy; flashy, showy.

espalhar, *vb.* spread, scatter.

espanador, *n.m.* duster.

espanar, *vb.* dust.

espancar, *vb.* beat, thrash.

Espanha, *n.f.* Spain.

espanhol -la, **1.** *adj.* Spanish. **2.** *n.* Spaniard; Spanish (language).

espantalho, *n.m.* scarecrow.

espantar, *vb.* frighten; amaze.

espanto, *n.m.* fear; astonishment.

espantoso, *adj.* frightening; astonishing.

esparadrapo, *n.m.* adhesive tape.

espargir -zir, *vb.* scatter; sprinkle.

espargo, *n.m.* asparagus.

esparramar, *vb.* spread, scatter.

esparrela, *n.f.* snare.

esportiva

esparso, *adj.* scattered.

espasmo, *n.m.* spasm.

espatifar, *vb.* shatter; squander.

espátula, *n.f.* spatula; letter-opener.

espaventar, *vb.* scare.

espavorir, *vb.* frighten.

especial, *adj.* special.

especialidade, *n.f.* specialty.

especialista, *n.m.f.* specialist.

especialização, *n.f.* specialization.

especializar, *vb.* specialize.
e.-se em, specialize in.

especialmente, *adv.* especially.

especiaria, *n.f.* spice.

espécie, *n.f.* species; kind; *(com.)* specie. **causar e.,** cause discussion.

especificação, *n.f.* specification.

especificar, *vb.* specify.

específico, *adj.* specific.

espécime, *n.m.* specimen.

especioso, *adj.* specious.

espectador -ra, *n.* spectator.

espectro, *n.m.* specter; spectrum.

especulador -ra, *n.m.* speculator.

especular, 1. *adj.* specular. **2.** *vb.* speculate.

espelhar, *vb.* mirror.

espelho, *n.m.* mirror. **e. retrovisor,** *n.m.* rearview mirror.

espelunca, *n.f.* cave; *(sl.)* dive.

espera, *n.f.* wait.

esperança, *n.f.* hope.

esperançoso, *adj.* hopeful.

esperar, *vb.* hope (for); wait (for); expect. **espera aí!,** hold on!

esperma, *n.m.* sperm.

espernear, *vb.* kick one's legs; *(coll.)* complain.

espertalhão -lhona, *n.m. (coll.)* shrewd customer.

esperteza, *n.f.* shrewdness.

esperto, *adj.* shrewd.

espesso, *adj.* thick.

espessura, *n.f.* thickness.

espetacular, *adj.* spectacular.

espetáculo, *n.m.* spectacle; something spectacular.

espetar, *vb.* stab.

espeto, *n.m.* skewer; thin person.

espevitado, *adj.* lively; saucy.

espia, *n.m.f.* spy.

espiantar, *vb. (coll.)* get away.

espião -piã, *n.* spy.

espiar, *vb.* spy, look; watch.

espicaçar, *vb.* peck; pierce; goad.

espichar(-se), *vb.* stretch.

espiga, *n.f.* ear of corn.

espigão, *n.m.* spike.

espinafração, *n.f. (coll.)* scolding.

espinafrar, *vb. (coll.)* scold.

espinafre, *n.m.* spinach.

espingarda, *n.f.* shotgun, rifle.

espinha, *n.f.* spine; pimple.

espinhaço, *n.m. (coll.)* spinal column; mountain chain.

espinheiro, *n.m.* thornbush.

espinho, *n.m.* thorn.

espinhoso, *adj.* thorny.

espionagem, *n.f.* espionage.

espiral, *adj., n.f.* spiral.

espírita, *adj.-n.f.* spiritualist.

espiritismo, *n.m.* spiritualism.

espírito, *n.m.* spirit; mind; wit. **e. de porco,** *(coll.)* contrariness; spoilsport; **E. Santo,** Holy Spirit.

espiritual, *adj.* spiritual.

espirituoso, *adj.* witty.

espirrar, *vb.* sneeze. —**espirro,** *n.m.*

esplanada, *n.f.* esplanade.

esplêndido, *adj.* splendid.

esplendor, *n.m.* splendor.

espoleta, *n.f.* fuse.

espoliar, *vb.* plunder.

espólio, *n.m.* spoils; estate.

esponja, *n.f.* sponge; parasite; *(coll.)* boozer.

esponsais, *n.m.pl.* betrothal; wedding.

espontaneidade, *n.f.* spontaneity.

espontâneo, *adj.* spontaneous.

espora, *n.f.* spur; stimulus.

esporádico, *adj.* sporadic.

esporo, *n.m.* spore.

esporrar-se, *vb. (vulg.)* ejaculate.

esporro, *n.m. (vulg.)* chewing-out.

esporte, *n.m.* sport.

esportista, *n.m.f.* sportsman, -woman.

esportiva, *n.f.* sportsmanship. **perder a e.,** *(coll.)* be a poor sport.

esportivo, *adj.* sportive, sports.
esposa, *n.f.* wife.
esposo, *n.m.* husband; *(pl.)* husband and wife.
espraiar, *vb.* scatter.
espreguiçadeira, *n.f.* lounge chair.
espreguiçar-se, *vb.* stretch one's limbs.
espreitar, *vb.* spy on.
espremer, *vb.* wring, squeeze.
espuma, *n.f.* foam. —**espumar**, *vb.*
espumoso, -mante, *adj.* foamy.
espúrio, *adj.* spurious.
esputinique, *n.m.* sputnik.
esquadra, *n.f.* fleet; squad.
esquadrão, *n.m.* squadron.
esquadria, *n.f.* door casing.
esquadrilha, *n.f.* flotilla; squadron.
esquadrinhar, *vb.* scrutinize.
esquálido, *adj.* squalid; emaciated.
esquartejar, *vb.* quarter.
esquecidiço, *adj.* forgetful.
esquecer(-se), *vb.* forget. **e.(-se) de**, forget to.
esquecido, *adj.* forgotten; forgetful.
esquecimento, *n.m.* forgetfulness; oblivion.
esqueleto, *n.m.* skeleton.
esquema, *n.m.* scheme.
esquentar, *vb.* heat, warm. **e.-se**, get angry.
esquerda, *n.f.* left.
esquerdista, *adj., n.m.f.* leftist.
esquerdo, *adj.* left.
esqui, *n.m.* ski; skiing. **e. aquático**, water skiing.
esquiar, *vb.* ski.
esquife, *n.m.* coffin.
esquilo, *n.m.* squirrel.
esquimó, *adj., n.m.f.* Eskimo.
esquina, *n.f.* street corner.
esquisitice, *n.f.* strangeness.
esquisito, *adj.* strange, odd.
esquivar, *vb.* dodge.
esquivo, *adj.* elusive.
esquizofrênico, *adj.* schizophrenic.
esse, *n.m.* the letter s.
esse, -sa, *dem.adj. & pron.* that; that one; *(pl.)* those.
essência, *n.f.* essence.
essencial, *adj.* essential.

esta, *dem. adj. & pron.* fem. of **este**.
estabanado, *adj.* reckless.
estabelecer, *vb.* establish.
estabelecimento, *n.m.* establishment.
estabilidade, *n.f.* stability.
estabilizar, *vb.* stabilize.
estábulo, *n.m.* stable, barn.
estaca, *n.f.* stake; pile.
estacada, *n.f.* stockade.
estação, *n.f.* station; season. **e. de águas**, spa, resort; **e. rodoviária**, *n.f.* bus station.
estacar, *vb.* stop; stake.
estacionamento, *n.m.* parking; parking lot.
estacionar, *vb.* park (car).
estacionário, *adj.* stationary.
estada, *n.f.* stay; stop.
estádio, *n.m.* stadium.
estadista, *n.m.f.* statesman, -woman.
estado, *n.m.* state; status. **e. civil**, marital status; **e. de sítio**, state of siege; **em e. interessante**, pregnant.
estado-maior, *n.m.* (mil.) general staff.
Estados Unidos, *n.m.pl.* United States.
estadual, *adj.* state.
estadunidense, *adj., n.m.f.* U.S. citizen.
estafa, *n.f.* toil; fatigue. —**estafar(-se)**, *vb.*
estafado, *adj.* tired.
estafermo, *n.m.* fool; scarecrow.
estafeta, *n.m.* messenger.
estagiário -ria, *n.* apprentice, intern.
estágio, *n.m.* stage; period; internship.
estagflação, *n.f.* stagflation.
estagnação, *n.f.* stagnation.
estagnado, *adj.* stagnant.
estagnar, *vb.* stagnate; stop up.
estalagem, *n.f.* inn.
estalar, *vb.* crack, snap.
estaleiro, *n.m.* shipyard.
estalo, -lido, *n.m.* snap, crack, click.
estamento, *n.m.* estate.
estampa, *n.f.* print.
estampado, *n.m.* print (cloth).
estampar, *vb.* print; stamp.

estampido, *n.m.* crash.

estancar, *vb.* stanch. **e.-se,** run dry.

estância, *n.f.* residence; stay; lumberyard; cattle ranch.

estandardizar, *vb.* standardize.

estandarte, *n.m.* standard, banner.

estanho, *n.m.* tin.

estanque, 1. *adj.* water-tight. **2.** *n.m.* draining; monopoly.

estante, *n.m.* bookcase.

estapafúrdio, *adj.* (coll.) extravagant; odd.

estar, *vb.* be. **e. com,** have.

estardalhaço, *n.m.* noise; ostentation.

estarrecer, *vb.* frighten, appall.

estatal, *adj.* state.

estatelar-se, *vb.* fall flat on the ground/floor.

estática, *n.f.* static. **—estático,** *adj.*

estatística, *n.f.* statistic(s).

estatístico, *adj.* statistical.

estátua, *n.f.* statue.

estatuir, *vb.* establish, ordain.

estatura, *n.f.* stature.

estatuto, *n.m.* statute.

estável, *adj.* stable.

este, *n.m.* east.

este, esta, *dem. adj. & pron.* this; this one; latter; (pl.) these.

esteio, *n.m.* prop, stay.

esteira, *n.f.* mat; wake; track.

esteiro, *n.m.* narrow estuary.

estêncil, *n.m.* stencil.

estender, *vb.* extend, stretch. **e.-se,** extend.

estenógrafo -fa, *n.* stenographer.

esterco, *n.m.* manure; garbage.

estéreo, *n.m.* stereo.

estereofônico, *adj.* stereophonic.

estereótipo, *n.m.* stereotype. **—estereotipar,** *vb.*

estéril, *adj.* sterile.

esterilidade, *n.f.* sterility.

esterilizar, *vb.* sterilize.

estertor, *n.m.* stertor.

estética, *n.f.* esthetics.

esteticista, *n.m.f.* estheticist; cosmetician.

estético, *adj.* esthetic; cosmetic.

estetoscópio, *n.m.* stethoscope.

estiada, -agem, *n.f.* dry weather.

estiar, *vb.* dry up (weather).

estibordo, *n.m.* starboard.

esticar, *vb.* stretch.

estigma, *n.m.* stigma.

estilha, *n.f.*, **estilhaço,** *n.m.* splinter.

estilhaçar, *vb.* splinter; shatter.

estilingue, *n.m.* sling, slingshot.

estilístico, *adj.* stylistic.

estilizar, *vb.* stylize.

estilo, *n.m.* style.

estima, *n.f.* esteem.

estimação, *n.f.* estimation; esteem.

estimado, *adj.* esteemed; dear (letters).

estimar, *vb.* esteem; estimate.

estimativa, *n.f.* estimate.

estimular, *vb.* stimulate.

estímulo, *n.m.* stimulus.

estio, *n.m.* summer.

estiolar, *vb.* wither, fade.

estipêndio, *n.m.* stipend.

estipulação, *n.f.* stipulation.

estipular, *vb.* stipulate.

estirar, *vb.* stretch. **e. as pernas,** stretch one's legs.

estirpe, *n.f.* lineage.

estivador, *n.m.* stevedore.

estival, *adj.* estival, summer.

estocada, *n.f.* jab, thrust.

estofa, *n.f.* stuff, material.

estofar, *vb.* upholster.

estofo, *n.m.* padding.

estóico, *adj., n.m.* stoic.

estojo, *n.m.* case.

estola, *n.f.* stole.

estômago, *n.m.* stomach.

estontear, *vb.* daze. **e.-se,** be stunned.

estopim, *n.m.* fuse.

estoque, *n.m.* stock.

estore, *n.m.* windowshade.

estória, *n.f.* story.

estorvar, *vb.* obstruct.

estorvo, *n.m.* obstruction.

estourar, *vb.* explode, blow up; burst with anger.; break into; (sl.) fizzle.

estouro, *n.m.* burst; stampede; scolding; (sl.) really something.

estouvado, *adj.* scatterbrained.

estraçalhar, *vb.* shatter.

estrada, *n.f.* road, highway. **e. de ferro,** railroad; **e. de rodagem,** highway.

estrado, *n.m.* platform.

estragar, *vb.* spoil, ruin.

estrago, *n.m.* damage.

estrangeiro -ra, 1. *adj.* foreign. **2.** *n.* foreigner, stranger; *n.m.* abroad.

estrangular, *vb.* strangle.

estranhar, *vb.* find strange.

estranheza, *n.f.* strangeness.

estranho, 1. *adj.* strange. **2.** *n.m.* stranger.

estratagema, *n.m.* stratagem.

estratégia, *n.f.* strategy.

estratégico, *adj.* strategic.

estratificar, *vb.* stratify.

estrato, *n.m.* stratum.

estrear, *vb.* debut; use for the first time.

estrebaria, *n.f.* stable.

estrebuchar, *vb.* toss about.

estréia, *n.f.* debut, premiere.

estreitar, *vb.* narrow; tighten.

estreito, *adj.* narrow; close.

estrela, *n.f.* star. **e. cadente,** falling star; **e. de cinema,** movie star.

estrelado, *adj.* starry; fried (eggs).

estrelar, *vb.* shine; star (film).

estremecer, *vb.* shake, tremble.

estremunhar, *vb.* awaken suddenly; startle.

estrepar-se, *vb.* (*sl.*) get fouled up.

estrépito, *n.m.* noise, racket.

estrepitoso, *adj.* noisy.

estressado, *adj.* stressed.

estresse, *n.m.* stress.

estria, *n.f.* groove. —**estriar,** *vb.*

estribado, *adj.* well-founded; (*coll.*) well-heeled.

estribar, *vb.* prop, rest. **e.(-se) em,** be based on.

estribeira, *n.f.* stirrup. **perder as estribeiras,** lose one's cool.

estribilho, *n.m.* refrain, chorus.

estribo, *n.m.* stirrup. **estar com o pé no e.,** be about to leave.

estridente, *adj.* strident.

estrilar, *vb.* (*sl.*) get mad.

estrilo, *n.m.* (*sl.*) shout, cry. **dar o e.,** get mad.

estripulia, *n.f.* (*coll.*) mischief; disorder.

estrito, *adj.* strict.

estrofe, *n.f.* strophe, stanza.

estróina, *adj., n.m.f.* bohemian, profligate.

estrondo, *n.m.* loud noise, boom.

estrondoso, *adj.* loud, booming.

estropiar, *vb.* mangle; bungle.

estropício, *n.m.* damage.

estrume, *n.m.* manure.

estrupício, *n.m.* (*coll.*) uproar; blunder; lot.

estrutura, *n.f.* structure. —**estruturar,** *vb.*

estrutural, *adj.* structural.

estuário, *n.m.* estuary.

estudante, *n.m.f.* student. —**estudantil,** *adj.*

estudar, *vb.* study. —**estudo,** *n.m.*

estúdio, *n.m.* studio.

estudioso, 1. *adj.* studious. **2.** *n.m.* scholar.

estufa, *n.f.* hothouse.

estulto, *adj.* stupid.

estupefato, *adj.* stupefied.

estupefazer, *vb.* stupefy.

estupendo, *adj.* stupendous.

estupidez, *n.f.* stupidity.

estúpido, *adj.* stupid; boorish.

estupor, *n.m.* stupor.

estupro, *n.m.* rape. —**estuprar,** *vb.*

estuque, *n.m.* stucco. —**estucar,** *vb.*

estúrdio, *adj.* profligate; mischievous.

esvaecer, *vb.* vanish. **e.-se,** fade away.

esvair-se, *vb.* vanish; faint.

esvaziar, *vb.* empty, drain.

esverdeado, *adj.* greenish.

esvoaçar, *vb.* flutter.

eta, *interj.* wow!; what a . . .!

etapa, *n.f.* stage; stopping place; daily ration.

etário, *adj.* age.

éter, *n.m.* ether.

etéreo, *adj.* ethereal.

eternidade, *n.f.* eternity.

eterno, *adj.* eternal.

ética, *n.f.* ethics.

ético, *adj.* ethical.

etimologia, *n.f.* etymology.

etiqueta, *n.f.* tag; etiquette.

etnia, *n.f.* ethnic group.

étnico, *adj.* ethnic.

eu, *pron.* I.

Eucaristia, *n.f.* Eucharist.

eufemismo, *n.m.* euphemism.

euforia, *n.f.* euphoria.

eunuco, *n.m.* eunuch.

Europa, *n.f.* Europe.

europeu -péia, *adj., n.* European.

evacuar, *vb.* evacuate.

evadir, *vb.* evade. **e.-se**, escape.

evanescente, *adj.* evanescent.

Evangelho, *n.m.* Gospel.

evangélico, *adj.* evangelical; Protestant.

evangelista, *n.m.f.* evangelist.

evangelizar, *vb.* evangelize.

evaporar(-se), *vb.* evaporate.

evasão, *n.f.* evasion; escape.

evasiva, *n.f.* subterfuge.

evasivo, *adj.* evasive.

evencer, *vb.* (*jur.*) evict.

evento, *n.m.* event.

eventual, *adj.* fortuitous.

evicção, *n.f.* (*jur.*) eviction.

evidência, *n.f.* evidence. **—evidenciar**, *vb.*

evidente, *adj.* evident, manifest.

evitar, *vb.* avoid.

evocar, *vb.* evoke.

evolução, *n.f.* evolution.

evolucionário, *adj.* evolutionary.

evoluir, *vb.* evolve.

exacerbar, *vb.* exacerbate.

exagerar, *vb.* exaggerate.

exagero, *n.m.* exaggeration.

exalar, *vb.* exhale; emit.

exaltado, *adj.* exaggerated; ardent; testy.

exaltar, *vb.* exalt; excite; anger. **e.-se**, get excited; get mad.

exame, *n.m.* examination.

examinando -da, *n.* examinee.

examinar, *vb.* examine.

exangue, *adj.* bloodless; weak.

exasperar, *vb.* exasperate.

exatidão, *n.f.* exactness.

exato, *adj.* exact.

exaurir, *vb.* exhaust.

exaustão, *n.f.* exhaustion.

exaustar, *vb.* exhaust.

exaustivo, *adj.* exhaustive.

exausto, *adj.* exhausted.

exaustor, *n.m.* air vent.

exceção, *n.f.* exception.

excedente, *adj., n.m.* excess.

exceder, *vb.* excede. **e.-se**, overdo.

excelência, *n.f.* excellence. **por e.**, par excellence; **Vossa E.**, Your Excellency.

excelente, *adj.* excellent.

excelso, *adj.* exalted; sublime.

excêntrico, *adj.* eccentric.

excepcional, *adj.* exceptional; handicapped.

excerto, *n.m.* excerpt.

excessivo, *adj.* excessive.

excesso, *n.m.* excess.

exceto, *prep.* except.

excetuar, *vb.* except.

excitar, *vb.* excite; arouse; irritate.

exclamação, *n.f.* exclamation.

exclamar, *vb.* exclaim.

excluir, *vb.* exclude.

exclusão, *n.f.* exclusion.

exclusive, *adv.* exclusive of.

exclusivo, *adj.* exclusive.

excomungado, *adj.* excommunicated; (*coll.*) damned.

excomungar, *vb.* excommunicate.

excomunhão, *n.f.* excommunication.

excremento, *n.m.* excrement.

excrescência, *n.f.* excrescence, growth.

excretar, *vb.* excrete.

excruciante, *vb.* excruciating.

exculpar, *vb.* exculpate.

excursão, *n.f.* excursion.

execução, *n.f.* execution.

executar, *vb.* execute.

executivo -va, *adj., n.* executive.

exemplar, **1.** *adj.* exemplary. **2.** *n.m.* exemplar; copy (book).

exemplificar, *vb.* exemplify.

exemplo, *n.m.* example. **por e.**, for example.

exéquias, *n.f.pl.* funereal rites.

exercer, *vb.* exercise; perform; practice.

exercício, *n.m.* exercise; fiscal year.

exercitar, *vb.* exercise; practice.

exército, *n.m.* army.

exibição, *n.f.* exhibition.

exibir, *vb.* exhibit.

exigência, *n.f.* exigency; demand.

exigente, *adj.* demanding.
exigir, *vb.* demand.
exíguo, *adj.* meager.
exilado -da, *n.* exile (person).
exilar, *vb.* exile. **e.-se,** go into exile.
exílio, *n.m.* exile.
exímio, *adj.* skilled; distinguished.
eximir, *vb.* exempt. **e-se de,** shirk.
existência, *n.f.* existence.
existencial, *adj.* existential.
existente, *adj.* existent.
existir, *vb.* exist.
êxito, *n.m.* success; result.
êxodo, *n.m.* exodus.
exonerar, *vb.* discharge (employee).
exorbitante, *adj.* exorbitant.
exorcismar, *vb.* exorcise.
exorcismo, *n.m.* exorcism.
exortar, *vb.* exhort.
exótico, *adj.* exotic.
expandir, *vb.* expand. **e.-se,** air one's feelings.
expansão, *n.f.* expansion.
expansivo, *adj.* effusive, outgoing.
expatriado -da, *n.* expatriate.
expatriar, *vb.* exile. **e.-se,** go into exile.
expectativa, *n.f.* expectation.
expectorar, *vb.* expectorate.
expedição, *n.f.* expedition; dispatch; shipment.
expediente, *n.m.* business hours; daily work routine; official correspondence; device.
expedir, *vb.* ship, send; issue.
expelir, *vb.* expel.
experiência, *n.f.* experience; experiment.
experiente, *adj.* experienced.
experimentado, *adj.* experienced.
experimental, *adj.* experimental.
experimentar, *vb.* try, try on; experiment; experience.
experimento, *n.m.* experiment; experience.
experto -a, *n.m.* expert.
expiar, *vb.* expiate, atone for.
expirar, *vb.* expire; exhale.
explicação, *n.f.* explanation.
explicar, *vb.* explain.

explicitar, *vb.* make explicit.
explícito, *adj.* explicit.
explodir, *vb.* explode.
exploração, *n.f.* exploration; exploitation.
explorador -ra, *n.* explorer; exploiter.
explorar, *vb.* explore; exploit.
exploratório, *adj.* exploratory.
explosão, *n.f.* explosion.
explosivo, *adj.* explosive.
expoente, *n.m.* exponent.
expor, *vb.* expose; exhibit; state; reveal. **e.-se,** take risks.
exportador -ra, 1. *adj.* exporting. **2.** *n.* exporter.
exportar, *vb.* export.
exposição, *n.f.* exposition, exhibition.
expressão, *n.f.* expression; squeezing.
expressar, *vb.* express.
expresso, *n.m.* express.
exprimir, *vb.* express.
expropriar, *vb.* appropriate.
expulsão, *n.f.* expulsion.
expulsar, *vb.* expel.
expurgar, *vb.* purge; expurgate.
exsudar, *vb.* exude.
êxtase, *n.m.* ecstasy.
extasiado -tático, *adj.* ecstatic.
extasiar, *vb.* elate. **e.-se,** be ecstatic.
extemporâneo, *adj.* extemporaneous.
extensão, *n.f.* extension; expanse; extent.
extenso, -sivo, *adj.* extensive.
extenuar, *vb.* exhaust.
exterior, 1. *adj.* exterior, outside; foreign. **2.** *n.m.* exterior, outside; overseas.
exterminar, *vb.* exterminate.
extermínio, *n.m.* extermination.
externato, *n.m.* day school.
externo, *adj.* external, outer.
extinção, *n.f.* extinction.
extinguir, *vb.* extinguish.
extinto, *adj.* extinguished; extinct; dead.
extintor, *n.m.* fire extinguisher.
extirpar, *vb.* extirpate.
extorquir, *vb.* extort.
extorsão, *n.f.* extortion.
extra, *adj., n.m.* extra.
extra-, *pref.* extra-.

extração, *n.f.* extraction; drawing (lottery).

extradição, *n.f.* extradition.

extraditar, *vb.* extradite.

extrair, *vb.* extract.

extra-oficial, *adj.* unofficial.

extraordinário, *adj.* extraordinary.

extrato, *n.m.* extract; abstract.

extravagância, *n.f.* extravagance.

extravagante, *adj.* extravagant.

extravasar, *vb.* overflow.

extraviar, *vb.* lead astray; embezzle. **e.-se**, go astray.

extravio, *n.m.* going astray; embezzlement.

extremado, *adj.* distinguished.

extremar, *vb.* exalt. **e.-se**, distinguish oneself.

extremidade, *n.f.* extremity.

extremismo, *n.m.* extremism.

extremo, *adj.*, *n.m.* extreme. **E. Oriente**, Far East.

extremoso, *adj.* affectionate.

extrovertido, 1. *adj.* extroverted. **2.** *n.m.* extrovert.

exuberância, *n.f.* exuberance.

exuberante, *adj.* exuberant.

exultar, *vb.* exult.

exumar, *vb.* exume.

ex-voto, *n.m.* votive offering.

F

fã, *n.m.f.* fan.

fábrica, *n.f.* factory.

fabricante, *n.m.f.* manufacturer.

fabricar, *vb.* manufacture. **—fabricação**, *n.f.*, **fabrico**, *n.m.*

fábula, *n.f.* fable.

fabuloso, *adj.* fabulous.

faca, *n.f.* knife.

facada, *n.f.* stab; *(sl.)* request for money.

facadista, *n.m.f.* *(sl.)* sponger.

façanha, *n.f.* feat, exploit.

facão, *n.m.* big knife; sword.

facção, *n.f.* faction.

face, *n.f.* face; cheek.

faceiro, *adj.* foppish; content.

faceta, *n.f.* facet.

fachada, *n.f.* façade; *(sl.)* face.

fácil, *adj.* easy.

facilidade, *n.f.* facility, ease.

facilitar, *vb.* facilitar.

facínora, *adj.*, *n.m.* criminal.

fac-símile, *n.m.* facsimile.

factível, *adj.* feasible.

faculdade, *n.f.* faculty; college. **fazer f.**, go to college.

facultativo, *adj.* optional.

facundo, *adj.* eloquent.

fada, *n.f.* fairy. **conto de fadas**, fairy tale.

fadar, *vb.* fate.

fadiga, *n.f.* fatigue.

fado, *n.m.* fate; Portuguese folk song.

fagote, *n.m.* bassoon.

fagueiro, *adj.* affectionate.

fagulha, *n.f.* spark.

faina, *n.f.* chore, task.

faisão, *n.m.* pheasant.

faísca, *n.f.* spark. **—faiscar**, *vb.*

faixa, *n.f.* band; banner; zone; group; lane. **f. de segurança**, crosswalk; **f. etária**, age group.

fala, *n.f.* speech, talk.

falácia, *n.f.* fallacy.

falador -deira, *adj.* talkative.

falange, *n.f.* phalanx.

falante, 1. *adj.* talking. **2.** *n.m.f.* speaker. **f. nativo**, native speaker.

falar, *vb.* speak, talk; say. **falou!**, *(sl.)* you said it!

falastrão -trona, 1. *adj.* talkative. **2.** *n.* chatterbox.

falatório, *n.m.* murmuring.

falaz, *adj.* fallacious.

falcão, *n.m.* falcon, hawk.

falcatrua, *n.f.* trickery, fraud.

falecer, *vb.* die, pass away.

falecido, *adj.* late, deceased.

falência, *n.f.* bankruptcy.

falha, *n.f.* flaw.

falhar, *vb.* fail.

fálico, *adj.* phallic.

falir, *vb.* go bankrupt.

falível, *adj.* fallible.

falo, *n.m.* phallus.

falsear, *vb.* deceive; err.

falsete, *n.m.* falsetto.

falsidade, *n.f.* falseness.

falsificar, *vb.* falsify.

falso, *adj.* false.

falta, *n.f.* lack, absence; mistake. **por f. de**, for want of; **sem f.**, without fail.

faltar, *vb.* be lacking; fail. **f. (a)**,

be absent (from); **faltam dez para as cinco**, it's ten minutes to five.

fama, *n.f.* fame, reputation.

famélico, *adj.* famished.

famigerado, *adj.* notorious.

família, *n.f.* family.

familiar, 1. *adj.* familiar. 2. *n.m.f.* family member.

familiaridade, *n.f.* familiarity.

familiarizar, *vb.* familiarize.

faminto, *adj.* hungry.

famoso, *adj.* famous.

fanático, 1. *adj.* fanatical. 2. *n.m.* fanatic; fan.

fanatismo, *n.m.* fanaticism.

fanfarra, *n.f.* fanfare.

fanfarrão -rona, 1. *adj.* boastful. 2. *n.* braggart.

fanhoso, *adj.* twangy, nasal.

faniquito, *n.m.* fit.

fantasia, *n.f.* fantasy; Carnival costume.

fantasiar, *vb.* fancy. **f.-se**, dress in Carnival costume.

fantasioso, *adj.* fanciful.

fantasma, *n.m.* ghost, phantom.

fantástico, *adj.* fantastic.

fantoche, *n.m.* puppet.

faraó, *n.m.* Pharaoh.

farda, *n.f.* uniform.

fardar(-se), *vb.* dress in a uniform.

fardo, *n.m.* burden; bundle.

farejar, *vb.* scent. **—farejo**, *n.m.*

farelo, *n.m.* chaff, bran.

farfalhar, *vb.* rustle; jabber; brag.

faringe, *n.f.* pharynx.

farinha, *n.f.* flour; manioc flour.

fariseu, *n.m.* pharisee; hypocrite.

farmacêutico -ca, 1. *adj.* pharmaceutical. 2. *n.* pharmacist.

farmácia, *n.f.* pharmacy.

faro, *n.m.* sense of smell; scent.

faroeste, *n.m.* (*coll.*) cowboy movie.

farofa, *n.f.* toasted manioc flour, meat, raisins, etc.; boasting.

farofeiro -ra, 1. *adj.* boastful. 2. *n.* braggart; (*sl.*) beach picknicker.

farol, *n.m.* lighthouse; head-

light. **fazer f.**, (*sl.*) show off, boast.

faroleiro -ra, 1. *adj.* (*sl.*) boastful. 2. *n.* lighthouse operator; (*sl.*) braggart; show-off.

farpa, *n.f.* barb.

farra, *n.f.* (*coll.*) spree, orgy; fun. **cair na f.**, go on a binge.

farrapo, *n.m.* tatter; ragamuffin.

farrear, *vb.* (*coll.*) carouse.

farrista, *n.m.f.* (*coll.*) reveler.

farroupilha, *n.m.* ragamuffin.

farsa, *n.f.* farce.

farsante, *n.m.f.* farse actor; impostor.

farsista, *n.m.f.* prankster; clown.

fartadela, *n.f.* glut; abundance.

fartar, *vb.* glut. **f.-se**, gorge oneself; become sated.

farto, *adj.* sated; fed up.

fartum, *n.m.* stench.

fartura, *n.f.* abundance.

fascinação, *n.f.* fascination.

fascinante, *adj.* fascinating.

fascinar, *vb.* fascinate.

fascínio, *n.m.* fascination.

fascismo, *n.m.* fascism.

fascista, *adj.*, *n.m.f.* fascist.

fase, *n.f.* phase.

fastidioso, *adj.* dull, boring.

fastio, *n.m.* boredom; aversion.

fatal, *adj.* fatal; fated.

fatalidade, *n.f.* fatality; fate; disaster.

fatia, *n.f.* slice, piece.

fatigar, *vb.* tire. **f.-se**, get tired.

fatiota, *n.f.* man's suit.

fato, *n.m.* fact. (*P.*) man's suit. **de f.**, indeed.

fator, *n.m.* factor.

fatura, *n.f.* invoice, bill.

faturar, *vb.* invoice; (*coll.*) make a mint; earn, win; have sex (with).

fausto, 1. *adj.* happy. 2. *n.m.* luxury; ostentation.

fava, *n.m.* bean. **favas contadas**, (*coll.*) sure thing; **mandar às favas**, send to blazes.

favela, *n.f.* slum, shantytown.

favelado -da, *n.* slumdweller.

favo, *n.m.* honeycomb.

favor, *n.m.* favor. **a f. de**, in favor of; **fazer** o **favor de**, be so kind as to; **por f.**, please.

favorável, *adj.* favorable.

favorecer, *vb.* favor.

favorito, *adj.* favorite.

faxina, *n.f.* clean-up.

faxineiro -ra, *n.* janitor.

faz-de-conta, *n.m.* make-believe.

fazedor -ra -deira, *n.m.* maker.

fazenda, *n.f.* hacienda; property; treasury; cloth.

fazendeiro -ra, *n.* rancher, planter.

fazer, *vb.* make; do. **f.que**, pretend that; **faz três anos**, three years ago.

fazer-se, *vb.* become.

faz-tudo, *n.m.* factotum.

fé, *n.f.* faith; *(sl.)* bet.

fealdade, *n.f.* ugliness.

febre, *n.f.* fever.

febril, *adj.* feverish.

fechado, *adj.* closed; dense; overcast; reserved.

fechadura, *n.f.* lock.

fechamento, *n.m.* closing.

fechar, *vb.* close; cut off (car); turn red (light); become overcast.

fecho, *n.m.* fastener. **f. éclair**, zipper.

fecundar, *vb.* fertilize; conceive.

fecundo, *adj.* fecund, fertile.

fedentina, *n.f.* stink.

feder, *vb.* stink.

federação, *n.f.* federation.

federal, *adj.* federal.

federativo, *adj.* federative.

fedido, *adj.* stinking.

fedor, *n.m.* stench.

fedorento, *adj.* stinking.

feérico, *adj.* fairylike.

feição, *n.f.* feature; form; manner.

feijão, *n.m.* beans.

feijoada, *n.f.* typical dish of black beans, rice, meats, etc.

feio, *adj.* ugly; improper.

feira, *n.f.* open-air market; fair. **f.-livre**, open-air market.

feirante, *n.m.f.* feira merchant.

feitiçaria, *n.f.* witchcraft.

feiticeiro -ra, 1. *adj.* bewitching. **2.** *n.* sorcerer, witch.

feitiço, *n.m.* magic spell.

feitio, *n.m.* cut, shape, style.

feito, 1. *adj.* made; done;

grown. **2.** *n.m.* act, fact. **3.** *conj. (coll.)* like.

feitor, *n.m.* foreman.

feitura, *n.f.* making.

feiúra, *n.f.* ugliness.

feixe, *n.m.* sheaf.

fel, *n.m.* bile, gall.

felicidade, *n.f.* happiness. **felicidades!**, *(sl.)* so long!

felino, *adj.* feline.

feliz, *adj.* happy. **F. Ano Novo!**, Happy New Year!; **F. Natal!**, Merry Christmas.

felizardo -da, *n.* lucky dog.

felpudo, *adj.* fluffy.

feltro, *n.m.* felt.

fêmea, *n.f.* female.

femeeiro, *adj.* woman-chasing.

feminidade, -nilidade, *n.f.* femininity.

feminino, *adj.* feminine.

feminismo, *n.m.* feminism.

feminista, *adj., n.m.f.* feminist.

fenda, *n.f.* crack. **—fender**, *vb.*

fenecer, *vb.* wither; die.

fênix, *n.m.* phoenix.

feno, *n.m.* hay.

fenomenal, *adj.* phenomenal.

fenômeno, *n.m.* phenomenon.

fera, *n.f.* wild animal. **ficar uma f.**, get mad.

féretro, *n.m.* coffin; bier.

féria, *n.f.* wage; income; *(pl.)* vacation.

feriado, *n.m.* holiday.

ferir, *vb.* wound. **—ferida**, *n.f.*, **ferimento**, *n.m.*

fermentar, *vb.* ferment.

fermento, *n.m.* ferment, yeast.

ferocidade, *n.f.* ferocity.

feroz, *adj.* ferocious.

ferrabrás, *n.m.* braggart.

ferradura, *n.f.* horseshoe.

ferragem, *n.f.* hardware.

ferramenta, *n.f.* tool.

ferrão, *n.m.* spike; stinger.

ferrar, *vb.* shoe (horses); brand. **f. no sono**, fall/be fast asleep.

ferraria, *n.f.* forge; ironworks.

ferreiro, *n.m.* blacksmith.

ferrenho, *adj.* ironlike; stubborn.

ferro, *n.m.* iron; clothes iron; *(sl.)* money. **a f. e fogo**, by hook or crook.

ferrolho, *n.m.* door bolt.

ferrovia, *n.f.* railroad.

ferroviário -ria, 1. *adj.* railroad.
2. *n.* railroad employee.
ferrugem, *n.f.* rust.
ferrugento, *adj.* rusty.
fértil, *adj.* fertile.
fertilidade, *n.f.* fertility.
fertilizante, *n.m.* fertilizer.
fertilizar, *vb.* fertilize.
fervente, *adj.* boiling; fervent.
ferver, *vb.* boil.
fervor, *n.m.* fervor.
fervura, *n.f.* boiling.
festa, *n.f.* party; feast; holiday;
  (pl.) fondling. **Boas Festas!,**
  Happy Holidays!
festança, *n.f.* celebration; big
  party.
festão, *n.m.* big party; festoon.
festejar, *vb.* celebrate; fete.
festim, *n.m.* small party; banquet; blank cartridge.
festival, *n.m.* festival.
festividade, *n.f.* festivity.
festivo, *adj.* festive.
fetiche, *n.m.* fetish.
fétido, *adj.* fetid.
feto, *n.m.* fetus.
feudal, *adj.* feudal.
fevereiro, *n.m.* February.
fezes, *n.f.pl.* feces; dregs.
fiado, 1. *adj.* spun; on credit. **2.**
  n.m. yarn.
fiador -ra, *n.* guarantor.
fiambre, *n.m.* cold meats.
fiança, *n.f.* bail, bond.
fiapo, *n.m.* small thread, lint.
fiar, *vb.* spin (thread); entrust;
  saw; sell on credit.
fiasco, *n.m.* fiasco.
fibra, *n.f.* fiber. **f. de vidro,**
  fiberglass.
ficar, *vb.* stay; continue; be
  located; become. **f. com,** keep,
  take; **f. de,** agree to.
ficção, *n.f.* fiction.
ficha, *n.f.* token; index card; record.
fichar, *vb.* index.
fichário, *n.m.* file cabinet; card
  file.
fichinha, *n.m. (sl.)* unimportant
  person.
fictício, *adj.* fictitious.
fidalgo -ga, *adj., n.* noble.
fidedigno, *adj.* reliable, trustworthy.
fidelidade, *n.f.* faithfulness.

fiel, *adj.* faithful.
figa, *n.f.* good-luck fist gesture/
  charm.
fígado, *n.m.* liver.
figo, *n.m.* fig.
figueira, *n.f.* fig tree.
figura, *n.f.* figure; picture. *(sl.)*
  real character.
figurado, *adj.* figurative.
figurão, *n.m. (coll.)* bigwig.
figurar, *vb.* figure. **f.-se,** imagine.
figurinha, *n.f. (coll.)* oddball.
figurino, *n.m.* fashion plate;
  pattern.
fila, *n.f.* line, file, row.
filamento, *n.m.* filament.
filante, *n.m.f. (coll.)* moocher.
filantropia, *n.f.* philanthropy.
filantropo, *n.m.* philanthropist.
filão, *n.m.* vein, lode.
filar, *vb.* seize; observe; (coll.)
  bum; cheat.
filarmônico, *adj.* philharmonic.
filatelia, *n.f.* stamp-collecting.
filé, *n.m.* filet.
fileira, *n.f.* row.
filha, *n.f.* daughter. **minha f.,**
  dear (f.).
filharada, *n.f.* brood.
filho, *n.m.* son; *(pl.)* one's children; **meu f.,** darling, friend
  (m.).
filhote, *n.m.* cub, pup; native;
  protégé.
filiação, *n.f.* parentage.
filial, 1. *adj.* filial. **2.** *n.f.* branch
  office.
filigrana, *n.f.* filigree.
filmagem, *n.f.* filming.
filmar, *vb.* film.
filme, *n.m.* film. **f. de mocinho,**
  cowboy movie.
filmoteca, *n.f.* film library.
filó, *n.m.* netting.
filologia, *n.f.* philology.
filosofar, *vb.* philosophize.
filosofia, *n.f.* philosophy.
filosófico, *adj.* philosophical.
filósofo -fa, *n.* philosopher.
filtro, *n.m.* filter. **—filtrar,** *vb.*
fim, *n.m.* end, finish; aim. **f. de
  semana,** weekend; **f. do mundo,**
  middle of nowhere; **a f. de,** in
  order to; *(sl.)* game for; **sem f.,**
  endless; **ser o f.(da picada),**
  (coll.) be the last straw.

fímbria, n.f. hem, fringe.

finado, adj., n.m. dead, deceased.

final, **1.** adj. final. **2.** n.m. end.

finalidade, n.f. finality; purpose.

finalista, n.m.f. finalist.

finalizar, vb. finalize, end.

finanças, n.f.pl. finances.

financeira, n.f. finance company.

financeiro -ra, **1.** adj. financial. **2.** n. financier.

financiamento, n.m. financing.

financiar, vb. finance.

financista, n.m.f. financier.

finar, vb. end; die.

finca-pé, n.m. stubbornness. **fazer f.**, insist; be stubborn.

fincar, vb. thrust, stick. **f.-se**, stand firm.

findar, vb. finish, end.

findo, adj. ended, over.

fineza, n.f. fineness; elegance; courtesy.

fingido, adj. feigned; hypocritical.

fingidor -ra, n. feigner.

fingimento, n.m. pretense.

fingir, vb. pretend. **f.-se**, pretend to be.

finlandês -desa, **1.** adj. Finnish. **2.** n. Finn; n.m. Finnish.

Finlândia, n.f. Finland.

fino, adj. fine; thin; polite. **ser o f.**, (sl.) be terrific.

finório, **1.** adj. shrewd. **2.** n.m. sharpie.

finta, n.f. feint; trick; tax. **—fintar**, vb.

finura, n.f. fineness; courtesy; cunning.

fio, n.m. thread, string; wire; cutting edge. **f. dental**, dental floss; (sl.) brief bikini; **a f.**, on end.

firma, n.f. firm, company; signature.

firmamento, n.m. heavens.

firmar, vb. fix, secure; lean on; hold up; affirm; sign.

firme, adj. firm, solid.

firmeza, n.f. firmness, stability.

firula, n.f. (sl.) ornamentation.

fiscal, **1.** adj. fiscal. **2.** n.m.f. inspector.

fiscalizar, vb. inspect.

fisco, n.m. treasury.

fisga, n.f. harpoon.

fisgar, vb. harpoon; catch.

física, n.f. physics.

físico, **1.** adj. physical. **2.** n.m. physique; physicist.

fisiologia, n.f. physiology.

fisiológico, adj. physiological.

fisionomia, n.f. physiognomy.

fissão, n.f. fission.

fissura, n.f. fissure.

fita, n.f. ribbon; tape; movie; pretense. **f. durex**, Scotch tape.

fitar, vb. stare at.

fivela, n.f. buckle.

fixador, n.m. fixative. **f. de cabelo**, hair spray.

fixar, vb. fix, set. **f.-se**, become fixed; settle; stare.

fixo, adj. fixed, set.

flácido, adj. flabby.

flagelado -da, n. disaster victim.

flagelar, vb. scourge, torture.

flagelo, n.m. scourge; torment; disaster.

flagrante, **1.** adj. flagrant; red-handed. **2.** n.m. instant; snapshot. **em f.**, in the act.

flagrar, vb. burn; catch in the act.

flamingo, n.m. flamingo.

flâmula, n.f. pennant.

flanar, vb. loiter.

flanco, n.m. flank.

flanela, n.f. flannel.

flauta, n.f. flute. **levar na f.**, (coll.) not take seriously.

flautear, vb. (coll.) loaf.

flautim, n.m. piccolo.

flecha, n.f. arrow.

flecheiro, n.m. archer.

flectir, vb. flex.

flertar, vb. flirt.

flerte, n.m. flirtation.

fleuma, n.f. phlegm; sluggishness.

flexão, n.f. inflection.

flexionar, vb. bend; inflect.

flexível, adj. flexible.

fliperama, n.m. pinball arcade.

floco, n.m. flake, tuft. **f. de neve**, snowflake.

flor, n.f. flower. **a fina f.**, the cream; **à f. de**, on the surface of; **em f.**, in bloom.

floreado, adj. flowery.

floreio, n.m. flourish.

floreira, *n.f.* flower vase.

floreiro -ra, *n.* florist; *n.m.* vase.

florescer, *vb.* flower; flourish.

floresta, *n.f.* forest.

florido, *adj.* in bloom; flowery.

florista, *n.m.f.* florist.

flotilha, *n.f.* flotilla.

fluência, *n.f.* fluency.

fluente, *adj.* fluent.

fluidez, *n.f.* fluidity.

fluido, *adj.*, *n.m.* fluid.

fluir, *vb.* flow.

fluminense, 1. *adj.* pert. to Rio de Janeiro state. **2.** *n.m.f.* Rio state native.

fluorescente, *adj.* fluorescent.

flutuante, *adj.* floating.

flutuar, *vb.* float; fluctuate.

fluxo, *n.m.* flow, flux.

fobia, *n.f.* phobia.

foca, *n.f.* (*zool.*) seal; *n.m.f.* (*journ.*) cub reporter.

focal, *adj.* focal.

focalizar, *vb.* focus on.

focar, *vb.* focus (on).

focinho, *n.m.* snout.

foco, *n.m.* focus.

foder, *vb.* (*vulg.*) have sex (with); mess up; pester.

fofo, *adj.* fluffy; (*coll.*) cute.

fofoca, *n.f.* (*sl.*) gossip. —**fofocar**, *vb.*

fofoqueiro -ra, 1. *adj.* (*sl.*) gossipy. **2.** *n.* (*sl.*) gossiper.

fogão, *n.m.* stove.

fogaréu, *n.m.* bonfire.

fogo, *n.m.* fire. **fogos de artifício**, fireworks; **pegar f.**, catch fire. **ser f. (na roupa)**, (*coll.*) be rough; be hard to beat.

fogoso, *adj.* fiery.

fogueira, *n.f.* bonfire.

foguete, *n.m.* rocket; firecracker.

foice, *n.m.* scythe.

folclore, *n.m.* folklore.

folclórico, *adj.* folk.

fole, *n.m.* bellows.

fôlego, *n.m.* breath; scope. **tomar f.**, catch one's breath.

folga, *n.f.* rest; leisure; playtime. **dia de f.**, day off.

folgado, *adj.* idle, carefree; lazy; baggy. (*coll.*) fresh.

folgança, *n.f.* rest; frolic.

folgar, *vb.* relax; idle; be happy; frolic; loosen.

folgazão -zona, 1. *adj.* playful. **2.** *n.* merrymaker.

folguedo, *n.m.* fun, frolic.

folha, *n.f.* leaf; page, sheet; newspaper.

folhagem, *n.f.* foliage.

folhear, *vb.* leaf through.

folhetim, *n.m.* serial story.

folheto, *n.m.* leaflet.

folhinha, *n.f.* small calendar.

folia, *n.f.* frolic.

folião -ona, *n.m.* frolicker.

fome, *n.f.* hunger; famine. **estar com f.**, be hungry; **passar f.**, starve.

fomentar, *vb.* foment, promote.

fomento, *n.m.* promotion.

fone, *n.m.* earphone; receiver; phone; phone number. **fones de ouvido**, earphones.

fonética, *n.f.* phonetics.

fonoaudiologia, *n.f.* speech therapy.

fonógrafo, *n.m.* phonograph.

fonologia, *n.f.* phonology.

fonte, *n.f.* fountain; source; print font. **f. limpa/fidedigna**, reliable source.

fora, 1. *adv.* out, away. **2.** *prep.* except. **3.** *interj.* get out! **f. de**, outside; besides; **cair f.** or **dar o f.**, (*sl.*) run away; leave; **dar um f.**, (*sl.*) blunder; **estar por f.**, (*sl.*) be out of style or in the dark.

foragido, *adj.*, *n.m.* fugitive.

forasteiro -ra, *n.* outsider; stranger.

forca, *n.f.* gallows.

força, *n.f.* force, strength. **f. aérea**, air force; **f. de vontade**, willpower; **à f.**, by force; **à f. de**, by dint of; **fazer f.**, make an effort; **por f.**, inevitably.

forçar, *vb.* force; rape.

forças armadas, *n.f.pl.* armed forces.

força-tarefa, *n.f.* task force.

forçoso, *adj.* forceful; forcible; inevitable.

forense, *adj.* forensic.

forja, *n.f.* forge. —**forjar**, *vb.*

forma, *n.f.* form, shape. **da mesma f.**, likewise; **de f. que**, so that; **de qualquer f.,** anyway; **estar em f.,** be in shape.

fôrma, *n.f.* mold, pattern.

formação, *n.f.* formation; training; background.

formal, *adj.* formal.

formalidade, *n.f.* formality.

formalizar, *vb.* formalize.

formando -da, *n.* graduating student.

formão, *n.m.* chisel.

formar, *vb.* form, shape; educate. **f.-se,** graduate.

formato, *n.m.* format.

formatura, *n.f.* graduation.

formidável, *adj.* formidable; (coll.) excellent.

formiga, *n.f.* ant.

formigar, *vb.* swarm; tingle.

formigueiro, *n.m.* anthill.

formoso, *adj.* beautiful.

formosura, *n.f.* beauty.

fórmula, *n.f.* formula.

formular, *vb.* formulate.

formulário, *n.m.* blank form.

fornecer, *vb.* furnish, supply.

fornicar, *vb.* fornicate.

fornido, *adj.* supplied; robust.

forno, *n.m.* oven, furnace. **f. de microondas,** microwave oven.

foro, *n.m.* rent; jurisdiction; privilege; forum; court.

forragear, *vb.* forage; steal.

forragem, *n.f.* forage, fodder.

forrar, *vb.* cover, line; **f.-se,** dress warmly; (sl.) eat one's fill.

forro, *n.m.* covering, lining.

forró, forrobodó, *n.m.* (sl.) popular dance; ruckus.

fortalecer, *vb.* fortify.

fortaleza, *n.f.* fortress; fortitude.

forte, 1. *adj.* strong. **2.** *n.m.* fort; forte; strong person.

fortificação, *n.f.* fortification.

fortificar, *vb.* fortify.

fortuito, *adj.* fortuitous.

fortuna, *n.f.* fortune; luck.

fórum, *n.m.* forum, courthouse.

fosco, *adj.* dull, tarnished.

fósforo, *n.m.* match; phosphorus.

fosquinha, *n.f.* grimace; pretense.

fossa, *n.f.* hole; dimple; (sl.) de-

pression. **estar na f.,** (sl.) be in the dumps.

fóssil, *n.m.* fossil.

fosso, *n.m.* moat.

foto, *n.f.* photo.

fotocópia, *n.f.* photocopy.
—**fotocopiar,** *vb.*

fotografia, *n.f.* photograph.
—**fotografar,** *vb.*

fotográfico, *n.f.* photographic.

fotógrafo -fa, *n.f.* photographer.

fotonovela, *n.f.* photo-frame magazine story.

foz, *n.f.* mouth (river).

fração, *n.f.* fraction.

fracassar, *vb.* fail.

fracasso, *n.m.* failure.

fraco, 1. *adj.* weak. **2.** *n.m.* weak person; weakness.

frade, *n.m.* monk, friar.

fragata, *n.f.* frigate.

frágil, *adj.* fragile.

fragmentário, *adj.* fragmentary.

fragmento, *n.m.* fragment.
—**fragmentar,** *vb.*

fragrância, *n.f.* fragrance.

fragrante, *adj.* fragrant.

frágua, *n.f.* forge.

frajola, *adj.* (sl.) elegant.

fralda, *n.f.* diaper; shirttail.

framboesa, *n.f.* raspberry.

França, *n.f.* France.

francês -cesa, 1. *adj.* French. **2.** *n.* Frenchman, -woman; *n.m.* French.

franco, 1. *adj.* frank. **2.** *n.m.* franc.

franco-atirador, *n.m.* sniper; free-lancer.

frango, *n.m.* chicken. **f. assado,** roast chicken.

frangote, *n.m.* lad.

franja, *n.f.* fringe; bangs.

franquear, *vb.* frank; free; grant; cross.

franqueza, *n.f.* frankness.

franquia, *n.f.* franchise; exemption; postage.

franzino, *adj.* thin, slender.

franzir, *vb.* wrinkle.

fraque, *n.m.* cutaway (coat).

fraqueza, *n.f.* weakness.

frasco, *n.m.* flask, jar.

frase, *n.f.* sentence; phrase. **f. feita,** idiom, cliché.

fraseado, *n.m.* phrasing.

frasear, *vb.* phrase.

fraseologia, *n.f.* phraseology.
fraternal, *adj.* fraternal.
fraternidade, *n.f.* brotherhood.
fraterno, *adj.* fraternal.
fratura, *n.f.* fracture. —**fraturar,** *vb.*
fraude, *n.f.* fraud.
fraudulento, *adj.* fraudulent.
freada, *n.f.* braking.
frege, *n.m.* (coll.) greasy spoon; commotion.
freguês -guesa, *n.* customer; parishioner.
freguesia, *n.f.* clientele; parish.
frei, *n.m.* Fra (title).
freio, *n.m.* brake; bridle bit.
freira, *n.f.* nun.
freire, *n.m.* monk.
freixo, *n.m.* ash tree.
fremir, *vb.* rustle; roar; tremble; flutter. —**frêmito,** *n.m.*
frenesi, *n.m.* frenzy.
frenético, *adj.* frenzied.
frente, *n.f.* front. **à f. de,** in front of; **de f.,** facing; **em frente,** straight ahead; **em f. de,** across from, in front of; **fazer f. a,** face up to; **na f.,** in front; **para a f.,** onward; **pela f.,** ahead.
freqüência, *n.f.* frequency. **com f.,** frequently.
freqüentar, *vb.* frequent; attend.
freqüente, *adj.* frequent.
fresco, 1. *adj.* fresh; cool; (sl.) effeminate; affected. **2.** *n.m.* (sl.) homosexual.
frescura, *n.f.* freshness; coolness; (sl.) effeminacy; affectation; nonsense.
fresta, *n.f.* crack, gap, slit.
fretar, *vb.* charter. **vôo fretado,** charter flight.
frete, *n.m.* freight; freight charge.
freudiano, *adj.* Freudian.
frevo, *n.m.* fast Carnival dance.
fria, *n.f.* (sl.) jam, mess.
friagem, *n.f.* cold, chilliness.
frialdade, *n.f.* coldness.
fricção, *n.f.* friction; rubbing.
friccionar, *vb.* rub.
fricote, *n.m.* prissiness.
frieira, *n.f.* chilblain; athlete's foot.
frieza, *n.f.* coldness.

frigideira, *n.f.* frying pan; omelet.
frigidez, *n.f.* frigidity.
frígido, *adj.* frigid.
frigir, *vb.* fry.
frigorífico, *n.m.* coolant; meat locker; meat-packing plant.
frincha, *n.f.* crack.
frio, 1. *adj.* cold, cool; (sl.) false, stolen. **2.** *n.m.* cold.
frioleira, *n.f.* trifle; stupidity.
friorento, *adj.* sensitive to cold.
frisar, *vb.* curl, frizz; stress.
fritada, *n.f.* omelet, soufflé.
fritar, *vb.* fry.
frito, *adj.* fried. **estar f.,** (coll.) be in a jam.
fritura, *n.f.* fried food.
friúra, *n.f.* coldness.
frívolo, *adj.* frivolous.
fronde, *n.f.* frond.
frondoso, *adj.* leafy, dense.
fronha, *n.f.* pillowcase.
frontal, *adj.* frontal.
fronte, *n.f.* forehead.
fronteira, *n.f.* border; frontier. —**fronteiriço,** *adj.*
frontispício, *n.m.* frontispiece; face.
frota, *n.f.* fleet.
frouxo, 1. *adj.* loose; weak; (coll.) cowardly. **2.** *n.m.* **f. de riso,** fit of laughter.
frugal, *adj.* frugal.
fruição, *n.f.* fruition.
fruir, *vb.* enjoy.
frustração, *n.f.* frustration.
frustrado, *adj.* frustrated.
frustrar, *vb.* frustrate. **f.-se,** get frustrated; fail.
fruta, *n.f.* fruit.
fruta-pão, *n.f.* breadfruit.
fruteira, *n.f.* fruit tree.
fruteiro -ra, *n.* fruit vendor.
fruto, *n.m.* fruit; offspring; result.
fubá, *n.m.* corn meal; rice flour.
fubeca, *n.f.* (sl.) beating.
fubecar, *vb.* (sl.) beat.
fubica, *n.f.* (sl.) jalopy.
fuçar, *vb.* grub; (sl.) mix up; meddle.
fuças, *n.f.pl.* (sl.) snout; face.
fuga, *n.f.* escape, flight; fugue.
fugaz, *adj.* fleeting.
fugidio, *adj.* fugitive; shy.

fugir, vb. flee, run away; evade.

fugitivo -va, adj., n. fugitive.

fulano -na, n. so-and-so.

fulcro, n.m. fulcrum.

fuleiro, adj. (sl.) crummy.

fulgor, n.m. shine, glow.

fuligem, n.f. soot.

fuliginoso, adj. sooty.

fulo, adj. furious.

fulvo, adj. tawny.

fumaça, n.f. smoke; (pl.) airs.

fumaceira, n.f. smoke cloud.

fumacento, -rento, adj. smoky.

fumante, n.m.f. smoker.

fumar, vb. smoke (cigarette).

fumegar, vb. smoke.

fumigar, vb. fumigate.

fumo, n.m. smoke; tobacco; (sl.) marijuana.

funâmbulo -la, n. tightrope walker.

função, n.f. function; social event.

funcional, adj. functional.

funcionalismo. n.m. civil service.

funcionar, vb. function, run, work.

funcionário -ria, n. official. f. público -ca, civil servant.

funda, n.f. sling, slingshot.

fundação, n.f. foundation; base.

fundador -dora, 1. adj. founding. **2.** n. founder.

fundamental, adj. fundamental.

fundamentar, vb. found, base.

fundamento, n.m. foundation; (pl.) basics.

fundar, vb. found, establish.

fundear, vb. anchor.

fundição, n.f. foundry; melting.

fundir, vb. fuse; melt; smelt.

fundo, 1. adj. deep; (sl.) clumsy. **2.** n.m. bottom, back; base; background; fund. **a f.**, in depth; **no f.**, at bottom.

fundura, n.f. depth.

fúnebre, adj. funeral.

funeral, adj., n.m. funeral.

funesto, adj. fatal; ill-fated; evil.

fungar, vb. sniff; whine.

fungo, n.m. fungus.

funil, n.m. funnel.

furacão, n.m. hurricane.

furado, adj. holey; (sl.) crummy.

furão, n.m. (coll.) pushy person.

furar, vb. pierce. (coll.) crash; (vulg.) deflower.

furgão, n.m. baggage car.

fúria, n.f. fury, rage.

furibundo, adj. raging.

furioso, adj. furious.

furna, n.f. cave.

furo, n.m. hole; (journ.) scoop.

furor, n.m. furor; (coll.) success.

furtar, vb. steal. **f.-se**, evade.

furtivo, adj. furtive.

furto, n.m. theft.

fusão, n.f. fusion; melting.

fusco, adj. dusky.

fuselagem, n.f. fuselage.

fusível, n.m. fuse.

fuso, n.m. spindle. **f. horário**, time zone.

fuste, n.m. rod, shaft.

fustigar, vb. flog.

futebol, n.m. soccer. **f. americano**, football.

futicar, -tucar, vb. (coll.) fool with; meddle.

fútil, adj. futile.

futrica, n.f. (coll.) gossip. —**futricar**, vb.

futuro, adj., n.m. future. **f. do pretérito**, (gram.) conditional.

fuxico, n.m. (coll.) gossip. —**fuxicar**, vb.

fuxiqueiro -ra, 1. adj. (coll.) gossipy. **2.** n. (coll.) gossiper.

fuzarca, n.f. (coll.) revelry; uproar.

fuzil, n.m. rifle.

fuzilar, vb. shoot; execute.

fuzileiro, n.m. rifleman. **f. naval**, marine.

fuzuê, n.m. (sl.) party; ruckus.

G

gabar, vb. praise. **g.-se**, boast.

gabaritado, adj. well-qualified.

gabarito, n.m. gauge; standard; quality.

gabinete, n.m. office; dressing room; cabinet.

gabola, n.m.f. braggart.

gadanho, n.m. claw; fingernail.

gado, n.m. cattle, livestock.

gafanhoto, n.m. grasshopper.

gafe, n.f. gaffe.

gafieira, n.f. (coll.) seedy dance hall/dance.

gagá, adj. senile.

gago, 1. adj. stuttering. **2.** n.m. stutterer.

gagueira, n.f. stutter.

gaguejar, vb. stutter.

gaiato, 1. adj. playful. **2.** n.m. joker.

gaio, n.m. jay.

gaiola, n.f. small cage; jail; n.m. small riverboat.

gaita, n.f. fife; harmonica; (sl.) money. **g. de boca**, harmonica; **g. de foles**, bagpipe.

gaitada, n.f. (coll.) guffaw.

gaja, n.f. (P., coll.) woman.

gajo, n.m. (P., coll.) fellow.

gala, n.f. gala; (vulg.) semen.

galã, n.m. lover; romantic male lead.

galalau, n.m. (coll.) tall man.

galantaria, n.f. gallantry.

galante, adj. gallant, elegant.

galantear, vb. court; flirt; adorn.

galanteio, n.m. flirtatious remark; flattery.

galão, n.m. stripe, braid; gallon.

galáxia, n.f. galaxy.

galé, n.f. galley; n.m. galley slave. **n.m.pl.** forced labor.

galeão, n.m. galleon.

galego -ga, adj. n. Galician (coll., derog.) Portuguese person.

galeote, n.m. galley slave.

galeria, n.f. gallery; mall; fans. **g. de arte**, art gallery.

Gales, País de G., n. Wales.

galês -lesa, adj. n. Welsh.

galeto, n.m. fried chicken.

galgar, vb. climb; cross; jump.

galgo, n.m. greyhound.

galhardete, n.m. pennant.

galhardia, n.f. gallantry; elegance.

galhardo, adj. gallant; elegant; generous.

galho, n.m. branch; horn; (sl.) problem. **quebrar um g.**, (sl.) solve a problem.

galhofa, n.f. joke; mockery.

galhofeiro -ra, 1. adj. playful. **2.** n. joker; mocker.

galhudo, 1. adj. branchy;

horned; (sl.) cuckolded. **2.** n.m. (sl.) cuckold.

galicismo, n.m. gallicism.

galinha, n.f. chicken, hen; (coll.) coward; (sl.) easy lay.

galinheiro, n.m. chicken coop; (sl.) peanut gallery.

Galiza, n.f. Galicia.

galo, n.m. rooster; (coll.) lump on the head.

galocha, n.f. galosh.

galopar, vb. gallop. **—galope**, n.m.

galpão, n.m. covered area; stable.

galvanizar, vb. galvanize.

gama, n.f. gamut; scale; range; n.m. gamma.

gamão, n.m. backgammon.

gamado, adj. (sl.) in love.

gamar-se, vb. (sl.) fall in love with.

gamo, n.m. deer, buck.

gana, n.f. desire, longing.

Gana, n.m. Ghana.

ganância, n.f. greed; lucre.

gancho, n.m. hook; (coll.) part-time job.

gandaia, n.f. ragpicking; leisure; revelry.

gangorra, n.f. seesaw.

ganha-pão, n.m. livelihood.

ganhar, vb. win; earn; gain; get; reach.

ganho, 1. adj. won; earned; gained. **2.** n.m. gain.

ganir, vb. howl. **—ganido**, n.m.

ganso, n.m. goose.

garagem, n.f. garage.

garanhão, n.m. studhorse; (coll.) stud.

garantir, vb. guarantee. **—garantia**, n.f.

garapa, n.f. sugar-cane juice.

garatujar, vb. scribble. **—garatuja**, n.f.

garbo, n.m. elegance.

garboso, adj. elegant.

garça, n.f. heron.

garçom, n.m. waiter.

garçonete, n.f. waitress.

garfo, n.m. fork.

gargalhada, n.f. guffaw. **—gargalhar**, vb.

gargalo, *n.m.* bottleneck.

garganta, *n.f.* throat; gorge; *(coll.)* boasting. *n.m. (coll.)* braggart. **molhar a g.,** drink.

gargarejar, *vb.* gargle. —**gargarejo,** *n.m.*

gari, *n.m.* trash collector.

garimpar, *vb.* prospect for gold.

garimpeiro, *n.m.* gold/diamond miner.

garimpo, *n.m.* gold/diamond field.

garnisé, *adj.* bantam.

garoa, *n.f.* mist.

garota, *n.f.* girl; girlfriend.

garotada, *n.f.* group of kids.

garoto, 1. *adj.* mischievous. **2.** *n.m.* boy; kid.

garra, *n.f.* claw; *(sl.)* drive; *(pl.)* clutches.

garrafa, *n.f.* bottle. **g. térmica,** thermos.

garrafal, *adj.* large.

gárrulo, *adj.* talkative; songful.

garupa, *n.f.* hindquarters.

gás, *n.m.* gas; *(coll.)* pep; fart. **g. lacrimogêneo,** tear gas.

gasolina, *n.f.* gasoline. **posto de g.,** gas station.

gasosa, *n.f.* (lemon) soda pop.

gastador -ra -deira, 1. *adj.* free-spending. **2.** *n.* spendthrift.

gastar, *vb.* spend; waste; wear out.

gasto, 1. *adj.* spent; worn out. **2.** *n.m.* expense; wear.

gastrônomo -ma, *n.f.* gourmet.

gata, *n.f.* female cat; *(sl.)* attractive female.

gatão, *n.m. (sl.)* handsome male.

gatilho, *n.m.* trigger.

gatinha, *n.f.* female kitten; *(sl.)* attractive girl. **de gatinhas,** on all fours.

gato, *n.m.* cat; tomcat; error; *(sl.)* thief; *(sl.)* handsome male.

gato-pingado, *n.m. (coll.)* nobody; habitual attender.

gatuno, *n.m.* thief.

gaúcho -cha, *adj. n.m.* gaucho; *n.* Rio Grande do Sul native.

gaudério, *n.m.* reveler; loafer.

gáudio, *n.m.* delight.

gávea, *n.f.* crow's-nest.

gaveta, *n.f.* drawer.

gavião, *n.m.* hawk; *(sl.)* Don Juan.

gaze, *n.f.* gauze.

gazear, -zetear, *vb. (sl.)* cut class.

gazeta, *n.f.* gazette; *(sl.)* truancy. **fazer g.,** *(sl.)* cut class.

gazeteiro, 1. *adj. (sl.)* truant. **2.** *n.m.* hack newspaper writer; newsboy; *(sl.)* truant.

gazua, *n.f.* lock jimmy.

gê, *n.m.* the letter g.

geada, *n.f.* frost.

geladeira, *n.f.* refrigerator.

gelado, *adj.* ice-cold, frozen.

gelar, *vb.* freeze, ice; *(sl.)* cold-shoulder; *(sl.)* fizzle.

gelatina, *n.f.* gelatin.

geléia, *n.f.* jelly, jam.

geleira, *n.f.* glacier; ice floe.

geleiro, *n.m.* iceman.

gelo, *n.m.* ice.

gema, *n.f.* yolk. **da g.,** genuine.

gêmeo -mea, *n.* twin; *(m.pl., cap.)* Gemini.

gemer, *vb.* moan; lament; creak. —**gemido,** *n.m.*

gene, *n.m.* gene.

genealogia, *n.f.* genealogy.

genebra, *n.m.* gin (drink); *(cap.)* Geneva.

general, *n.m.* general (rank).

generalização, *n.f.* generalization.

generalizar, *vb.* generalize.

genérico, *adj.* generic.

gênero, *n.m.* genus, kind; gender; genre. **g. humano,** humankind; *(pl.)* goods. **g. alimentícios,** foodstuff.

generosidade, *n.f.* generosity.

generoso, *adj.* generous.

gênese, *n.f.* genesis; *n.m., (cap.)* Genesis.

genética, *n.f.* genetics.

genético, *adj.* genetic.

gengibre, *n.m.* ginger.

gengiva, *n.f.* gum (mouth).

genial, *adj.* brilliant; genial; *(sl.)* terrific.

gênio, *n.m.* genius; genie; temperament; temper.

genioso, *adj.* grouchy.

genital, *adj.* genital.

genitália, *n.f.* genitalia.

genitor, *n.m.* father.

genitora, *n.f.* mother.

genocídio, n.m. genocide.

Gênova, n. Genoa.

genro, n.m. son-in-law.

gentalha, n.f. riffraff.

gente, 1. n.f. people; a g., (coll.) we, us; one; da g., our. g. bem, (sl.) high society. 2. interj. gosh!

gentil, adj. gentle; kind, polite.

gentileza, n.f. courtesy. por g., please.

gentinha, n.f. riffraff.

gentio -ia, adj., n. gentile, heathen.

genuíno, adj. genuine.

geografia, n.f. geography.

geográfico, adj. geographical.

geologia, n.f. geology.

geológico, adj. geological.

geometria, n.f. geometry.

geométrico, adj. geometrical.

geração, n.f. generation.

gerador, 1. adj. generative. 2. n.m. generator; progenitor.

geral, adj. general. em g., generally, in general.

gerar, vb. generate; beget.

gerência, n.f. management.

gerente, 1. adj. managerial, managing. 2. n.m.f. manager.

geringonça, n.f. contraption; jargon.

gerir, vb. administer, run.

germânico, adj. Germanic.

germe, n.m. germ.

germinar, vb. germinate.

gerúndio, n.m. present participle.

gesso, n.m. plaster, gypsum.

gestação, n.f. gestation.

gestante, n.f. pregnant woman.

gesto, n.m. gesture. —gesticular, vb.

giba, n.f. hump.

gibi, n.m. comic book.

gigante -ta, adj., n. giant.

gigantesco, adj. gigantic.

gigolô, n.m. gigolo.

gilete, n.f. razor blade; (sl.) bisexual.

gim, n.m. gin (drink).

ginasial, adj. pert. to ginásio, high school.

ginasiano -na, n. high school student.

ginásio, n.m. gymnasium; high school.

ginasta, n.m.f. gymnast.

ginástica, n.f. gymnastics.

gincana, n.f. auto rally.

ginecologia, n.f. gynecology.

ginete, n.m. steed; (South) horseman.

ginga, n.f., gingado, n.m. swing, sway. —gingar, vb.

gira, adj. (sl.) crazy.

girafa, n.f. giraffe; beanpole.

girar, vb. gyrate, spin. não g. bem, be screwy.

girassol, n.m. sunflower.

giratório, adj. revolving.

gíria, n.f. slang.

giro, n.m. turn; walk.

giz, n.m. chalk.

glacê, n.m. icing.

glaciar, n.m. glacier.

gladiador, n.m. gladiator.

glândula, n.f. gland.

gleba, n.f. land.

glissar, vb. skid.

global, adj. global; overall.

globo, n.m. globe, ball. g. ocular, eyeball.

glória, n.f. glory.

glorificar, vb. glorify.

glorioso, adj. glorious.

glosa, n.f. gloss, comment. —glosar, vb.

glossário, n.m. glossary.

glutão -tona, 1. adj. gluttonous. 2. n. glutton.

godo, n.m. Goth.

goela, n.f. gullet.

gogó, n.m. Adam's apple.

goiaba, n.f. guava.

goaiabada, f. guava paste.

goiano -na, 1. adj. pert. to Goiás state. 2. n. Goiás native.

gol, n.m. (sport.) goal.

gola, n.f. collar.

gole, n.m. swallow, gulp.

goleiro, n.m. (sport.) goalie.

golfada, n.f. gush; vomit.

golfar, vb. gush, spurt.

golfe, n.m. golf.

golfinho, n.m. dolphin; miniature golf.

golfo, n.m. gulf.

golpe, n.m. blow, hit, stroke; coup; job (crime). g. de estado, coup d'état; g. do baú, marrying into money; de um g., in one stroke.

golpear, vb. hit, strike.

golpista, 1. *adj.* advocating a coup. **2.** *n.m.* coup advocate; *(coll.)* swindler.

goma, *n.f.* gum. **g.de mascar,** chewing gum.

gomo, *n.m.* bud; section (of an fruit).

gomoso, *adj.* gummy.

gongo, *n.m.* gong.

gonorréia, *n.f.* gonorrhea.

gonzo, *n.m.* hinge.

gorar, *vb.* fail to develop (egg); fizzle.

gordo, 1. *adj.* fat. **2.** *n.m.* fat person.

gordura, *n.f.* fat, grease; lard.

gorduroso, *adj.* greasy.

gorila, *n.m.* gorilla; *(sl.)* military man who takes power by coup.

gorjear, *vb.* chirp. —**gorjeio,** *n.m.*

gorjeta, *n.f.* tip, gratuity.

gorro, *n.m.* cap.

gosma, *n.f.* mucus, phlegm.

gostar (de), *vb.* like.

gosto, *n.m.* taste; liking. **bom/mau g,** good/bad taste.

gostosão, *n.m.* *(sl.)* handsome man.

gostoso, *adj.* tasty; delightful; attractive.

gostosura, *n.f.* *(coll.)* delight.

gota, *n.f.* drop, drip.

goteira, *n.f.* gutter; roof leak.

gotejar, *vb.* drip.

gótico, *adj.* Gothic.

governador -ra, *n.* governor.

governamental, *adj.* governmental.

governanta, *n.f.* governess.

governar, *vb.* govern, run.

governo, *n.m.* government; regime.

gozação, *n.f.* *(sl.)* joke, teasing.

gozado, *adj.* *(coll.)* funny; *(coll.)* strange.

gozador -ra, *n.* *(coll.)* loafer; *(sl.)* joker.

gozar, *vb.* enjoy; *(coll.)* poke fun at, tease; *(vulg.)* come.

gozo, *n.m.* joy; enjoyment; something funny; *(vulg.)* orgasm.

Graal, *n.m.* Grail.

Grã-Bretanha, *n.f.* Great Britain.

graça, *n.f.* grace; charm; wit, funniness; first name; **de g,** free; **ter g.,** be fun(ny); *(pl.)* **graças a,** thanks to; **graças a Deus,** thank God.

gracejar, *vb.* jest. —**gracejo,** *n.m.*

gracinha, *n.f.* *(coll.)* cute person/thing.

gracioso, *adj.* gracious; graceful; free.

graçola, *n.f.* *(coll.)* (coarse) joke.

gradação, *n.f.* gradation.

gradativo, *adj.* gradual.

grade, *n.f.* grate; *(pl., sl.)* jail.

gradiente, *n.m.* gradient.

grado, *n.m.* **de bom g.,** willingly; **de mau g.,** unwillingly.

graduação, *n.f.* gradation; graduation; rank; university study.

graduado, *adj.* graded; graduated; eminent.

gradual, *adj.* gradual.

graduar, *vb.* grade; graduate; classify. **g.-se,** graduate.

grafar, *vb.* write down; spell.

grafia, *n.f.* spelling.

gráfica, *n.f.* print shop.

gráfico, 1. *adj.* graphic; spelling. **2.** *n.m.* graph; printer.

grã-fino -na, 1, *adj.* upper-class. **2.** *n.* socialite.

grafito, *n.m.* graffito; *(pl.)* graffiti.

gralha, *n.f.* crow; *(coll.)* chatterbox.

grama, *n.f.* grass; *n.m.f.* gram.

gramado, *n.m.* lawn; soccer field.

gramática, *n.f.* grammar; grammar book.

gramatical, *adj.* grammatical.

gramático -ca, *n.* grammarian.

grampeador, *n.m.* stapler.

grampo, *n.m.* staple. —**grampear,** *vb.*

grana, *n.f.* *(sl.)* money.

granada, *n.f.* grenade.

grande, *adj.* big; great, grand. **um g. homem,** a great man; **um homem g.,** a large man.

grandeza, *n.f.* greatness; largeness.

grandiloqüente, *adj.* grandiloquent.

grandiosidade, *n.f.* grandeur.

grandioso, *adj.* grandiose.

granel, *n.m.* granary. **a g.,** in abundance.

granito, *n.m.* granite.

granizo, *n.m.* hail. **—granizar**, *vb.*

granja, *n.f.* small farm.

granjear, *vb.* till (land); attract.

grão, *n.m.* grain, kernel.

grasnar, *vb.* quack; croak. **—grasnada**, *n.f.*

grassar, *vb.* spread.

gratidão, *n.f.* gratitude.

gratificação, *n.f.* gratification; gratuity.

gratificar, *vb.* tip, remunerate; thank.

grátis, *adv.* gratis.

grato, *adj.* grateful; gratifying.

gratuito, *adj.* gratis; gratuitous.

grau, *n.m.* degree; grade. **colar g.,** get a degree; **primeiro g.,** elementary school; **segundo g.,** high school.

graúdo, 1. *adj.* large; important. **2.** *n.m.* important person.

graúna, *n.f.* grackle.

gravação, *n.f.* engraving; recording.

gravador, *n.m.* engraver (m.); tape recorder.

gravadora, *n.f.* engraver (f.); recording company.

gravame, *n.m.* grievance; gravamen.

gravanço, *n.m.* garbanzo.

gravar, *vb.* engrave; tape-record; remember; burden.

gravata, *n.f.* necktie.

grave, *adj.* grave, serious.

graveto, *n.m.* kindling.

gravidade, *n.f.* gravity.

grávida, *adj.* pregnant.

gravidez, *n.f.* pregnancy.

gravitar, *vb.* gravitate.

gravura, *n.f.* engraving; print, picture.

graxa, *n.f.* grease; shoe polish.

graxento, *adj.* greasy.

Grécia, *n.f.* Greece.

gregário, *adj.* gregarious.

grego -ga, *adj., n.* Greek.

grei, *n.f.* flock; congregation.

grelha, *n.f.* grill. **—grelhar**, *vb.*

grêmio, *n.m.* guild, society.

grenha, *n.f.* mop of hair.

greta, *n.f.* crack. **—gretar**, *vb.*

greve, *n.f.* strike. **g. de fome,** hunger strike; **entrar em g.,** go out on strike.

grevista, *n.m.f.* striker.

grifar, *vb.* italicize.

grifo, *n.m.* italics.

grilado, *adj.* (*sl.*) upset.

grilar, *vb.* (*sl.*) upset, spoil. **g.-se,** get upset, worry.

grileiro -ra, *n.* squatter.

grilhão, *n.m.* shackle.

grilo, *n.m.* cricket; (*coll.*) land with a false title; (*sl.*) annoyance; (*sl.*) problem.

grimpa, *n.f.* weather vane; crest; (*sl.*) head.

grinalda, *n.f.* garland.

gringo -ga, *n.* foreigner (esp. fair-haired).

gripar-se, *vb.* get the flu.

gripe, *n.f.* flu, cold.

grisalho, *adj.* gray, gray-haired.

gritadeira, *n.f.* outcry.

gritar, *vb.* shout, scream, yell. **—grito**, *n.m.*

gritaria, *n.f.* shouting.

Groenlândia, *n.f.* Greenland.

grogue, 1. *adj.* groggy, tipsy. **2.** *n.m.* grog.

groselha, *n.f.* currant; gooseberry.

grosseiro, *adj.* crude, coarse, rude.

grosseria, *n.f.* coarseness; impoliteness.

grosso, *adj.* thick; rough; deep (voice); great; gross.

grossura, *n.f.* thickness; roughness.

grotesco, *adj.* grotesque.

grou, *n.m.* (*ornith.*) crane.

grua, *n.f.* crane, derrick.

grudar, *vb.* glue, stick.

grude, *n.m.* glue, paste; (*sl.*) chow.

grumete, *n.m.* apprentice sailor.

grunhir, *vb.* grunt, grumble. **—grunhido**, *n.m.*

grupamento, *n.m.* grouping.

grupo, *n.m.* group; office suite; (*sl.*) lies. **g. escolar,** elementary school.

gruta, *n.f.* grotto, cave.

guaraná, *n.m.* a tropical fruit; guaraná soft drink.

guarani, *adj., n.m.* Guarani.

guarda, *n.f.* guard; custody. **g. civil,** civil guard; **g. nacional,** national guard; *n.m.* policeman.

guarda-chuva, *n.m.* umbrella.

guarda-costas, *n.m.* coastguard cutter; bodyguard.

guarda-florestal, *n.m.* forest ranger.

guarda-livros, *n.m.* bookkeeper.

guarda-louça, *n.m.* china cupboard.

guarda-móis, *n.m.* furniture storage facility.

guardanapo, *n.m.* napkin.

guarda-pó, *n.m.* smock, duster.

guardar, *vb.* guard; keep; put away.

guarda-roupa, *n.m.* clothes closet, wardrobe.

guardião-diã, *n.* guardian; custodian.

guarida, *n.f.* den; shelter.

guarnecer, *vb.* equip; man; edge, garnish.

guarnição, *n.f.* garrison; crew; edging, garnish.

guatemalteco -ca, *adj. n.* Guatemalan.

gude, *n.m.* marbles (game). **bola de g.,** marble.

guedelha, *n.f.* mop of hair.

guei, *n.m.* gay, homosexual.

guelra, *n.f.* gill.

guerra, *n.f.* war. **g. civil,** civil war; **g. fria,** cold war.

guerrear, *vb.* war, fight.

guerreiro -ra, *n.* warrior.

guerrilha, *n.f.* guerrilla (war).

guerrilheiro -ra, *n.* guerrilla fighter.

gueto, *n.m.* ghetto.

guia, *n.m.* guide; *n.f.* guidance.

Guiana, *n.f.* Guyana.

guiar, *vb.* guide; drive; head (for).

guidom, *n.m.* handlebar.

guilhotina, *n.f.* guillotine; paper cutter.

guimba, *n.f.* (*sl.*) cigarette butt.

guinar, *vb.* veer. —**guinada,** *n.f.*

guinchar, *vb.* screech; tow.

guincho, *n.m.* screech; windlass; tow truck.

guindar, *vb.* hoist.

guindaste, *n.m.* crane, derrick.

Guiné, *n.f.* Guinea.

guisa, *n.f.* **à g. de,** in the guise of, in the manner of.

guisar, *vb.* stew. —**guisado,** *n.m.*

guitarra, *n.f.* (electric) guitar; (*sl.*) counterfeiting press.

guitarrista, *n.m.f.* guitarist; (*sl.*) counterfeiter.

guizo, *n.m.* jingle bell.

gula, *n.f.* gluttony.

gulodice, *n.f.* gluttony; sweet.

guloseima, *n.f.* sweet, delicacy.

guloso, *adj.* gluttonous.

gume, *n.m.* cutting edge; acumen.

guri, *n.m.* (*coll.*) boy; kid.

guria, *n.f.* (*coll.*) girl; girlfriend.

gusano, *n.m.* maggot.

gutural, *adj.* guttural.

H

hábil, *adj.* skillful, able; clever.

habilidade, *n.f.* skill, capability, ability.

habilidoso, *adj.* skilled, skillful.

habilitação, *n.f.* qualification; aptitude, capability.

habilitar, *vb.* qualify, enable, prepare, train.

habitação, *n.f.* habitation, house, dwelling.

habitante, *n.m.f.* inhabitant.

habitar, *vb.* inhabit, live in.

hábito, *n.m.* habit (also dress), custom, practice.

habitual, *adj.* habitual.

habituar, *vb.* habituate. **h.-se,** become accustomed.

haitiano -na, *adj., n.m.f.* Haitian.

hálito, *n.m.* breath.

hall, *n.m.* entry hall, foyer.

halo, *n.m.* halo.

haltere, *n.m.* dumbbell, weight.

halterofilia, *n.f.,* **-filismo,** *n.m.* weightlifting.

hambúrguer, *n.m.* hamburger.

hangar, *n.m.* hangar.

harém, *n.m.* harem.

harmonia, *n.f.* harmony.

harmônica, *n.f.* harmonica; accordeon.

harmonioso, *adj.* harmonious.

harmonizar, *vb.* harmonize.

harpa, *n.f.* harp.

hasta, *n.f.* auction.

haste, *n.f.* rod, pole; flagpole.

hastear, *vb.* raise, hoist.

haurir, *vb.* drain; suck in; draw.

Havaí, *n.m.* Hawaii.

havaiano -na, *adj., n.* Hawaiian.

haver, 1. *impers. vb.* be, there to be; ago. **há dois carros lá,** there are two cars there; **haja o que houver,** come what may; **não há de quê,** you're welcome; **morreu há três anos,** he died three years ago; **o que é que há?,** what's new? **2.** *aux. vb.* have. **eles haviam chegado,** they had arrived; **h. de** + *infin.,* must, shall, be supposed to. **3.** *n.m. (pl.)* property, chattel.

haxixe, *n.m.* hashish.

hebdomadário, *adj., n.m.* weekly.

hebraico -ca, 1. *adj.* Hebraic. **2.** *n.* Hebrew.

hebreu -éia, *adj., n.* Hebrew *n.m.* Hebrew (language).

hediondo, *adj.* heinous, hideous.

hedonismo, *n.m.* hedonism.

hein, *interj.* huh? what?; isn't that so?

hélice, *n.f.* helix; airplane propeller.

helicóptero, *n.m.* helicopter.

hélio, *n.m.* helium.

heliografia, *n.f.* blueprint.

hem, *interj.* huh?; isn't that so?

hemeroteca, *n.f.* newspaper or periodical library.

hemisfério, *n.m.* hemisphere.

hemofilia, *n.f.* hemophilia.

hemofílico, 1. *adj.* hemophilic. **2.** *n.m.* hemophiliac.

hemorragia, *n.f.* hemorrhage.

hemorróidas, *n.f.pl.* hemorrhoids.

hena, *n.f.* henna.

henequém, *n.m.* henequen.

hepatite, *n.f.* hepatitis.

hera, *n.f.* ivy.

heráldica, *n.f.* heraldry.

herança, *n.f.* inheritance; heritage.

herdar, *vb.* inherit.

herdeiro -ra, *n.* heir.

hereditariedade, *n.f.* heredity.

hereditário, *adj.* hereditary.

herege, *n.m.f.* heretic.

heresia, *n.f.* heresy.

hermético, *adj.* hermetic.

hérnia, *n.f.* hernia.

herói, *n.m.* hero.

heróico, *adj.* heroic.

heroína, *n.f.* heroine; heroin.

heroísmo, *n.m.* heroism.

hesitação, *n.f.* hesitation.

hesitar, *vb.* hesitate.

heterodoxo, *adj.* heterodox.

heterogeneidade, *n.f.* heterogeneity.

heterogêneo, *adj.* heterogeneous.

heterossexual, *adj.* heterosexual.

heureca, *interj.* eureka!

hiato, *n.m.* hiatus.

hibernar, *vb.* hibernate.

híbrido, *adj.* hybrid.

hidrante, *n.m.* fire hydrant.

hidratar, *vb.* hydrate.

hidráulico, *adj.* hydraulic.

hidravião, *n.m.* hydroplane, seaplane.

hidrelétrica, *n.f.* hydroelectric plant.

hidrelétrico, *adj.* hydroelectric.

hidrofobia, *n.f.* hydrophobia, rabies.

hidrogênio, *n.m.* hydrogen.

hidropisia, *n.f.* dropsy.

hiena, *n.f.* hyena.

hierarquia, *n.f.* hierarchy.

hierárquico, *adj.* hierarchical.

hieroglífico, *adj., n.m.* hieroglyphic.

hífen, *n.m.* hyphen.

higiene, *n.f.* hygiene.

higiênico, *adj.* hygienic.

hilário, *adj.* hilarious.

hímen, *n.m.* hymen.

hindi, *n.m.* Hindi.

hindu, *adj., n.m.f.* Hindu.

hino, *n.m.* hymn, anthem.

hipérbole, *n.f.* hyperbole.

hipermercado, *n.m.* large supermarket.

hipertensão, *n.f.* hypertension.

hipertenso, *adj.* hypertensive.

hípico, *adj.* pert. to horses.

hipismo, *n.m.* horse racing.

hipnose, *n.f.* hypnosis.

hipnótico, *adj.* hypnotic.

hipnotismo, *n.m.* hypnotism.

hóspede

hipnotizar, vb. hypnotize.
hipocondríaco -ca, adj. n. hypochondriac.
hipocrisia, n.f. hypocrisy.
hipócrita, 1. adj. hypocritical. **2.** n.m.f. hypocrite.
hipodérmico, adj. hypodermic.
hipódromo, n.m. race track.
hipoteca, n.f. mortgage. —**hipotecar,** vb.
hipótese, n.f. hypothesis.
hipotético, adj. hypothetical.
hirto, adj. stiff, rigid.
hispânico, adj. Hispanic.
hispanismo, n.m. Hispanicism.
hispano-americano -na, adj. n. Spanish American.
histeria, n.f. hysteria.
histérico, adj. hysterical.
história, n.f. history; story. **h. em quadrinhos,** comic strip.
historiador -ra, n. historian.
histórico, 1. adj. historic, historical. **2.** n.m. record.
hodierno, adj. modern.
hodômetro, n.m. odometer.
hoje, n., adv. today. **h. à/de noite,** tonight; **h. à/de tarde,** this afternoon; **h. de manhã,** this morning; **h. em dia,** nowadays.
Holanda, n.f. Holland.
holandês -esa, 1. adj. Dutch. **2.** n. Dutchman; n.m. Dutch (language).
holocausto, n.m. holocaust.
holofote, n.m. searchlight, floodlight.
holograma, n.m. hologram.
homem, n.m. man; (coll.) the devil; (pl.) mankind, (sl.) police. **h. de bem,** man of honor; **h. de negócios,** businessman.
homem-de-palha, n.m. straw man.
homem-rã, n.m. frogman.
homenagear, vb. honor, pay homage to.
homenagem, n.f. homage.
homenzarrão, n.m. large man.
homicida, n.m.f. murderer.
homicídio, n.m. homicide.
homiziar, vb. harbor; hide. **h.-se,** flee.
homogeneidade, n.f. homogeneity.

homogeneizar, vb. homogenize.
homogêneo, adj. homogeneous.
homologar, vb. approve.
homólogo, n. homologue, counterpart.
homossexual, adj., n.m.f. homosexual.
homossexualismo, n.m. homosexuality.
hondurenho -nha, adj. n. Honduran.
honestidade, n.f. honesty.
honesto, adj. honest; decent; chaste.
honra, n.f. honor. —**honrar,** vb.
honradez, n.f. integrity, honesty.
honrado, adj. honorable, honest.
honraria, n.f. honor, distinction.
honroso, adj. honorable.
hóquei, n.m. hockey.
hora, n.f. hour; time. **h. H,** zero hour; **h. marcada,** appointment; **estar na h. (de),** be time (to); **fazer h.,** kill time; **que horas são?,** what time is it?
horário, n.m. schedule; time. **h. nobre,** (TV) prime time.
horda, n.f. horde.
horizontal, adj. horizontal.
horizonte, n.m. horizon.
hormônio, n.m. hormone.
horóscopo, n.m. horoscope.
horrendo, adj. horrendous.
horripilante, adj. hair-raising, scary.
horripilar, vb. terrify.
horrível, adj. horrible.
horror, n.m. horror. **que h.!** how terrible!
horrorizar, vb. horrify; appall.
horroroso, adj. horrible, awful.
horta, n.f. vegetable garden.
hortaliça, n.f. vegetable.
hortelã, n.f. mint.
hortelão -loa, n. vegetable gardener.
hortênsia, n.f. hydrangea.
horticultura, n.f. horticulture.
horto, n.m. small vegetable garden.
hospedagem, n.f. lodging.
hospedar, vb. lodge, put up.
hospedaria, n.f. inn, hostel.
hóspede, n.m.f. guest, lodger.

hospedeira, n.f. hostess. **h. do ar,** (P.) stewardess.
hospedeiro, 1. adj. hospitable. **2.** n.m. host; innkeeper.
hospício, n.m. insane asylum; hospice.
hospital, n.m. hospital.
hospitaleiro, adj. hospitable.
hospitalidade, n.f. hospitality.
hospitalizar, vb. hospitalize.
hoste, n.f. host; army.
hóstia, n.f. (eccles.) host.
hostil, adj. hostile.
hostilidade, n.f. hostility.
hotel, n.m. hotel.
hoteleiro -ra, 1. adj. hotel. **2.** n. hotel owner/administrator.
humanidade, n.f. humanity; (pl.) humanities.
humanismo, n.m. humanism.
humanitário, adj. n.m. humanitarian.
humanitarismo, n.m. humanitarianism.
humanizar, vb. humanize.
humano, adj. human; humane. **ser h.,** human being.
humildade, n.f. humility, humbleness.
humilde, adj. humble.
humilhar, vb. humiliate, humble.
humor, n.m. humor; mood. **bom/mau h.,** good/bad humor.
humorismo, n.m. humor, comedy.
humorista, n.m.f. humorist.
humorístico, adj. humorous.
húngaro -ra, adj., n. Hungarian.
Hungria, n.f. Hungary.

I

i, n.m. the letter i.
ialorixá, n.f. Afro-Brazilian priestess.
ianque, adj., n.m.f. Yankee.
iate, n.m. yacht.
ibérico -ca, adj., n. Iberian.
ibero-americano -na, adj., n. Latin American.
içar, vb. hoist.
ícone, n.m. icon.
iconoclasta, n.m.f. iconoclast.
icterícia, n.f. jaundice.

ida, n.f. departure, going.
idade, n.f. age.
ideal, adj. ideal.
idealismo, n.m. idealism.
idealista, 1. adj. idealistic. **2.** n.m.f. idealist.
idealizar, vb. idealize.
idéia, n.f. idea; (coll.) head, mind. **fazer i.,** realize, understand.
idem, pron. (L.) the same, ditto.
idêntico, adj. identical.
identidade, n.f. identity.
identificação, n.f. identification.
identificar, vb. identify.
ideologia, n.f. ideology.
ideológico, adj. ideological.
idílio, n.m. idyll.
idioma, n.m. language.
idiomático, adj. idiomatic.
idiota, n.m.f. idiot.
idiotice, n.f. idiocy.
idiotismo, n.m. idiocy; idiom.
idolatrar, vb. idolize.
ídolo, n.m. idol.
idôneo, adj. competent.
idoso, adj. aged, old.
iene, n.m. yen (money).
ignaro, adj. ignorant.
ígneo, adj. igneous.
ignição, n.f. ignition.
ignóbil, adj. ignoble.
ignominioso, adj. ignominious.
ignorância, n.f. ignorance.
ignorante, 1. adj. ignorant. **2.** n.m. ignoramus.
ignorar, vb. not know; ignore.
ignoto, adj. unknown.
igreja, n.f. church.
igrejinha, n.f. chapel; (coll.) clique.
igual, 1. adj. equal; the same; (pl.) alike. **2.** n.m.f. peer.
igualar, vb. equal; equate.
igualdade, n.f. equality.
igualitário -ria, adj., n. egalitarian.
iguaria, n.f. food, dish.
iídiche, n.m. Yiddish.
ilegal, adj. illegal.
ilegítimo, adj. illegitimate.
ilegível, adj. illegible.
ileso, adj. unharmed.
ilha, n.f. island.
ilharga, n.f. flank.

ilhéu -lhoa, 1. adj. island. **2.** n. islander; n.f. islet.

ilícito, adj. illicit.

iludir, vb. deceive. **i.-se,** fool oneself.

iluminação, n.f. illumination.

iluminar, vb. illuminate; clarify; inform.

ilusão, n.f. illusion.

ilusório, adj. illusory.

ilustração, n.f. illustration; enlightenment; fame.

ilustrar, vb. illustrate; enlighten; glorify. **i.-se,** become famous.

ilustre, adj. illustrious.

ímã, n.m. magnet.

imaculado, adj. immaculate.

imagem, n.f. image.

imaginação, n.f. imagination.

imaginar, vb. imagine.

imaginário, adj. imaginary.

imantar, vb. magnetize.

imaturo, adj. immature.

imbecil, adj., n.m.f. imbecile.

imberbe, adj. beardless.

imbuir, vb. imbue.

imediato, 1. adj. immediate. **2.** n.m. (naut.) mate.

imensidade, -dão, n.f. immensity.

imenso, adj. immense.

imergir, vb. immerse.

imersão, n.f. immersion.

imerso, adj. immersed.

imigração, n.f. immigration.

imigrante, adj., n.m.f. immigrant.

imigrar, vb. immigrate.

iminente, adj. imminent.

imiscuir-se, vb. meddle.

imitação, n.f. imitation.

imitador -ra, n. imitator.

imitar, vb. imitate.

imo, n.m. core, heart.

imobiliária, n.f. real estate agency.

imobiliário, adj. real estate.

imobilizar, vb. immobilize.

imoral, adj. immoral.

imoralidade, n.f. immorality.

imortal, adj., n.m.f. immortal.

imortalidade, n.f. immortality.

imortalizar, vb. immortalize.

imóvel, 1. adj. immobile. **2.** n.m. (coll.) building; (pl.) real estate.

impacto, n.m. impact.

ímpar, adj. uneven, odd (number).

impasse, n.m. impasse.

impávido, adj. intrepid.

impecável, adj. impeccable.

impedimento, n.m. impediment.

impedir, vb. impede; stop; forbid.

impelir, vb. impel.

impensado, adj. unintended; unforseen.

imperador, n.m. emperor.

imperar, vb. reign; dominate; predominate.

imperativo, adj., n.m. imperative.

imperatriz, n.f. empress.

imperceptível, adj. imperceptible.

imperdoável, adj. inexcusable.

imperfeição, n.f. imperfection, flaw.

imperfeito, adj., n.m. imperfect.

imperial, adj. imperial.

imperialismo, n.m. imperialism.

império, n.m. empire.

imperioso, adj. imperious.

imperito, adj. inexperienced; ignorant.

impermeabilizar, vb. waterproof.

impermeável, 1. adj. impermeable. **2.** n.m. raincoat.

impertinente, adj. impertinent.

impérvio, adj. impervious.

ímpeto, n.m. impetus.

impetrar, vb. plead for; enter (appeal, petition).

impetuoso, adj. impetuous.

impingir, vb. strike; foist.

ímpio, adj. impious.

implacável, adj. implacable.

implantar, vb. implant, plant. **i.-se,** get established.

implemento, n.m. implement.

implicância, n.f. implication; annoyance; (coll.) ill will.

implicar, vb. implicate; imply; involve; entangle; be incompatible; annoy. **i. com,** pick on.

implícito, adj. implicit.

implorar, vb. implore.

imponente, adj. imposing.

impor, vb. impose; instill; command; bestow; deceive.

importação, n.f. import, importation.

importador -ra, 1. adj. importing. 2. n. importer; n.f. import company.

importância, n.f. importance; sum. **não ter i.**, not matter.

importante, adj. important.

importar, vb. import; bring; cause; involve; matter. **i.-se com**, care about; **i. em**, amount to.

importunar, vb. importune.

importuno, adj. annoying.

imposição, n.f. imposition.

impossibilitar, vb. preclude.

impossível, adj. impossible.

imposto, n.m. tax. **i. de renda**, income tax.

impostor -ra, n. impostor.

imprecar, vb. curse.

impregnar, vb. impregnate; imbue.

imprensa, n.f. press; printing press; printing.

imprescindível, adj. indispensable.

impressão, n.f. impression; printing; printout. **i. digital**, fingerprint.

impressionante, adj. impressive.

impressionar, vb. impress; affect. **i.-se**, be impressed/affected.

impresso, 1. adj. printed. 2. n.m. printed form; (pl.) printed matter.

impressor -ra, n. printer (person); n.f. printer (machine). **i. matricial**, dot-matrix printer.

imprestável, adj. useless.

impreterível, adj. undeferrable; inevitable.

imprevidente, adj. improvident.

imprevisão, n.f. lack of foresight.

imprimir, vb. print.

impropério, n.m. insult.

impróprio, adj. improper.

improvidente, adj. improvident.

improvisar, vb. improvise.

improviso, n.m. impromptu piece. **de i.**, suddenly.

impudente, adj. impudent.

impudicícia, n.f. immodesty.

impudico, adj. immodest; shameless.

impudor, n.m. shamelessness.

impugnar, vb. refute; oppose.

impulsionar, vb. propel; stimulate.

impulsivo, adj. impulsive.

impulso, n.m. impulse; impetus.

impune, adj. unpunished.

impunidade, n.f. impunity.

imputar, vb. impute.

imundície, n.f. filth; garbage.

imundo, adj. filthy, dirty.

imune, adj. immune.

imunidade, n.f. immunity.

imunizar, vb. immunize.

in-, pref. un-, in-.

inabalável, adj. unshakable.

inábil, adj. unskilled; incapable.

inabilidade, n.f. incapability.

inabilitar, vb. disqualify; incapacitate.

inacreditável, adj. incredible.

inadvertência, n.f. inadvertence.

inadvertido, adj. inadvertent.

inalar, vb. inhale.

inana, n.f. (sl.) trouble.

inane, adj. inane.

inanimado, adj. inanimate.

inato, adj. innate.

inaudito, adj. unheard of.

inauguração, n.f. inauguration.

inaugurar, vb. inaugurate.

incabível, adj. inappropriate; absurd.

incandescente, adj. incandescent.

incaico, adj. Incan.

incansável, adj. tireless.

incapacitar, vb. incapacitate.

incauto, adj. careless, unwary.

incendiar, vb. set fire to. **i.-se**, catch fire.

incendiário -ria, 1. adj. incendiary. 2. n. firebug; agitator.

incêndio, n.m. fire, conflagration.

incenso, n.m. incense; flattery.

incentivar, vb. motivate.

incentivo, n.m. incentive.

incessante, adj. incessant.

incesto, n.m. incest.

inchação, *n.f.* swelling; *(coll.)* arrogance.
inchaço, *n.m.* swelling.
inchar, *vb.* swell. **i.-se**, bloat; become arrogant.
incidência, *n.f.* incidence.
incidental, *adj.* incidental.
incidente, *n.m.* incident.
incidir, *vb.* happen. **i. em**, incur.
incinerar, *vb.* incinerate.
incipiente, *adj.* incipient.
incisão, *n.f.* incision.
incisivo, *adj.* incisive.
incitar, *vb.* incite.
inclinação, *n.f.* inclination.
inclinar, *vb.* incline, bow; prepare. **i.-se**, slope; bend; be inclined.
ínclito, *adj.* illustrious.
incluir, *vb.* include.
inclusão, *n.f.* inclusion.
inclusive, *adv.* even; inclusive; including.
inclusivo, *adj.* inclusive.
incluso, *adj.* included.
incógnito, *adj., n.m.* unknown.
incólume, *adj.* unharmed.
incombustível, *adj.* fireproof.
incomodar, *vb.* bother. **i.-se**, trouble oneself; get irked, mind.
incômodo, 1. *adj.* uncomfortable. 2. *n.m.* inconvenience.
inconfidência, *n.f.* disloyalty.
incongruente, *adj.* incongruent.
inconsciência, *n.f.* unconsciousness.
inconsciente, *adj., n.m.* unconscious.
inconseqüente, *adj.* inconsequent; imprudent.
inconstante, *adj.* changeable.
inconveniente, 1. *adj.* inconvenient; unsuitable. 2. *n.m.* obstacle; difficulty; objection.
incorporar, *vb.* incorporate.
incorrer em, *vb.* incur, fall into.
incrementar, *vb.* develop; *(sl.)* jazz up.
incremento, *n.m.* increment; development.
increpar, *vb.* censure.
incriminar, *vb.* incriminate, criminalize.
incrível, *adj.* incredible.
incrustar, *vb.* encrust, embed.
incubar, *vb.* hatch.

inculcar, *vb.* inculcate; implant; indicate; show.
inculto, *adj.* uncultivated; uncultured.
incumbência, *n.f.* mission, charge.
incumbir, *vb.* commission; be obliged.
incúria, *n.f.* negligence.
incursão, *n.f.* incursion.
incutir, *vb.* instill.
inda, *var. of* **ainda.**
indagação, *n.f.* investigation, inquiry.
indagar, *vb.* investigate, inquire.
indébito, *adj.* undue.
indeciso, *adj.* undecided.
indefeso, *adj.* defenseless, helpless.
indefinido, *adj.* indefinite.
indelével, *adj.* indelible.
indenização, -dade, *n.f.* indemnity.
indenizar, *n.f.* indemnify.
independência, *n.f.* independence.
independente, *adj.* independent.
independer, *vb.* be independent, not depend.
indeterminado, *adj.* indeterminate.
indevassável, *adj.* unexposed to view, private.
indevido, *adj.* undue, improper.
indiano -na, *adj., n.* Indian, Hindu. **fila i.**, single file.
Indias, *n.f.pl.* Indies. **I. Ocidentais**, West Indies.
indicação, *n.f.* indication.
indicado, *adj.* appropriate, logical.
indicar, *vb.* indicate, point out; designate.
indicativo, *adj., n.m.* indicative.
índice, *n.m.* index; forefinger.
indiciar, *vb.* indict; accuse; show.
indício, *n.m.* indication, sign.
indiferença, *n.f.* indifference.
indiferente, *adj.* indifferent; all the same; unimportant.
indígena, 1. *adj.* indigenous. 2. *n.m.f.* native.
indigente, *adj.* indigent.
indigestão, *n.f.* indigestion.

indigesto, *adj.* indigestible; (*coll.*) annoying, unsavory.

indignado, *adj.* indignant.

indignar, *vb.* make indignant. **i.-se,** become indignant.

indigno, *adj.* unworthy; despicable.

índio -dia, *adj., n.* Indian.

indireta, *n.f.* hint, innuendo.

indiscutível, *adj.* unquestionable.

indispensável, *adj.* indispensable.

indispor, *vb.* disarrange; indispose; upset.

indisposto, *adj.* indisposed; ill-humored.

individual, *adj.* individual.

indivíduo, *n.m.* individual; (*coll.*) guy.

índole, *n.f.* nature, character.

indolente, *adj.* indolent.

indômito, *adj.* untamed; unbeaten; arrogant.

indonésio -sia, *adj., n.* Indonesian.

indubitável, *adj.* doubtless.

indução, *n.f.* induction.

indulgência, *n.f.* indulgence.

indulgente, *adj.* indulgent.

indultar, *vb.* pardon. —**indulto,** *n.m.*

indumentária, *n.f.* clothing, apparel.

indústria, *n.f.* industry.

industrial, 1. *adj.* industrial. **2.** *n.m.f.* industrialist.

industrialização, *n.f.* industrialization.

industrializar, *vb.* industrialize.

industrioso, *adj.* industrious.

induzir, *vb.* induce.

inebriar, *vb.* inebriate. **i.-se,** get drunk.

inédito, *adj.* unpublished; unprecedented.

inefável, *adj.* ineffable, indescribable..

inepto, *adj.* inept.

inequívoco, *adj.* unmistakable.

inércia, *n.f.* inertia.

inerente, *adj.* inherent.

inerme, *adj.* unarmed, defenseless.

inerte, *adj.* inert.

inesgotável, *adj.* inexhaustible.

inesperado, *adj.* unexpected.

inesquecível, *adj.* unforgettable.

inevitável, *adj.* inevitable.

inexperiente, -perto, *adj.* unexperienced.

inexplicável, *adj.* inexplicable.

infame, *adj.* infamous.

infâmia, *n.f.* infamy.

infância, *n.f.* infancy.

infanta, *n.f.* infanta.

infante, 1. *adj.* infant. **2.** *n.m.* infant; infante.

infantil, *adj.* infantile, childish; children's.

infatigável, *adj.* tireless.

infausto, *adj.* unlucky.

infecção, *n.f.* infection.

infeccionar, *vb.* infect.

infeccioso, *adj.* infectious.

infelicitar, *vb.* make unhappy; deflower.

infeliz, *adj.* unhappy, unfortunate.

inferência, *n.f.* inference.

inferior, *adj.* inferior; lower.

inferioridade, *n.f.* inferiority.

inferir, *vb.* infer.

infernal, *adj.* infernal; (*sl.*) terrific.

infernar, *vb.* torment.

inferninho, *n.m.* (*coll.*) small nightclub.

inferno, *n.m.* hell.

infestar, *vb.* infest.

infidelidade, *n.f.* infidelity.

infiel, 1. *adj.* unfaithful. **2.** *n.m.f.* infidel.

infiltrar, *vb.* infiltrate.

ínfimo, *adj.* lowest, inferior.

infindo, *adj.* endless.

infinidade, *n.f.* infinitude.

infinitivo, *adj., n.m.* infinitive.

infinito, 1. *adj.* infinite. **2.** *n.m.* infinitive.

inflação, *n.f.* inflation.

inflamação, *n.f.* inflammation.

inflamar, *vb.* inflame.

inflar, *vb.* inflate, puff up; make/become proud.

inflexão, *n.f.* inflection.

infligir, *vb.* inflict.

influência, *n.f.* influence. —**influenciar,** *vb.*

influente, *adj.* influential.

influenza, *n.f.* influenza.

influir, *vb.* flow in; influence; inspire; excite; matter. **i. em,** influence. **i.-se**, become enthusiastic.

influxo, n.m. influx; influence.

informação, n.f. information; intelligence.

informal, adj. informal.

informante, n.m.f. informer, informant.

informar, vb. inform, notify; report. **i.-se (de)**, find out about.

informática, n.f. computer science.

informativo, adj. informative.

informe, 1. adj. shapeless. **2.** n.m. information.

infortúnio, n.m. misfortune.

infração, n.f. infraction.

infra-estrutura, n.f. infrastructure.

infravermelho, adj. infrared.

infringir, vb. infringe, violate.

infundir, vb. infuse, inspire.

infusão, n.f. infusion.

ingenuidade, n.f. naiveté.

ingênuo, adj. naive, ingenuous.

ingerir, vb. ingest; inject. **i.-se em**, interfere in.

inglês -glesa, 1. adj. English. **2.** n. Englishman -woman; n.m. English. **para inglês ver**, (coll.) just for show.

ingrato, 1. adj. ungrateful. **2.** n.m. ingrate.

ingrediente, n.m. ingredient.

íngreme, adj. steep; arduous.

ingressar em, vb. enter; join.

ingresso, n.m. entrance, admission.

inhaca, n.f. (coll.) body odor; bad luck.

inhame, n.m. type of yam.

inibição, n.f. inhibition.

inibir, vb. inhibit.

iniciação, n.f. initiation.

inicial, adj., n.f. initial.

iniciar, vb. initiate. **i.-se**, be initiated.

iniciativa, n.f. initiative.

início, n.m. beginning, start.

inimigo, n.m. enemy.

inimizade, n.f. enmity.

iníquo, adj. iniquitous; inequitable.

injeção, n.f. injection, shot; (coll.) annoyance.

injetar, vb. inject; make/

become bloodshot; (coll.) annoy.

injúria, n.f. insult. **—injuriar**, vb.

inocência, n.f. innocence.

inocente, adj. innocent.

inocular, vb. innoculate.

inócuo, adj. innocuous.

inóspito, adj. inhospitable.

inovação, n.f. innovation.

inovar, vb. innovate.

inoxidável, adj. rustproof, stainless.

inquérito, n.m. inquiry, examination; inquest.

inquietar, vb. disturb, trouble, worry.

inquieto, adj. restless, uneasy.

inquilino -na, n. tenant.

inquirição, n.f. inquiry.

inquirir, vb. inquire.

inquisição, n.f. inquisition.

insaciável, adj. insatiable.

insânia, insanidade, n.f. insanity.

insano, adj. insane; arduous.

insatisfeito, adj. dissatisfied.

inscrever, vb. inscribe; register; write; draw. **i.-se**, register.

inscrição, n.f. inscription; registration.

inseguro, adj. insecure.

inseminação, n.f. insemination.

insensato, adj. senseless, foolish.

insensível, adj. insensitive.

insepulto, adj. unburied.

inserção, n.f. insertion.

inserir, vb. insert.

inseticida, n.f. insecticide.

inseto, n.m. insect.

insidioso, adj. insidious.

insigne, adj. illustrious.

insígnia, n.f. insignia.

insignificante, adj. insignificant.

insincero, adj. insincere.

insinuação, n.f. insinuation.

insinuar, vb. insinuate; instill; slip into. **i.-se**, penetrate; ingratiate oneself; **i.-se em**, creep into.

insípido, adj. insipid.

insistência, n.f. insistence.

insistente, adj. insistent.

insistir, vb. insist; persist. **i. em**, insist on.

insofrível, *adj.* insufferable.
insolação, *n.f.* sunstroke.
insolente, *adj.* insolent.
insólito, *adj.* unusual.
insolúvel, *adj.* insoluble.
insone, **1.** *adj.* sleepless. **2.** *n.m.f.* insomniac.
insônia, *n.f.* insomnia.
insosso, *adj.* insipid.
inspeção, *n.f.* inspection.
inspecionar, *vb.* inspect.
inspetor -ra, *n.* inspector.
inspiração, *n.f.* inspiration.
inspirar, *vb.* inspire. **i.-se**, be/become inspired.
instabilidade, *n.f.* instability.
instalação, *n.f.* installation; equipment.
instalar, *vb.* install. **i.-se**, settle.
instância, *n.f.* urging. **em última i.**, as a last resort.
instantâneo, **1.** *adj.* instant, instantaneous. **2.** *n.m.* snapshot.
instante, **1.** *adj.* urgent; impending. **2.** *n.m.* instant.
instar, *vb.* urge; be imminent.
instaurar, *vb.* institute, establish.
instável, *adj.* unstable.
instigar, *vb.* instigate; urge.
instintivo, *adj.* instinctive.
instinto, *n.m.* instinct.
institucional, *adj.* institutional.
instituição, *n.f.* institution.
instituir, *vb.* institute; designate; train; schedule.
instituto, *n.m.* institute.
instrução, *n.f.* instruction, education.
instruir, *vb.* instruct, educate; prepare for trial. **i.-se**, receive instruction.
instrumental, *adj.* instrumental.
instrumento, *n.m.* instrument.
instrutivo, *adj.* instructive.
instrutor -ra, **1.** *adj.* instructive. **2.** *n.* instructor.
insubordinação, *n.f.* insubordination.
insubordinar, *vb.* cause to revolt. **i.-se**, rebel.
insucesso, *n.m.* failure.
insular, **1.** *adj.* insular. **2.** *n.m.f.* islander. **3.** *vb.* insulate, isolate.
insulina, *n.f.* insulin.

insulto, *n.m.* insult. **—insultar**, *vb.*
insultuoso, *adj.* insulting.
insuperável, *adj.* insurmountable.
insuportável, *adj.* unbearable.
insurgente, *adj.*, *n.m.f.* insurgent.
insurreição, *n.f.* insurrection.
insurreto, *adj.*, *n.m.* insurgent.
intato, *adj.* intact.
íntegra, *n.f.* totality. **na i.**, in full.
integração, *n.f.* integration.
integral, *adj.* integral, whole.
integrante, *adj.*, *n.m.f.* constituent.
integrar, *vb.* integrate; make complete; make up. **i.-se**, integrate oneself.
integridade, *n.f.* integrity; wholeness.
íntegro, *adj.* upright; whole.
inteirar, *vb.* complete; inform. **i.-se**, find out.
inteireza, *n.f.* entirety; uprightness.
inteiro, *adj.* entire.
intelecto, *n.m.* intellect.
intelectual, *adj.*. *n.m.f.* intellectual.
inteligência, *n.f.* intelligence.
inteligente, *adj.* intelligent.
inteligível, *adj.* intelligible.
intempérie, *n.f.* bad weather.
intenção, *n.f.* intention.
intencional, *adj.* intentional.
intendente, *n.m.f.* comptroller; quartermaster.
intensidade, *n.f.* intensity.
intensificar, *vb.* intensify.
intensivo, *adj.* intensive.
intenso, *adj.* intense.
intentar, *vb.* plan, attempt.
intento, *n.m.* intent.
inter-, *pref.* inter-.
intercalar, *vb.* intercalate, interpolate.
intercâmbio, *n.m.* interchange. **—intercambiar**, *vb.*
interceder, *vb.* intercede.
interceptar, *vb.* intercept.
interdição, *n.f.* interdiction; prohibition; closing.
interditar, *vb.* interdict, prohibit; close down.

interdito, 1. *adj.* prohibited. **2.** *n.m.* prohibition.

interessado, *adj.* interested; biased.

interessante, *adj.* interesting.

interessar, *vb.* interest; profit. **i.-se,** take an interest.

interesse, *n.m.* interest.

interesseiro, *adj.* self-seeking.

interface, *vb.* interface. **—interfacear,** *vb.*

interferência, *n.f.* interference.

interferir, *vb.* interfere, intervene.

interfone, *n.m.* intercom.

ínterim, *n.m.* interim. **—interino,** *adj.*

interior, 1. *adj.* interior, inner. **2.** *n.m.* interior.

interjeição, *n.f.* interjection.

interlocutor -ra, *n.* interlocutor.

interlúdio, *n.m.* interlude.

intermediário, *adj.* intermediary.

intermédio, 1. *adj.* intermediate. **2.** *n.m.* intermediary; intermediation; interlude.

interminável, *adj.* interminable.

intermissão, *n.f.* intermission.

intermitente, *adj.* intermittent.

internacional, *adj.* international.

internar, *vb.* intern, enroll. **i.-se,** enter.

internato, *n.m.* boarding school.

interno, 1. *adj.* internal; boarding. **2.** *n.m.* boarding student.

interpelar, *vb.* question, quiz.

interpolar, *vb.* interpolate; intersperse.

interpretação, *n.f.* interpretation.

interpretar, *vb.* interpret.

intérprete, *n.m.f.* interpreter.

interrogação, *n.f.* interrogation; question mark.

interrogar, *vb.* interrogate.

interrogativo, *adj.* interrogative.

interrogatório, *n.m.* interrogatory.

interromper, *vb.* interrupt.

interrupção, *n.f.* interruption.

interruptor, *n.m. (elec.)* switch.

interseção, *n.f.* intersection.

interstício, *n.m.* interstice.

interurbano, 1. *adj.* interurban. **2.** *n.m.* long-distance call.

intervalo, *n.m.* interval; intermission.

intervenção, *n.f.* intervention; participation. **i. cirúrgica,** operation.

interventor -ra, *n.* temporary federally appointed governor.

intervir, *vb.* intervene; participate; happen.

intestino, *n.m.* intestine.

intimação, *n.f.* intimation, summons; announcement.

intimar, *vb.* intimate, notify, summon.

intimidade, *n.f.* intimacy.

intimidar, *vb.* intimidate.

íntimo, 1. *adj.* intimate, close. **2.** *n.m.* innermost part; close friend.

intolerante, *adj.* intolerant.

intra-, *pref.* intra-.

intragável, *adj.* intolerable.

intransigente, *adj.* intransigent.

intransitável, *adj.* impassable.

intransitivo, *adj.* intransitive.

intratável, *adj.* intractable.

intravenoso, *adj.* intravenous.

intrépido, *adj.* intrepid.

intricado, -trincado, *adj.* intricate.

intriga, *n.f.* intrigue, plot; gossip. **—intrigar,** *vb.*

intrínseco, *adj.* intrinsic.

introdução, *n.f.* introduction.

introdutório, -tivo, *adj.* introductory.

introduzir, *vb.* introduce; insert. **i.-se,** penetrate; take root.

intróito, *n.m.* beginning.

intrometer, *vb.* insert. **i.-se,** meddle.

intrometido, 1. *adj.* meddlesome. **2.** *n.m.* meddler.

intromissão, *n.f.* meddling.

introspectivo, *adj.* introspective.

introvertido, 1. *adj.*, introverted. **2.** *n.m.* introvert.

intrujão, *n.m.* swindler; *(coll.)* fence.

intrujar, *vb.* swindle; lie.

intrusão, *n.f.* intrusion.

intruso, 1. *adj.* intruding; meddlesome. **2.** *n.m.* intruder; meddler.

intuição, *n.f.* intuition.

intuir, *vb.* intuit.

inumano, *adj.* inhuman, inhumane.

inumerável, *adj.* innumerable.

inundação, *n.f.* flood. —**inundar,** *vb.*

inusitado, *adj.* unusual.

inútil, *adj.* useless.

inutilizar, *vb.* make useless.

invadir, *vb.* invade.

invalidar, *vb.* invalidate.

inválido, *adj., n.m.* invalid.

invariável, *adj.* invariable.

invasão, *n.f.* invasion.

invasor -ra, 1. *adj.* invading. **2.** *n.* invader.

invectiva, *n.f.* invective.

inveja, *n.f.* envy. —**invejar,** *vb.*

invejoso, *adj.* envious.

invenção, *n.f.* invention.

invencível, *adj.* invincible.

inventar, *vb.* invent.

inventário, *n.m.* inventory. —**inventariar,** *vb.*

inventiva, -vidade, *n.f.* inventiveness.

inventivo, *adj.* inventive.

invento, *n.m.* invention.

inverno, *n.m.* winter.

inverossímil, *adj.* implausible.

inversão, *n.f.* inversion; investment; homsexuality.

inverso, *adj., n.m.* inverse.

inverter, *vb.* invert; invest.

invertido, *n.m.* homosexual.

invés, *n.m.* wrong side; contrary.

investida, *n.f.* attack.

investigação, *n.f.* investigation; research.

investigador -ra, *n.* investigator; researcher.

investigar, *vb.* investigate; research.

investimento, *n.m.* investment.

investir, *vb.* invest; attack.

inveterado, *adj.* inveterate.

invicto, *adj.* undefeated.

invisível, *adj.* invisible.

invocação, *n.f.* invocation; *(sl.)* nagging.

invocar, *vb.* invoke; *(sl.)* nag.

invólucro, *n.m.* wrapper.

invulgar, *adj.* uncommon.

iodo, *n.m.* iodine.

ioga, *n.f.* yoga.

iogurte, *n.m.* yogurt.

íon, *n.m.* ion.

iorubano, *adj., n.m.* Yoruban.

ípsilon, *n.m.* the letter y.

ir, *vb.* go. **i.(-se) embora,** go away. **como vai?,** how are you?; **i. andando/indo/levando,** *(coll.)* be getting by.

ira, *n.f.* ire, anger.

Irã, *n.m.* Iran.

iraniano -na, *adj., n.* Iranian.

iracundo, *adj.* irate.

Iraque, *n.m.* Iraq.

iraquiano -na, *adj., n.* Iraqi.

irascível, *adj.* irascible.

íris, *n.m.* iris.

Irlanda, *n.f.* Ireland.

irlandês -desa, 1. *adj.* Irish. **2.** *n.* Irishman -woman; *n.m.* Irish (language).

irmã, *n.f.* sister; nun.

irmandade, *n.f.* brotherhood.

irmão, *n.m.* brother.

ironia, *n.f.* irony.

irônico, *adj.* ironic.

irracional, *adj.* irrational.

irradiar, *vb.* irradiate, radiate; broadcast.

irreal, *adj.* unreal.

irregular, *adj.* irregular.

irrelevante, *adj.* irrelevant.

irrequieto, *adj.* restless.

irresistível, *adj.* irresistible.

irresoluto, *adj.* irresolute.

irresponsável, *adj.* irresponsible.

irreverente, *adj.* irreverent.

irrigação, *n.f.* irrigation.

irrigar, *vb.* irrigate.

irritação, *n.f.* irritation.

irritar, *vb.* irritate; annoy.

irrupção, *n.f.* irruption; invasion.

isca, *n.f.* bait.

isenção, *n.f.* exemption.

isento, *adj.* exempt. —**isentar,** *vb.*

Islã, -lame, *n.m.* Islam.

islâmico, *adj.* islamic.

Islândia, *n.f.* Iceland.

isolamento, *n.m.* isolation; insulation.

isolar, *vb.* isolate; insulate.

isopor, *n.m.* styrofoam.

isqueiro, *n.m.* cigarette lighter.
israelense, *adj.*, *n.m.f.* Israeli.
israelita, *adj.*, *n.m.f.* Israelite.
isso, *neut. dem. pron.* that; that thing. **i. mesmo**, (*coll.*) exactly; **por i.**, therefore.
istmo, *n.m.* isthmus.
isto, *neut. dem. pron.* this.
Itália, *n.f.* Italy.
italiano -na, *adj.*, *n.* Italian.
itálico, *adj.*, *n.m.* italic(s).
itinerário, *n.m.* itinerary.
Iugoslávia, *n.f.* Yugoslavia.
iugoslavo -va, *adj.*, *n.* Yugoslav.

J

já, **1.** *adv.* already; now. **j.**, **j.**, right away; **j. não**, no longer; **j. que**, since. **2. j. . . j.**, now . . . now.
jabaculê, *n.m.* (*sl.*) bribe.
jaburu, *n.m.* jabiru stork; tall, clumsy person.
jabuti, *n.m.* type of land turtle.
jabuticaba, *n.f.* jaboticaba fruit.
jaca, *n.f.* jack fruit.
jaça, *n.f.* flaw.
jacarandá, *n.m.* jacaranda.
jacaré, *n.m.* alligator. **fazer j.**, (*coll.*) body surf; surf.
jacinto, *n.m.* hyacinth.
jactância, *n.f.* boasting; conceit.
jactancioso, *adj.* boastful; arrogant.
jactar-se, *vb.* boast.
jacu, *n.m.* (*coll.*) hillbilly.
jade, *n.m.* jade.
jaez, *n.m.* harness; sort.
jaguar, *n.m.* jaguar.
jagunço, *n.m.* thug, hoodlum.
jaleco, *n.m.* jacket.
jamais, *adv.* never.
jamba, *n.f.* door jamb.
jamegão, *n.m.* (*coll.*) signature.
janeiro, *n.m.* January.
janela, *n.f.* window.
jangada, *n.f.* raft.
janota, *n.m.* dandy, fop.
janta, *f.* (*coll.*) dinner.
jantar, **1.** *n.m.* dinner. **2.** *vb.* dine.
Japão, *n.m.* Japan.
japona, *n.f.* jacket.
japonês -nesa, *a.*, *n.* Japanese; *n.m.* Japanese (language).

jaqueta, *n.f.* jacket.
jararaca, *n.f.* pit viper; vicious hag.
jarda, *n.f.* yard (measure).
jardim, *n.m.* garden; park. **j. do Eden**, garden of Eden; **j. zoológico**, zoo.
jardim-de-infância, *n.f.* kindergarten.
jardinagem, *n.f.* gardening.
jardinar, *vb.* garden.
jardineiro -ra, *n.* gardener.
jargão, *n.m.* jargon.
jarra, *n.f.* vase.
jarro, *n.m.* pitcher.
jasmim, *n.m.* jasmine.
jato, jacto, *n.m.* jet; jet plane; gush.
jaula, *n.f.* large cage.
javali, *n.m.* wild boar.
jazer, *vb.* lie; be buried.
jazida, *n.f.* ore deposit.
jazigo, *n.m.* tomb; ore deposit.
jeca, *n.m.f.* hillbilly.
jeitão, *n.m.* personal style.
jeito, *n.m.* way; air; nature; (*coll.*) talent. **dar um j.**, find a way, fix it; **de j. nenhum**, by no means; **não tem jeito**, it's no use; **sem j.**, embarrassed, ill-at-ease.
jeitoso, *adj.* skillful, talented.
jejum, *n.m.* fast. **-jejuar**, *vb.*
jenipapo, *n.m.* genipap fruit.
jerico, *n.m.* donkey.
jerimum, *n.m.* pumpkin.
jérsei, *n.m.* jersey.
jesuíta, *n.m.* Jesuit.
Jesus, *n.m.* Jesus. **J. Cristo**, Jesus Christ.
jia, *n.f.* bullfrog.
jibóia, *n.f.* boa constrictor.
jiló, *n.m.* type of nightshade fruit.
jipe, *n.m.* jeep.
jirau, *n.m.* raised platform.
joalharia, -lheria, *n.f.* jewelry store.
joalheiro -ra, *n.* jeweler.
joaninha, *n.f.* ladybug.
joão-ninguém, *n.m.* (*coll.*) unimportant person.
joça, *n.f.* (*sl.*) thingamajig.
jocoso, *adj.* jocose.
joelho, *n.m.* knee.
jogada, *n.f.* play (in a game).

jogador -ra, *n.* player; gambler.
jogar, *vb.* play (game); gamble; throw; toss. **j. fora**, throw out.
jogatina, *n.f.* gambling.
jogo, *n.m.* game; match; gambling; fun; tossing; set. **j. de azar**, game of chance; **j. de damas**, checkers; **j. de palavras**, play on words; **j. de salão**, parlor game; **jogos Olímpicos**, Olympic games.
jogo-do-bicho, *n.m.* illegal numbers game.
jogral, *n.m.* minstrel; reciter; choral recitation.
joguete, *n.m.* laughingstock.
jóia, **1.** *adj.* (*sl.*) terrific. **2.** *n.f.* jewel; initiation fee.
joio, *n.m.* darnel grass.
jóquei, *n.m.* jockey.
Jordânia, *n.f.* Jordan (country).
Jordão, *n.m.* Jordan (river).
jorna, *n.f.* (*coll.*) daily wages.
jornada, *n.f.* (day's) journey.
jornal, *n.m.* newspaper; diary; newscast; day's pay.
jornaleiro, *n.m.* newsboy; day laborer.
jornalismo, *n.m.* journalism.
jornalista, *n.m.f.* journalist.
jorrar, *vb.* gush; bulge.
jorro, *n.m.* gush, spurt.
jota, *n.m.* the letter j.
jovem, **1.** *adj.* young. **2.** *m.f.* young person.
jovial, *adj.* jovial.
juazeiro, *n.m.* jujube tree.
juba, *n.f.* lion's mane.
jubilação, *n.f.* jubilation; retirement.
jubilar(-se), *vb.* jubilate; retire.
jubileu, *n.m.* jubilee.
júbilo, *n.m.* jubilation.
jubiloso, *adj.* jubilant.
judaico, *adj.* Judaic.
judaísmo, *n.m.* Judaism.
judeu -dia, **1.** *adj.* Jewish. **2.** *n.* Jew.
judiação, *n.f.* (*coll.*) mockery; abuse.
judiar (com/de), *vb.* (*coll.*) mock; abuse
judicial, *adj.* judicial.
judiciário, *adj.* judiciary.
judicioso, *adj.* judicious.
judô, *n.m.* judo.
jugo, *n.m.* yoke.

juiz, -íza, *n.* judge; referee.
juizado, *n.m.* judgeship.
juízo, *n.m.* judgment; sense. **j. de valor**, value judgment; **j. final**, Last Judgment; **criar/tomar j.**, get some sense; **perder o j.**, lose one's mind.
julgamento, *n.m.* judgment trial; sentence.
julgar, *vb.* judge; sentence; deem.
julho, *n.m.* July.
jumento, *n.m.* donkey.
junção, *n.f.* junction.
junco, *n.m.* (*bot.*) rush; (*naut.*) junk.
jungir, *vb.* yoke.
junho, *n.m.* June.
junino, *adj.* June.
júnior, *adj.* junior.
junta, *n.f.* junction; joint; meeting; board, junta; pair; team (oxen).
juntar, *vb.* join; gather. **j.-se**, gather; (*coll.*) cohabit.
junto, **1.** *adj.* together; nearby. **2.** *adv.* together, jointly. **j. a/de**, beside; vis-à-vis.
juntura, *n.f.* juncture.
Júpiter, *n.m.* Jupiter.
jurado -da, *n.* juror.
juramento, *n.m.* oath.
jurar, *vb.* swear; testify.
jurema, *n.f.* type of acacia.
júri, *n.m.* jury.
jurídico, *adj.* juridical.
jurisdição, *n.f.* jurisdiction.
jurisprudência, *n.f.* jurisprudence.
jurista, *m.f.* jurist.
juros, *n.m.pl.* (*com.*) interest.
jururu, *adj.* sad, blue.
jus, *n.m.* right. **fazer j. a**, deserve.
jusante, *n.f.* ebb tide; **a j.**, downstream.
justa, *n.f.* joust; (*sl.*) police.
justapor, *vb.* juxtapose.
justar, *vb.* joust.
justeza, *n.f.* exactness.
justiça, *n.f.* justice; legal profession; the law; judiciary.
justiçar, *vb.* execute; torture.
justiceiro, *adj.* just; severe.
justificação, *n.f.* justification.
justificar, *vb.* justify; absolve; prove.

justificativa, *n.f.* justification.
justo, 1. *adj.* just, fair; exact; tight. **2.** *n.m.* just person.
juta, *n.f.* jute.
juvenil, *adj.* juvenile.
juventude, *n.f.* youth; young people.

L

la, form of dir. obj. pron. **a** after vb. ending in **r, s,** or **z.**
lá, *adv.* over there.
lã, *n.f.* wool.
labareda, *n.f.* flame.
lábia, *n.f.* cunning; gift of gab.
lábio, *n.m.* lip; labium.
labioso, *adj.* thick-lipped; sly; fast-talking.
labirinto, *n.m.* labyrinth, maze.
labor, *n.m.* labor. **—laborar,** *vb.*
laboratório, *n.m.* laboratory.
laborioso, *adj.* laborious; hardworking.
labrego, 1. *adj.* boorish. **2.** *n.m.* peasant; boor.
labutar, *vb.* toil.
laca, *n.f.* lacquer. **—laquear,** *vb.*
lacaio, *n.m.* lackey.
laçar, *vb.* lasso; snare.
lacerar, *vb.* lacerate.
laço, *n.m.* bow; lasso; snare.
lacônico, *adj.* laconic; brief.
lacrar, *vb.* seal with wax.
lacre, *n.m.* sealing wax.
lacrimogêneo, *adj.* producing tears.
lacrimoso, *adj.* tearful.
lácteo, *adj.* milky. **Via Láctea,** Milky Way.
laticínio, *n.m.* dairy product.
lacuna, *n.f.* gap, lacuna; space.
ladainha, *n.f.* litany; long, boring talk.
ladeira, *n.f.* hill.
ladino, *adj.* shrewd.
lado, *n.m.* side; direction. **ao l. de,** next to; **de lado,** aside; **por um/outro l.,** on the one/other hand.
ladrão, -dra, 1. *adj.* thieving. **2.** *n.* thief.
ladrar, *vb.* bark, yelp. **—ladrido,** *n.m.*
ladrilho, *n.m.* tile.

ladroeira, -oíce, *n.f.* theft, thievery.
lagarta, *n.f.* caterpillar.
lagartixa, *n.f.* small lizard.
lagarto, *n.m.* lizard.
lago, *n.m.* lake.
lagoa, *n.f.* lagoon; lake.
lagosta, *n.f.* lobster.
lagostim, *n.m.* crawfish.
lágrima, *n.f.* tear.
lagrimejar, *vb.* shed tears; water (eyes).
laia, *n.f.* sort, ilk.
laico, *adj.* lay, secular.
laivo, *n.m.* stain; trace.
laje, *n.f.* flagstone; slab.
lajedo, *n.m.* paved floor.
lama, *n.f.* mud.
lamaçal, *n.m.* bog, mire.
lamacento, *adj.* muddy.
lambada, *n.f.* lashing; swig; popular dance.
lambedor -ra, 1. *adj.* licking; *(coll.)* bootlicking. **2.** *n.* licker; *(coll.)* bootlicker.
lambe-lambe, *n.m.* *(coll.)* sidewalk photographer.
lamber, *vb.* lick.
lambido, *adj.* affected.
lambiscar, *vb.* snack; nibble.
lambisgóia, *n.f.* busybody.
lambreta, *n.f.* motor scooter.
lambris, *n.m.* wainscot.
lambujem, *n.f.* tidbits; small profit. **de l.,** to boot.
lambuzar, *vb.* smear, dirty.
lameiro, *n.m.* swamp.
lamentar, *vb.* lament, regret. **—lamento,** *n.m.*
lâmina, *n.f.* blade; slide.
laminar, *vb.* laminate.
lâmpada, *n.f.* lamp; light bulb; lantern.
lampeiro, *adj.* cheerful, lively.
lampejar, *vb.* flash. **—lampejo,** *n.m.*
lampião, *n.m.* lantern; street lamp.
lamúria, *n.f.* lament. **—lamuriar,** *vb.*
lança, *n.f.* lance, spear. **quebrar lanças por,** stand up for.
lança-chamas, *n.m.* flamethrower.
lançador -ra, *n.* bidder.
lançamento, *n.m.* throw; launch; introduction. **plata-**

forma/rampa de l., launching pad.

lança-perfume, *n.m.* Carnival perfume squirter.

lançar, *vb.* throw; launch; introduce; bid. **l. mão de**, take hold of.

lance, *n.m.* throwing; risk; happening; play; situation; bid. **l. de olhos**, glance.

lanceiro, *n.m.* lancer.

lanceta, *n.f.* lancet.

lancha, *n.f.* motor boat; *(sl.)* big foot/shoe.

lanche, *n.m.* snack. **—lanchar**, *vb.*

lanchonete, *n.f.* luncheonette.

lancinar, *vb.* pierce; torment.

lanço, *n.m.* throw; gush; bid; flight (stairs).

languescer, *vb.* languish.

languidez, *n.f.* languor.

lânguido, *adj.* languid.

lanhar, *vb.* slash; wound. **—lanho**, *n.m.*

lanterna, *n.f.* lantern; flashlight.

lanugem, *n.f.* fuzz.

lapa, *n.f.* grotto.

lapela, *n.f.* lapel.

lapidar, **1.** *adj.* lapidary; concise. **2.** *vb.* lapidate; cut and polish.

lápis, *n.m.* pencil. **l. de sobrancelha**, eyebrow pencil.

lapiseira, *n.f.* pencil box; mechanical pencil.

lapso, *n.m.* lapse, slip.

lar, *n.m.* home, hearth.

laranja, *n.f.* orange.

laranjada, *n.f.* orangeade.

laranjeira, *n.f.* orange tree.

larápio -pia, *n.* pilferer.

lareira, *n.f.* hearth.

larga, *n.f.* loosening; largesse; **à l.**, loose; comfortably; **dar largas a**, give free rein to.

largar, *vb.* let go; abandon; leave.

largo, *adj.* wide, broad; vast. **ao l. de**, far from.

largueza, *n.f.* width; generosity; ease.

largura, *n.f.* width.

laringe, *n.m./f.* larynx.

laringite, *n.f.* laryngitis.

las, *form of dir. obj. pron.* **as** *after vb. ending in* **r**, **s**, *or* **z**.

lasanha, *n.f.* lasagna.

lasca, *n.f.* chip, sliver.

lascado, *adj. (coll.)* fast.

lascar, *vb.* chip; split. **ser de l.**, *(sl.)* be murder.

lascívia, *n.f.* lasciviousness.

lascivo, *adj.* lascivious.

lassidão, *n.f.* lassitude.

lasso, *adj.* lax; tired.

lástima, *n.f.* pity.

lastimar, *vb.* regret; grieve; pity. **l.-se**, complain.

lastimoso, *adj.* lamentable; plaintive.

lastro, *n.m.* ballast; base.

lata, *n.f.* tin can, can; *(sl.)* face.

latagão -gona, *n.* husky person.

latão, *n.m.* brass.

látego, *n.m.* whip.

latejar, *vb.* throb. **—latejo**, *n.m.*

latente, *adj.* latent.

lateral, *adj.* lateral.

látex, *n.m.* latex.

latifúndio, *n.m.* large landed estate.

latim, *n.m.* Latin. **perder o seu l.**, waste one's breath.

latino, *adj.* Latin.

latino-americano -na, *adj., n.* Latin American.

latir, *vb.* bark. **—latido**, *n.m.*

latitude, *n.f.* latitude.

lato, *adj.* broad, vast.

latrina, *n.f.* latrine.

latrocínio, *n.m.* armed robbery.

lauda, *n.f.* page.

laudatório, *adj.* laudatory.

laureado, *adj.* laureate.

lauto, *adj.* lavish.

lavabo, *n.m.* washbasin.

lavadeira, -vandeira, *n.f.* laundress.

lavadora, *n.f.* washing machine.

lavagem, *n.f.* washing; enema. **l. a seco**, dry cleaning; **l. cerebral**, brainwashing.

lavanderia, *n.f.* laundry.

lavar, *vb.* wash. **l.-se**, wash oneself.

lavatório, *n.m.* lavatory.

lavoura, *n.f.* farming.

lavra, *n.f.* farming; mine.

lavradio, 1. *adj.* arable. **2.** *n.m.* farming.

lavrador -ra, *n.* farmer, peasant.

lavrar, *vb.* till; carve; draft; embroider; explore.

laxante, laxativo, *n.m.* laxative.

lazareto, *n.m.* leper hospital.

lazer, *n.m.* leisure.

leal, *adj.* loyal; honest.

lealdade, *n.f.* loyalty.

leão, *n.m.* lion. **l. de chácara,** bouncer.

lebre, *n.f.* hare.

lecionar, *vb.* teach.

ledo, *adj.* cheerful.

legação, *n.f.* legation.

legado, *n.m.* legate.

legal, *adj.* legal; *(sl.)* terrific.

legalizar, *vb.* legalize.

legar, *vb.* bequeath.

legenda, *n.f.* inscription; subtitle; legend.

legião, *n.f.* legion.

legislação, *n.f.* legislation.

legislador -ra, *n.* legislator.

legislar, *vb.* legislate.

legislativo, *adj.* legislative.

legislatura, *n.f.* legislature.

legitimidade, *n.f.* legitimacy.

legitimar, *vb.* legitimate.— **legítimo,** *adj.* legitimate.

legível, *adj.* legible.

légua, *n.f.* league (distance).

legume, *n.m.* legume, vegetable.

lei, *n.f.* law.

leiaute, *n.m.* layout.

leigo -ga, 1. *adj.* lay. **2.** *n.* layman.

leilão, *n.m.* auction. —**leiloar,** *vb.*

leiloeiro -ra, *n.* auctioneer.

leitão -toa, *n.* suckling pig.

leite, *n.m.* milk. **l. condensado,** condensed milk; **l. de magnésia,** milk of magnesia; **l. em pó,** powdered milk; **l. evaporado,** evaporated milk; **l. desnatado/ magro,** skim milk.

leiteira, *n.f.* milkmaid; creamer.

leiteiro, *n.m.* milkman.

leiteria, *n.f.* dairy.

leito, *n.m.* bed.

leitor -ra, *n.* reader.

leitoso, *adj.* milky.

leitura, *n.f.* reading.

lema, *n.m.* motto.

lembrança, *n.f.* remembrance; souvenir; *(pl.)* regards.

lembrar, *vb.* remember; remind.

lembrete, *n.m.* memo.

leme, *n.m.* helm.

lenço, *n.m.* handkerchief. **l. de papel,** facial tissue.

lençol, *n.m.* sheet; water table. **em maus lençóis,** in a jam.

lenda, *n.f.* legend.

lendário, *adj.* legendary.

lengalenga, *n.f.* monotonous story.

lenha, *n.f.* firewood, wood; *(coll.)* beating; *(sl.)* murder.

lenhador -ra, *n.* woodcutter.

lenho, *n.m.* log.

lenocínio, *n.m.* pandering.

lente, *n.f.* lens; *n.m.f.* professor, teacher. **l. de contato,** contact lens.

lentejoula, *n.f.* sequin.

lentidão, *n.f.* slowness.

lentilha, *n.f.* lentil.

lento, *adj.* slow.

leoa, *n.f.* lioness.

leopardo, *n.m.* leopard.

lépido, *n.m.* cheerful; joking; agile.

lepra, *n.f.* leprosy.

leproso -sa, 1. *adj.* leprous. **2.** *n.* leper.

leque, *n.m.* fan.

ler, *vb.* read.

lerdo, *adj.* heavy; stupid.

léria, *n.f.* *(coll.)* hooey.

lero-lero, *n.m.* *(sl.)* idle talk.

lesão, *n.f.* lesion; hurt.

lesar, *vb.* injure; damage; spout nonsense.

lésbica, *adj., n.f.* lesbian.

lesco-lesco, *n.m.* *(sl.)* daily grind.

leseira, *n.f.* laziness; foolishness.

lesma, *n.f.* *(zool.)* slug; *(sl.)* slowpoke.

leso, *adj.* crazy.

leste, *n.m.* east.

letal, *adj.* lethal.

letargia, *n.f.* lethargy.

letárgico, *adj.* lethargic.

letargo, *n.m.* lethargy.

letivo, *adj.* scholastic, academic.

letra, *n.f.* letter; type; lyrics; (*pl.*) literature. **l. de fôrma** or **de imprensa,** block letter; **l. maiúscula/minúscula,** capital/small letter.

letrado -da, 1. *adj.* learned. **2.** *n.* scholar; lawyer.

letreiro, *n.m.* sign; label; caption.

léu, *n.m.* opportunity. **ao l.,** aimlessly; at random; bare.

leucemia, *n.f.* leukemia.

leva, *n.f.* recruitment; group.

levadiço, *adj.* liftable. **ponte levadiça,** drawbridge.

levado, *adj.* naughty, mischievous.

levantamento, *n.m.* raising; survey; uprising.

levantar, *vb.* raise; incite; collect; recruit; arise. **l.-se,** rise; revolt.

levante, *n.m.* uprising; east.

levar, *vb.* carry, take, take away; lead; use; have; spend. **l. a,** cause to; lead to; **l. a mal,** take amiss; **l. em conta,** take into account.

leve, *adj.* light.

lêvedo, *n.m.* yeast.

leveza, *n.f.* lightness.

leviano, *adj.* frivolous.

léxico, *n.m.* lexicon.

lha, *contr. of* **lhe(s) + a.**

lhama, *n.m.* llama.

lhaneza, *n.f.* candor.

lhano, *adj.* candid; friendly.

lhas, *contr. of* **lhe(s) + as.**

lhe, *indir. obj. pron.* to you (*s.*), to him, to her, to it.

lhes, *indir. obj. pron.* to you (*pl.*), to them.

lho, *contr. of* **lhe(s) + o.**

lhos, *contr. of* **lhe(s) + os.**

liame, *n.m.* bond, tie.

liana, *n.f.* liana (vine).

libanês -nesa, *adj., n.* Lebanese.

Líbano, *n.m.* Lebanon.

libelo, *n.m.* opening statement; accusation.

libélula, *n.f.* dragonfly.

liberação, *n.f.* liberation.

liberal, *adj., n.m.f.* liberal.

liberar, *vb.* liberate.

liberdade, *n.f.* freedom, liberty.

libertação, *n.f.* liberation.

libertar, *vb.* liberate, free.

libertinagem, *n.f.* libertinage.

libertino -na, *adj., n.* libertine.

liberto -ta, 1. *adj.* freed. **2.** *n.* freedman -woman.

Líbia, *n.f.* Libya.

libido, *n.f.* libido.

libra, *n.f.* pound; (*cap.*) Libra. **l. esterlina,** pound sterling.

lição, *n.f.* lesson.

licença, *n.f.* license, permission; permit; leave. **com l.?** or **dá l.?,** excuse me.

licenciado -da, *n.* licentiate.

licenciar, *vb.* license; furlough. **l.-se,** take a leave; get a licentiate degree.

licenciatura, *n.f.* licentiate degree.

licencioso, *adj.* licentious.

liceu, *n.m.* lycée.

lícito, *adj.* licit, legal.

licor, *n.m.* liqueur.

lida, *n.f.* chore; (*coll.*) reading.

lidar, *vb.* fight; toil; cope.

lide, *n.f.* chore; conflict.

líder, *n.m.f.* leader.

liderança, *n.f.* leadership.

liderar, *vb.* lead.

lídimo, *adj.* legitimate.

lido, *adj.* well-read.

liga, *n.f.* league; alloy; garter.

ligação, *n.f.* connection, liaison.

ligadura, *n.f.* bandage; ligature.

ligar, *vb.* tie, connect. **l. para,** (*coll.*) phone; care about; **não l. para,** (*coll.*) ignore.

ligeiro, *adj.* light; fast.

lilás, *n.m.* lilac.

lima, *n.f.* file (tool); lime.

limão, *n.m.* lemon.

limar, *vb.* file; polish.

limeira, *n.f.* lime tree.

limiar, *n.m.* threshold.

limitação, *n.f.* limitation.

limite, *n.m.* limit. —**limitar,** *vb.*

limo, *n.m.* slime; moss.

limoeiro, *n.m.* lemon tree.

limonada, *n.f.* lemonade.

limpa, *n.f.* cleaning.

limpar, *vb.* clean; rob, clean out.

limpeza, *n.f.* cleanliness; cleaning; robbery; (*sl.*) pennilessness.

límpido, *adj.* limpid, clear.

limpo, *adj.* clean; free; trustworthy; *(sl.)* broke. **tirar a l.,** clear up.

lince, *n.m.* lynx.

linchar, *vb.* lynch.

lindar, *vb.* border (on).

linde, *n.m.* border.

lindo, *adj.* pretty. **l. de morrer,** *(sl.)* simply gorgeous.

linear, -neal, *adj.* linear.

linfa, *n.f.* lymph.

lingote, *n.m.* ingot.

língua, *n.f.* tongue; language. **l. românica/neo-latina,** Romance language; **ter a l. comprida,** *(coll.)* be talkative.

linguado, *n.m.* sole, flounder.

linguagem, *n.f.* language.

linguajar, *n.m.* dialect.

linguarudo, *adj.* talkative.

lingüiça, *n.f.* sausage. **encher l.,** *(coll.)* beat around the bush.

lingüista, *n.m.f.* linguist.

lingüística, *n.f.* linguistics.

linha, *n.f.* line; thread; decorum. **l. aérea,** airline; **l. dura,** hard line; **entrar na l.,** fall into line; **sair da l.,** step out of line.

linha-dura, *adj.* hard-line.

linhagem, *n.f.* lineage.

linho, *n.m.* flax; linen.

linóleo, *n.m.* linoleum.

liqüidação, *n.f.* liquidation; sale.

liqüidar, *vb.* liquidate, settle; sell off; kill.

liqüidificador, *n.m.* blender.

líqüido, **1.** *adj.* liquid; net. **2.** *n.m.* liquid.

lira, *n.f.* lyre; lira.

lírica, *n.f.* lyric poetry.

lírico, *adj.* lyrical; operatic.

lírio, *n.m.* lily.

lirismo, *n.m.* lyricism.

Lisboa, *n.* Lisbon.

lisboeta, **1.** *adj.* pert. to Lisbon. **2.** *n.m.f.* native of Lisbon.

liso, *adj.* smooth; straight (hair); *(sl.)* broke.

lisonja, *n.f.* flattery.

lisonjear, *vb.* flatter.

lista, *n.f.* list; stripe. **l. telefônica,** phone directory.

listão, *n.m.* political blacklist.

listra, *n.f.* stripe.

listrado, *adj.* striped.

litania, *n.f.* litany.

liteira, *n.f.* litter.

literal, *adj.* literal.

literário, *adj.* literary.

literato -ta, *n.* man/woman of letters.

literatura, *n.f.* literature. **l. de cordel,** chapbook poetry.

litígio, *n.m.* lawsuit, litigation.

litoral, **1.** *adj.* coastal. **2.** *n.m.* coast, seaboard.

litorâneo, *adj.* coastal.

litorina, *n.f.* self-propelled railroad car.

litro, *n.m.* liter.

liturgia, *n.f.* liturgy.

lívido, *adj.* livid.

living, *n.m.* living room.

livrar, *vb.* free; deliver; save. **l.-se,** get rid (of); escape.

livraria, *n.f.* bookstore.

livre, *adj.* free. **amor l.,** free love; **ao ar l.,** open-air; **luta l.,** wrestling.

livreiro -ra, *n.* bookseller.

livro, *n.m.* book. **l. brochado,** paperback; **l. de bolso,** pocket book; **l. de cabeceira,** favorite book; **l. de ponto,** timecard.

lixa, *n.f.* sandpaper. —**lixar,** *vb.*

lixadeira, *n.f.* sander.

lixeira, *n.f.* trash heap.

lixeiro, *n.m.* trash collector.

lixívia, *n.f.* lye.

lixo, *n.m.* trash, garbage.

lo, *form of dir. obj. pron.* **o** *after vb. ending in* r, s, *or* z.

loa, *n.f.* praise.

lobisomem, *n.m.* werewolf.

lobo, *n.m.* lobe.

lobo, *n.m.* wolf.

lôbrego, *adj.* dark, gloomy.

lóbulo, *n.m.* lobe.

loca, *n.f.* cave, den.

locador -ra, *n.* lessor.

locadora, *n.f.* rental agency.

local, **1.** *adj.* local. **2.** *n.m.* place, locale.

localidade, *n.f.* locality.

localização, *n.f.* localization; location.

localizar, *vb.* localize; locate.

loção, *n.f.* lotion.

locatário -ria, *n.* lessee, renter.

locomotiva, *n.f.* locomotive.

locução, *n.f.* expression.

locutor -ra, *n.* radio/TV announcer.

lodo, *n.m.* mud.

logaritmo, *n.m.* logarithm.

lógica, *n.f.* logic.

lógico, *adj.* logical.

logístico, *adj.* logistical.

logo, 1. *adv.* right away; soon; later, afterward; right. **até l!** so long!; **l. mais,** soon. **2.** *conj.* therefore. **l. que,** as soon as.

logradouro, *n.m.* public place.

lograr, *vb.* dupe; attain, get to.

logro, *n.m.* deception.

loja, *n.f.* store, shop; lodge.

lojista, *n.m.f.* shopkeeper.

lomba, *n.f.* ridge.

lombo, *n.f.* loin, sirloin; back.

lombriga, *n.f.* worm.

lona, *n.f.* canvas.

Londres, *n.* London.

longe, *adv.* far. **ao l.,** far away. **de l. em l.,** once in a great while.

longevidade, *n.f.* longevity.

longínquo, *adj.* remote, distant.

longitude, *n.f.* longitude.

longo, *adj.* long. **ao l. de,** all along.

lontra, *n.f.* otter.

loquaz, *adj.* loquacious.

lorde, *n.m.* lord, noble.

lorota, *n.f. (coll.)* lie, fib.

los, *form of dir. obj. pron.* **os** *after vb. ending in* **r, s,** *or* **z.**

losango, *n.m.* lozenge, diamond.

lotação, *n.f.* capacity; *n.f.m.* small bus.

lotado, *adj.* full, crowded.

lotar, *vb.* fill up.

lote, *n.m.* lot.

lotear, *vb.* parcel out.

loteria, *n.f.* lottery.

loto, *n.m.* lotus.

louca, *n.f.* **dar a l,** *(sl.)* go haywire.

louça, *n.f.* china, dishes.

loução -çã, *adj.* fresh; elegant.

louco -ca, 1. *adj.* crazy; extraordinary. **l. por,** *(coll.)* crazy about. **2.** *n.* madman -woman.

loucura, *n.f.* insanity; *(coll.)* sensation.

louro, 1. *adj.* blond. **2.** *n.m.* laurel, bay.

lousa, *n.f.* slate, blackboard.

louvaminhar, *vb.* flatter.

louvar, *vb.* praise. **—louvação,** *n.f.,* **louvor,** *n.m.*

lua, *n.f.* moon; mood.

lua-de-mel, *n.f.* honeymoon.

luar, *n.m.* moonlight.

lúbrico, *adj.* lecherous.

lubrificante, *n.m.* lubricant.

lubrificar, *vb.* lubricate.

lúcido, *adj.* lucid.

lucrativo, *adj.* lucrative.

lucro, *n.m.* profit. **—lucrar,** *vb.*

ludibriar, *vb.* deceive; mock.

lúdico, *adj.* playful.

lufada, *n.f.* gust.

lufa-lufa, *n.f. (coll.)* bustle.

lugar, *n.m.* place. **dar l. a,** give rise to; **em l. de,** instead of.

lugar-comum, *n.m.* commonplace.

lugarejo, *n.m.* village.

lúgubre, *adj.* gloomy; dismal.

lula, *n.f.* squid.

lume, *n.m.* fire; light.

luminar, *n.m.* luminary.

luminoso, 1. *adj.* luminous. **2.** *n.m.* neon sign.

lunar, *adj.* lunar.

lunático, *adj., n.m.* lunatic.

lundu, *n.m.* African dance; peevishness.

luneta, *n.f.* eyeglass.

lupa, *n.f.* magnifying glass.

lupanar, *n.m.* brothel.

lúrido, *adj.* pale; dark.

lusco-fusco, *n.m.* dusk.

lusitano -na, *adj., n.* Portuguese.

luso-brasileiro -ra, *adj.* Luso-Brazilian, Portuguese-Brazilian.

lustrar, *vb.* polish, shine.

lustre, *n.m.* luster; glory; chandelier.

lustro, *n.m.* luster; five-year period.

lustroso, *adj.* shiny.

luta, *n.f.* struggle, fight; work. **—lutar,** *vb.*

lutador -ra, *n.* fighter.

luterano -na, *adj., n.* Lutheran.

luto, *n.m.* mourning.

luva, *n.f.* glove; *(pl.)* premium payment.

luxento, *adj.* prissy.

luxo, *n.m.* luxury; *(coll.)* fussiness. **de l.,** de luxe.

luxuoso, *adj.* luxurious.

luxúria, *n.f.* lust.

luz, *n.f.* light; *(pl.)* knowledge.

à l. de, in light of ; dar à l., give birth to; ver a l., be born; vir à l., come to light.

luzido, adj. bright; showy.

luzir, vb. shine; excel.

M

ma, contr. of me + a.

má, adj. f.s. bad, evil.

maca, n.f. stretcher.

maça, n.f. mace, club.

maçã, n.f. apple.

macabro, adj. macabre.

macaca, n.f. monkey (f.); bad luck. **m. de auditório,** (sl.) groupie.

macacão, n.m. overalls.

macaco -ca, n. monkey; n.m. jack. **vá pentear macacos!,** go fly a kite!

maçada, n.f. annoyance.

macambúzio, adj. sad.

maçaneta, n.f. knob.

maçante, adj. annoying.

macaquear, vb. ape, mimic.

macaquice, n.f. mimicry, clowning.

macaquinho, n.m. small monkey. **ter macaquinhos no sótão,** have bats in one's belfry.

maçar, vb. hammer; annoy.

macaréu, n.m. tidal bore.

maçarico, n.m. blowtorch.

maçaroca, n.f. ear of corn.

macarrão, n.m. macaroni; noodles.

Macau, n.m. Macao.

macaxeira, n.f. kind of manioc.

macete, n.m. small mallet; (sl.) trick, key.

machado, n.m. ax.

machão, n.m. (sl.) he-man.

machete, n.m. machete.

machismo, n.m. male chauvinism.

machista, adj., n.m. male chauvinist.

macho, 1. adj. male, masculine. **2.** n.m. male, man.

machucar, vb. hurt; crush. **m.-se,** get hurt.

maciço, 1. adj. massive, solid. **2.** n.m. massif; dense woods.

macieira, n.f. apple tree.

maciez, n.f. softness.

macilento, adj. gaunt.

macio, adj. soft.

maciota, n.f. **na m.,** easily.

maço, n.m. mallet; mace; pile; pack.

maçom -ção, n.m. Mason.

maconha, n.f. marijuana.

maconheiro -ra, n. marijuana smoker.

maçônico, adj. Masonic.

má-criação, n.f. rudeness.

macróbio -bia, n. oldster.

maçudo, adj. heavy; boring.

macular, vb. stain.

macumba, n.f. an Afro-Brazilian religion.

macumbeiro -ra, n. Afro-Brazilian priest -ess.

madeira, n.f. wood; (pl., mus.) woodwinds. **m. compensada,** plywood.

madeiramento, n.m. woodwork.

madeiro, n.m. log, beam.

madeixa, n.f. tress, lock; skein.

madrasta, n.f. stepmother.

madre, n.f. nun; mother superior; uterus.

madrepérola, n.f. mother-of-pearl.

madressilva, n.f. honeysuckle.

Madri, n. Madrid.

madrigal, n.m. madrigal.

madrinha, n.f. godmother; maid of honor.

madrugada, n.f. early morning.

madrugar, vb. get up early.

madurar, vb. ripen, mature.

madureza, n.f. ripeness, maturity.

maduro, adj. ripe; mature.

mãe, 1. n.f. mother. **2.** adj. (sl.) tremendous.

mãe-de-santo, n.f. Afro-Brazilian priestess.

maestro, n.m. maestro, conductor.

má-fé, n.f. bad faith.

magazine, n.m. department store.

magia, n.f. magic. **m. negra,** black magic.

mágico, 1. adj. magic. **2.** n.m. magician.

magistério, n.m. teaching; teachers.

magistrado, n.m. magistrate.

magistral, *adj.* masterly, excellent.

magnânimo, *adj.* magnanimous.

magnata, *n.m.* magnate.

magnésio, *n.m.* magnesium.

magnético, *adj.* magnetic.

magnetizar, *vb.* magnetize; attract.

magnificar, *vb.* magnify.

magnificência, *n.f.* magnificence.

magnífico, *adj.* magnificent.

magnitude, *n.f.* magnitude.

magno, *adj.* great.

mago, *n.m.* magician; *(cap., pl.)* Magi.

mágoa, *n.f.* bruise; sorrow.

magoar, *vb.* hurt, grieve.

magote, *n.m.* group; pile.

magricela, 1. *adj.* skinny. **2.** *n.m.f.* skinny person.

magro, *adj.* thin, skinny; meager.

maia, *adj.* , *n.m.f.* Maya.

maio, *n.m.* May.

maiô, *n.m.* women's bathing suit.

maionese, *n.f.* mayonnaise; salad.

maior, *adj.* bigger, biggest; major; adult.

maioral, *n.m.* head, leader.

maioria, *n.f.* majority, most.

maioridade, *n.f.* age of majority.

mais, 1. *adj.* more, most; so; else; plus. **2.** *adv.* more, most; any more. **a m.**, extra; **m. ou menos,** more or less; so-so.

maisena, *n.f.* cornstarch.

mais-que-perfeito, *adj.* , *n.m.* pluperfect.

maiúsculo, *adj.* capital (letter).

majestade, *n.f.* majesty.

majestoso, *adj.* majestic.

major, *n.m.* major (rank).

majoração, *n.f.* increase. —**majorar,** *vb.*

majoritário, *adj.* majority.

mal, 1. *n.m.* evil; harm; woe; sickness. **2.** *adv.* badly; hardly; ill. **de m.**, on bad terms; **não faz m.**, it doesn't matter. **3.** *conj.* as soon as.

mala, *n.f.* suitcase; bag; mail.

malabarismo, *n.m.* juggling.

malabarista, *n.m.f.* juggler.

mal-acabado, *adj.* badly finished; odd-looking.

malagueta, *n.f.* hot red pepper.

malandro, *n.m.* bum, rogue, trickster.

mal-assombrado, *adj.* haunted.

mal-aventurado, *adj.* unlucky.

malbaratar, *vb.* sell cheaply; waste.

malcheiroso, *adj.* smelly.

mal-comportado, *adj.* badly behaved.

malcontente, *adj.* discontented.

malcriado, *adj.* rude; ill-mannered.

maldade, *n.f.* evil.

maldição, *n.f.* curse.

maldito, *adj.* cursed, damned.

maldizente, 1. *adj.* defaming. **2.** *n.m.* defamer.

maldizer, *vb.* defame; curse.

mal-educado, *adj.* ill-mannered, impolite.

maléfico, *adj.* evil, harmful.

mal-entendido, *n.m.* misunderstanding.

mal-estar, *n.m.* indisposition; discomfort.

maleta, *n.f.* handbag, attaché case.

malevolente, *adj.* malevolent.

malfadado, *adj.* ill-fated, unlucky.

malfeito, *adj.* badly done; wrong.

malfeitor, *n.m.* malefactor.

malgastar, *vb.* waste, squander.

malgrado, *prep.* despite.

malha, *n.f.* mesh, knitwear; mail; stitch.

malhado, *adj.* spotted, speckled.

malhar, *vb.* hammer, beat; backbite.

malharia, *n.f.* knitwear mill.

malho, *n.m.* (sledge) hammer.

mal-humorado, *adj.* ill-humored.

malícia, *n.f.* malice; mischief; craft.

malicioso, *adj.* mischievous; sly.

maligno, *adj.* malignant; harmful.

má-língua, *n.m.f.* gossiper.

maloca, *n.f.* Indian hut or village; hideout; gang.

malograr, *vb.* fail; spoil.

malogro, *n.m.* failure.

malote, *n.m.* mailbag, mailpouch.

malquerer, *vb.* wish ill.

malquisto, *adj.* disliked, hated.

malta, *n.f.* group, gang.

maltrapilho, 1. *adj.* ragged. **2.** *n.m.* ragamuffin.

maltratar, *vb.* mistreat, abuse; spoil.

maluco, *adj.* crazy.

maluquice, *n.f.* insanity.

malvado, *adj.* mean, evil.

malversar, *vb.* mismanage; embezzle.

mama, *n.f.* breast.

mamadeira, *n.f.* baby bottle.

mamãe, *n.f.* mama, mom. **a m.,** *(sl.)* I, me (f.).

mamão, *n.m.* papaya.

mamar, *vb.* suckle; suck. **dar de m. a,** breast-feed.

mamata, *n.f. (sl.)* public corruption, racket.

mambembe, *adj. (sl.)* seedy, two-bit.

mameluco -ca, *n. (hist.)* mestizo.

mamífero, *n.m.* mammal.

mamilo, *n.m.* nipple; breast.

maminha, *n.f.* nipple; male breast.

mamona, *n.f.* castor bean.

mana, *n.f. (coll.)* sister.

manada, *n.f.* herd, flock.

manancial, *n.m.* fountain, spring.

manar, *vb.* flow, spring, emanate.

mancada, *n.f. (coll.)* blunder.

mancar, *vb.* cripple; limp; renege.

mancar-se, *vb.* go lame; *(sl.)* get wise.

manceba, *n.f.* concubine, mistress.

mancebia, *n.f.* concubinage.

mancebo, *n.m.* lad; servant.

mancha, *n.f.* stain, spot. **—manchar,** *vb.*

manchete, *n.f.* headline.

manco, *adj.* cripple, lame.

mancomunar, *vb.* collude.

mandachuva, *n.m. (coll.)* boss, bigshot.

mandado, *n.m.* order, decree; errand.

mandamento, *n.m.* commandment.

mandão -dona, *adj.* bossy.

mandar, *vb.* order, command, rule; send. **m. dizer,** send word; **m. fazer,** have made; **que é que você manda?,** how can I help you?

mandatário, *n.m.* agent, representative.

mandato, *n.m.* mandate.

mandíbula, *n.f.* mandible, jaw.

mandinga, *n.f.* sorcery.

mandioca, *n.f.* manioc, cassava.

mando, *n.m.* command, power.

mandrião, *adj.* lazy.

manducar, *vb.* chew; eat.

mané, *n.m.* fool.

maneira, *n.f.* manner; *(pl.)* manners. **à m. de,** in the manner of; **de m. nenhuma!,** by no means! **de m. que,** so as to; **de qualquer m.,** anyway.

maneirar, *vb. (sl.)* get by; simmer down.

maneiro, *adj.* handy, easy; agile; *(sl.)* terrific.

maneiroso, *adj.* polite, mannerly.

manejar, *vb.* handle, control. **—manejo,** *n.m.*

manequim, *n.m.f.* mannequin, model.

manga, *n.f.* sleeve; mango. **botar as mangas de fora,** let one's hair down.

manganês, *n.m.* manganese.

mangar, *vb.* mock, make fun (of).

mangue, *n.m.* mangrove; *(sl.)* red-light district; mess.

mangueira, *n.f.* hose; mango tree.

manha, *n.f.* skill; cunning; bad habit; whining.

manhã, *n.f.* morning. **de m.,** in the morning.

manhãzinha, *n.f.* early morning.

manhoso, *adj.* skillful; sly; whiny.

mania, *n.f.* mania; idiosyncrasy; hobby.

maníaco, 1. *adj.* maniacal. **2.** *n.m.* maniac.

maniatar, *vb.* tie the hands of; restrain.

manicômio, *n.m.* insane asylum.

manicur- -ra, *n.* manicurist.

manifestação, *n.f.* manifestation; public demonstration.

manifestante, *n.m.f.* demonstrator.

manifestar, *vb.* manifest; declare; demonstrate. **m.-se,** be manifest.

manifesto, *n.m.* manifesto; manifest.

manilha, *n.f.* bracelet, anklet; shackle.

manipular, *vb.* manipulate.

manivela, *n.f.* crank, handle.

manjar, 1. *n.m.* food; delicacy. **2.** *vb.* eat; *(sl.)* understand; *(sl.)* recognize.

manjedoura, *n.f.* manger, trough.

mano, *n.m.* *(coll.)* brother.

manobra, *n.f.* maneuver. —**manobrar,** *vb.*

manobrista, *n.m.f.* parking valet.

manopla, *n.f.* gauntlet.

manquejar, *vb.* limp.

mansão, *n.f.* mansion.

mansidão, *n.f.* tameness, gentleness.

mansinho, *adj.* **de m.,** *(coll.)* on the sly.

manso, *adj.* tame, meek, gentle.

manta, *n.f.* blanket; shawl; kerchief; school (fish).

manteiga, *n.f.* butter.

manteigueira, *n.f.* butter dish.

mantel, *n.m.* tablecloth.

manter, *vb.* maintain.

manteúdo, *adj.* kept; supported.

mantimento, *n.m.* sustenance; *(pl.)* foodstuffs.

manto, *n.m.* cape, cloak; mantle.

manual, 1. *adj.* manual. **2.** *n.m.* handbook, manual.

manufatura, *n.f.* manufacture. —**manufaturar,** *vb.*

manuscrito, *n.m.* manuscript.

manusear, *vb.* handle, thumb, finger.

manuseio, *n.m.* handling.

manutenção, *n.f.* maintenance.

mão, *n.f.* hand; coat (paint); direction. **m. de ferro,** iron hand; **m. única/dupla,** one/two way traffic; **abrir m. de,** give up; **à m.,** by hand; at hand; **dar uma m. a,** help; **de m. cheia,** firstrate; **de segunda m.,** secondhand; **meter a m. em,** hit.

mão-de-obra, *n.f.* labor; manpower; labor force.

maometano -na, *adj., n.* Muslim.

mapa, *n.m.* map.

mapa-múndi, *n.m.* world map.

maqueta, *n.f.* scale model.

maquiagem, -quilagem, *n.f.* makeup, cosmetics.

maquiar-se, -quilar-se, *vb.* put on makeup.

máquina, *n.f.* machine; *(coll.)* camera. **m. de costura,** sewing machine; **m. de escrever,** typewriter; **m. de lavar,** washing machine; **m. de lavar pratos,** dishwasher; **m. fotográfica,** camera.

maquinar, *vb.* machinate; plot.

maquinaria, -nária, *n.f.* machinery.

maquinista, *n.m.f.* machinist; train engineer.

mar, *n.m.* sea. **fazer-se ao m.,** put to sea.

maracujá, *n.m.* passion fruit.

marajá, *n.m.* maharajah; double-dipper.

maranhense, 1. *adj.* of/pert. to the state of Maranhão. **2.** *n.m.f.* Maranhão native.

maratona, *n.f.* marathon.

maravilha, *n.f.* marvel, wonder. —**maravilhar-se,** *vb.*

maravilhoso, *adj.* marvelous, wonderful.

marca, *n.f.* mark; brand. **m. registrada,** registered trademark.

marcação, *n.f.* marking; scoring. **estar de m. com,** *(coll.)* pick on.

marcado, *adj.* marked, pronounced.

marcador, *n.m.* marker; scoreboard.

marcar, *vb.* mark; brand; score;

schedule. **m. um encontro,** make an appointment.

marceneiro, *n.m.* cabinet-maker.

marcha, *n.f.* march; gear. **m. à ré,** reverse gear.

marchante, *n.m.f.* cattle dealer.

marchar, *vb.* march.

marcial, *adj.* martial.

marciano -na, *adj., n.* Martian.

marco, *n.m.* marker, landmark; boundary; Deutsche mark.

março, *n.m.* March.

maré, *n.f.* tide; streak. **m. alta/baixa,** high/low tide.

mareado, *adj.* seasick.

marear, *vb.* steer a ship; make seasick.

marechal, *n.m. (mil.)* marshal.

marejar, *vb.* ooze out. **m.-se,** fill with tears.

maremoto, *n.m.* seaquake.

maresia, *n.f.* marshy smell.

marfim, *n.m.* ivory.

margarida, *n.f.* daisy.

margarina, *n.f.* margarine.

margear, *vb.* border, skirt.

margem, *n.f.* margin, edge, bank.

marginal, 1. *adj.* marginal. **2.** *n.m.f.* vagrant, derelict.

maricas, *n.m.* sissy, pantywaist.

marido, *n.m.* husband.

marimacho, *n.m.* mannish woman, tomboy.

marimbondo, *n.m.* wasp.

marinha, *n.f.* navy. **m. mercante,** merchant marine.

marinheiro, *n.m.* sailor.

marinho, *adj.* marine.

marionete, *n.f.* marionette.

mariposa, *n.f.* moth.

marisco, *n.m.* shellfish or mollusk; mussel.

marítimo, 1. *adj.* maritime. **2.** *n.m.* seaman.

marmanjo, *n.m.* man; grown boy.

marmelada, *n.f.* quince marmalade; *(sl.)* racket.

marmelo, *n.m.* quince.

marmita, *n.f.* lunch pail, mess kit.

mármore, *n.m.* marble. **—marmóreo,** *adj.*

marmota, *n.f.* ground hog.

marola, *n.f.* large wave.

maroto, *adj.* roguish, naughty.

marquês -quesa, *n.* marquis -quise.

marreco, *n.m.* teal.

marreta, *n.f.* sledge hammer.

marretar, *vb.* sledge, pound.

Marrocos, *n.m.* Morocco.

marrom, *adj.* brown.

marroquino -na, *adj., n.* Moroccan.

Marte, *n.m.* Mars.

martelo, *n.m.* hammer. **—martelar,** *vb.*

mártir, *n.m.f.* martyr.

martírio, *n.m.* martyrdom.

marujo, *n.m.* sailor.

marulho, *n.m.* tossing of the sea.

marxismo, *n.m.* Marxism.

marxista, *adj., n.m.f.* Marxist.

mas, 1. *conj.* but. **2.** *n.m.* problem, drawback. **3.** *contr. of* **me** + **as.**

mascar, *vb.* chew.

máscara, *n.f.* mask. **—mascarar,** *vb.*

mascarado -da, *n.* masquerader.

mascate, *n.m.* peddler.

mascavado, *adj.* brown, unrefined.

mascote, *n.m.* mascot.

masculinidade, *n.f.* masculinity.

masculino, *adj.* masculine, male.

másculo, *adj.* masculine.

masmorra, *n.f.* dungeon.

masoquismo, *n.m.* masochism.

má-sorte, *n.f.* bad luck.

massa, *n.f.* dough; pasta; mass; *(pl.)* masses; **m. cinzenta,** gray matter; **m. crítica,** critical mass; **cultura de m.,** mass culture.

massacre, *n.m.* massacre. **—massacrar,** *vb.*

massagem, *n.f.* massage. **—massagear,** *vb.*

massapé, *n.m.* rich, black soil.

mastigar, *vb.* chew.

mastim, *n.m.* mastiff.

mastro, *n.m.* mast.

masturbar-se, *vb.* masturbate.

mata, *n.f.* forest, jungle.

matador -ra, *n.* killer.

matadouro, *n.m.* slaughter-house.

matagal, *n.m.* thick forest.

matança, *n.f.* killing.

matar, *vb.* kill, murder; cut (classes). **m.-se**, commit suicide.

mate, *n.m.* maté; checkmate.

mateiro, *n.m.* woodsman.

matemática, *n.f.* mathematics.

matemático -ca, **1.** *adj.* mathematical. **2.** *n.* mathematician.

matéria, *n.f.* matter; subject; course. **em m. de**, as for.

material *adj.*, *n.m.* material.

materialismo, *n.m.* materialism.

matéria-prima, *n.f.* raw material.

maternal, *adj.* maternal.

maternidade, *n.f.* maternity; maternity hospital.

materno, *adj.* maternal.

matilha, *n.f.* pack, gang.

matinal, *adj.* morning.

matinê, *n.f.* matinee.

matiz, *n.m.* blend of colors; nuance, shade.

matizar, *vb.* blend or shade colors.

mato, *n.m.* brush; countryside. **estar no m. sem cachorro**, *(coll.)* be up the creek without a paddle; **ser m.**, *(coll.)* abound.

mato-grossense, **1.** *adj.* pert. to the state of Mato Grosso. **2.** *n.m.f.* Mato Grosso native.

mato-grossense-do-sul, **1.** *adj.* pert. to the state of Mato Grosso do Sul. **2.** *n.m.f.* Mato Grosso do Sul native.

matoso, *adj.* woody, brushy.

matraca, *n.f.* rattle.

matraquear, *vb.* rattle; chatter.

matreiro, *adj.* shrewd, sly.

matriarca, *n.f.* matriarch.

matrícula, *n.f.* enrollment.

matricular, *vb.* enroll. **m.-se**, enroll oneself.

matrimônio, *n.m.* matrimony.

matriz, **1.** *adj.* main. **2.** *n.f.* matrix; womb; mother church; head office.

matrona, *n.f.* matron.

maturidade, *n.f.* maturity.

matutar, *vb.* ponder, mull over.

matutino, **1.** *adj.* morning. **2.** *n.m.* morning paper.

matuto, *n.m.* hillbilly.

mau, má, *adj.* bad, evil.

mau-olhado, *n.m.* evil eye.

mausoléu, *n.m.* mausoleum.

mavioso, *adj.* sweet-sounding, soft.

maxila, *n.f.* maxilla, jawbone.

máxime, *adv.* mainly, especially.

máximo, *adj.*, *n.m.* maximum.

maxixe, *n.m.* a Brazilian ballroom dance.

mazanza, *adj.* lazy.

mazela, *n.f.* wound; illness; annoyance; blot.

mazorca, *n.f.* commotion.

me, **1.** *obj. pron.* me; to me. **2.** *reflex. pron.* myself.

meada, *n.f.* skein.

meados, *n.m.pl.* middle (of a month).

meão, -ã, *adj.* average, mean.

mecânica, *n.f.* mechanics.

mecânico, **1.** *adj.* mechanical. **2.** *n.m.* mechanic.

mecanismo, *n.m.* mechanism.

mecanizar, *vb.* mechanize.

mecha, *n.f.* wick.

medalha, *n.f.* medal.

medalhão, *n.m.* medallion.

média, *n.f.* average, mean; large café au lait.

mediação, *n.f.* mediation.

mediador -ra, *n.* mediator.

mediano, *adj.* median, medium.

mediante, **1.** *adj.* intervening. **2.** *prep.* by means of.

mediar, *vb.* mediate; halve; lie between; intervene.

medicamento, *n.m.* medicine, medication.

medicar, *vb.* medicate.

medicastro, *n.m.* quack doctor.

medicina, *n.f.* medicine (field).

médico -ca, **1.** *adj.* medical. **2.** *n.* doctor, physician.

medida, *n.f.* measure; measurment; extent. **à m. que**, as, while; **na m. em que**, to the extent that; **sob m.**, custom-made.

medidor, *n.m.* gauge, meter.

medieval, *adj.* medieval.

médio, *adj.* medium; middle.
  classe média, middle class;
  Idade Média, Middle Ages;
  Oriente Médio, Middle East.
mediocre, *adj.* mediocre.
medir, *vb.* measure. **m. as palavras**, weigh one's words.
meditabundo, *adj.* meditative.
meditação, *n.f.* meditation.
meditar, *vb.* meditate.
Mediterrâneo, *adj., n.m.* Mediterranean.
médium, *n.m.f.* medium (spiritualism).
medo, *n.m.* fear. **meter m.**, frighten; **ter m.**, be afraid.
medonho, *adj.* frightful, awful.
medrar, *vb.* grow; thrive.
medroso, *adj.* fearful, afraid.
medula, *n.f.* medulla; marrow; core.
medusa, *n.f.* jellyfish.
meeiro, 1. *adj.* halvable. 2. *n.m.* half-owner; sharecropper.
megafone, *n.m.* megaphone.
megera, *n.f.* shrew.
meia, *n.f.* sock, stocking.
meia-idade, *n.f.* middle age.
meia-noite, *n.f.* midnight.
meia-tigela, *n.f.* **de m.**, mediocre.
meigo, *adj.* loving, tender, affectionate.
meio, 1. *adj.* half, middle. 2. *adv.* half; somewhat. 3. *n.m.* middle, center; means; midst; environment. **no m. de**, in the midst of; **por m. de**, by means of.
meio-ambiente, *n.m.* environment.
meio-dia, *n.m.* noon, midday.
meio-fio, *n.m.* curb.
meio-termo, *n.m.* middle of the road.
meirinho, 1. *adj.* merino. 2. *n.m.* bailiff.
mel, *n.m.* honey; syrup.
melaço, *n.m.* molasses.
melado, 1. *adj.* sticky, gooey. 2. *n.m.* molasses.
melancia, *n.f.* watermelon.
melancolia, *n.f.* melancholy.
  —melancólico, *adj.*
melão, *n.m.* melon; honeydew.
melar, *vb.* honey-coat; become sticky; *(sl.)* fizzle.

meleca, *n.f. (sl.)* booger; junk.
melena, *n.f.* mop of hair.
melhor, *adj., adv.* better, best.
melhora, *n.f.* improvement.
melhoramento, *n.m.* improvement.
melhorar, *vb.* improve.
melhoria, *n.f.* improvement.
melindrar, *vb.* offend. **m.-se**, take offense.
melindre, *n.m.* delicacy; affectation; touchiness.
melindroso, *adj.* delicate; affected; touchy.
melodia, *n.f.* melody.
melódico, *adj.* melodic.
melodrama, *n.m.* melodrama.
melro, *n.m.* blackbird.
membrana, *n.f.* membrane.
membro, *n.m.* member; limb; *(coll.)* penis.
memento, *n.m.* memento; notebook.
memorando, *n.m.* memorandum, memo.
memória, *n.f.* memory *(also comput.)*; memoir. **m. de acesso aleatório**, random-access memory; **de m.**, by heart.
memorial, 1. *adj.* memorable. 2. *n.m.* memorial; notebook; memoir.
memorizar, *vb.* memorize; remember.
menção, *n.f.* mention.
mencionar, *vb.* mention.
mendigar, *vb.* beg.
mendigo -ga, *n.* beggar.
menear, *vb.* shake, wiggle.
  —meneio, *n.m.*
menestrel, *n.m.* minstrel.
menina, *n.f.* girl. **m. do olho**, pupil of the eye. **m. dos olhos**, apple of one's eye.
meninada, *n.f.* group of children.
meninice, *n.f.* childhood; childishness.
menino, *n.m.* boy; child.
meninote -ta, *n.* adolescent.
menopausa, *n.f.* menopause.
menor, 1. *adj.* smaller, smallest; minor; underage. 2. *n.m.f.* minor.
menoridade, *n.f.* minority (age).
menos, 1. *adj., adv.* less, least.

2. *prep.* minus; except. **a m. que**, unless; **muito m.** or **quanto m.**, let alone; **pelo m.**, at least.

menoscabar, *vb.* belittle; under-value; despise.

menosprezar, *vb.* disdain, scorn. **—menosprezo**, *n.m.*

mensageiro -ra, *n.* messenger.

mensagem, *n.f.* message.

mensal, *adj.* monthly.

mensalidade, *n.f.* monthly allowance or fee.

menstruação, *n.f.* menstruation.

menstruar, *vb.* menstruate.

mênstruo, *n.m.* menses.

menta, *n.f.* mint.

mental, *adj.* mental.

mentalidade, *n.f.* mentality.

mente, *adj.* mind. **em m.**, in mind.

mentecapto, *adj.* crazy.

mentir, *vb.* lie.

mentira, *n.f.* lie, falsehood. **m.! você're kidding!**

mentiroso, 1. *adj.* lying. **2.** *n.m.* liar.

mentol, *n.m.* menthol.

mentor -ra, *n.* mentor.

menu, *n.m.* menu.

mequetrefe, *n.m.* (coll.) meddler; scoundrel.

mercado, *n.m.* market. **m. negro/paralelo**, black market.

mercador, *n.m.* merchant.

mercadoria, *n.f.* merchandise.

mercancia, *n.f.* merchandise.

mercante, *adj.*, *n.m.f.* merchant.

mercantil, *adj.* mercantile.

mercar, *vb.* buy; buy and sell.

mercê, *n.f.* favor; mercy. **m. de**, thanks to; **à m. de**, at the mercy of.

mercearia, *n.f.* grocery store.

mercenário -ria, *adj.*, *n.* mercenary.

mercúrio, *n.m.* mercury.

merda, *n.f.* (vulg.) excrement.

merecedor -ra, *adj.* deserving.

merecer, *vb.* deserve, merit.

merenda, *n.f.* snack; picnic lunch; school lunch.

merendar, *vb.* eat a snack or school lunch.

merendeira, *n.f.* lunchbox, picnic basket.

merengue, *n.m.* meringue.

meretrício, *n.m.* prostitution.

meretriz, *n.f.* prostitute.

mergulhador -ra, *n.* diver.

mergulhar, *vb.* dive. **—mergulho**, *n.m.*

meridiano, *adj.*, *n.m.* meridian.

meridional, *adj.* meridional; southern.

mérito, *n.m.* merit, worth.

mero, *adj.* mere.

mês, *n.m.* month.

mesa, *n.f.* table; desk; board; mesa.

mesada, *n.f.* monthly allowance.

mesa-de-cabeceira, *n.f.* night table.

mesa-de-trabalho, *n.f.* desk.

mesa-redonda, *n.f.* round table.

mesclar, *vb.* mix. **—mescla**, *n.f.*

mesmice, *n.f.* sameness.

mesmo, 1. *adj.* same; self. **2.** *n.m.* same. **3.** *adv.* really, indeed; exactly; even. **m. que**, even if; **agora m.**, right now; **aqui m.**, right here; **é m.?** really?; **é isso m.**, that's right.

mesquinho, *adj.* stingy; petty.

mesquita, *n.f.* mosque.

messe, *n.f.* field ready for harvesting; harvest.

Messias, *n.m.* Messiah.

mestiçagem, *n.f.* miscegenation; mixed-race people.

mestiço -ça, 1. *adj.* mixed-race. **2.** *n.* person of mixed race.

mestre -tra, 1. *adj.* main. **2.** *n.* teacher; master.

mestre-escola, *n.m.* schoolmaster.

mestre-sala, *n.m.* lead male Carnival dancer.

mesura, *n.f.* bow, curtsy. **—mesurar**, *vb.*

mesurado, *adj.* moderate; obsequious.

meta, *n.f.* goal, aim.

metabolismo, *n.m.* metabolism.

metade, *n.f.* half.

metafísica, *n.f.* metaphysics.

metáfora, *n.f.* metaphor.

metal, *n.m.* metal; (pl.) brass section.

metálico, *adj.* metallic.

metalurgia, *n.f.* metallurgy.

metalúrgico -ca, 1. *adj.* metallurgical. **2.** *n.* metallurgist; metal worker.

metamorfose, *n.f.* metamorphosis.

metamorfosear, *vb.* metamorphose.

metediço, *adj.* meddlesome.

meteorito, *n.m.* meteorite.

meteoro, *n.m.* meteor.

meteorologia, *n.f.* meteorology.

meter, *vb.* put, put in. **m.-se,** get in; **m.-se a,** set oneself up as; **m.-se com,** become involved with.

meticuloso, *adj.* meticulous.

metido, *adj.* nosy.

metódico, *adj.* methodical.

metodista, *adj.; n.m.f.* Methodist.

método, *n.m.* method.

metodologia, *n.f.* methodology.

metralhador, *n.m.* machine gun.

metralhar, *vb.* machine-gun.

métrico, *adj.* metric.

metro, *n.m.* meter; meter stick.

metrô, *n.m.* subway.

metrônomo, *n.m.* metronome.

metrópole, *n.f.* metropolis.

metropolitano, *adj.* metropolitan.

meu, minha, 1. *adj.* my; of mine. **2.** *pron.* mine.

mexer, *vb.* move, stir, shake; mix up. **m. com,** deal with; fool with; tease; **m. em,** touch; fool with.

mexericar, *vb.* gossip. —**mexerico,** *n.m.*

mexeriqueiro -ra, *n.* gossiper.

mexicano -na, *adj., n.* Mexican.

mexido, *adj.* mixed, scrambled.

mexilhão, *n.m.* mussel.

mezanino, *n.m.* mezzanine.

mezinha, *n.f.* home remedy.

miar, *vb.* meow. —**miau, míado,** *n.m.*

miçanga, *n.f.* small glass bead.

micção, *n.f.* urination.

mico, *n.m.* monkey.

micróbio, *n.m.* microbe.

microcomputador, *n.m.* microcomputer.

microcosmo, *n.m.* microcosm.

microfilme, *n.m.* microfilm. —**microfilmar,** *vb.*

microfone, *n.m.* microphone.

microonda, *n.f.* microwave.

microprocessador, *n.m.* (*comput.*) microprocessor.

microscópio, *n.m.* microscope.

mictar, *vb.* urinate.

mictório, *n.m.* public urinal.

micuim, *n.m.* tick, mite.

mídia, *n.f.* communications media.

migalha, *n.f.* crumb.

migração, *n.f.* migration.

migrador -ra, -grante, 1. *adj.* migrating. **2.** *n.* migrant.

migrar, *vb.* migrate.

mijar, *vb.* (*vulg.*) piss. —**mijo,** *n.m.*

mil, *adj.* thousand. —**milhar,** *n.m.*

milagre, *n.m.* miracle.

milagroso, *adj.* miraculous.

milênio, *n.m.* millennium.

milésimo, *adj.* thousandth.

milha, *n.f.* mile.

milhão, *n.m.* million.

milharal, *n.m.* cornfield.

milho, *n.m.* corn.

milícia, *n.f.* militia.

milico, *n.m.* (*coll.*) military man.

miligrama, *n.m.* milligram.

mililitro, *n.m.* milliliter.

milímetro, *n.m.* millimeter.

milionário -ria, *n.* millionaire.

milionésimo, *adj.* millionth.

militante, *adj.* militant; active.

militar, 1. *adj.* military. **2.** *n.m.* military man.

mil-réis, *n.m.* old Brazilian monetary unit.

mim, *prep. pron.* me.

mimar, *vb.* pamper.

mimeógrafo, *n.m.* mimeograph. —**mimeografar,** *vb.*

mímica, *n.f.* mimicry.

mimoso, *adj.* delicate, dainty.

mina, *n.f.* mine; (*sl.*) girl.

minar, *vb.* mine.

mineiro -ra, 1. *adj.* pert. to Minas Gerais state. **2.** *n.* miner; Minas Gerais native.

mineração, *n.f.* mining.

mineral, *adj., n.m.* mineral.

minerar, *vb.* mine.

minério, *n.m.* mineral, ore.

mingau, *n.m.* porridge, mush.

míngua, *n.f.* lack, scarcity. **à m.,** in poverty; **à m. de,** for want of.

minguar, vb. wane, decrease.
minha, adj., pron. fem. of meu.
minhoca, n.f. earthworm.
miniatura, n.f. miniature.
mínimo, 1. adj. minimal, least. 2. n.m. minimum; the least.
ministério, n.m. ministry, department.
ministrar, vb. minister.
ministro -tra, n. government minister.
minoração, n.f. reduction.
minorar, vb. reduce.
minoria, n.f. minority.
minoritário, adj. minority.
minúcia, n.f. minute detail.
minucioso, adj. detailed.
minueto, n.m. minuet.
minúsculo, adj. lower-case.
minuto, n.m. minute.
miolo, n.m. core; (pl.) brains.
míope, adj. myopic, near-sighted.
mira, n.f. sight; gunsight.
mirabolante, adj. showy, gaudy.
mirada, n.f. look.
miragem, n.f. mirage.
mirar, vb. look, look at.
miríade, n.f. myriad.
mirim, adj. small.
mirrado, adj. skinny, shriveled.
misantropo -pa, n. misanthrope.
miscelânea, n.f. miscellany.
miscigenação, n.f. miscegenation.
miserável, adj. miserable.
miséria, n.f. misery; pittance. **fazer misérias**, (sl.) do wonders.
misericórdia, n.f. mercy.
misericordioso, adj. merciful.
mísero, adj. miserable, wretched.
missa, n.f. mass. **m. do galo**, midnight mass.
missal, n.m. missal.
missão, n.f. mission.
misse, n.f. beauty queen.
míssil, n.m. missile.
missionário -ria, n. missionary.
mister, n.m. trade, métier; necessity. **ser m.**, be necessary.
mistério, n.m. mystery.
misterioso, adj. mysterious.

misticismo, n.m. mysticism.
místico -ca, 1. adj. mystical. 2. n. mystic.
mistificar, vb. mystify.
misto, 1. adj. mixed. **m. quente**, toasted ham and cheese sandwich. 2. n.m. mixture.
mistura, n.f. mixture.
misturar, vb. mix.
mítico, adj. mythical.
mitigar, vb. mitigate.
mito, n.m. myth.
mitologia, n.f. mythology.
mitológico, adj. mythological.
miudeza, n.f. smallness; trifle.
miúdo, adj. small, minute; petty.
mixórdia, n.f. mess, hodgepodge.
mo, contr. of me + o.
mó, n.f. millstone.
moagem, n.f. grinding, milling.
móbile, n.m. mobile.
mobília, n.f. furniture.
mobiliado, adj. furnished.
mobiliária, n.f. furniture store.
mobilidade, n.f. mobility.
mobilizar, vb. mobilize.
moça, n.f. young lady; (coll.) virgin; (sl.) prostitute.
moçada, n.f. young people.
Moçambique, n.m. Mozambique.
moçambicano -na, adj., n. Mozambican.
mocambo, n.m. hut, shack.
moção, n.f. motion.
mocetão -tona, n. handsome young person.
mochila, n.f. backpack, knapsack.
mocho, n.m. owl.
mocidade, n.f. youth.
mocinho, n.m. film hero, good guy.
moço, 1. adj. young. 2. n.m. young man; waiter.
mocotó, n.m. calf's foot.
moda, n.f. fashion, style. **na m.**, in style.
modalidade, n.f. modality.
modelar, vb. model, mold.
modelo, n.m. model; pattern; n.f. fashion model.
moderação, n.f. moderation.
moderado, adj. moderate.
moderar, vb. moderate.

modernidade, n.f. modernity.

modernismo, n.m. modernism.

modernizar, vb. modernize.

moderno, adj. modern; (coll.) young.

modéstia, n.f. modesty.

modesto, adj. modest.

módico, adj. small, moderate.

modificar, vb. modify.

modinha, n.f. simple song.

modismo, n.m. idiom.

modista, n.m.f. fashion designer.

modo, n.m. mode, manner, way; (pl.) manners. **de m. geral,** in general; **de m. que,** so that; **de outro m.,** otherwise.

modorra, n.f. drowsiness.

modular, 1. adj. modular. **2.** vb. modulate.

módulo, n.m. module.

moeda, n.f. coin; currency. **casa da m.,** mint; **m. falsa,** counterfeit.

moedeiro, n.m. coiner, minter. **m. falso,** counterfeiter.

moedor, n.m. grinder.

moenda, n.f. mill.

moer, vb. grind, mill.

mofa, n.f. mockery.

mofado, adj. musty, moldy.

mofar, vb. mock; mold.

mofento, adj. moldy.

mofino, adj. unhappy, miserable.

mofo, n.m. mold, mildew.

moganga, n.f. grimace, face.

mogno, n.m. mahogany.

moinho, n.m. mill. **m. de vento,** windmill.

moita, 1. n.f. thicket. **ficar na m.,** (sl.) keep quiet. **2.** interj. (sl.) keep quiet!

mola, n.f. (mech.) spring.

molambo, n.m. rag, tatter.

molar, n.m. molar.

moldar, vb. mold, shape.

molde, n.m. mold; pattern.

moldura, n.f. picture frame.

mole, adj. soft; lazy; (sl.) easy.

molécula, n.f. molecule.

moleira, n.f. fontanel.

moleirão -rona, 1. adj. (coll.) lazy. **2.** n. (coll.) lazy person.

moleiro, n.m. miller.

molejo, n.m. wiggle, sway.

molenga, 1. adj. (coll.) lazy. **2.** n.m.f. (coll.) lazy person.

moleque -leca, 1. adj. mischievous. **2.** n. street urchin; rascal.

molestar, vb. annoy, molest.

moléstia, n.f. disease, illness.

molesto, adj. annoying.

moleza, n.f. softness; laziness; (sl.) ease.

molhado, adj. wet. **—molhar,** vb.

molho, n.m. cluster, bundle.

molho, n.m. sauce, dressing.

molinete, n.m. windlass; turnstile; fishing reel.

molusco, n.m. mollusk.

momentâneo, adj. momentary.

momento, n.m. moment; momentum.

momo, n.m. grimace; mimicry.

monarca, n.m. monarch.

monarquia, n.f. monarchy.

monção, n.f. monsoon.

mondrongo, n.m. (coll.) ugly person.

monetário, adj. monetary.

monge, n.m. monk, friar.

mongolóide, adj. Mongoloid.

monitor, n.m. monitor (also comput.); tutor.

monja, n.f. nun.

mono, n.m. monkey.

monóculo, n.m. monocle.

monocultura, n.f. monoculture.

monogamia, n.f. monogamy.

monógamo, adj. monogamous.

monografia, n.f. monograph.

monograma, n.m. monogram.

monolítico, adj. monolithic.

monólogo, n.m. monologue. **—monologar,** vb.

monopólio, n.m. monopoly.

monopolizar, vb. monopolize.

monótono, adj. monotonous.

monotrilho, n.m. monorail.

monsenhor, n.m. monsignor.

monstro, n.m. monster; (coll.) star, giant.

monstruosidade, n.f. monstrosity.

monstruoso, adj. monstrous.

monta, n.f. amount, sum. **de m.,** of importance.

montagem, n.f. assembly; montage. **linha de m.,** assembly line.

montanha, n.f. mountain. **m. russa**, roller coaster.

montanhês -nhesa, n. mountaineer.

montanhismo, n.m. mountain climbing.

montanhoso, adj. mountainous, hilly.

montante, 1. adj. mounting. **2.** n.m. sum.

montão, n.m. pile; lot.

montar, vb. mount; ride on; stage; set up; assemble. **montar a cavalo**, ride a horse.

montaria, n.f. mount, saddle horse.

monte, n.m. mountain; hill; lot.

montepio, n.m. life insurance fund.

monturo, n.m. dump; dunghill.

monumental, adj. monumental.

monumento, n.m. monument.

moqueca, n.f. Afro-Brazilian fish dish.

mor, adj. chief, grand.

morada, n.f. residence, home.

moradia, n.f. abode, dwelling.

morador -ra, n. dweller.

moral, 1. adj. moral. **2.** n.f. morals; moral (story); n.m. morality, morale.

moralidade, n.f. morality.

morango, n.m. strawberry.

morar, vb. reside, live.

moratória, n.f. moratorium.

mórbido, adj. morbid.

morcego, n.m. (zool.) bat.

mordaça, n.f. muzzle.

mordaz, adj. mordacious, caustic.

mordedor -ra, n. biter; (coll.) moocher.

mordedura, n.f. bite.

morder, vb. bite; (coll.) put the bite on.

mordida, n.f. bite; (coll.) request for money.

mordomia, n.f. stewardship; (pl.) perks; (sl.) liberties.

mordomo, n.m. majordomo, steward, butler.

moréia, n.f. moray.

moreno -na, 1. adj. dark-complexioned, brunet(te). **2.** n.m. brunet(te).

morfina, n.f. morphine.

morfologia, n.f. morphology.

morgado, n.m. primogeniture; eldest son.

moribundo, adj. moribund.

moringa, n.f. water jug; (sl.) head.

mormaço, n.m. mugginess.

mormente, adv. mainly.

morno, adj. lukewarm, tepid.

moroso, adj. sluggish, slow.

morrer, vb. die.

morrinha, 1. adj. (sl.) stingy; annoying. **2.** n.f. sadness; n.m.f. (sl.) pest.

morro, n.m. hill; hillside slum.

morsa, n.f. walrus.

morsegar, vb. dent.

mortal, adj. mortal.

mortalha, n.f. shroud.

mortalidade, n.f. mortality; death rate.

mortandade, n.f. carnage.

morte, n.f. death; **ser de m.**, (sl.) be murder.

morteiro, n.m. mortar.

mortificar, vb. mortify.

morto, adj. dead.

mos, contr. of **me** + **os**.

mosaico, adj., n.m. mosaic.

mosca, n.f. fly; bull's-eye.

Moscou -covo, n. Moscow.

mosquete, n.m. musket.

mosqueteiro, n.m. musketeer.

mosquiteiro, n.m. mosquito net.

mosquito, n.m. mosquito.

mossa, n.f. bruise, dent.

mostarda, n.f. mustard.

mosteiro, n.m. monastery.

mostra, n.f. showing. **à m.**, on view.

mostrador, n.m. dial; face; counter.

mostrar, vb. show.

motejar, vb. mock; joke.

motim, n.m. mutiny, riot.

motivação, n.f. motivation.

motivar, vb. motivate.

motivo, n.m. reason; motive; motif.

moto, -toca, n.f. (coll.) motorcycle.

motocicleta, n.f. motorcycle.

motoneta, n.f. motor scooter.

motor, adj., n.m. motor.

motorista, n.m.f. driver, motorist.

motriz, adj. fem. of **motor**.

mouco, *adj.* deaf.
mourejar, *vb.* work hard, drudge.
mourisco, *adj.* Moorish.
mouro -ra, **1.** *adj.* Moorish. **2.** *n.* Moor.
movediço, *adj.* moving, shifting.
móvel, **1.** *adj.* movable. **2.** *n.m.* piece of furniture.
mover, *vb.* move.
movimentado, *adj.* lively, bustling.
movimentar, *vb.* move.
movimento, *n.m.* movement; activity.
mu, *n.m.* mule (m.).
muamba, *n.f.* contraband; *(sl.)* loot; gear.
mucama, *n.f.* *(hist.)* female house slave.
muco, *n.m.* mucus.
muçulmano -na, *adj., n.* Muslim.
muda, *n.f.* move, change; plant cutting.
mudança, *n.f.* change; move; gearshift.
mudar, *vb.* change; move. **m.-se**, change residence; **m. de idéia**, change one's mind; **m. de roupa**, change clothes.
mudo, *adj.* mute, silent.
mugir, *vb.* moo. —**mugido**, *n.m.*
mui, *adv.* very.
muito, **1.** *adj.* much; *(pl.)* many. **muitas vezes**, often. **2.** *adv.* very. **m. bem**, very well, great.
mula, *n.f.* mule (f.).
mulato -ta, *adj., n.* mulatto.
muleta, *n.f.* crutch.
mulher, *n.f.* woman; wife.
mulher-da-vida, *n.f.* *(coll.)* prostitute.
mulherengo, *adj.* given to womanizing.
mulo, *n.m.* mule (m.).
multa, *n.f.* fine. —**multar**, *vb.*
multidão, *n.f.* crowd, multitude.
multiplicação, *n.f.* multiplication.
multiplicar, *vb.* multiply.
múltiplo, *adj.* multiple.
múmia, *n.f.* mummy.
mundana, *n.f.* prostitute.

mundano, *adj.* mundane, worldly.
mundial, *adj.* world, worldwide.
mundo, *n.m.* world.
munheca, *n.f.* wrist.
munição, *n.f.* munition.
municipal, *adj.* municipal.
municipalidade, *n.f.* city council; city hall.
município, *n.m.* county.
munir, *vb.* provision, arm.
muque, *n.m.* brawn, muscle.
muquirana, **1.** *adj.* *(sl.)* stingy. **2.** *n.f.* *(entom.)* louse; *n.m.f.* *(sl.)* miser; oaf.
mural, *n.m.* mural.
muralha, *n.f.* wall; rampart.
murchar, *vb.* wilt.
murcho, *adj.* wilted.
muriçoca, *n.f.* mosquito.
murmurar, *vb.* murmur, mumble. —**murmúrio**, *n.m.*
muro, *n.m.* wall.
murro, *n.m.* sock, punch.
musa, *n.f.* Muse.
músculo, *n.m.* muscle.
museu, *n.m.* museum.
musgo, *n.m.* moss.
música, *n.f.* music; song.
musical, *adj.* musical.
músico, *n.m.* musician.
mutação, *n.f.* mutation, change.
mutilar, *vb.* mutilate.
mutirão, *n.m.* community work project.
mutreta, *n.* *(sl.)* trick.
mútuo, *adj.* mutual.
muxoxo, *n.m.* kiss, pout.

N

na, **1.** *contr. of* **em** + **a.** in the, on the, at the, into the; in the one (that), etc.; *(pl.)* in the; in those. **2.** *nas. dir. obj. pron.* her, you *(f.s.)*; it; *(pl.)* them, you *(f.pl.)*.
nabo, *n.m.* turnip.
nação, *n.f.* nation.
nácar, *n.m.* mother-of-pearl.
nacional, *adj.* national.
nacionalidade, *n.f.* nationality.
nacionalismo, *n.m.* nationalism.
nacionalizar, *vb.* nationalize.

naco, *n.m.* chunk, piece.

Nações Unidas, *n.f.pl.* United Nations.

nada, 1. *indef. pron.* nothing. **de n.,** you're welcome. **que nada!,** nonsense! not at all! **2.** *n.m.* nothingness; *(coll.)* nobody. **3.** *adv.* (not) at all, in no way.

nadar, *vb.* swim.

nádega, *n.f.* buttock; *(pl.)* hips.

nafta, *n.f.* naphtha.

naftalina, *n.f.* mothball(s).

nagô, *adj., n.m.f.* Yoruba.

náilon, *n.m.* nylon.

naipe, *n.m.* suit (cards).

nalgum, nalguma, *contr. of* em + algum, etc.

namorada, *n.f.* girlfriend.

namoradeiro -ra, 1. *adj.* flirtatious. **2.** *n.* flirt.

namorado, *n.m.* boyfriend.

namorador -ra, *adj.* flirtatious.

namorar, *vb.* court, go (steady) with.

namorico, *n.m.* flirtation.

namoro, *n.m.* going steady.

nanico, *adj.* small.

não, 1. *interj.* no. **2.** *adv.* not. **a n. ser,** except; **a n. ser que,** unless; **n. é?,** isn't that so?; **n. faz mal,** it's all right, never mind; **pois n!,** certainly!

não-, *pref.* non-.

naquele, naquela, *contr. of* em + aquele, *etc.* in that, in that one; *(pl.)* in those.

naquilo, *contr. of* em + aquilo in that, in that thing.

narcisismo, *n.m.* narcissism.

narciso, *n.m.* narcissus, daffodil.

narcotizar, *vb.* drug.

narcotráfico, *n.m.* drug smuggling.

narcotraficante, *n.m.f.* drug smuggler.

narigão, *n.m.* big nose.

narigudo, *adj.* big-nosed.

narina, *n.f.* nostril.

nariz, *n.m.* nose. **meter o n. (em),** meddle (in).

narração, *n.f.* narration.

narrador -ra, *n.* narrator.

narrar, *vb.* narrate.

narrativo, *adj.* narrative. —**narrativa,** *n.f.*

nas, *contr. of* em + as. in the,

on the, at the; in the ones (that).

nasal, *adj., n.f.* nasal.

nasalizar, *vb.* nasalize.

nascente, 1. *adj.* rising. **2.** *n.m.* east; *n.f.* headwaters.

nascer, 1. *n.m.* birth. **n. do sol,** sunrise. **2.** *vb.* be born; originate; rise (sun, moon).

nascimento, *n.m.* birth.

nata, *n.f.* cream.

natação, *n.f.* swimming.

natal, 1. *adj.* natal. **2.** *n.m.* *(cap.)* Christmas.

natalício, 1. *adj.* natal. **2.** *n.m.* birthday.

natalidade, *n.f.* birth rate.

natalino, *adj.* Christmas.

natimorto, *n.m.* stillborn baby.

natividade, *n.f.* Nativity.

nativo -va, *adj., n.* native.

nato, *adj.* born; congenital.

natural, 1. *adj.* natural. **filho n.,** bastard. **2.** *n.m.* native; temperament.

naturalismo, *n.m.* naturalism.

naturalizar, *vb.* naturalize. **n.-se,** become naturalized.

natureza, *n.f.* nature. **n. morta,** still life.

nau, *n.f.* ship, vessel.

naufragar, *vb.* shipwreck; fail.

naufrágio, *n.m.* shipwreck.

náufrago -ga, *n.* shipwrecked person.

náusea, *n.f.* nausea.

nauseabundo, *adj.* nauseating.

nausear, *vb.* nauseate.

nauta, *n.m.* sailor.

náutico, *adj.* nautical.

naval, *adj.* naval.

navalha, *n.f.* razor.

nave, *n.f.* ship; *(arch.)* nave. **n. espacial,** space ship.

navegação, *n.f.* navigation, sailing.

navegante, -gador, *n.m.* navigator.

navegar, *vb.* navigate, sail.

navio, *n.m.* ship. **deixar/ficar a ver navios,** leave/be left high and dry.

Nazaré, *n.* Nazareth.

nazismo, *n.m.* Nazism.

nazista, *adj., n.m.f.* Nazi.

neblina, *n.f.* fog, mist.

nebuloso, adj. cloudy; nebulous.

necessário, adj. necessary.

necessidade, n.f. necessity, need. **fazer n.**, (coll.) go to the bathroom.

necessitado, 1. adj. needy, poor. **2.** n.m.pl. the needy, the poor.

necessitar, vb. need; be needy.

necrologia, n.f. necrology, obituary.

necrológico, 1. adj. necrological. **2.** n.m. obituary; eulogy.

necrópole, n.f. cemetery.

necrotério, n.m. morgue.

nédio, adj. shiny; plump.

nefando, adj. nefarious.

nefasto, adj. ominous; tragic.

nega, n.f. (coll.) darling (f.); (sl.) black woman.

negaça, n.f. enticement; deception.

negação, n.f. negation.

negacear, vb. entice; deceive.

negar, vb. deny; negate. **n.-se**, refuse.

negativa, n.f. negative, denial.

negativo, 1. adj. negative. **2.** n.m. negative (also photog.). **3.** adv. (coll.) no.

negligenciar, vb. neglect.

negligente, adj. negligent.

nego, n.m. (coll.) dear (m.); (sl.) black man; (sl.) guy.

negociação, n.f. negotiation.

negociador -ra, n. negotiator.

negociante, n.m.f. businessman -woman.

negociar, vb. negotiate; do business.

negociata, n.f. shady deal.

negócio, n.m. business; deal; affair; (sl.) thingamajig; (vulg.) penis. **n. da China**, good deal; **a negócios**, on business.

negrejar, vb. turn black.

negrito, n.m. bolface type; Negrito.

negro, 1. adj. black; Negro. **2.** n.m. blackness; black person.

negrura, n.f., **-grume**, n.m. blackness.

nele, nela, contr. of em + ele, etc. in him/her, in it; (pl.) in them.

nem, 1. adv. not; not even. **n. que**, even if; **n. sempre**, not al-

ways; **n. sequer**, not even; **n. todos**, not everyone; **que n.**, just like; **2.** conj. nor; neither . . .nor. **nem. . .nem**, neither . . .nor.

nenê, -nen, n.m. baby.

nenhum, 1. adj. no, none, not any. **2.** pron. no one.

neófito, n.m. neophyte.

neônio, n.m. neon.

neozelandês -esa, adj., n. New Zealander.

nepotismo, n.m. nepotism.

nervo, n.m. nerve.

nervosidade, n.f., **-sismo**, n.m. nervousness.

nervoso, adj. nervous.

néscio, adj. stupid, foolish.

nesga, n.f. piece.

nesse, nessa, contr. of em + esse, etc. in that, in that one; (pl.) in those.

neste, nesta, contr. of em + este, etc. in this, in this one; (pl.) in these.

neta, n.f. granddaughter.

neto, n.m. grandson.

neurologia, n.f. neurology.

neurose, n.f. neurosis.

neurótico, adj., n.m. neurotic.

neutralidade, n.f. neutrality.

neutralizar, vb. neutralize.

neutro, adj. neutral; neuter.

nevada, n.f. snowfall.

nevado, adj. snow-covered.

neve, n.f. snow. —**nevar**, vb.

névoa, n.f. fog, mist.

nevoeiro, n.m. fog.

nevoento, adj. foggy; snowy.

nexo, n.m. connection.

nhandu, n.m. rhea.

nhoque, n.m. gnocchi.

nicaraguano -na, -güense, adj., n. Nicaraguan.

nicho, n.m. niche.

nigeriano -na, adj., n. Nigerian.

nímio, adj. excessive.

ninar, vb. lull to sleep; sleep. **canção de n.**, lullaby.

ninfa, n.f. nymph.

ninguém, indef. pron. no one, nobody.

ninharia, n.f. trifle; pittance.

ninho, n.m. nest.

níquel, n.m. nickel.

nisso, *contr. of* **em + isso.** in that, in that thing.

nisto, *contr. of* **em + isto.** in this, in this thing.

nitidez, *n.f.* clarity; brightness.

nítido, *adj.* clear-cut; bright.

nitro, *n.m.* saltpeter.

nível, *n.m.* level; standard. **n. de vida,** standard of living.

nivelar, *vb.* level.

no, 1. *contr. of* **em + o.** in the, on the, at the, into the; in the one (that); *(pl.)* in the; in those. **2.** *nas. dir. obj. pron.* him, you *(m.s.)*; it; *(pl.)* them, you *(m.pl.)*.

nó, *n.m.* knot; node; crux; knuckle. **n. de Adão,** Adam's apple.

nobre, *adj., n.m.f.* noble.

nobreza, *n.f.* nobility.

noção, *n.f.* notion.

nocaute, *n.m.* knockout. **—nocautear,** *vb.*

nocivo, *adj.* noxious.

noctâmbulo -la, *n.* sonambulist, sleepwalker.

nódoa, *n.f.* stain, blot. **—nodoar,** *vb.*

nodoso, *adj.* knotty.

nogueira, *n.f.* walnut tree.

noite, *n.f.* night, evening. **à/de n.,** at night; **boa n.,** good night; **da n. para o dia,** overnight.

noitinha, *n.f.* nightfall.

noiva, *n.f.* fiancée; bride.

noivado, *n.m.* engagement, betrothal.

noivar, *vb.* become/be engaged; spend one's honeymoon.

noivo, *n.m.* fiancé; groom; *(pl.)* engaged couple; bride and groom.

nojento, *adj.* nauseating.

nojo, *n.m.* nausea; disgust; mourning.

no-la, *contr. of* **nos + a.**

no-las, *contr. of* **nos + as.**

no-lo, *contr. of* **nos + o.**

no-los, *contr. of* **nos + os.**

nômade, 1. *adj.* nomadic. **2.** *n.m. & f.* nomad.

nome, *n.m.* name; noun. **n. de família,** surname; **n. feio,** curse word; **de n.,** by name. **em n. de,** in the name of, on behalf of;

como/qual é o seu n., what's your name?

nomeação, *n.f.* appointment.

nomear, *vb.* name; appoint.

nomenclatura, *n.f.* nomenclature.

nominal, *adj.* nominal.

nonada, *n.f.* trifle.

nonagésimo, *adj.* ninetieth.

nono, *adj., n.m.* ninth.

nora, *n.f.* daughter-in-law.

nordeste, *adj., n.m.* northeast.

nordestino -na, 1. *adj.* northeastern. **2. n.** northeasterner.

nórdico -ca, *adj., n.* Nordic, Norse.

norma, *n.f.* norm, rule.

normal, *adj.* normal.

normalizar, *vb.* normalize.

normativo, *adj.* normative.

noroeste, *adj., n.m.* northwest.

norte, 1. *adj.* north. **2.** *n.m.* north; direction, bearings.

norte-americano -na, *adj., n.* North American, American.

nortear, *vb.* head north; orient.

nortista, 1. *adj.* northern. **2.** *n.m.f.* northerner.

Noruega, *n.f.* Norway.

norueguês -guesa, *adj., n.* Norwegian.

nos, 1. *contr. of* **em + os.** in the, on the, at the; in the ones (that). **2.** *dir. obj. pron.* us. **3.** *indir. obj. pron.* to us, for us, us. **4.** *refl. pron.* ourselves.

nós, 1. *subj. pron.* we. **2.** *prep. pron.* us.

nosocômio, *n.m.* hospital.

nosso, nossa, 1. *poss. adj.* our. **2.** *poss. pron.* ours. **Nossa Senhora,** Our Lady; **Nossa Senhora!,** or **Nossa!,** heavens!

nostalgia, *n.f.* nostalgia.

nostálgico, *adj.* nostalgic.

nota, *n.f.* note; grade; bill; banknote; news item; **uma n.,** *(sl.)* a pretty penny.

notação, *n.f.* notation.

notar, *vb.* note, notice.

notário, *n.m.* notary.

notável, *adj.* notable.

notícia, *n.f.* news; word.

noticiar, *vb.* report.

noticiário, *n.m.* newscast; *(journ.)* news section.

noticioso, *adj.* informative.

objetiva

notificar, vb. notify.
notoriedade, n.f. notoriety.
notório, adj. public, widely known.
noturno, 1. adj. nocturnal, night. 2. n.m. nocturne; night train.
noutro, noutra, contr. of em + outro, etc. in another; (pl.) in other.
nova, n.f. news.
Nova Guiné, n.f. New Guinea.
Nova Inglaterra, n.f. New England.
Nova Iorque, n. New York.
nova-iorquino -na, 1. adj. pert. to New York. 2. n. New Yorker.
novato -ta, 1. adj. inexperienced. 2. n.m. novice; freshman.
Nova Zelândia, n.f. New Zealand.
nove, adj. nine. cheio de n. horas, finicky.
novecentos, adj. nine hundred.
novel, adj. novel, new; inexperienced.
novela, n.f. novelette; novel; soap opera.
novelesco, adj. novelistic; fantastic.
novelista, n.m.f. novelette writer; novelist.
novelística, n.f. fiction.
novelo, n.m. ball of yarn.
novembro, n.m. November.
novena, n.f. novena.
noventa, adj. ninety.
noviciado, n.m. novitiate.
noviço -ça, n. novice.
novidade, n.f. newness; news.
novilho, n.m. calf.
novo, adj. new; young. n. em folha, brand new.
Novo Mundo, n.m. New World.
novo-rico, adj. nouveau riche.
Novo Testamento, n.m. New Testament.
noz, n.f. nut; walnut.
noz-moscada, n.f. nutmeg.
nu, nua, adj. naked, nude. a olho n., with the naked eye; n. em pelo, stark naked; verdade n. e crua, naked truth.
nuança, n.f. nuance.

nublado, adj. cloudy.
nuca, n.f. nape.
nuclear, adj. nuclear.
núcleo, n.m. nucleus.
nudez, n.f. nudity.
nudista, n.m.f. nudist.
nulidade, n.f. nullity; nonentity.
nulificar, vb. nullify.
nulo, adj. null, void; worthless; nonexistent; inept; inert.
num, numa, contr. of em + um, etc. in a, on a, at a.
numerador, n.m. numerator.
numerar, vb. number.
numérico, adj. numerical.
número, n.m. number, numeral; quantity; size; issue. ser um n., be a funny person.
numeroso, adj. numerous.
nunca, adv. never; ever. n. jamais, never again.
nupcial, adj. nuptial.
núpcias, n.f.pl. nuptials, wedding.
nutrição, n.f. nutrition.
nutricionista, n.m.f. nutritionist.
nutrimento, n.m. nutrient, nourishment.
nutrir, vb. nourish; be nutritious; foster.
nutritivo, adj. nutritious.
nuvem, n.f. cloud.

O

o, 1. def. art. the. 2. dir. obj. pron. him, it, you (m.s.). 3. rel. pron. the one (that).
ó, 1. n.m. the letter o. 2. interj. oh! hey! look!
oba, interj. wow! gee!; hi!
obcecar, vb. blind; obfuscate.
obedecer, vb. obey.
obediência, n.f. obedience.
obediente, adj. obedient.
obeso, adj. obese.
óbice, n.m. impediment.
óbito, n.m. death.
obituário, adj., n.m. obituary.
objeção, n.f. objection.
objetar, vb. object.
objetiva, n.f. (opt., phot.) objective.

objetivo, 1. adj. objective. **2.** n.m. objective, aim.
objeto, n.m. object.
obliquo, adj. oblique; (gram.) object.
obliterar, vb. obliterate.
oblívio, n.m. oblivion.
oboé, n.m. oboe.
óbolo, n.m. small donation.
obra, n.f. work, opus; deed; (coll.) excrement.
obra-prima, n.f. masterpiece.
obrar, vb. work, produce; (coll.) defecate.
obreiro -ra, 1. adj. working. **2.** n. worker.
obrigação, n.f. obligation.
obrigado -da, 1. adj. obliged, obligated. **2.** interj. thank you!; no thank you!
obrigar, vb. oblige, obligate.
obrigatório, adj. obligatory.
obscenidade, n.f. obscenity.
obsceno, adj. obscene.
obscuridade, n.f. obscurity.
obscuro, adj. obscure. —**obscurecer,** vb.
obsedar, vb. obsess.
obsequiar, vb. oblige; present.
obséquio, n.m. favor, kindness.
obsequioso, n.f. obsequious.
observação, n.f. observation.
observador -ra, 1. adj. observant. **2.** n. observer.
observância, n.f. observance.
observar, vb. observe
observatório, n.m. observatory.
obsessão, n.f. obsession.
obsessivo, adj. obsessive.
obsoleto, adj. obsolete.
obstáculo, n.m. obstacle.
obstante, adj. obstructive. **não o.,** nevertheless; despite.
obstar, vb. impede.
obstetrícia, n.f. obstetrics.
obstinado, adj. obstinate, stubborn.
obstinar-se, vb. be obstinate.
obstrução, n.f. obstruction; occlusion.
obstruir, vb. obstruct; occlude.
obter, vb. obtain.
obturação, n.f. (dent.) filling.
obturar, vb. (dent.) fill (a cavity).
obus, n.m. howitzer.
óbvio, adj. obvious, evident.

ocasião, n.f. occasion, opportunity.
ocasional, adj. random, accidental.
ocasionar, vb. occasion.
ocaso, n.m. sunset; west.
Oceânia, -ania, n.f. Oceania.
oceânico, adj. oceanic.
oceano, n.m. ocean.
ocidental, adj. occidental, western.
ocidente, n.m. occident, west.
ócio, n.m. leisure; spare time; laziness.
ocioso, 1. adj. idle; lazy. **2.** n.m. idler.
oco, adj., n.m. hollow.
ocorrência, n.f. occurrence.
ocorrer, vb. occur.
octogésimo, adj. eightieth.
octópode, n.m. octopus.
ocular, adj. ocular.
oculista, n.m.f. oculist.
óculo, n.m. telescope; (pl.) eyeglasses.
ocultar, n.f. conceal.
oculto, adj. hidden; occult. **às ocultas,** secretly.
ocupação, n.f. occupation.
ocupado, adj. occupied, busy.
ocupar, vb. occupy. **o.-se em/de/com,** busy oneself with.
ode, n.f. ode.
odiar, vb. hate. —**ódio,** n.m.
odioso, adj. odious.
odisséia, n.f. odyssey.
odontologia, n.f. dentistry.
odor, n.m. odor.
odre, n.m. wineskin.
oeste, adj., n.m. west.
ofegar, vb. pant.
ofender, vb. offend.
ofensa, n.f. offense.
ofensivo, adj. offensive. —**ofensiva,** n.f.
oferecer, vb. offer. **o.-se,** present itself; offer (to); occur.
oferecimento, n.m. offer, offering.
oferenda, n.f. offering.
oferendar, vb. make an offering.
oferta, n.f. offer, offering; present; sale item.
ofertar, vb. offer, present.
oficial, 1. adj. official. **2.** n.m. (mil.) officer.
oficializar, vb. officialize.

oficiante, *n.m.* (*eccles.*) officiant.

oficina, *n.f.* workshop, shop, garage.

ofício, *n.m.* trade, profession; function; office; official letter. **Santo O.**, Inquisition.

oficioso, *adj.* obliging; disinterested; unofficial, informal.

ofsete, *n.m.* offset printing.

oftalmologista, *n.m.f.* ophthalmologist.

ofuscar, *vb.* obfuscate.

ogiva, *n.f.* nose cone; (*arch.*) ogive.

ogro, *n.m.* ogre.

oh, *interj.* oh!

oi, *interj.* hi! hello!

oitava, *n.f.* (*mus.*) octave.

oitavo, *adj.*, *n.m.* eighth.

oitenta, *adj.* eighty.

oiticica, *n.f.* a certain oil-bearing tree.

oito, *adj.* eight.

oitocentos, *adj.* eight hundred.

ojeriza, *n.f.* ill will.

OK, *n.m.* (*sl.*) okay, all right.

olá, *interj.* hello! hi!

olaria, *n.f.* pottery factory.

oleiro, *n.m.* potter.

óleo, *n.m.* oil.

oleoso, *adj.* oily.

olfato, *n.m.* sense of smell.

olhada, *n.f.* glance, look. **dar uma o.**, take a glance.

olhadela, *n.f.* glance.

olhar, **1.** *n.m.* look, regard. **2.** *vb.* look, look at, watch. **o. para.**, look at.

olheiras, *n.f.* dark circles under the eyes.

olho, *n.m.* eye. **o.!**, watch out! beware!

olho-d'água, *n.m.* spring, fountain.

oligarquia, *n.f.* oligarchy.

olimpíadas, *n.f.pl.* Olympic games, Olympiad.

olímpico, *adj.* Olympian; Olympic.

Olimpo, *n.m.* Olympus.

oliva, *n.f.* olive.

oliveira, *n.f.* olive tree.

olmo, *n.m.* elm.

olvidar, *vb.* forget.

ombro, *n.m.* shoulder. **encolher os/dar de ombros**, shrug.

omelete, *n.f.* omelet.

ominoso, *adj.* ominous.

omissão, *n.f.* omission.

omitir, *vb.* omit.

onça, *n.f.* wildcat, jaguar; ounce. **do tempo da onça**, from a long time ago.

oncologia, *n.f.* oncology.

onda, *n.f.* wave; (*coll.*) fuss, to-do; (*sl.*) fad; (*sl.*) affectation. **o. curta**, shortwave; **estar na o.**, (*sl.*) be in style; **fazer o.**, make a fuss.

onde, *adv.* where; whereto. **onde quer que**, wherever; **de o.**, from where; **para o.**, whereto; **por o.**, by which route.

ondear, *vb.* wave, roll, undulate.

ondulação, *n.f.* undulation, wave.

ondulado, *adj.* wavy, curly.

ondular, *vb.* wave, undulate, roll.

onerar, *vb.* burden.

ônibus, *n.m.* bus. **ô. espacial**, space shuttle; **pegar o ô.**, catch the bus.

onipotente, *adj.* omnipotent.

onipresente, *adj.* omnipresent.

onírico, *adj.* oneiric.

onisciente, *adj.* omniscient.

onívoro, *adj.* omnivorous.

ônix, *n.m.* onyx.

onomatopéia, *n.f.* onomatopoeia.

ontem, *adv.* yesterday. **ontem à/de noite**, last night; **o. à/de tarde**, yesterday afternoon; **o. de manhã**, yesterday morning.

ônus, *n.m.* onus, burden.

onze, *adj.* eleven.

onzeneiro -ra, *n.* usurer; busybody.

opa, *interj.* wow! gee!; hi!

opaco, *adj.* opaque.

opala, *n.f.* opal.

opção, *n.f.* option.

opcional, *adj.* optional.

ópera, *n.f.* opera.

operação, *n.f.* operation.

operar, *vb.* operate, work; operate on. **o.-se**, be operated on.

operário -ria, *n.* worker.

operoso, *adj.* industrious.

opinar, *vb.* opine.

opinião, *n.f.* opinion.

opiniático, -ioso, *adj.* opinionated.

ópio, *n.m.* opium.

opíparo, *adj.* sumptuous.

oponente, 1. *adj.* opposing. **2.** *n.m.f.* opponent.

opor, *vb.* oppose. **o.-se**, be opposed.

oportunidade, *n.f.* opportunity.

oportunista, *n.m.f.* opportunist.

oportuno, *adj.* opportune.

oposição, *n.f.* opposition.

opositor -ra, 1. *adj.* opposing. **2.** *n.* opponent; rival candidate.

oposto, *adj.*, *n.m.* opposite.

opressão, *n.f.* oppression.

opressivo, *adj.* oppressive.

opressor -ra, 1. *adj.* oppressive. **2.** *n.* oppressor.

oprimir, *vb.* oppress.

optar, *vb.* opt.

optativo, *adj.* optional; optative.

óptica, ótica, *n.f.* optics; optic; optical shop.

óptico, ótico, 1. *adj.* optical. **2.** *n.m.* optician.

optometrista, *n.m.f.* optometrist.

opulento, *adj.* oppulent.

ora, 1. *adv.* now. **2.** *conj.* but; either, now. **o. . ..o.**, either . . . or, now. . .now. **3.** *interj.* now then! well! **o. bolas!**, golly! **o. essa!**, wow! gee!

oração, *n.f.* prayer; oration; *(gram.)* clause.

oráculo, *n.m.* oracle.

orador -ra, *n.m.* orator.

oral, *adj.* oral.

orar, *vb.* pray; beg for; orate.

oratória, *n.f.* oratory.

oratório, 1. *adj.* oratorical. **2.** *n.m.* oratory; oratorio.

orbe, *n.m.* orb; earth; field.

órbita, *n.f.* orbit.

orçamental, *adj.* budgetary.

orçamento, *n.m.* budget. —**orçar**, *vb.*

ordeiro, *adj.* orderly.

ordem, *n.f.* order. **em o.**, in order.

ordenado, *n.m.* salary.

ordenança, *n.m.f.* *(mil.)* orderly.

ordenar, *vb.* order, arrange; *(eccles.)* ordain.

ordenhar, *vb.* milk.

ordinário, *adj.* ordinary; shoddy; rude; mediocre.

orégão, *n.m.* oregano.

orelha, *n.f.* ear; cover flap (book).

orelhão, *n.m.* *(sl.)* phone booth.

orelheira, *n.f.* earflap (of a cap).

orelhudo, *adj.* large-eared.

orfanato, *n.m.* orphanage.

órfão -fã, *n.f.* orphan.

orfeão, *n.m.* glee club, choir. —**orfeônico**, *adj.*

orgânico, *adj.* organic.

organismo, *n.m.* organism.

organização, *n.f.* organization.

organizar, *vb.* organize.

órgão, *n.m.* organ (also mus.).

orgasmo, *n.m.* orgasm.

orgia, *n.f.* orgy.

orgulhar, *vb.* fill with pride. **o.-se (de)**, pride oneself (on).

orgulho, *n.m.* pride.

orgulhoso, *adj.* proud.

orientação, *n.f.* orientation.

orientador -ra, 1. *adj.* orienting, guiding. **2.** *n.* director, guide.

oriental, *adj.* oriental, eastern.

orientar, *vb.* orient, guide. **o.-se**, get oriented.

oriente, *n.m.* orient, east. **O. Médio**, Middle East.

orifício, *n.m.* orifice.

origem, *n.f.* origin.

original, *adj.* original.

originalidade, *n.f.* originality.

originar, *vb.* originate. **o.-se**, derive.

originário, *adj.* originating; primitive.

oriundo, *adj.* native.

orixá, *n.m.* Afro-Brazilian divinity.

orla, *n.f.* edge, rim. **o. marítima**, coastal strip.

orlar, *vb.* edge; verge on.

ornamentação, *n.f.* ornamentation.

ornamentar, *vb.* adorn.

ornamento, *n.m.* ornament.

ornar, *vb.* adorn.

ornato, *n.m.* decoration.

ornitologia, *n.f.* ornithology.

ornitorrinco, *n.m.* platypus.

orquestra, *n.f.* orchestra.

orquestrar, *vb.* orchestrate.

orquídea, *n.f.* orchid.

ortodoxo, *adj.* orthodox.

ortografia, *n.f.* orthography, spelling.

ortopédico, *adj.* orthopedic.

orvalho, *n.m.* dew.

os, **1.** *def. art.* the. **2.** *dir. obj. pron.* them, you (m.pl.). **3.** *rel. pron.* those (that).

oscilação, *n.f.* oscillation.

oscilar, *vb.* oscillate; waver; shake.

oscular, *vb.* kiss. —**ósculo**, *n.m.*

osmose, *n.f.* osmosis.

ossada, *n.f.* pile of bones; skeleton; remains.

ósseo, *adj.* bony.

osso, *n.m.* bone. **em carne e o.**, in the flesh; **o. difícil de roer**, *(coll.)* hard nut to crack.

ossudo, *adj.* big-boned, bony.

ostensivo, *adj.* ostensible.

ostentação, *n.f.* ostentation.

ostentar, *vb.* show off, flaunt.

ostentoso, *adj.* ostentatious.

ostra, *n.f.* oyster.

ostracismo, *n.m.* ostracism.

otário, *n.m. (sl.)* sucker, fool.

otimismo, *n.m.* optimism.

otimista, **1.** *adj.* optimistic. **2.** *n.m.f.* optimistic.

ótimo, *adj.* excellent.

ou, *conj.* or, either. **o. seja**, in other words.

ouriçar, *vb.* bristle; **o.-se**, *(sl.)* get excited.

ouriço, *n.m.* burr; hedgehog. **o. do mar**, sea urchin.

ourives, *n.m.* goldsmith, silversmith.

ouro, *n.m.* gold.

ousadia, *n.f.* audacity; gall.

ousado, *adj.* daring; impudent.

ousar, *vb.* dare.

outeiro, *n.m.* small hill.

outono, *n.m.* autumn, fall.

outorgar, *vb.* grant; approve.

outrem, *pron.* someone else.

outro, *indef. art., pron.* other, other one; another.

outrora, *adv.* formerly.

outrossim, *adv.* also.

outubro, *n.m.* October.

ouvido, *n.m.* ear; sense of hearing.

ouvinte, *n.m.f.* listener; auditor (of a course).

ouvir, *vb.* hear, listen. **o. dizer/falar**, hear tell.

ovação, *n.f.* ovation.

ovacionar, *vb.* applaud.

ovário, *n.m.* ovary.

ovelha, *n.f.* ewe, sheep.

ovni (objeto voador não identificado), *n.m.* u.f.o.

ovo, *n.m.* egg; ovum; *(pl., vulg.)* testicles; **ovos duros**, hard-boiled eggs; **ovos fritos/estrelados**, fried eggs; **ovos mexidos**, scrambled eggs.

oxalá, *interj. (P.)* let's hope!; if only!

oxidar, *vb.* oxidize, rust.

oxigenar, *vb.* oxygenate; peroxide.

oxigênio, *n.m.* oxygen.

ozônio, *n.m.* ozone.

P

pá, *n.f.* shovel; paddle. **da p. virada** *(coll.)* naughty.

paca, **1.** *n.f. (zool.)* paca. **2.** *adv.(sl.)* galore; very.

pacato, *adj.* peaceful, quiet.

pachola, **1.** *adj.* vain; stylish. **2.** *n.m.f.* idler.

pachorra, *n.f.* sluggishness.

paciência, *n.f.* patience; solitaire (game).

paciente, *adj., n.m.f.* patient.

pacificar, *vb.* pacify.

pacífico, **1.** *adj.* peaceful. **2.** *n.m.(cap.)* Pacific.

pacifista, *adj., n.m.f.* pacifist.

paço, *n.m.* palace.

paçoca, *n.f.* manioc-meal and meat dish.

pacote, *n.m.* package, bundle; *(pl., sl.)* money.

pacto, *n.m.* pact.

pactuar, *vb.* make a pact.

padaria, *n.f.* bakery; *(sl.)* buttocks.

padecer, *vb.* suffer.

padeiro, *n.m.* baker.

padrão, **1.** *adj.* standard. **2.** *n.m.* pattern; standard.

padrasto, *n.m.* stepfather.

padre, *n.m.* priest.

padre-nosso, *n.m.* Lord's Prayer.

padrinho, *n.m.* godfather; best man.

padroeiro -ra, 1. *adj.* patron. 2. *n.* patron saint.

padronizar, *vb.* standardize.

paga, *n.f.* pay.

pagador -ra, *n.* payer.

pagadoria, *n.f.* pay office/window.

pagamento, *n.m.* payment.

pagão -gã, *adj., n.* pagan.

pagar, *vb.* pay. **p. o pato**, (*coll.*) suffer the consequences.

pagável, *adj.* payable, due.

página, *n.f.* page. **p. de rosto**, title page.

pago, 1. *adj.* paid. 2. *n.m.* pay.

pagode, *n.m.* pagoda; revelry; type of samba.

pagodeiro -ra, *n.* reveler.

pagodeira, *n.f.* revelry.

pai, *n.m.* father; (*cap.*) God; (*pl.*) parents.

pai-de-santo, *n.m.* Afro-Brazilian priest.

pai-dos-burros, *n.m.* (*coll.*) dictionary.

paina, *n.f.* kapok.

painço, *n.m.* millet.

painel, *n.m.* panel; dashboard.

paio, *n.m.* pork sausage.

paiol, *n.m.* powder magazine; storehouse.

pairar, *vb.* hover; flutter.

país, *n.m.* country, nation.

paisagem, *n.f.* landscape, scenery.

paisagista, *n.m.f.* landscapist; landscape architect.

paisana, *n.f.* civilian clothes.

paisano -na, *n.* civilian; compatriot.

Países Baixos, *n.m.pl.* Holland.

paixão, *n.f.* passion; (*cap.*) Passion.

paixonite, *n.f.* (*coll.*) lovesickness.

pajé, *n.m.* shaman.

pajear, *vb.* serve; take care of.

pajem, *n.m.* page, attendant.

palacete, *n.m.* small palace, mansion.

palaciano, 1. *adj.* palatial. 2. *n.m.* courtier.

palácio, *n.m.* palace.

paladar, *n.m.* palate.

palanque, *n.m.* stage.

palavra, *n.f.* word; promise; speech; floor (debate). **p.?** really?; **p.!** honest!; **palavras cruzadas**, crossword puzzle. **estar com a p. na boca**, have the word on the tip of one's tongue; **tirar a p. da boca de**, take the word right out of (someone's) mouth; **a última p.**, the last word.

palavrão, *n.m.* four-letter word.

palavreado, *n.m.* chatter; wordiness.

palavrear, *vb.* chatter.

palavrório, *n.m.* chatter; wordiness.

palavroso, *adj.* wordy.

palco, *n.m.* stage.

palerma, 1. *adj.* stupid. 2. *n.m.f.* idiot.

Palestina, *n.f.* Palestine.

palestino -na, *adj., n.* Palestinian.

palestra, *n.f.* talk, lecture.

paleta, *n.f.* palette; shoulder blade.

paletó, *n.m.* coat; jacket.

palha, *n.f.* straw; trifle. **p. de aço**, steel wool; **fogo de p.**, temporary enthusiasm; **por dá cá aquela p.**, for no reason.

palhaçada, *n.f.* clowning.

palhaço, *n.m.* clown.

palheiro, *n.m.* hayloft.

palheta, *n.f.* (*mus.*) reed; pick; blade; palette.

palhoça, *n.f.* thatched hut.

paliativo, *adj., n.m.* palliative.

paliçada, *n.f.* palisade.

palidez, *n.f.* paleness.

pálido, *adj.* pale.

palitar, *vb.* pick (teeth).

paliteiro, *n.m.* toothpick holder.

palito, *n.m.* toothpick; match; skinny person.

palma, *n.f.* palm; (*pl.*) applause. **bater palmas**, applaud; **levar/ganhar a p.**, be victorious; **sua alma, sua p.**, it's your funeral.

palmada, *n.f.* slap, spank.

palmar, 1. *adj.* obvious. 2. *n.m.* palm grove.

palmatória, *n.f.* ferule. **dar a mão à p.**, admit mistakes.

palmeira, *n.f.* palm tree.

palmilha, *n.f.* insole.

palmito, *n.m.* palmetto; heart of palm.

palmo, *n.m.* palm (measure).

palpável, *adj.* palpable.

pálpebra, *n.f.* eyelid.

palpitar, *vb.* palpitate.

palpite, *n.m.* palpitation; *(coll.)* hunch; tip.

palpiteiro -ra, *n.* tipster; buttinsky.

palra, *n.f.* chatter.

palrar, -rear, *vb.* chatter; blab.

paludismo, *n.m.* malaria.

palustre, *adj.* swampy.

pamonha, *n.f.* corn and cinnamon cake; *n.m.f.* dunce.

pampa, 1. *adj.* white-faced; piebald. 2. *n.m.f. pl.* pampas; **às pampas**, *(coll.)* galore; very.

panacéia, *n.f.* panacea.

Panamá, *n.m.* Panama.

panamenho -nha, *adj., n.* Panamanian.

pan-americano, *adj.* Pan-American.

panar, *vb.* bread.

pança, *n.f.* paunch.

pancada, 1. *adj. (coll.)* crazy. 2. *n.f.* blow, hit; squall.

pancrácio, *n.m.* idiot.

pançudo, *adj.* paunchy.

pandarecos, *n.m. pl.* pieces.

pândega, *n.f.* revelry.

pândego, 1. *adj.* carousing; merry. 2. *n.m.* carouser.

pandeiro, *n.m.* tambourine.

pandemônio, *n.m.* pandemonium.

pandorga, *n.f.* kite (toy).

pandulho, *n.m. (coll.)* belly.

pane, *n.f.* breakdown.

panela, *n.f.* pan, pot; clique.

panelinha, *n.f.* clique.

panfleto, *n.m.* pamphlet; lampoon.

pânico, *n.m.* panic.

panificação, *n.f.* bakery; breadmaking.

panificador -ra, *n.* baker; *n.f.* bakery.

pano, *n.m.* cloth; *(naut.)* sail; *(sl.)* clothes. **p. de boca**, stage curtain; **a todo p.** full speed; **botar panos quentes em**, *(coll.)* compromise; **dar p. para mangas**, *(coll.)* create a fuss; **por**

baixo do p., under the counter.

panorama, *n.m.* panorama; survey.

panorâmico, *adj.* panoramic, overall.

panqueca, *n.f.* pancake.

pantalha, *n.f.* lampshade.

pantanal, *n.m.* large swamp; *(cap.)* lowlands in Mato Grosso.

pântano, *n.m.* swamp.

pantanoso, *adj.* swampy.

panteão, *n.m.* pantheon.

pantera, *n.f.* panther.

pantomima, *n.f.* pantomime.

panturrilha, *n.f.* calf (leg).

pão, *n.m.* bread, loaf; *(sl.)* cute guy. **p. integral**, whole-wheat bread; **P. de Açúcar**, Sugar Loaf; **p. p., queijo queijo**, *(coll.)* outspokenly; **comer o p. que o diabo amassou**, *(coll.)* have a hard life; **ganhar o p.**, earn one's living.

pão-de-ló, *n.m.* sponge cake.

pão-duro, *(coll.)* 1. *adj.* stingy. 2. *n.m.f.* tightwad.

pãozinho, *n.m.* roll, bun.

Papa, *n.m.* Pope.

papa, *n.f.* pap, mush. **não ter papas na língua**, be outspoken.

papada, *n.f.* double chin.

papaguear, -guear, *vb.* chatter.

papagaio, 1. *n.m.* parrot; kite (toy); *(coll.)* chatterbox; *(coll.)* IOU. 2. *interj.* gee! wow!

papai, *n.m.* papa, daddy. **o p.**, *(sl.)* yours truly (m.); **P. Noel**, Santa Claus.

papa-jantares, *n.m.f. (coll.)* freeloader.

papalvo, *n.m.* fool.

papa-moscas, *n.m.f. (coll.)* lamebrain.

papão, *n.m.* boogeyman.

papar, *vb. (coll.)* eat.

paparicar, *vb. (coll.)* pamper.

papear, *vb. (coll.)* chat; *(sl.)* sweet-talk.

papeira, *n.f.* goiter; mumps.

papel, *n.m.* paper; role; *(pl.)* documents. **fazer/desempenhar um p.**, play a role.

papelada, *n.f.* pile of papers; *(coll.)* red tape.

papelão, *n.m.* cardboard; *(coll.)* spectacle.

papelaria, *n.f.* stationery store.
papel-carbono, *n.m.* carbon paper.
papeleiro -ra, *n.* stationer.
papeleta, *n.f.* slip of paper.
papel-moeda, *n.m.* banknote.
papo, *n.m.* craw; goiter; *(coll.)* belly; *(coll.)* chat; *(coll.)* hot air. **p. firme**, *(sl.)* straight talk; **p. furado**, *(sl.)* lies; **bater (um) p.**, *(coll.)* chat; **de p. para o ar**, *(coll.)* loafing; **estar em papos de aranha**, *(coll.)* be in a jam.
papoula, *n.f.* poppy.
papudo, *adj.* double-chinned; *(coll.)* boastful.
paquera, *n.m.* *(sl.)* woman-chaser; *n.f.* woman-chasing.
paquerar, *vb.* *(sl.)* flirt (with), try to pick (someone) up.
paquete, *n.m.(naut.)* liner; *(coll.)* menstruation. **estar de p.**, *(coll.)* have one's period.
Paquistão, *n.m.* Pakistan.
par, **1.** *adj.* like; even (number); **2.** *n.m.* pair; peer; partner. **a p. de**, up-to-date on; **de p. em p.**, wide open; **sem p.**, peerless.
para, **1.** *prep.* for; to, toward. **p. cá/lá**, this/that way; **p. onde?**, whereto?; **de lá para cá**, back and forth; **estar p.**, be about to. **2.** *conj.* in order to. **p. que**, in order that.
parabenizar, *vb.* congratulate.
parabéns, *n.m.pl.* congratulations.
parábola, *n.f.* parable.
pára-brisa, *n.m.* windshield.
pára-choque, *n.m.* bumper (car).
parada, *n.f.* stop; stopping place; parade; bet; *(sl.)* challenge; hard task; *(sl.)* really something. **p. de ônibus**, bus stop.
paradeiro, *n.m.* whereabouts.
paradigma, *n.m.* paradigm.
parado, *adj.* stopped; still; standing; *(sl.)* crazy (about).
paradoxal, *adj.* paradoxical.
paradoxo, *n.m.* paradox.
paraense, **1.** *adj.* of/pert. to the state of Pará. **2.** *n.m.f.* Pará native.
parafernália, *n.f.* paraphernalia.

parafina, *n.f.* paraffin.
paráfrase, *n.f.* paraphrase.
—**parafrasear**, *vb.*
parafuso, *n.m.* screw, bolt. **ter um p. frouxo/de menos**, *(coll.)* have a screw loose.
paragem, *n.f.* stopping place; place.
parágrafo, *n.m.* paragraph.
Paraguai, *n.m.* Paraguay.
paraguaio -ia, *adj.*, *n.* Paraguayan.
paraibano, **1.** *adj.* of/pert. to Paraíba state. **2.** *n.m.* Paraíba native.
paraíso, *n.m.* paradise.
pára-lama, *n.m.* fender (car).
paralelepípedo, *n.m.* paving stone.
paralelo, *adj.*, *n.m.* parallel.
paralelogramo, *n.m.* parallelogram.
paralisar, *vb.* paralyze.
paralisia, *n.f.* paralysis.
paralítico -ca, *adj.*, *n.* paralytic.
paramento, *n.m.* vestment; adornment.
parâmetro, *n.m.* parameter.
páramo, *n.m.* high plain.
paranaense, **1.** *adj.* of/pert. to Paraná state. **2.** *n.m.f.* Paraná native.
paraninfar, *vb.* give a graduation speech.
paraninfo, *n.m.* graduation speaker.
paranóia, *n.f.* paranoia.
paranóico -ca, *adj.*, *n.* paranoid.
parapeito, *n.m.* parapet; rampart.
paraplégico -ca, *adj.*, *n.* paraplegic.
parapsicologia, *n.f.* parapsychology.
pára-quedas, *n.m.* parachute.
pára-quedista, *n.m.f.* parachutist.
parar, *vb.* stop; stay (at). **p. de**, quit.
pára-raios, *n.m.* lightning rod.
parasítico, *adj.* parasitic.
parasito, *n.m.* parasite.
pára-sol, *n.m.* parasol.
paratropa, *n.f.* paratroops.
parceiro -ra, *n.* partner.
parcela, *n.f.* parcel, small part.
parcelar, *vb.* parcel.

parceria, n.f. partnership.

parche, n.m. (med.) compress.

parcial, adj. partial.

parcialidade, n.f. partiality.

parcimônia, n.f. parsimony.

parcimonioso, adj. parsimonious.

parco, adj. meager; frugal.

pardal, n.m. sparrow.

pardavasco -ca, adj., n. mulatto.

pardieiro, n.m. shack.

pardo -da, 1. adj. brownish. **2.** n. mulatto.

parecença, n.f. likeness.

parecer, 1. n.m. appearance; opinion. **2.** vb. seem, look; look like. **p.-se com,** resemble, look like.

parecido, adj. similar, like.

paredão, n.m. high wall.

parede, n.f. wall; strike.

paredro, n.m. director; bigwig.

parelha, n.f. pair; partner. **correr parelhas com,** rival.

parelho, adj. similar.

parental, adj. parental.

parente, 1. adj. related. **2.** n.m.f. relative.

parentela, n.f. kin.

parentesco, n.m. kinship.

parêntese, -sis, n.m. parenthesis.

páreo, n.m. race, contest.

pareô, n.m. pareu.

pária, n.m. pariah.

paridade, n.f. parity.

parir, vb. give birth (to).

parlamentar, 1. adj. parliamentary. **2.** n.m.f. member of parliament. **3.** vb. discuss, parley.

parlamentário -ria, 1. adj. parliamentary. **2.** n. negotiator.

parlamento, n.m. parliament.

parnasiano -na, adj., n. Parnassian.

Parnaso, n.m. Parnassus; poetry.

pároco, n.m. parish priest.

paródia, n.f. parody.
—parodiar, vb.

parola, -lagem, n.f. idle talk.

paróquia, n.f. parish.

paroquial, adj. parish, parochial.

paroquiano -na, n. parishioner.

paroxismo, n.m. paroxysm, spasm.

parque, n.m. park.

parquete, -quê, n.m. parquet.

parquímetro, n.m. parking meter.

parra, n.f. grape leaf.

parreira, n.f. grapevine.

parrudo, adj. (sl.) brawny.

parte, n.f. part; role; report; place; (jur.) party; (pl.) talents; genitalia. **à p.,** apart, aside; **da p. de,** on the part of; **dar p.,** inform; **ter p. com,** have a pact with; **tomar p. em,** take part in.

parteira, n.f. midwife.

partição, n.f. partition, division.

participação, n.f. participation; announcement. **p. nos lucros,** profit sharing.

participante, 1. adj. participating. **2.** n.m.f. participant.

participar, vb. participate; announce. **p. de/em,** participate in.

partícipe, adj., n.m.f. participant.

particípio, n.m. (past) participle.

partícula, n.f. particle.

particular, 1. adj. particular; private; peculiar. **2.** n.m. particular; private conversation. **em p.,** in private; in particular.

particularidade, n.f. detail; circumstance.

partida, n.f. departure; game, match; shipment; record; gang; prank.

partidário -ria, adj., n. partisan.

partido, n.m. party, faction; advantage; decision; (coll.) marriage catch. **tirar p. de,** take advantage of; **tomar o p. de,** take the side of.

partilha, n.f. apportionment; portion.

partilhar, vb. (jur.) apportion; share.

partir, vb. divide; break; depart; start. **a p. de,** as of.

partitura, n.f. (mus.) score.

parto, n.m. childbirth.

parturição, n.f. parturition.

parturiente, 1. adj. parturient. **2.** n.f. woman in childbirth.

parvo, 1. adj. small; silly. **2.** n.m. fool.

parvoíce, n.f. stupidity; silliness.

párvulo, 1. adj. small. **2.** n.m. small boy.

pascer, vb. graze; delight.

Páscoa, n.f. Easter; Passover.

pasmaceira, n.f. amazement; apathy.

pasmar, vb. amaze; be amazed. **p.-se,** be amazed.

pasmo, n.m. 1. adj. amazed. **2.** n.m. amazement; awe.

pasmoso, adj. amazing.

paspalhão -lhona, 1. adj. foolish. **2.** n. fool.

pasquim, n.m. lampoon, pasquinade.

passa, n.f. raisin.

passada, n.f. step; fast trip; (pl.) efforts.

passadeira, n.f. long rug; ironing woman; ironer.

passadiço, 1. adj. transitory. **2.** n.m. corridor; walk.

passado, 1. adj. past; ago; aged; overdone; upset. **bem/mal p.,** well-done/rare (meat). **2.** n.m. past; (pl.) ancestors.

passador -ra, n. passer; (sl.) smuggler; (sl.) pusher; n.m. colander.

passageiro -ra, 1. adj. transitory. **2.** n. passenger.

passagem, n.f. passage; fare, ticket; crossing. **de p.,** in passing; **dar p.,** make way; **estar de p.,** be passing through; **p. de nível,** level crossing.

passante, 1. adj. exceeding. **2.** n.m.f. passer-by.

passaporte, n.m. passport.

passar, vb. pass; go; carry; spend (time); iron; experience; apply; show; assign; elapse; get along. **p.-se,** happen. **não p. de,** be no more than; **p. a ferro,** iron; **p. por alto,** overlook; **p. a limpo,** make a clean copy of; **p. bem/mal,** be fine/ill; **p. de,** exceed; **p. fome,** starve.

passarada, n.f., **-redo,** n.m. flock of birds.

passarela, n.f. (theat.) runway.

passarinho, n.m. bird.

pássaro, n.m. bird.

passatempo, n.m. pastime.

passe, n.m. pass.

passear, vb. walk, stroll; ride; tour.

passeata, n.f. walk; public demonstration.

passeio, n.m. walk; ride; excursion; promenade; sidewalk. **dar um p.,** take a walk.

passional, adj. passionate; of passion.

passista, n.m.f. Carnival dancer.

passível, adj. sensitive. **p. de,** subject to.

passivo, 1. adj. passive. **2.** n.m. liability.

passo, n.m. pace, step; situation; passageway; (cap., pl.) Stations of the Cross; **ao p. que,** whereas; **marcar p.,** mark time.

pasta, n.f. paste; briefcase; file folder; portfolio. **p. dentifrícia/de dentes,** toothpaste.

pastagem, n.f. pasture, grass.

pastar, vb. graze; (fig.) feast.

pastel, n.m. turnover; pastel.

pastelão, n.m. large pie; slapstick comedy.

pastelaria, n.f. pastry; pastry shop.

pasteurizar, vb. pasteurize.

pastilha, n.f. tablet, pill.

pasto, n.m. pasture; feeding.

pastor -ra, n. shepherd -ess; pastor.

pastoral, adj. pastoral.

pastorear, vb. herd, shepherd.

pastoril, adj. pastoral, rustic.

pata, n.f. paw; (coll.) foot.

pataca, n.f. old coin; money.

pata-choca, n.f. fat, lazy woman.

patacudo, adj. (coll.) wealthy.

patada, n.f. kick; blunder; ingratitude.

patamar, n.m. staircase landing.

patavina, n.f. (coll.) nothing.

patear, vb. stamp one's feet.

patente, 1. adj. patent. **2.** n.f. patent; charter; rank.

patentear, vb. patent; make plain. **p.-se,** be evident.

paternal, adj. paternal.

paternidade, n.f. paternity.

paterno, adj. paternal.

pateta, *n.m.f.* nitwit.

patético, *adj.* pathetic.

patíbulo, *n.m.* scaffold, gallows.

patife, *n.m.* scoundrel.

patim, *n.m.* skate. —**patinar**, *vb.*

patinação, -nagem, *n.f.* skating.

patinador -ra, *n.* skater.

patinete, *n.m.* scooter.

patinhar, *vb.* splash about.

pátio, *n.m.* patio.

pato, *n.m.* duck; (*coll.*) sucker.

patologia, *n.f.* pathology.

patos, *n.m.* pathos.

patranha, *n.f.* lie, whopper.

patrão, *n.m.* owner, boss (*m.*).

pátria, *n.f.* native land.

patriarca, *n.m.* patriarch.

patrício -cia, 1. *adj.* patrician. 2. *n.* patrician; compatriot.

patrimônio, *n.m.* patrimony; estate.

patriota, *n.m.f.* patriot.

patriotada, -tice, *n.f.* flag-waving.

patrioteiro, *adj.* chauvinistic.

patriótico, *adj.* patriotic.

patriotismo, *n.m.* patriotism.

patroa, *n.f.* owner, boss (*f.*); (*coll.*) wife.

patrocinador -ra, *n.* sponsor. —**patrocinar**, *vb.*

patrocínio, *n.m.* sponsorship.

patronagem, *n.f.* patronage.

patrono, *n.m.* patron.

patrulha, *n.f.* patrol. —**patrulhar**, *vb.*

patuscada, *n.f.* revelry.

pau, 1. *adj.* (*coll.*) boring. 2. *n.m.* wood; stick; club; (*coll.*) cruzado -zeiro; (*sl.*) skirmish; (*vulg.*) penis; (*pl.*) clubs (cards). **levar p.**, (*sl.*) flunk; **meter/baixar o p. em**, (*coll.*) clobber; run down.

pau-a-pique, *n.m.* wattle.

pau-brasil, *n.m.* brazilwood.

pau-d'água, *n.m.* (*coll.*) drunkard.

pau-de-arara, *n.m.f.* (*coll.*) Northeasterner.

pau-de-cabeleira, *n.m.f.* (*coll.*) chaperon.

pau-de-fogo, *n.m.* (*sl.*) firearm.

paul, *n.m.* swamp.

paulada, *n.f.* blow with a stick.

paulatino, *adj.* slow, gradual.

pauleira, *n.f.* (*sl.*) fight. **som p.** (*sl.*) hard rock music.

paulificação, *n.f.* (*coll.*) annoyance.

paulificar, *vb.* (*coll.*) annoy.

paulista, 1. *adj.* of/pert. to São Paulo state. 2. *n.m.f.* native of São Paulo state.

paulistano -na, 1. *adj.* of/pert. to the city of São Paulo. 2. *n.* native of the city of São Paulo.

pau-mandado, *n.m.* henchman.

paupérrimo, *adj.* extremely poor.

pausa, *n.f.* pause. —**pausar**, *vb.*

pausado, *adj.* slow.

pauta, *n.f.* guide line; (*mus.*) staff; list; agenda.

pautar, *vb.* rule (paper); regulate.

pauzinhos, *n.m.pl.* (*coll.*) gossip; (*pl.*) chopsticks. **mexer os p.**, (*coll.*) pull strings.

pavão, *n.m.* peacock.

pavilhão, *n.m.* pavillion; banner.

pavimentar, *vb.* pave; floor.

pavimento, *n.m.* pavement; floor, story.

pavio, *n.m.* wick, fuse. **de fio a p.**, from end to end.

pavonada, *n.f.* showing off; vanity.

pavonear-se, *vb.* strut, show off.

pavor, *n.m.* fear.

pavoroso, *adj.* frightful.

paz, *n.f.* peace. **deixar em p.**, leave alone; **fazer as pazes**, make peace.

pé, *n.m.* foot; bottom; foothold; basis; tree. **ao p. da letra**, word for word; **dar no p.**, (*coll.*) run away; leave; **estar com um p. na cova**, have a foot in the grave; **não ter pés nem cabeça**, lack rhyme or reason; **negar a pés juntos**, deny flatly.

pê, *n.m.* the letter p.

peanha, *n.f.* bracket, shelf.

peão, *n.m.* pedestrian; foot soldier; pawn (chess); peon.

peça, *n.f.* piece; part; room; (*theat.*) play; (*coll.*) prank.

pecadilho, *n.m.* peccadillo.

pecado, *n.m.* sin.

pecador -ra, *n.* sinner.

pecaminoso, *adj.* sinful.

pecar, *vb.* sin, err.

pecha, *n.f.* flaw.

pechincha, *n.f.* bargain; windfall.

pechinchar, *vb.* bargain, haggle.

peco, 1. *adj.* withered. 2. *(bot.)* blight.

peçonha, *n.f.* poison, venom.

pecuária, *n.f.* cattle-raising.

pecuário, 1. *adj.* cattle. 2. *n.m.* cattle rancher.

pecuarista, *n.m.f.* cattle rancher.

peculiar, *adj.* peculiar.

peculiaridade, *n.f.* peculiarity.

pecúlio, *n.m.* savings.

pecúnia, *n.f.* money.

pedaço, *n.m.* piece; *(coll.)* attractive woman. **cair aos pedaços**, fall to pieces.

pedágio, *n.m.* toll (road).

pedagogia, *n.f.* pedagogy.

pedagogo, *n.m.* pedagogue.

pé-d'água, *n.m.* sudden downpour.

pedal, *n.m.* pedal. —**pedalar**, *vb.*

pedante, 1. *adj.* pedantic. 2. *n.m.f.* pedant.

pé-de-boi, *n.m. (coll.)* hard worker.

pé-de-cabra, *n.m.* crowbar.

pé-de-meia, *n.m.* savings.

pé-de-moleque, *n.m.* peanut brittle.

pederasta, *n.m.* pederast; homosexual.

pederneira, *n.f.* flint.

pedestal, *n.m.* pedestal.

pedestre, *adj., n.m.f.* pedestrian.

pé-de-vento, *n.m.* gust of wind.

pediatra, *n.m.f.* pediatrician.

pedicuro, *n.m.* podiatrist.

pedido, *n.m.* request.

pedinchão -chona, 1. *adj.* begging. 2. *n.* beggar; importuner.

pedinchar, *vb.* beg; importune.

pedinte, *n.m.f.* beggar.

pedir, *vb.* ask (for); request; demand; beg. **p. contas**, demand an explanation; **p. desculpas**, apologize.

pedra, *n.f.* rock, stone; blackboard. **p. angular**, cornerstone; **p. de gelo**, ice cube.

pedrada, *n.f.* blow with a stone.

pedra-sabão, *n.f.* soapstone.

pedregoso, *adj.* rocky.

pedregulho, *n.m.* gravel.

pedreira, *n.f.* stone quarry.

pedreiro, *n.m.* bricklayer, mason.

pedrês, *adj.* spotted.

pé-duro, 1. *adj. (sl.)* shoddy. 2. *n.m. (coll.)* poor devil.

pé-frio, *n.m. (coll.)* jinx; bad luck.

pega, *n.f.* catch; handle; *n.m.* skirmish.

pegada, *n.f.* footstep, track.

pegadiço, *adj.* sticky; annoying.

pegado, *adj.* near, close.

pegajoso, *adj.* sticky; annoying.

pega-ladrão, *n.m.* burglar alarm.

pega-pega, *n.m.* scuffle.

pega-pra-capar, *n.m. (sl.)* skirmish.

pegar, *vb.* catch; grab; catch on; pick up; understand; start; stick. **p.-se a**, stick to; **p. em**, grab, pick up.

peia, *n.f.* shackle; obstacle.

peidar, *vb. (vulg.)* fart. —**peido**, *n.m.*

peitar, *vb.* bribe. —**peita**, *n.f.*

peitilho, *n.m.* shirt front.

peito, *n.m.* chest, breast; courage. **dar o p.**, suckle; **meter os peitos**, *(sl.)* exert oneself; **no p.**, *(sl.)* the hard way; **tomar a p.**, take to heart.

peitoril, *n.m.* sill, parapet.

peituda, *adj. (coll.)* busty.

peitudo, *adj. (coll.)* gutsy.

peixada, *n.f.* fish stew; fish fry.

peixão, *n.m. (coll.)* attractive woman.

peixaria, *n.f.* fish market.

peixe, *n.m.* fish. **vender o seu p.**, *(coll.)* speak one's piece.

peixe-espada, *n.m.* swordfish.

peixeira, *n.f.* fishwife; knife.

peixeiro -ra, *n.* fishmonger.

peixinho, *n.m. (coll.)* pet, favorite.

pejar, *vb.* clog, fill. **p.-se**, be embarrassed.

pejo, *n.m.* embarrassment; bashfulness.

pejorativo, *adj.* pejorative, derogatory.

pela, *contr. of* por + a.

pelada, *n.f.* informal soccer match.

pelado, *adj.* hairless; *(coll.)* naked.

pelanca, *n.f.* loose skin.

pelar, *vb.* skin, peel; rob.

pelas, *contr. of* por + as.

pele, *n.f.* skin; pelt, fur.

peleja, *n.f.* fight; match.

pelejador -ra, *n.* fighter.

pelejar, *vb.* fight; compete.

pelica, *n.f.* kid leather.

pelicano, *n.m.* pelican.

película, *n.f.* membrane; *(phot.)* film.

pelintra, *n.m.f.* shabby, pretentious person; fop.

pelo, *contr. of* por + o.

pêlo, *n.m.* hair, fuzz. **em p.,** *(coll.)* naked.

pelos, *contr. of* por + os.

pelota, *n.f.* pellet; ball.

pelotão, *n.m.* platoon.

pelourinho, *n.m.* pillory.

peltre, *n.m.* pewter.

peludo, *adj.* hairy, shaggy.

pelve, -vis, *n.f.* pelvis.

pena, *n.f.* feather; pen; punishment; pity. **valer a p.,** be worthwhile; **p. de morte,** death penalty; **que p.!,** too bad!; **ter p. de,** pity.

penacho, *n.m.* plume, tuft.

penado, *adj.* suffering.

penal, *adj.* penal.

penalidade, *n.f.* penalty, punishment.

pênalti, *n.m. (sport.)* penalty.

penar, 1. *n.m.* suffering. **2.** *vb.* pain; suffer.

penca, *n.f.* bunch (fruit). **em p.,** galore.

pendão, *n.m.* banner.

pendência, *n.f.* fight.

pendente, 1. *adj.* hanging; pending. **2.** *n.m.* pendant.

pender, *vb.* hang; tilt; tend.

pendor, *n.m.* propensity; slope.

pêndulo, *n.m.* pendulum.

pendura, *n.f.* hanging. **na p.,** *(coll.)* penniless.

pendurar, *vb.* hang; *(coll.)* pawn.

penduricalho, *n.m.* trinket.

penedo, *n.m.* rock, cliff.

peneira, *n.f.* sieve.

peneirar, *vb.* sift.

penetra, *n.m.f. (coll.)* intruder, crasher.

penetrar, *vb.* penetrate; *(coll.)* crash.

penha, *n.f.* cliff.

penhasco, *n.m.* crag.

penhor, *n.m.* pledge; pawn.

penhorar, *vb. (jur.)* seize; pawn; pledge.

penhorista, *n.m.f.* pawnbroker.

penicilina, *n.f.* penicillin.

penico, *n.m.* bedpan. **pedir p.,** *(coll.)* give up.

península, *n.f.* peninsula.

pênis, *n.m.* penis.

penitência, *n.f.* penitence; penance.

penitenciária, *n.f.* penitentiary.

penitente, *adj.* penitent.

penoso, *adj.* distressing; annoying.

pensador -ra, *n.* thinker.

pensamento, *n.m.* thought.

pensão, *n.f.* boardinghouse; board; allowance.

pensar, *vb.* think; consider; intend; dress (wound).

pensativo, *adj.* pensive.

pênsil, *adj.* hanging.

pensionato, *n.m.* boarding school.

pensionista, *n.m.f.* pensioner; boarder.

penso, 1. *adj.* hanging. **2.** *n.m.* dressing (wound).

pentágono, *n.m.* pentagon

pente, *n.m.* comb.

penteadeira, *n.f.* dressing table.

penteado, *n.m.* hair-do.

penteador -ra, *n.* comber; *n.m.* peignoir.

pentear, *vb.* comb.

pentelho, *n.m. (vulg.)* pubic hair *(coll.)* jerk.

penugem, *n.f.* fuzz, down.

penúltimo, *adj.* next-to-last.

penúria, *n.f.* penury.

pepino, *n.m.* cucumber.

pepita, *n.f.* nugget.

pequenez, *n.f.* smallness.

pequenino, *adj.* very little.

pequena, *n.f. (sl.)* girlfriend.

pequeno, *adj.* little, small.

Pequim, *n.* Beijing.

pêra, *n.f.* pear.

peralta, 1. adj. mischievous. **2.** n.m.f. little rascal; dandy.

perante, prep. before, in the presence of.

pé-rapado, n.m. (coll.) poor devil.

perca, n.f. (ichth.) perch, bass.

percalço, n.m. drawback, hitch.

perceber, vb. perceive; notice; understand.

percentagem, n.f. percentage.

percepção, n.f. perception.

perceptivo, adj. perceptive.

percevejo, n.m. bedbug; thumbtack.

percha, n.f. gymnastic bar.

percolar, vb. percolate.

percorrer, vb. go over/through; look over.

percurso, n.m. course, route.

percussão, n.f. percussion.

percutir, vb. strike, hit.

perda, n.f. loss.

perdão, 1. n.m. pardon, forgiveness. **2.** interj. sorry!

perdedor -ra, n. loser.

perder, vb. lose; miss; waste; ruin. **p.-se,** go astray. **p. o juízo,** lose one's mind.

perdição, n.f. perdition.

perdigão, n.m. male partridge.

perdiz, n.f. partridge.

perdoar, vb. pardon, forgive.

perdulário -ria, 1. adj. wasteful. **2.** n. wastrel.

perdurar, vb. endure, last long.

pereba, n.f. sore.

perecer, vb. perish; die.

peregrinação, n.f. pilgrimage.

peregrinar, vb. go on a pilgrimage.

peregrino -na, n. pilgrim.

pereira, n.f. pear tree.

peremptório, adj. peremptory.

perene, adj. perennial.

perereca, adj. small and lively.

perfazer, vb. add up to; accomplish.

perfeccionista, n.m.f. perfectionist.

perfeição, n.f. perfection.

perfeito, 1. adj. perfect; (gram.) preterite. **2.** n.m. (gram.) preterite.

perfídia, n.f. treachery.

pérfido, adj. perfidious.

perfil, n.m. profile. —**perfilar,** vb.

perfume, n.m. perfume—**perfumar,** vb.

perfunctório, adj. perfunctory.

perfuração, n.f. perforation; drilling.

perfurar, vb. perforate; drill.

perfuratriz, -dora, n.f. drilling machine.

pergaminho, n.m. parchment.

pérgula, n.f. arbor.

pergunta, n.f. question.

perguntar, vb. ask a question; ask.

perícia, n.f. expertise, skill.

periferia, n.f. periphery.

periférico, adj., n.m. peripheral.

perífrase, n.f. periphrasis.

perigo, n.m. danger.

perigoso, adj. dangerous.

periódico, 1. adj. periodic. **2.** n.m. periodical.

periodismo, n.m. journalism.

periodista, n.m.f. journalist.

período, n.m. period; (gram.) clause, sentence.

peripécia, n.f. vicissitude.

periquito, n.m. parakeet.

perito, adj., n.m. expert.

perjurar, vb. renounce; commit perjury.

perjúrio, n.m. perjury.

perjuro -ra, 1. adj. perjuring. **2.** n. perjurer.

permanecer, vb. remain, stay.

permanência, n.f. permanence; stay.

permanente, adj., n.f. permanent.

permear, vb. permeate; put/come between; occur.

permeio, adv. in the middle de p., in between.

permissão, n.f. permission; permit.

permissível, adj. permissible.

permissivo, adj. permissive.

permitir, vb. permit, allow.

permuta, n.f. exchange, barter.

permutação, n.f. permutation.

permutar, vb. exchange, barter.

perna, n.f. leg. **de pernas para o ar,** (coll.) topsy-turvy; **estirar/desenferrujar as pernas,** stretch one's legs; **passar a p.**

em, *(coll.)* trick; cheat on; **trocar pernas,** *(coll.)* stagger.

pernambucano -na, 1. *adj.* of/ pert. to Pernambuco state. **2.** *n.* Pernambuco native.

perneira, *n.f.* legging.

perneta, *n.m.f.* one-legged person.

pernicioso, *adj.* pernicious.

pernil, *n.m.* shank; haunch (ham).

pernilongo, 1. *adj.* long-legged. **2.** *n.m.* yellow-fever mosquito.

pernoitar, *vb.* stay overnight.

pernóstico, *adj.* pretentious; arrogant.

peroba, *n.f.* type of timber tree; *n.m.f.* nuisance.

pérola, *n.f.* pearl.

peroração, *n.f.* peroration; speech.

perorar, *vb.* give a long speech.

perpassar, *vb.* pass through/ over.

perpendicular, *adj.* perpendicular.

perpetrar, *vb.* perpetrate.

perpetuar, *vb.* perpetuate.

perpetuidade, *n.f.* perpetuity.

perpétuo, *adj.* perpetual.

perplexo, *adj.* perplexed.

perrengue, *adj.* weak; sickly; cowardly.

perro, 1. *adj.* stubborn. **2.** *n.m.* dog.

persa *adj.*, *n.m.f.* Persian.

perscrutar, *vb.* investigate.

perseguição, *n.f.* pursuit; persecution.

perseguir, *vb.* pursue; persecute.

perseverar, *vb.* persevere.

persianas, *n.f.pl.* Venetian blinds.

pérsico, *adj.* Persian.

persignar-se, *vb.* make the sign of the cross.

persistente, *adj.* persistent.

persistir, *vb.* persist.

personagem, *n.m.f.* character, personage.

personalidade, *n.f.* personality.

personalizar, *vb.* personalize.

personificar, *vb.* personify.

perspectiva, *n.f.* perspective; prospect.

perspicaz, *adj.* astute.

perspiração, *n.f.* perspiration.

persuadir, *vb.* persuade. **p.-se,** become convinced.

persuasão, *n.f.* persuasion.

persuasiva, *n.f.* persuasiveness.

persuasivo, *adj.* persuasive.

pertencer, *vb.* belong; pertain.

pertences, *n.m.pl.* belongings.

pertinaz, *adj.* persistent.

pertinência, *n.f.* pertinence.

pertinente, *adj.* pertinent.

perto, *adv.* nearby. **p. de,** close to, near (to).

perturbar, *vb.* disturb, perturb. **p.-se,** get upset.

peru, *n.m.* turkey; *(coll.)* kibitzer; *(vulg.)* penis.

perua, *n.f.* turkey (f.); *(coll.)* prostitute; *(coll.)* station wagon.

peruano -na, *adj.*, *n.* Peruvian.

peruar, *vb. (coll.)* look on.

peruca, *n.f.* wig.

pervagar, *vb.* cross back and forth; wander.

perversão, *n.f.* perversion.

perverso, *adj.* perverse.

perverter, *vb.* pervert.

pervertido -da, 1. *adj.* perverted. **2.** *n.* pervert.

pesadelo, *n.m.* nightmare.

pesado, *adj.* heavy; rich (food); rough; annoying; crude; *(coll.)* unlucky.

pêsames, *n.m.pl.* condolences.

pesar, 1. *n.m.* sorrow. **2.** *vb.* weigh. **p. na balança,** carry weight; **em que pese a,** despite.

pesaroso, *adj.* sorry; sorrowful.

pesca, *vb.* fishing.

pescador -ra, *n.* fisherman -woman.

pescar, *vb.* fish; *(coll.)* understand.

pescaria, *n.f.* fishing; *(sl.)* cheating (exams).

pescoço, *n.m.* neck.

peso, *n.m.* weight; peso; *(coll.)* bad luck. **p. bruto,** gross weight; **p. líquido,** net weight.

pespegar, *vb.* strike, deal.

pesquisa, *n.f.* research, investigation.

pesquisador -ra, *n.* researcher.

pesquisar, *vb.* research.

pêssego, *n.m.* peach.

pessimismo, *n.m.* pessimism.

pessimista, 1. *adj.* pessimistic. **2.** *n.m.f.* pessimist.

péssimo, *adj.* very bad.

pessoa, *n.f.* person.

pessoal, 1. *adj.* personal. **2.** *n.m.* personnel; *(coll.)* folks.

pestana, *n.f.* eyelash; *(coll.)* nap.

pestanejar, *vb.* wink, blink.

peste, *n.f.* plague; scoundrel. **da p.,** *(coll.)* terrible; extraordinary.

pestilência, *n.f.* pestilence.

peta, *n.f. (coll.)* fib, lie.

pétala, *n.f.* petal.

petardo, *n.m.* petard.

peteca, *n.f.(sport.)* hand shuttlecock.

peteleco, *n.m.* fillip.

petição, *n.f.* petition, request; application. **em p. de miséria,** in a miserable state.

peticego, *adj.* nearsighted.

peticionário -ria, *n.* petitioner.

petimetre, *n.m.* dandy, fop.

petiscar, *vb.* nibble.

petisco, *n.m.* tidbit, goody.

petiz, *n.m.f. (coll.)* small child.

petrechos, *n.m.pl.* equipment, gear.

petrificar, *vb.* petrify.

petroleiro, 1. *adj.* petroleum. **2.** *n.m.* oil tanker.

petróleo, *n.m.* petroleum, oil.

petrolífero, *adj.* oil-yielding.

petulante, *adj.* petulant.

pevide, *n.f.* pip, seed.

pexote, *n.m.* novice; *(sport.)* bad player.

pez, *n.m.* tar, pitch.

pia, *n.f.* sink.

piada, *n.f.* joke; chirp.

pianista, *n.m.f.* pianist.

piano, *n.m.* piano.

pianola, *n.f.* player piano.

pião, *n.m.* top (toy).

piar, *vb.* chirp, peep; *(sl.)* speak.

piauiense, 1. *adj.* of/pert. to Piauí state. **2.** *n.m.f.* Piauí native.

pica, *n.f. (vulg.)* penis.

picada, *n.f.* prick; sting; path; nose dive; peak.

picadeira, *n.f.* pickaxe.

picadeiro, *n.m.* circus arena.

picadinho, *n.m.* hash; chopped meat and vegetables.

picado, 1. *adj.* offended; excited. **2.** *n.m.* hash.

picante, *adj.* spicy; biting; racy.

picão, *n.m.* pickaxe.

pica-pau, *n.m.* woodpecker.

picar, *vb.* prick; sting; peck; chop up; bite; itch. **p.-se,** take offense; *(sl.)* shoot drugs.

picaresco, *adj.* picaresque, roguish.

picareta, *n.f.* pick; *n.m.f. (coll.)* con artist.

pícaro -ra, 1. roguish. **2.** *n.* rogue.

piçarra, *n.f.* shale; slate; quarry.

pichar, *vb.* smear with pitch; paint grafitti (on); *(coll.)* run down.

piche, *n.m.* pitch, tar.

picles, *n.m.pl.* pickles.

pico, *n.m.* peak; sting; *(sl.)* fix (drugs).

picolé, *n.m.* popsicle.

pictórico, *adj.* pictorial.

picuinha, *n.f.* chirp; quip; gibe.

pidão -dona, 1. *adj.* begging. **2.** *n.* beggar.

piedade, *n.f.* piety; pity.

piedoso, *adj.* pious; compassionate.

piegas, *adj.* maudlin; finicky.

pifão, *n.m. (sl.)* drunken spree.

pifar, *vb. (sl.)* break down; fizzle.

pigarrear, *vb.* clear one's throat.

pigmentação, *n.f.* pigmentation.

pigmento, *n.m.* pigment.

pigmeu -méia, *adj., n.* Pygmy.

pijama, *n.m.* pajamas.

pilantra, *n.m.f. (coll.)* scoundrel.

pilão, *n.m.* wooden mortar; pestle, crusher; pylon.

pilar, 1. *n.m.* pillar. **2.** *vb.* crush.

pileque, *n.m. (sl.)* drunken binge.

pilha, *n.f.* pile; *(elec.)* battery.

pilhagem, *n.f.* pillaging; loot.

pilhar, *vb.* pillage; *(coll.)* catch.

pilhéria, *n.f.* joke. **—pilheriar,** *vb.*

pilotar, *vb.* pilot.

pilotis, *n.m.pl. (arch.)* stilts.

piloto, *n.m.* pilot; race-car driver.

pílula, n.f. pill.

pimenta, n.f. pepper, chili pepper.

pimenta-do-reino, n.f. black pepper.

pimenta-malagueta, n.f. red pepper.

pimentão, n.m. pimento; red pepper.

pimpão -pona, n. swaggerer.

pimpolho, n.m. sprout; young lad.

pinacoteca, n.f. art museum/collection.

pináculo, n.m. pinnacle.

pinça, n.f. tweezers; pincers.

pincaro, n.m. pinnacle.

pincel, n.m. brush.

pincelada, n.f. brush stroke.

pinchar, vb. throw; (coll.) jump.

pindaíba, n.m. (sl.) pennilessness.

pinga, n.f. drop; (sl.) brandy, liquor.

pingar, vb. drip; trickle; (coll.) chip in.

pingente, n.m. pendant; trinket; straphanger.

pingo, n.m. drip, drop; dab; small person.

pingue-pongue, n.m. ping-pong.

pingüim, n.m. penguin.

pinha, n.f. pine cone; type of tropical fruit.

pinheiro, n.m. pine tree.

pinho, n.m. pine; (coll.) guitar.

pinicar, vb. peck; pinch.

pino, n.m. (mech.) pin, bolt; apex. **a p.,** straight up.

pinóia, n.f. (coll.) junk; (coll.) annoyance.

pinote, n.m. leap, jump. **dar o p.,** (sl.) run away.

pinta, n.f. spot; beauty mark; (coll.) looks.

pinta-braba, n.m.f. (sl.) shady character.

pintado, adj. painted; spotted.

pintalgar, vb. speckle.

pintar, vb. paint; (coll.) appear; (coll.) act up. **p. o diabo/o sete,** (coll.) raise hell.

pinto, n.m. chick; kid. **como um p.,** soaking wet.

pintor -ra, n. painter.

pintura, n.f. painting.

pio, 1. adj. pious. **2.** n.m. chirp, peep, hoot. **nem um pio,** not a peep.

piolho, n.m. (entom.) louse.

pioneiro -ra, n. pioneer.

pior, adj. adv. worse; worst.

piorar, vb. worsen.

pipa, n.f. cask; kite (toy).

piparote, n.m. fillip, thump.

pipi, n.m. (coll.) penis; urine. **fazer p.,** pee.

pipoca, n.f. popcorn. **pipocas!,** shucks!

pipocar, vb. pop; bubble.

pique, n.m. piquancy; rush. **a p.,** vertically; **a p. de,** about to; **ir a p.,** (naut.) sink.

piquenique, n.m. picnic.

piqueta, n.f. picket.

piquete, n.m. shift (workers); picket line.

piqueteiro -ra, n. picketer.

pira, n.f. pyre; **dar o p.,** (sl.) run away.

pirado, adj. (sl.) crazy.

pirâmide, n.f. pyramid.

piranha, n.f. piranha.

pirão, n.m. manioc mush.

pirar, vb. (sl.) run away.

pirata, n.m. pirate. —**piratear,** vb.

pirataria, -tagem, n.f. piracy.

pires, n.m. saucer.

pirilampo, n.m. firefly.

piroca, n.f. (vulg.) penis.

pirraça, n.f. stubbornness; spite.

pirracento, adj. stubborn; spiteful.

pirralho -ha, n. child; brat.

pirueta, n.f. pirouette.

pirulito, n.m. lollipop, sucker.

pisada, n.f. footstep.

pisar, vb. step (on).

pisca, n.f. speck; spark.

piscadela, n.f. winking, blinking.

pisca-pisca, n.m. turn signal (car).

piscar, vb. wink, blink; twinkle.

piscina, n.f. swimming pool.

piso, n.m. floor.

pisotear, vb. trample.

pista, n.f. trail; clue; track; lane; runway; dance floor.

pistão, n.m. piston; trumpet.

pistola, *n.f.* pistol.

pistolão, *(coll.)* influential backer, connections.

pistoleiro, *n.m.* gunman.

pistom, *n.m.* trumpet.

pitada, *n.f.* pinch, dab.

pitanga, *n.f.* a tropical fruit.

pitar, *vb.* smoke (pipe).

piteira, *n.f.* cigarette holder.

pitéu, *n.m.* delicacy, tidbit.

pito, *n.m. (coll.)* scolding.

pitomba, *n.f.* soapberry; *(sl.)* punch, blow.

pitoresco, *adj.* picturesque.

pitu, *n.m.* prawn.

pivete, *n.m.* mischievous child; *(sl.)* child thief.

pivô, *n.m.* pivot; support; kingpin.

pixaim, *n.m.* tight curly hair.

placa, *n.f.* plate; plaque, sign; license plate.

placar, *n.m.* placar; badge; scoreboard.

plácido, *adj.* placid.

plaga, *n.f.* region.

plagiar, *vb.* plagiarize.

plágio, *n.m.* plagiarism.

plaina, *n.f.* plane (tool).

plana, *n.f.* category.

planador, *n.m.* glider.

planalto, *n.m.* plateau; *(cap.)* Brazilian executive branch.

planar, *vb.* glide (plane).

planejador -ra, *n.* planner.

planejamento, *n.m.* planning. **p. familiar**, family planning.

planejar, *vb.* plan.

planeta, *n.m.* planet.

planetário, **1.** *adj.* planetary. **2.** *n.m.* planetarium.

plangente, *adj.* plaintive.

planger, *vb.* knell; weep.

planície, *n.f.* plain; prairie.

planificação, *n.f.* planning.

planificador -ra, *n.* planner.

planificar, *vb.* plan.

plano, **1.** *adj.* level, flat. **2.** *n.m.* plan; plane, level.

planta, *n.f.* plant; plan; sole (foot).

plantação, *n.f.* planting; plantation.

plantador -ra, *n.* planter.

plantão, *n.m.* guard duty, duty; one on duty. **de p.**, on duty.

plantar, *vb.* plant; set up; implant.

plantio, *n.m.* planting; planted area.

plantonista, *n.m.f.* one on duty.

planura, *n.f.* plateau; plain.

plaqueta, *n.f.* platelet.

plasma, *n.m.* plasma.

plasmar, *vb.* mold, shape.

plástica, *n.f.* plastic surgery.

plástico, *adj., n.m.* plastic.

plataforma, *n.f.* platform; launching pad; **p. giratória** turntable; *(coll.)* appearance. **p. continental**, continental shelf.

plátano, *n.m.* plane tree; sycamore.

platéia, *n.f.* audience; orchestra seats.

platina, *n.f.* platinum; platen.

platô, *n.m.* plateau.

platônico, *adj.* platonic.

plausível, *adj.* plausible.

plebe, *n.f.* masses.

plebeu -béia, *adj., n.* plebeian.

plebiscito, *n.m.* plebiscite.

pleitear, *vb. (jur.)* plead, argue.

pleito, *n.m. (jur.)* plea; lawsuit; contest.

plenária, *n.f.* plenary session.

plenário, *adj., n.m.* plenary.

plenilúnio, *n.m.* full moon.

plenitude, *n.f.* plenitude.

pleno, *adj.* full, complete. **em plena rua**, in the middle of the street; **em p. dia**, in broad daylight.

pletora, *n.f.* plethora.

plexo, *n.m.* network.

plissar, *vb.* crimp, pleat.

pluma, *n.f.* feather, plume; pen.

plumagem, *n.f.* plumage.

plumitivo, *n.m.* hack writer.

plural, *adj., n.m.* plural.

pluralidade, *n.f.* plurality.

pluralismo, *n.m.* pluralism.

pluralizar, *vb.* pluralize.

pneu, *n.m.* tire. **p. sobressalente**, spare tire.

pneumático, **1.** *adj.* pneumatic. **2.** *n.m.* tire (car).

pneumonia, *n.f.* pneumonia.

pó, *n.m.* powder; dust; *(sl.)* cocaine. **em p.**, powdered.

pobre, **1.** *adj.* poor; wretched. **2.** *n.m.f.* pauper.

pobretão -tona, *n.* pauper; wretch.
pobreza, *n.f.* poverty.
poça, *n.f.* puddle, pool.
poção, *n.f.* potion.
pocilga, *n.f.* pigsty.
poço, *n.m.* well; pool; pit. **p. de petróleo,** oil well.
poda, *n.f.* pruning.
podar, *vb.* prune.
poder, **1.** *n.m.* power; ability; strength. **no p.,** in power. **2.** *vb.* be able, can, may.
poderio, *n.m.* power, authority.
poderoso, *adj.* powerful.
pódio, *n.m.* podium.
podre, **1.** *adj.* rotten. **p. de rico,** filthy rich. **2.** *n.m.* rottenness; (*pl.*) vices.
podridão, *n.f.* rottenness.
poeira, *n.f.* dust.
poeirento, *adj.* dusty.
poema, *n.m.* poem.
poente, **1.** *adj.* setting (sun). **2.** *n.m.* sunset; west.
poesia, *n.f.* poetry; poem.
poeta, *n.m.f.* poet.
poetar, -tizar, *vb.* poetize.
poético, *adj.* poetic.
poetisa, *n.f.* poetess.
poial, *n.m.* stone bench/slab.
pois, **1.** *adv.* so, then. **p. é,** that's right; **p. não,** certainly. **2.** *conj.* for, since.
polaina, *n.f.* legging.
polar, *adj.* polar.
polarizar, *vb.* polarize.
polca, *n.f.* polka.
poldro, *n.m.* colt.
polé, *n.f.* pulley.
polegada, *n.f.* inch.
polegar, *n.m.* thumb.
poleiro, *n.m.* perch; (*theat.*) gallery.
polêmica, *n.f.* polemic.
pólen, *n.m.* pollen.
polia, *n.f.* pulley.
polícia, *n.f.* police.
policial, **1.** *adj.* police. **2.** *n.m.f.* policeman -woman.
polidez, *n.f.* politeness.
polido, *adj.* polished; polite.
poliglota, *adj.*, *n.m.f.* polyglot.
polígono, *n.m.* polygon.
pólio, poliomielite, *n.f.* polio.
polir, *n.m.* polish.

politeama, *n.m.* variety theater.
politécnico, *adj.* polytechnic.
política, *n.f.* politics; policy.
político -ca, **1.** *adj.* political. **2.** *n.* politician.
politiqueiro -ra, *n.* petty politician.
politizar, *vb.* politicize.
pólo, *n.m.* pole; polo.
polonês -nesa, **1.** *adj.* Polish. **2.** *n.* Pole; *n.m.* Polish (language).
Polônia, *n.f.* Poland.
polpa, *n.f.* pulp, fleshy part.
poltrão -trona, *n.m.* coward.
poltrona, *n.f.* armchair.
poluição, *n.f.* pollution.
poluir, *vb.* pollute.
poluto, *adj.* polluted; corrupt.
polvilho, *n.m.* powder. —**polvilhar,** *vb.*
polvo, *n.m.* octopus.
pólvora, *n.f.* gunpowder.
polvorosa, *n.f.* fuss, stir.
polvoroso, *adj.* dusty.
pomada, *n.f.* pomade.
pomar, *n.m.* orchard.
pombal, *n.m.* dovecote.
pombo -ba, *n.* pigeon, dove.
pomo, *n.m.* pome.
pomo-de-adão, *n.m.* Adam's apple.
pompa, *n.f.* pomp.
pompom, *n.m.* pompon.
pomposo, *adj.* pompous.
pômulo, *n.m.* cheek.
ponche, *n.m.* punch (drink).
poncheira, *n.f.* punchbowl.
poncho, *n.m.* poncho.
ponderado, *adj.* judicious.
ponderar, *vb.* ponder.
ponderoso, *adj.* ponderous.
pônei, *n.m.* pony.
ponta, *n.f.* point, tip, end; bit; cigarette butt. **de p.,** (*coll.*) at odds.
ponta-cabeça, *n.f.* **de p.,** head first.
pontada, *n.f.* pang; prick.
pontal, *n.m.* point of land.
pontão, *n.m.* pontoon.
pontapé, *n.m.* kick.
pontaria, *n.f.* aim; marksmanship.
ponte, *n.f.* bridge. **p. aérea,** airlift; shuttle.

pontear, vb. dot; baste; finger (guitar); (sport.) lead.

ponteiro, n.m. pointer; clock hand; (sport.) leader.

pontiagudo, adj. sharp-pointed.

pontífice, n.m. pontiff, Pope.

pontilhado, adj. dotted. **linha p.,** dotted line.

pontinho, n.m. dot; fine stitch; (pl.) ellipsis.

ponto, n.m. dot; period; stitch; place; stop. **p. de exclamação,** exclamation point; **p, de interrogação,** question mark; **p. de ônibus,** bus stop; **p. e vírgula,** semicolon; **a p. de,** about to; **assinar o p.,** sign in; **dois pontos,** colon; **entregar os pontos,** (coll.) give up; **fazer p. em,** (coll.) hang out at.

ponto-de-vista, n.m. point of view.

pontuação, n.f. punctuation.

pontual, adj. punctual.

pontuar, vb. punctuate.

pontudo, adj. pointed, sharp.

popa, n.f. (naut.) stern. **de vento em p.,** quite well.

populaça, n.f. populace, rabble.

população, n.f. population.

populacho, n.m. rabble.

popular, 1. adj. popular; folk; democratic. **2.** n.m. commoner.

popularidade, n.f. popularity.

popularizar, vb. popularize.

populoso, adj. populous.

pôquer, n.m. poker (game).

por, prep. for; through; via; around; because of; by; per. **p. enquanto,** for now; **p. exemplo,** for example; **p. que,** why?

pôr, vb. put, place, set; lay; put on. **p.-se,** become, get; set (sun). **p.- se a,** start to.

porão, n.m. (naut.) hold; basement.

porquê, n.m. electric eel.

porca, n.f. sow; nut (screw).

porcalhão -lhona, 1. adj. sloppy. **2.** n. slob.

porção, n.f. portion; serving; lot.

porcaria, n.f. junk; poor job; smut.

porcelana, n.f. porcelain.

porcentagem, n.f. percentage.

porco, 1. adj. filthy. **2.** n.m. pig; slob.

porco-espinho, n.m. porcupine.

porém, **1.** n.m. drawback. **2.** conj. but, however.

porfia, n.f. dispute; insistence.

porfiado, adj. stubborn.

porfiar, vb. argue; persist.

pormenor, n.m. detail. **—pormenorizar,** vb.

pornô, n.f. (sl.) porno, porn.

pornochanchada, n.f. soft-porn movie.

pornografia, n.f. pornography.

pornográfico, adj. pornographic.

poro, n.m. pore.

pororoca, n.f. tidal bore.

poroso, adj. porous.

porquanto, conj. inasmuch as.

por quê ?, adv. why?

porque, conj. because.

porquê, n.m. reason, why.

porqueiro -ra, n. swineherd.

porquinho-da-índia, n.m. guinea pig.

porra, 1. n.f. (vulg.) semen; penis. **a p. de,** the damned. **2.** interj. (vulg.) hell! damn it!

porrada, n.f. (vulg.) punch, blow; lot.

porre, n.m. (coll.) drunken binge.

porrete, n.m. club, stick.

porrista, n.m.f. (coll.) drunkard.

porta, n.f. door; gate.

porta-aviões, n.m. aircraft carrier.

porta-bandeira, n.m.f. flagbearer.

portada, n.f. portal; frontispiece.

portador -ra, n. messenger; bearer.

porta-estandarte, n.m.f. flagbearer.

portagem, n.f. toll.

portal, n.m. portal.

porta-luvas, n.m. glove compartment.

porta-malas, n.m. trunk (car).

portanto, conj. therefore.

portão, n.m. gate, entrance.

portar, vb. carry. **p.-se,** behave.

portaria, n.f. reception desk; edict.

porta-seios, *n.m.* bra.
portátil, *adj.* portable.
porta-voz, *n.m.* megaphone; *n.m.f.* spokesperson.
porte, *n.m.* portage; cargo; postage; mien.
porteiro -ra, *n.* doorkeeper; janitor.
portento, *n.m.* wonder.
pórtico, *n.m.* portico; gate.
portinhola, *n.f.* small door; carriage door.
porto, *n.m.* port, harbor; port wine; *(cap.)* Oporto.
Porto-Rico, *n.m.* Puerto Rico.
porto-riquenho -nha, *adj., n.* Puerto Rican.
portuário, 1. *adj.* port. **2.** *n.m.* longshoreman.
portuga, *n.m.f. (derog.)* Portuguese.
português -guesa, *adj., n.* Portuguese; *n.m.* Portuguese (language).
porventura, *adv.* perhaps.
porvir, *n.m.* future.
pós-, *pref.* post-
posar, *vb.* pose. **—pose,** *n.f.*
pós-datar, *vb.* postdate.
pós-escrito, *n.m.* postscript.
pós-graduação, *n.f.* graduate study.
pós-graduado -da, *adj., n.* postgraduate.
pós-guerra, *n.m.* post-war period.
posição, *n.f.* position; standing.
positivo, *adj.* positive.
posologia, *n.f.* dosage indication.
pospor, *vb.* postpone.
possante, *adj.* powerful.
posse, *n.f.* possession; inauguration. **tomar p.,** take office.
posseiro -ra, *n.* squatter.
possessão, *n.f.* possession.
possessivo, *adj.* possessive.
possesso, *adj.* possessed.
possessor -ra, *n.* possessor.
possibilidade, *n.f.* possibility.
possibilitar, *vb.* make possible.
possível, *adj.* possible.
possuir, *vb.* possess.
posta, *n.f.* slice; postal service.
postal, 1. *adj.* postal. **2.** *n.m.* postcard.

postar, *vb.* station; mail. **p.-se,** post oneself.
poste, *n.m.* post, pole.
pôster, *n.m.* poster.
postergar, *vb.* postpone.
posteridade, *n.f.* posterity.
posterior, 1. *adj.* later. **2.** *(coll.)* buttocks.
postiço, *adj.* false, artificial.
postigo, *n.m.* hatch; peephole.
posto, 1. *adj.* put. **2.** *n.m.* post, station; position; job; place. **p. de gasolina,** gas station; **p. de ônibus,** bus stop; **p. de socorro,** first-aid station. **3.** *conj.* **p. que,** although.
postremo, *adj.* last.
postulado, *n.m.* postulate.
postulante, *n.m.f.* candidate.
postular, *vb.* postulate.
póstumo, *adj.* posthumous.
postura, *n.f.* posture; position; attitude; ordinance.
potável, *adj.* potable.
pote, *n.m.* jug; pot.
potência, *n.f.* potency; power.
potencial, *adj., n.m.* potential.
potencialidade, *n.f.* potentiality.
potente, *adj.* potent.
potiguar, 1. *adj.* of/pert. to Rio Grande do Norte state. **2.** *n.m.f.* Rio Grande do Norte native.
potoca, *n.f.* fib, lie.
potro, *n.m.* colt; bronco.
pouca-vergonha, *n.f.* shamelessness.
pouco, 1. *adj.* little; *(pl.)* few. **2.** *adv.* little; not much; not very. **3.** *n.m.* little. **por p.,** almost; **um p. (de),** a little/bit (of).
poupança, *n.f.* savings. **caderneta de p.,** savings account.
poupar, *vb.* save; spare.
pousada, *n.f.* inn.
pousar, *vb.* set down; land; stay.
pouso, *n.m.* landing; resting place.
povão, *n.m. (sl.)* commonfolk.
povaréu, *n.m.* populace.
povo, *n.m.* people; commonfolk.
povoação, *n.f.* village, town.
povoado, *n.m.* village.
povoar, *vb.* populate.
praça, *n.f.* plaza, square; city;

(mil.) private. **sentar p.,** join the military.

prado, *n.m.* meadow.

praga, *n.f.* curse; plague.

pragmático, *adj.* pragmatic.

praia, *n.f.* beach, shore.

praiano -na, 1. *adj.* beach, shore. **2.** *n.* beach/shore resident.

prancha, *n.f.* board, plank; surfboard.

prancheta, *n.f.* small board; drafting table.

prantear, *vb.* weep, mourn.

pranto, *n.m.* weeping.

prata, *n.f.* silver; silverware.

prateado, *adj.* silver (color).

prateleira, *n.f.* shelf.

prática, *n.f.* practice; experience; lecture.

praticante, 1. *adj.* practicing. **2.** *n.m.f.* trainee.

praticar, *vb.* practice; do; commit; teach; converse.

prático, 1. *adj.* practical; experienced. **2.** *n.m. (naut.)* pilot; expert.

pratinho, *n.m.(coll.)* piece of gossip.

prato, *n.m.* plate; dish; *(mus.)* cymbal.

praxe, *n.f.* practice; custom. **de p.,** usual.

prazenteiro, *adj.* jolly; pleasant.

prazer, 1. *n.m.* pleasure. **muito p.** or **p. em conhecê-lo/la,** pleased to meet you. **2.** *vb.* please.

prazo, *n.m.* term, period. **a/de longo/curto p.,** long-/short-term; **a p.,** on time (installments).

pré, *n.m. (mil.)* daily pay. **praça de p.,** private.

preá, *n.m.* cavy.

preamar, *n.m.* high tide.

preâmbulo, *n.m.* preamble.

precário, *adj.* precarious.

precatado, *adj.* cautious.

precatar, *vb.* warn. **p.-se,** beware.

precaução, *n.f.* precaution.

precaver, *vb.* warn. **p.-se,** beware.

prece, *n.f.* prayer; plea.

precedência, *n.f.* precedence.

precedente, 1. *adj.* preceding. **2.** *n.m.* precedent.

preceder, *vb.* precede.

preceito, *n.m.* precept.

preceituar, *vb.* prescribe.

precioso, *adj.* precious.

precipício, *n.m.* precipice.

precipitação, *n.f.* precipitation; haste.

precipitado, *adj.* hasty.

precipitar, *vb.* precipitate; hurl down.

precipitoso, *adj.* steep; rash.

precisão, *n.f.* precision; need.

precisar, *vb.* need; specify. **p. de,** need.

preciso, *adj.* necessary; precise.

preclaro, *adj.* illustrious.

preço, *n.m.* price.

precoce, *adj.* precocious.

pré-colombiano, *adj.* Pre-Columbian.

preconceito, *n.m.* prejudice; preconception.

preconizar, *vb.* commend.

precursor -ra, *n.* precursor.

predatório, *adj.* predatory.

predecessor -ra, *n.* predecessor.

predestinar, *vb.* predestine.

predial, *adj.* building; land.

prédica, *n.f.* preaching.

predicado, *n.m.* attribute; *(gram.)* predicate.

predição, *n.f.* prediction.

predicar, *vb.* preach.

predileto, *adj.* favorite.

prédio, *n.m.* building.

predizer, *vb.* predict.

predominar, *vb.* predominate; rule.

predomínio, *n.m.* predominance.

preeminente, *adj.* preeminent.

preencher, *vb.* fill out; fulfill.

prefácio, *n.m.* preface.

prefeito -ta, *n.* mayor.

prefeitura, *n.f.* city hall.

preferência, *n.f.* preference; priority. **de p.,** preferably.

preferir, *vb.* prefer; choose.

preferível, *adj.* preferable.

prefixo, *n.m.* prefix.

prega, *n.f.* pleat. —**preguear,** *vb.*

pregação, *n.f.* preaching.

pregadeira, *n.f.* cushion.

pregado, *adj. (coll.)* tired out.

pregador -ra, n. preacher.

pregão, n.m. vendor's cry; proclamation; (pl.) banns.

pregar, vb. preach; nail, fasten; stick; (coll.) tire out. **p. uma partida,** play a trick; **não p. olho,** not sleep a wink.

prego, nail; (coll.) pawnshop. **dar o p.,** (coll.) tire out; **pôr no p.,** (coll.) pawn.

pregoeiro, n.m. town crier; auctioneer.

preguiça, n.f. laziness; (zool.) sloth. **estar com p.,** be lazy.

preguiçoso, adj. lazy.

pré-histórico, adj. prehistoric.

preia-mar, n.m. high tide.

prejudicar, vb. damage, harm.

prejudicial, adj. harmful.

prejuízo, n.m. damage; prejudice.

preleção, n.f. lecture.

preliminar, adj., n.f. preliminary.

prelo, n.m. printing press.

prelúdio, n.m. prelude.

prematuro, adj. premature.

premeditar, vb. premeditate.

premente, adj. pressing.

premer, -mir, vb. press.

premiado -da, n. prize-winner.

premiar, vb. award a prize to, reward.

prêmio, n.m. prize; premium.

premissa, n.f. premise.

premonição, n.f. premonition.

prenda, n.f. gift; token; talent.

prendado, adj. talented.

prendedor, n.m. clip, pin.

prender, vb. fasten; join; catch; arrest; captivate; delay. **p.-se,** get stuck; stick.

prenhe, adj. pregnant; full.

prenhez, n.f. pregnancy.

prensa, n.f. press; printing press.

prensar, vb. press, squeeze.

prenúncio, n.m. prediction.

preocupação, n.f. preoccupation; worry.

preocupado, adj. preoccupied; worried.

preocupar, vb. preoccupy; worry. **p.-se com,** worry about.

preparação, n.f. preparation.

preparar, vb. prepare; equip; teach.

preparativos, n.m.pl. preparations.

preparatório, adj. preparatory.

preparo, n.m. preparation; preparedness.

preponderância, n.f. preponderance.

preposição, n.f. preposition.

prerrogativa, n.f. prerogative.

presa, n.f. prey; seizure; booty; tusk; claw; prisoner (f.).

presbiteriano -na, adj., n. Presbyterian.

presciente, adj. prescient.

prescindir de, vb. dispense with.

prescrever, vb. prescribe.

prescrição, n.f. prescription.

presença, n.f. presence; appearance; demeanor.

presenciar, vb. witness.

presente, 1. adj. present. **ter p.,** bear in mind. **2.** n.m. present; gift; present tense; (pl.) those present.

presentear, vb. present, offer.

presepada, vb. bragging.

presepeiro, n.m. braggart.

presépio, n.m. nativity scene.

preservação, n.f. preservation.

preservar, vb. preserve.

preservativo, n.m. condom.

presidência, n.f. presidency.

presidencial, adj. presidential.

presidente, 1. adj. presiding. **2** n.m.f. president.

presidiário, n.m. convict.

presídio, n.m. presidio; penitentiary.

presidir, vb. preside (over).

presilha, n.f. loop; barrette.

preso -sa, 1. adj. arrested; caught. **2.** n. prisoner.

pressa, n.f. haste. **às pressas,** hurriedly; **estar com p.,** be in a hurry.

pressagiar, vb. presage.

presságio, n.m. omen.

pressão, n.f. pressure; snap. **p. arterial/sanguínea,** blood pressure.

pressentimento, n.m. premonition.

pressentir, vb. foresee; suspect.

pressionar, vb. press, pressure.

pressuposto, n.m. presupposition; plan.

pressuroso, adj. hasty; eager.

prestação, *n.f.* installment (payment); reckoning.

prestamista, *n.m.f.* money-lender.

prestar, *vb.* give, render; be any good. **p.-se,** lend it-/oneself. **p. atenção,** pay attention; **p. contas,** give an account; **p. serviço,** render service.

prestes, *adj., adv.* ready (to).

prestidigitador -ra, *n.* prestidigitator.

prestígio, *n.m.* prestige.

prestigioso, *adj.* prestigious.

préstimo, *n.m.* use; aid.

prestimoso, *adj.* helpful; useful.

presumido, *adj.* presumptuous; conceited.

presumir, *vb.* presume; be presumptuous.

presunção, *n.f.* presumption; conceit.

presunçoso, *adj.* presumptuous.

presunto, *n.m.* ham; *(sl.)* corpse.

pretendente, *n.m.f.* candidate; *n.m.* suitor.

pretender, *vb.* intend; claim; seek to.

pretensão, *n.f.* pretension; airs.

pretenso, *adj.* supposed.

preterir, *vb.* omit; bypass.

pretérito, *adj., n.m.* preterite.

pretexto, *n.m.* pretext.

pretidão, *n.f.* blackness.

preto, 1. *adj.* black; Negro; dismal. **2.** *n.m.* black; Black.

prevalecer, *vb.* prevail.

prevaricar, *vb.* betray a trust; commit adultery.

prevenção, *n.f.* prevention; warning; bias. **estar de p. com,** *(coll.)* pick on.

prevenir, *vb.* prevent; forewarn; advise. **p.-se,** be wary.

preventivo, *adj.* preventive.

prever, *vb.* foresee.

previdência, *n.f.* foresight. **p. social,** social welfare.

previdente, *adj.* provident; far-sighted.

prévio, *adj.* previous; prior.

previsão, *n.f.* forecast; foresight. **p. do tempo,** weather forecast.

previsível, *adj.* foreseeable.

prezado -da, *adj.* esteemed; dear (letters).

prezar, *vb.* value, prize. **p.-se,** pride oneself.

primar, *vb.* excel.

primário, *adj.* primary; primitve.

primata, *n.m. (zool.)* primate.

primavera, *n.f.* spring.

primazia, *n.f.* primacy.

primeiranista, *n.m.f.* freshman.

primeiro -ra, 1. *adj.* first; chief. **2.** *adv.* first. **p. ministro -ra,** prime minister.

primitivo, *adj.* primitive; original.

primo -ma, 1. *adj.* prime. **2.** *n.* cousin.

primogênito -ta, *adj., n.* first-born.

primor, *n.m.* excellence; beauty.

primordial *adj.* primordial; primary.

primoroso, *adj.* excellent; beautiful.

princesa, *n.f.* princess.

principal, *adj., n.m.f.* principal.

príncipe, 1. *adj.* first. **2.** *n.m.* prince.

principiante, 1. *adj.* beginning. **2.** *n.m.f.* beginner.

principiar, *vb.* begin.

princípio, *n.m.* beginning; principle. **em p.,** in principle; **no p.,** in the beginning.

prioridade, *n.f.* priority.

prisão, *n.f.* prison; imprisonment. **p. de ventre,** constipation; **p. perpétua,** life imprisonment.

prisioneiro -ra, *n.* prisoner.

prisma, *n.m.* prism; standpoint.

privação, *n.f.* privation; hardship.

privacidade, *n.f.* privacy.

privada, *n.f.* latrine.

privado, 1. *adj.* private; deprived. **2.** *n.m.* intimate.

privar, *vb.* deprive; associate closely. **p.-se de,** forgo.

privativo, *adj.* private.

privilegiado, *adj.* privileged; exceptional.

privilégio, *n.m.* privilege; prerogative.

pró, 1. *n.m.* advantage. **em p.**

de, for the benefit of; **o p. e o contra,** the pro and con. **2.** *adv.* pro, for.

proa, *n.f.* bow, prow.

probabilidade, *n.f.* probability.

problema, *n.m.* problem.

problemático, *adj.* problematical.

probo, *adj.* upright.

procedência, *n.f.* (place of) origin.

procedente, *adj.* coming (from); logical.

proceder, 1. *vb.* behavior; procedure. **2.** *vb.* proceed; originate; behave.

procedimento, *n.m.* procedure; proceeding.

procela, *n.f.* sea storm.

prócer, *n.m.* luminary.

processamento, *n.m.* processing. **p. de dados,** data processing; **unidade central de p.** *(comput.)* c.p.u.

processar, *vb.* sue, prosecute; process. **p.-se,** occur.

processo, *n.m.* process; lawsuit.

procissão, *n.f.* procession.

proclamação, *n.f.* proclamation.

proclamar, *vb.* proclaim.

procrastinar, *vb.* procrastinate.

procriar, *vb.* procreate, breed.

procura, *n.f.* search; demand. **à p. de,** in search of; **oferta e p.,** supply and demand.

procuração, *n.f.* power of attorney; proxy.

procurador -ra, *n.* attorney; proxy.

procurar, *vb.* look for; seek (to); look up.

prodigalizar, *vb.* squander.

prodígio, *n.m.* marvel.

pródigo -ga, *adj., n.* prodigal.

produção, *n.f.* production; product. **p. em série,** mass production.

produtivo, *adj.* productive.

produto, *n.m.* product; profit. **p. nacional bruto,** gross national product.

produtor -ra, 1. *adj.* producing. **2.** *n.* producer.

produzir, *vb.* produce.

proeminente, *adj.* prominent.

proêmio, *n.m.* preface.

proeza, *n.f.* heroic deed.

profanar, *vb.* profane.

profanidade, *n.f.* profanity.

profano, *adj.* profane; secular.

profecia, *n.f.* prophecy.

proferir, *vb.* pronounce; deliver (speech).

professar, *vb.* profess; teach; take religious vows.

professor -ra, *n.* teacher; professor.

professorado, *n.m.* teaching career, professorship; faculty.

profeta, *n.m.* **-tisa,** *n.f.* prophet -ess.

profético, *adj.* prophetic.

profetizar, *vb.* prophesy.

proficiência, *n.f.* proficiency.

proficiente, *adj.* proficient.

profícuo, *adj.* useful, advantageous.

profissão, *n.f.*, profession.

profissional, *adj., n.m.f.* professional.

prófugo, *adj.* fugitive.

profundidade, *n.f.* depth; profundity.

profundo, *adj.* deep; profound.

profusão, *n.f.* profusion.

progênie, *n.f.* progeny.

progenitor -ra, *n.* progenitor; *(m.pl.)* ancestors.

prognosticar, *vb.* prognosticate.

prognóstico, *n.m.* prognosis, forecast.

programa, *n.m.* program; plan; date. **p. de índio,** *(sl.)* boring time; **fazer um p.,** go out on the town.

programação, *n.f.* programming.

programador -ra, *n.* programmer.

programar, *vb.* program; plan.

progredir, *vb.* progress.

progressão, *n.f.* progression.

progressivo, *adj.* progressive.

progresso, *n.m.* progress.

proibição, *n.f.* prohibition.

proibido, *adj.* prohibited, forbidden.

proibir, *vb.* prohibit, forbid.

projeção, *n.f.* projection.

projetar, *vb.* project.

projetil, -jétil, *n.m.* projectile.

projetista, *n.m.f.* planner, designer.

projeto, n.m. project; plan. **p. de lei,** bill.

projetor, n.m. projector.

prol, n.m. benefit. **em p. de,** in behalf of.

prole n.f. progeny.

proletariado, n.m. working class.

proletário -ria, n. worker.

proliferação, n.f. proliferation.

proliferar, vb. proliferate.

prolífico, adj. prolific.

prolixo, adj. prolix, verbose.

prólogo, n.m. prologue.

prolongar, vb. prolong.

promessa, n.f. promise; pledge; votive offering.

prometer, vb. promise.

promíscuo, adj. promiscuous; indiscriminately mixed.

promissão, n.f. promise. **Terra da P.,** Promised Land.

promissor, adj. promising.

promontório, n.m. promontory.

promoção, n.f. promotion.

promotor -ra, n. promoter; prosecutor. **p. público -ca,** district attorney.

promover, vb. promote.

promulgar, vb. promulgate.

pronome, n.m. pronoun.

prontidão, n.f. readiness; (sl.) pennilessness.

prontificar, vb. get ready.

pronto, 1. adj. ready; prompt; alert; finished; (sl.) broke. **e p.,** and that's all. **2.** interj. hello! (telephone).

pronto-socorro, n.m. first-aid clinic.

pronúncia, n.f. pronunciation.

pronunciamento, n.m. proclamation; pronouncement.

pronunciar, vb. pronounce; deliver (speech); declare.

propaganda, n.f. advertising; advertisement; propaganda.

propagar, vb. propagate.

propalar, vb. disclose; publish.

propelir, vb. propel.

propender, vb. incline.

propensão, n.f. propensity.

propenso, adj. inclined, prone.

propício, adj. propitious.

propina, n.f. tip; bribe; fee.

propínquo, adj. near, close.

proponente, n.m.f. proponent.

propor, vb. propose; suggest; nominate; intend.

proporção, n.f. proportion.

proporcional, adj. proportional.

proporcionar, vb. provide; adjust.

proposição, n.f. proposition.

propositado, -sital, adj. deliberate.

propósito, n.m. purpose. **a p.,** by the way; **a p. de,** apropos of; **de p.,** on purpose.

proposta, n.f. proposal.

propriedade, n.f. property; capability; ownership; propriety.

proprietário -ria, n. proprietor, owner.

próprio, adj. proper; suitable; own; oneself, himself, etc.

propulsar, vb. propel.

prorrogar, vb. defer; prolong.

prorromper, vb. burst out.

prosa, 1. adj. conceited. **2.** n.f. prose; chat; chit-chat; (coll.) boasting; n.m.f. (coll.) talker.

prosador -ra, n. prose writer.

prosaico, adj. prosaic.

prosápia, n.f. lineage; pride.

proscrever, vb. proscribe.

proscrito, 1. adj. proscribed; exiled. **2.** n.m. exile (person).

proseador -ra, 1. adj. talkative. **2.** n. conversationalist.

prosear, vb. talk, chat.

prosista, n.m.f. prose writer; talker, chatterer.

prosódia, n.f. phonology; prosody.

prosopopéia, n.f. personification; (coll.) haughtiness.

prospectar, vb. prospect.

prospectivo, adj. prospective.

prospecto, n.m. prospectus.

prospector -ra, n. prospector.

prosperar, vb. prosper.

prosperidade, n.f. prosperity.

próspero, adj. prosperous.

prossecução, n.f. continuation.

prosseguimento, n.m. continuation.

prosseguir, vb. proceed (with).

prostíbulo, n.m. brothel.

prostituição, n.f. prostitution.

prostituir, vb. prostitute. **p.-se,** prostitute oneself.

prostituta, n.f. prostitute.

prostrar, vb. prostrate.

protagonista, *n.m.f.* protagonist.

proteção, *n.f.* protection.

proteger, *vb.* protect.

protegido -da, *n.* protégé.

proteína, *n.f.* protein.

protelar, *vb.* postpone.

protestante, *adj. n.m.f.* Protestant.

protestar, *vb.* protest.

protesto, *n.m.* protest.

protetor -ra, *n.* protector.

protocolo, *n.m.* protocol; official register.

protótipo, *n.m.* prototype.

protuberância, *n.f.* protuberance.

prova, *n.f.* proof; exam; ordeal; taste. **à p. de água**, waterproof.

provar, *vb.* prove; try; taste; try on.

provável, *adj.* probable.

proveito, *n.m.* profit, benefit. **tirar p. de**, take advantage of.

proveitoso, *adj.* profitable.

proveniência, *n.f.* origin.

proveniente, *adj.* coming from.

prover, *vb.* provide. -

proverbial, *adj.* proverbial.

provérbio, *n.m.* proverb.

proveta, *n.f.* test tube.

providência, *n.f.* providence; lucky occurrence. **tomar providências**, take necessary measures.

providenciar, *vb.* make arrangements (to), take steps (to get).

providente, *adj.* provident; prudent.

província, *n.f.* province.

provinciano, *adj.* provincial.

provir, *vb.* proceed (from).

provisão, *n.f.* provision.

provisório, *adj.* provisional, temporary.

provocação, *n.f.* provocation.

provocar, *vb.* provoke.

proxeneta, *n.m.f.* pimp, procuress.

proximidade, *n.f.* proximity; closeness; *(pl.)* outskirts.

próximo, **1.** *adj.* next; close; coming. **2.** *adv.* nearby; past. **3.** *n.m.* fellow being.

prudência, *n.f.* prudence.

prudente, *adj.* prudent.

prumo, *n.m.* plumb, bob. **a p.**, straight up.

prurido, *n.m.* desire.

pseudônimo, *n.m.* pseudonym.

psicanálise, *n.f.* psychoanalysis.

psicanalista, *n.m.f.* psychoanalyst.

psicologia, *n.f.* psychology.

psicológico, *adj.* psychological.

psicólogo -ga, *n.* psychologist.

psicopata, *n.m.f.* psychopath.

psicose, *n.f.* psychosis.

psicótico -ca, *adj., n.* psychotic.

psique, *n.f.* psyche.

psiquiatra, *n.m.f.* psychiatrist.

psiquiatria, *n.f.* psychiatry.

psiquiátrico, *adj.* psychiatric.

psíquico, *adj.* psychic.

psiu, *interj. (coll.)* psst! yoohoo!; sh!

pua, *n.f.* drill; sharp point.

puberdade, *n.f.* puberty.

púbere, *adj.* pubscent.

púbico, *adj.* pubic.

publicação, *n.f.* publication.

publicar, *vb.* publish; publicize.

publicidade, *n.f.* publicity.

publicitário -ria, **1.** *adj.* advertising. **2.** *n.* advertising person.

público, *adj., n.m.* public.

pudendo, *adj.* shameful. **partes pudendas**, genitals.

pudera, *interj.* no wonder!

pudibundo, *adj.* modest.

pudicícia, *n.f.* modesty; chastity.

púdico, *adj.* modest; chaste.

pudim, *n.m.* pudding.

pudor, *n.m.* decency, modesty; shyness.

pueril, *adj.* childish.

puerilidade, *n.f.* childishness.

pugilato, *n.m.* fistfight.

pugilismo, *n.m.* boxing.

pugilista, *n.m.* boxer.

pugna, *n.f.* fight.

pugnacidade, *n.f.* pugnacity.

puir, *vb.* fray.

pujança, *n.f.* strength, vigor.

pujante, *adj.* strong, vigorous.

pular, *vb.* jump; dance.

pulcro, *adj.* beautiful.

pulga, *n.f.* flea.

pulha, **1.** *adj.* roguish. **2.** *n.m.* scoundrel.

pulmão, *n.m.* lung.

pulo, *n.m.* jump. **dar um p. em**, (*coll.*) stop/drop by.

pulôver, *n.m.* pullover sweater.

púlpito, *n.m.* pulpit.

pulsar, *vb.* pulsate, throb.

pulseira, *n.f.* bracelet.

pulso, *n.m.* wrist; pulse; strength. **a p.**, by force.

pulular, *vb.* swarm.

pulverizar, *vb.* pulverize.

punção, *n.f.* punch, puncture.

punctura, *n.f.* puncture.

pundonor, *n.m.* punctilio.

pungente, *adj.* painful; heart-rending.

pungir, *vb.* prick; distress.

punhado, *n.m.* handful.

punhal, *n.m.* dagger.

punhalada, *n.f.* stab.

punheta, (*vulg.*) masturbation.

punho, *n.m.* fist; cuff; handle; handwriting.

punição, *n.f.* punishment.

punir, *vb.* punish.

punitivo, *adj.* punitive.

pupila, *n.f.* pupil (eye).

purê, *n.m.* purée. **p. de batatas**, mashed potatoes.

pureza, *n.f.* purity.

purga, *n.f.* purge.

purgante, *n.m.* laxative.

purgar, *vb.* purge, cleanse.

purgatório, *n.m.* purgatory.

purificar, *vb.* purify.

purista, *n.m.f.* purist.

puritano -na, **1.** *adj.* Puritan; puritanical. **2.** *n.* Puritan; prude.

puro, *adj.* pure; clean; chaste; complete.

puro-sangue, *adj.*, *n.m.f.* thoroughbred.

púrpura, *n.f.* purple. —**purpúreo**, *adj.* .

pus. *n.m.* pus.

pusilânime, *adj.* cowardly.

puta, *n.f.* (*vulg.*) whore.

pútrido, *adj.* putrid.

puxa, *interj.* wow! gee!; heck! (also **p. vida!**).

puxada, *n.f.* pulling in (fish net).

puxado, *adj.* affected; fancy; (*coll.*) expensive; difficult.

puxador, *n.m.* handle.

puxão, *n.m.* pull, tug.

puxar, *vb.* pull; hail; mention;

call for; provoke; strike up; favor; (*sl.*) smoke (marijuana). **p. a**, take after; **p. saco**, (*sl.*) polish the apple.

puxa-saco, *n.m.* (*sl.*) apple-polisher.

Q

Q.I., *n.m.* I.Q.

quadra, *n.f.* city block; fourspot; quatrain; period ;(*sport.*) court.

quadrado, **1.** *adj.* square; squared; stupid; (*sl.*) square. **raiz quadrada**, square root. **2.** *n.* square; squared number; quad; (*sl.*) square.

quadragésimo, *adj.* fortieth.

quadrante, *n.m.* quadrant; dial.

quadrar, *vb.* square; suit.

quadrigêmeo -mea, *n.* quadruplet.

quadril, *n.m.* hip, haunch.

quadrilha, *n.f.* quadrille; square dance; gang.

quadrilheiro, *n.m.* gangster.

quadrinhos, *n.m.pl.* comic strip; comics.

quadro, *n.m.* picture; painting; frame; blackboard; bulletin board; list; cadre; team; chart. **q. negro**, blackboard.

quadro-vivo, *n.m.* tableau.

quadruplicar, *vb.* quadruple. —**quádruplo**, *adj.*, *n.m.*

quaisquer, *adj. pl. of* qualquer.

qual, **1.** *adj.* which, what. **2.** *interrog. pron.* which, which one, what; **3.** *rel. pron.* which, whichever. **o q., a q., os quais, as quais**, which, that, who, whom; **cada q.**, each one; **seja q. for**, whichever it may be. **4.** *conj.* as, like. **5.** *interj.* nonsense!

qualidade, *n.f.* quality; characteristic; capacity.

qualificação, *n.f.* qualification.

qualificado, *adj.* qualified; aggravated (crime).

qualificar, *vb.* qualify; label. **q.-se**, be qualified.

qualitativo, *adj.* qualitative.

qualquer, *adj.* any, whichever, either. **q. coisa**, anything; **q.**

um/uma, anyone; **de q. jeito/modo/maneira/forma,** anyhow.

quando, 1. *adv.* when. **de vez em quando,** once in a while. **2.** *conj.* when; whenever; whereas; even though; even if. **q. de,** at the time of, during.

quantia, *n.f.* sum.

quantidade, *n.f.* quantity, amount.

quantioso, *adj.* considerable; numerous; valuable.

quantificar, *vb.* quantify.

quantitativo, *adj.* quantitative.

quanto, 1. *adj.* as much as, whatever; *(pl.)* as many as. **2.** *rel. pron.* all that, everything that; *(pl.)* all those that. **3.** *adj. & pron.* how much? *(pl.)* how many? **4.** *adv.* how, as. **q. a,** as for; **q. antes,** as soon as possible; **q. mais,** let alone; all the more; **q. mais ... (tanto) mais ...,** the more ... the more ...; **tanto q.,** as much as.

quão, *adv.* how; as.

quarenta, *adj.* forty.

quarentão -tona, *n.* person in his/her forties.

quarentena, *n.f.* quarantine; forty days.

Quaresma, *n.f.* Lent.

quaresmal, *adj.* Lenten.

quarta, *n.f.* Wednesday.

quarta-feira, *n.f.* Wednesday.

quartanista, *n.m.f.* fourth-year student.

quarteirão, *n.m.* city block.

quartel, *n.m.* barracks; quarter.

quartel-general, *n.m.* military headquarters.

quarteto, *n.m.* quartet; quatrain.

quarto, 1. *adj.* fourth. **2.** *n.m.* quarter, fourth; bedroom, room; quarter hour; watch; deathwatch; *(pl.)* hindquarters.

quartzo, *n.m.* quartz.

quase, *adv.* almost; quasi.

quatorze, *adj.* fourteen.

quatro, *adv.* four.

quatrocentos, *adj.* four hundred.

que, 1. *adj.* what, which. **2.** *adv.* what, how. **3.** *rel. pron.* that,

which, who, whom. **4.** *relater* that. **5.** *interrog. pron.* what? which? **6.** *conj.* than; for. **que nem,** just like. **7.** *prep.* except.

quê, *stressed form of interrog. pron.* **que,** *used esp. at the end of a sentence.* **2.** *n.m.* anything, something; charm. **não há de q.,** don't mention it; **como q.,** as the devil; **sem q. nem para q.,** for no good reason **3.** *interj.* what!

quê, *n.f.* the letter q.

quebra, *n.f.* break; breaking; bankruptcy; violation. **de q.,** to boot.

quebra-cabeça, *n.m.* puzzle, riddle; jigsaw puzzle.

quebra-costela, *n.m. (coll.)* bear hug.

quebrada, *n.f.* gorge.

quebradiço, *adj.* breakable.

quebrado, *adj.* broken; worn-out; *(coll.)* broke.

quebradura, *n.f.* break.

quebra-galho, *n.m. (sl.)* problem-solver; trouble-shooter.

quebra-gelos, *n.m. (naut.)* ice-breaker.

quebra-luz, *n.m.* lampshade.

quebra-mar, *n.m.* breakwater.

quebra-nozes, *n.m.* nutcracker.

quebrantar, *vb.* break; violate; tame; surpass; weaken; calm.

quebranto, *n.m.* fatigue; evil-eye illness.

quebra-pau, *n.m. (sl.)* skirmish.

quebra-quebra, *n.m.* trashing and looting.

quebrar, *vb.* break; violate; interrupt; tame; go bankrupt.

queda, *n.f.* fall; descent; ruin; slope; bent.

queda-d'água, *n.f.* waterfall.

queda-de-braço, *adj.* arm wrestling.

quedar, *vb.* stop, stay.

quedê, *interrog. (coll.)* where is/are?

quedo, *adj.* quiet, still.

quefazeres, *n.m.pl.* affairs; chores.

queijo, *n.m.* cheese.

queima, *n.f.* burn, burning; *n.m.* fire sale.

queimadura, *n.f.* burn.

queimar, *vb.* burn; destroy;

(coll.) sell cheaply; *(sl.)* criticize; *(sl.)* shoot.

queima-roupa, *n.f.* à q., pointblank; suddenly.

queixa, *n.f.* complaint.

queixar-se, *vb.* complain.

queixo, *n.m.* chin. **bater o q.**, shiver.

queixoso, *adj.* complaining. —**queixume**, *n.m.*

quem, **1.** *interrog. pron.* who? whom? **2.** *rel. pron.* who, whom; one who. **de quem**, whose, of whom; **q. quer que seja**, whoever; **seja q. for**, whoever it may be.

quengo, *n.m. (coll.)* head.

Quênia, *n.m.* Kenya.

quentão, *n.m.* hot alcoholic drink.

quente, *adj.* hot; fresh (news); *(sl.)* sexy; *(sl.)* genuine; *(sl.)* neat.

quentura, *n.f.* heat.

quer, *conj.* q. . . q. . ., whether . . . or . . .

querela, *n.f. (jur.)* charge; dispute.—e. —**querelar**, *vb.*

querer, *vb.* want; intend; require; please + vb.; love. **como quiser**, as you wish; **não q.** + vb., refuse to; **q. bem**, love; **q. mal**, hate; **q. dizer**, mean; **sem q.**, unintentionally.

querido -da, **1.** *adj.* dear. **2.** *n.* darling.

quermesse, *n.f.* charity bazaar.

querosene, *n.m.* kerosene.

querubim, *n.m.* cherub.

quesito, *n.m.* query.

questão, *n.f.* question, issue; dispute; lawsuit. **fazer q. de**, insist on.

questionar, *vb.* question.

questionário, *n.m.* questionnaire.

quiabo, *n.m.* okra.

quiçá, *adv.* perhaps.

quicar, *vb.* bounce; *(coll.)* get mad.

quíchua, *adj.. n.m.* Quechua.

quício, *n.m.* hinge.

quieto, *adj.* quiet, still.

quietude, *n.f.* quietude.

quilate, *n.m.* carat; quality.

quilha, *n.f.* keel.

quilo, *n.m.* kilo.

quilograma, *n.m.* kilogram.

quilombo, *n.m. (hist.)* runawayslave refuge.

quilométrico, *adj.* kilometric; long.

quilômetro, *n.m.* kilometer.

quilowatt, *n.m.* kilowatt.

quimbanda, *n.m.* an Afro-Brazilian religion.

quimera, *n.f.* chimera.

química, *n.f.* chemistry.

químico -ca, **1.** *adj.* chemical. **2.** *n.* chemist.

quimioterapia, *n.f.* chemotherapy.

quina, *n.f.* edge, corner; fivespot.

quinau, *n.m.* correction.

quindim, *n.m.* coy movement; coconut candy.

quinhão, *n.m.* share, portion.

quinhentos, *adj.* five hundred.

quinina, *n.f.* quinine.

quino, *n.m.* lotto, keno.

qüinquagésimo, *adj.* fiftieth.

quinquilharia, *n.f.* knickknack.

quinta, *f.* farm; Thursday.

quinta-feira, *n.f.* Thursday.

quinteto, *n.m.* quintet.

quinto, *adj.. n.m.* fifth.

quinze, *adj.* fifteen.

quinzena, *n.f.* group of fifteen; fortnight.

quinzenal, *adj.* fortnightly. —**quinzenário**, *n.m.*

quiosque, *n.m.* kiosk.

qüiproquó, *n.m.* confusion; mixup.

quiquiriqui, *n.m.* cock-a-doodle-doo.

quiromante, *n.m.f.* fortuneteller.

quisto, *n.m.* cyst.

quitação, *n.f.* release from a debt; receipt of payment.

quitanda, *n.f.* vegetable market; small grocery.

quitandeiro -ra, *n.* greengrocer.

quitar, *vb.* free from a debt; leave.

quite, *adj.* paid-up, even.

quitute, *n.m.* delicacy; tenderness.

quixotesco, *adj.* quixotic.

quizila, *n.f.* aversion; annoyance; quarrel.

quizilar, *vb.* annoy. **q.-se,** get irked.

quizilento, *adj.* annoying.

quociente, *n.m.* quotient. **q. de inteligência,** I.Q.

quorum, *n.m.* (L.) quorum.

quota, *n.f.* quota; dues, share; marginal note.

quotidiano, 1. *adj.* everyday. **2.** *n.m.* daily paper.

quotista, *n.m.f.* shareholder.

R

rã, *n.f.* frog.

rabada, *n.f.* tail; oxtail stew; (coll.)

rabanada, *n.f.* (coll.) huffy gesture.

rabanete, *n.m.* radish.

rabear, *vb.* wag one's tail; wiggle.

rabeca, *n.f.* fiddle.

rabecão, *n.m.* contrabass; (sl.) coroner's van.

rabeira, *n.f.* (coll.) tail end.

rabicho, *n.m.* pigtail.

rábido, *adj.* rabid.

rabino, *n.m.* rabbi.

rabiscar, *vb.* scribble, scrawl. —**rabisco,** *n.m.*

rabo, *n.m.* tail; butt; corner (eye); **de cabo a r.,** from one end to the other; **pegar em r. de foguete,** (coll.) take on a hard task.

rabo-de-cavalo, *n.m.* (coll.) ponytail.

rabo-de-galo, *n.m.* (coll.) cocktail.

rabo-de-palha, *n.m.* **ter r.,** (coll.) have a blot on one's reputation.

rabo-de-saia, *n.m.* (coll.) woman, dame.

rabudo, *adj.* long-tailed.

rabugem, *n.f.* mange; grouchiness.

rabugento, *adj.* grouchy.

rábula, *n.m.f.* shyster; untrained lawyer.

raça, *n.f.* race; people; (coll.) guts. **de r.,** thoroughbred; **na r.,** (coll.) with great effort.

ração, *n.f.* ration.

racha, *n.f.* split. —**rachar,** *vb.*

rachadura, *n.f.* split.

racial, *adj.* racial.

raciocinar, *vb.* reason. —**raciocínio,** *n.m.*

racional, *adj.* rational.

racionalizar, *vb.* rationalize.

racionar, *vb.* ration.

racismo, *n.m.* racism.

racista, *adj.; n.m.f.* racist.

raconto, *n.m.* tale.

radar, *n.m.* radar.

radiação, *n.f.* radiation.

radiador, *n.m.* radiator.

radial, *adj.* radial.

radialista, *n.m.f.* broadcaster.

radiante, *adj.* radiant.

radiar, *vb.* radiate.

radical, 1. *adj.* radical. **2.** *n.m.* (gram.) root.

radicar, *vb.* root. **r.-se,** take root; settle.

rádio, *n.m.* radio; (anat.) radius; radium; *n.f.* radio station.

radioamador -ra, *n.* radio amateur.

radioatividade, *n.f.* radioactivity.

radioativo, *adj.* radioactive.

radiodifusão, *n.f.* broadcasting.

radiografia, *n.f.* radiograph; x-ray.

radiograma, *n.m.* radiogram.

radiola, *n.f.* radio-phonograph.

radiologia, *n.f.* radiology.

radionovela, *n.f.* radio soap opera.

radiopatrulha, *n.f.* patrol-car system; squad car.

radioso, *adj.* radiant.

radiouvinte, *n.m.f.* radio listener.

ragu, *n.m.* ragout; (sl.) food.

raia, *n.f.* line; limit. **fechar a r.,** bring up the rear.

raiar, *vb.* streak; shine; dawn.

rainha, *n.f.* queen.

raio, *n.m.* ray; radius; lightning. **o r. de...,** the blasted. . .

raiom, *n.m.* rayon.

raiva, *n.f.* anger, rage; rabies. **estar com r.,** be angry.

raivoso, *adj.* angry; rabid.

raiz, *n.f.* root. **r. quadrada/ cúbica,** square/cube root.

rajada, *n.f.* gust; blast.

ralador, *n.m.* grater.

ralar, *vb.* grate; torment.
ralé, *n.f.* riffraff.
ralear, *vb.* thin out.
ralhar, *vb.* scold.
ralo, *adj.* thin, sparse; watery.
rama, *n.f.* branch. **pela r.,** superficially.
ramada, -magem, *n.f.* branches.
ramal, *n.m.* extension; branch.
ramalhete, *n.m.* twig; small bouquet.
rameira, *n.f.* whore.
ramerrão, *n.m.* routine, grind.
ramificação, *n.f.* ramification.
ramificar, *vb.* branch out.
ramo, *n.m.* branch; bouquet; field.
rampa, *n.f.* ramp.
rancho, *n.m.* group; Carnival dancers; chow; shack.
rancor, *n.m.* rancor.
rancoroso, *adj.* rancorous.
rançoso, *adj.* rancid.
randevu, *n.m.* rendezvous for illicit sex.
ranger, *vb.* gnash; creak; grate. **—rangido,** *n.m.*
ranheta, 1. *adj.* grouchy. **2.** *n.m.f.* grouch.
ranho, *n.m.* (coll.) snot.
ranhura, *n.f.* slot, groove.
ranzinza, *adj.* grouchy.
rapacidade, *n.f.* rapacity.
rapadura, *n.f.* brown sugar lump.
rapagão, *n.m.* husky young man.
rapapé, *n.m.* bow, curtsy.
rapar, *vb.* scrape; rasp; shave.
rapariga, *n.f.* prostitute, concubine; (P.) young lady.
rapaz, *n.m.* young man.
rapaziada, *n.f.* group of young men.
rapazola, *n.m.* grown boy.
rapé, *n.m.* snuff.
rapidez, *n.f.* rapidity.
rápido, *adj., adv.* fast.
rapina, *n.f.* rapine. **ave de r.,** bird of prey.
raposa, *n.f.* fox.
rapsódia, *n.f.* rhapsody.
raptar, *vb.* abduct.
rapto, *n.m.* abduction; rapture.
raquítico, *adj.* rickety.
raquitismo, *n.m.* rickets.
rarear, *vb.* rarefy.

raridade, *n.f.* rarity.
raro, *adj.* rare.
rascar, *vb.* scrape.
rascunho, *n.m.* rough draft.
rasgado, *adj.* torn; free; vast; lively.
rasgão, rasgo, *n.m.* tear.
rasgar, *vb.* tear; strum.
raso, *adj.* flat; shallow; ordinary.
raspadura, *n.f.* scraping; erasure.
raspar, *vb.* scrape, scratch. **—raspão,** *n.m.*
rasteira, *n.f.* **passar uma r. em,** (coll.) trip.
rasteiro, *adj.* creeping; humble; plain.
rastejar, *vb.* track; creep.
rasto, *n.m.* track, trace.
rata, *n.f.* (coll.) goof.
ratazana, *n.f.* rat; *n.m.f. (sl.)* thief.
ratear, *vb.* apportion.
ratificar, *vb.* ratify.
rato, *n.m.* rat; thief. **r. de biblioteca,** bookworm; **r. de igreja,** religious fanatic.
ratoeira, *n.f.* mousetrap.
ravina, *n.f.* mountain stream; ravine.
razão, *n.f.* reason; right; rate. **à r. de,** at the rate of; **dar r. a,** agree with; **em r. de,** by reason of; **ter r.,** be right.
razoável, *adj.* reasonable.
ré, *n.f.* defendant (f.); stern. **à r.,** in reverse.
re-, *pref.* re-.
reabilitar, *vb.* rehabilitate.
reação, *n.f.* reaction. **r. em cadeia,** chain reaction.
reacionário -ria, *adj., n.* reactionary.
reagir, *vb.* react.
real, 1. *adj.* real; royal. **2.** *n.m.* real (old currency; *pl.* **réis**).
realçar, *vb.* highlight, enhance.
realce, *n.m.* highlight; distinction.
realejo, *n.m.* hand organ; harmonica.
realeza, *n.f.* royalty.
realidade, *n.f.* reality. **na r.,** in reality.
realismo, *n.m.* realism.

realista, 1. *adj.* realist; realistic. **2.** *n.m.f.* realist.

realização, *n.f.* accomplishment.

realizar, *vb.* accomplish, realize.

reator, *n.m.* reactor. **r. nuclear/atômico,** nuclear/atomic reactor.

reaver, *vb.* retrieve.

rebaixar, *vb.* lower, reduce.

rebanho, *n.m.* flock, herd.

rebarbativo, *adj.* disagreeable.

rebater, *vb.* repel; rebut; discount.

rebelar-se, *vb.* rebel.

rebelde, *n.m.f.* rebel.

rebeldia, *n.f.* rebellion.

rebenque, *n.m.* small whip.

rebentar, *vb.* burst; sprout.

rebento, *n.m.* bud, shoot; offspring.

rebite, *n.m.* rivet. —**rebitar,** *vb.*

reboar, *vb.* echo. —**rebôo,** *n.m.*

rebocador, *n.m.* plasterer; tugboat.

rebocar, *vb.* plaster; tow.

reboco, *n.m.* plaster.

rebolado, *n.m.* sway. **perder o r.,** *(sl.)* be embarrassed.

rebolar, *vb.* wiggle; *(sl.)* work.

reboque, *n.m.* towing; trailer.

rebordosa, *n.f. (coll.)* rebuke; jam; ruckus.

rebuçar, *vb.* cover.

rebuço, *n.m.* collar; pretense.

rebuliço, *n.m.* uproar.

rebuscado, *adj.* recherché.

rebuscar, *vb.* ransack; search.

recado, *n.m.* message; errand.

recaída, *n.f.* relapse.

recalcar, *vb.* trample; insist on; repress.

recalcitrante, *adj.* recalcitrant.

recalque, *n.m.* trampling; repression.

recâmara, *n.f.* small interior bedroom.

recanto, *n.m.* nook.

recapitular, *vb.* review.

recatado, *adj.* modest, retiring.

recato, *n.m.* modesty; caution.

recauchutar, *vb.* retread (tires).

recear, *vb.* fear. —**receio,** *n.m.*

recebedoria, *n.f.* cashier's window; treasury.

receber, *vb.* receive.

recebimento, *n.m.* receiving, reception.

receita, *n.f.* recipe; prescription.

receitar, *vb.* prescribe.

recém-, *pref.* recently, newly.

recensão, *n.f.* book review; census.

recenseamento, *n.m.* census.

recente, *adj.* recent.

receoso, *adj.* fearful.

recepção, *n.f.* reception.

recepcionar, *vb.* receive (guests).

recepcionista, *n.m.f.* receptionist.

receptáculo, *n.m.* receptacle.

receptar, *vb.* deal in stolen goods.

receptivo, *adj.* receptive.

receptor, *n.m.* receiver.

recessão, *n.f.* recession.

recessivo, *adj.* recessive.

recesso, *n.m.* recess; retreat.

rechaçar, *vb.* reject.

rechear, *vb.* stuff, fill.

recheio, recheado, *n.m.* stuffing.

rechinar, *vb.* creak; hiss; sizzle.

rechonchudo, *adj.* chubby.

recibo, *n.m.* receipt.

reciclar, *vb.* recycle.

recife, *n.m.* reef.

recinto, *n.m.* premises; enclosure.

recipiente, *n.m.* receptacle.

recíproco, *adj.* reciprocal.

recital, *n.m.* recital.

recitar, *vb.* recite.

reclamação, *n.f.* complaint.

reclamante, *n.m.f.* complainer.

reclamar, *vb.* complain; demand.

reclame, *n.m.* advertisement.

reclamo, *n.m.* complaint.

reclinar, *vb.* recline; bend. **r.-se,** lean; lie.

recluso -sa, 1. *adj.* secluded. **2.** *n.* recluse.

recobrar, *vb.* recover. **r.-se,** recuperate.

recobrir, *vb.* re-cover; coat.

recolher, *vb.* gather, collect. **r.-se,** retire.

recolhido, *adj.* withdrawn.

recolhimento, *n.m.* withdrawal; seclusion.

recomeçar, vb. resume.

recomendação, n.f. recommendation.

recomendar, vb. recommend; send regards. **r.-se**, merit distinction.

recompensa, n.f. reward; award; recompense. **—recompensar**, vb.

recôncavo, n.m. cavern; environs; Bahian coastal region.

reconciliar, vb. reconcile. **r.-se**, be reconciled.

recôndito, 1. adj. hidden. **2.** n.m. nook.

reconduzir, vb. send back; reappoint.

reconfortar, vb. comfort; refresh.

reconhecer, vb. recognize, acknowledge; examine.

reconhecido, adj. recognized; grateful.

reconhecimento, n.m. recognition; examination; reconnaissance; gratitude.

recopilar, vb. compile; summarize.

recordar, vb. recall. **r.-se de**, remember.

recorde, récorde, n.m. (sport.) record.

recordista, n.m.f. record holder.

reco-reco, n.m. (mus.) notched noisemaker.

recorrer, vb. go over. **r. a**, resort to.

recortar, vb. cut out, clip.

recorte, n.m. clipping.

recostar, vb. lean, lay. **r.-se**, lie down.

recosto, n.m. seat back; slope.

recreação, n.f. recreation.

recrear, vb. amuse. **r.-se**, have fun.

recreio, n.m. recreation; playtime.

recriminação, n.f. recrimination.

recrudescer, vb. intensify.

recruta, n.m. recruit. **—recrutar**, vb.

recrutamento, n.m. recruitment, draft.

recuar, vb. move back, recoil; retreat.

recuo, n.m., **recueta**, n.f. recoil; retreat.

recuperar, vb. regain. **r.-se**, recover.

recurso, n.m. recourse; resource.

recusar, vb. refuse. **r.-se**, decline.

redação, n.f. editing; editorial staff or room; composition.

redargüir, vb. retort.

redator -ra, n. editor.

rede, n.f. net; network; hammock; trap.

rédea, n.f. reins.

redemoinho, n.m. whirlwind; whirlpool.

redenção, n.f. redemption.

redentor -ra, n. redeemer.

redigir, vb. write, draft.

redil, n.m. sheepfold.

redimir, vb. redeem.

redobrar, vb. redouble.

redondeza, n.f. roundness; environs.

redondo, adj. round.

redor, n.m. **ao/em r.**, around.

redução, n.f. reduction.

redundante, adj. redundant.

redundar, vb. result.

reduto, n.m. redoubt.

reduzir, vb. reduce.

reembolsar, vb. reimburse.

reembolso, n.m. repayment. **r. postal**, c.o.d.

reentrância, n.f. recess.

reescalonar, vb. reschedule (debt).

refazer, vb. remake, redo. **r.-se**, rest up.

refeição, n.f. meal.

refeitório, n.m. dining hall.

refém, n.m.f. hostage.

referência, n.f. reference.

referendo, n.m. referendum.

referir, vb. relate; refer; assign. **r-se a**, refer to.

refestelar-se, vb. relax; stretch out.

refinamento, n.m. refinement.

refinar, vb. refine.

refinaria, n.f. refinery.

refletido, adj. reflected; prudent.

refletir, vb. reflect; think. **r.-se**, be manifest.

refletor, n.m. reflector.

reflexão, *n.f.* reflection; thought.

reflexionar, *vb.* reflect, ponder.

reflexivo, *adj.* reflexive.

reflexo, 1. *adj.* reflected. **2.** *n.m.* reflection; reflex.

refluxo, *n.m.* ebb.

refocilar, *vb.* reinvigorate; recover. **r.-se,** relax.

refogar, *vb.* sauté.

reforçar, *vb.* reinforce. **r.-se,** gain strength.

reforço, *n.m.* reinforcement.

reforma, *n.f.* reform; reformation; remodeling; retirement; renewal.

reformação, *n.f.* reformation.

reformar, *vb.* reform; remodel; renew. **r.-se,** *(mil.)* retire.

refrão, *n.m.* proverb; refrain.

refratário, 1. *adj.* refractory. **2.** *n.m.* draft dodger.

refrear, *vb.* restrain.

refrescar, *vb.* refresh; cool off.

refresco, *n.m.* refreshment; fruit juice.

refrigeração, *n.f.* refrigeration; air-conditioning.

refrigerador, *n.m.* refrigerator.

refrigerante, *n.m.* soda pop.

refrigerar, *vb.* refrigerate.

refugiar-se, *vb.* take refuge.

refúgio, *n.m.* refuge.

refugo, *n.m.* refuse, rubbish.

refulgir, *vb.* shine brightly.

refundir, *vb.* recast; correct. **r.-se,** melt; become.

refutar, *vb.* refute.

regaço, *n.m.* lap.

regador, *n.m.* waterer; watering can.

regalar, *vb.* regale.

regalia, *n.f.* privilege.

regalo, *n.m.* regalement; present.

regar, *vb.* water.

regatear, *vb.* haggle.

regedor, *n.m.* governor.

regência, *n.f.* regency.

regenerar, *vb.* regenerate.

regente, *n.m.* regent; maestro.

reger, *vb.* govern, direct.

região, *n.f.* region.

regime, *n.m.* regime; diet.

regimento, *n.m.* regiment. **—regimentar,** *vb.*

régio, *adj.* regal.

regional, *adj.* regional.

registrar, *vb.* register; record.

registro, *n.m.* registration; registry; record.

rego, *n.m.* furrow.

regozijar-se, *vb.* rejoice.

regozijo, *n.m.* rejoicing.

regra, *n.f.* rule; *(pl.)* menses. **via de r.,** as a rule.

regredir, *vb.* regress.

regressão, *n.f.* regression.

regressar, *vb.* return. **—regresso,** *n.m.*

regressivo, *adj.* regressive.

régua, *n.f.* ruler.

regueira, *n.f.,* **-ro,** *n.m.* stream.

regulamento, *n.m.* regulation.

regular, 1. *adj.* regular; so-so. **2.** *vb.* regulate. **não r. bem,** *(coll.)* be crazy.

regurgitar, *vb.* regurgitate.

rei, *n.m.* king. **Reis Magos,** Magi.

reide, *n.m.* raid.

reinado, *n.m.* reign; *(coll.)* kingdom.

reinar, *vb.* reign.

reino, *n.m.* kingdom. **R. Unido,** United Kingdom.

réis, *n.m. pl. of* **real** (old currency).

reisado, *n.m.* Epiphany folk pageant.

reiterar, *vb.* reiterate.

reitor, *n.m.* rector, university president.

reitoria, *n.f.* university president's office.

reivindicar, *vb.* demand, claim. **—reivindicação,** *n.f.*

rejeição, *n.f.* rejection.

rejeitar, *vb.* reject.

rejuvenescer, *vb.* rejuvenate.

relação, *n.f.* relation, -ship; list. **relações exteriores,** foreign affairs; **relações públicas,** public relations; **ter relações,** *(coll.)* have sex.

relacionamento, *n.m.* relationship.

relacionar, *vb.* relate; list. **r.-se,** be related; get acquainted.

relâmpago, *n.m.* lightning.

relampaguear, -pejar, *vb.* lighten.

relance, *n.m.* glance. **—relancear,** *vb.*

relapso, *adj.* relapsing; impenitent.

relatar, *vb.* relate, tell.

relatividade, *n.f.* relativity.

relativo, *adj.* relative.

relato, *n.m.* account, report.

relatório, *n.m.* report.

relaxação, *n.f.,* **-amento,** *n.m.* relaxation; depravity.

relaxar, *vb.* relax; slacken; exempt. **r.-se,** become lax.

relegar, *vb.* relegate.

relento, *n.m.* dew. **ao r.,** outdoors.

reles, *adj.* petty, cheap.

relevante, *adj.* relevant.

relevar, *vb.* distinguish; relieve; forgive. **r.-se,** distinguish oneself.

relevo, *n.m.* relief, distinction. **pôr em r.,** distinguish.

relha, *n.f.* plowshare.

relho, *n.m.* leather whip.

religião, *n.f.* religion.

religioso, *adj., n.m.* religious.

relinchar, *vb.* neigh. **—relincho,** *n.m.*

relíquia, *n.f.* relic; keepsake.

relógio, *n.m.* clock; watch. **r. de pulso,** wristwatch; **r. de sol,** sundial.

relojoaria, *n.f.* watchmaking; watchmaking or repair shop.

relojoeiro -ra, *n.* watchmaker/-repairer.

relutante, *adj.* reluctant.

relutar, *vb.* be reluctant.

reluzir, *vb.* glitter.

relva, *n.f.* lawn.

remanescente, *adj.* remaining.

remanescer, *vb.* remain.

remanso, *n.m.* backwater; tranquility.

remar, *vb.* row.

remarcar, *vb.* re-mark; mark down.

rematado, *adj.* outright.

rematar, *vb.* finish. **—remate,** *n.m.*

remediar, *vb.* remedy.

remédio, *n.m.* remedy, medicine. **não tem r.,** *(coll.)* it's no use.

remelexo, *n.m.* swaying.

remendar, *vb.* mend, patch.

remendo, *n.m.* patch.

remessa, *n.f.* sending; shipment.

remetente, *n.m.f.* sender.

remeter, *vb.* send, remit; refer.

remexer, *vb.* stir, shake; fool (with). **r.-se,** wiggle.

reminiscência, *n.f.* reminiscence.

remir, *vb.* redeem; expiate; pay off.

remissão, *n.f.* remission; cross-reference.

remissivo, *adj.* cross-referenced.

remisso, *adj.* remiss.

remitir, *vb.* forgive; relinquish; abate.

remo, *n.m.* oar.

remoção, *n.f.* removal.

remoçar, *vb.* rejuvenate.

remodelar, *vb.* remodel.

remoinho, *n.m.* whirlpool; whirlwind.

remontar a, *vb.* go back to (in time).

remoque, *n.m.* taunt.

remorso, *n.m.* remorse.

remoto, *adj.* remote.

remover, *vb.* remove.

remunerar, *vb.* remunerate.

renascença, *n.f.* Renaissance; rebirth.

renascimento, *n.m.* Renaissance; rebirth.

renda, *n.f.* income; lace. **imposto de r.,** income tax.

render, *vb.* yield; subdue; relieve; render; give way. **r.-se,** surrender.

rendimento, *n.m.* yield, income.

rendoso, *adj.* profitable.

renegado, *n.m.* renegade.

renegar, *vb.* renounce; reject.

renhir, *vb.* dispute; fight.

renomeado, *adj.* renowned.

renome, *n.m.* renown.

renovação, *n.f.* renovation; renewal.

renovar, *vb.* renovate; renew.

renque, *n.m.* row.

rentabilidade, *n.f.* profitability.

rentável, *adj.* profitable.

rente, *adj., adv.* close, near.

renúncia, *n.f.* renunciation; resignation.

renunciar, *vb.* renounce; resign.

reparação, *n.f.* reparation.

reparar, *vb.* repair; recover; atone for; notice. **r. em,** notice.

reparo, *n.m.* repair; observation; remark.

repartição, *n.f.* division; office.

repartimento, *n.m.* compartment; bedroom.

repartir, *vb.* divide; distribute; share. **r.-se,** divide.

repassar, *vb.* go over; soak.

repasto, *n.m.* repast; feast.

repatriar, *vb.* repatriate.

repelão, *n.m.* pull, tug.

repelente, *adj.* repellent.

repelir, *vb.* repel.

repente, *n.m.* sudden act/remark. **de r.,** suddenly.

repentino, *adj.* sudden.

repercussão, *n.f.* repercussion.

repercutir, *vb.* echo; have repercussions.

repertório, *n.m.* repertory, repertoire.

repeteco, *n.m. (sl.)* repeat, seconds.

repetição, *n.f.* repetition.

repetir, *vb.* repeat.

repetitivo, *adj.* repetitive.

repicar, *vb.* ring.

repimpar, *vb.* glut. **r.-se,** stuff oneself; relax.

repique, *n.m.* peal.

repisar, *vb.* repeat, harp on.

repleto, *adj.* replete.

réplica, *n.f.* reply; replica.

replicar, *vb.* reply.

repolho, *n.m.* cabbage.

repontar, *vb.* retort.

repor, *vb.* replace; restore.

reportagem, *n.f.* report, story.

reportar-se a *vb.* refer to.

repórter, *n.m.f.* reporter.

repositório, *n.m.* repository.

repostar, *vb.* reply.

repousar, *vb.* repose, rest.

repreender, *vb.* reprimand. —**repreensão,** *n.f.*

represa, *n.f.* dam; reservoir.

represália, *n.f.* reprisal.

represar, *vb.* dam up.

representação, *n.f.* representation; performance.

representante, *n.m.f.* representative.

representar, *vb.* represent; perform.

representativo, *adj.* representative.

repressão, *n.f.* repression.

reprimenda, *n.f.* reprimand.

reprimir, *vb.* repress.

reprise, *n.f.* reprise; rerun.

réprobo, *n.m.* reprobate.

reprochar, *vb.* reproach. —**reproche,** *n.m.*

reprodução, *n.f.* reproduction.

reprodutivo, *adj.* reproductive.

reproduzir, *vb.* reproduce.

reprovação, *n.f.* flunk; disapproval.

reprovar, *vb.* flunk; reprove.

reptar, *vb.* challenge.

reptil, réptil, *n.m.* reptile.

repto, *n.m.* challenge.

república, *n.f.* republic; student co-op house.

republicano, *adj., n.m.* republican.

repudiar, *vb.* repudiate.

repúdio, *n.m.* repudiation.

repugnância, *n.f.* repugnance.

repugnante, *adj.* repugnant.

repugnar, *vb.* be repugnant; reject.

repulsa, *n.f.* repulse; abhorrence.

repulsar, *vb.* repel; reject.

repulsivo, *adj.* repulsive.

reputação, *n.f.* reputation.

reputar, *vb.* consider; credit; value.

repuxar, *vb.* jerk; recoil; gush.

repuxo, *n.m.* fountain; recoil. **aguentar o r.,** *(coll.)* bear up.

requebrar, *vb.* sway. **r.-se,** wiggle.

requebro, *n.m.* sway; amorous gesture.

requeijão, *n.m.* cream cheese.

requerer, *vb.* request; apply for; demand.

requerimento, *n.m.* petition, application.

requestar, *vb.* solicit; woo.

requintado, *adj.* refined, dainty.

requinte, *n.m.* refinement, daintiness.

requisição, *n.f.* requisition; request.

requisitar, *vb.* requisition; demand.

requisito, *n.m.* requirement.

rés, *adj., adv.* close, low.

rês, *n.f.* head of cattle.

rescaldar, *vb.* scald; parch.

rescindir, *vb.* rescind; annul.

rés-do-chão, *n.m.* ground floor.

resenha, *n.f.* book review; report; list.

resenhar, *vb.* review; report; list.

reserva, *n.f.* reservation; reserve.

reservado, 1. *adj.* reserved. **2.** *n.m.* booth; bathroom.

reservar, *vb.* reserve.

resfriado, 1. *adj.* having a cold. **2.** *n.m.* cold.

resfriar, *vb.* chill. **r.-se**, catch a cold.

resgatar, *vb.* ransom; redeem.

resgate, *n.m.* ransom; redemption.

resguardar, *vb.* safeguard, protect; observe.

resguardo, *n.m.* defense; caution; decorum; secret.

residência, *n.f.* residence.

residencial, *adj.* residential.

residente, *adj., n.m.f.* resident.

residir, *vb.* reside.

resíduo, *n.m.* residue.

resignação, *n.f.* resignation.

resignado, *adj.* long-suffering.

resignar, *vb.* resign. **r.-se**, resign oneself.

resiliente, *adj.* resilient.

resina, *n.f.* resin, rosin.

resistência, *n.f.* resistance.

resistente, *adj.* resistant.

resistir, *vb.* resist, endure.

resma, *n.f.* ream (paper).

resmungar, *vb.* mumble; grumble. **—resmungo**, *n.m.*

resolução, *n.f.* resolution; resolve.

resoluto, *adj.* resolute.

resolver, *vb.* resolve; decide; dissolve. **r.-se**, decide.

respaldar, *vb.* level; support.

respaldo, *n.m.* chair back; support.

respectivo, *adj.* respective.

respeitar, *vb.* respect; concern.

respeitável, *adj.* respectable.

respeito, *n.m.* respect. **a r. de** or **com r. a**, with respect to.

respeitoso, *adj.* respectful.

respingar, *vb.* splash; spark; be recalcitrant.

respiração, *n.f.* breathing.

respiradouro, *n.m.* vent.

respirar, *vb.* breathe.

respiratório, *adj.* respiratory.

respiro, *n.m.* breathing; breather.

resplandecente, *adj.* resplendent.

resplandecer, *vb.* glow, shine.

resplendor, *n.m.* brightness; glory.

respondão -dona, 1. *adj.* backtalking. **2.** *n.* backtalker.

responder, *vb.* answer, respond. **r. por**, answer for.

responsabilidade, *n.f.* responsibility.

responsabilizar, *vb.* make responsible. **r.-se**, take responsibility.

responsável, *adj.* responsible.

resposta, *n.f.* answer, response.

resquício, *n.m.* trace, vestige.

ressabiado, *adj.* easily offended; fearful.

ressabido, *adj.* learned; experienced.

ressaca, *n.f.* surf, breaker; *(coll.)* hangover.

ressaibo, *n.m.* bad taste; trace; resentment.

ressaltar, *vb.* bound; highlight; stand out.

ressalva, *n.f.* exception; errata.

ressalvar, *vb.* except; protect; correct.

ressarcir, *vb.* indemnify.

ressecar, -quir, *vb.* parch, dry.

ressentido, *adj.* resentful.

ressentimento, *n.m.* resentment.

ressentir, *vb.* resent. **r.-se**, be sentful; feel the effects.

ressoar, *vb.* resound.

ressonância, *n.f.* resonance.

ressurgir, *vb.* reappear; revive.

ressurreição, *n.f.* resurrection.

ressuscitar, *vb.* resuscitate; resurrect.

restabelecer, *vb.* re-establish; restore. **r.-se**, recover.

restante, *adj., n.m.* remainder.

restar, *vb.* remain.

restaurante, *n.m.* restaurant.

restaurar, *vb.* restore.

réstia, *n.f.* ray, beam.

restinga, *n.f.* shoal, reef.

restituição, *n.f.* restoration; refund.

restituir, *vb.* restore; return; refund.

resto, *n.m.* rest, remainder; *(pl.)* remains. **de r.,** besides.

restrição, *n.f.* restriction.

restringir, *vb.* restrict.

restrito, *adj.* restricted.

resultado, *n.m.* result. —**resultar**, *vb.*

resumir, *vb.* summarize; abridge.

resumo, *n.m.* summary, résumé. **em r.,** in brief.

resvalar, *vb.* slip, slide.

reta, *n.f.* straight line.

retaguarda, *n.f.* rear guard.

retalhar, *vb.* shred, tear.

retalho, *n.m.* scrap, remnant. **a r.,** at retail.

retaliar, *vb.* retaliate.

retângulo, *n.m.* rectangle.

retardado, 1. *adj.* retarded. **2.** *n.m.* mental retard.

retardar, *vb.* retard; delay.

retardatário, 1. *adj.* late. **2.** *n.m.* late-comer.

retenção, *n.f.* retention; detention.

retentiva, *n.f.* retention.

reter, *vb.* retain; detain.

retesar, *vb.* stiffen.

reticência, *n.f.* reticence; *(pl.)* ellipsis.

reticencioso, *adj.* reticent.

retidão, *n.f.* rectitude.

retificar, *vb.* rectify; overhaul.

retinir, *vb.* ring, clang; resound.

retinto, *adj.* dark-colored.

retirada, *n.f.* retreat; withdrawal; emigration.

retirante, *n.m.f.* migrant from the Northeast interior.

retirar, *vb.* withdraw; depart. **r.-se**, retreat, leave.

retiro, *n.m.* seclusion; retreat.

reto, 1. *adj.* straight, right; upright. **2.** *n.m.* rectum.

retocar, *vb.* retouch. —**retoque**, *n.m.*

retorcer, *vb.* twist, contort. **r.-se**, writhe.

retórico, *adj.* rhetorical.

retornar, *vb.* return; restore.

retorno, *n.m.* return.

retorquir, *vb.* retort, reply.

retração, *n.f.* contraction; shrinkage.

retraído, *adj.* reserved; secluded.

retraimento, *n.m.* reserve; timidity; seclusion.

retrair, *vb.* retract; shrink; hide.

retrair-se, *vb.* retreat; contract; hide.

retranca, *n.f.* (coll.) **na r.,** on the defensive.

retrasado, *adj.* before last (year, month).

retratar, *vb.* portray; photograph; retract.

retrato, *n.m.* portrait; photograph.

retrete, *n.f.* rest room.

retribuição, *n.f.* repayment; reward.

retribuir, *vb.* repay; reward.

retroalimentação, *n.f.* feedback.

retroativo, *adj.* retroactive.

retroceder, *vb.* retreat, recede.

retrocesso, *n.m.* recession.

retrógrado, 1. *adj.* backward, reactionary. **2.** *n.m.* reactionary.

retrospectivo, *adj.* retrospective.

retrovisor, *adj.* rear-view. **espelho r.,** rear-view mirror.

retrucar, *vb.* reply, retort.

retumbar, *vb.* resound, echo.

réu, *n.m.* defendant.

reumatismo, *n.m.* rheumatism.

reunião, *n.f.* meeting; get-together; party. **r. de cúpula,** summit meeting.

reunir, *vb.* gather, assemble. **r.-se**, meet, get together.

revelação, *n.f.* revelation; development.

revelar, *vb.* reveal; develop (film).

revelia, *n.f.* rebellion; default.

revendedor, *n.m.* dealer; car dealer.

reverberar, *vb.* reflect; shine.

reverência, *n.f.* reverence.

reverenciar, *vb.* revere.

reverendo, *n.m.* reverend.

reverente, *adj.* reverent.

reversão, *n.f.* reversion.

reversível, *adj.* reversible.

reverso, *adj., n.m.* reverse.

reverter, vb. revert.

revertério, n.m. (sl.) reversal; fit.

revés, n.m. reverse, setback. **ao r.,** backwards, just the opposite.

revestir, vb. clothe; dress in; cover.

revezar, vb. alternate. **r.-se,** take turns.

revidar, vb. retort; retaliate.

revigorar, vb. reinvigorate.

revirar, vb. turn over/around.

reviravolta, n.f. reversal, about-face.

revisão, n.f. revision; review; proofreading.

revisar, vb. revise; review; proofread.

revisor, n.m. reviser; proof-reader.

revista, n.f. magazine, review; revue.

revistar, vb. review; inspect.

reviver, vb. revive.

revogar, vb. revoke.

revolta, n.f. revolt.

revoltado -da, 1. adj. rebellious. **2.** n. rebel.

revoltar, vb. stir to revolt; outrage. **r.-se,** revolt.

revolução, n.f. revolution.

revolucionar, vb. stir to revolt; revolutionize. **r.-se,** rebel.

revolucionário -ria, adj., n. revolutionary.

revolver, vb. revolve; stir; rummage; dig; roll.

revólver, n.m. revolver.

reza, n.f. prayer.

rezar, vb. pray.

rezingar, vb. growl, grumble.

riacho, n.m. creek, brook.

ribalta, n.f. footlights.

ribamar, n.m. seashore.

ribanceira, n.f. (steep) river bank.

ribeirão, n.m. stream.

ribeiro, n.m. creek, stream.

ribombar, vb. resound, boom.

ricaço -ça, n. (coll.) rich person.

ricino, n.m. castor bean. **óleo de r.,** castor oil.

rico, adj. rich.

ricochetear, vb. ricochet. **—ricochete,** n.m.

ridicularizar, -larizar, vb. ridicule.

ridículo, adj. ridiculous.

rifa, n.f. raffle. **—rifar,** vb.

rifão, n.m. proverb.

rifle, n.m. repeating rifle.

rígido, adj. rigid.

rigor, n.m. rigor. **a/de r.,** formal, de rigueur.

rigoroso, adj. rigorous.

rijo, adj. rigid.

rim, n.m. kidney.

rima, n.f. rhyme. **—rimar,** vb.

rímel, n.m. mascara.

rincão, n.m. glen; corner.

rinchar, vb. neigh. **—rincho,** n.m.

ringue, n.m. boxing ring.

rinha, n.f. fight. **—rinhar,** vb.

rinoceronte, n.m. rhinoceros.

rinque, n.m. rink.

rio, n.m. river; (cap.) Rio de Janeiro.

rio-grandense-do-norte, 1. adj. pert. to Rio Grande do Norte. **2.** n.m.f. Rio Grande do Norte native.

rio-grandense-do-sul, 1. adj. pert. to Rio Grande do Sul. **2.** n.m.f. Rio Grande do Sul native.

ripa, n.f. lath, slat.

riqueza, n.f. riches, wealth.

rir, vb. laugh. **r.(-se) de,** laugh at.

risada, n.f. laugh, laughter.

risca, n.f. line, stripe; part (hair). **à r.,** to the letter.

riscar, vb. line; cross out; sketch.

risco, n.m. risk; mark; sketch. **correr um r.,** run a risk.

risível, adj. laughable.

riso, n.m. laughter.

risonho, adj. smiling; happy.

ríspido, adj. severe, harsh.

riste, n.m. em r., at the ready, poised.

ritmo, n.m. rhythm.

rito, n.m. rite.

ritual, adj., n.m. ritual.

rival, adj., n.m.f. rival. **—rivalizar,** vb.

rivalidade, n.f. rivalry.

rixa, n.f. fight. **—rixar,** vb.

robô, n.m. robot.

robótica, n.f. robotics.

robustecer, *vb.* strengthen.

robusto, *adj.* robust, strong.

roca, *n.f.* distaff.

roça, *n.f.* farm field; countryside.

roçado, *n.m.* cleared land; farm field.

roçar, *vb.* touch lightly; rub; clear (land).

roceiro -ra, 1. *adj.* country. **2.** *n.* rustic; small farmer.

rocha, *n.f.* rock, boulder.

rochedo, *n.m.* cliff.

rochoso, *adj.* rocky.

rocio, *n.m.* dew.

roda, *n.f.* wheel; circle; group. **r. gigante**, ferris wheel.

rodagem, *n.f.* rotation; wheeling. **estrada de r.**, highway.

rodapé, *n.m.* baseboard; footnote.

rodar, *vb.* roll; ride around; *(sl.)* flunk; film.

roda-viva, *n.f. (coll.)* bustle, rat race.

rodear, *vb.* surround.

rodeio, *n.m.* circumlocution; roundup.

rodela, *n.f.* round slice, wheel.

rodízio, *n.m.* rotation; work shift.

rodo, *n.m.* squeegee. **a r.**, galore.

rodopiar, *vb.* spin. —**rodopio**, *n.m.*

rodovia, *n.f.* highway.

rodoviária, *n.f.* bus station; trucking company.

rodoviário, *adj.* of or for a highway.

roedor, *n.m.* rodent.

roer, *vb.* gnaw.

rogar, *vb.* beg, plead. **fazer-se r./de rogado**, wait to be coaxed.

rogo, *n.m.* plea.

rojão, *n.m.* skyrocket. **agüentar o r.**, stick it out.

rol, *n.m.* roll, roster.

rola, *n.f.* turtledove.

rolamento, *n.m.* ball bearing.

rolante, *adj.* rolling. **escada r.**, escalator.

rolar, *vb.* roll, turn.

roldana, *n.f.* pulley.

roleta, *n.f.* roulette.

rolha, *n.f.* cork; *(coll.)* censorship.

roliço, *adj.* round; chubby.

rolo, *n.m.* roll; roller; *(sl.)* row; disorder. **r. compressor**, steam roller.

Roma, *n.* Rome.

romã, *n.f.* pomegranate.

romance, *n.m.* novel; romance.

românico, *adj.* Romance.

romano -na, *adj., n.* Roman.

romântico, *adj., n.m.* romantic.

romantismo, *n.m.* romanticism.

romaria, *n.f.* pilgrimage.

romeiro -ra, *n.* pilgrim.

romper, *vb.* break, tear. —**rompimento**, *n.m.*

roncar, *vb.* snore; roar.

ronco, *n.m.* snore, snoring. **puxar r.**, *(sl.)* snooze.

ronda, *n.f.* patrol, rounds.

rondar, *vb.* patrol, make the rounds.

ronronar, *vb.* purr. —**ronrom**, *n.m.*

roque, *n.m.* rook; rock music/ song.

roqueiro -ra, *n.* rock musician/ fan.

rosa, 1. *adj.* pink, rose-colored. **2.** *n.f.* rose.

rosado, *adj.* pink; rosé (wine).

rosário, *n.m.* rosary.

rosbife, *n.m.* roast beef.

rosca, *n.f.* screw thread.

roseira, *n.f.* rosebush.

rosnar, *vb.* growl, snarl.

rossio, *n.m.* public square.

rosto, *n.m.* face; title page.

rota, *n.f.* route.

rotação, *n.f.* rotation.

rotatividade, *n.f.* **de alta r.**, high-turnover.

rotativo, *adj.* rotating.

roteiro, *n.m.* itinerary; outline; script.

rotina, *n.f.* routine.

rotineiro, *adj.* customary.

rótula, *n.f.* kneecap.

rótulo, *n.m.* label. —**rotular**, *n.m.*

rotundo, *adj.* rotund.

roubalheira, *n.f.* robbery.

roubar, *vb.* rob, steal.

roubo, *n.m.* robbery, theft.

rouco, *adj.* hoarse.

roupa, *n.f.* clothes. **r. branca,**

underwear; **r. de cama**, bed linen.

roupão, *n.m.* robe, dressing gown.

rouparia, *n.f.* wardrobe.

rouxinol, *n.m.* nightingale.

roxo, *adj.* purple.

rua, *n.f.* street.

ruão, *adj.* roan.

rubi, *n.m.* ruby.

rubor, *n.m.* redness; blush.

ruborizar-se, *vb.* blush.

rubrica, *n.f.* rubric.

ruço, 1. *adj.* gray. 2. *n.m.* dense fog.

rude, *adj.* rude, coarse.

rudez, **-deza**, *n.f.* rudeness, coarseness.

rudimentário, *adj.* rudimentary.

rufião, *n.m.* ruffian; pimp.

ruga, *n.f.* wrinkle.

ruge, *n.m.* rouge.

rugir, *vb.* roar. —**rugido**, *n.m.*

rugoso, *adj.* wrinkled.

ruibarbo, *n.m.* rhubarb.

ruído, *n.m.* noise, sound.

ruidoso, *adj.* noisy.

ruim, *adj.* bad; evil.

ruína, *n.f.* ruin.

ruindade, *n.f.* wickedness.

ruir, *vb.* fall down.

ruivo, *adj.* red-headed.

rum, *n.m.* rum.

rumar, *vb.* head (for).

ruminar, *vb.* ruminate.

rumo, *n.m.* direction.

rumor, *n.m.* noise; rumor.

rumorejar, *vb.* make noise.

ruptura, *n.f.* rupture, break.

rural, *adj.* rural.

rusga, *n.f.* row, fight.

russo -sa, *adj.*, *n.* Russian; *n.m.* Russian (language).

rústico, *adj. n.m.* rustic.

rutilar, *vb.* gleam, shine.

S

sabá, *n.m.* Sabbath.

sábado, *n.m.* Saturday.

sabão, *n.m.* soap; *(coll.)* scolding.

sabatina, *n.f.* weekly quiz; discussion session.

sabedor -ra, 1. *adj.* knowledgeable. 2. *n.* learned person; sage.

sabedoria, *n.f.* wisdom, knowledge.

sabença, *n.f.* *(coll.)* knowledge.

saber, 1. *n.m.* knowledge. 2. *vb.* know, find out; know how. **s. a**, taste like; **a s.**, namely. **sei lá!**, how should I know?

sabe-tudo, *n.m.f.* *(coll.)* know-it-all.

sabiá, *n.m.* Brazilian thrush.

sabichão -chona, **-dão -dona**, *n.* know-it-all.

sabido, *adj.* knowing; smart; shrewd.

sábio -bia, 1. *adj.* wise. 2. *n.* sage; scholar.

sabonete, *n.m.* bar of soap.

saboneteira, *n.f.* soapdish.

sabor, *n.m.* taste, flavor. **ao s. de**, at the whim of.

saborear, *vb.* savor.

saboroso, *adj.* tasty, flavorful.

sabotagem, *n.f.* sabotage. —**sabotar**, *vb.*

sabre, *n.m.* saber.

sabugo, *n.m.* pith; corncob.

sabujice, *n.f.* fawning.

sabujo, *n.m.* bloodhound; bootlicker.

saca, *n.f.* large sack, purse; pulling.

sacada, *n.f.* balcony; pull.

sacado -da, *n.* *(com.)* drawee.

sacana, 1. *adj.* *(vulg.)* immoral; mean, dirty. 2. *n.m.f.* *(vulg.)* homosexual; scoundrel.

sacanagem, *n.f.* *(vulg.)* immorality; homosexuality; dirty trick.

sacar, *vb.* take out, draw; *(sport.)* serve; *(sl.)* understand, know.

saçaricar, *vb.* *(coll.)* wiggle. —**saçarico**, *n.m.*

sacarina, *n.f.* saccharin.

saca-rolha, *n.m.* corkscrew.

sacerdócio, *n.m.* priesthood.

sacerdote, *n.m.* priest.

sacerdotisa, *n.f.* priestess.

sací(-pererê), *n.m.* one-legged goblin.

saciar, *vb.* satiate; satisfy.

saco, *n.m.* sack, bag; *(vulg.)* scrotum; *(sl.)* patience; *(sl.)* bummer. **s. de água quente**, hot-water bottle; **s. de dormir**, sleeping bag; **encher o s. de**, (sl.) get on the nerves of; **estar de s. cheio**, (sl.) be fed up; **puxar o s. de**, (sl.) lick the boots of.

sacola, n.f. bag, pouch.

sacolejar, vb. shake, jolt. —**sacolejo**, n.m.

sacramental, adj. sacramental; traditional.

sacramentar, vb. administer sacraments to; make sacred; (coll.) legalize.

sacramento, n.m. sacrament.

sacrificar, vb. sacrifice.

sacrificial, adj. sacrificial.

sacrifício, n.m. sacrifice.

sacrilégio, n.m. sacrilege.

sacripanta, n.m.f. scoundrel.

sacristão, n.m. sacristan, sexton.

sacro, adj. sacred.

sacrossanto, adj. sacrosanct.

sacudida, -didela, n.f. shake, jolt.

sacudido, adj. shaken; brusque; agile.

sacudir, vb. shake, jolt; throw off. **s.-se**, wiggle.

sádico -ca, 1. adj. sadistic. 2. n. sadist.

sadio, adj. healthy, sound, wholesome.

sadismo, n.m. sadism.

safadeza, n.f. (coll.) shamelessness; dirty trick.

safado, 1. adj. (coll.) shameless; angry. 2. n.m. (coll.) scoundrel.

safanão, n.m. push, shove; slap.

safar, vb. pull out; disentangle; steal. **s.-se**, get away. **s. onça**, (sl.) get by, manage.

safardana, n.m.f. scoundrel.

safira, n.f. sapphire.

safra, n.f. harvest.

saga, n.f. saga.

sagaz, adj. sagacious.

Sagitário, n.m. Sagittarius.

sagrado, adj. sacred, holy.

saguão, n.m. lobby, foyer.

saia, n.f. skirt; (coll.) dame.

saibro, n.m. gravel and sand mixture.

saída, n.f. departure; sally; exit; way out; outlet; (elec.) output;

sales; remark. **(logo) de s.** right off the bat.

saída-de-praia, n.f. beach robe.

saído, adj. protruding; forward; (coll.) meddlesome.

saiote, n.m. short skirt; kilt.

sair, vb. leave; go out; escape; come out; be published. **s.-se com**, blurt out; **s. a**, take after.

sal, n.m. salt; wit.

sala, n.f. room; living room; hall. **s. de aula**, classroom; **s. de estar/visita**, parlor, living room; **s. de jantar**, dining room.

salada, n.f. salad; confusion. **s. russa**, tossed salad.

saladeira, n.f. salad bowl.

salafrário -ria, n. (coll.) scoundrel.

salamaleque, n.m. fawning.

salamandra, n.f. salamander.

salame, n.m. salami.

salão, n.m. salon; hall, **s. de beleza**, beauty salon; **s. nobre**, auditorium.

salariado -ria, n. wage earner.

salarial, adj. wage.

salário, n.m. wages. **s. mínimo**, minimum wage.

salchicha, n.f. sausage.

saldar, vb. pay up, settle; balance.

saldo, n.m. (com.) balance.

saleiro, n.m. salt shaker.

saleta, n.f. small room.

salgadinhos, n.m.pl. salty snacks.

salgado, adj. salty; witty; sarcastic; (coll.) expensive.

salgar, vb. salt.

salgueiro, n.m. willow. **s. chorão**, weeping willow.

saliência, n.f. salience; protuberance.

salientar, vb. emphasize, stress.

saliente, adj. salient; protruding.

salina, n.f. salt marsh; salt works.

salino, adj. saline; coastal.

salitre, n.m. nitrate, saltpeter.

saliva, n.f. saliva.

salivar, vb. salivate.

salmão, n.m. salmon.

salmo, n.m. psalm.

salmoura, n.f. brine.

salobro, adj. salty, briny.

saloia, n.f. (P.) peasant girl/woman.

saloio, 1. adj. (P.) rustic; sly. **2.** n.m. (P.) peasant man/boy.

salpicar, vb. spatter; besmirch.

salsa, n.f. parsley.

salseiro, n.m. downpour; brawl.

salsicha, n.f. sausage.

saltar, vb. jump; get off/out (of); assault; skip over; (sl.) bring. **s. à vista,** stand out.

salteador, n.m. highwayman.

saltear, vb. assault, hold up.

saltimbanco, n.m. traveling entertainer; mountebank.

saltitar, vb. hop, skip.

salto, n.m. jump; bounce; waterfall; shoe heel. **s. mortal,** somersault.

salubre, adj. salubrious, healthy.

salutar, adj. salutary.

salva, n.f. salvo; applause; tray.

salvação, n.f. salvation; rescue; greeting.

salvador, n.m. savior.

salvadorenho -nha, 1. adj. of/pert. to El Salvador. **2.** n. El Salvador native.

salvaguarda, n.f. safeguard; safe-conduct.

salvaguardar, vb. safeguard, protect.

salvamento, n.m. salvation; rescue.

salvar, vb. save; fire a salvo; greet.

salva-vidas, n.m.f. lifeguard. n.m. life preserver.

salve, interj. hail!

salvo, 1. adj. safe. **2.** prep. except, save.

salvo-conduto, n.m. safe-conduct.

samambaia, n.f. fern.

samba, n.m. samba. **—sambar,** vb.

sambista, n.m.f. samba dancer.

sanar, vb. cure.

sanativo, adj. curative.

sanatório, n.m. sanatarium, nursing home.

sancão, n.f. sanction.

sancionar, vb. sanction.

sandália, n.f. sandal.

sandeu -dia, adj. foolish, stupid.

sandice, n.f. silliness.

sanduíche, n.m.f. sandwich. **s. americano,** ham-and-egg sandwich.

saneamento, n.m. sanitation.

sanear, vb. sanitize; remedy.

sanfona, n.f. concertina, accordion.

sangrar, vb. bleed.

sangrento, adj. bloody.

sangria, n.f. bleeding; bloodshed; sangría.

sangue, n.m. blood. **a s. frio,** in cold blood.

sanguessuga, n.f. leech.

sanguinário, adj. bloodthirsty, cruel; bloody.

sanguíneo, adj. blood; sanguine; blood-colored.

sanguinolento, adj. bloodthirsty.

sanha, n.f. anger, wrath.

sanidade, n.f. health, hygiene.

sanitário, 1. adj. sanitary. **2.** n.m. bathroom.

santa, 1. adj. holy, blessed; saint (f.). **2.** n.f. saint.

santarrão -rona, 1. adj. sanctimonious. **2.** n. sanctimonious person.

santidade, n.f. sanctity, holiness.

santificar, vb. sanctify.

santo, 1. adj. holy, blessed; saint (before a masc. name beginning with a vowel or h). **2.** n.m. saint.

santuário, n.m. sanctuary, shrine.

são, adj. saint (before a masc. name except those beginning with a vowel or h).

são, sã, adj. healthy, sound. **s. e salvo,** safe and sound.

sapa, n.f. sapping, undermining.

sapatão, n.m. big shoe; (sl.) lesbian.

sapataria, n.f. shoe store; shoe-repair shop.

sapateiro -ra, n. cobbler; shoe salesclerk.

sapato, n.m. shoe.

sapeca, adj. (coll.) flirtatious; mischievous.

sapecar, vb. scorch; botch; (coll.) flirt; (coll.) beat.
sapiência, n.f. wisdom.
sapo, n.m. toad; (sl.) kibitzer.
saque, n.m. sacking; (sport.) serve.
saquear, vb. sack, plunder.
sarabatana, n.f. blowgun.
saracotear, vb. sway, wiggle. —**saracoteio**, n.m.
saraiva, n.f. hail.
sarampo, n.m. measles.
sarapintar, vb. speckle.
sarar, vb. heal.
sarará, n.m.f. light-skinned mulatto.
sarau, n.m. soirée.
saravá, interj. hail! greetings!
sarça, n.f. bramble.
sarcasmo, n.m. sarcasm.
sarcástico, adj. sarcastic.
sarda, n.f. freckle.
sardento, adj. freckled.
sardinha, n.f. sardine.
sargento, n.m. sergeant; vise.
sarilho, n.m. reel, winch; (coll.) confusion.
sarjeta, n.f. gutter.
sarmento, n.m. vine shoot.
sarna, n.f. itch, mange.
sarrafo, n.m. slat, lath.
sarro, n.m. tartar, deposit; (sl.) fun. tirar um s., (sl.) get one's kicks.
satanás, n.m. Satan.
satânico, adj. satanic.
satélite, adj., n.m. satellite.
sátira, n.f. satire.
satírico, 1. adj. satirical. 2. n.m. satirist.
satirizar, vb. satirize.
satisfação, n.f. satisfaction; reparation; explanation.
satisfatório, adj. satisfactory.
satisfazer, vb. satisfy.
saturar, vb. saturate.
saudação, n.f. salutation, greeting.
saudade, n.f. longing, nostalgia. estar com saudades de, miss, long for.
saudar, vb. salute, greet.
saudável, adj. healthful.
saúde, 1. n.f. health. 2. interj. cheers!; Gesundheit!
saudita, adj., n.m.f. Saudi.

saudoso, adj. longing, nostalgic.
saúva, n.f. leaf-cutting ant.
saveiro, n.m. small fishing/transport boat.
saxofone, n.m. saxophone.
se, 1. conj. if. s. bem que, even though. 2. pron. one, you; your-, her-, him-, it- oneself; (pl.) themselves; each other.
sé, n.f. (eccles.) cathedral; see.
seara, n.f. grainfield; harvest.
sebe, n.f. hedge.
sebo, n.m. tallow, grease; (coll.) used-book store.
seboso, -bento, adj. greasy; filthy.
seca, n.f. drought; drying.
secador, n.m. dryer.
secar, vb. dry.
secção, seção, n.f. section.
secessão, n.f. secession.
seco, 1. adj. dry; arid; barren; lean; (coll.) longing. 2. n.m.pl. dry goods. s. e molhados, groceries.
secreção, n.f. secretion.
secretaria, n.f. secretariat; administrative office.
secretária, n.f. secretary (f.); desk. s. eletrônica, answering machine.
secretariado, n.m. secretariat.
secretário, n.m. secretary (m.). s. de estado, secretary of state.
secreto, adj. secret.
sectário -ria, n. follower.
secular, adj. secular; age-old.
século, n.m. century; epoch; secular life.
secundar, vb. support, aid.
secundário, adj. secondary.
secura, n.f. dryness; sterility; (coll.) craving, sexual desire.
seda, n.f. silk. rasgar s., (coll.) be overly solicitous.
sedar, vb. calm, soothe.
sedativo, adj., n.m. sedative.
sede, n.f. headquarters; home office.
sede, n.f. thirst. estar com s., be thirsty.
sedentário, adj. sedentary.
sedento, n.m. thirsty; eager.
sedição, n.f. sedition.
sedimento, n.m. sediment.
sedoso, adj. silky.

sedução, *n.f.* seduction.
sedutor -ra, **1.** *adj.* seductive. **2.** *n.* seducer.
seduzir, *vb.* seduce.
sega, *n.f.* harvest, reaping.
segadeira, *n.f.* scythe.
segador -ra, *n.* reaper, harvester.
segadora, *n.f.* (*mech.*) reaper.
segar, *vb.* harvest, reap; mow down.
segmento, *n.m.* segment.
segredar, *vb.* tell a secret; whisper
segredo, *n.m.* secret; lock combination.
segregação, *n.f.* segregation.
segregar, *vb.* segregate; secrete.
seguida, *n.f.* **em s.**, right away.
seguido, *adj.* consecutive, running.
seguidor -ra, *n.* follower.
seguimento, *n.m.* pursuit; continuation. **dar s. a**, proceed with.
seguinte, **1.** *adj.* following, next. **no dia s.**, the next day. **2.** *n.m.* the following.
seguir, *vb.* follow; continue.
segunda, *n.f.* Monday.
segunda-feira, *n.f.* Monday.
segundanista, *n.m.f.* sophomore.
segundo, **1.** *adj.* second. **de segunda mão**, second-hand. **2.** *n.m.* second, instant. **3.** *adv.* secondly. **4.** *prep.* according to; as.
segurador -ra, *n.* insurer.
seguradora, *n.f.* insurance company.
segurança, *n.f.* safety; security; protection; *n.m.f.* security guard.
segurar, *vb.* hold; grasp; secure; insure.
seguro, **1.** *adj.* safe, secure; firm; certain. **2.** *n.m.* insurance.
seio, *n.m.* breast; bosom; sinus.
seis, *adj.* six.
seiscentos, *adj.* six hundred.
seita, *n.f.* sect; party; denomination.
seiva, *n.f.* sap; vigor.
seixo, *n.m.* pebble.
sela, *n.f.* saddle.
selar, *vb.* stamp; seal; saddle.

seleção, *n.f.* selection; (*sport.*) all-star team.
selecionar, *vb.* select, pick.
seleta, *n.f.* anthology.
seletivo, *ajd.* selective.
seleto, *adj.* select, choice.
selim, *n.m.* bicycle seat.
selo, *n.m.* seal; stamp; postage stamp.
selva, *n.f.* rainforest, jungle.
selvagem, **1.** *adj.* savage, wild. **2.** *n.m.f.* savage.
sem, *prep.* without. **s. que**, without.
semáforo, *n.m.* semaphore.
semana, *n.f.* week.
semanal, *adj.* weekly.
semanário, *adj.*, *n.m.* weekly.
semântica, *n.f.* semantics.
semblante, *n.m.* face, countenance.
semeada, *n.f.* sown field.
semear, *vb.* sow.
semelhança, *n.f.* similarity. **à s. de**, like.
semelhante, **1.** *adj.* similar; such. **2.** *n.m.f.* fellow being.
semelhar, *vb.* resemble.
sêmen, *n.m.* semen.
semente, *n.f.* seed.
sementeira, *n.f.* sown field; seedbed; spread.
semestre, *n.m.* semester.
sem-fim, **1.** *adj.* endless. **2.** *n.m.* endless quantity.
semicondutor, *n.m.* semiconductor.
seminário, *n.m.* seminary.
seminarista, *n.m.* seminarian.
seminu -nua, *adj.* half-naked.
sem-número, *n.m.* vast number.
semovente, *adj.* self-moving.
sempiterno, *adj.* everlasting.
sempre, *adv.* always, ever. **nem s.**, not always; **para s.**, forever.
sem-vergonha, **1.** *adj.* shameless. **2.** *n.m.f.* shameless person.
senado, *n.m.* senate.
senador -ra, *n.* senator.
senão, **1.** *conj.* otherwise; except. **2.** *n.m.* flaw.
senda, *n.f.* path, trail.
sendeiro, *n.m.* old nag.
senectude, *n.f.* old age.
senha, *n.f.* password.
senhor, *n.m.* mister; sir; master;

gentleman; (cap.) God, Lord. **o s.**, you (m.s.).

senhora, n.f. Mrs., ma'am; mistress; lady. **Nossa S.**, Our Lady.; **a s.**, you (f.s.).

senhorear, vb. dominate.

senhoria, n.f. lordship; domain; landlady. **Vossa S.**, you (formal letters).

senhorial, adj. lordly; manorial.

senhoril, adj. noble, majestic.

senhorio, n.m. lordship; property; landlord.

senhorita, n.f. miss.

senil, adj. senile.

senilidade, n.f. senility.

sensaboria, n.f. insipidness, dullness.

sensação, n.f. sensation.

sensacional, adj. sensational.

sensatez, n.f. sensibleness.

sensato, adj. sensible.

sensibilidade, n.f. sensitivity.

sensibilizar, vb. sensitize; touch.

sensível, adj. sensitive.

senso, n.m. sense. **s. comum**, common sense.

sensual, adj. sensual, sensuous.

sensualidade, n.f. sensuality.

sentada, n.f. sitting.

sentado, adj. sitting, seated.

sentar, vb. seat; sit. **s.-se**, sit down.

sentença, n.f. sentence; maxim.

sentenciar, vb. sentence, convict.

sentido, 1. adj. grieved; sad. 2. n.m. sense; feeling; meaning; direction. 3. interj. attention!

sentimental, adj. sentimental.

sentimentalidade, n.f. sentimentality.

sentimento, n.m. sentiment.

sentinela, n.f. sentry; watch; wake.

sentir, vb. feel, sense; smell; regret.

senzala, n.f. (hist.) slave quarters.

separação, n.f. separation.

separar, vb. separate.

separata, n.f. offprint.

séptico, adj. septic.

septuagésimo, adj. seventieth.

sepulcro, n.m. sepulcher, tomb.

sepultar, vb. bury, inter.

sepultura, n.f. grave, tomb.

sequaz, n.m.f. follower.

seqüela, n.f. sequel; gang.

seqüência, n.f. sequence.

sequer, adv. even. **nem s.**, not even.

seqüestrador -ra, n. kidnapper.

seqüestrar, vb. kidnap; hijack; seize.

seqüestro, n.m. kidnapping; hijacking; seizure.

sequidão, n.f. dryness.

sequioso, adj. thirsty; avid.

séquito, n.m. entourage.

ser, 1. n.m. being; essence. **s. humano**, human being. 2. vb. be. **s. de**, belong to; **a não s.**, except; **a não s. que**, unless; **pode s.**, maybe.

serafim, n.m. seraph.

serão, n.m. night work; soirée.

sereia, n.f. siren, mermaid.

serelepe, adj. lively.

serenar, vb. calm; mist.

serenata, n.f. serenade.

sereno, 1. adj. serene, calm; clear. 2. n.m. night dew; outdoors.

seresta, n.f. (coll.) serenade.

sergipano -na, 1. adj. of/pert. to Sergipe state. 2. n. Sergipe native.

serial, adj. serial.

série, n.f. series; grade (school).

seriedade, n.f. seriousness.

seringa, n.f. syringe; latex.

seringal, n.m. rubber plantation.

seringueira, n.f. rubber tree.

seringueiro, n.m. rubber tapper.

sério, adj. serious; sober. **levar/tomar a s.** take seriously.

sermão, n.m. sermon.

serôdio, adj. late.

serpente, n.f. serpent, snake.

serpentear, -pear, vb. snake, wind.

serpentina, n.f. coil; streamer; candelabrum.

serra, n.f. saw; mountain range.

serrador -ra, n. sawyer.

serradura, -ragem, n.f. sawing; sawdust.

serralheiro, n.m. locksmith.

serralho, n.m. seraglio; brothel.

serrania, n.f. mountain range.

serrano -na, 1. *adj.* mountain. **2.** *n.* highlander.

serrar, *vb.* saw.

serraria, *n.f.* sawmill.

serrote, *n.m.* handsaw.

sertanejo -ja, 1. *adj.* backwoods **2.** *n.* backlander.

sertania, *n.f.* hinterland.

sertão, *n.m.* backlands (esp. of northeast Brazil).

servente, *n.m.f.* servant; assistant.

serventia, *n.f.* utility.

serviçal, 1. *adj.* helpful, **2.** *n.m.f.* servant; assistant.

serviço, *n.m.* service; work; job; cover charge; toilet.

servidão, *n.f.* servitude.

servidor, *n.m.* servant.

servil, *adj.* servile.

servir, *vb.* serve; be useful. **s.-se de,** make use of. **s. de,** serve as.

servo -va, *n.m.* serf; servant.

sésamo, *n.m.* sesame.

sesmaria, *n.f.* land grant.

sessão, *n.f.* session.

sessenta, *adj.* sixty.

sesta, *n.f.* siesta.

seta, *n.f.* arrow, dart.

sete, *adj.* seven.

setecentos, *adj.* seven hundred.

setembro, *n.m.* September.

setenta, *adj.* seventy.

setentrional, *adj.* northern.

sétimo, *adj.* seventh.

setor, *n.m.* sector.

seu, sua, 1. *adj.* your; her, his, its; their; (name-calling) you ... **2.** *pron.* yours; hers, his, its; theirs. **3.** *n.m.* title used before a man's first name.

severidade, *n.f.* severity.

severo, *adj.* severe, harsh.

sevícias, *n.f.pl.* ill-treatment, abuse.

sexagésimo, *adj.* sixtieth.

sexo, *n.m.* sex. **belo s.,** fair sex.

sexta, *n.f.* Friday.

sexta-feira, *n.f.* Friday.

sexto, *adj.* sixth.

sexual, *adj.* sexual.

sexualidade, *n.f.* sexuality.

sezão, *n.f.* intermittent fever.

shopping, *n.m.* shopping center.

show, *n.m.* show.

si, *pron.* her-, him-, it-, oneself; yourself; themselves; yourselves; you. (after a preposition).

sibilar, *vb.* whistle, hiss. —**sibilo,** *n.m.*

sicrano -na, *n.* so-and-so.

sideral, *adj.* sidereal.

siderurgia, *n.f.* steel production.

siderúrgica, *n.f.* steel mill.

siderúrgico, *adj.* pert. to steel production.

sidra, *n.f.* cider.

sifão, *n.m.* siphon.

sífilis, *n.f.* syphilis.

sigilo, *n.m.* secrecy; secret.

sigla, *n.f.* initials.

signatário, *n.m.* signatory, signer.

significação, *n.f.* meaning, significance.

significado, *n.m.* meaning.

significar, *vb.* mean, signify.

significativo, *adj.* meaningful, significant.

signo, *n.m.* sign.

sílaba, *n.f.* syllable.

silenciador, *n.m.* silencer; muffler.

silenciar, *vb.* silence; hush.

silêncio, *n.m.* silence.

silencioso, *adj.* silent.

silhueta, *n.f.* silhouette.

silício, *n.m.* silicon.

silo, *n.m.* silo.

silvar, *vb.* whistle, hiss. —**silvo,** *n.m.*

silvestre, *adj.* sylvan; rural.

silvícola, *n.m.f.* forest-dweller; Indian.

silvicultura, *n.f.* forestry.

sim, *adv.* yes.

simbiose, *n.f.* symbiosis.

simbólico, *adj.* symbolic.

simbolizar, *vb.* symbolize.

símbolo, *n.m.* symbol.

simétrico, *adj.* symmetrical.

similar, *adj.* similar.

símile, *n.m.* simile.

simpatia, *n.f.* liking, friendliness.

simpático, *adj.* nice, likable.

simpatizar com, *vb.* like, take to.

simples, *adj.* simple; single; mere.

simplicidade, *n.f.* simplicity.

simplificar, *vb.* simplify.
simplório, *n.m.* simpleton.
simpósio, *n.m.* symposium.
simulacro, *n.m.* simulacrum.
simular, *vb.* simulate.
simultâneo, *adj.* simultaneous.
sina, *n.f.* fate.
sinagoga, *n.f.* synagogue.
sinal, *n.m.* signal, sign; traffic signal; deposit; mole. **por s.,** incidentally.
sinaleira, *n.f.*, **-ro**, *n.m.* traffic signal.
sinalização, *n.f.* road signs and signals.
sinalizador, *n.m.* flare.
sinceridade, *n.f.* sincerity.
sincero, *adj.* sincere.
sincronizar, *vb.* synchronize.
sindical, *adj.* trade-union.
sindicalista, *n.m.f.* union member.
sindicalizar, *vb.* unionize.
sindicato, *n.m.* labor union.
síndico, *n.m.* agent; tenants' representative.
sinecura, *n.f.* sinecure.
sineta, *n.f.* small bell; doorbell.
sinete, *n.m.* seal, signet.
sinfonia, *n.f.* symphony.
singeleza, *n.f.* simplicity.
singelo, *adj.* simple; single.
singrar, *vb.* sail.
singular, *adj.* singular.
sinistrado, *n.m.* injured party; total loss.
sinistro, **1.** *adj.* sinister; disastrous. **2.** *n.m.* disaster; damage; loss.
sino, *n.m.* bell.
sinônimo, *n.m.* synonym.
sinopse, *n.f.* synopsis.
sintaxe, *n.f.* syntaxis.
síntese, *n.f.* synthesis.
sintético, *adj.* synthetic.
sintetizar, *vb.* synthesize.
sintoma, *n.m.* symptom.
sintonia, *n.f.* syntony. **em s. com,** in tune with.
sintonizar, *vb.* tune (in).
sinuca, *n.f.* pool, snooker. **em s.,** (*sl.*) in a jam.
sinuoso, *adj.* sinuous.
sinusite, *n.f.* sinusitis.
sirena, **-ne**, *n.f.* siren (alarm).
sirgo, *n.m.* silkworm.
siri, *n.m.* crab.

sirigaita, *n.f.* (*coll.*) old biddy; hussy.
sírio -ria, *adj.*, *n.* Syrian.
sísmico, *adj.* seismic.
siso, *n.m.* sense, judgment. **dente do s.,** wisdom tooth.
sistema, *n.m.* system. **s. operacional,** operating system.
sistemático, *adj.* systematic.
sistematizar, *vb.* systematize.
sistêmico, *adj.* systemic.
sisudo, *adj.* sensible, prudent.
sitiar, *vb.* besiege.
sítio, *n.m.* siege; site; small farm. **estado de s.,** state of siege.
situação, *n.f.* situation; position; party in power.
situar, *vb.* situate.
slide, *n.m.* slide, transparency.
smoking, *n.m.* tuxedo.
só, **1.** *adj.* alone; only; lonely. **a sós,** all alone. **2.** *adv.* only, just.
soalho, *n.m.* wooden floor.
soar, *vb.* sound; ring.
sob, *prep.* under, below; subject to.
sobejar, *vb.* be left over; be more than enough.
sobejo, **1.** *adj.* excessive. **2.** *n.m.pl.* leftovers.
soberania, *n.f.* sovereignty.
soberano -na, *adj.*, *n.* sovereign.
soberbia, **-berba**, *n.f.* haughtiness.
soberbo, *adj.* haughty; superb.
sobra, *n.f.* excess; (*pl.*) leftovers. **de s.,** extra, to spare.
sobraçar, *vb.* carry under the arm.
sobrado, **1.** *adj.* leftover. **2.** *n.m.* wooden floor; storied house.
sobranceiro, *adj.* lofty; haughty.
sobrancelha, *n.f.* eyebrow.
sobrar, *vb.* be left over.
sobre, *prep.* over, above; on; about.
sobreabundante, *adj.* superabundant.
sobreaviso, *n.m.* precaution. **de s.,** on one's guard.
sobrecapa, *n.f.* book jacket.
sobrecarga, *n.f.* overload. **—sobrecarregar**, *vb.*
sobrecasaca, *n.f.* frock coat.

sobredito, *adj.* aforementioned.
sobre-humano, *adj.* superhuman.
sobreloja, *n.f.* mezzanine.
sobremaneira, -modo, *adv.* exceedingly.
sobremesa, *n.f.* dessert.
sobrenatural, *adj., n.m.* supernatural.
sobrenome, *n.m.* surname.
sobreolhar, *vb.* look down on.
sobrepairar, *vb.* hover over.
sobrepor, *vb.* superimpose, overlap.
sobrepujar, *vb.* surpass, excel.
sobrescrito, *n.m.* envelope.
sobressair, *vb.* stand out.
sobressaltar, *vb.* startle. **s.-se,** be startled.
sobressalto, *n.m.* shock.
sobretaxa, *n.f.* surcharge.
sobretudo, 1. *n.m.* overcoat. **2.** *adv.* above all, especially.
sobrevir, *vb.* occur.
sobrevivência, *n.f.* survival.
sobrevivente, 1. *adj.* surviving. **2.** *n.m.f.* survivor.
sobreviver, *vb.* survive.
sobrevoar, *vb.* fly over.
sobriedade, *n.f.* sobriety.
sobrinha, *n.f.* niece.
sobrinho, *n.f.* nephew.
sóbrio, *adj.* sober; somber.
socapa, *n.f.* disguise; pretense. **à s.,** stealthily.
socavar, *vb.* excavate, undermine.
social, *adj.* social; sociable.
socialismo, *n.m.* socialism.
socialista, *adj., n.m.f.* socialist.
socializar, *vb.* socialize.
sociedade, *n.f.* society; company; partnership; association. **s. anônima,** corporation.
sócio -cia, *n.* member; partner.
sociologia, *n.f.* sociology.
sociológico, *adj.* sociological.
soco, *n.m.* sock, punch.
soçobrar, *vb.* sink; capsize.
socorro, *n.m.* help. **—socorrer,** *vb.*
soda, *n.f.* soda.
sódio, *n.m.* sodium.
soer, *vb.* be wont to.
soerguer, *vb.* lift slightly.
soez, *adj.* vile, low.
sofá, *n.m.* sofa.

sofisticação, *n.f.* sophistication.
sofisticado, *adj.* sophisticated.
sofrê, *n.m.* Brazilian oriole.
sofrear, *vb.* rein in.
sofredor -ra, *n.* sufferer.
sôfrego, *adj.* greedy; impatient.
sofrer, *vb.* suffer; undergo.
sofrimento, *n.m.* suffering. **—sofrido,** *adj.*
sofrível, *adj.* bearable.
soga, *n.f.* hemp rope.
sogra, *n.f.* mother-in-law.
sogro, *n.m.* father-in-law.
soja, *n.f.* soy.
sol, *n.m.* sun. **fazer s.,** be sunny.
sola, *n.f.* sole (shoe).
solapa, *n.f.* **à s.,** furtively.
solapar, *vb.* undermine; hide.
solar, 1. *adj.* solar. **2.** *n.m.* manor house. **3.** *vb.* sole; solo.
solavanco, *n.m.* jolt, bump.
soldada, *n.f.* wages, pay.
soldado, *n.m.* soldier.
soldar, *vb.* solder, weld.
soldo, *n.m. (mil.)* pay.
soledade, *n.f.* solitude, loneliness.
soleira, *n.f.* doorstep.
solene, *adj.* solemn.
solenidade, *n.f.* solemnity.
solerte, *adj.* cunning.
soletrar, *vb.* spell out.
solicitar, *vb.* solicit; apply (for).
solícito, *adj.* solicitous.
solidão, *n.f.* solitude; loneliness.
solidariedade, *n.f.* solidarity.
solidário, *adj.* united.
solidificar, *vb.* solidify.
sólido, *adj.* solid.
solista, *n.m.f.* soloist.
solitário, 1. *adj.* solitary; deserted. **2.** *n.m.* solitary (ring).
solo, *n.m.* ground; floor; soil; solo.
solta, -tura, *n.f.* release; loosening.
soltar, *vb.* release; loosen; blurt out.
solteiro -ra, 1. *adj.* unmarried. **2.** *n.m.* bachelor; *n.f.* spinster.
solto, *adj.* loose, free.
solução, *n.f.* solution.
soluço, *n.m.* sob; hiccup. **—soluçar,** *vb.*
solucionar, *vb.* solve.
solúvel, *adj.* soluble.
solvente, *adj., n.m.* solvent.

solver, *vb.* solve; dissolve; pay up.

som, *n.m.* sound; (*sl.*) music.

soma, *n.f.* sum, amount.

somar, *vb.* add, total; come to.

sombra, *n.f.* shade; shadow; eye shadow. **s. e água fresca**, (*sl.*) easy life; **nem por sombras**, not by a long shot; **sem s. de dúvida**, without a shadow of a doubt.

sombrear, *vb.* shade.

sombrinha, *n.f.* parasol.

sombrio, *adj.* somber, gloomy.

somenos, *adj.* worthless, inferior.

somente, *adv.* only.

somítico, *adj.* stingy.

sonâmbulo -la, *n.* sleepwalker.

sonante, *adj.* sounding. **moeda s.**, hard cash.

sondar, *vb.* sound, probe. —**sonda, -dagem**, *n.f.*

soneca, *n.f.* nap.

sonegar, *vb.* evade (taxes); pilfer.

soneto, *n.m.* sonnet.

sonhador -ra, *n.* dreamer.

sonhar, *vb.* dream. **s. com**, dream of.

sonho, *n.m.* dream; doughnut.

sônico, *adj.* sonic.

sono, *n.m.* sleep; sleepiness. **estar com s.**, be sleepy.

sonolência, *n.f.* sleepiness.

sonolento, *adj.* sleepy.

sonoro, *adj.* sonorous; talking; voiced.

sonso, *adj.* sly.

sopa, *n.f.* soup; (*coll.*) cinch. **dar s.**, (*sl.*) flirt.

sopapo, *n.m.* bounce, slap.

sopé, *n.m.* foot (hill, wall).

sopear, *vb.* trample.

sopeira, *n.f.* soup tureen.

sopesar, *vb.* weigh with the hand.

soprano, *n.m.f.* soprano.

soprar, *vb.* blow (on); whisper.

sopro, *n.m.* blow; (*mus.*) wind.

sórdido, *adj.* sordid.

soro, *n.m.* whey; serum.

sóror, *n.f.* sister (used with a nun's name).

sorrateiro, *adj.* sly, sneaky.

sorrelfa, *n.f.* **à s.**, sneakily.

sorridente, *adj.* smiling.

sorrir, *vb.* smile. —**sorriso**, *n.m.*

sorte, *n.f.* luck; lot; sort. **de s. que**, in such a way that.

sortear, *vb.* draw lots; raffle.

sorteio, *n.m.* drawing, raffle.

sortilégio, *n.m.* sorcery, spell.

sortimento, *n.m.* assortment, selection.

sorumbático, *adj.* sad, glum.

sorvedouro, *n.m.* whirlpool.

sorver, *vb.* sip; suck; absorb.

sorvete, *n.m.* ice cream, sherbet.

sorveteria, *n.f.* ice-cream parlor.

sorvo, *n.m.* sip.

sósia, *n.m.f.* double, look-alike.

soslaio, *adv.* **de s.**, sideways, askance.

sossegar, *vb.* calm, quiet. —**sossego**, *n.m.*; **sossegado**, *adj.*

sota, *n.f.* rest; queen (cards).

sotaina, *n.f.* cassock.

sótão, *n.m.* attic.

sotaque, *n.m.* accent, pronunciation.

sotavento, *n.m.* leeward.

soterrar, *vb.* bury.

soturno, *adj.* gloomy.

soutien, *n.m.* (*F.*) bra.

sova, *n.f.* beating.

sovaco, *n.m.* armpit.

sovar, *vb.* knead; beat.

soviético -ca, *adj. n.* Soviet.

sovina, **1.** *adj.* miserly. **2.** *n.m.f.* miser.

sozinho, *adj.* alone.

sua, *adj., pron. fem.* of **seu.**

suado, *adj.* sweaty.

suar, *vb.* sweat.

suave, *adj.* soft; smooth; mild.

suavidade, *n.f.* softness; smoothness; mildness.

suavizar, *vb.* soften.

subalimentação, *n.f.* undernourishment.

subconsciente, *adj.* subconscious. —**subconsciência**, *n.f.* **subdesenvolvido**, *adj.* underdeveloped.

subdesenvolvimento, *n.m.* underdevelopment.

subentender, *vb.* understand, assume.

subestimar, *vb.* underestimate, underrate.

subida, n.f. rise, ascent.
subir, vb. go up, rise; climb; get in/on; raise.
subitâneo, adj. sudden.
súbito, 1. adj. sudden. 2. adv. suddenly. **de s.**, suddenly.
subjacente, adj. underlying.
subjetivo, adj. subjective.
subjugar, vb. subjugate.
subjuntivo, adj., n.m. subjunctive.
sublevação, n.f. uprising.
sublevar-se, vb. revolt.
sublimar, vb. sublimate.
sublime, adj. sublime.
subliminar, adj. subliminal.
sublinhar, vb. underline.
sublocar, vb. sublease.
submarino, 1. adj. underwater. 2. n.m. submarine.
submergir, vb. submerge.
submersão, n.f. submersion.
submerso, adj. submerged.
submeter, vb. submit; subdue. **s.-se**, surrender.
submisso, adj. submissive.
submundo, n.m. underworld.
subnutrição, n.f. malnutrition.
subnutrir, vb. undernourish.
subordinar, vb. subordinate. **s.-se**, surrender.
subornar, vb. bribe. —**suborno**, n.m.
subproduto, n.m. by-product.
sub-reptício, adj. surreptitious.
subscrever, vb. subscribe (to); undersign.
subscrição, n.f. subscription.
subseqüente, adj. subsequent.
subserviente adj. subservient.
subsidiar, vb. subsidize.
subsídio, n.m. subsidy; (pl.) information.
subsistência, n.f. subsistence.
subsolo, n.m. subsoil; basement.
substância, n.f. substance.
substancial, -cioso, adj. substantial.
substanciar, vb. nourish; strengthen; summarize.
substantificar, vb. substantiate.
substantivo, adj., n.m. substantive; noun.
substituição, n.f. substitution.
substituir, vb. substitute. —**substituto**, n.m.

subterfúgio, n.m. subterfuge.
subterrâneo, 1. adj. underground. 2. n.m. cave; subway.
subtítulo, n.m. subtitle.
subtração, n.f. subtraction.
subtrair, vb. subtract.
suburbano -na, 1. adj. suburban. 2. n. suburbanite.
subúrbio, n.m. suburb.
subvenção, n.f. subsidy.
subvencionar, vb. subsidize.
subversão, n.f. subversion.
subversivo -va, adj., n. subversive.
subverter, vb. subvert.
sucata, n.f. scrap metal.
sucção, n.f. suction.
sucedâneo, adj., n.m. substitute.
suceder, vb. follow; happen.
sucedido, 1. adj. **bem/mal s.**, successful/unsuccessful. 2. n.m. happening.
sucessão, n.f. succession.
sucessivo, adj. successive.
sucesso, n.m. success; occurrence.
sucessor -ra, 1. adj. succeeding. 2. n. successor.
súcia, n.f. gang, pack.
sucinto, adj. succinct.
suco, n.m. juice.
suculento, adj. juicy.
sucumbir, vb. succumb.
sucursal, n.f. branch office.
sudário, n.m. shroud.
sudeste, sueste, adj. southeast.
súdito -ta, n. subject, citizen.
sudoeste, n.m. southwest.
Suécia, n.f. Sweden.
sueco -ca, 1. adj. Swedish. 2. n. Swede; n.m. Swedish (language).
suéter, n.m. sweater.
suficiente, adj. sufficient.
sufixo, n.m. suffix.
sufocar, vb. suffocate; stifle.
sufoco, n.m. (sl.) hassle; bind.
sufrágio, n.m. suffrage; prayers for the dead.
sugar, vb. suck; extort.
sugerir, vb. suggest.
sugestão, n.f. suggestion.
sugestivo, adj. suggestive.
Suíça, n.f. Switzerland.
suíças, n.f.pl. sideburns.
suíço -ça, adj., n. Swiss.

suíno, *n.m.* swine.

sujar, *vb.* dirty; defecate.

sujeição, *n.f.* subjection.

sujeira, *n.f.* filth; dirty trick.

sujeitar, *vb.* subject. **s.-se a,** subject oneself to.

sujeito, **1.** *adj.* subject. **s. a,** subject to. **2.** *n.m. (gram.)* subject; *(coll.)* fellow.

sujo, *adj.* dirty.

sul, *adj.* south.

sul-americano -na, *adj., n.* South American.

sulco, *n.m.* furrow. —**sulcar,** *vb.*

súlfur, *n.m.* sulfur.

sulista, **1.** *adj.* southern. **2.** *n.m.f.* southerner.

sultão, *n.m.* sultan.

suma, *n.f.* summary. **em s.,** in short.

sumário, **1.** *adj.* summary; brief. **2.** *n.m.* summary.

sumiço, *n.m.* disappearance.

sumir, *vb.* disappear.

sumo, **1.** *adj.* supreme. **2.** *n.m.* juice; top.

sunga, *n.f.* trunks; jockstrap.

suntuoso, *adj.* sumptuous.

suor, *n.m.* sweat.

super-, *pref.* super-, over-.

superabundante, *adj.* overabundant.

superar, *vb.* overcome; surpass.

superávit, *n.m.* surplus.

supercondutor, *n.m.* superconductor.

superestimar, *vb.* overestimate, overrate.

superestrutura, *n.f.* superstructure.

superficial, *adj.* superficial.

superfície, *n.f.* surface.

supérfluo, *adj.* superfluous.

super-homem, *n.m.* superman.

superintendente, *n.m.f.* superintendent.

superior, **1.** *adj.* superior; upper. **2.** *n.m.f.* superior.

superioridade, *n.f.* superiority.

superlativo, *adj.* superlative.

supermercado, *n.m.* supermarket.

superpopulação, *n.f.* overpopulation.

superpovoar, *vb.* overpopulate.

supersônico, *adj.* supersonic.

superstição, *n.f.* superstition.

supersticioso, *adj.* superstitious.

supervisão, *n.f.* supervision.

supervisar, -visionar, *vb.* supervise.

supervisor -ra, *n.* supervisor.

supetão, *n.f.* **de s.** suddenly.

supimpa, *adj. (coll.)* terrific.

suplantar, *vb.* supplant.

suplementar, **1.** *adj.* supplementary. **2.** *n.m.* supplement.

suplemento, *n.m.* supplement.

suplente, *n.m.f.* substitute.

supletivo, *adj.* supplementary.

súplica, *n.f.* entreaty, appeal.

suplicar, *vb.* beseech, implore.

suplício, *n.m.* torture.

supor, *vb.* suppose.

suportar, *vb.* tolerate; support.

suporte, *n.m.* prop, stand.

suposição, *n.f.* supposition.

supositório, *n.m.* suppository.

supracitado, -dito, -mencionado, *adj.* aforementioned.

supra-sumo, *n.m.* utmost, height.

supremacia, *n.f.* supremacy.

supremo, *adj.* supreme.

suprimir, *vb.* suppress; eliminate.

suprir, *vb.* supply; make up for.

surdez, *n.f.* deafness; voicelessness.

surdina, *n.f. (mus.)* mute. **em s.,** softly.

surdir, *vb.* emerge.

surdo, *adj.* deaf; muffled; voiceless.

surdo-mudo, *n.m.* deaf mute.

surgir, *vb.* emerge, appear.

surpreendente, *adj.* surprising.

surpreender, *vb.* surprise.

surpresa, *n.f.* surprise.

surra, *n.f.* beating.

surrado, *adj.* beaten; worn.

surrar, *vb.* beat; wear out.

surripiar, -rupiar, *vb.* pilfer.

surtida, *n.f.* sortie.

surtir, *vb.* cause.

surto, *n.m.* impulse; outbreak.

suruba, *n.f. (vulg.)* penis; orgy.

sururu, *n.m. (coll.)* brawl.

suscetível, *adj.* susceptible.

suscitar, *vb.* provoke.

suspeita, *n.f.* suspicion.

suspeitar, *vb.* suspect.

suspeito, adj., n.m. suspect.
suspeitoso, adj. suspicious.
suspender, vb. suspend; pull up.
suspensão, n.f. suspension.
suspenso, adj. suspended.
suspensórios, n.m.pl. suspenders.
suspicaz, adj. suspicious.
suspirar, vb. sigh. —**suspiro**, n.m.
sussurrar, vb. whisper. —**sussurro**, n.m.
sustar, vb. stop.
sustenido, n.m. (mus.) sharp.
sustentar, vb. support; sustain; affirm.
sustento, n.m. support; sustenance.
suster, vb. support; restrain.
susto, n.m. scare, fright.
sutil, adj. subtle.
sutiã, n.m. bra.
sutileza, n.f. subtlety.
sutura, n.f. suture.

T

ta, contr. of **te** + **a**.
tá (for **está**), interj. (coll.) OK! yep! **t.?**, OK? all right?
taba, n.f. Indian village.
tabaco, n.m. tobacco.
tabaréu -roa, n. (coll.) hick, rube.
tabefe, n.m. (coll.) punch, sock.
tabela, n.f. table, list.
tabelião, n.m. notary.
taberna, n.f. tavern.
tabique, n.m. partition.
tablado, n.m. stage, platform.
tablete, n.m. tablet, pill.
tabu, n.m. taboo.
tábua, n.f. board, plank; list, table.
tabuleiro, n.m. tray; game board.
tabuleta, n.f. sign.
taça, n.f. goblet; trophy cup.
tacanho, adj. petty; stingy; narrow-minded.
tacha, n.f. tack.
tachar, vb. criticize; brand.
tácito, adj. tacit.
taciturno, adj. taciturn.
taco, n.m. (sport.) cue, stick, club.

tagarela, 1. adj. talkative. 2. n.m.f. chatterbox.
tagarelar, vb. chatter, gab.
tagarelice, n.f. chatter, talkativeness.
Tailândia, n.f. Thailand.
taipa, n.f. mud wall; lath-and-plaster wall.
tal, 1. adj. such. **que t.?**, how about? what do you think?. 2. n.m.f. the one; (sl.) the greatest. 3. pron. this, that. **e t.**, and the like.
talagada, n.f. swig.
talante, n.m. will, desire.
talão, n.m. stub, ticket. **t. de cheques**, checkbook.
talco, n.m. talc, talcum powder.
taleiga, n.f. sack, bag.
talento, n.m. talent.
talentoso, adj. talented.
talha, n.f. carving; large jug.
talhador -ra, n. carver, engraver.
talhar, vb. carve.
talharim, n.m. thin noodles.
talhe, n.m. figure, shape, cut.
talheres, n.m.pl. silverware.
talho, n.m. carving, cutting; cut, chop; form.
talião, n.m. lei/pena de t., an eye for an eye.
talismã, n.m. talisman.
talo, n.m. stalk, stem.
talvez, adv. perhaps, maybe.
tamanco, n.m. clog.
tamanduá, n.m. anteater.
tamanho, 1. adj. so great/big; such. 2. n.m. size.
também, adv. also, too; either. **t. não**, not either.
tambor, n.m. drum.
tamborete, n.m. stool.
tamborim, n.m. tabor.
tamis, n.m. cloth strainer.
tampa, n.f. lid, cover, cap.
tampão, n.m. plug; tampon.
tampar, vb. cover, cap, plug.
tampinha, n.f. bottle cap; n.m.f. (coll.) runt.
tampouco, adv. either, neither.
tanajura, n.f. female sauba ant; (coll.) large-bottomed female.
tanga, n.f. loincloth; string bikini. **de t.**, (sl.) flat broke.
tangente, adj., n.f. tangent.

tanger, *vb.* play, strum, ring.

tangerina, *n.f.* tangerine.

tangível, *adj.* tangible.

tanoeiro, *n.m.* cooper.

tanque, *n.m.* tank; washtub, sink.

tanto, *adj.,* *pron.* so much, as much; *(pl.)* so many, as many. **t. faz,** it makes no difference; **t. melhor,** so much the better; **t. quanto/como,** as much as; **tanto. . .quanto/como,** both . . .and. . .; **um t.,** somewhat.

tão, *adv.* so; such; as.

tapa, *n.f.* slap; sock.

tapado, *adj.* covered; *(coll.)* stupid.

tapar, *vb.* cover; plug; hide.

tapear, *vb.* *(coll.)* cheat, gyp.

tapeçaria, *n.f.* tapestry; rugs.

tapera, *n.f.* abandoned dwelling(s); ruins.

tapete, *n.m.* rug, carpet; tapestry.

tapume, *n.m.* fence; hedge.

taquara, *n.f.* bamboo.

taquigrafia, *n.f.* shorthand.

tara, *n.f.* flaw, physical or moral defect.

tarado, 1. *adj.* defective; crazy; perverted; *(coll.)* infatuated. **2.** *n.m.* madman; pervert.

taramela, *n.f.* wooden catch or latch.

tardança, *n.f.* delay, tardiness.

tardar, *vb.* delay, be late. **o mais t.,** at the latest.

tarde, 1. *n.f.* afternoon. **2.** *adv.* late.

tardinha, *(coll.)* late afternoon.

tardio, *adj.* late, slow.

tardo, *adj.* slow, sluggish.

tareco, *n.m.* thing; *(pl.)* belongings.

tarefa, *n.f.* task, job.

tarifa, *n.f.* tariff, rate; rate schedule.

tarimba, *n.f.* bunk; army life; experience.

tarja, *n.f.* trim; black mourning border.

tarjado, *adj.* black-bordered.

tartamudear, *vb.* stutter, stammer. **—tartamudez,** *n.f.*

tartamudo, 1. *adj.* stuttering, stammering. **2.** *n.m.* stutterer, stammerer.

tartaruga, *n.f.* turtle, tortoise.

tarugo, *n.m.* dowel, peg.

tas, *contr. of* **te + as.**

tasca, *n.f.* tavern.

tataraneto -ta, *n.m.* great-great-great-grandchild.

tataravó, *n.f.* great-great-great-grandmother.

tataravô, *n.m.* great-great-great-grandfather.

tatear, *vb.* grope.

tática, *n.f.* tactics.

tático, *adj.* tactical.

tato, *n.m.* touch, feel; tact.

tatu, *n.m.* armadillo.

tatuagem, *n.f.* tatoo. **—tatuar,** *vb.*

tavolagem, *n.f.* casino; gambling.

taxa, *n.f.* tax; rate; charge, fee.

taxar, *vb.* tax; fix the price of.

táxi, *n.m.* taxi.

taxista, *n.m.f.* taxi driver.

Tchad, *n.m.* Chad.

tchau, *interj.* ciao, goodbye.

Tchecoslováquia, *n.f.* Czechoslovakia.

te, *obj. pron.* you (*s.*); to you (*s.*); yourself; to yourself.

té (*for* **até**), *prep.* until.

tê, *n.m.* the letter t.

tear, *n.m.* loom.

teatral, *adj.* theatrical.

teatro, *n.m.* theater.

teatrólogo, *n.m.* playwright.

tecelagem, *n.f.* weaving; textile mill.

tecer, *vb.* weave.

tecido, *n.m.* fabric, cloth; tissue.

tecla, *n.f.* key.

teclado, *n.m.* keyboard.

técnica, *n.f.* technique.

técnico -ca, 1. *adj.* technical. **2.** *n.* technician; coach.

tecnologia, *n.f.* technology. **t. de ponta,** high tech.

teco, *n.m.* (*sl.*) shot, bullet.

teco-teco, *n.m.* single-engine airplane.

tédio, *n.m.* tedium, boredom.

tedioso, *adj.* tedious.

teia, *n.f.* web. **t. de aranha,** spider web.

teima, teimosia, *n.f.* stubbornness.

teimar, *vb.* be stubborn, persist.

teimoso, *adj.* stubborn, persistent.

teixo, *n.m.* yew.

tela, *n.f.* screen; canvas; cloth; *(sl.)* movie.

telecomando, *n.m.* remote control.

telecomunicação, *n.f.* telecommunication.

teleférico, *n.m.* cable lift.

telefonar, *vb.* telephone.

telefone, *n.m.* telephone. **—telefônico,** *adj.*

telefonema, *n.m.* telephone call.

telefonista, *n.m.f.* telephone operator.

telégrafo, *n.m.* telegraph.

telegrama, *n.m.* telegram.

teleguiado, *adj.* guided (missile).

telenovela, *n.f.* TV soap opera.

telepatia, *n.f.* telepathy.

telescópio, *n.m.* telescope.

telespectador -ra, *n.* TV viewer.

televisão, *n.f.* television; TV set.

televisionar, *vb.* televise.

televisor, *n.m.* TV set.

telha, *n.f.* roofing tile; *(coll.)* head.

telhado, *n.f.* roof.

tema, *n.m.* theme, subject.

temer, *vb.* fear. **—temor,** *n.m.*

temeridade, *n.f.* temerity.

temeroso, *adj.* fearful; frightening.

temperamental, *adj.* temperamental.

temperamento, *n.m.* temperament.

temperar, *vb.* season; moderate.

tempero, *n.m.* seasoning, spice, dressing.

tempestade, *n.f.* storm, tempest.

tempestuoso, *adj.* tempestuous.

templo, *n.m.* temple, church.

tempo, *n.m.* time; weather; tense; tempo. **a t.,** on time; **matar t.,** kill time; **t. integral,** full time.

têmpora, *n.f. (anat.)* temple.

temporada, *n.f.* season; period of time.

temporal, *n.m.* storm.

temporário, *adj.* temporary.

tenacidade, *n.f.* tenacity.

tenaz, *adj.* tenacious.

tenção, *n.f.* intention.

tencionar, *vb.* intend.

tenda, *n.f.* tent; stall.

tendão, *n.m.* tendon.

tendência, *n.f.* tendency.

tender, *vb.* stretch; tend, lean.

tenebroso, *adj.* dark, gloomy.

tenente, *n.m.* lieutenant.

tênis, *n.m.* tennis; sneaker.

tenor, *n.m.* tenor.

tenro, *adj.* tender; young.

tensão, *n.f.* tension.

tenso, *adj.* tense.

tentação, *n.f.* temptation.

tentáculo, *n.m.* tentacle.

tentador -ra, *adj.* tempting.

tentar, *vb.* tempt; try.

tentativo, *adj.* tentative.

tentear, *vb.* probe, experiment; grope.

tento, *n.m.* attention; goal; score.

tênue, *adj.* tenuous.

teologia, *n.f.* theology.

teor, *n.m.* tenor; manner; intent.

teoria, *n.f.* theory.

teórico -ca, **1.** *adj.* theoretical. **2.** *n.* theoretician.

teorizar, *vb.* theorize.

tépido, *adj.* tepid, lukewarm.

ter, *vb.* **1.** have; own; be (age); consider; for there to be. **ter que/de,** have to, must; **t. razão,** be right; **ir t. com,** go meet; **não tem de que,** you're welcome; **não ter nada com** or **não ter nada a ver com,** have nothing to do with; **vai ter,** you're going to get it! **2.** *aux. vb.* have. **eles tinham chegado,** they had arrived.

terapêutico, *adj.* therapeutic.

terapia, *n.f.* therapy.

terça, *n.f.* Tuesday.

terça-feira, *n.f.* Tuesday.

terceiro, *adj.; n.m.* third. **T. Mundo,** Third World.

terço, *n.m.* third; small rosary.

terebintina, *n.f.* turpentine.

tergiversar, *vb.* tergiversate.

térmico, *adj.* thermal. **garrafa térmica,** thermos.

terminação, *n.f.* termination, ending.

terminal, *adj., n.m.* terminal.

terminar, *vb.* finish, end, terminate.

término, *n.m.* terminus; limit; close.

terminologia, *n.f.* terminology.

termo, *n.m.* term; limit; end.

termonuclear, *adj.* thermonuclear.

terneiro, *n.m.* calf.

terno, *n.m.* man's suit.

ternura, *n.f.* tenderness.

terra, *n.f.* earth; land; ground; dirt; country. **T. da Promissão,** Promised Land; **t. natal,** native land.

terreiro, *n.m.* public square; yard; Afro-Brazilian place of worship.

terremoto, *n.m.* earthquake.

terreno, *n.m.* terrain, ground; lot. **ganhar/perder t.,** gain/lose ground.

térreo, 1. *adj.* ground. **2.** *n.m.* ground floor.

terrestre, *adj.* terrestrial, earth; earthy.

terrificar, *vb.* terrify.

terrífico, terrificante, *adj.* terrifying.

territorial, *adj.* territorial.

território, *n.m.* territory.

terrível, *adj.* terrible, horrible.

terror, *n.m.* terror.

terrorismo, *n.m.* terrorism.

terrorista, *n.m.f.* terrorist.

terso, *adj.* clean, glossy; pure, correct.

tertúlia, *n.f.* get-together; literary gathering.

tesão, *n.m.* stiffness; *(vulg.)* erection; sexual desire; turn-on.

tese, *n.f.* thesis.

teso, *adj.* tense, stiff, rigid; *(sl.)* broke.

tesoura, *n.f.* scissors.

tesourar, *vb.* clip, snip; *(coll.)* run down.

tesouraria, *n.f.* treasury.

tesoureiro -ra, *n.* treasurer.

tesouro, *n.m.* treasure, treasury.

tessitura, *n.f.* range, register; contexture.

testa, *n.f.* forehead, brow; head.

testa-de-ferro, *n.m.* figurehead.

testamento, *n.m.* testament, will.

testar, *vb.* test; bequeath.

teste, *n.m.* test, exam.

testemunha, *n.f.* witness. **t. ocular,** eyewitness.

testemunhar, *vb.* witness; testify.

testemunho, *n.m.* testimony.

testicular, *vb.* testify; attest.

testículo, *n.m.* testicle.

tesura, *n.f.* stiffness; *(sl.)* pennilessness.

teta, *n.f.* teat, nipple.

tetéia, *n.f.* trinket; *(coll.)* cutie-pie.

teto, *n.m.* ceiling.

tétrico, *adj.* gloomy, sad.

teu, tua, 1. *adj.* your; of yours. **2.** *pron.* yours.

teúdo, *adj.* kept. **teúda e manteúda,** kept (woman).

teutônico, *adj.* Teutonic, German.

tevê, *n.f. (coll.)* TV.

têxtil, *adj.* textile.

texto, *n.m.* text.

textura, *n.f.* texture.

texugo, *n.m.* badger.

tez, *n.f.* complexion, skin.

ti, *prep. pron.* you; yourself.

tia, *n.f.* aunt.

tição, *n.m.* coal, ember.

tico, *n.m. (coll.)* bit, dab.

tifo, *n.m.* typhus; typhoid fever.

tigela, *n.f.* bowl, dish.

tigre, *n.m.* tiger.

tijolo, *n.m.* brick.

tijuco, *n.m.,* **tijuca,** *n.f.* bog; mud.

til, *n.m.* tilde.

tilintar, *vb.* jingle, tinkle.

timão, *n.m.* helm, rudder; direction.

timbrado, *adj.* letterhead (paper).

timbre, *n.m.* seal, stamp; timbre; point of honor.

time, *n.m.* team.

timidez, *n.f.* timidity.

tímido, *adj.* timid, shy.

timoneiro, *n.m.* helmsman.

tímpano, *n.m.* eardrum; kettledrum.

tina, *n.f.* tub.

tingir, *vb.* tint, dye.

tinhoso, *adj.* scabby; repugnant.

tinir, *vb.* tinkle; shiver; be hungry.

tino, *n.m.* judgment, sense.

tinta, *n.f.* ink; paint.

tinteiro, *n.m.* inkwell.

tintim, *n.m.* **t. por t.,** blow by blow.

tinto, *adj.* red, wine-colored.

tintura, *n.f.* tincture, dye.

tinturaria, *n.f.* dry cleaner.

tintureiro -ra, *n.* dyer; dry cleaner; *n.m.* (*sl.*) paddy wagon.

tio, *n.m.* uncle.

típico, *adj.* typical.

tiple, *n.m.* treble.

tipo, *n.m.* type; (*coll.*) fellow.

tipóia, *n.f.* sling.

tique, *n.m.* tic.

tique-taque, *n.m.* ticktock.

tira, *n.f.* strip; *n.m.* (*sl.*) police detective, cop.

tiracolo, *n.m.* shoulder strap. **a t.,** on one's shoulder; (*sl.*) in tow.

tirada, *n.f.* tirade; long stretch.

tira-dentes, *n.m.* (*coll.*) dentist.

tiragem, *n.f.* printing, edition.

tira-gosto, *n.m.* hors-d'oeuvre.

tirania, *n.f.* tyranny.

tirânico, *adj.* tyrannical.

tirano, 1. *adj.* tyrannical. **2.** *n.m.* tyrant.

tirão, *n.m.* pull, tug; long stretch.

tirar, *vb.* take out/off/away; draw, pull; win; check out; take (*phot.*; course); print.

tiririca, *adj.* (*sl.*) furious.

tiritar, *vb.* shiver, shake.

tiro, *n.m.* shot; throw. **t. e queda,** (*sl.*) sure thing.

tirocínio, *n.m.* training; practice; experience.

tiroteio, *n.m.* shooting, gunfire.

tísica, *n.f.* tuberculosis, consumption.

tísico, *adj., n.m.* consumptive.

tisna, *n.f.* soot, grime.

tisnar, *vb.* blacken, dirty.

tisne, *n.m.* grime.

titã, *n.m.* titan.

titânico, *adj.* titanic.

títere, *n.m.* puppet.

titereiro -ra, -teriteiro -ra, *n.* puppeteer.

titia, *n.f.* (*coll.*) auntie; old maid.

titica, *n.f.* (*coll.*) excrement; junk.

titio, *n.m.* (*coll.*) uncle.

titubear, *vb.* stagger; stammer.

titular, 1. *adj.* titular. **2.** *vb.* entitle.

título, *n.m.* title; caption; deed, bond; degree. **a t. de,** in the capacity of.

to, *contr. of* te + o.

toa, *n.f.* (*naut.*) tow. **à t.,** aimlessly; at random; carelessly; in vain; idle.

toada, *n.f.* tune.

toalete, *n.f.* toilette; *n.m.* toilet, bathroom.

toalha, *n.f.* towel; tablecloth.

toca, *n.f.* hole; lair.

toca-discos, *n.m.* record player, turntable.

tocado, *adj.* (*coll.*) tipsy.

tocador -ra, *n.* player (instrument); herder.

toca-fitas, *n.m.* tape deck.

tocaia, *n.f.* ambush.

tocante, *adj.* touching. **no t. a,** concerning.

tocar, *vb.* touch; abut; affect; play (instrument, song); ring; touch up; herd; get going. **t. em,** touch on; **t. para,** head for; (*coll.*) phone; **pelo que me toca,** as far as I'm concerned.

tocha, *n.f.* torch.

toco, *n.m.* stump; stub.

todavia, *adv., conj.* nevertheless, yet.

todo, 1. *adj.* all; every; whole. **t. dia** or **todos os dias,** every day; **t. (o) mundo,** everyone; **o dia t.** or **o dia todo,** all day. **2.** *n.m.* all, whole; (*pl.*) all, everyone. **3.** *adv.* all, entirely.

todo-poderoso, *adj.* almighty.

toga, *n.f.* toga; robe.

toldo, *n.m.* awning.

toleima, *n.f.* foolishness.

tolerância, *n.f.* tolerance.

tolerante, *adj.* tolerant.

tolerar, *vb.* tolerate.

tolete, *n.m.* (*vulg.*) turd.

tolher, *vb.* hinder, restrain.

tolice, *n.f.* foolishness; stupid act/remark.

tolo, 1. *adj.* foolish, silly. **2.** *n.m.* fool.

tom, *n.m.* tone; *(mus.)* key.

tomada, *n.f.* capture; socket; plug.

tomar, *vb.* take; seize, capture; drink.

tomara, *interj.* I hope so! **t. que**, I hope that.

tomate, *n.m.* tomato.

tombadilho, *n.m.* ship deck.

tombar, *vb.* topple; fall; register; protect as a monument.

tombo, *n.m.* fall.

tomo, *n.m.* tome, volume.

tona, *n.f.* surface. **à t.**, on the surface; afloat.

tonel, *n.m.* barrel.

tonelada, *n.f.* ton.

tônica, *n.f.* stressed syllable; tonic water.

tônico, 1. *adj.* stressed, tonic. **2.** *n.m.* tonic.

tonsila, *n.f.* tonsil.

tonto, *adj.* dizzy; foolish, silly. **às tontas**, dizzily, rashly.

tontura, *n.f.* dizziness.

topar, *vb.* run across; bump into; stub; *(sl.)* be game, agree (to). **t. com**, come upon.

topázio, *n.m.* topaz.

tope, -po, *n.m.* top, summit.

topete, *n.m.* forelock; *(coll.)* nerve, gall.

tópico, 1. *adj.* topical. **2.** *n.m.* topic; newspaper commentary; cliché.

toque, *n.m.* touch; playing, call (instrument). **t. de recolher**, curfew; **a t. de caixa**, *(coll.)* in a great hurry.

Tóquio, *n.* Tokyo.

tora, *n.f.* large slice; log; *(coll.)* nap.

toranja, *n.f.* grapefruit.

tórax, *n.m.* thorax, chest.

torcedor -ra, *n. (sport.)* rooter, fan.

torcedura, *n.f.* twist; sprain.

torcer, *vb.* twist; sprain; *(sport.)* root, cheer.

torcida, *n.f. (sport.)* cheering; fans.

tordo, *n.m.* thrush.

tormenta, *n.f.* storm; turmoil.

tormento, *n.m.* torment.

tormentoso, *adj.* stormy; tormenting.

tornado, *n.m.* tornado.

tornar, *vb.* make, render; return; retort. **t.-se**, become; **t. a fazer**, do again.

tornassol, *n.m.* litmus.

tornear, *vb.* lathe, shape.

torneio, *n.m.* tournament; lathing.

torneira, *n.f.* faucet. **abrir/fechar a t.**, turn on/off the faucet.

torneiro, *n.m.* turner, lather.

torniquete, *n.m.* turnstile; tourniquet.

torno, *n.m.* lathe; vise; peg; round. **em t. (de)**, around; about.

tornozelo, *n.m.* ankle.

toro, *n.m.* log; torso.

toró, *n.m.* rainshower.

toronja, *n.f.* grapefruit.

torpe, *adj.* vile; obscene.

torpedeiro, *n.m.* torpedo boat.

torpedo, *n.m.* torpedo.

torpeza, *n.f.* turpitude; vile action.

torrada, *n.f.* toast (bread).

torradeira, *n.f.* toaster.

torrão, *n.m.* clod; lump; earth, land. **t. natal**, native land.

torrar, *vb.* toast, roast; *(sl.)* squander.

torre, *n.f.* tower, steeple; rook.

torrencial, *adj.* torrential.

torrente, *n.f.* torrent.

torresmo, *n.m.* crackling.

tórrido, *adj.* torrid.

torso, *n.m.* torso.

torta, *n.f.* pie; cake.

torto, *adj.* crooked; cross-eyed; one-eyed. **a t. e a direito**, every which way.

tortuoso, *adj.* tortuous.

tortura, *n.f.* torture. —**torturar**, *vb.*

torvar, *vb.* upset, become upset.

torvelinho, *n.m.* whirlwind; whirlpool.

torvo, *adj.* grim, frightful.

tos, *contr. of* te + os.

tosão, *n.m.* fleece.

tosar, *vb.* shear, clip.

tosco, *adj.* crude, rough.

tosquiar, *vb.* shear.

tossir, vb. cough. —**tosse**, n.f.

tostão, n.m. old Brazilian coin; plugged nickel.

tostar, vb. toast.

total, adj., n.m. total.

totalidade, n.f. totality.

totalitário, adj. totalitarian.

totalizar, vb. totalize; total.

totem, n.m. totem.

touca, n.f. bonnet, cap.

toucado, n.m. hairdo, coiffure.

toucador, n.m. dressing table; boudoir.

toucar, vb. fix the hair.

toucinho, n.m. salt pork.

toupeira, n.f. mole; (coll.) idiot.

tourada, n.f. bullfight.

tourear, vb. fight bulls.

toureiro, **-reador**, n.m. bull-fighter.

touro, n.m. bull.

tóxico, 1. adj. toxic. 2. n.m. poison.

toxicômano -na, n. drug addict.

toxina, n.f. toxin.

trabalhador -ra, 1. adj. hard-working. 2. n. worker.

trabalhar, vb. work; function.

trabalhista, 1. adj. labor. 2. n.m.f. laborite.

trabalho, n.m. work; job. **dar t.**, be troublesome.

trabalhoso, adj. laborious, arduous.

trabucar, vb. work hard.

traça, n.f. moth; silverfish.

traçado, n.m. tracing, sketch; plan.

tração, n.f. traction, pull, drive.

traçar, vb. trace; sketch; draw; plan; (sl.) eat/drink up.

traço, n.m. trace, line; stroke; feature; vestige.

traço-de-união, n.m. hyphen.

tradição, n.f. tradition.

tradicional, adj. traditional.

trado, n.m. auger.

tradução, n.f. translation.

tradutor -ra, n. translator.

traduzir, vb. translate.

tráfego, n.m. traffic; transit; commerce.

traficante, n.m.f. trafficker.

traficar, vb. traffic, deal.

tráfico, n.m. trade, trafficking; traffic.

tragada, n.f. swallow; puff.

tragar, vb. swallow; inhale; (coll.) stomach.

tragédia, n.f. tragedy.

trágico, adj. tragedy.

trago, n.m. swallow; drink.

traição, n.f. betrayal, treason.

traiçoeiro, adj. treacherous, disloyal.

traidor -ra, n. traitor.

trair, vb. betray; be unfaithful to.

trajar, vb. wear. **t.-se**, dress.

traje, n.m. dress, attire. **t. a rigor**, formal attire; **trajes menores**, underwear.

trajeto, n.m. route, course.

trajetória, n.f. trajectory.

tralha, n.f. small fish net; (coll.) junk; (pl.) belongings.

trama, n.f. weave; plot; intrigue.

tramar, vb. plot, conspire.

trambolhão, n.m. fall, tumble.

tramela, n.f. wooden latch or catch.

tramitar, vb. go through the proper channels.

trâmites, n.m.pl. proper channels or procedures.

tramóia, n.f. trick, ruse.

trampolim, n.m. diving board; springboard.

trampolinar, vb. (coll.) trick, swindle.

trampolineiro -ra, n. swindler, con artist.

tranca, n.f. door bolt, crossbar; hindrance.

trança, n.f. braid. —**trançar**, vb.

trancar, vb. lock, bar; lock up.

tranco, n.m. jolt, jerk. **aos trancos e barrancos**, jolted every which way.

tranqüilidade, n.f. tranquility.

tranqüilo, 1. adj. tranquil, calm; sure. 2. adv. surely; easily.

trans-, pref. trans-.

transa, n.f. (sl.) dealings, matter; deal; thing; love affair.

transação, n.f. transaction, deal; dealing.

transacionar, vb. transact.

transar, vb. (sl.) have dealings; arrange; sell; spend; have sex (with).

transatlântico, *n.m.* ocean liner.

transbordar, *vb.* overflow, spill.

transbordo, *n.m.* overflow; transshipment.

transcendência, *n.f.* transcendence.

transcendente, -dental, *adj.* transcendent; important.

transcender, *vb.* transcend.

transcorrer, *vb.* pass by, elapse.

transcrever, *vb.* transcribe.

transcrição, *n.f.* transcription.

transcrito, *n.m.* transcript.

transcurso, *n.m.* passing, elapsing.

transe, *n.m.* trance; crisis, ordeal.

transeunte, *n.m.f.* pedestrian, passerby.

transexual, *adj., n.m.f.* transsexual.

transferência, *n.f.* transfer.

transferir, *vb.* transfer.

transformação, *n.f.* transformation.

transformador, *n.m.* transformer.

transformar, *vb.* transform. **t.-se (em)**, become.

transfusão, *n.f.* transfusion.

transgredir, *vb.* transgress.

transgressão, *n.f.* transgression.

transição, *n.f.* transition.

transiente, *adj.* passing, transient.

transigir, *vb.* compromise. —**transigência**, *n.f.*

transir, *vb.* transfix; overwhelm.

transistor, *n.m.* transistor; transistor radio.

transitar, *n.m.* transit.

transitivo, *adj.* transitive.

trânsito, *n.m.* transit, passage; transition; traffic.

transitório, *adj.* transitory.

transmissão, *n.f.* transmission; broadcast.

transmissor, *n.m.* transmitter.

transmitir, *vb.* transmit; broadcast.

transparecer, *vb.* show through.

transparência, *n.f.* transparence; transparency.

transparente, *adj.* transparent.

transpirar, *vb.* perspire.

transplantar, *vb.* transplant. —**transplante**, *n.m.*

transpor, *vb.* transpose; pass over.

transportadora, *n.f.* hauling company.

transportar, *vb.* transport.

transporte, *n.m.* transportation.

transtornar, *vb.* upset, overturn, overthrow. —**transtorno**, *n.m.*

transversal, **1.** *adj.* transverse, cross. **2.** *n.f.* cross street.

transviar, *vb.* lead astray, pervert.

trapaça, *n.f.* swindle, trick. —**trapacear**, *vb.*

trapaceiro -ra, *n.* swindler, trickster.

trapalhada, *n.f.* mess; swindle.

trapalhão -lhona, *n.* ragamuffin; bungler; swindler.

trapézio, *n.m.* trapeze.

trapo, *n.m.* rag; wreck (person).

traque, *n.m. (vulg.)* fart. —**traquear**, *vb.*

traquejado, *adj.* persecuted, chased; experienced.

traquejar, *vb.* persecute, chase.

traquejo, *n.m.* experience, skill.

traquinas, *adj.* mischievous.

trás, *adv., prep.* behind, back; after. **para t.**, backward; **por t. de**, in back of.

traseira, *n.f. (coll.)* rump.

traseiro, **1.** *adj.* back, rear. **2.** *n.m. (coll.)* rump.

trasladar, *vb.* transfer; postpone; translate; copy. **t.-se**, move.

traslado, *n.m.* transfer; copy; model.

traspassar, *vb.* pass over, cross; pierce; hurt; violate; transfer; transcribe; cede; sell; translate.

traste, *n.m.* household article; good-for-nothing.

tratado, *n.m.* treaty; treatise.

tratamento, *n.m.* treatment; cure; address; title.

tratante, *n.m.f.* swindler, crook, rascal.

tratar, *vb.* treat; deal with; address. **t.-se**, take care of oneself; **t.(-se) de**, be about, be a matter of; **t. com,** deal with; **t. de,** deal with; try to.

trato, *n.m.* treatment; usage; deal; behavior; manners.

trator, *n.m.* tractor.

traulitada, *n.f. (coll.)* beating.

trauma, *n.f.* trauma.

trava, *n.f.* hindrance; brake; connection.

travação, *n.f.* hindrance; connection.

trava-língua, *n.m.* tongue twister.

travanca, *n.f.* hindrance.

travão, *n.m.* brake; fetter.

travar, *vb.* link; hinder; brake; clench. **t. conversa com,** engage in conversation.

trave, *n.f.* beam, crossbar; goal post.

través, *n.m.* slant. **de t.,** askance.

travessa, *n.f.* beam; crosspiece; railroad tie; cross street; serving dish.

travessão, *n.m.* crossbar; dash.

travesseiro, *n.m.* pillow.

travessia, *n.f.* crossing, voyage.

travesso, *adj.* mischievous, naughty.

travessura, *n.f.* mischief, prank.

travesti, *n.m.f.* transvestite.

trazer, *vb.* bring; carry; wear; cause.

trecho, *n.m.* space; excerpt.

treco, *n.m. (sl.)* thing; *(pl.)* belongings.

tréfego, *adj.* lively, brisk; tricky.

trégua, *n.f.* truce, lull.

treinador -ra, *n.* trainer.

treinamento, treino, *n.m.* training; exercise; practice.

treinar, *vb.* train, coach; exercise; practice.

trejeito, *n.m.* gesture; twitch; grimace.

trela, *n.f.* leash; permission; prank; *(coll.)* conversation.

trem, *n.m.* train; gear; *(coll.)* thing; *(coll.)* belongings. **t. de aterrissagem,** landing gear; **t. de vida,** lifestyle.

trema, *n.m.* dieresis, umlaut.

tremelicar, *vb.* shiver.

tremeluzir, *vb.* flicker.

tremendo, *adj.* tremendous; terrible; terrific.

tremer, *vb.* shake, tremble.

tremor, *n.m.* tremor.

trempe, *n.f.* trivet.

tremular, *vb.* quiver; hesitate.

trêmulo, *adj.* shaking, tremulous.

trenó, *n.m.* sleigh, sled.

trepada, *n.f.* climb; *(vulg.)* copulation.

trepar, *vb.* climb, mount; *(vulg.)* have sex.

trepidar, *vb.* shake; shiver; hesitate.

trépido, *adj.* tremulous, afraid.

três, *adj.* three.

tresandar, *vb.* stink, reek.

tresloucar, *vb.* rave, go mad.

tresnoitar, *vb.* spend a sleepless night.

tresvariar, *vb.* rave, be crazy.

treta, *n.f.* trick, deception.

trevas, *n.f.pl.* darkness.

trevo, *n.m.* clover; trefoil; cloverleaf.

treze, *adj.* thirteen.

trezentos, *adj.* three hundred.

triagem, *n.f.* triage.

triângulo, *n.m.* triangle.

tribal, *adj.* tribal.

tribo, *n.f.* tribe.

tribunal, *n.m.* tribunal, court.

tribuna, *n.f.* rostrum, dais.

tributar, *vb.* tax; pay taxes; pay tribute; render.

tributário, *adj., n.m.* tributary.

tributo, *n.m.* tribute; tax.

triciclo, *n.m.* tricycle.

tricô, *n.m.* knitting.

tricotar, *vb.* knit.

trigêmeo -mea, *n.* triplet.

trigésimo, *adj.* thirtieth.

trigo, *n.m.* wheat.

trigonometria, *n.f.* trigonometry.

trigueiro, *adj.* brunet.

triguenho, *adj.* swarthy, dark.

trilar, *vb.* trill, warble. **—trilo,** *n.m.*

trilha, *n.f.* track, trail, path. **t. sonora,** sound track.

trilhado, *adj.* trodden; well-known.

trilhão, *n.m.* trillion.

trilhar, *vb.* thrash; trample; track; follow.

trilho, *n.m.* track, trail, way.

trilogia, *n.f.* trilogy.

trimestre, *n.m.* trimester, quarter.

trinar, *vb.* trill, warble. —**trinado,** *n.m.*

trinca, *n.f.* threesome; three of a kind.

trincar, *vb.* bite, chew.

trinchar, *vb.* carve (meat).

trincheira, *n.f.* trench; foxhole.

trinco, *n.m.* latch, catch.

trindade, *n.f.* trinity; *(cap.)* Trinidad.

trineto -ta, *n.* great-great-grandchild.

trinta, *adj.* thirty.

trio, *n.m.* trio. **t. elétrico,** carnival music truck.

tripa, *n.f.* entrails, tripe.

tripeça, *n.f.*, **tripé,** *n.m.* tripod.

triplo, *adj.* triple. —**triplicar,** *vb.*

tripó, *n.m.* three-legged stool.

tripulação, *n.f.* crew.

tripulante, *n.m.f.* crew member.

tripular, *vb.* man.

triquetraque, *n.m.* firecracker.

trisavó, *n.f.* great-great-grandmother.

trisavô, *n.m.* great-great-grandfather.

triste, *adj.* sad.

tristeza, *n.f.* sadness.

tristonho, *adj.* sad.

triturar, *vb.* grind, pulverize.

triunfal, *adj.* triumphal.

triunfante, *adj.* triumphant.

triunfo, *n.m.* triumph. —**triunfar,** *vb.*

trivial, 1. *adj.* trivial. **2.** *n.m.* simple homecooking.

triz, *n.m.* **por um t.,** just barely.

troar, *vb.* thunder, roar. **troada,** *n.f.*

troca, *n.f.* exchange, trade; change.

troça, *n.f.* mockery. **fazer t. de,** make fun of.

trocadilho, *n.m.* pun.

trocado, *n.m.* small change.

trocador -ra, *n.f.* fare collector (bus).

trocar, *vb.* exchange, trade; change. **t. de roupa,** change clothes.

troçar, *vb.* mock.

trocista, *n.m.f.* mocker; joker.

troco, *n.m.* change (money); exchange.

troço, *n.m.* *(coll.)* thing; *(sl.)* big shot; *(coll., pl.)* belongings.

troféu, *n.m.* trophy.

Tróia, *n.f.* Troy.

troiano -na, *adj., n.* Trojan.

trole, *n.m.* handcar.

trolebus, *n.m.* electric bus.

trolha, *n.f.* trowel.

tromba, *n.f.* trunk, snout.

trombada, *n.f.* collision, crash.

trombar, *vb.* collide, crash.

trombeta, *n.f.* trumpet, bugle.

trombone, *n.m.* trombone.

trompa, *n.f.* French horn; *(anat.)* tube.

tronar, *vb.* thunder, roar.

tronco, *n.m.* trunk, stalk; torso.

troncudo, *adj.* heavy-set.

trono, *n.m.* throne.

tropa, *n.f.* troop; herd.

tropeçar, *vb.* trip, stumble. —**tropeção,** *n.m.*

tropeço, *n.m.* stumble; stumbling block.

trôpego, *adj.* staggering, hobbling.

tropeiro, *n.m.* muleteer, cattle driver.

tropel, *n.m.* trample; multitude; uproar.

tropical, *adj.* tropical.

trópico, *n.m.* tropic; *(pl.)* tropics.

trotar, *vb.* trot.

trote, *n.m.* trot; hazing; telephone prank.

trouxa, *n.f.* bundle; *n.m. (sl.)* sucker, chump.

trova, *n.f.* ballad.

trovador, *n.m.* troubadour; popular poet.

trovão, *n.m.* thunder. —**trovejar, trovoar,** *vb.*

trovoada, *n.f.* thunderclap; racket, uproar.

truão, *n.m.* clown.

trucidar, *vb.* slaughter; behead.

truncar, *vb.* truncate.

trunfo, *n.m.* trump; *(coll.)* big shot.

truque, *n.m.* trick.

truta, *n.f.* trout.

tu, *pron.* you *(s.).*

tua, *pron. fem. of* **teu.**

tuba, *n.f.* tuba.

tubarão, *n.m.* shark.

tubérculo, *n.m.* tuber; tubercle.

tuberculose, *n.f.* tuberculosis.

tubo, *n.m.* tube, pipe; *(pl., sl.)* big bucks.

tubulação, *n.f.* tubing, pipes.

tucano, *n.m.* toucan.

tudo, 1. *neut. adj.* all. **t. isso** *or* **isso t.,** all of that. **2.** *neut. pron.* everything; everyone.

tufão, *n.m.* typhoon.

tufo, *n.m.* tuft.

tulipa, *n.f.* tulip.

tumba, *n.f.* tomb.

tumor, *n.m.* tumor.

túmulo, *n.m.* tomb, grave.

tumulto, *n.m.* tumult.

tumultuoso, *adj.* tumultuous.

tunante, *n.m.* idler.

túnel, *n.m.* tunnel.

túnica, *n.f.* tunic.

tupi, *adj., n.m.* Tupi Indian.

turba, *n.f.* mob, rabble.

turbamulta, *n.f.* mob; crowd.

turbante, *n.m.* turban.

turbar, *vb.* muddy; confuse; agitate.

turbilhão, *n.m.* whirlwind; whirlpool.

turbina, *n.f.* turbine.

turbulência, *n.f.* turbulence.

turbulento, *adj.* turbulent.

turco -ca, 1. *adj.* Turkish. **2.** *n.* Turk; Turkish.

turfe, *n.m.* turf, horse racing.

turismo, *n.m.* tourism.

turista, *n.m.f.* tourist. —**turístico,** *adj.*

turma, *n.f.* group; class; group of friends.

turno, *n.m.* turn; shift.

turquesa, *adj., n.f.* turquoise.

Turquia, *n.f.* Turkey.

turvar, *vb.* muddy; confuse.

turvo, *adj.* muddy, cloudy; confused.

tuta-e-meia, *n.f.* trifle.

tutano, *n.m.* marrow; *(coll.)* intelligence; talent.

tutear, *vb.* address as **tu.**

tutela, *n.f.* tutelage; guardianship.

tutor -ra, *n.* guardian; tutor.

tutu, *n.m.* dish of beans and manioc starch; *(coll.)* big shot; *(sl.)* money.

U

u, *n.m.* the letter u.

uai, *interj.* oh! gee!

úbere, 1. *adj.* fruitful, abundant. **2.** *n.m.* udder.

ubíquo, *adj.* ubiquitous.

uca, *n.f.* *(sl.)* brandy; booze.

Ucrânia, *n.f.* Ukraine.

uca, *n.* cane brandy.

ué, *interj.* wow! gee!

ufanar-se, *vb.* be proud; boast.

ufanismo, *n.m.* patriotic bragging.

ui, *interj.* ouch! ooh!

uirapuru, *n.m.* Amazonian wren.

uísque, *n.m.* whisky.

uivar, *vb.* howl. —**uivo,** *n.m.* howl.

úlcera, *n.f.* ulcer.

ulterior, *adj.* later; further.

ultimar, *vb.* finish.

últimas, *n.f.pl.* one's last legs; *(coll.)* latest news.

ultimato, *n.m.* ultimatum.

último, *adj.* last, final; latest. **por ú,** finally.

ultra-, *pref.* ultra-.

ultrajar, *vb.* offend, outrage.

ultraje, *n.m.* offense, outrage.

ultramar, *n.m.* overseas. —**ultramarino,** *adj.*

ultrapassar, *vb.* pass, overtake.

ululante, *adj.* howling; glaring.

ulular, *vb.* ululate, howl; yell.

um, uma, 1. *indef. art.* a; an; *(pl.)* some. **2.** *adj., n.m.* one.

umbanda, *n.m.* an Afro-Brazilian religion.

umbigo, *n.m.* navel.

umbral, *n.m.* doorpost; threshold.

ume, *n.m.* alum.

umedecer, *vb.* humidify.

umidade, *n.f.* humidity.

úmido, *adj.* humid.

unânime, *adj.* unanimous.

unção, *n.f.* unction, anointment.

ungir, *vb.* anoint; give extreme unction to; correct, improve.

ungüento, *n.m.* ointment.

unha, *n.f.* fingernail, toenail;

claw. **com unhas e dentes,** tooth and nail; **unha e carne,** hand and glove.

unha-de-fome, *n.m.f.* tightwad.

união, *n.f.* union.

União Soviética, *n.f.* Soviet Union.

único, *adj.* only, sole; unique. **filho ú,** only child.

unidade, *n.f.* unit; unity.

unido, *adj.* united.

unificar, *n.f.* unify.

uniforme, *adj., n.m.* uniform.

unir, *vb.* unite, join. **u.-se,** unite; wed.

unissex, *adj.* unisex.

uníssono, *n.m.* unison.

unitário, *adj.* unitary.

universal, *adj.* universal.

universidade, *n.f.* university.

universitário -ria, 1. *adj.* university. **2.** *n.* university student/professor.

universo, *n.m.* universe.

uno, *adj.* single, one.

untar, *vb.* anoint, grease.

untura, *n.f.* anointment, greasing.

urânio, *n.m.* uranium.

Urano, *n.m.* Uranus.

urbanismo, *n.m.* urbanism, city planning.

urbanizar, *vb.* urbanize.

urbano, *adj.* urban; urbane.

urbe, *n.f.* city, urb.

urdidura, *n.f.* weaving; plot.

urdir, *vb.* weave; plot.

urgência, *n.f.* urgency; emergency.

urgente, *adj.* urgent, pressing.

urgir, *vb.* urge, drive; be urgent.

urina, *n.f.* urine.

urinar, *vb.* urinate.

urinol, *n.m.* chamberpot; *(P.)* urinal.

urna, *n.f.* urn; ballot box; *(pl.)* polls.

urrar, *n.f.* roar; scream. **—urro,** *n.m.*

ursada, *n.f. (coll.)* double-cross.

urso -sa, *n.f.* bear.

urtiga, *n.f.* nettle.

urubu, *n.m.* black vulture, turkey buzzard.

urucubaca, *n.f. (coll.)* bad luck.

Uruguai, *n.m.* Uruguay.

uruguaio -ia, *adj., n.* Uruguayan.

urze, *n.f.* heather.

usado, *adj.* used; second-hand.

usança, *n.f.* usage; custom.

usar, *vb.* use; wear; be used to.

useiro, *adj.* accustomed. **u. e vezeiro em,** in the habit of.

usina, *n.f.* plant, mill. **u. de açúcar,** sugar mill; **u. hidrelétrica,** hydroelectric power plant; **u. nuclear,** nuclear plant.

usinar, *vb.* tool, machine, process.

uso, *n.m.* use; usage, custom.

usual, *adj.* usual.

usuário -ria, *n.* user.

usufruir, *vb.* usufruct; enjoy.

usufruto, *n.f.* usufruct; enjoyment.

usura, *n.f.* usury.

usurário -ria, *n.* usurer; miser.

usurpar, *vb.* usurp.

utensílio, *n.m.* utensil.

útero, *n.m.* uterus.

útil, *adj.* useful, helpful.

utilidade, *n.f.* usefulness, utility.

utilitário, *adj.* utilitarian.

utilizar, *vb.* utilize, use.

utopia, *n.f.* utopia.

utópico, *adj.* utopian. **—utopista,** *m.f.*

uva, *n.f.* grape; *(sl.)* attractive female.

V, W

vaca, *n.f.* cow; *(sl.)* slut; *(coll.)* collection (money). **voltar à v. fria,** *(coll.)* get back to the subject.

vacância, *n.f.* vacancy.

vacilar, *vb.* vacillate; *(sl.)* make a slip-up.

vacina, *n.f.* vaccine.

vacinação, *n.f.* vaccination.

vacinar, *vb.* vaccinate.

vacum, *adj.* bovine.

vácuo, 1. *adj.* vacuous. **2.** *n.m.* vacuum.

vadear, *vb.* ford.

vadiar, *vb.* loaf, fool around.

vadio, 1. *adj.* loafing. **2.** *n.m.* loafer, vagrant.

vaga, *n.f.* wave; opening, vacancy; parking place.

vagabunda, *n.f. (coll.)* tramp, whore.

vagabundear, *vb.* wander; loaf.

vagabundo, 1. *adj.* vagabond; loafing; fickle; shoddy. **2.** *n.m.* tramp, bum.

vagalhão, *n.m.* large wave.

vaga-lume, *n.m.* firefly; *(coll.)* usher.

vagamundo, *n.m.* vagabond.

vagão, *n.m.* railroad car.

vagar, 1. *n.m.* slowness; leisure. **2.** *vb.* vacate; roam.

vagaroso -rento, *adj.* slow.

vagem, *n.f.* green beans.

vagina, *n.f.* vagina.

vago, *adj.* vague; vacant, empty.

vaguear, *vb.* roam, idle.

vaiar, *vb.* hiss, boo. —**vaia,** *n.f.*

vaidade, *n.f.* vanity.

vaidoso, *adj.* vain.

vaivém, *n.m.* to-and-fro, swing.

vala, *n.f.* ditch.

valdevinos, *n.m.* vagrant, scamp.

vale, *n.m.* valley, vale; voucher. **v. postal,** money order.

valentão -tona, 1. *adj.* rowdy; boastful. **2.** *n.* ruffian; braggart.

valente, *adj.* valiant, brave.

valentia, *n.f.* valor, courage.

valer, *vb.* be worth, equal; aid; be valid. **v. a pena,** be worthwhile; **para v.,** *(coll.)* for real, really; a lot; **vale tudo,** anything goes. **v.-se de,** avail oneself of.

valeta, *n.f.* ditch, gutter.

valete, *n.m.* (cards) jack, knave.

valhacouto, *n.m.* den; shelter.

valia, *n.f.* worth, value.

validade, -dez, *n.f.* validity.

validar, *vb.* validate.

válido, *adj.* valid; able-bodied.

valioso, *adj.* valuable.

valise, *n.f.* valise.

valor, *n.m.* value, worth; *(pl.)* securities. **não dar v. a,** take for granted.

valorizar, *vb.* valorize, appreciate.

valoroso, *adj.* valorous, brave.

valsa, *n.f.* waltz. —**valsar,** *vb.*

válvula, *n.f.* valve. **v. de escape,** safety valve.

vampiro -resa, *n.* vampire.

vândalo, *n.m.* vandal.

vanglória, *n.f.* vainglory.

vangloriar-se, *vb.* boast.

vanglorioso, *adj.* boastful.

vanguarda, *n.f.* vanguard.

vantagem, *n.f.* advantage; *(coll.)* boasting. **contar v.,** *(coll.)* brag.

vantajoso, *adj.* advantageous, profitable.

vão, vã, 1. *adj.* vain, idle. **2.** *n.m.* space, gap.

vapor, *n.m.* steam, vapor; steamship. **a todo v.,** full speed.

vaporizar, *vb.* vaporize. **v.-se,** evaporate.

vaporoso, *adj.* vaporous.

vaqueiro, *n.m.* cowboy.

vaquejada, *n.f.* roundup.

vaquinha, *n.f. (coll.)* collection. **fazer uma v.,** pass the hat.

vara, *n.f.* rod, wand; pole; jurisdiction; drove. **v. de condão,** magic wand.

varadouro, *n.m.* shipyard.

varal, *n.m.* pole; clothesline.

varanda, *n.f.* veranda, porch.

varão, *n.m.* man, male.

varapau, *n.m. (coll.)* beanpole.

varar, *vb.* pierce, cross; beach.

varejar, *vb.* search; hurl; retail; beat; blow.

varejista, *n.m.f.* retailer.

varejo, *n.m.* retail; search. **a v.,** at retail.

vareta, *n.f.* rod.

várgea, -gem, *n.f., var. of* **várzea.**

variação, *n.f.* variation.

variado, *adj.* varied; *(coll.)* fickle.

variante, *adj., n.f.* variant.

variar, *vb.* vary; go mad.

variável, *adj., n.f.* variable.

varicela, *n.f.* chickenpox.

variedade, *n.f.* variety; fickleness.

variegar, *vb.* variegate.

vários, *adj., pron. pl.* several, various.

varíola, *n.f.* smallpox.

varja, *n.f., var. of* **várzea.**

varonil, *adj.* manly, virile.

varredura, *n.f.* sweepings.

varrer, *vb.* sweep.

varrido, *adj.* swept; crazy, raving. **um doido/louco v.**, raving madman.

Varsóvia, *n.* Warsaw.

várzea, *n.f.* meadow; lowland.

vasa, *n.f.* mud; bog; degradation.

vasca, *n.f.* convulsion; agony; *(pl.)* nausea.

vascolejar, *vb.* shake, stir.

vasconço, *adj., n.m.* Basque.

vasculhar, *vb.* sweep; search.

vaselina, *n.f.* vaseline.

vasilha, *n.f.* bowl, container; barrel.

vaso, *n.m.* vase; vessel; toilet.

vasqueiro, *adj.* scarce; critical.

vassalo -la, *n.* vassal.

vassoura, *n.f.* broom; *(sl.)* coquette.

vassourada, *n.f.* cleaning; purge.

vastidão, *n.f.* vastness.

vasto, *adj.* vast.

vatapá, *n.m.* Afro-Brazilian dish of shrimp, coconut milk, etc.

vate, *n.m.* bard, poet.

vaticano, *adj., n.m.* Vatican.

vaticinar, *vb.* prophesy.

vaticínio, *n.m.* prophecy.

vau, *n.m.* ford; chance.

vazadouro, *n.m.* cesspool, sewer.

vazamento, *n.m.* leak; emptying; founding.

vazante, **1.** *adj.* ebbing; emptying. **2.** *n.f.* ebb tide.

vazão, *n.m.* outflow; emptying; outlet; solution.

vazar, *vb.* empty; leak; ebb; cast; hollow; pierce.

vazio, **1.** *adj.* empty. **2.** *n.m.* vacuum, void.

vê, *n.m.* the letter v.

veado, *n.m.* deer; *(sl.)* homosexual.

vedar, *vb.* prohibit; impede; close.

vedete, *n.f.* movie star, star.

veemente, *adj.* vehement.

vegetação, *n.f.* vegetation.

vegetal, *adj., n.m.* vegetable.

vegetar, *vb.* vegetate.

vegetariano -na, *adj., n.* vegetarian.

veia, *n.f.* vein; bent; mood.

veicular, **1.** *adj.* vehicular. **2.** *vb.* transport; convey.

veículo, *n.m.* vehicle.

veiga, *n.f.* plain; lowland.

veio, *n.m.* vein, lode; brook; essence.

vela, *n.f.* sail; candle; vigil. **barco à v.**, sailboat; **fazer-se à v.**, set sail.

velar, *vb.* veil; fog; watch.

veleidade, *n.f.* whim.

veleidoso, *adj.* capricious.

veleiro, *n.m.* sailboat, sailing ship.

velejar, *vb.* sail.

veleta, *n.f.* weathervane; fickle person.

velhaco, **1.** *adj.* sly, crooked. **2.** *n.m.* rogue, crook.

velhice, *n.f.* old age.

velho -lha, **1.** *adj.* old. **2.** *n.* old person.

velo, *n.m.* fleece.

velocidade, *n.f.* velocity, speed.

velocímetro, *n.m.* speedometer.

velocino, *n.m.* fleece.

velocípede, *n.m.* tricycle.

velório, *n.m.* wake, vigil.

veloz, *adj.* fast, swift.

veludo, *adj., n.m.* velvet.

vencedor -ra, **1.** *adj.* winning. **2.** *n.* winner.

vencer, *vb.* win, defeat; fall due.

vencimento, *n.m.* victory; expiration; due date; pay.

venda, *n.f.* sale; small store; blindfold. **à v.**, on sale.

vendar, *vb.* blindfold.

vendaval, *n.m.* gale.

vendedor -ra, *n.* vendor, salesperson.

vender, *vb.* sell; have in abundance. **v.-se**, sell out.

veneno, *n.m.* poison.

venenoso, *adj.* poisonous.

venerando -rável, *adj.* venerable.

venerar, *vb.* venerate.

venéreo, *adj.* venereal.

veneta, *n.f.* fit of madness; whim; *(coll.)* head.

Veneza, *n.* Venice.

veneziana, *n.f.* Venetian blind, louver; shutter.

venezuelano -na, *adj., n.* Venezuelan.

vênia, *n.f.* permission; pardon; bow.

venta, *n.f.* nostril; *(pl.)* nose.

ventania, *n.f.* high wind.

ventar, *vb.* blow (the wind).

ventilação, *n.f.* ventilation.

ventilador, *n.m.* fan, ventilator.

ventilar, *n.m.* ventilate.

vento, *n.m.* wind. **bons ventos o levem!** Godspeed! good riddance.

ventoso, *adj.* windy; vain; haughty; flatulent.

ventre, *n.m.* belly; womb.

ventríloquo -qua, *n.* ventriloquist.

ventura, *n.f.* venture; happiness; luck. **à v.,** at random.

venturoso, *adj.* happy; lucky.

ver, 1. *n.m.* opinion. **a meu v.,** in my opinion. **2.** *vb.* see. **v.-se,** find oneself. **não ter nada a/que ver com,** have nothing to do with.

veracidade, *n.f.* veracity.

veraneio, *n.m.* summer vacation.

veranista, *n.m.f.* summer vacationer.

verão, *n.m.* summer. —**veranear,** *vb.*

veraz, *adj.* veracious.

verba, *n.f.* allocation, allowance.

verbal, *adj.* verbal.

verbalizar, *vb.* verbalize.

verbete, *n.m.* dictionary entry.

verbo, *n.m.* verb; Word.

verborragia, -réia, *n.f.* verbiage.

verboso, *adj.* verbose.

verdade, *n.f.* truth. **na v.,** in fact; **ser v.,** be true; **não é v.?,** isn't that so?

verdadeiro, *adj.* true, real.

verde, *adj.* green.

verdejar, *vb.* turn green.

verdor, *n.m.* greenness.

verdugo, *n.m.* executioner.

verdura, *n.f.* greenness; vegetation; *(pl.)* vegetables.

vereador -ra, *n.* city councilman -woman.

vereda, *n.f.* path.

veredicto, *n.m.* verdict.

verga, *n.f.* twig, rod; spar; lintel.

vergar, *vb.* bend, bow; conquer; humble.

vergonha, *n.f.* shame, disgrace; embarrassment; *(pl.)* genitals.

vergonhoso, *adj.* shameful.

vergôntea, *n.f.* shoot, sprout.

verídico, *adj.* veridical.

verificação, *n.f.* verification.

verificar, *vb.* verify, check. **v.-se,** occur.

verme, *n.m.* worm.

vermelho, *adj.* red. —**vermelhidão,** *n.f.*

vernáculo, *adj., n.m.* vernacular.

verniz, *n.m.* varnish.

vero, *adj.* true, real.

verossímil, *adj.* plausible.

verossimilhança, *n.f.* verisimilitude.

verrina, *n.f.* diatribe.

verruga, *n.f.* wart.

verruma, *n.f.* auger.

versado, *adj.* versed, experienced.

versão, *n.f.* version.

versar, *vb.* examine, study; train. **v. sobre,** deal with, be about.

versátil, *adj.* versatile; fickle.

versejar, *vb.* versify, rhyme.

versículo, *n.m.* subsection; *(Bib.)* verse.

versificar, *vb.* versify.

verso, *n.m.* verse.

vértebra, *n.f.* vertebra.

vertente, *n.f.* slope; watershed.

verter, *vb.* pour, spill; translate. **v. lágrimas,** shed tears.

vertical, *adj.* vertical.

vértice, *n.m.* apex, summit.

vertigem, *n.f.* dizziness, vertigo.

vertiginoso, *adj.* dizzy.

verve, *n.f.* verve.

vesgo, *adj.* cross-eyed.

vesícula, *n.f.* vesicle, bladder. **v. biliar,** gall bladder.

vespa, *n.f.* wasp.

véspera, *n.f.* eve.

vespertino, 1. *adj.* evening. **2.** *n.m.* evening newspaper.

vestes, *n.f.pl.* clothing.

vestiário, *n.m.* cloakroom; dressing room; wardrobe attendant.

vestibular, *n.m.* college entrance exam.

vestíbulo, *n.m.* vestibule, lobby.

vestido, *n.m.* dress, gown; clothing.

vestidura, *n.f.* clothing.

vestígio, *n.m.* vestige.

vestimenta, *n.f.* vestment.

vestir, *vb.* dress; wear; cover. **v.-se**, get dressed.

vestuário, *n.m.* wardrobe; clothing.

veterano, *adj.*, *n.m.* veteran.

veterinário -ria, 1. *adj.* veterinary. **2.** *n.* veterinarian.

veto, *n.m.* veto. **—vetar**, *vb.*

vetusto, *adj.* old; venerable.

véu, *n.m.* veil; velum.

vexação, *n.f.* vexation.

vexame, *n.m.* vexation; shame; scandal.

vexar, *vb.* vex; make ashamed.

vez, *n.f.* time, instance; turn; chance. **às vezes**, sometimes; **de uma v.**, at one time; for good; **de v.** or **de uma v. para sempre**, once and for all; **de v. em quando**, once in a while; **em v. de**, instead of; **fazer as vezes de**, take the place of; **era uma v.**, once upon a time; **muitas vezes**, often; **outra v.**, again.

vezeiro, *adj.* accustomed.

vezo, *n.m.* bad habit; habit.

via, 1. *n.f.* way; road; manner; (anat.) canal. **em vias de**, about to; **v. aérea**, airmail; **v. de regra**, usually; **por v. das dúvidas**, just in case. **2.** *prep.* via.

viação, *n.f.* means of transportation; transportation system.

viaduto, *n.m.* viaduct.

viagem, *n.f.* trip, voyage; (pl.) travels. **boa v.!**, bon voyage! **v. de ida e volta**, round trip.

viajante, *n.m.f.* traveler.

viajar, *vb.* travel, voyage.

viandas, *n.f.pl.* victuals, food.

viandante, *n.m.f.* traveler.

viatura, *n.f.* vehicle.

viável, *adj.* passable; viable.

víbora, *n.f.* viper.

vibração, *n.f.* vibration; thrill.

vibrador, *n.m.* vibrator.

vibrar, *vb.* vibrate; brandish; ring; strum; thrill.

viçar, *vb.* flourish, thrive.

vicário, *adj.* vicarious.

vice-, *pref.* vice-.

vicejar, *vb.* flourish, thrive, bloom.

vice-rei, *n.m.* viceroy.

viciado -da, *n.* addict.

viciar, *vb.* addict; corrupt; invalidate; falsify.

vício, *n.m.* vice, bad habit.

vicioso, *adj.* vicious; corrupt.

viço, *n.m.* lushness; exuberance; vigor.

viçoso, *adj.* lush; exuberant; vigorous; inexperienced.

vida, *n.f.* life, living; (coll.) prostitution. **boa v.**, easy life; **danado/contente da v.**, (coll.) very angry/happy.

vidão, *n.m.* (coll.) easy life.

vide, *n.f.* grapevine.

videira, *n.f.* vine.

vidente, *adj.*, *n.m.f.* clairvoyant.

vídeo, *n.m.* video.

videocassete, *n.m.* videocassette; VCR.

videoclube, *n.m.* video rental club.

videodisco, *n.m.* videodisk.

videojogo, *n.m.* videogame.

videoteipe, *n.m.* videotape.

vidraça, *n.f.* window pane.

vidrado, 1. *adj.* glassy; (sl.) in love, crazy about. **2.** *n.m.* glaze.

vidrar, *vb.* glaze; become glassy; (sl.) flip over.

vidro, *n.m.* glass; pane; vial.

vieira, *n.f.* scallop.

viela, *n.f.* alley, lane.

viés, *n.m.* bias. **de/ao v.**, on the bias, obliquely.

Vietnã, *n.m.* Vietnam.

vietnamita, *adj.*, *n.m.f.* Vietnamese.

viga, *n.f.* beam, rafter.

vigarice, *n.f.* (coll.) swindle; crookedness.

vigário, *n.m.* vicar. **conto do v.**, (coll.) con game.

vigarista, *n.m.f.* (coll.) con artist, crook.

vigente, *adj.* in effect, valid.

viger, *vb.* be in force.

vigésimo, *adj.*, *n.m.* twentieth.

vigia, *n.m.* sentry, guard; *n.f.* watch, lookout; porthole.

vigiar, *vb.* watch, guard.

vigilante, *adj.* vigilant, watchful.

vigília, *n.f.* sleeplessness; vigil.

vigor, *n.m.* vigor; validity. **em v.,** in force.

vigorar, *vb.* be in effect.

vigoroso, *adj.* vigorous.

vil, *adj.* vile, low, contemptible.

vila, *n.f.* village; villa.

vilania, *n.f.* villainy.

vilão -lã -loa, 1. *adj.* villainous; rustic; coarse. **2.** *n.* villain; peasant; boor.

vilarejo, vilela, *n.m.* small village.

vilegiatura, *n.f.* vacation.

vileza, *n.f.* vileness, villainy.

vilipendiar, *vb.* vilify.

vime, *n.m.* wicker.

vinagre, *n.m.* vinager.

vinco, *n.m.* crease, wrinkle; groove.

vincular, *vb.* tie, link. —**vinculação,** *n.f.*

vínculo, *n.m.* tie, bond.

vinda, *n.f.* coming, arrival.

vindicar, *vb.* vindicate; claim, demand.

vindima, *n.f.* vintage; harvest.

vindimar, *vb.* harvest; kill.

vindita, *n.f.* revenge.

vindouro, *adj.* coming, future.

vingador -ra, *n.* avenger.

vingança, *n.f.* vengeance, revenge.

vingar, *vb.* avenge; attain; succeed; thrive. **v.-se,** avenge oneself.

vingativo, *adj.* vindictive.

vinha, *n.f.* vineyard; vine.

vinhedo, *n.m.* large vineyard.

vinheta, *n.f.* vignette; logo.

vinho, *n.m.* wine. **v. tinto,** red wine.

vinil, *n.m.* vinyl.

vinte, *adj.* twenty.

vintém, *n.m.* former Brazilian coin.

vintena, *n.f.* score (twenty).

viola, *n.f.* small guitar; viola.

violação, *n.f.* violation.

violão, *n.m.* guitar.

violar, *vb.* violate; rape.

violeiro -ra, *n.* guitar player; guitar maker.

violência, *n.f.* violence.

violentar, *vb.* violate; force; rape.

violento, *adj.* violent.

violeta, *adj., n.f.* violet.

violinista, *n.m.f.* violinist.

violino, *n.m.* violin, fiddle.

violoncelo, *n.m.* cello.

violonista, *n.m.f.* guitar player

viperino, *adj.* viperish.

viquingue, *n.m.* Viking.

vir, *vb.* come. **que vem,** coming, next.

viração, *n.f.* breeze.

vira-casaca, *n.m.f.* turncoat.

virada, *n.f.* turning; turnabout.

virador -ra, *n.* (*coll.*) go-getter; *n.m.* railroad turntable.

viragem, *n.f.* turning.

vira-lata, *n.m.* mongrel; bum.

virar, *vb.* turn; turn over; become. **v.-se,** turn, turn over/around; (*coll.*) struggle, get by.

virgem, *adj., n.f.* virgin; (*cap.*) Virgin; Virgo. **v.!,** or **v. Maria!,** heavens!

virgindade, *n.f.* virginity.

vírgula, *n.f.* comma.

viril, *adj.* virile.

virilha, *n.f.* groin.

virtual, *adj.* virtual.

virtude, *n.f.* virtue. **em v. de,** due to.

virtuoso, 1. *adj.* virtuous. **2.** *n.m.* virtuoso.

virulento, *adj.* virulent.

vírus, *n.m.* virus; computer virus.

visado, *adj.* certified; visaed.

visagem, *n.f.* grimace; ghost; (*sl.*) grandstanding.

visão, *n.f.* vision; apparition.

visar, *vb.* certify; visa; aim. **v. a,** aim to, intend.

vísceras, *n.f.pl.* viscera, entrails.

visconde, *n.m.* viscount.

viseira, *n.f.* visor.

visgo, *n.m.* mistletoe; lure.

visibilidade, *n.f.* visibility.

visionário -ria, *adj., n.* visionary.

visita, *n.f.* visit; visitor. **fazer uma v. a,** pay a visit to, visit.

visitante, 1. adj. visiting. **2.** n.m.f. visitor.

visitar, vb. visit.

visível, adj. visible.

vislumbrar, vb. glimpse; suspect; look like; glimmer; loom.

vislumbre, n.m. glimpse; glimmer; trace.

viso, n.m. appearance; trace; hillock.

visor, n.m. view finder.

víspora, n.f. lotto.

vista, n.f. sight, vision; view. **até a v.,** so long; **à v.,** in cash; **dar a v.,** attract attention; **em v. de,** in view of; **ponto de v.,** point of view.

visto, 1. adj. seen. **v. que,** inasmuch as; **haja v.,** as shown by; **pelo v.,** apparently. **2.** n.m. visa.

vistoria, n.f. inspection.

vistoriador -ra, n. inspector.

vistoriar, vb. inspect.

vistoso, adj. showy, flashy.

visual, 1. adj. visual. **2.** n.m. (sl.) appearance; view.

visualizar, vb. visualize.

vital, adj. vital.

vitalicidade, n.f. life tenure.

vitalício, adj. lifelong.

vitalidade, n.f. vitality.

vitamina, n.f. vitamin; (pl.) fruit or vegetable milkshake.

vitela, n.f. veal.

vitelo, n.m. calf.

vítima, n.f. victim.

vitimar, vb. victimize.

vitória, n.f. victory.

vitorioso, adj. victorious.

vitral, n.m. stained-glass window.

vitrine, -na, n.f. display window.

vitrola, n.f. phonograph.

vitualhas, n.f.pl. victuals, provisions.

vituperar, vb. vituperate.

vitupério, n.m. vituperation.

viúva, n.f. widow.

viuvez, n.f. widowhood.

viúvo, n.m. widower.

viva, interj. viva! hurrah!

vivacidade, n.f. vivacity; cunning.

vivaldino, adj. (sl.) sly.

vivar, vb. cheer.

vivaz, adj. vivacious; long-lasting; strong.

viveiro, n.m. vivarium; hotbed.

vivência, n.f. living, existence; experience.

vivenda, n.f. dwelling; way of life; subsistence.

vivente, 1. adj. living. **2.** n.m.f. living being.

viver, vb. live.

víveres, n.m.pl. provisions, food.

viveza, n.f. liveliness.

vivido, adj. experienced.

vívido, adj. vivid.

vivo, adj. live, alive; lively; vivid; (coll.) shrewd.

vizinhança, n.f. neighborhood, vicinity; nearness.

vizinho, 1. adj. near, neighboring. **2.** n.m. neighbor.

voador -ra, 1. adj. flying. **2.** n. flier.

voar, vb. fly.

vocabulário, n.m. vocabulary.

vocábulo, n.m. word, term.

vocação, n.f. vocation, calling.

vocacional, adj. vocational.

vocal, adj. vocal.

vocalista, n.m.f. vocalist.

você, pron. you (s.).

vocês, pron. you (pl.).

vociferar, vb. vociferate, cry out.

vodu, n.m. voodoo.

voejar, vb. flutter.

voga, n.f. vogue, fashion.

vogal, n.f. vowel; n.m.f. voting member.

vogar, vb. sail; row; be in vogue; matter. **não v.,** (coll.) not work.

vo-la, contr. of **vos** + **a.**

volante, 1. adj. flying; movable; changeable. **2.** n.m. steering wheel; race-car driver; broadside; lackey.

volantim, n.m. tightrope walker.

volátil, adj. flying; volatile.

vo-las, contr. of **vos** + **as.**

vôlei, voleibol, n.m. volleyball.

volição, n.f. volition.

vo-lo, contr. of **vos** + **o.**

vo-los, contr. of **vos** + **os.**

volta, n.f. return; turn. **às voltas com,** tied up with; **dar uma v.,**

go for a walk/ride; **estar de v.**, be back; **por v. de**, at around; **v. e meia**, often.

volta-face, *n.f.* about-face.

voltar, *vb.* go/come back, return; turn. **v.-se para**, turn around/toward; **v. a fazer**, do again; **v. a si**, come to.

voltear, *vb.* circle; spin; turn; flutter. —**volteio**, *n.m.*

volume, *n.m.* volume; book.

volumoso, *adj.* voluminous.

voluntário -ria, 1. *adj.* voluntary. **2.** *n.* volunteer.

voluntarioso, *adj.* stubborn, whimsical.

volúpia, *n.f.* sensuality; pleasure.

voluptuoso, *adj.* voluptuous.

volúvel, *adj.* fickle.

volver, *vb.* return, turn.

vomitar, *vb.* vomit. —**vômito**, *n.m.*

vontade, *n.f.* will; desire; whim. **à v.**, at ease; in abundance; **boa v.**, goodwill; **cheio de vontades**, spoiled; **estar com v. de**, feel like; **fazer as vontades de**, humor.

vôo, *n.m.* flight.

voragem, *n.f.* vortex.

voraz, *adj.* voracious.

vórtice, *n.m.* vortex.

vos, 1. *obj. pron.* you (*pl.*), to you (*pl.*). **2.** *reflex. pron.* yourselves.

vós, *subj. pron.* you (*pl.*).

vosso, *poss. adj., pron.* your, yours (pl.).

votação, *n.f.* voting; vote.

votante, 1. *adj.* voting. **2.** *n.m.f.* voter.

votar, *vb.* vote; vow; award. **v.-se**, devote oneself.

voto, *n.m.* vote; vow; desire.

vovó, *n.f.* grandma.

vovô, *n.m.* grandpa.

voz, *n.f.* voice; word. **em v. alta**, aloud.

vozearia, *n.f.*, **vozerio**, *n.m.* clamor, shouting.

vozear, *vb.* cry, shout.

vulcânico, *adj.* volcanic.

vulcão, *n.m.* volcano.

vulgar, *adj.* vulgar, common, coarse.

vulgaridade, *n.f.* vulgarity; coarseness.

vulgo, *n.m.* common people; (*coll.*) alias.

vulnerável, *adj.* vulnerable.

vulto, *n.m.* volume; bulk; figure; important person; importance.

vultoso, *adj.* large, bulky.

watt, *n.m.* watt.

X

xá, *n.m.* shah.

xadrez, *n. m.* chess; checkered pattern; (*sl.*) jail. **2.** *adj.* checkered.

xadrezado, *adj.* checkered.

xadrezista, *n.m.f.* chess player.

xale, *n.m.* shawl.

xamã, *n.m.* shaman.

xampu, *n.m.* shampoo.

Xangai, *n.* Shanghai.

xangô, *n. m.* (Northeast) an Afro-Brazilian religion.

xará, *n.m.f.* namesake.

xaropada, *n.f.* dose of medicinal syrup; (*coll.*) bother, bore.

xarope, *n.m.* medicinal syrup; (*coll.*) bore, drag.

xaropear, *vb.* (*coll.*) annoy, bore.

xaroposo, *adj.* syrupy; (*coll.*) boring, annoying.

xaveco, *n.m.*(*sl.*) swindle; (*coll.*) hag.

xepa, *n.f.* (*coll.*) chow; table scraps.

xeque, *n.m.* sheik; check (chess).

xeque-mate, *n.m.* checkmate.

xereta, *n.m.f.* (*coll.*) snoop; bootlicker.

xeretear, *vb.* (*coll.*) pry; flatter.

xerez, *n.m.* sherry.

xerife, *n.m.* sheriff.

xerocar, *vb.* (*sl.*) xerox, copy.

xerox, *n.m.* (*sl.*) copy machine; (Xerox) copy.

xi, *interj.* gee!

xícara, *n.f.* cup.

xicrinha, *n.f.* (*coll.*) demitasse.

xilindró, *n.m.* (*sl.*) jail.

xilofone, *n.m.* xylophone.

xilogravura, *n.f.* woodcut.

xingar, *vb.* curse, swear (at).

xinxim, *n.m.* stewed chicken dish.

xiquexique, *n.m.* a type of cactus.

xis, *n.m.* the letter x; *(coll.)* crux.

xixi, *n.m. (coll.)* urine. **fazer x.,** pee.

xodó, *n.m. (coll.)* sweetheart; *(coll.)* love affair.

xoxota, *n.f. (vulg.)* vagina.

Z

zagueiro, *n.m.* fullback (soccer).

zambo, *n.m.* zambo, person of mixed African and Amerindian ancestry.

zanga, *n.f.* anger.

zangado, *adj.* angry.

zangão, *n.m.* drone; parasite.

zangar, *vb.* anger. **z.-se,** get mad.

zanzar, *vb. (coll.)* wander.

zarabatana, *n.f.* blowgun.

zarco, *adj.* blue-eyed.

zarolho, *adj.* one-eyed; cross-eyed.

zarpar, *vb.* sail; *(coll.)* leave.

zá, *interj.* bang! wham!

zé, *m. (coll.)* man-on-the-street; *(coll.)* mack (term of address); *(cap.)* Joe.

zê, *n.m.* the letter z.

zebra, *f.* zebra; *(coll.)* fool; *(sl.)* upset, surprise reversal.

zelador, *n.m.* janitor.

zelar, *vb.* take care of; be zealous about; be jealous of.

zelo, *n.m.* zeal; *(pl.)* jealousy.

zeloso, *adj.* zealous; jealous.

zé-mané, *n.m. (sl.)* sucker, fool.

zênite, *n.m.* zenith.

zé-pereira, *n.m.* drummer; Carnival drumbeat.

zé-povinho, *m. (coll.)* average Joe.

zero, *n.m.* zero; nothing; nonentity. **reduzir a z.,** bankrupt.

zero-quilômetro, *n.m. (sl.)* brand new.

ziguezague, *n.m.* zigzag. **—ziguezaguear,** *vb.*

zinco, *n.m.* zinc.

zinho, *n.m. (coll.)* guy.

zíper, *n.m.* zipper.

zoada, *n.f.* buzz; noise.

zodíaco, *n.m.* zodiac.

zoeira, *n.f.* buzz; noise.

zombador -ra, -beteiro -ra, *n.* mocker.

zombar de, *vb.* make fun of.

zombaria, *n.f.* mockery.

zona, *n.f.* zone, area; *(sl.)* red-light district; *(sl.)* mess; *(sl.)* commotion.

zonzo, *adj.* dizzy.

zôo, *n.m.* zoo.

zoologia, *n.f.* zoology.

zoológico, *adj.* zoological.

zorro, 1. *adj.* foxy, sly. **2.** *n.m.* fox.

zuarte, *n.m.* denim.

zumbi, *n.m.* zombie.

zumbido, *n.m.* buzz.

zumbir, *vb.* buzz; whisper.

zunir, *vb.* whistle (the wind); hum. **—zunido,** *n.m.*

zunzum, zunzunzum, *n.m.* buzz; *(coll.)* gossip; *(sl.)* commotion.

zureta, *adj. (coll.)* crazy.

zurrar, *vb.* bray. **—zurro,** *n.m.*

zurzir, *vb.* beat; criticize.

ENGLISH-PORTUGUESE

A

a, *indef. art.* um, uma.
abandon, **1.** *n.* abandono. *m.* **2.** *vb.* abandonar.
abandonment, *n.* abandono *m.*
abase, *vb.* humilhar, aviltar.
abasement, *n.* humilhação, degradação, *f.*
abash, *vb.* envergonhar.
abate, *vb.* diminuir; minguar.
abbess, *n.* abadessa *f.*
abbey, *n.* abadia *f.*, convento, mosteiro *m.*
abbot, *n.* abade *m.*
abbreviate, *vb.* abreviar.
abbreviation, *n.* abreviatura *f.*
abdicate, *vb.* abdicar.
abdomen, *n.* abdome *m.*
abduct, *vb.* seqüestrar.
aberration, *n.* aberração *f.*
abet, *vb.* apoiar, acumpliciar-se com.
abeyance, *n.* suspensão *f.*
abhor, *vb.* aborrecer, detestar.
abhorrent, *adj.* abominável.
abide, *vb.* suportar, tolerar. a. by, conformar-se com.
abiding, *adj.* permanente.
ability, *n.* capacidade, aptidão *f.*
abject, *adj.* abjeto.
ablaze, *adj., adv.* em chamas, ardente.
able, *adj.* capaz, competente. be a., poder.
abnegation, *n.* abnegação *f.*
abnormal, *adj.* anormal.
aboard, *adv.* a bordo.
abode, *n.* domicílio *m.*
abolish, *vb.* abolir.
abolition, *n.* abolição *f.*
abominate, *vb.* abominar, odiar.
aborigine, *n.* aborígine *m.f.*
abort, *vb.* abortar.
abortion, *n.* aborto *m.*
abortive, *adj.* abortivo.
abound, *vb.* abundar.
about, **1.** *adv.* quase, cerca de; por aí; de pé. **a. to,** a ponto de;

all a., por todas as partes. **2.** *prep.* de, sobre, acerca de; ao redor de, em torno de; por; cerca de.
about-face, *n., interj.* meia-volta *f.*
above, **1.** *adv.* em cima, acima. **2.** *prep.* sobre, por cima de; mais que; além de. **a. all,** sobretudo. **3.** *adj.* supradito.
aboveboard, **1.** *adj.* sincero. **2.** *adv.* às claras.
above-mentioned, *adj.* supracitado.
abrade, *vb.* desgastar, raspar.
abrasion, *n.* abrasão *f.*
abrasive, *adj.* abrasivo; cáustico.
abreast, *adv.* lado a lado; **a. of,** a par de.
abridge, *vb.* abreviar, resumir.
abridgment, *n.* abreviação *f.*, resumo *m.*
abroad, *adv.* no exterior, no estrangeiro.
abrogate, *vb.* ab-rogar.
abrupt, *adj.* abrupto; repentino; íngreme.
abscess, *n.* abscesso *m.*
abscond, *vb.* fugir.
absence, *n.* ausência, falta *f.*
absent, **1.** *adj.* ausente. **be a.,** faltar. **2.** *vb.* **absent oneself,** ausentar-se.
absent-minded, *adj.* distraído.
absolute, *adj.* absoluto.
absolution, *n.* absolvição *f.*
absolve, *vb.* absolver.
absorb, *vb.* absorver.
absorption, *n.* absorção *f.*
abstain, *vb.* abster-se de.
abstinent, *adj.* abstinente, abstêmio.
abstract, **1.** *adj.* abstrato. **2.** *n.* resumo *m* **3.** *vb.* abstrair.
abstraction, *n.* abstração *f.*
absurd, *adj.* absurdo.
absurdity, *n.* absurdo *m.*.
abundance, *n.* abundância *f.*
abundant, *adj.* abundante.

abuse, 1. *n.* abuso *m.* **2.** *vb.* abusar de; maltratar.

abusive, *adj.* abusivo.

abut (on), *vb.* confinar com.

abutment, *n.* pilar, contraforte *m.*

abyss, *n.* abismo *m.*

academic, *adj.* acadêmico.

academy, *n.* academia *f.*

accede, *vb.* aceder, consentir.

accelerate, *vb.* acelerar.

accelerator, *n.* acelerador *m.*

accent, 1. *n.* (mark) acento *m.*; (pronunciation) sotaque *m.*

acute a., acento agudo; **circumflex a.,** acento circunflexo, (*coll.*) chapeuzinho *m.* **grave a.,** acento grave. **2.** *vb.* acentuar.

accentuate, *vb.* acentuar.

accept, *vb.* aceitar.

acceptable, *adj.* aceitável.

acceptance, *n.* aceitação *f.*

access, *n.* acesso *m.*, entrada *f.*

accessible, *adj.* acessível.

accessory, 1. *adj.* acessório. **2.** *n.* acessório *m.*; cúmplice *m.f.*

accident, *n.* acidente *m.* **by a.,** por acaso.

accidental, *adj.* acidental, casual.

acclaim, 1. *n.* aclamação *f.* **2.** *vb.* aclamar.

acclamation, *n.* aclamação *f.*

acclimate, *vb.* aclimar, **become acclimated,** aclimar-se.

accolade, *n.* honra *f.*, elogio *m.*

accommodate, *vb.* acomodar.

accommodating, *adj.* acomodatício, complacente.

accommodation, *n.* acomodação *f.*; (*pl.*) acomodações *f.pl.*

accompaniment, *n.* acompanhamento *m.*

accompanist, *n.* (*mus.*) acompanhador *m.*, acompanhante *m.f.*

accompany, *vb.* acompanhar.

accomplice, *n.* cúmplice *m.f.*

accomplish, *vb.* realizar.

accomplished, *adj.* consumado.

accomplishment, *n.* realização *f.*; façanha *f.*

accord, 1. *n.* acordo *m.* **2.** *vb.* outorgar; concordar.

accordance, *n.* acordo *m.* **in a. with,** de acordo com.

according to, *prep.* segundo; de acordo com, conforme.

accordingly, *adv.* desta maneira, assim.

accordion, *n.* acordeão *m.*, sanfona *f.*

accost, *vb.* aproximar-se de (alguém); dirigir-se a.

account, 1. *n.* relato *m.*; (*com.*) conta *f.* **on a. of,** por causa de; **on no a.,** de maneira alguma; **on one's own a.,** por conta própria; **settle accounts with,** acertar contas com; **take into a.,** levar em conta. **2.** *vb.* **a. for,** prestar contas de; explicar.

accountable, *adj.* responsável.

accountant, *n.* contador *m.*, contabilista *m.f.*

accounting, *n.* contabilidade *f.*

accredit, *vb.* acreditar; dar crédito a; equiparar (escola).

accrue, *vb.* advir; acumular-se.

acculturation, *n.* aculturação *f.*

accumulate, *vb.* acumular(-se).

accuracy, *n.* exatidão, precisão *f.*

accurate, *adj.* exato; acurado.

accuse, *vb.* acusar.

accustom, *vb.* acostumar.

ace, *n.* ás *m.*

ache, 1. *n.* dor *f.*

achieve, *vb.* realizar, atingir.

achievement, *n.* realização, façanha *f.*

acid, *n.* ácido *m.*

acknowledge, *vb.* reconhecer, acusar.

acknowledgment, *n.* reconhecimento *m.*

acorn, *n.* bolota *f.*

acoustics, *n.* acústica *f.*

acquaint, *vb.* familiarizar. **be acquainted with,** conhecer.

acquaintance, *n.* conhecimento *m.*; (person) conhecido -da. **make the a. of,** conhecer.

acquiesce, *vb.* aquiescer, consentir.

acquire, *vb.* adquirir.

acquisition, *n.* aquisição *f.*

acquit, *vb.* absolver.

acquittal, *n.* absolvição *f.*

acre, *n.* acre *m.*

acrid, *adj.* acre.

acrimonious, *adj.* acrimonioso.

acrimony, *n.* acrimônia *f.*

acrobat, n. acrobata m.f.

across, 1. adv. através; no outro lado. 2. prep. através de; no outro lado de.

act, 1. n. ação f.; ato m. 2. vb. agir; representar, atuar; portar-se.

acting, 1. adv. interino. 2. n. ação f.; representação, atuação f.

action, n. ação f. **take a.**, tomar medidas.

activate, vb. ativar.

active, adj. ativo.

activist, n. ativista m.f.

activity, n. atividade f.

actor, n. ator m.

actress, n. atriz f.

actual, adj. real, verdadeiro.

actuality, n. realidade f.

actually, adv. de fato, na verdade.

acumen, n. acume m.

acupuncture, n. acupuntura f.

acute, adj. agudo; perspicaz.

adage, n. adágio.

adamant, adj. firme, inflexível.

Adam's apple, n. pomo-de-adão m.

adapt, vb. adaptar(-se).

adaptable, adj. adaptável.

adaptation, n. adaptação f.

adapter, n. adaptador m.

add, vb. adicionar; acrescentar. **a. up**, somar.

addendum, n. adenda f., adendo m.

addict, n. viciado m. **drug a.**, toxicômano.

addicted to, adj. viciado em; entregue a.

addiction, n. vício m.

addition, n. adição, soma f. **in a.**, além disso; **in a. to**, além de.

additional, adj. adicional.

additive, adj., n. aditivo m.

addle, vb. confundir.

address, 1. n. (house) endereço m.; (speech) discurso m. 2. vb. (person) dirigir-se a; (letter) endereçar.

addressee, n. destinatário m.

adduce, vb. aduzir.

adept, adj. perito, versado.

adequacy, n. suficiência f.

adequate, adj. adequado, suficiente.

adhere, vb. aderir.

adherence, n. aderência, adesão f.

adherent, n. aderente m.f., partidário m.

adhesive, adj. adesivo. **a. tape**, esparadrapo m.

adjacent, adj. contíguo, adjacente.

adjective, adj., n. adjetivo m.

adjoin, vb. ser contíguo; confinar (com).

adjoining, adj. contíguo, vizinho.

adjourn, vb. suspender, levantar (a sessão).

adjunct, adj., n. adjunto m.

adjust, vb. ajustar; arrumar; adaptar-se.

adjustment, n. ajuste m.; adaptação f.

ad-lib, vb. (coll.) improvisar.

administer, vb. administrar.

administration, n. administração f.; governo m.

administrative, adj. administrativo.

administrator, n. administrador m.

admirable, adj. admirável.

admiral, n. almirante m.

admiration, n. admiração, estima f.

admire, vb. admirar, apreciar.

admirer, n. admirador, pretendente m.

admissible, adj. admissível.

admission, n. admissão f.; entrada f.

admit, vb. admitir; aceitar.

admittance, n. entrada f.

admixture, n. mistura.

admonish, vb. admoestar.

adolescence, n. adolescência f.

adolescent, adj., n. adolescente m.f.

adopt, vb. adotar.

adopted, adoptive, adj. adotivo.

adoption, n. adoção f.

adorable, adj. adorável, encantador.

adore, vb. adorar.

adorn, vb. adornar.

adornment, n. adorno m.

adrift, adv. à deriva.

adroit, adj. destro, hábil.

adulate, vb. adular, bajular.

adulation, n. adulação, bajulação.

adult, adj., n. adulto m.

adulterate, vb. adulterar.

adulterer, n. adúltero m.

adulteress, n. adúltera f.

adultery, n. adultério m.

advance, 1. n. avanço; adiantamento m.; antecipação f. **in a.,** com antecedência. **2.** vb. avançar; adiantar.

advanced, adj. avançado, adiantado.

advancement, n. adiantamento m.; progresso m.

advantage, n. vantagem f. **take a. of,** aproveitar(-se de).

advantageous, adj. vantajoso.

advent, n. advento m.

adventure, n. aventura f.

adventurer, n. aventureiro m.

adventurous, adventuresome, adj. aventuroso.

adverb, n. advérbio m.

adversary, n. adversário m.

adverse, adj. adverso.

adversity, n. adversidade f.

advert to, vb. referir-se a.

advertise, vb. anunciar, fazer propaganda (para).

advertisement, n. anúncio m., propaganda f.

advertiser, n. anunciante m.f.

advertising agency, n. agência de publicidade f.

advice, n. conselho m.

advisable, adj. aconselhável.

advise, vb. aconselhar; avisar.

advisement, n. consideração f. **take under a.,** submeter a estudo.

adviser, advisor, n. conselheiro m.; assessor m.

advisory, adj. consultivo.

advocacy, n. advocacia f.; defesa f.

advocate, 1. n. advogado m.; defensor m. **2.** vb. advogar.

aegis, n. égide f.

aerate, vb. arejar, ventilar.

aerial, 1. adj. aéreo. **2.** n. antena f.

aerobic, adj. aeróbio.

aerosol, n. aerossol m.

aerospace, 1. adj. aeroespacial. **2.** n. aeroespaço m.

aesthetic, adj. estético.

aesthetics, n. estética f.

afar, adv. longe. **from a.,** de longe.

affable, adj. afável.

affair, n. assunto m.; (pl.) afazeres m.pl. **love a.,** caso m.

affect, 1. n. afeto m. **2.** vb. afetar; comover; fingir.

affectation, n. afetação f., fingimento m.

affected, adj. afetado, fingido.

affection, n. afeição f.; carinho m.

affectionate, adj. afetuoso, carinhoso.

affidavit, n. declaração f., depoimento m.

affiliate, 1. n. pessoa ou organização afiliada f. **2.** vb. afiliar (-se).

affiliation, n. afiliação f.

affinity, n. afinidade f.

affirm, vb. afirmar.

affirmative, 1. n. afirmativa f. **2.** adj. afirmativo.

affix, vb. afixar, pregar.

afflict, vb. afligir. **be afflicted with,** sofrer de.

affliction, n. aflição f.; doença f.

affluence, n. afluência f.

affluent, adj. afluente.

afford, vb. proporcionar. **be able to a.,** ter os meios para.

affront, 1. n. afronta f. **2.** vb. afrontar.

Afghanistan, n. Afeganistão m.

afield, adv. longe de casa. **far a.,** longe.

afire, adv. em chamas.

aflame, adv em chamas.

afloat, 1. adj. flutuante; a bordo. **2.** adv. à tona, à deriva.

aforementioned, adj. supracitado.

aforethought, adj. premeditado.

afoul, adv. em colisão. **run a. of,** meter-se em dificuldades com.

afraid, adj. amedrontado. **be a. of,** ter medo de.

African, adj., n. africano m.

Afro-Brazilian, adj. n. afro-brasileiro m.

aft, adv. (naut.) à popa, à ré.

after, 1. adv. depois; atrás. **2.**

prep. depois de; atrás de; à maneira de. **3.** *conj.* depois que.

afterlife, *n.* além-túmulo *m.*

aftermath, *n.* resultado *m.*; consequência *f.*

afternoon, *n.* tarde *f.* **good a.,** boa tarde.

afterward, *adv.* depois, mais tarde.

again, *adv.* outra vez, de novo.

against, *prep.* contra.

agape, *adj., adv.* boquiaberto.

age, 1. *n.* idade *f.*; época *f.* **of a.,** maior de idade; **old a.,** velhice *f.* **2.** *vb.* envelhecer.

aged, *adj.* velho, idoso.

ageism, *n.* discriminação contra os idosos.

ageless, *adj.* que não envelhece.

agency *n.* agência *f.* **travel a.,** agência de viagens.

agenda, *n.* ordem do dia *f.*; agenda *f.*

agent, *n.* agente *m.*

agglomerate, 1. *n.* aglomerado *m.* **2.** *vb.* aglomerar(-se).

agglutinate, *vb.* aglutinar.

aggrandize, *vb.* engrandecer.

aggravate, *vb.* agravar; irritar.

aggravation, *n.* agravamento *m.*; irritação *f.*

aggregate, 1. *n.* agregado *m.* **2.** *vb.* agregar(-se).

aggression, *n.* agressão *f.*

aggressive, *adj.* agressivo.

aggressiveness, *n.* agressividade *f.*

aggressor, *n.* agressor *m.*

aghast, *adj.* horrorizado.

agile, *adj.* ágil.

agility, *n.* agilidade *f.*

agitate, *vb.* agitar.

agitator, *n.* agitador *m.*

agnostic, *adj.* agnóstico *m.*

ago, 1. *adj.* passado. **2.** *adv.* há, faz; atrás. **two days a.,** há/faz dois dias.

agonize, *vb.* agonizar.

agony, *n.* agonia *f.*; angústia *f.*

agrarian, *adj.* agrário.

agree, *vb.* concordar; consentir (em).

agreeable, *adj.* agradável; conveniente.

agreement, *n.* acordo *m.*; convênio *m.*; *(gram.)* concordância *f.*

agricultural, *adj.* agrícola.

agriculture, *n.* agricultura *f.*

aground, *adj.* encalhado.

ahead, *adv.* adiante. **straight a.,** em frente; **be a.,** estar na dianteira; **go a.,** prosseguir.

aid, 1. *n.* ajuda *f.* **2.** *vb.* ajudar.

aide, *n.* ajudante, assistente *m.f.*

AIDS, *n.* AIDS *f.*

ail, *vb.* afligir; estar doente.

ailing, *adj.* doente.

ailment, *n.* doença *f.*

aim, 1. *n.* pontaria *f.*; propósito *m.* **2.** *vb.* apontar; pretender.

aimless, *adj.* sem rumo; a esmo.

air, 1. *n.* ar *m.*; aparência *f.*; melodia *f.*; *(pl.)* afetação *f.* **in the open a.,** ao ar livre. **2.** *adj.* aéreo. **3.** *vb.* arejar.

air base, *n.* base aérea *f.*

air-conditioned, *adj.* refrigerado.

air-conditioner, *n.* condicionador do ar *m.*

air-conditioning, *n.* ar condicionado *m.*

aircraft, *n.* aeronave *f.*; avião *m.*

aircraft carrier, *n.* porta-aviões *m.*

air force, *n.* força aérea *f.*

airlift, *n.* ponte aérea *f.*

airline, *n.* linha aérea *f.*

airmail, *n.* via aérea *f.*

airplane, *n.* avião, aeroplano *m.*

airport, *n.* aeroporto *m.*

air raid, *n.* ataque aéreo *m.*

air-raid shelter, *n.* abrigo antiaéreo *m.*

airsick, *adj.* enjoado.

airtight, *adj.* hermético.

aisle, *n.* passagem, coxia *f.*; (church) nave *f.*

ajar, *adj.* entreaberto.

akin, *adj.* aparentado; afim.

alarm, 1. *n.* alarme, alarma *m.*; susto *m.* **2.** *vb.* alarmar.

alarm clock, *n.* despertador *m.*

alas, *interj.* ai! ai de mim!

albino, *n.* albino, sararáú *m.*

album, *n.* álbum *m.*

alchemy, *n.* alquimia *f.*

alcohol, *n.* álcool *m.*

alcoholic, 1. *adj.* alcoólico. **2.** *n.* alcoólatra *m.f.*

alcove, *n.* alcova *f.*, recanto *m.*

ale, *n.* cerveja inglesa *f.*

alert, 1. *n.* alerta *m.* **2.** *adj.* alerta. **3.** *vb.* alertar.

alfalfa, *n.* alfafa *f.*

alga, *n.* alga *f.*

algebra, *n.* álgebra *f.*

Algeria, *n.* Argélia *f.*

Algerian, *n.*, *adj.* argelino -na.

Algiers, *n.* Argel.

alias, *n.* vulgo *m.*

alien, 1. *adj.* estrangeiro, alheio. **2.** *n.* estrangeiro, forasteiro *m.*

alienate, *vb.* alienar, alhear.

alight, *vb.* apear-se; pousar.

align, *vb.* alinhar.

alike, *adj.* parecido, semelhante.

alimentary, *adj.* alimentar, alimentício. **a. canal,** tubo digestivo.

alimony, *n.* alimentos *m.pl.*

alive, *adj.* vivo; animado.

all, 1. *pron.* tudo; todo; todos. **after a.,** afinal de contas; **not at a.,** de modo algum. **2.** *adj.* todo. **3.** *adv.* todo. **a. of a sudden,** de repente.

allay, *vb.* aquietar.

allegation, *n.* alegação *f.*

allege, *vb.* alegar.

allegiance, *n.* fidelidade, obediência *f.*

allegory, *n.* alegoria *f.*

allergic, *adj.* alérgico.

allergy, *n.* alergia *f.*

alleviate, *vb.* aliviar.

alley, *n.* beco *m.*, viela *f.*

alliance, *n.* aliança *f.*

alligator, *n.* jacaré *m.*

allocate, *vb.* distribuir.

allocation, *n.* distribuição *f.*; verba *f.*

allot, *vb.* distribuir.

allotment, *n.* distribuição *f.*; parcela *f.*

all-out, *adj.* total, completo.

allow, *vb.* permitir, deixar; admitir.

allowance, *n.* pensão, mesada *f.*; concessão *f.* **make a. for,** levar em conta.

alloy, *n.* liga, mistura *f.*

all-powerful, *adj.* todo-poderoso.

all right, 1. *adj.* satisfatório. **2.** *interj.* está bem; não faz mal; *(sl.)* falou!

all-round, *adj.* completo, acabado.

allude, *vb.* aludir.

allure, 1. *n.* fascinação *f.* **2.** *vb.* aliciar, seduzir, fascinar.

alluring, *adj.* encantador, aliciante.

allusion, *n.* alusão *f.*

ally, 1. *n.* aliado *f.* **2.** *vb.* aliar.

almanac, *n.* almanaque *m.*

almighty, *adj.* todo-poderoso.

almond, *n.* amêndoa *f.*

almost, *adv.* quase, por pouco.

alms, *n.* esmola *f.*

aloft, *adv.* em cima, no alto.

alone, *adj.*, *adv.* só, sozinho; a sós. **leave a.,** deixar em paz.

along, 1. *adv.* **a. with,** com, junto de; **all a.,** o tempo todo; **get a.,** ir embora; arranjar-se; **get a. with,** dar-se (bem) com. **2.** *prep.* por, ao longo de.

alongside, 1. *adv.* ao lado. **2.** *prep.* ao lado de.

aloof, *adj.* afastado.

aloud, *adv.* em voz alta.

alphabet, *n.* alfabeto *m.*

alphabetical, *adj.* alfabético.

Alps, *n.pl.* Alpes *m.pl.*

already, *adv.* já.

also, *adv.* também.

altar, *n.* altar *m.*

altar boy, *n.* acólito *m.*

alter, *vb.* alterar.

altercation, *n.* altercação, disputa *f.*

alternate, 1. *adj.* alternado, alterno. **2.** *n.* substituto *m.* **3.** *vb.* alternar.

alternative, 1. *adj.* alternativo. **2.** *n.* alternativa *f.*

although, *conj.* embora, ainda que, se bem que.

altitude, *n.* altitude, altura *f.*

alto, *n.* alto *m.*

altogether, *adv.* totalmente.

altruism, *n.* altruísmo *m.*

alum, *n.* alume *m.*, pedra-ume *f.*

aluminum, *n.* alumínio *m.*

alumnus, *n.* ex-aluno *m.*

always, *adv.* sempre.

amalgamate, *vb.* amalgamar.

amass, *vb.* amontoar.

amateur, *adj.*, *n.* amador *m.*

amaze, *vb.* pasmar, espantar.

amazement, *n.* pasmo, espanto *m.*

amazing, *adj.* espantoso, assombroso.

amazon, *n.* amazona *f.*

Amazon, *n.* (region) Amazônia *f.*; (river) Amazonas *m.*

Amazonian, *adj.* amazônico.

ambassador, *n.* embaixador *m.*

amber, 1. *adj.* ambarino. **2.** *n.* âmbar *m.*

ambidextrous, *adj.* ambidestro.

ambiguous, *adj.* ambíguo.

ambition, *n.* ambição *f.*

ambitious, *adj.* ambicioso.

ambivalent, *adj.* ambivalente.

ambrosia, *n.* ambrosia *f.*

ambulance, *n.* ambulância, *f.*

ambush, 1. *n.* emboscada, tocaia. **2.** *vb.* emboscar-se; tocaiar.

ameliorate, *vb.* melhorar.

amen, *interj.* amém!

amenable, *adj.* dócil; receptivo.

amend, 1. *n.* reparação *f.* **make amends,** reparar. **2.** *vb.* emendar.

amendment, *n.* emenda *f.*

amenity, *n.* amenidade *f.*

American, *adj.*, *n.* americano, norte-americano *m.*

Amerind, *n.* ameríndio *m.*

Amerindian, *adj.* ameríndio.

amiable, *adj.* amável.

amicable, *adj.* amigável.

amid, *prep.* no meio de, entre.

amiss, 1. *adj.* errado. **2.** *adv.* mal. **take a.,** levar a mal.

amity, *n.* amizade, cordialidade *f.*

ammonia, *n.* amoníaco *m.*

ammunition, *n.* munição *f.*

amnesia, *n.* amnésia *f.*

amnesty, 1. *n.* anistia *f.* **2.** *vb.* anistiar.

among, *prep.* entre, em meio de.

amorous, *adj.* amoroso.

amortize, *vb.* amortizar.

amount, 1. *n.* quantidade; (money) soma, quantia, importância *f.* **2. a. to,** montar a; importar em.

amp, ampere, *n.* ampere *m.*

amphetamine, *n.* anfetamina *f.*

amphibian, *adj.*, *n.* anfíbio *m.*

amphitheater, *n.* anfiteatro *m.*

ample, *adj.* amplo; abundante; suficiente.

amplifier, *n.* amplificador *m.*

amplify, *vb.* amplificar.

amputate, *vb.* amputar.

amuck, amok, *adv.* freneticamente. **run a.,** atacar às cegas.

amulet, *n.* amuleto *m.*

amuse, *vb.* divertir. **a. oneself,** divertir-se.

amusement, *n.* diversão *f.*, divertimento *m.*

amusing, *adj.* divertido, engraçado.

an, *indef. art.* um, uma.

anachronism, *n.* anacronismo *m.*

anaesthetic, *adj.*, *n.* anestésico *m.*

anal, *adj.* anal.

analogous, *adj.* análogo.

analogy, *n.* analogia *f.*

analysis, *n.* análise *f.*

analyst, *n.* analista *m.f.*

analytical, *adj.* analítico.

analyze, *vb.* analizar.

anarchy, *n.* anarquia *f.*

anatomy, *n.* anatomia *f.*

ancestor, *n.* antepassado, ancestral *m.*

ancestral, *adj.* ancestral.

ancestry, *n.* ascendência, linhagem *f.*

anchor, 1. *n.* âncora *f.* **2.** *vb.* ancorar.

anchorage, *n.* ancoradouro *m.*

anchovy, *n.* enchova, anchova *f.*

ancient, *adj.*, *n.* antigo, ancião *m.*

and, *conj.* e.

Andean, *adj.* andino.

anecdote, *n.* anedota *f.*

anemia, *n.* anemia *f.*

anemic, *adj.* anêmico.

anew, *adv.* de novo.

angel, *n.* anjo *m.*

angelic, *adj.* angélico.

anger, 1. *n.* raiva, cólera *f.* **2.** *vb.* enfurecer.

angle, *n.* ângulo *m.* **right a.,** ângulo reto.

Anglican, *adj.*, *n.* anglicano *m.*

Anglicism, *n.* anglicismo *m.*

Anglo-Saxon, *adj.*, *n.* anglo-saxão -xã.

Angolan, *adj.*, *n.* angolano *m.*

angry, *adj.* raivoso, zangado. **get/be a.,** ficar/estar com raiva.

anguish, *n.* angústia *f.*

anguished, *adj.* angustiado.

animal, *adj., n.* animal *m.*

animate, 1. *adj.* animado. **2.** *vb.* animar.

animated, *adj.* animado; vivo.

animation, *n.* animação *f.*; vivacidade *f.*

animosity, *n.* animosidade *f.*

ankle, *n.* tornozelo *m.*

annals, *n.pl.* anais *m.pl.*

annex, 1. *n.* anexo *m.* **2.** *vb.* anexar.

annihilate, *vb.* aniquilar.

anniversary, *n.* aniversário *m.*; (wedding) bodas *f.pl.*

annotate, *vb.* anotar.

announce, *vb.* anunciar; participar.

announcement, *n.* anúncio, aviso *m.*; participação *f.*

announcer, *n.* anunciador *m.*; (rad., TV) locutor *m.*

annoy, *vb.* incomodar, aborrecer.

annoyance, *n.* aborrecimento *m.*

annoying, *adj.* aborrecido, maçante.

annual, 1. *adj.* anual. **2.** *n.* anuário *m.*

annuity, *n.* anuidade *f.*

annul, *vb.* anular, invalidar.

anoint, *vb.* ungir, untar.

anomalous, *adj.* anômalo.

anomaly, *n.* anomalia *f.*

anonymity, *n.* anonimato *m.*

anonymous, *adj.* anônimo.

another, *adj., pron.* outro.

answer, 1. *n.* resposta *f.*; solução *f.* **2.** *vb.* responder.

ant, *n.* formiga *f.*

antagonism, *n.* antagonismo *m.*

antagonist, *n.* antagonista *m.f.*

antagonistic, *adj.* antagônico.

antagonize, *vb.* contrariar.

antarctic, *adj.* antártico.

Antarctica, *n.* Antártica *f.*

ante, 1. *n.* parada. **2.** *vb.* apostar.

anteater, *n.* tamanduá *m.*

antecedent, *adj., n.* antecedente *m.*

antelope, *n.* antílope *m.f.*

antenna, *n.* antena *f.*

anteroom, *n.* antecâmara, antesala *f.*

anthem, *n.* hino *m.*

anthology, *n.* antologia *f.*

anthropologist, *n.* antropólogo *m.*

anthropology, *n.* antropologia *f.*

anti-, *pref.* anti-.

anti-aircraft, *adj.* antiaéreo.

antibiotic, *adj., n.* antibiótico *m.*

antibody, *n.* anticorpo *m.*

anticipate, *vb.* antecipar.

antics, *n.pl.* travessuras *f.pl.*

antidote, *n.* antídoto *m.*

Antilles, *n.pl.* Antilhas *f.pl.*

antipathy, *n.* antipatia *f.*

antiquated, *adj.* antiquado.

antique, *n.* antiguidade, antigualha *f.*

antiquity, *n.* antiguidade.

antiseptic, *adj., n.* anti-séptico *m.*

antithesis, *n.* antítese *f.*

antler, *n.* chifre *m.*, aspa *f.*

anus, *n.* ânus *m.*

anvil, *n.* bigorna *f.*

anxiety, *n.* ansiedade, ânsia *f.*

anxious, *adj.* ansioso, inquieto; desejoso.

any, 1. *indef. adj. & pron.* algum; qualquer; todo; nenhum. **2.** *adv.* **a.** longer/more, mais.

anybody, *pron.* = anyone.

anyhow, *adv.* de qualquer maneira; seja como for.

anyone, *pron.* alguém; qualquer um.

anything, *pron.* qualquer coisa; alguma coisa.

anyway, *pron.* = anyhow.

anywhere, *adv.* em qualquer lugar. **not a.,** em lugar nenhum.

apart, *adv.* à parte. **take a.,** desmontar.

apartment, *n.* apartamento *m.*

apathetic, *adj.* apático.

apathy, *n.* apatia *f.*

ape, 1. *n.* macaco. **2.** *vb.* macaquear, imitar.

apéritif, *n.* aperitivo *m.*, abrideira *f.*

aphorism, *n.* aforismo *m.*

aphrodisiac, *adj.*, *n.* afrodisíaco *m.*

apiary, *n.* apiário *m.*, colmeia *f.*

apiece, *adv.* (por, para) cada um.

apocalypse, *n.* apocalipse *m.*

apocryphal, *adj.* apócrifo.

apogee, *n.* apogeu *m.*

apologetic, *adj.* apologético.

apologize, *vb.* pedir desculpas.

apology, *n.* desculpa; apologia.

apoplexy, *n.* apoplexia *f.*

apostle, *n.* apóstolo *m.*

apostrophe, *n.* apóstrofo *m.*

appall, *vb.* horrorizar.

apparatus, *n.* aparelho; aparato.

apparel, *n.* roupa *f.*

apparent, *adj.* aparente, evidente.

apparition, *n.* aparição *f.*, fantasma *m.*

appeal, **1.** *n.* apelo *m.*; (*jur.*) apelação *f.*; atrativo *m.* **2.** apelar.

appear, *vb.* aparecer; (seem) parecer.

appearance, *n.* aparecimento *m.*; aparência *f.*

appease, *vb.* apaziguar.

appellation, *n.* apelativo *m.*

append, *vb.* juntar, anexar.

appendage, *n.* apêndice *m.*

appendectomy, *n.* apendicectomia *f.*

appendicitis, *n.* apendicite *f.*

appendix, *n.* apêndice *m.*

appetite, *n.* apetite *m.*

appetizer, *n.* aperitivo *m.*; entrada *f.*

appetizing, *adj.* apetitoso.

applaud, *vb.* aplaudir, bater palmas.

applause, *n.* aplauso *f.*

apple, *n.* maçã *f.* **a. of the eye**, menina dos olhos.

appliance, *n.* eletrodoméstico *m.*

applicant, *n.* requerente *m.f.*; candidato *m.*

application, *n.* aplicação *f.*, uso *m.*; petição *f.*

applied, *adj.* aplicado.

apply, *vb.* aplicar. **a. for**, pedir, solicitar.

appoint, *vb.* nomear.

appointment, *n.* nomeação *f.*; encontro marcado, compromisso *m.*

apportion, *vb.* repartir, ratear.

appraisal, *n.* avaliação, apreciação *f.*

appraise, *vb.* avaliar.

appreciable, *adj.* apreciável.

appreciate, *vb.* apreciar; agradecer; subir (price).

appreciation, *n.* apreciação *f.*, apreço *m.*; (prices) alta *f.*

apprehend, *vb.* apreender; prender.

apprehension, *n.* apreensão *f.*

apprehensive, *adj.* apreensivo.

apprentice, *n.* aprendiz *m.f.*

apprenticeship, *n.* aprendizagem *f.*; aprendizado *m.*

apprise, *vb.* informar.

approach, **1.** *n.* aproximação *f.*; abordagem *f.* **2.** *vb.* aproximar-se de; abordar.

appropriate, **1.** *adj.* apropriado. **2.** *vb.* apropriar-se de.

approval, *n.* aprovação *f.*

approve, *vb.* aprovar.

approximate, **1.** *adj.* aproximado. **2.** *vb.* aproximar-se.

appurtenance, *n.* pertence, acessório *m.*

apricot, *n.* abricó, damasco *m.*

April, *n.* abril *m.*

apron, *n.* avental *m.*

apropos, *adv.* a propósito.

apt, *adj.* apto. **a. to**, capaz de.

aptitude, *n.* aptidão, aptitude *f.*

aquamarine, *n.* água-marinha *f.*

aquarium, *n.* aquário *m.*

Aquarius, *n.* Aquário *m.*

aquatic, *adj.* aquático.

aqueduct, *n.* aqueduto *m.*

Arab, Arabian, *adj.*, *n.* árabe *m.f.*

Arabic, **1.** *adj.* arábico. **2.** *n.* árabe (language).

arable, *adj.* arável.

arbiter, *n.* árbitro *m.*

arbitrary, *adj.* arbitrário.

arbitrate, *vb.* arbitrar.

arbitration, *vb.* arbitragem *f.*

arbitrator, *n.* arbitrador *m.*

arbor, *n.* caramanchão *m.*

arc, *n.* arco *m.*

arcade, *n.* arcada, galeria *f.*

arch, *n.* arco; abóbada *f.*

archaeologist, *n.* arqueólogo *m.*

archaeology, *n.* arqueologia *f.*

archaic, *adj.* arcaico.

archbishop, *n.* arcebispo *m.*

archdiocese, *n.* arquidiocese *f.*

archer, *n.* arqueiro, flecheiro *m.*

archetype, *n.* arquétipo *m.*

archipelago, *n.* arquipélago *m.*

architect, *n.* arquiteto -ta.

architectural, *adj.* arquitetônico.

architecture, *n.* arquitetura *f.*

archive, *n.* arquivo *m.*

arctic, *adj.* ártico.

ardent, *adj.* ardente.

ardor, *n.* ardor *m.*

arduous, *adj.* árduo.

area, *n.* área *f.*; região *f.*; campo *m.*

area code, *n.* código de discagem direta à distância, DDD *m.*

arena, *n.* arena *f.*

Argentine, Argentinean, *adj., n.* argentino *m.*

argue, *vb.* argumentar; discutir.

argument, *n.* argumento *m.*; discussão *f.*

arid, *adj.* árido.

arise, *vb.* levantar-se; surgir.

aristocracy, *n.* aristocracia *f.*

aristocrat, *n.* aristocrata *m.f.*

aristocratic, *adj.* aristocrático.

arithmetic, *n.* aritmética *f.*

ark, *n.* arca *f.*

arm, 1. *n.* braço *m.*; (*mil.*) arma *f.* **2.** *vb.* armar.

armadillo, *n.* tatu *m.*

armament, *n.* armamento *m.*

armchair, *n.* poltrona *f.*

armed forces, *n.pl.* forças armadas *f.pl.*

armful, *n.* braçada *f.*

armistice, *n.* armistício, *m.*

armor, *n.* armadura *f.*

armored, *adj.* blindado.

armory, *n.* armaria *f.*; arsenal *m.*

armpit, *n.* axila *f.*; sovaco *m.*

army, *n.* exército *m.*

aroma, *n.* aroma *m.*

around, 1. *adv.* em volta; em redor; por aí. **2.** *prep.* em volta de, ao redor de; cerca de; por; (*time*) por volta de.

arouse, *vb.* despertar; estimular.

arraign, *vb.* chamar a juízo; acusar.

arrange, *vb.* arranjar, arrumar.

arrangement, *n.* arranjo; (*pl.*) preparativos *m.pl.*

array, 1. *n.* ordem *f.*; pompa *f.* **2.** *vb.* adornar.

arrears, *n.pl.* dívidas *f.pl.* **in a.,** em atraso.

arrest, 1. prisão *f.* **2.** *vb.* parar; prender.

arrival, *n.* chegada *f.*

arrive, *vb.* chegar.

arrogance, *n.* arrogância *f.*

arrogant, *adj.* arrogante.

arrow, *n.* flecha, seta *f.*

arsenal, *n.* arsenal *m.*

arsenic, *n.* arsênico *m.*

arson, *n.* incêndio premeditado.

art, *n.* arte *f.* **a. gallery,** galeria de arte; **fine arts,** belas artes.

artery, *n.* artéria *f.*

artful, *adj.* manhoso, astucioso.

arthritis, *n.* artrite *f.*

artichoke, *n.* alcachofra *f.*

article, *n.* artigo.

articulate, *vb.* articular.

artifact, *n.* artefato *m.*

artifice, *n.* artifício *m.*

artificial, *adj.* artificial.

artillery, *n.* artilharia *f.*

artisan, *n.* artesão -sã.

artist, *n.* artista *m.f.*

artistic, *adj.* artístico.

artistry, *n.* arte *f.*

artless, *adj.* ingênuo.

as, 1. *adv.* tão. **a. . .a.,** tão . . .quanto/como; **a. for,** quanto a; **a. long a.,** enquanto; contanto que; **a. much (. . .) as,** tanto (..) quanto/como; **a. of,** a partir de; **a. soon a.,** assim que; **a. well,** também; **a. well as,** tanto (. . .) quanto/como; **a. yet,** até agora. **2.** *conj.* como. **a. if,** como se. **3.** *prep.* como.

asbestos, *n.* asbesto *m.*

ascend, *vb.* ascender, subir.

ascendance, -dancy, *n.* ascendência *f.*

ascendant, *adj.* ascendente.

ascent, *n.* subida *f.*

ascertain, *vb.* verificar, averiguar.

ascribe, *vb.* atribuir.

ash, *n.* cinza *f.*

ashamed, adj. envergonhado.

ashen, adj. cinzento, pálido.

ashore, adv. em terra. **go a.,** desembarcar.

ashtray, n. cinzeiro m.

Asian, Asiatic, adj., n. asiático m.

aside, 1. n. (theat.) aparte m. **2.** adv. de lado; à parte. **a. from,** fora, à parte de.

asinine, adj. asinino.

ask, vb. perguntar; convidar; pedir. **a. for,** pedir.

askance, adv. de soslaio, de esguelha.

asleep, adj. adormecido. **fall a.,** pegar no sono.

asp, n. áspide m.f.

asparagus, n. aspargo m.

aspect, n. aspecto m.

aspersion, n. difamação f.

asphalt, n. asfalto m.

asphyxiate, vb. asfixiar.

aspiration, n. aspiração f.

aspire, vb. aspirar.

aspirin, n. aspirina f.

ass, n. asno, burro m.; (vulg.) cu m.

assail, vb. acometer; criticar.

assailant, n. assaltante m.f.

assassin, n. assassino m.

assassinate, vb. assassinar.

assassination, n. assassínio m.

assault, 1. n. assalto m. **2.** vb. assaltar.

assay, vb. aquilatar; testar.

assemblage, n. assembléia, f.

assemble, vb. armar, montar; reunir(-se).

assembly, n. assembléia f. **a. line,** linha de montagem.

assent, 1. n. assentimento m. **2.** vb. assentir.

assert, vb. afirmar. **a. oneself,** impor-se.

assertion, n. asserção, afirmação f.

assess, vb. taxar; avaliar.

asset, n. qualidade, vantagem f.

assets, n.pl. ativo m., bens m.pl.

assiduous, adj. assíduo.

assign, vb. designar; distribuir; passar.

assignment, n. designação f.; tarefa f.

assimilate, vb. assimilar.

assist, vb. ajudar, auxiliar.

assistance, n. ajuda, assistência f.

assistant, n. ajudante, assistente m.f.

associate, 1. n. sócio m. **2.** vb. associar.

association, n. associação f.

assort, vb. classificar.

assorted, adj. variado.

assortment, n. classificação f.; sortimento m.

assuage, vb. aplacar, mitigar.

assume, vb. assumir; supor.

assuming, adj. presunçoso. **a. that,** supondo que.

assumption, n. assunção f.; suposição f.

assurance, n. segurança, garantia f.

assure, vb. assegurar, garantir.

asterisk, n. asterisco m.

astern, adv. à popa.

asthma, n. asma f.

astigmatism, n. astigmatismo m.

astir, adv. em movimento.

astonish, vb. espantar, pasmar.

astonishment, n. espanto, pasmo m.

astound, vb. estarrecer, pasmar.

astray, adv. extraviado. **lead a.,** extraviar.

astride, adv. escarranchado.

astringent, adj., n. adstringente m.

astrology, n. astrologia f.

astronaut, n. astronauta m.f.

astronomical, adj. astronômico.

astronomy, n. astronomia f.

astute, adj. astucioso, perspicaz.

astuteness, n. astúcia f.

Asunción, n. Assunção.

asunder, adv. aos pedaços.

asylum, n. asilo m.

at, prep. a; em.

atheist, n. ateu -téia.

Athens, n. Atenas.

athlete, n. atleta m.f.

athletic, adj. atlético.

athletics, n. atletismo, esporte m.

Atlantic, 1. adj. atlântico. **2.** n. Atlântico m.

atlas, *n.* atlas *m.*

atmosphere, *n.* atmosfera *f.*; ambiente *f.*

atoll, *n.* atol *m.*

atom, *n.* átomo.

atomic, *adj.* atômico.

atomic bomb, *n.* bomba atômica *f.*

atomic energy, *n.* energia atômica *f.*

atone for, *vb.* expiar, reparar.

atop, *prep.* em cima de, no alto de.

atrocious, *adj.* atroz.

atrocity, *n.* atrocidade *f.*

atrophy, **1.** *n.* atrofia *f.* **2.** *vb.* atrofiar.

attach, *vb.* atar, ligar; anexar.

attaché, *n.* adido *m.*

attached, *adj.* anexo; afeiçoado.

attachment, *n.* ligação *f.*; afeto *m.*; acessório *m.*

attack, **1.** *n.* ataque *m.* **2.** *vb.* atacar.

attain, *vb.* atingir; conseguir.

attainment, *n.* consecução *f.*

attempt. **1.** *n.* tentativa *f.* **2.** *vb.* tentar, procurar.

attend, *vb.* assistir, freqüentar. **a. to**, aplicar-se a.

attendance, *n.* assistência, freqüência *f.*

attendant, **1.** *adj.* concomitante. **2.** *n.* assistente *m.f.*; servidor *m.*

attention, *n.* atenção *f.* **pay a.**, prestar atenção.

attentive, *adj.* atencioso.

attenuate, *vb.* atenuar.

attest (to), *vb.* atestar.

attic, *n.* sótão, ático *m.*

attire, **1.** *n.* vestimenta *f.* **2.** *vb.* vestir.

attitude, *n.* atitude *f.*

attorney, *n.* advogado *n.*

attract, *vb.* atrair.

attraction, *n.* atração *f.*, atrativo *m.*

attractive, *adj.* atraente, atrativo.

attribute, **1.** *n.* atributo *m.* **2.** *vb.* atribuir.

attune, *vb.* harmonizar.

auburn, *adj.* castanho avermelhado.

auction, **1.** *n.* leilão *m.*, hasta *f.* **2.** *vb.* leiloar.

auctioneer, *n.* leiloeiro *m.*

audacious, *adj.* audaz, ousado.

audible, *adj.* audível.

audience, *n.* audiência *f.*; público *m.*

audit, **1.** *n.* balanço *m.*, auditoria *f.* **2.** *vb.* fiscalizar; freqüentar como ouvinte.

audition, *n.* audição *f.*; prova *f.*

auditor, *n.* auditor *m.*; ouvinte (de aulas) *m.*

auditorium, *n.* auditório, salão nobre *m.*

auger, *n.* verruma *f.*, trado *m.*

augment, *vb.* aumentar.

augmentative, *adj.* aumentativo.

augur, *vb.* augurar, agourar.

augury, *n.* augúrio, agouro *m.*

august, **1.** *adj.* augusto. **2.** *n. (cap.)* agosto *m.*

aunt, *n.* tia *f.*

auntie, *n.* titia *f.*

aura, *n.* aura *f.*

auspice, *n.* auspício *m.*

auspicious, *adj.* auspicioso.

austere, *adj.* austero.

austerity, *n.* austeridade *f.*

Australian, *adj.*, *n.* australiano *m.*

Austrian, *adj.*, *n.* austríaco *m.*

authentic, *adj.* autêntico.

author, *n.* autor -ra.

authoritarian, *adj.* autoritário.

authority, *n.* autoridade, *f.*

authorize, *vb.* autorizar.

authorship, *n.* autoria *f.*

auto, *n.* automóvel *m.*

autobiography, *n.* autobiografia *f.*

autocratic, *adj.* autocrático.

autograph, **1.** *n.* autógrafo *m.* **2.** *vb.* autografar.

automatic, *adj.* automático.

automation, *n.* automação, automatização *f.*

automobile, **1.** *adj.* automobilístico. **2.** *n.* automóvel *m.*

autonomous, *adj.* autônomo.

autonomy, *n.* autonomia *f.*

autopsy, *n.* autópsia *f.*

autumn, *n.* outono *m.*

auxiliary, *adj.* auxiliar.

avail, **1.** *n.* utilidade *f.* **to no a.**, em vão. **2. a. oneself of**, valer-se.

availability, n. disponibilidade f.

available, adj. disponível.

avalanche, n. avalancha f.

avant-garde, adj. de vanguarda.

avarice, n. avareza f.

avaricious, adj. avaro, avarento.

avenge, vb. vingar.

avenger, n. vingador m.

avenue, n. avenida f.

average, 1. adj. médio. **2.** n. média f. **3.** vb. tirar/fazer uma média.

averse, adj. avesso, averso.

aversion, n. aversão f.

avert, vb. desviar; evitar.

aviary, n. aviário m.; passareira f.

aviation, n. aviação f.

aviator, n. aviador m.

avid, adj. ávido, sôfrego.

avocado, n. abacate m.

avocation, n. passatempo m.

avoid, vb. evitar.

avow, vb. admitir, confessar.

avowal, n. confissão f.

await, vb. esperar, aguardar.

awake, adj. acordado.

awaken, vb. acordar; estimular.

award, 1. n. prêmio m. **2.** vb. conferir.

aware, adj. ciente, a par.

awareness, n. consciência f., conhecimento m.

away, 1. adv. longe; fora; à distância. **2.** adj. afastado; ausente.

awe, n. admiração, reverência f.

awesome, adj. aterrador; impressionante.

awful, adj. horrível; espantoso.

awhile, adv. por algum tempo.

awkward, adj. desajeitado; embaraçoso.

awl, n. sovela f.

awning, n. toldo m.

awry, adv. torto; errado; mal.

ax, axe, n. machado m.

axiom, n. axioma m.

axis, n. eixo m.

axle, n. eixo m.

ayatollah, n. aiatolá m.

Azores, n.pl. Açores m.pl.

Azorean, adj., n. açoriano m.

Aztec, adj., n. asteca m.f.

azure, adj. azul-celeste.

B

baa, 1. n. balido m. **2.** vb. balir.

babble, 1. n. murmúrio m.; tagarelice f. **2.** vb. murmurar; tagarelar.

baboon, n. mandril m.

baby, n. bebê, nenê m.

babyish, adj. infantil.

baby sitter, n. baby-sitter m.f.; babá f.

baccalaureate, n. bacharelado m.

bachelor, m. solteiro m.; (acad.) bacharel m.f.

back, 1. adj. traseiro. **2.** n. costas f.pl.; (animal) lombo m.; (chair) espaldar m.; reverso m.; fundo m. **3.** vb. apoiar; recuar. **4.** adv. atrás; de volta. **in b. of,** atrás de.

backbone, n. espinha dorsal, coluna vertebral f.

backer, n. partidário -ria.; financiador -ra.

backfire, vb. sair o tiro pela culatra.

background, n. fundo m.; formação f.; antecedentes m.pl.

backing, n. apoio m.

backlash, n. reação contrária f.

backlog, n. acumulação de trabalho por fazer f.

backpack, n. mochila f.

backside, n. traseiro m.

backtalk, n. resposta insolente f.

backtrack, vb. retroceder; desandar.

backward, 1. adj. atrasado; para trás; às avessas. **2.** adv. para trás.

backwardness, n. atraso m.

backwoods, n. interior, sertão m.

backwoodsman, n. sertanejo m.

back yard, n. quintal m.

bacon, n. bacon, toucinho defumado m.

bad, 1. adj. mau, ruim. **2.** n. mal m.

badge, n. distintivo m.; crachá m.

badger, 1. n. texugo m. **2.** vb. apoquentar.

badly, adv. mal.

badness, n. maldade, ruindade f.

baffle, vb. deixar perplexo.

bag, 1. n. saco m. , bolsa f. 2. vb. ensacar; abiscoitar.

baggage, n. bagagem f. **b. cart,** carrinho m. **b. check,** talão de bagagem m. ; **b. rack,** bagageiro m.

baggy, adj. largo, folgado.

bagpipe, n. gaita de foles f.

bail, 1. n. fiança f. **go b. for,** afiançar. 2. vb. (water) baldear. **b. out,** saltar de pára-quedas.

bailiff, n. alguazil m.

bait, 1. n. isca f. , engodo m. 2. vb. iscar.

bake, vb. cozer no forno. **baked,** ao forno.

baker, n. padeiro m.

bakery, n. padaria f.

baking powder, n. fermento em pó m.

baking soda, n. bicarbonato de sódio m.

balance, 1. n. equilíbrio m. ; balança f. (fin.) balanço m. ; (com.) saldo m. 2. vb. equilibrar; contrabalançar; saldar.

balance sheet, n. balancete m.

balcony, n. terraço, balcão m. , sacada f.

bald, adj. careca, calvo.

baldness, n. calvície f.

bale, 1. n. bala f. , fardo m. 2. vb. embalar.

balk, vb. empacar.

ball, n. bola f. ; (yarn) novelo m. ; (dance) baile m.

ballad, n. balada f. ; modinha f.

ballast, n. lastro m.

ball bearing, n. rolamento m.

ballerina, n. bailarina f.

ballet, n. balé, bailado m.

ballistic, adj. balístico.

balloon, n. balão m.

ballot, 1. n. cédula f. ; voto m. **b. box,** urna f. 2. vb. votar.

balloting, n. votação f.

ballpoint pen, n. esferográfica f.

ballroom, n. salão de baile m.

balm, n. bálsamo m.

balmy, adj. fragrante; refrescante.

baloney, n. (sl.) papo m. , chute m.

bamboo, n. bambu m.

ban, 1. n. proibição f. 2. vb. proibir.

banal, adj. banal.

banana, n. banana f.

band, 1. n. bando m. ; banda f. ; faixa f. 2. vb. **b. together,** associar-se.

bandage, 1. n. bandagem f. ; band-aid m. 2. vb. enfaixar.

bandana, n. lenço m.

bandit, n. bandido m. ; cangaceiro m.

bandstand, n. coreto m.

bane, n. veneno m. ; ruína f.

bang, 1. n. estrondo m. ; pancada f. ; (pl.) franja f. 2. vb. bater ruidosamente; martelar. 3. interj. bum!, bumba!

banish, vb. banir, desterrar.

banister, n. balaustrada f. ; corrimão m.

bank, 1. n. banco m. ; (river) margem f. ; ladeira f. 2. vb. depositar no banco. **b. on,** contar com.

bank account, n. conta bancária f.

bankbook, n. caderneta de banco f.

bank clerk, n. bancário -ria.

banker, n. banqueiro m.

bankrupt, 1. adj. falido 2. vb. levar à bancarrota.

bankruptcy, n. bancarrota, falência f.

banner, n. bandeira f. ; faixa f.

banquet, n. banquete m.

banter, 1. n. gracejo m. 2. vb. gracejar.

baptism, n. batismo m. ; batizado m.

Baptist, adj., n. batista m.f.

baptize, vb. batizar.

bar, 1. n. barra f. ; lingote m. ; obstáculo m. ; (jur.) advocacia f. ; (door) tranca f. ; (drink) bar m. ; (counter) balcão m. ; faixa f. 2. vb. trancar; proibir.

barb, 1. n. farpa f. 2. vb. farpar. **barbed wire,** arame farpado m.

barbarian, n. bárbaro -ra.

barbarism, n. barbarismo m. ; barbárie f.

barbarous, adj. bárbaro.

barbecue, 1. n. churrasco m. ; (grill) churrasqueira f. 2. vb. fazer churrasco.

bar bell, *n.* haltere *m.*
barber, *vb.* barbeiro *m.*
barbershop, *n.* barbearia *f.*
barbiturate, *n.* barbiturato *m.*
bare, **1.** *adj.* nu, despido. **2.** *vb.* despir.
barefoot, *adj.* descalço.
barely, *adv.* apenas.
bargain, **1.** *n.* negócio *m.*; pechincha *f.* **2.** *vb.* negociar; pechinchar.
barge, **1.** *n.* barcaça, chata *f.* **2.** *vb.* **b. into**, embarafustar em.
baritone, *n.* barítono *m.*
bark, **1.** *n.* (tree) casca *f.*; (dog) latido *m.* **2.** *vb.* latir.
barley, *n.* cevada *f.*
barn, *n.* celeiro, estábulo *m.*
barnyard, *n.* terreiro, quintal *m.*
barometer, *n.* barômetro *m.*
baron, *n.* barão *m.*
baroness, *n.* baronesa *f.*
baroque, *adj.*, *n.* barroco *m.*
barracks, *n.pl.* caserna *f.*, quartel *m.*
barrage, *n.* barragem *f.*
barrel, *n.* barril *m.*; (gun) cano *m.*
barren, *adj.* estéril.
barrette, *n.* presilha *f.*
barricade, *n.* barricada *f.*
barrier, *n.* barreira *f.*, obstáculo *m.*
bartender, *n.* garçom (de bar) *m.*
barter, **1.** *n.* troca *f.* **2.** *vb.* trocar, permutar.
base, **1.** *n.* baixo, vil. **2.** *n.* base *f.* **3.** *vb.* basear. **be based on**, basear-se em.
baseball, *n.* beisebol *m.*
basement, *n.* subsolo *m.*
bash, **1.** *n.* pancada *f.*; (sl.) festão *m.* **2.** *vb.* espancar.
bashful, *adj.* tímido, acanhado.
basic, *adj.* básico, fundamental.
basin, *n.* bacia *f.*
basis, *n.* base *f.*
bask, *vb.* aquecer-se ao sol.
basket, *n.* cesta *f.*
basketball, *n.* basquete *m.*, basquetebol -ca.
Basque, *adj.*, *n.* basco -ca.
bass, *n.* (fish) perca *f.*; (mus.) baixo *m.* **b. viol**, contrabaixo *m.*
bassoon, *n.* fagote *m.*

bastard, *n.* bastardo -da.
baste, *vb.* (sew) alinhavar; (food) regar.
bastion, *n.* bastião, baluarte *m.*
bat, *n.* (animal) morcego *m.*; bastão *m.*
batch, *n.* fornada *f.*; porção *f.*
bath, *n.* banho *m.*
bathe, *vb.* banhar(-se).
bather, *n.* banhista *m.f.*
bathing cap, *n.* touca de banho *f.*
bathing resort, *n.* balneário *m.*
bathing suit, *n.* (women) maiô *m.*; (men) calção *m.*
bathrobe, *n.* roupão de banho *m.*
bathroom, *n.* banheiro *m.*, (P.) casa de banho *f.*
bathtub, *n.* banheira *f.*
baton, *n.* bastão *m.*; (mus.) batuta *f.*
battalion, *n.* batalhão *m.*
batter, **1.** *n.* (food) massa *f.* **2.** *vb.* bater (em).
battery, *n.* bateria *f.*; (elec.) pilha *f.*
battle, **1.** *n.* batalha *f.* **2.** *vb.* batalhar.
battlefield, *n.* campo de batalha *m.*
battleship, *n.* encouraçado *m.*
bauble, *n.* bugiganga *f.*
bawdy, *adj.* indecente, obsceno.
bawl, *vb.* berrar. **b. out**, descompor.
bay, **1.** *n.* baía *f.* **2.** *vb.* latir, ladrar.
bayonet, *n.* baioneta *f.*
bazaar, *n.* bazar *m.* **charity b.**, quermesse *f.*
bazooka, *n.* bazuca *f.*
be, *vb.* ser; estar.
beach, *n.* praia *f.*
beacon, *n.* farol *m.*
bead, *n.* conta *f.*
beak, *n.* bico *m.*
beam, **1.** *n.* viga *f.*; (light) raio *m.* **2.** *vb.* transmitir; brilhar; sorrir.
beaming, *adj.* radiante; sorridente.
bean, *n.* feijão *m.*; fava *f.*; vagem *f.*
beanpole, *n.* (coll.) varapau *m.*
bear, **1.** *n.* urso -sa. **2.** *vb.* levar; agüentar; (child) dar à luz. **b.**

down, esforçar-se muito; **b. in mind,** ter em mente; **b. out,** confirmar; **b. up,** resistir.

bearable, adj. suportável.

beard, n. barba f.

bearded, adj. barbado, barbudo.

bearer, n. portador -ra.

bearing, n. porte m.; posição f.; relação f. **get one's bearings,** orientar-se.

beast, n. besta f.; bruto m.

beastly, adj. bestial.

beat, 1. n. batida, pancada f.; (mus.) compasso m.; (drum) toque m.; (policeman's) ronda f. **2.** vb. bater (em), golpear; surrar; vencer; (heart) bater.

beaten, adj. batido; derrotado; trilhado.

beating, n. surra f.

beautiful, adj. belo, bonito.

beautify, vb. embelezar.

beauty, n. beleza f.; beldade f. **b. parlor,** salão de beleza m.

beaver, n. castor m.

because, conj. porque. **b. of,** por, por causa de.

beckon, vb. chamar com gesto.

become, vb. tornar-se, ficar; ficar bem.

becoming, adj. apropriado. **be b.,** assentar bem.

bed, n. cama f.; (river) leito m.

bedbug, n. percevejo m.

bedridden, adj. acamado.

bedrock, n. leito de rocha firme m.; (fig.) alicerce m.

bedroom, n. quarto m.

bedside, n. cabeceira f.

bedspread, n. colcha f.

bee, n. abelha f.

beef, n. carne de boi f.; (sl.) bronca f.

beefsteak, n. bife m.

beehive, n. colmeia f., cortiço m.

beer, n. cerveja f., chope m.

beet, n. beterraba f.

beetle, n. besouro m.

befall, vb. acontecer a.

befitting, adj. conveniente; condizente.

before, 1. adv. antes. **2.** prep. antes de; diante de; perante. **3.** conj. antes que.

beforehand, adv. de antemão, antecipadamente.

befriend, vb. tornar-se amigo de.

befuddle, vb. confundir, aturdir.

beg, vb. rogar, suplicar; mendigar.

beget, vb. gerar; puxar.

beggar, n. mendigo -ga.

begin, vb. começar. **b. to,** começar a.

beginner, n. principiante m.f.

beginning, n. princípio, começo m.

begrudge, vb. invejar; dar de má vontade.

behalf, n. favor. m. **in b. of,** a favor de; **on b. of,** em nome de.

behave, vb. portar-se, comportar-se.

behavior, n. comportamento m., conduta f.

behead, vb. degolar.

behest, n. mandado m., ordem f.

behind, 1. n. (coll.) traseiro m. **2.** adv. atrás, para trás. **be b.,** estar atrasado. **3.** prep. atrás de.

behold, 1. vb. contemplar. **2.** interj. eis (aqui); eis que.

beholden, adj. obrigado, devedor.

beige, n. bege.

being, n. existência f.; ser m. **human b.,** ser humano m.

belabor, vb. repisar, ridicularizar.

belated, adj. tardio.

belch, 1. n. arroto m. **2.** vb. arrotar.

beleaguer, vb. sitiar, assediar.

belfry, n. campanário m., torre f.

Belgian, adj., n. belga m.f.

Belgium, n. Bélgica f.

belie, vb. desmentir.

belief, n. opinião f.; crença f.

believable, adj. crível, acreditável.

believe, vb. crer, acreditar; achar. **make b.,** fazer de conta.

believer, n. crente m.f.; devoto -ta m.

belittle, vb. menosprezar.

bell, n. sino m.; (door) campainha, sineta f.

bellboy, n. moço de recados, mensageiro m.

belligerent, adj. beligerante.

bellow, 1. berro m. **2.** vb. berrar.

bellows, n. fole m.

bell tower, n. campanário m.

belly, n. barriga f.; ventre m.

belong, vb. pertencer.

belongings, n.pl. pertences m.pl., posses f.pl.

beloved, adj. querido, caro.

below, 1. adv. embaixo, abaixo. **2.** prep. debaixo de, sob.

belt, n. cinto m.; faixa f.; (sl.) tapa m.; (sl.) (liquor) talagada f. **2.** vb. (sl.) dar um tapa em.

bemoan, vb. lamentar.

bench, n. banco m.

bend, 1. n. curva, volta f. **2.** vb. curvar, dobrar.

beneath, prep. sob, debaixo de.

benediction, n. bênção f.

benefactor -tress, n. benfeitor -ra.

beneficial, adj. benéfico; útil.

beneficiary, n. beneficiário -ria.

benefit, 1. n. benefício m.; proveito m. **2.** vb. favorecer; beneficiar(-se).

benevolence, n. benevolência f.

benevolent, adj. benevolente.

benign, adj. benigno.

bent, 1. adj. curvado; torto. **b. on,** resolvido a. **2.** n. propensão f.

bequeath, vb. legar.

bequest, n. herança f.

berate, vb. repreender.

beret, n. boina f.

berry, n. **mulberry,** amora f.; **raspberry,** framboesa f.; **strawberry,** morango m.

berserk, adj. louco, frenético.

berth, n. (bed) beliche m.; (dock) ancoradouro m.; vaga f.

beseech, vb. suplicar, rogar.

beset, vb. assediar.

beside, prep. ao lado de.

besides, 1. adv. além disso. **2.** prep. além de.

besiege, vb. sitiar, assediar.

besmirch, vb. manchar.

best, adj., adv. melhor. **at b.,** no melhor dos casos; **do one's b.,** fazer o máximo, caprichar.

best man, n. padrinho (de casamento) m.

bestow, vb. conferir.

bet, 1. n. aposta f. **2.** vb. apostar. **I'll b. that,** vai ver que.

Bethlehem, n. Belém.

betoken, vb. indicar.

betray, vb. trair, atraiçoar.; enganar; revelar.

betrayal, n. traição f.

betrothed, adj. noivo. **become b.,** ficar noivo.

betrothal, n. noivado m.

better, 1. adj., adv. melhor. **2.** vb. melhorar.

between, 1. adv. no meio. **2.** prep. entre; no meio de.

beverage, n. bebida f.

beware, 1. vb. ter/tomar cuidado. **2.** interj. cuidado!

bewilder, vb. confundir, aturdir.

bewitch, vb. enfeitiçar.

beyond, 1. n. além m. **2.** adv. além. **3.** prep. além de.

bias, 1. n. preconceito m.; (sewing) viés m. **2.** vb. predispor, influenciar.

bib, n. babadouro m.

Bible, n. Bíblia f.

biblical, adj. bíblico.

bibliography, n. bibliografia f.

bicarbonate, n. bicarbonato m.

bicentennial, adj., n. bicentenário m.

bicker, vb. discutir, altercar.

bicycle, n. bicicleta f.

bid, 1. n. lanço m., oferta f.; convite m. **2.** vb. oferecer; mandar.

bidder, n. arrematante m.f.; lançador -ra.

bide, vb. aguardar.

bidet, n. bidê m.

biennial, adj. bienal.

bier, n. esquife, ataúde m.

bifocal, adj. bifocal.

big, adj. grande.

bigamist, n. bígamo -ma.

bigamy, n. bigamia f.

bigger, adj. maior.

biggest, adj. maior.

bigot, n. intolerante m.f.

bigoted, adj. intolerante.

bigotry, *n.* intolerância *f.*; preconceito *m.*

big shot, *n.* mandachuva *m.*

big toe, *n.* dedão *m.*

bigwig, *n.* mandachuva *m.*

bikini, *n.* biquíni *m.*

bilateral, *adj.* bilateral.

bile, *n.* bílis *f.*

bilingual, *adj.* bilíngüe.

bilk, *vb.* lograr, tapear.

bill, **1.** *n.* conta, nota *f.*; fatura *f.*; (money) nota *f.*; cartaz *m.*; volante *m.*; projeto de lei *m.*; (beak) bico *m.* **2.** *vb.* cobrar.

billboard, *n.* outdoor *m.*

billfold, *n.* carteira *f.*

billiards, *n.pl.* bilhar *m.*

billion, *n.* bilhão *m.*

bill of exchange, *n.* letra de câmbio *f.*

bill of health, *n.* atestado de saúde *m.*

bill of lading, *n.* conhecimento de embarque *m.*

bill of sale, *n.* escritura de venda *f.*

billow, *vb.* enfunar-se.

billy club, *n.* cassetete *m.*

billy goat, *n.* bode *m.*

bimonthly, *adj.* bimestral, bimensal.

bin, *n.* caixa *f.*; depósito *m.*

binary, *adj.* binário.

bind, *vb.* amarrar; obrigar; encadernar.

binding, *n.* encadernação *f.*

binge, *n.* (*sl.*) farra *f.*; bebedeira *f.*

binoculars, *n.* binóculo *m.*

biodegradable, *adj.* biodegradável.

biography, *n.* biografia *f.*

biologist, *n.* biólogo -ga.

biology, *n.* biologia *f.*

bird, *n.* pássaro *m.*; ave *f.* **b. of prey**, ave de rapina *f.*

bird cage, *n.* gaiola *f.*

birdseed, *n.* alpiste *m.*, -sta *f.*

birth, *n.* nascimento *m.*; parto *m.* **by b.**, de nascença; **give b. to**, dar à luz.

birth certificate, *n.* certidão de nascimento *f.*

birth control, *n.* controle de natalidade *m.*

birthday, *n.* aniversário, natalício *m.*

birthmark, *n.* sinal *m.*

birthrate, *n.* natalidade *f.*

bisect, *n.* dividir ao meio.

bisexual, *adj.*, *n.* bissexual *m.f.*

bishop, *n.* bispo *m.*

bishopric, *n.* bispado *m.*

bison, *n.* bisão *m.*

bit, *n.* pedacinho, bocado *m.*; broca *f.*; (horse) bocado *m.*; (*comput.*) bit *m.* **a b.**, um pouco.

bitch, *n.* cadela *f.*

bite, **1.** *n.* mordida *f.*; picada *f.*; (food) bocado *m.* **2.** *vb.* morder; picar.

biting, *adj.* penetrante; mordaz.

bitter, *adj.* amargo.

bitterness, *n.* amargura *f.*

bivouac, **1.** *n.* bivaque *m.* **2.** *vb.* bivacar.

biweekly, **1.** *adj.* quinzenal. **2.** *n.* quinzenário *m.*

bizarre, *adj.* esquisito.

blab, *vb.* (*sl.*) fofocar; dar com a língua nos dentes.

blabbermouth, *n.* língua-de-trapo *m f.*

black, **1.** *adj.* preto, negro. **2.** *n.* (person) preto -ta, negro -gra.

blackberry, *n.* amora preta *f.*

blackbird, *n.* melro *m.*

blackboard, *n.* quadro-negro *m.*, lousa *f.*

blacken, *vb.* enegrecer, escurecer.

black eye, *n.* tapa-olho *m.*

black hole, *n.* buraco negro *m.*

black list, *n.* lista negra *f.*, listão *m.*

blackmail, **1.** *n.* chantagem *f.* **2.** *vb.* chantagear.

black market, *n.* mercado negro/paralelo *m.*

blackness, *n.* negrura *f.*, negrume *m.*

blackout, *n.* blecaute *m.*; desmaio *m.*

blacksmith, *n.* ferreiro *m.*

bladder, *n.* bexiga *f.*

blade, *n.* lâmina, folha *f.*

blame, **1.** *n.* culpa *f.* **2.** *vb.* culpar. **be to b. for**, ter a culpa de.

bland, *adj.* brando; insosso.

blank, **1.** *adj.* branco; em branco; (cartridge) de festim. **2.** *m.* lacuna *f.*; cartucho de festim.

blunt

blanket, *n.* cobertor *m.*

blare, 1. *n.* clangor *m.* 2. *vb.* clangorar.

blasphemy, *n.* blasfêmia *f.*

blast, 1. *n.* rajada *f.*; (horn) toque *m.*; explosão *f.* **full b.**, a todo o vapor. 2. *vb.* fazer explodir. **b. off**, arrancar.

blastoff, *n.* lançamento *m.*

blatant, *adj.* manifesto, flagrante.

blaze, 1. *n.* chama *f.*; incêndio *m.* 2. *vb.* arder.

blazing, *adj.* flamejante; resplandecente.

bleach, 1. *n.* branqueamento *m.* 2. *vb.* branquear.

bleachers, *n.pl.* arquibancadas *f.pl.*

bleak, *adj.* árido; desolado; triste.

bleary, *adj.* turvo.

bleat, 1. *n.* balido *m.* 2. *vb.* balir.

bleed, *vb.* sangrar.

blemish, *n.* mancha *f.*; jaça *f.*

blend, 1. *n.* mistura *f.* 2. *vb.* misturar(-se).

blender, *n.* liqüidificador *m.*

bless, *vb.* abençoar, benzer.

blessed, *adj.* bendito.

blessing, *n.* bênção *f.*

blight, 1. *n.* praga *f.* 2. *vb.* empestar; frustrar.

blimp, *n.* dirigível *m.*

blind, 1. *adj.* cego. 2. *vb.* cegar.

blind alley, *n.* beco sem saída *m.*

blinders, *n.pl.* antolhos *m.pl.*

blindfold, 1. *n.* venda *f.* 2. *vb.* vendar.

blindness, *n.* cegueira *f.*

blink, 1. *n.* piscadela *f.* 2. *vb.* piscar.

blinker, *n.* (car) pisca-pisca *m.*

bliss, *n.* felicidade *f.*

blister, *n.* bolha *f.*

blithe, *adj.* alegre.

blizzard, *n.* nevasca *f.*

bloat, *vb.* inchar.

bloc, *n.* bloco *m.*

block, 1. *n.* bloco *m.*; (street) quarteirão *m.*, quadra *f.*; (wood) cepo *m.* 2. *vb.* bloquear; obstruir.

blockade, 1. *n.* bloqueio *m.* 2. *vb.* bloquear.

blond, *adj.* louro, loiro *m.*

blood, *n.* sangue *m.*; parentesco *m.*

bloodhound, *n.* sabujo *m.*

bloodless, *adj.* exangue; sem derramamento de sangue.

bloodletting, *n.* sangria *f.*

blood pressure, *n.* pressão arterial/sangüínea.

bloodshed, *n.* derramamento de sangue *m.*; carnificina *f.*

bloodshot, *adj.* (eye) injetado.

bloodthirsty, *adj.* sangüinário, sangüinolento.

blood type, *n.* tipo sangüíneo *m.*

blood vessel, *n.* vaso sangüíneo *m.*

bloody, *adj.* ensangüentado; sangrento.

bloom, 1. *n.* flor *f.*; florescência *f.* 2. *vb.* florescer.

blooming, *adj.* em flor.

blossom, 1. *n.* flor *f.* 2. *vb.* florescer.

blot, 1. *n.* mancha *f.*, borrão *m.* 2. *vb.* manchar, borrar.

blotch, *n.* mancha (na pele) *f.*

blotter, *n.* mata-borrão *m.*

blouse, *n.* blusa *f.*

blow, 1. *n.* golpe *m.*; sopro *m.* 2. *vb.* soprar; (horn) tocar. **b. one's nose**, assoar o nariz; **b. up**, explodir.

blowout, *n.* pneu furado *m.*; (*sl.*) festão *m.*

blowtorch, *n.* maçarico *m.*

blowup, *n.* explosão *f.*; acesso de raiva *m.*; (*phot.*) ampliação *f.*

blubber, 1. *n.* gordura de baleia *f.* 2. *vb.* chorar.

bludgeon, 1. *n.* cacete *m.* 2. *vb.* maçar.

blue, 1. *adj.* azul; triste. 2. *n.pl.* tristeza *f.*

bluebird, *n.* azulão *m.*

bluejay, *n.* gaio *m.*

blueprint, *n.* heliografia, cianotipia *f.*

bluff, 1. *n.* blefe *m.* 2. *vb.* blefar.

blunder, 1. *n.* erro *m.*, mancada *f.* 2. *vb.* errar, dar uma mancada.

blunt, 1. *adj.* embotado; brusco. 2. *vb.* embotar.

blur, 1. *n.* falta de clareza *f.* **2.** *vb.* embaçar.

blush, 1. *n.* rubor *m.* **2.** *vb.* corar.

bluster, 1. *n.* fanfarronada *f.* **2.** *vb.* fanfarronar.

boar, *n.* javali *m.*

board, 1. *n.* tábua, prancha *f.*; (game) tabuleiro *m.*; pensão *f.*; conselho *m.* room and b., casa e comida *f.* **2.** abordar; (house) hospedar.

boarder, *n.* pensionista *m.f.*; agregado -da.

boarding house, *n.* pensão *f.*

boarding pass, *n.* cartão de embarque *m.*

boarding school, *n.* internato *m.*

board of directors, *n.* conselho diretor *m.*, junta diretora *f.*

boast, 1. *n.* bazófia *f.* **2.** *vb.* gabar-se, jactar-se, contar vantagem.

boastful, *adj.* jactancioso.

boat, *n.* barco, bote *m.*, lancha *f.*

bob, *vb.* flutuar; cortar rente.

bobbin, *n.* bobina *f.*

bobby pin, *n.* grampo (de cabelo) *m.*

bode, *vb.* augurar.

bodice, *n.* corpinho, corpete *m.*

bodily, *adj.* corpóreo.

body, *n.* corpo *m.*; (dead) cadáver *m.*

bodyguard, *n.* guarda-costas *m.*

bog, 1. *n.* pântano, brejo *m.* **2.** *vb.* **b. down,** atolar-se.

boggle, *vb.* confundir, deixar perplexo.

bogus, *adj.* falso, (sl.) fajuto, frio.

bogyman, *n.* bicho-papão *m.*

bohemian, *adj., n.* boêmio -mia.

boil, 1. *n.* fervura *f.*; (med.) furúnculo *m.* **2.** *vb.* ferver; aferventar.

boiler, *n.* caldeira *f.*

boisterous, *adj.* barulhento.

bold, *adj.* arrojado; (type) negrito.

boldness, *n.* arrojo *m.*, audácia *f.*

Bolivian, *adj., n.* boliviano -a.

bologna, *n.* salsichão *m.*

bolster, 1. *n.* travesseiro *m.* **2.** *vb.* apoiar, reforçar.

bolt, 1. *n.* perno *m.*; (door) ferrolho *m.*; (lightning) raio *m.* **2.** *vb.* aferrolhar.

bomb, 1. *n.* bomba *f.* **2.** *vb.* bombardear.

bombard, *vb.* bombardear.

bombastic, *adj.* bombástico.

bomber, *n.* (plane) bombardeiro *m.*

bombing, *n.* bombardeio *m.*

bombshell, *n.* bomba *f.*

bonbon, *n.* bombom *m.*

bond, *n.* vínculo *m.*; (com.) título, bônus *m.*; (pl.) cativeiro *m.*

bondage, *n.* escravidão *f.*

bonded, *adj.* garantido.

bone, 1. *n.* osso *m.* **2.** *vb.* desossar.

bonfire, *n.* fogueira *f.*

bonnet, *n.* touca *f.*; toucado *m.*

bonus, *n.* bonificação *f.*, abono *m.*

bony, *adj.* ossudo.

book, 1. *n.* livro *m.* **2.** *vb.* reservar; contratar.

bookbinding, *n.* encadernação *f.*

bookcase, *n.* prateleira, estante *f.*

bookkeeper, *n.* guarda-livros *m.f.*

bookkeeping, *n.* contabilidade *f.*

booklet, *n.* livrinho, folheto *m.*

book review, *n.* resenha, recensão *f.*

bookseller, *n.* livreiro -ra.

bookshelf, *n.* prateleira, estante *f.*

bookstand, *n.* banca de livros *f.*

bookstore, *n.* livraria *f.*

bookworm, *n.* rato de biblioteca, c.d.f. *m.*

boom, *n.* estrondo *m.*; (naut.) botaló *m.*; boom *m.*

boomerang, *n.* bumerangue *m.*

boon, *n.* dádiva *f.*, benefício *m.*

boor, *n.* rústico, grosseiro *m.*

boost, 1. *n.* ajuda *f.*; aumento *m.* **2.** *vb.* ajudar; alçar; fomentar.

booster, *n.* fomentador -ra; (sport.) torcedor -ra.

boot, *n.* bota *f.*

bootblack, *n.* engraxate *m.*

booth, *n.* cabine *f.*; barraca *f.*

bootlicker, *n. (sl.)* puxa-saco *m.*

booty, *n.* despojos *m.pl.*, presa *f.*

border, **1.** *adj.* fronteiriço. **2.** *n.* fronteira *f.* **3.** *vb.* **b. on**, confinar com.

borderline, **1.** *adj.* fronteiriço; duvidoso. **2.** *n.* fronteira.

bore, **1.** *n.* chateação *f.*; (person) chato *m.* **2.** *vb.* chatear, aborrecer; *(mech.)* perfurar.

bored, *adj.* aborrecido, chateado.

boredom, *n.* tédio, aborrecimento *m.*

boring, *adj.* chato, monótono.

born, *adj.* nascido; nato. **be b.**, nascer.

borrow, *n.* pedir/tomar emprestado.

bosom, *n.* seio, peito *m.*

boss, *n.* chefe *m.f.*, patrão -troa.

bossy, *adj.* mandão.

botanical, *adj.* botânico.

botany, *n.* botânica *f.*

botch, **1.** *n.* trabalho mal feito. **2.** *vb.* fazer um trabalho mal feito.

both, *adj., pron.* ambos -bas; os dois, as duas. **b. . . . and**, tanto . . . como.

bother, **1.** *n.* incômodo *m.*; aborrecimento *m.* **2.** *vb.* incomodar, amolar; preocupar. **b. about**, preocupar-se com.

bothersome, *adj.* incômodo.

bottle, **1.** *n.* garrafa *f.* **2.** *vb.* engarrafar.

bottom, *n.* fundo *m.*; (buttocks) traseiro *m.*

bough, *n.* galho, ramo *m.*

boulder, *n.* penedo *m.*, pedra grande *f.*

boulevard, *n.* bulevar *m.*

bounce, **1.** *n.* pulo, salto *m.* **2.** *vb.* pular, saltar; fazer pular.

bouncer, *n.* leão-de-chácara *m.*

bound, **1.** *adj.* amarrado; preso. **b. for**, com destino a. **2.** *n.* limite *m.*; salto *m.* limitar (com); saltar.

boundary, *n.* fronteira *f.*, limite *m.*

bountiful, *adj.* liberal; abundante.

bounty, *n.* generosidade *f.*; recompensa *f.*

bouquet, *n.* buquê, ramalhete *m.*

bourgeois, *adj., n.* burguês *m.*

bourgeoisie, *n.* burguesia *f.*

bout, *n.* contenda *f.*; *(med.)* ataque *m.*

bow, **1.** *n.* saudação, mesura *f.*; (ship) proa *f.*; (archery, violin) arco *m.*; (ribbon) laço *m.* **2.** *vb.* curvar(-se); fazer mesura.

bowels, *n.* intestinos *m.pl.*, entranhas *f.pl.*

bowl, *n.* tigela *f.*; (wash) bacia *f.*

bowlegged, *adj.* cambaio.

bowling, *n.* boliche *m.*

bow tie, *n.* gravata borboleta *f.*

box, **1.** *n.* caixa *f.*; *(theat.)* camarote *m.* **2.** *vb.* encaixotar; *(sport.)* boxear.

boxcar, *n.* vagão *m.*

boxer, *n.* boxeador *m.*

boxing, *n.* boxe *m.*

box office, *n.* bilheteria *f.*, guichê *m.*

boy, *n.* menino *m.* (older) rapaz, moço *m.*

boycott, **1.** *n.* boicote *m.* **2.** *vb.* boicotar.

boyfriend, *n.* namorado *m.*

boy scout, *n.* escoteiro *m.*

bra, *n.* sutiã *m.*

brace, *n.* - esteio, suporte *m.*; grampo *m.*; *(pl.)* suspensórios *m.pl.* **2.** *vb.* reforçar.

bracelet, *n.* bracelete *m.*, pulseira *f.*

bracket, *n.* suporte *m.*; faixa *f.*; *(pl.)* colchetes *m.pl.*

brad, *n.* preguinho, grampo *m.*

brag, **1.** *n.* gabolice *f.* **2.** *vb.* gabar-se, contar vantagem.

braggart, *n.* faroleiro *m.*, gabola *m.f.*, fanfarrão -rona.

braid, **1.** *n.* trança *f.* **2.** *vb.* trançar.

brain, *n.* cérebro *m.*; *(sl.)* cuca *f.*

brainwashing, *n.* lavagem cerebral *f.*

brainy, *adj.* inteligente.

brake, **1.** *n.* freio *m.*, *(P.)* trava *f.* **2.** *vb.* frear.

bran, *n.* farelo *m.*

branch, **1.** *n.* galho, ramo *m.* **b.**

office, filial *f.* 2. *vb.* ramificar-se. **b. out**, estender-se.

brand, 1. *n.* marca *f.* 2. *vb.* marcar; *(fig.)* tachar.

branding iron, *n.* ferrete *m.*

brandish, *vb.* brandir.

brand-new, *adj.* novo em folha.

brandy, *n.* brande *m.*, aguardente *f.*

brash, *adj.* impetuoso.

brass, *n.* latão, bronze *m.*

brassiere, *n.* sutiã *m.*

brat, *n.* criança traquinas *f.*, capeta *m.*

bravado, *n.* bravata *f.*

brave, *adj.* bravo, valente, corajoso.

bravery, *n.* bravura, valentia, coragem *f.*

brawl, 1. *n.* baderna, briga *f.* 2. *vb.* brigar.

brawn, *n.* músculo *m.*; muque *m.*

brawny, *adj.* forte.

bray, 1. *n.* zurro *m.* 2. *vb.* zurrar.

brazen, *adj.* descarado, desavergonhado.

Brazil, *n.* Brasil *m.*

Brazilian, *adj.*, *n.* brasileiro -ra.

Brazil nut, *n.* castanha-do-pará *f.*

brazilwood, *n.* pau-brasil *m.*

breach, 1. *n.* brecha *f.*; infração *f.* 2. *vb.* abrir brecha em; quebrar.

bread, *n.* pão *m.*

breaded, *adj.* à milanesa.

breadth, *n.* largura *f.*

break, 1. *n.* quebra *f.*; ruptura *f.*; intervalo *m.*; folga *f.*; oportunidade *f.* **give a b.**, dar uma colher de chá. 2. *vb.* quebrar; violar.

breakable, *adj.* quebradiço, frágil.

breakdown, *n.* colapso *m.*; pane, avaria *f.*; classificação *f.*

breakfast, 1. *n.* café da manhã, café, *(P.)* pequeno almoço *m.* 2. *vb.* tomar o café da manhã.

breakthrough, *n.* progresso, avanço *m.*

breakup, *n.* desintegração, dissolução *f.*

breakwater, *n.* quebra-mar *m.*

breast, *n.* peito, seio *m.*

breast-feed, *vb.* amamentar.

breath, *n.* fôlego *m.*; hálito *m.*; sopro *m.* **catch one's b.**, tomar fôlego; **hold one's b.**, prender a respiração; **out of b.**, esbaforido.

breathe, *vb.* respirar.

breather, *n.* descanso *m.*, folga *f.*

breathing, *n.* respiração *f.*

breeches, *n.pl.* calça(s) *f.(pl.)*

breed, 1. *n.* raça *f.* 2. *vb.* procriar; engendrar; criar; educar.

breeder, *n.* criador -ra.

breeding, *n.* reprodução *f.*; criação *f.*; educação *f.*

breeze, *n.* brisa *f.*

brevity, *n.* brevidade *f.*

brew, 1. *n.* bebida *f.*; cerveja *f.* 2. *vb.* fazer (cerveja); preparar (chá, etc.).

brewer, *n.* cervejeiro *m.*

brewery, *n.* cervejaria *f.*

bribe, 1. *n.* suborno *m.*, *(sl.)* bola *f.* 2. *vb.* subornar.

bribery, *n.* suborno *m.*

brick, *n.* tijolo *m.*

bricklayer, *n.* pedreiro *m.*

bridal, *adj.* nupcial.

bride, *n.* noiva *f.*

bridegroom, *n.* noivo *m.*

bridesmaid, *n.* dama de honor/honra *f.*

bridge, *n.* ponte *f.*; (cards) bridge *m.*

bridle, *n.* brida, rédea *f.*

brief, 1. *adj.* breve. 2. *n.* auto *m.* 3. *vb.* dar instruções, informar.

briefcase, *n.* pasta, maleta *f.*

briefing, *n.* instruções *f.pl.*

brier, *n.* sarça *f.*

brigade, *n.* brigada *f.*

bright, *adj.* brilhante, claro.

brighten, *vb.* abrilhantar; alegrar.

brightness, *n.* brilho *m.*, claridade *f.*

brilliance, *n.* brilho *m.*; inteligência *f.*

brilliant, *adj.* brilhante.

brim, *n.* borda *f.*; (hat) aba *f.*

brine, *n.* salmoura *f.*; água salgada *f.*

bring, *vb.* trazer. **b. about**, efetuar; **b. up**, criar.

brink, *n.* beira *f.*

briny, *adj.* salgado.

brisk, *adj.* vivo, enérgico.

bristle, *n.* cerda *f.*

Britain, *n.* Grã-Bretanha *f.*

British, *adj.* britânico.

Briton, *n.* britânico -ca.

brittle, *adj.* frágil, quebradiço.

broach, *vb.* mencionar, abordar.

broad, *adj.* largo, amplo.

broadcast, 1. *n.* transmissão *f.* **2.** *vb.* transmitir.

broadcasting, *n.* radiodifusão *f.*

broaden, *vb.* alargar, ampliar.

broadminded, *adj.* tolerante, liberal.

broccoli, *n.* brócolis *m.pl.*

brochure, *n.* brochura *f.* ; prospecto *m.*

broil, *vb.* grelhar, assar.

broiler, *n.* grelha, assadeira *f.*

broke, *adj. (sl.)* duro, limpo.

broken, *adj.* quebrado; (car, machine) enguiçado.

broken-hearted, *adj.* abatido.

broker, *n.* corretor *m.*

brokerage, *n.* corretagem *f.*

bronchitis, *n.* bronquite *f.*

bronze, *n.* bronze *m.*

brooch, *n.* broche *m.*

brood, 1. *n.* ninhada, cria *f.* **2.** *vb.* cismar.

brook, *n.* riacho, córrego *m.*

broom, *n.* vassoura *f.*

broth, *n.* caldo *m.*

brothel, *n.* bordel *m.*

brother, *n.* irmão *m.*

brotherhood, *n.* fraternidade *f.* ; (religious) confraria *f.*

brother-in-law, *n.* cunhado *m.*

brotherly, *adj.* fraternal.

brow, *n.* testa, fronte *f.* ; sobrancelha *f.*

browbeat, *vb.* intimidar.

brown, *adj.* marrom, castanho; moreno.

browse, *vb.* folhear (livros).

bruise, 1. *n.* contusão *f.* **2.** *vb.* contundir.

brunet, *adj., n.* moreno -na; de cabelos castanhos.

brunt, *n.* impacto *m.* , maior peso ou parte.

brush, 1. *n.* escova *f.* ; (paint) pincel *m.* ; mato *m.* **2.** *vb.* escovar.

brusque, *adj.* brusco.

Brussels, *n.* Bruxelas.

brutal, *adj.* brutal.

brutality, *n.* brutalidade *f.*

brutalize, *vb.* brutalizar.

brute, *adj., n.* bruto *m.*

bubble, 1. *n.* bolha, borbulha *f.* **2.** *vb.* borbulhar.

bubble gum, *n.* chiclete *m.* , goma de mascar *f.*

buck, 1. *n.* (deer) gamo, cervo *m.* ; corcovo *m.* ; (money) prata *f.* **2.** *vb.* corcovear.

bucket, *n.* balde *m.* , caçamba *f.*

buckle, 1. *n.* fivela *f.* **2.** *vb.* afivelar. **b. down,** empenhar-se.

buckwheat, *n.* trigo sarraceno *m.*

bud, 1. *n.* botão *m.* ; broto *m.* **2.** *vb.* brotar.

Buddhism, *n.* budismo *m.*

buddy, *n.* amigo *m.* , *(sl.)* chapa *m.*

budge, *vb.* mover(-se).

budget, 1. *n.* orçamento *m.* **2.** *vb.* orçar.

buff, *vb.* polir.

buffalo, *n.* búfalo *m.*

buffer, *n.* pára-choque *m.*

buffet, *n.* (food) bufê *m.* ; (furniture) aparador *m.*

buffoon, *n.* bufão *m.*

bug, 1. *n.* inseto, bicho *m.* ; *(sl.)* entusiasta *m.f.* ; *(sl.)* sistema de escuta clandestina *m.* **2.** *vb. (sl.)* amolar; instalar sistema de escuta clandestina em; escutar clandestinamente.

buggy, *n.* carruagem *m.* ; carrinho (para bebês) *m.*

bugle, *n.* corneta *f.* , clarim *m.*

build, 1. *n.* construção *f.* ; talhe *m.* **2.** *vb.* construir.

builder, *n.* construtor *m.*

building, *n.* edifício, prédio *m.*

built-in, *n.* embutido.

bulb, *n.* lâmpada *f.* ; *(bot.)* bulbo *m.*

Bulgarian, *adj., n.* búlgaro *m.*

bulge, 1. *n.* bojo *m.* , saliência *f.* **2.** *vb.* bojar(-se).

bulging, *adj.* bojudo, protuberante.

bulk, *n.* volume *m.* ; massa *f.* ; grosso *m.* ; maioria *f.*

bulky, *adj.* volumoso, avultado.

bull, *n.* touro *m.* ; *(sl.)* (bunk) chute *m.*

bulldozer, n. buldôzer m.

bullet, n. bala f.

bulletin, n. boletim m. **b. board,** quadro de avisos m.

bulletproof, adj. à prova de bala.

bullfight, n. tourada f.

bullfighter, n. toureiro m.

bullfighting, n. tauromaquia f.

bullring, n. praça de touros f.

bull's-eye, n. mosca f.

bully, n. valentão, bamba m.

bulwark, n. baluarte m.

bum, 1. n. vagabundo, malandro m. **2.** vb. (cigarette, etc.) filar.

bump, 1. n. baque m.; pancada f.; (swelling) inchaço m. **2.** vb. **b. into,** dar com, chocar em; **b. off,** (sl.) dar cabo de.

bumper, n. pára-choque m.

bumpkin, n. caipira, jeca m.f.

bun, n. pãozinho m.; (hair) carrapicho m.

bunch, 1. n. cacho m., penca f.; porção f.

bundle, 1. n. trouxa f.; fardo m.; molho m. **b. up,** agasalhar.

bungalow, n. bangalô m.

bungle, 1. n. erro m.; trabalho mal feito m. **2.** vb. estragar; fazer serviço mal feito.

bunk, n. beliche m.; (sl.) papo m.

bunny, n. coelhinho m.

buoy, n. bóia f.

buoyant, adj. flutuante; alegre, vivaz.

burden, 1. n. carga f., fardo m.; ônus m. **2.** vb. carregar.

burdensome, adj. pesado.

bureau, n. (furniture) cômoda f.; agência f., departamento m.

bureaucracy, n. burocracia f.

bureaucrat, n. burocrata m.f.

bureaucratic, adj. burocrático.

burglar, n. ladrão, gatuno m.

burglar alarm, n. pega-ladrão m.

burglarize, vb. roubar, limpar.

burglary, n. roubo m.

burial, n. enterro m.

burlap, n. aniagem f.

burlesque, 1. adj. burlesco. **2.** n. paródia f.; revista teatral f. **3.** vb. parodiar.

burly, adj. corpulento.

Burma, n. Birmânia f.

burn, 1. n. queimadura f. **2.** vb. queimar; arder.

burner, n. bico de gás m.

burning, 1. adj. ardente. **2.** n. queima f.

burp, 1. n. arroto m. **2.** vb. arrotar.

burrow, 1. n. toca f. **2.** vb. fazer toca.

burst, 1. n. estouro m.; (gunfire) rajada f. **2.** vb. estourar; rebentar. **b. into,** irromper em.

bury, n. enterrar.

bus, n. ônibus m. **catch the b.,** pegar o ônibus.

bush, n. arbusto m.; (forest) mato m.

bushel, n. alqueire m.

bushy, adj. matoso; cerrado.

business, n. negócio(s) m.(pl.), comércio m.; empresa f.; profissão f. **b. hours,** expediente m.

businessman, n. homem de negócios, negociante m.

businesswoman, n. mulher de negócios f.

bust, 1. n. busto m.; peitos m.pl. **2.** vb. (coll.) quebrar.

bustle, n. alvoroço m., azáfama f.

busy, 1. adj. ocupado; (street) movimentado. **2.** vb. **b. oneself,** ocupar-se.

busybody, n. bisbilhoteiro -ra, xereta m.f.

but, 1. prep. exceto. **2.** conj. mas, porém; senão.

butcher, n. açougueiro m.; (fig.) assassino m. **b.'s shop,** açougue m.

butchery, n. chacina, carnificina f.

butler, n. mordomo m.

butt, 1. n. fundo m. (cigarette) ponta f.; traseiro m., (coll.) bunda f. **2.** vb. dar cabeçada.

butter, n. manteiga f.

butterfly, n. borboleta f.

buttocks, n.pl. nádegas f.pl.; traseiro m.

button, 1. n. botão m. **2.** vb. abotoar.

buttonhole, n. casa de botão f.; botoeira f.

buttress, 1. *n.* apoio, suporte *m.* **2.** *vb.* reforçar, apoiar.

buxom, *adj.* robusto; peituda.

buy, 1. *n.* compra *f.* **2.** *vb.* comprar.

buyer, *n.* comprador -ra.

buzz, 1. *n.* zumbido, zunido *m.* **2.** *vb.* zumbir, zunir.

by, *prep.* por; (near) perto de, ao lado de; (time) para. **b. and b.,** daqui/daí a pouco.

bye-bye, *interj.* até logo!, tchau!

bygone, *adj.* passado.

bylaw, *n.* estatuto, regulamento *m.*

bypass, 1. *n.* desvio *m.* **2.** *vb.* desviar.

by-product, *n.* subproduto *m.*

bystander, *n.* circunstante *m.f.*

byte, *n.* byte *m.*

C

cab, *n.* carro de praça, táxi *m.*

cabaret. *n.* cabaré *m.*

cabbage, *n.* repolho *m.*

cabin, *n.* cabana *f.* ; (ship) camarote *m.*

cabinet, *n.* gabinete *m.* ; armário *m.*

cabinetmaker, *n.* marceneiro *m.*

cable, *n.* cabo *m.* ; cabograma *m.*

cacao, *n.* cacau *m.*

cache, *n.* esconderijo *m.* ; mantimentos escondidos *m.pl.*

cackle, 1. *n.* cacarejo *m.* **2.** *vb.* cacarejar.

cactus, *n.* cacto *m.*

cad, *n.* velhaco *m.* ; grosseirão *m.*

cadaver, *n.* cadáver *m.*

cadence, *n.* cadência *f.*

cadet, *n.* cadete *m.*

cadre, *n.* quadro *m.*

caesarean section, *n.* cesariana *f.*

café, *n.* café *m.*

cafeteria, *n.* restaurante *m.*

caffeine, *n.* cafeína *f.*

cage, *n.* (bird) gaiola *f.* ; (large) jaula *f.*

cagey, *adj.* astucioso, esperto.

cajole, *vb.* lisonjear.

cake, *n.* bolo *m.*

calamity, *n.* calamidade *f.*

calcium, *n.* cálcio *m.*

calculate, *vb.* calcular.

calculating, *adj.* calculista.

calculation, *n.* cálculo *m.*

calculator, *n.* calculadora *f.*

calculus, *n.* cálculo *m.*

caldron, *n.* caldeira *f.*, caldeirão *m.*

calendar, *n.* calendário *m.*

calf, *n.* bezerro *m.* ; barriga (da perna) *f.*

caliber, *n.* calibre *m.* ; qualidade *f.*

calibrate, *vb.* calibrar.

calico, *n.* chita *f.*

caliper, *n.* compasso de calibre, calibrador *m.*

calisthenics, *n.* calistenia *f.*

calk, *vb.* calafetar.

calking, *n.* calafeto *m.*

call, 1. *n.* chamada *f.*, -do *m.* ; grito *m.* ; visita *f.* ; (phone) ligação *f.*, telefonema *m.* **2.** *vb.* chamar; gritar; (phone) ligar (para), telefonar (para); convocar. **c. off,** cancelar; **c. on,** visitar.

caller, *n.* visitante *m.f.* ; chamador -ra.

calling, *n.* vocação *f.* **c. card,** cartão de visita *m.*

callous, *adj.* caloso; insensível.

callow, *adj.* inexperiente.

callus, *n.* calo *m.*, calosidade *f.*

calm, 1. *adj.* calmo, tranqüilo. **2.** *n.* calma *f.* **3.** *vb.* acalmar.

calorie, *n.* caloria *f.*

calumniate, *vb.* caluniar.

Calvary, *n.* Calvário *m.*

camaraderie, *n.* camaradagem *f.*

Cambodia, *n.* Camboja *m.*

camel, *n.* camelo *m.*

camellia, *n.* camélia *f.*

cameo, *n.* camafeu *m.*

camera, *n.* máquina (fotográfica), câmara *f.*

Cameroons, *n.* Camarões *m.pl.*

camouflage, 1. *n.* camuflagem *f.* **2.** camuflar.

camp, 1. *n.* campo *m.* ; acampamento *m.* **2.** *vb.* acampar, fazer camping.

campaign, 1. *n.* campanha *f.* **2.** *vb.* fazer campanha.

campfire, *n.* fogueira *f.*

camping, *n.* camping *m.*

campus, *n.* campus *m.*, cidade universitária *f.*

can, *vb.* (be able) poder.

can, 1. *n.* lata *f.* **c. opener,** abridor de lata *m.* **2.** *vb.* enlatar.

Canaan, *n.* Canaã *m.*

Canada, *n.* Canadá *m.*

Canadian, *adj., n.m.f.* canadense.

canal, *n.* canal *m.*

canard, *n.* boato falso *m.*

canary, *n.* canário *m.*

canasta, *n.* canastra *f.*

cancan, *n.* cancã *m.*

cancel, *vb.* cancelar.

cancellation, *n.* cancelamento *m.*

cancer, *n.* câncer *m.*; (*cap.*) Câncer, Caranguejo *m.*

cancerous, *adj.* canceroso.

candelabrum, *n.* candelabro *m.*

candid, *adj.* franco, aberto.

candidacy, *n.* candidatura *f.*

candidate, *n.* candidato *m.*

candle, *n.* vela *f.*

candleholder, *n.* castiçal *m.*

candor, *n.* franqueza, sinceridade *f.*

candy, *n.* doce *m.*; bala *f.*; bombom *m.*

cane, *n.* bastão *m.*, bengala *f.*; (sugar) cana *f.*

canine, 1. *adj.* canino. **2.** *n.* cachorro *m.*; (tooth) canino *m.*

canister, *n.* lata *f.*; caixa de metralha *f.*

canker, *n.* úlcera *f.*

canned goods, *n.pl.* conservas *f.pl.*, enlatados *m.pl.*

cannery, *n.* fábrica de conservas *f.*

cannibal, *n.* antropófago, canibal *m.*

cannon, *n.* canhão *m.*

canny, *adj.* sagaz; prudente.

canoe, *n.* canoa *f.*

canon, *n.* cânon, -ne *m.*

canopy, *n.* dossel *m.*

cant, *n.* gíria *f.*; jargão *m.*

cantaloupe, *n.* cantalupo *m.*

cantankerous, *adj.* rabugento.

canteen, *n.* cantina *f.*

canter, 1. *n.* meio galope *m.* **2.** *vb.* andar a meio galope.

canvas, *n.* lona *f.*; (painting) tela *f.*

canyon, *n.* canhão *m.*

cap, 1. *n.* boné, gorro *m.*; touca *f.*; (lid) tampa *f.* **c. and gown,** borla e capelo *m.* **2.** *vb.* tampar.

capability, *n.* capacidade *f.*

capable, *adj.* capaz; hábil.

capacity, *n.* capacidade *f.*

cape, *n.* capa *f.*; (*geog.*) cabo *m.*

caper, *n.* cambalhota *f.*; travessura *f.*; (*bot.*) alcaparra *f.* **2.** *vb.* cambalhotar.

Cape Verde, *n.* Cabo Verde *m.*

capillary, 1. *adj.* capilar. **2.** *n.* vaso capilar *m.*

capital, 1. *adj.* principal; excelente; maiúsculo. **2.** *n.* (city) capital *f.*; (money) capital *m.*; (letter) maiúscula *f.*

capitalism, *n.* capitalismo *m.*

capitalist, *n.* capitalista *m.f.*

capitalize, *vb.* capitalizar; escrever com maiúscula.

capital punishment, *n.* pena capital/de morte *f.*

capitol, *n.* capitólio *m.*

capitulate, *vb.* capitular, render-se.

caprice, *n.* capricho *m.*

capricious, *adj.* caprichoso.

Capricorn, *n.* Capricórnio *m.*

capsize, *vb.* capotar, emborcar.

capsule, *n.* cápsula *f.*

captain, 1. *n.* capitão *m.* **2.** *vb.* capitanear, chefiar.

caption, *n.* título *m.*, legenda *f.*

captivate, *vb.* cativar.

captive, *adj., n.* cativo -va.

captivity, *n.* cativeiro *m.*

captor, *n.* captor, capturador *m.*

capture, 1. *n.* captura *f.* **2.** *vb.* capturar.

car, *n.* carro *m.*; (train) vagão *m.*

carafe, *n.* garrafa *f.*

caramel, *n.* caramelo *m.*

carat, *n.* quilate *m.*

caravan, *n.* caravana *f.*

carbine, *n.* carabina *f.*

carbohydrate, *n.* hidrato de carbono, carboidrato *m.*

carbon, *n.* carbono *m.* **c. paper,** papel carbono *m.*

carbonated, *adj.* carbonatado.

carbon dioxide, *n.* dióxido de carbono *m.*

carburetor, *n.* carburador *m.*

carcass, n. carcaça f.

carcinogen, n. carcinógeno m.

card, n. cartão m.; ficha f.; (playing) carta f. **play cards**, jogar cartas.

cardboard, n. cartão, papelão m., cartolina f.

cardiac, adj. cardíaco.

cardinal, **1.** adj. (point) cardeal; (number) cardinal. **2.** n. cardeal m.

cardiology, n. cardiologia f.

cardsharp, n. batoteiro -ra.

care, **1.** n. cuidado m., preocupação f. **in c. of**, aos cuidados de; **take c.**, ter/tomar cuidado; **take c. of**, cuidar de, tomar conta de. **2.** vb. cuidar (de); preocupar-se; importar-se. **c. about**, preocupar-se com; **c. for**, cuidar de/ gostar de.

career, n. carreira f.

carefree, adj. despreocupado.

careful, adj. cuidadoso. **be c.**, ter/tomar cuidado.

careless, adj. descuidado, negligente.

carelessness, n. descuido m.

caress, **1.** n. carícia f. **2.** vb. acariciar.

caretaker, n. guarda, zelador m.

cargo, n. carga f.

Caribbean, **1.** caribenho adj. **2.** n. mar das Caraíbas, Caribe m..

caricature, **1.** n. caricatura f. **2.** vb. caricaturar.

carload, n. carrada f.

carnage, n. carnificina f.

carnal, adj. carnal.

carnation, n. cravo m.

carnival, n. carnaval m.; parque de diversões m.

carnivorous, adj. carnívoro.

carol, n. canto, cântico (de Natal) m.

carom, **1.** n. carambola f. **2.** vb. carambolar.

carouse, vb. farrear.

carpenter, n. carpinteiro m.

carpentry, n. carpintaria f.

carpet, **1.** n. carpete, tapete m. **2.** vb. carpetar, atapetar.

carriage, n. carruagem f., coche m.; (bearing) porte m.

carrier, n. carregador m., por-

tador -ra. **c. pigeon**, pombo-correio m.

carrion, n. carniça f.

carrot, n. cenoura f.

carrousel, n. carrossel m.

carry, vb. levar, carregar. **c. out**, realizar.

cart, n. carreta f.; carroça f.

cartel, n. cartel m.

cartilage, n. cartilagem f.

carton, n. caixa de papelão f.

cartoon, n. cartum m.; desenho animado m.

cartoonist, n. cartunista m.f.

cartridge, n. cartucho m.

cartwheel, n. aú m.

carve, vb. talhar; (meat) trinchar.

carver, n. talhador -ra.

carving, n. talha f.

cascade, **1.** n. cascata f. **2.** vb. cascatear.

case, n. caso m.; caixa f.; estojo m. (jur.) causa f. **in any c.**, em todo o caso, seja como for; **in c.**, caso; **in c. of**, em caso de.

cash, **1.** n. dinheiro vivo m. **in c.**, à vista. **2.** vb. descontar (um cheque).

cashew, n. castanha de caju f.; (fruit) caju m.

cashier, **1.** n. caixa m. **2.** vb. demitir.

cashmere, n. caxemira f.

cash register, n. caixa registradora f.

casino, n. cassino m.

cask, n. barril, tonel m.

casket, n. caixão m.

cassava, n. mandioca f.

casserole, n. caçarola f.

cassette, n. cassete m.

cassock, n. batina f.

cast, **1.** n. lanço, lance m.; molde m.; elenco m.; gesso m.; caráter m. **2.** vb. lançar; fundir.

castanets, n.pl. castanholas f.pl.

castaway, n. náufrago -ga.

caste, n. casta f.

caster, n. rodízio (de móvel) m.

castigate, vb. castigar.

Castile, n. Castela f.

Castilian, adj. n. castelhano m.

castle, n. castelo m.

castor oil, n. óleo de rícino/ mamona m.

castrate, *vb.* castrar.

casual, *adj.* informal; casual.

casualty, *n.* vítima *f.*; *(mil.)* baixa *f.*

cat, *n.* gato -ta.

catacomb, *n.* catacumba *f.*

catalog, 1. *n.* catálogo *m.* **2.** *vb.* catalogar.

Catalonia, *n.* Catalunha *f.*

Catalonian, *adj., n.* catalão -lã.

catalyst, *n.* catalisador *m.*

catapult, *n.* catapulta *f.*

cataract, *n.* catarata *f.*

catastrophe, *n.* catástrofe *f.*

catch, *vb.* pegar, apanhar; agarrar; alcançar; atrair.

catchy, *adj.* atrativo.

catechism, *n.* catecismo *m.*

categorical, *adj.* categórico.

category, *n.* categoria *f.*

cater, *vb.* fornecer (alimentos). **c. to,** agradar.

caterpillar, *n.* lagarta *f.*; trator de lagarta *m.*

catharsis, *n.* catarse *f.*

cathedral, *n.* catedral *f.*

catheter, *n.* cateter *f.*

Catholic, 1. *adj.* católico. **2.** *n.* católico -ca.

Catholicism, *n.* catolicismo *m.*

catnap, *n.* soneca *f.*

catsup, *n.* ketchup *m.*

cattle, *n.* gado (vacum) *m.*

cattleman, *n.* pecuário, criador de gado *m.*

cattle raising, *n.* pecuária, criação de gado *f.*

catty, *adj.* rancoroso.

catty-cornered, *adj.* diagonal.

cauliflower, *n.* couve-flor *f.*

cause, 1. *n.* causa *f.* **2.** *vb.* causar.

caustic, *adj.* cáustico.

caution, 1. *n.* cautela *f.* **2.** *vb.* avisar, prevenir.

cautious, *adj.* cauteloso, cauto.

cavalcade, *n.* cavalgada *f.*

cavalier, *n.* cavaleiro *f.*

cavalry, *n.* cavalaria *f.*

cave, cavern, *n.* caverna *f.*

cave-in, *n.* desabamento *m.*

caviar, *n.* caviar *m.*

cavity, *n.* cavidade *f.*; *(dent.)* cárie *f.*

cease, *vb.* cessar.

cease-fire, *n.* cessar-fogo *m.*

cedar, *n.* cedro *m.*

cede, *vb.* ceder.

cedilla, *n.* cedilha *f.*

ceiling, *n.* teto *m.*

celebrant, *n.* celebrante *m.f.*

celebrate, *vb.* celebrar, comemorar.

celebrated, *adj.* célebre.

celebration, *n.* celebração, comemoração *f.*

celebrity, *n.* celebridade *f.*

celery, *n.* aipo *m.*

celestial, *adj.* celeste, celestial.

celibacy, *n.* celibato *m.*

celibate, *adj., n.* celibatário, solteiro *m.*

cell, *n.* cela *f.*; *(biol.)* célula *f.*

cellar, *n.* porão *m.*; adega *f.*

cello, *n.* violoncelo *m.*

cellophane, *n.* celofane *m.*

Celt, *n.* celta *m.f.*

Celtic, *adj.* celta, céltico.

cement, 1. *n.* cimento *m.* **2.** *vb.* cimentar.

cemetery, *n.* cemitério *m.*

censor, 1. *n.* censor *m.* **2.** *vb.* censurar.

censorship, *n.* censura *f.*

censure, 1. *n.* censura *f.* **2.** *vb.* censurar.

census, *n.* censo, recenseamento *m.*

cent, *n.* centavo *m.*

centennial, *adj., n.* centenário *m.*

center, 1. *n.* centro *m.* **2.** *vb.* centrar.

centigrade, *adj.* centígrado.

central, *adj.* central.

Central American, *adj., n.* centro-americano *m.*

centralize, *vb.* centralizar.

centrifuge, *n.* centrifuga *f.*

century, *n.* século *m.*

ceramic, *adj.* cerâmico.

ceramics, *n.* cerâmica *f.*

cereal, *adj., n.* cereal *m.*

ceremonial, *adj.* cermimonial.

ceremonious, *adj.* cerimonioso.

ceremony, *n.* cerimônia *f.*

certain, *adj.* certo, seguro. **be c.,** ter certeza; **for c.,** com certeza.

certainly, *adv.* claro; pois não.

certainty, *n.* certeza *f.*

certificate, *n.* certificado *m.*, certidão *f.*

certify, *vb.* certificar.

cervix, *n.* cerviz *f.*; (uterus) colo *m.*

cessation, *n.* cessação *f.*

cesspool, *n.* fossa, cloaca *f.*

Chad, *n.* Tchad *m.*

chafe, *vb.* esfregar; irritar-se.

chaff, *n.* alimpadura *f.*

chagrin, 1. *m.* desgosto *m.* **2.** *vb.* vexar.

chain, 1. *n.* cadeia, corrente *f.* **2.** *vb.* encadear, acorrentar.

chain reaction, *n.* reação em cadeia *f.*

chair, 1. *n.* cadeira *f.*; (university) cátedra *f.* **2.** *vb.* presidir (a).

chairman -woman -person, *n.* presidente *m./f.*; diretor -ra.

chairmanship, *n.* presidência *f.*; diretorado *m.*

chalet, *n.* chalé *m.*

chalice, *n.* cálice *m.*

chalk, *n.* giz *m.*

challenge, 1. *n.* desafio *m.* **2.** *vb.* desafiar.

challenger, *n.* desafiador -ra.

chamber, *n.* câmara *f.* **c. of commerce,** câmara de comércio *f.*

chameleon, *n.* camaleão *m.*

chamois, *n.* camurça *f.*

champagne, *n.* champanhe, champanha *f.*

champion, *n.* campeão -ã.

championship, *n.* campeonato *m.*

chance, 1. *adj.* fortuito. **2.** *n.* acaso *m.*; oportunidade, chance *f.* **by c,** por acaso; **take a c.,** arriscar-se. **3.** *vb.* acontecer por acaso. **c. upon,** topar com.

chancellor, *n.* chanceler *m.*

chandelier, *n.* lustre, candelabro *m.*

change, 1. *n.* mudança *f.*; (from payment) troco *m.*; (clothes) muda *f.* **small c,** trocado *m.* **2.** *vb.* mudar (de), trocar (de).

changeable, *adj.* mudável, mutável.

channel, 1. *n.* canal *m.* **2.** *vb.* canalizar.

chant, 1. *n.* canto *m.*, canção *f.* **2.** *vb.* cantar, entoar.

chaos, *n.* caos *m.*

chaotic, *adj.* caótico.

chap, 1. *n.* rachadura *f.*; (fellow) cara *m.* **2.** *vb.* rachar.

chapel, *n.* capela *f.*

chaperon, 1. *n.* pau-de-cabeleira *m.* **2.** *vb.* segurar a vela.

chaplain, *n.* capelão *m.*

chapter, *n.* capítulo *m.*

char, *vb.* queimar, carbonizar.

character, *n.* caráter *m.*; (play, novel) personagem *m./f.*; letra *f.*

characteristic, 1. *adj.* característico. **2.** *n.* característica *f.*

characterize, *vb.* caracterizar.

charade, *n.* charada *f.*

charcoal, *n.* carvão (vegetal) *m.* **c. burner,** carvoeiro *m.*

charge, 1. *n.* carga *f.*; preço *m.*; (attack) investida *f.*; (jur.) acusação *f.*; incumbência *f.* in **c. of,** encarregado de. **2.** *vb.* carregar; cobrar; atacar; (jur.) acusar; encarregar (de).

charge account, *n.* conta corrente *f.*

chargé d'affaires, *n.* encarregado de negócios *m.*

charger, *n.* cavalo de batalha *m.*

chariot, *n.* carro romano *m.*, biga *f.*

charisma, *n.* carisma *m.*

charitable, *adj.* caridoso, caritativo.

charity, *n.* caridade *f.*; esmola *f.*

charlatan, *n.* charlatão, impostor *m.*

charm, 1. *n.* charme, encanto *m.*; feitiço *m.*; amuleto *m.* **2.** *vb.* encantar.

charming, *adj.* encantador, charmoso.

chart, 1. *n.* carta *f.*, mapa *m.*; quadro *m.*, tabela *f.* **2.** *vb.* mapear, traçar.

charter, 1. *n.* carta *f.* **c. flight,** vôo fretado, charter *m.*; **c. member,** sócio fundador *m.* **2.** *vb.* fretar.

chase, 1. *n.* caça *f.*; perseguição *f.* **2.** *vb.* caçar, perseguir.

chasm, *n.* abismo *m.*

chassis, *n.* chassi *m.*

chaste, *adj.* casto.

chasten, *vb.* castigar, corrigir.

chastise, *vb.* castigar.

chastity, n. castidade f.

chat, 1. n. conversa f.; bate-papo m. **2.** vb. conversar, bater papo.

chattel, n. bem móvel m.

chatter, 1. n. tagarelice f. **2.** vb. tagarelar; (teeth) bater.

chatterbox, n. tagarela m.f.

chauffeur, n. chofer, motorista m.f.

chauvinism, n. chauvinismo m.

cheap, adj. barato; (quality) vagabundo.

cheapen, vb. baratear.

cheat, 1. n. trapaça f.; trapaceiro -ra f. **2.** vb. ludibriar, trapacear; (exams) colar.

cheater, n. trapaceiro -ra; (cards) batoteiro -ra; (exams) colador -ra.

cheating, n. trapaça f.; (cards) batota f.; (exams) cola f.

check, 1. n. checada f.; (bank) cheque m.; (bill) conta f.; (stub) talão m.; (pattern) xadrez m.; (chess) xeque m. **2.** vb. refrear; verificar, checar. **c. in,** registrar-se.

checkbook, n. talão de cheques m.

checkered, adj. enxadrezado; (fig.) acidentado.

checkers, n. jogo de damas.

checking account, n. conta corrente f.

checkmate, n. xeque-mate m.

checkup, n. checape m.

cheek, n. bochecha, face f.

cheer, 1. n. alegria f.; aplauso m. **2.** vb. animar; aplaudir. **c. for,** torcer por/para; **c. up,** (sl.) tirar/sair da fossa.

cheerful, adj. alegre.

cheers, interj. (toast) saúde!

cheese, n. queijo m.

chef, n. cozinheiro -ra.

chemical, 1. adj. químico. **2.** n. produto químico m.

chemistry, n. química f.

chemotherapy, n. quimioterapia f.

cherish, vb. querer, apreciar.

cherry, n. cereja f.

cherub, n. querubim m.

chess, n. xadrez m.

chest, n. peito, tórax m.; arca f.; (of drawers) cômoda f.

chestnut, n. castanha f.

chew, vb. mastigar, mascar.

chewing gum, n. chiclete m., goma de mascar f.

chic, adj. chique, elegante.

chicanery, n. chicana f.

chick, n. pinto m.

chicken, n. galinha f.; frango m.

chicken pox, n. catapora, varicela f.

chide, vb. repreender, ralhar.

chief, 1. adj. principal. **2.** n. chefe m.f.; (Indian) cacique m.

chieftain, n. chefe m.f.

child, n. criança f.; filho -lha.

childbirth, n. parto m.

childhood, n. meninice, infância f.

childish, adj. infantil, pueril.

childishness, n. puerilidade f.

Chilean, adj., n. chileno -na.

chili pepper, n. pimenta f.

chill, 1. n. frio m.; calafrio m. **2.** vb. esfriar.

chilly, adj. um tanto frio.

chime, 1. n. sino m. **2.** vb. repicar, soar. **c. in,** concordar (com).

chimera, n. quimera f.

chimney, n. chaminé f.

chimpanzee, n. chimpanzé m.

chin, n. queixo m.

china, n. porcelana, louça f.

Chinese, adj., n. chinês -esa.

chink, n. greta, racha f.

chip, 1. n. lasca f., cavaco m.; (computer) chip m. **2.** vb. lascar. **c. in,** (coll.) pingar.

chirp, 1. n. pio m. **2.** vb. piar.

chisel, 1. n. cinzel, formão m. **2.** vb. cinzelar.

chit-chat, n. conversa fiada f.; fofoca f.

chivalrous, adj. cavalheiresco, cavalheiroso.

chivalry, n. cavalaria f.; cavalheirismo m.

chive, n. cebolinho f.

chlorine, n. cloro m.

chloroform, n. clorofórmio m.

chlorophyll, n. clorofila f.

chock-full, adj. abarrotado, apinhado.

chocolate, n. chocolate m.

choice, 1. adj. seleto **2.** n. escolha f.; preferência f.; sortimento *m.*; alternativa *f.* **good c.!**, *(sl.)* boa pedida!; **multiple c.**, múltipla escolha *f.*

choir, *n.* coro *m.*

choke, *vb.* sufocar(-se), engasgar(-se).

choker, *n.* gargantilha *f.*

cholera, *n.* cólera *m.f.*

cholesterol, *n.* colesterol *m.*

choose, *vb.* escolher.

chop, 1. *n.* corte *m.*; (meat) costeleta *f.* **2.** *vb.* cortar.

choppy, *adj.* (sea) picado, encapelado.

chopsticks, *n.pl.* pauzinhos *m.pl.*

choral, *adj.* coral.

chorale, *n.* coral *m.*

chord, *n.* acorde *m.*

chore, *n.* tarefa *f.*

choreography, *n.* coreografia *f.*

chorus, *n.* coro *m.*; estribilho *m.*

chow, *n.* (*mil.*) gororoba *f.*

Christ, *n.* Cristo *m.*

christen, *vb.* batizar.

Christendom, *n.* cristandade *f.*

christening, *n.* batizado *m.*

Christian, *adj.*, *n.* cristão -tã.

Christianity, *n.* cristianismo *m.*

Christmas, *n.* Natal *m.* **C. eve,** véspera de Natal *f.*; **Merry C.!**, Feliz Natal!

chrome, *n.* cromo *m.*

chromosome, *n.* cromossomo *m.*

chronic, *adj.* crônico.

chronicle, *n.* crônica *f.*

chronological, *adj.* cronológico.

chrysalis, *n.* crisálida *f.*

chubby, *n.* rechonchudo, roliço.

chuck, *vb.* atirar, jogar.

chuckle, 1. *n.* risinho *m.* **2.** *vb.* rir entre os dentes.

chum, *n.* amigo -ga.

chummy, *adj.* íntimo.

chunk, *n.* pedaço, naco *m.*

church, *n.* igreja *f.* **go to c.**, ir à missa.

churchman, *n.* eclesiástico *m.*

churchyard, *n.* adro *m.*; cemitério *m.*

churn, 1. *n.* batedeira *f.* **2.** *vb.* bater; revolver(-se).

cicada, *n.* cigarra *f.*

cider, *n.* sidra *f.*

cigar, *n.* charuto *m.*

cigarette, *n.* cigarro *m.* **c. case,** cigarreira *f.*; **c. holder,** piteira *f.*; **c. lighter,** isqueiro *m.*

cinch, 1. *n.* cincha *f.*; (*sl.*) sopa *f.* **2.,** *vb.* cinchar.

cinder, *n.* cinza, brasa *f.*

cinema, *n.* cinema *m.*

cinnamon, *n.* canela *f.*

cipher, *n.* cifra *f.*; zero *m.*; código *m.*

circle, 1. *n.* círculo *m.* **2.** *vb.* rodear.

circuit, *n.* circuito *m.*

circuitous, *adj.* indireto; perifrástico.

circular, *adj.*, *n.* circular *f.*

circulate, *vb.* circular.

circulation, *n.* circulação *f.*; (*journ.*) tiragem *f.*

circulatory, *adj.* circulatório.

circumcise, *vb.* circuncidar.

circumcision, *n.* circuncisão *f.*

circumference, *n.* circunferência *f.*

circumflex, *adj.*, *n.* circunflexo *m.*

circumlocution, *n.* circunlóquio *m.*

circumscribe, *vb.* circunscrever.

circumspect, *adj.* circunspeto.

circumstance, *n.* circunstância *f.*

circumstantial, *adj.* circunstancial.

circumvent, *vb.* evadir, contornar.

circus, *n.* circo *m.*

cistern, *n.* cisterna *f.*

citadel, *n.* cidadela *f.*

citation, *n.* citação *f.*; intimação *f.*

cite, *vb.* citar; intimar.

citizen, *n.* cidadão -dã.

citizenship, *n.* cidadania *f.*

citrus *adj.* cítrico.

city, *n.* cidade *f.*

city council, *n.* câmara de vereadores, municipalidade *f.*

city hall, *n.* prefeitura *f.*

city planning, *n.* urbanismo *m.*

civic, *adj.* cívico.

civics, *n.pl.* educação cívica *f.*

civil, *adj.* civil; cortês; (*jur.*) cível. **c. rights,** direitos civis *m.pl.*; **c. servant,** funcionário público *m.*; **c. war,** guerra civil *f.*

civilian, *adj., n.* civil *m.f.* in **c. clothes,** à paisana.

civility, *n.* civilidade *f.*; cortesia *f.*

civilization, *n.* civilização *f.*

civilize, *vb.* civilizar.

clabber, 1. *n.* coalhada *f.* 2. *vb.* coalhar-se.

clad, *adj.* vestido.

claim, 1. *n.* pretensão *f.*; asserção *f.*; reivindicação *f.* 2. *vb.* pretender; reclamar; reivindicar.

claimant, *n.* demandante *m.f.*; requerente *m.f.*

claim check, *n.* comprovante *m.*

clairvoyant, 1. *adj.* clarividente. 2. *n.* vidente *m.f.*

clam, *n.* amêijoa *f.*

clamber, *vb.* subir com dificuldade.

clamor, 1. *n.* clamor *m.* 2. *vb.* clamar.

clamorous, *adj.* clamoroso.

clamp, 1. *n.* grampo *m.* 2. *vb.* segurar com grampo. **c. down on,** dar um aperto em.

clan, *n.* clã *m.*

clandestine, *adj.* clandestino.

clang, 1. *n.* tinido *m.* 2. *vb.* tinir, retinir.

clannish, *adj.* exclusivo, privativo.

clap, *vb.* bater palmas, aplaudir.

clapper, *n.* badalo *m.*

clarification, *n.* esclarecimento *m.*

clarify, *vb.* esclarecer, clarificar.

clarinet, *n.* clarineta *f.*, -te *m.*

clarity, *n.* claridade *f.*

clash, 1. *n.* choque *m.*; desavença *f.* 2. *vb.* chocar; (colors) não combinar.

clasp, 1. *n.* fecho *m.*; broche *m.*; (hand) aperto *m.* 2. *vb.* apertar; abraçar.

class, *n.* classe *f.*; (acad.) aula *f.* **c. struggle,** luta de classes *f.*

classic, *adj., n.* clássico *m.*

classical, *adj.* clássico.

classification, *n.* classificação *f.*

classify, *vb.* classificar.

classmate, *n.* colega *m.f.*

classroom, *n.* sala de aula *f.*

clatter, *n.* estrépito, barulho *m.*

clause, *n.* cláusula *f.*; (gram.) oração *f.*

claw, *n.* garra *f.*

clay, *n.* argila *f.*, barro *m.*

clean, 1. *adj.* limpo. 2. *vb.* limpar.

cleaner, *n.* limpador -ra; tintureiro -ra.

cleaning, *n.* limpeza *f.*

cleaning man -woman, *n.* faxineiro -ra.

cleanliness, *n.* limpeza *f.*, asseio *m.*

cleanse, *vb.* limpar, purificar.

cleanser, *n.* detergente *m.*

cleanup, *n.* limpeza *f.*, faxina *f.*

clear, 1. *n.* claro; nítido. 2. *vb.* clarear; desembaraçar; absolver.

clearance sale, *n.* liqüidação *f.*

clear-cut, *adj.* nítido.

clearing, *n.* clareira *f.*

clef, *n.* clave *f.*

clemency, *n.* clemência *f.*

clergy, *n.* clero *m.*

clergyman, *n.* clérigo *m.*

clerical, *adj.* de escritório; (eccles.) clerical.

clerk, *n.* empregado -da de escritório, banco, etc.; caixeiro -ra.

clever, *adj.* hábil, inteligente.

cliché, *n.* clichê *m.*

click, *n.* estalo, clique *m.*

client, *n.* cliente *m.f.*

clientele, *n.* clientela *f.*

cliff, *n.* penhasco, precipício *m.*

climate, *n.* clima *m.*

climatic, *adj.* climático.

climax, *n.* clímax *m.*

climb, 1. *n.* subida *f.* 2. *vb.* subir.

clinch, 1. *n.* aperto *m.* 2. *vb.* abraçar; fechar.

cling, *vb.* agarrar-se (a), aderir (a).

clinic, *n.* clínica *f.*

clink, 1. *n.* tinido *m.*; (sl.) cadeia *f.* 2. *vb.* tinir.

clip, 1. *n.* grampo *m.*, presilha *f.* **paper c.,** clipe *m.* 2. *vb.* grampear, prender; recortar.

clipper, *n.* (naut.) clíper *m.*

clipping, *n.* recorte *m.*

clique, *n.* panelinha *f.*

cloak, 1. n. capa f.; manto m. **2.** vb. encobrir.

clobber, vb. (sl.) surrar.

clock, n. relógio m. **alarm c.,** despertador m.

clockmaker, n. relojoeiro -ra.

clod, n. torrão m.; imbecil m.f.

clog, vb. entupir.

clog dance, n. sapateado m.

cloister, 1. n. claustro m. **2.** vb. enclausurar.

clone, n. clone m.

close, 1. adj. próximo; íntimo; fechado. **2.** adv. perto, rente. **c. to,** perto de. **3.** n. fim m. **4.** vb. fechar; encerrar.

closely, adv. de perto; estreitamente; cuidadosamente.

closeness, n. proximidade f.

closet, n. armário, guarda-roupa m.

clot, 1. n. coágulo m. **2.** vb. coagular-se.

cloth, n. pano, tecido m.; fazenda f.

clothe, vb. vestir.

clothes, clothing, n. roupa f.

clothes hanger, n. cabide m.

cloud, n. nuvem f. **c. up,** nublar-se.

cloudburst, n. aguaceiro m.

cloudiness, n. nebulosidade f.

cloudy, adj. nublado, nebuloso.

clove, n. cravo m.

clover, n. trevo m.

clown, n. palhaço m.

cloy, vb. saciar.

club, n. cacete m.; (social) clube m.; (pl.) (cards) paus m.pl.

clue, n. pista, deixa f.

clump, n. feixe, molho m.

clumsy, adj. desajeitado.

cluster, 1. n. grupo m.; magote m.; cacho m. **2.** vb. agrupar (-se).

clutch, 1. n. (car) embreagem f.; (pl.) garras f.pl. **2.** vb. agarrar.

clutter, vb. abarrotar.

coach, 1. n. coche m.; vagão m.; (sport.) treinador -ra. **2.** vb. (sport.) treinar.

coachman, n. cocheiro m.

coagulate, vb. coagular.

coal, n. carvão m.

coalesce, vb. coalescer, unir-se.

coalition, n. coalizão f.

coarse, adj. grosseiro, grosso; áspero.

coarseness, n. grosseria f.; aspereza f.

coast, 1. n. costa f., litoral m. **2.** vb. ir deslizando.

coastal, adj. costeiro, litorâneo.

coaster, n. descanso (para copos, etc.) m.

coast guard, n. guarda costeira f.

coat, 1. n. paletó m.; casaco m.; (paint) demão f.; camada f. **2.** vb. cobrir, revestir.

coat hanger, n. cabide m.

coat of arms, n. brasão m.

coax, vb. persuadir com lisonjas.

cob, n. sabugo m.

cobbler, n. sapateiro -ra; torta de frutas f.

cobblestone, n. paralelepípedo m.

cobweb, n. teia de aranha f.

cocaine, n. cocaína f.

cock, 1. n. galo m. **2.** vb. engatilhar.

cock-a-doodle-doo, n. cocorocó, quiquiriqui m.

cockpit, n. cabine f.

cockroach, n. barata f.

cocktail, n. coquetel, rabo-de-galo m.; batida f. **c. party,** coquetel m.

cocky, adj. convencido, arrogante.

cocoa, n. cacau m.; chocolate m.

coconut, n. coco m. **c. palm,** coqueiro m.

cocoon, n. casulo m.

cod, n. bacalhau m. **c. liver oil,** óleo de fígado de bacalhau m.

coddle, vb. mimar, afagar.

code, n. código m.

codify, vb. codificar; compilar.

coerce, vb. coagir.

coercion, n. coerção, coação f.

coercive, adj. coercivo, coativo.

coexist, vb. coexistir.

coexistence, n. coexistência f.

coffee, n. café m. **c. grower,** cafeicultor -ra m.; **c. growing,** cafeicultura f.; **c. plantation,** cafezal m.; **c. tree,** cafeeiro m.

coffee pot, *n.* cafeteira *f.*
coffer, *n.* cofre *m.*
coffin, *n.* caixão, ataúde *m.*
cog, *n.* dente de roda *m.*
cogent, *adj.* convincente.
cogitate, *vb.* cogitar, ponderar.
cognate, *n.* cognato *m.*
cognitive, *adj.* cognitivo.
cognizance, *n.* conhecimento *m.*
cognizant, *adj.* ciente.
cogwheel, *n.* roda dentada *f.*
coherence, *n.* coerência *f.*
coherent, *adj.* coerente.
cohesion, *n.* coesão *f.*
cohesive, *adj.* coeso, coesivo.
cohort, *n.* coorte *f.*
coiffure, *n.* penteado *m.* toucado *m.*
coil, 1. *n.* bobina *f.*, rolo *m.* **2.** *vb.* enrolar; enroscar-se.
coin, 1. *n.* moeda *f.* **2.** *vb.* cunhar.
coinage, *n.* cunhagem *f.*; neologismo *m.*
coincide, *vb.* coincidir.
coincidence, *n.* coincidência *f.*
coincidental, *adj.* coincidente.
coitus, *n.* coito *m.*
colander, *n.* coador *m.*
cold, 1. *adj.* frio. **be c.,** estar com frio; (weather) fazer/estar frio. **2.** *n.* frio *m.*; (med.) resfriado *m.*
cold blood, *m.* **in c.,** a sangue-frio.
cold-blooded, *adj.* friorento.
coldness, *n.* frio *m.*, frieza, frialdade *f.*
colic, *n.* cólica *f.*
coliseum, *n.* coliseu *f.*
collaborate, *vb.* colaborar.
collaborator, *n.* colaborador -ra.
collapse, 1. *n.* desabamento *m.*; colapso *m.* **2.** *vb.* desabar.
collar, *n.* colarinho *m.*, gola *f.*; (dog) coleira *f.*
collarbone, *n.* clavícula *f.*
collate, *vb.* colacionar; cotejar.
collateral, 1. *adj.* colateral; subsidiário. **2.** *n.* garantia *f.*
colleague, *n.* colega *m.f.*
collect, 1. *adj.* a cobrar **2.** *vb.* cobrar, coletar; arrecadar; colecionar; recolher.

collected, *adj.* reunido; calmo.
collection, *n.* coleção *f.*; coleta *f.*; arrecadação *f.*; cobrança *f.*
collective, *adj.* coletivo. **c. bargaining,** dissídio coletivo *m.*
collector, *n.* coletor -ra; colecionador -ra.
college, *n.* universidade *f.*; faculdade *f.*
collide, *vb.* colidir, chocar.
collision, *n.* colisão *f.*, choque *m.*
colloquial, *adj.* coloquial.
colloquium, *n.* colóquio *m.*
collusion, *n.* colusão *f.*, conluio *m.*
cologne, *n.* água-de-colônia *f.*
Colombian, *adj., n.* colombiano -na.
colon, *n.* (anat.) cólon *m.*; (gram.) dois pontos *m.pl.*
colonel, *n.* coronel *m.*
colonial, *adj.* colonial.
colonist, *n.* colono *m.*
colonize, *vb.* colonizar.
colony, *n.* colônia *f.*
color, 1. *adj.* em cores. **2.** *n.* cor *f.*; (pl.) bandeira *f.* **3.** *vb.* colorir.
coloration, *n.* colorido *m.*
color-blind, *adj.* daltônico.
color blindness, *n.* daltonismo *m.*
colorful, *adj.* colorido, pitoresco.
coloring, *n.* colorido *m.*
colorless, *adj.* incolor; sem graça.
colossal, *adj.* colossal.
colt, *n.* potro, poldro *m.*
column, *n.* coluna *f.*; crônica *f.*
columnist, *n.* colunista, cronista *m.f.*
coma, *n.* coma *m.f.*
comb, 1. *n.* pente *m.* **2.** *vb.* pentear.
combat, 1. *n.* combate *m.* **2.** *vb.* combater.
combatant, *n.* combatente *m.f.*
combination, *n.* combinação *f.*; (lock) segredo *m.*
combine, 1. *n.* consórcio *m.* **2.** *vb.* combinar.
combo, *n.* conjunto musical *m.*
combustible, *adj., n.* combustível *m.*
combustion, *n.* combustão *f.*

come, vb. vir. **c. about**, acontecer; **c. across**, deparar com; comunicar-se; **c. back**, voltar; **c. down**, descer; **c. in**, entrar; **c. out**, sair; **c. to**, voltar a si; **c. up**, subir; **c. upon**, dar com; **how c.?**, por quê?

comeback, n. retruque m.; volta f.; reabilitação f.

comedian -ienne, n. comediante m.f., cômico -ca.

comedy, n. comédia f.

comely, adj. bem parecido.

come-on, n. engodo, chamariz m.

comet, n. cometa m.

comfort, **1.** n. conforto m. **2.** vb. confortar.

comfortable, adj. confortável, cômodo.

comforter, n. acolchoado m.

comic, adj., n. cômico m.

comical, adj. cômico.

comic strip, n. história em quadrinhos, tira cômica f.

coming, **1.** adj. que vem, próximo. **2.** n. vinda, chegada f.

comma, n. vírgula f.

command, **1.** n. comando m., ordem f. **2.** vb. comandar; mandar.

commandant, n. comandante m.

commander, n. comandante m. **c. in chief**, comandante-em-chefe m.

commandment, n. mandamento m.

commando, n. comando m.

commemorate, vb. comemorar.

commemoration, n. comemoração f.

commence, vb. começar, iniciar(-se).

commencement, n. começo m.; formatura f.

commend, vb. encomendar, recomendar.

commendation, n. recomendação f.

commensurate, adj. comensurável; proporcionado.

comment, **1.** n. comentário m. **2.** vb. comentar.

commentary, n. comentário m.

commentator, n. comentarista m.f.

commerce, n. comércio m.

commercial, adj., n. comercial m.

commiserate, vb. comiserar-se.

commisary, n. comissário m.; reembolsável m.

commission, **1.** n. comissão f. **2.** vb. comissionar.

commissioner, n. comissário m.

commit, vb. cometer; comprometer; confiar. **c. oneself**, comprometer-se.

commitment, n. compromisso m.

committee, n. comitê m., comissão f.

commodity, n. mercadoria f.

commodore, n. comodoro m.

common, adj. comum; ordinário. **in c.**, em comum.

commoner, n. plebeu-béia.

commonplace, **1.** adj. comum, banal. **2.** n. lugar comum.

common sense, n. senso comum m.

commonwealth, n. comunidade f.; estado m.

commotion, n. desordem, confusão f.

communal, adj. comunal.

commune, **1.** n. comuna f. **2.** vb. comungar; conversar.

communicable, adj. transmissível.

communicate, vb. comunicar (-se).

communication, n. comunicação f.

communion, n. comunhão f.

communiqué, n. comunicado m.

communism, n. comunismo m.

communist, adj., n. comunista m.f.

community, n. comunidade f.

commute, vb. comutar; viajar diariamente para o trabalho.

commuter, n. viajante diário para o trabalho.

compact, **1.** adj. compacto. **2.** n. pacto m.; estojo de maquiagem m.

companion, n. companheiro -ra.

companionship, n. companheirismo m.

company, *n.* companhia *f.*; empresa *f.*; visita(s) *f.(pl.)*

comparable, *adj.* comparável.

comparative, *adj.* comparado.

compare, *vb.* comparar.

comparison, *n.* comparação *f.*

compartment, *n.* compartimento *m.*; cabine *f.*

compass, *n. (naut.)* bússola *f.*; compasso *m.*; âmbito *m.*

compassion, *n.* compaixão *f.*

compassionate, *adj.* compassivo.

compatible, *adj.* compatível.

compatriot, *n.* compatriota *m.f.*

compel, *vb.* obrigar, compelir.

compendium, *n.* compêndio *m.*

compensate, *vb.* compensar; remunerar.

compensation, *n.* compensação *f.*; remuneração *f.*

compete, *vb.* concorrer, competir.

competence, *n.* competência *f.*

competent, *adj.* competente.

competition, *n.* concorrência, competição *f.*; concurso *m.*

competitor, *n.* concorrente *m.f.*, competidor -ra.

compile, *n.* compilar.

complacency, *n.* satisfação *f.*; vaidade *f.*

complacent, *adj.* satisfeito; vaidoso.

complain, *vb.* reclamar, queixar-se.

complaint, *n.* queixa, reclamação *f.*

complement, 1. *n.* complemento *m.* **2.** *vb.* complementar.

complete, 1. *adj.* completo. **2.** *vb.* completar.

completeness, *n.* inteireza *f.*; totalidade *f.*

completion, *n.* terminação *f.*, acabamento *m.*

complex, *adj.,* *n.* complexo *m.*

complexion, *n.* tez, cútis *f.*

complexity, *n.* complexidade *f.*

compliance, *n.* cumprimento *m.*; obediência *f.*

compliant, *adj.* dócil, obediente.

complicate, *vb.* complicar.

complicated, *adj.* complicado.

complication, *n.* complicação *f.*

complicity, *n.* cumplicidade *f.*

compliment, 1. *n.* elogio *m.*; cumprimento *m.* **2.** *vb.* elogiar; cumprimentar.

complimentary, *adj.* lisonjeiro; gratuito.

comply, *vb.* cumprir.

component, *adj., n.* componente *m.*

compose, *vb.* compor.

composer, *n.* compositor -ra.

composite, *adj., n.* composto, compósito *m.*

composition, *n.* composição *f.*; redação *f.*

composure, *n.* compostura *f.*; calma *f.*

compound, 1. *adj.* composto. **2.** *n.* composto *n.*; recinto *m.*

comprehend, *vb.* compreender.

comprehensible, *adj.* compreensível.

comprehension, *n.* compreensão *f.*

comprehensive, *adj.* compreensivo.

compress, 1. *n.* compressa *f.* **2.** *vb.* comprimir.

compression, *n.* compressão *f.*

compressor, *n.* compressor *f.*

comprise, *vb.* incluir, abranger.

compromise, 1. *n.* acordo, compromisso *m.*, transigência *f.* **2.** *vb.* chegar a um acordo, transigir; comprometer.

compulsion, *n.* compulsão *f.*

compulsive, *adj.* compulsivo.

compulsory, *adj.* compulsório.

compunction, *n.* compunção *f.*

computation, *n.* computação *f.*, cômputo *n..*

compute, *vb.* computar, calcular.

computer, *n.* computador *m.*

computerize, *vb.* computadorizar.

computer science, *n.* informática *f.*

comrade, *n.* camarada *m.f.*

concave, *adj.* côncavo.

conceal, *vb.* esconder, ocultar.

concealment, *n.* ocultamento *m.*

concede, *vb.* conceder.

conceit, *n.* convencimento *m.*, vaidade *f.*

conceited, *adj.* convencido, vaidoso.

conceivable, *adj.* concebível.

conceive, *vb.* conceber; engravidar.

concentrate, *vb.* concentrar (-se).

concentration, *n.* concentração *f.*

concentric, *adj.* concêntrico.

concept, *n.* conceito *m.*

conception, *n.* concepção *f.*

conceptual, *adj.* conceptual.

concern, 1. *n.* interesse *m.*; preocupação *f.*; empresa *f.* 2. *vb.* concernir a; preocupar. c. oneself with, ocupar-se de; as far as I'm concerned, no que me diz respeito.

concerning, *prep.* no tocante a, no que diz respeito a.

concert, *n.* concerto *m.*

concerted, *adj.* combinado.

concertina, *n.* concertina, sanfona *f.*

concerto, *n.* concerto *m.*

concession, *n.* concessão *f.*

conciliate, *vb.* conciliar.

concise, *adj.* conciso.

conclude, *vb.* concluir.

conclusion, *n.* conclusão *f.*

concoct, *vb.* confeccionar; inventar.

concoction, *n.* mistura *f.*; invenção *f.*

concomitant, *adj.* concomitante.

concord, *n.* concórdia, harmonia *f.*

concordance, *n.* concordância *f.*

concrete, *adj., n.* concreto *m.*

concubine, *n.* concubina *f.*

concur, *vb.* concordar.

concurrence, *n.* consentimento *m.*

concurrent, *adj.* concorrente; simultâneo.

concussion, *n.* concussão *f.*; comoção cerebral *f.*

condemn, *vb.* condenar.

condemnation, *n.* condenação *f.*

condense, *vb.* condensar.

condenser, *n.* condensador *m.*

condescend, *vb.* dignar-se, baixar-se.

condescending, *adj.* arrogante.

condiment, *n.* condimento *m.*

condition, 1. *n.* condição *f.*, estado *m.* 2. *vb.* condicionar.

conditional, *adj.* condicional; (*gram.*) futuro do pretérito.

condolence, *n.* condolência *f.*, pêsame *m.*

condom, *n.* preservativo *m.*

condominium, *n.* condomínio *m.*

condone, *n.* perdoar, desculpar.

condor, *n.* condor *m.*

conducive, *adj.* conducente.

conduct, 1. *n.* conduta *f.*; direção *f.* 2. *vb.* conduzir; dirigir; guiar.

conductor, *n.* condutor *m.*; (*mus.*) maestro *m.*; (bus) cobrador *m.*

conduit, *n.* conduto *m.*

cone, *n.* cone *m.*

confection, *n.* confecção *f.*; confeito *m.*

confectionery, *n.* confeitaria *f.*

confederacy, *n.* confederação *f.*

confederate, 1. *adj., n.* confederado *m.* 2. *vb.* confederar (-se).

confederation, *n.* confederação, *f.*

confer, *vb.* conferir; conferenciar.

conference, *n.* reunião, conferência *f.*

confess, *vb.* confessar.

confession, *n.* confissão *f.*

confessional, 1. *adj.* confessional. 2. *n.* confessionário *m.*

confessor, *n.* confessor *m.*

confetti, *n.* confete *m.*

confidant -dante, *n.* confidente *m.f.*

confide, *vb.* confiar.

confidence, *n.* confiança *f.*

confident, *adj.* confiante.

confidential, *adj.* confidencial.

configuration, *n.* configuração *f.*

confine, 1. *n.* confins *m.pl.* 2. *vb.* encerrar.

confinement, *n.* prisão *f.*

confirm, *vb.* confirmar.

confirmation, *n.* confirmação *f.*

confiscate, *vb.* confiscar.

conflagration, *n.* conflagração *f.*

conflict, 1. *n.* conflito *m.* **2.** *vb.* conflitar.

conform, *vb.* conformar-se.

conformist, *n.* conformista *m.f.*

conformity, *n.* conformidade *f.*, conformismo *m.*

confound, *vb.* confundir.

confront, *vb.* confrontar; encarar.

confrontation, *n.* confrontação *f.*

confuse, *vb.* confundir.

confused, *adj.* confuso; confundido.

confusion, *n.* confusão *f.*

con game, *n.* conto do vigário *m.*

congenial, *adj.* agradável, simpático.

congenital, *adj.* congênito.

congest, *vb.* congestionar.

congestion, *n.* congestão *f.*

conglomerate, 1. *adj.*, *n.* conglomerado *m.* **2.** *vb.* conglomerar.

congratulate, *vb.* dar os parabéns a.

congratulations, *n.pl.* parabéns *m.pl.*

congregate, *vb.* congregar-se.

congregation, *n.* congregação *f.*

congress, *n.* congresso *m.*

congressional, *adj.* congressional.

congressman -woman, *n.* congressista *m.f.*

conjecture, 1. *n.* conjetura *f.* **2.** *vb.* conjeturar.

conjugal, *adj.* conjugal.

conjugate, *vb.* conjugar.

conjugation, *n.* conjugação *f.*

conjunction, *n.* conjunção *f.*

conjuncture, *n.* conjuntura *f.*

conjure, *vb.* conjurar; evocar; escamotear.

conk, 1. *n.* golpe na cabeça *m.* **2.** *vb.* bater (na cabeça). **c. out,** *(sl.)* pregar.

con man, *n.* vigarista *m.*

connect, *vb.* ligar, fazer conexão.

connection, *n.* conexão, ligação *f.*; *(pl.)* pistolão *m.*

connive, *vb.* ser conivente (em).

connoisseur, *n.* conhecedor -ra.

connotation, *n.* conotação *f.*

connote, *vb.* conotar.

conquer, *vb.* conquistar.

conqueror, *n.* conquistador -ra.

conquest, *n.* conquista *f.*

conscience, *n.* consciência *f.*

conscientious, *adj.* consciencioso.

conscious, *adj.*, *n.* consciente *m.*.

consciousness, *n.* consciência *f.*

conscript, 1. *n.* recruta *m.* **2.** *vb.* recrutar.

conscription, *n.* recrutamento *m.*

consecrate, *vb.* consagrar.

consecutive, *adj.* consecutivo.

consensus, *n.* consenso *m.*

consent, 1. *n.* consentimento *m.* **2.** *vb.* consentir.

consequence, *n.* conseqüência *f.*

consequent, *adj.* conseqüente.

conservation, *n.* conservação *f.*

conservationist, *n.* conservacionista *m.f.*

conservatism, *n.* conservantismo *m.*

conservative, *adj.*, *n.* conservador.

conservatory, *n.* conservatório *m.*

conserve, *vb.* conservar.

consider, *vb.* considerar.

considerable, *adj.* considerável.

considerate, *adj.* atencioso.

consideration, *n.* consideração *f.*

considering, 1. *prep.* em vista de. **2.** *conj.* considerando que.

consign, *vb.* consignar; entregar.

consignment, *n.* consignação *f.*

consist, *vb.* consistir. **c. of,** consistir em/de.

consistency, *n.* consistência *f.*

consistent, *adj.* consistente, constante.

consolation, *n.* consolação *f.*

console, 1. *n.* consolo *m.* **2.** *vb.* consolar.

consolidate, *vb.* consolidar.

consonant, *adj.*, *n.* consoante *f.*

consort, 1. *n.* consorte *m.f.* **2.** *vb.* associar-se.

consortium, *n.* consórcio *m.*

conspicuous, *adj.* conspícuo.

conspiracy, *n.* conspiração *f.*

conspirator, *n.* conspirador -ra.

conspire, vb. conspirar, tramar.

constable, n. policial m.

constant, adj. constante.

constellation, n. constelação f.

consternation, n. consternação f.

constipation, n. constipação, prisão de ventre f.

constituency, n. eleitorado m.

constituent, 1. adj. constituinte. **c. assembly,** assembléia constituinte f. **2.** n. eleitor -ra, constituinte m.f.

constitute, vb. constituir.

constitution, n. constituição f.

constitutional, 1. adj. constitucional. **c. convention,** constituinte f. **2.** n. passeio m.

constrain, vb. constranger, obrigar.

constraint, n. constrangimento m.; restrição f.

constrict, vb. constringir.

construct, 1. n. constructo m. **2.** vb. construir.

construction, n. construção f. **c. company,** construtora f.

constructive, adj. construtivo.

construe, vb. interpretar, explicar.

consul, n. cônsul m.

consulate, n. consulado m.

consult, vb. consultar.

consultant, n. consulente, consultante m.f.

consultation, n. consulta f.

consume, vb. consumir.

consumer, n. consumidor -ra.

consummate, 1. adj. consumado. **2.** vb. consumar.

consumption, n. consumo m.; consumpção f.

consumptive, adj., n. tísico m.

contact, 1. n. contato m. **2.** vb. entrar em contato com.

contact lens, n. lente de contato f.

contagious, adj. contagioso.

contain, vb. conter.

container, n. recipiente m.

contaminate, vb. contaminar.

contemplate, vb. contemplar.

contemporary, adj., n. contemporâneo m.

contempt, n. desprezo m.; (of court) contumácia f.

contemptible, adj. desprezível.

contemptuous, adj. desdenhoso.

contend, vb. asseverar; competir.

contender, n. contendor -ra.

content, 1. adj. contente. **2.** n. conteúdo m. **3.** vb. contentar.

contented, adj. contente.

contention, n. contenção f.

contentment, n. contentamento m.

contest, 1. n. concurso m. **2.** vb. contestar; disputar.

contestant, n. concorrente m.f.

context, n. contexto m.

contiguous, adj. contíguo.

continence, n. continência f.

continent, n. continente m.

continental, adj. continental.

contingency, n. contingência f.

contingent, adj., n. contingente m. **be c. upon,** depender de.

continual, adj. contínuo.

continuation, n. continuação f.

continue, vb. continuar.

continuity, n. continuidade f.

continuous, adj. contínuo.

contort, vb. retorcer, deformar.

contortion, n. contorção f.

contour, n. contorno m.

contraband, n. contrabando m.

contraception, n. anticoncepção f.

contraceptive, adj., n. anticoncepcional m.

contract, 1. n. contrato m. **2.** vb. contrair(-se); contratar.

contraction, n. contração f.

contractor, n. empreiteiro -ra.

contradict, vb. contradizer.

contradiction, n. contradição f.

contradictory, adj. contraditório.

contraption, n. geringonça f.

contrary, adj. contrário. **on the c.,** pelo contrário.

contrast, 1. n. contraste m. **2.** vb. contrastar.

contravene, vb. transgredir, contravir.

contretemps, n. contratempo m.

contribute, vb. contribuir.

contribution, n. contribuição f.

contributor, n. contribuinte m.f.; (journal) colaborador -ra.

contrite, adj. contrito.

contrition, *n.* contrição *f.*

contrivance, *n.* dispositivo *m.*; estratagema *m.*

contrive, *vb.* inventar, maquinar.

control, 1. *n.* controle *m.* **2.** *vb.* controlar.

controller, *n.* superintendente, fiscal *m.f.*

controversial, *adj.* controverso, controvertido.

controversy, *n.* controvérsia *f.*

contusion, *n.* contusão *f.*

conundrum, *n.* enigma *m.*

convalesce, *vb.* convalescer.

convalescence, *n.* convalescença *f.*

convalescent, *adj., n.* convalescente *m.f.*

convene, *vb.* convocar; reunir (-se).

convenience, *n.* conveniência *f.*; conforto *m.*

convenient, *adj.* conveniente; cômodo.

convent, *n.* convento, mosteiro *m.*

convention, *n.* convenção *f.*; congresso *m.*

conventional, *adj.* convencional.

converge, *vb.* convergir.

convergence, *n.* convergência *f.*

conversant with, *adj.* versado em.

conversation, *n.* conversação *f.*; (chat) conversa *f.*

conversational, *adj.* conversador; informal.

conversationalist, *n.(sl.)* (bom) papo *m.*

converse, 1. *adj., n.* contrário *m.* **2.** *vb.* conversar.

conversion, *n.* conversão *f.*

convert, 1. *n.* convertido *m.* **2.** *vb.* converter.

converter, *n.* (*elec.*) conversor *m.*

convertible, *adj.n.* conversível *m.*

convex, *adj.* convexo.

convey, *vb.* transportar; comunicar, veicular.

conveyance, *n.* transporte *m.*; veículo *m.*

conveyor, *n.* transportador *m.*

convict, 1. *n.* condenado. **2.** *vb.* condenar.

conviction, *n.* convicção *f.*; condenação *f.*

convince, *vb.* convencer.

convincing, *adj.* convincente.

convocation, *n.* convocação *f.*; assembléia *f.*

convoy, *n.* comboio *m.*

convulsion, *n.* convulsão *f.*

coo, 1. *n.* arrulho *m.* **2.** *vb.* arrulhar.

cook, 1. *n.* cozinheiro -ra. **2.** *vb.* cozinhar, cozer. **c. up,** (*sl.*) bolar.

cookbook, *n.* livro de receitas *m.*

cookery, *n.* culinária, cozinha *f.*

cookie, *n.* biscoito *m.*, bolacha *f.*

cooking, *n.* cozinha, culinária *f.*

cool, 1. *adj.* fresco; frio; calmo. **2.** *vb.* refrescar; esfriar, arrefecer.

coolness, *n.* fresco *m.*; serenidade *f.*

coop, 1. *n.f.* galinheiro *m.* **2.** *vb.* engaiolar; fechar.

cooperate, *vb.* cooperar.

cooperation, *n.* cooperação *f.*

cooperative, 1. *adj.* cooperativo. **2.** *n.* cooperativa *f.*

coordinate, 1. *n.* coordenada *f.* **2.** *vb.* coordenar.

coordination, *n.* coordenação *f.*

coordinator, *n.* coordenador -ra.

cop, *n.* guarda, policial *m.*

cope, *vb.* arranjar-se. **c. with,** lidar com.

copier, *n.* copiadora *f.*

copilot, *n.* co-piloto *m.*

copious, *adj.* copioso.

copper, *n.* cobre *m.*

copulate, *vb.* copular.

copy, 1. *n.* cópia *f.*; (book) exemplar *m.* **2.** *vb.* copiar.

copyright, *n.* copirraite *m.*

coquette, *n.* coquete *f.*

coral, *adj., n.* coral *m.*

cord, *n.* corda *f.*

cordial, *adj.* cordial.

cordon, *n.* cordão *f.*

corduroy, *n.* veludo cotelê *m.*

core, *n.* âmago *m.*; (fruit) caroço *m.*

coriander, *n.* coentro *m.*

cork, *n.* cortiça *f.*; (bottle) rolha *f.*

corkscrew, *n.* saca-rolha *f.*

corn, *n.* milho *m.*; (foot) calo *m.*

cornea, *n.* córnea *f.*

corner, *n.* canto *m.*; (street) esquina *f.*

cornerstone, *n.* pedra angular *f.*

cornet, *n.* cornetim *m.*, corneta *f.*

cornfield, *n.* milharal *m.*

cornice, *n.* cornija *f.*

corn meal, *n.* fubá *m.*

cornstalk, *n.* pé de milho *m.*

cornstarch, *n.* maisena *f.*

cornucopia, *n.* cornucópia *f.*

corny, *adj.* (*sl.*) rústico; piegas; cafona.

corollary, *n.* corolário *m.*

coronary, *adj.* coronário.

coronation, *n.* coroação *f.*

coroner, *n.* magistrado investigador de casos de morte suspeita.

corporal, **1.** *adj.* corporal, físico. **2.** *n.* cabo, caporal *m.*

corporate, *adj.* relativo a uma sociedade anônima.

corporation, *n.* sociedade anônima *f.*; corporação *f.*

corps, *n.* corpo *m.*

corpse, *n.* cadáver *m.*

corpulent, *adj.* corpulento.

corpuscle, *n.* corpúsculo *m.*

corral, **1.** *n.* curral *m.* **2.** *vb.* encurralar.

correct, **1.** *adj.* correto, certo. **2.** *vb.* corrigir.

correction, *n.* correção, emenda *f.*

correctness, *n.* correção *f.*

correlate, *vb.* correlatar, correlacionar.

correlation, *n.* correlação *f.*

correspond, *vb.* corresponder.

correspondence, *n.* correspondência *f.*

correspondent, *n.* correspondente *m.f.*

corresponding, *adj.* correspondente.

corridor, *n.* corredor *m.*

corroborate, *vb.* corroborar.

corrode, *vb.* corroer.

corrosion, *n.* corrosão *f.*

corrugate, *vb.* corrugar.

corrupt, **1.** *adj.* corrupto. **2.** *vb.* corromper.

corruption, *n.* corrupção *f.*

corsage, *n.* pequeno buquê usado ao ombro.

corset, *n.* espartilho *m.*

cortège, *n.* cortejo fúnebre *m.*; séquito *m.*

cortex, *n.* córtex, córtice *m.*

cosigner, *n.* avalista *m.f.*

cosmetic, *adj., n.* cosmético *m.*

cosmic, *adj.* cósmico.

cosmonaut, *n.* cosmonauta *m.f.*

cosmopolitan, *adj.* cosmopolita.

cosmos, *n.* cosmo, cosmos *m.*

cost, **1.** *n.* conta *f.*; preço de custo *m.* **c. of living,** custo de vida *m.*; **at all costs,** custe o que custar. **2.** *vb.* custar.

Costa Rican, *adj., n.* costarriquenho *m.*, costarriquense *m.f.*

costliness, *n.* carestia *f.*

costly, *adj.* caro, custoso.

costume, **1.** *n.* roupa *f.*, traje *m.*; fantasia *f.* **2.** *vb.* vestir; fantasiar.

cot, *n.* maca *f.*, catre *m.*

coterie, *n.* panelinha *f.*

cottage, *n.* casa de campo *f.*

cottage cheese, *n.* tipo de queijo ricota.

cotter pin, *n.* chaveta *f.*

cotton, *vb.* algodão *m.* **c. field,** algodoal *m.*; **c. gin,** descaroçador de algodão *m.*

couch, **1.** *n.* sofá *m.* **2.** *vb.* expressar, exprimir.

cougar, *n.* suçuarana *f.*, puma *m.*

cough, **1.** *n.* tosse *f.* **2.** *vb.* tossir.

council, *n.* conselho, (*P.*) concelho *m.*, câmara *f.*; (*eccles.*) consílio *m.*

councilman -woman, *n.* vereador -ra.

counsel, **1.** *n.* conselho *m.*; (*jur.*) advogado -da. **2.** *vb.* aconselhar.

counselor, *n.* conselheiro -ra; assessor -ra; (*jur.*) advogado -da.

count, **1.** *n.* conta *f.*; contagem *f.*; (title) conde *m.* **2.** *vb.* contar. **c. on,** contar com.

countdown, n. contagem regressiva f.

countenance, 1. n. semblante m. **2.** vb. aprovar.

counter-, pref. contra-.

counter, 1. n. balcão m.; mostrador m. **2.** vb. contrariar. **3.** adv. contra.

counteract, vb. agir contra, neutralizar.

counterattack, 1. n. contra-ataque m. **2.** vb. contra-atacar.

counterbalance, 1. n. contrapeso m. **2.** vb. contrabalançar.

counterfeit, 1. n. falsificação f.; moeda falsa f. **2.** vb. contrafazer; falsificar.

counterfeiter, n. contrafator m.; moedeiro falso m.

counterintelligence, n. contra-informação f.

countermand, vb. contramandar, contra-ordenar.

counterpart, n. contrapartida f., homólogo m.

counterpoint, n. contraponto m.

countess, n. condessa f.

countless, adj. inúmero.

country, n. país m.; (homeland) pátria f.; campo m.

countryman -woman, n. conterrâneo -nea m.f.

countryside, n. campo m.; paisagem f.

county, n. município m.

coup, n. golpe m. **c. d'état,** golpe de estado m.

coupe, coupé, n. cupê m.

couple, 1. n. casal m., dupla f. **2.** vb. juntar.

coupon, n. cupom m.

courage, n. coragem f., valor m.

corageous, adj. corajoso, valente.

courier, n. mensageiro -ra.

course, n. curso m.; caminho m.; (school) matéria f.; (meal) prato m.; (sport.) campo m. **in the c. of,** no decorrer de; **of c.,** claro.

court, 1. n. corte f., tribunal m.; (court) quadra f.; **pay c. to,** fazer a corte a. **2.** vb. cortejar, namorar.

courteous, adj. cortês.

courtesy, n. cortesia f.

courthouse, n. tribunal, fórum m.

court jester, n. bobo da corte m.

courtly, adj. cortesão, nobre.

court-martial, 1. n. conselho de guerra m. **2.** vb. submeter a conselho de guerra.

courtship, n. namoro m.

courtyard, n. pátio m.

cousin, n. primo -ma.

cove, n. angra, enseada f.

covenant, n. contrato, convênio m.

cover, 1. n. cobertura f.; tampa f.; cobertor m. **2.** vb. cobrir; tampar; incluir; proteger.

coverage, n. cobertura f.

cover charge, n. couvert m.; serviço m.

covering, n. revestimento m.

covert, adj. secreto, clandestino.

covet, vb. cobiçar.

covetous, adj. cobiçoso.

cow, n. vaca f.

coward, n. covarde m.f.

cowardice, n. covardia f.

cowardly, adj. covarde.

cowbell, n. chocalho, cincerro m.

cowboy, n. vaqueiro, (South) gaúcho m.

cower, vb. curvar-se.

cowhide, n. couro de vaca m.

cowl, n. capuz, capelo m.

coy, adj. reacatado, tímido.

coyote, n. coiote m.

cozy, adj. aconchegante.

crab, n. caranguejo m.; (coll.) ranheta m.f.

crabby, adj. (coll.) rabugento.

crack, 1. n. racha f.; (noise) estalo m. **2.** vb. rachar; estalar.

cracker, n. bolacha f.

crackle, 1. n. crepitação f. **2.** vb. crepitar.

cradle, n. berço m.

craft, n. arte f., ofício m.; astúcia f.; embarcação f.; avião m.

craftsman, n. artesão -sã, artífice m.f.

craftsmanship, n. artesanato f.

crafty, adj. astucioso.

crag, n. rochedo, penhasco m.

cram, n. abarrotar; (coll.) queimar as pestanas.

cramp, n. câimbra, cãibra f.

crane, n. guindaste m., grua f.; (ornith.) grou m.

cranium, n. crânio m.

crank, n. manivela f.; (coll.) ranheta m.f.

crankcase, n. cárter m.

cranky, adj. (coll.) ranzinza, rabugento.

cranny, n. fresta, greta f.

crap, n. (vulg.) excremento m.

crape, n. crepe m.

crash, 1. n. choque m., batida f.; estrondo m.; (fin.) craque m. 2. vb. chocar; falir.

crass, adj. crasso, grosseiro.

crate, n. caixote m.

crater, n. cratera f.

cravat, n. gravata f.

crave, vb. desejar; ansiar.

craven, adj. covarde.

craving, n. desejo m., ânsia f.

craw, n. papo m.

crawfish, n. lagostim m.

crawl, 1. n. arrastamento m. 2. vb. arrastar-se; (infant) engatinhar.

crayon, n. pastel m.

craze, 1. n. mania f.; coqueluche f. 2. vb. enlouquecer.

craziness, n. loucura f.

crazy, adj. louco, doido, maluco.

creak, 1. n. rangido, estalo m. 2. vb. ranger, estalar.

creaky, adj. rangente.

cream, n. creme m., nata f.

creamy, adj. cremoso.

crease, 1. n. vinco m.; dobra f. 2. vb. vincar; dobrar.

create, vb. criar.

creation, n. criação f.

creative, adj. criador, criativo.

creativity, n. criatividade f.

creator, n. criador -ra.

creature, n. criatura f.

crèche, n. presépio m.

credence, n. crédito m.

credentials, n. credenciais f.pl.

credibility, n. credibilidade f.

credible, adj. crível.

credit, 1. n. crédito m. on c., fiado; do c. to, honrar; give c. to, fazer justiça a; take c. for,

atribuir-se o mérito de. 2. vb. crer; atribuir; (com.) creditar.

credit card, n. cartão de crédito m.

creditor, n. credor -ra.

credulous, adj. crédulo.

creed, n. credo m.; profissão de fé f.

creek, n. riacho m.

creep, n. arrastar-se.

cremate, vb. cremar.

Creole, adj., n. crioulo (europeu nascido na América) m.

crepe, n. crepe m.; luto m. c. paper, papel crepom m.

crescent, n. crescente m.

crest, n. crista f.; cimo m.

crestfallen, adj. cabisbaixo.

cretin, n. cretino m.

crevasse, n. fenda f.

crevice, n. fissura f.

crew, n. tripulação f.

crib, n. caminha de criança f.

crick, n. torcicolo m.

cricket, n. grilo m.

crier, n. pregoeiro -ra.

crime, n. crime m.

criminal, 1. adj. criminoso, criminal. 2. n. criminoso -sa.

criminology, n. criminologia f.

crimp, 1. n. plissado m. 2. vb. plissar; frisar.

crimson, adj. carmesim.

cringe, vb. encolher-se, humilhar-se.

cripple, 1. n. aleijado -da. 2. vb. aleijar.

crippled, adj. aleijado.

crisis, n. crise f.

crisp, adj. fresco, crespo.

criterion, n. critério m.

critic, n. crítico -ca.

critical, adj. crítico.

criticism, n. crítica f.

criticize, vb. criticar; censurar.

critique, 1. n. crítica f. 2. vb. criticar.

croak, 1. n. coaxo m. 2. vb. coaxar; (sl.) bater as botas.

crochet, 1. n. crochê m. 2. vb. fazer crochê.

crock, n. pote ou jarro de barro m.

crockery, n. louça de barro f.

crocodile, n. crocodilo, jacaré m.

crony, n. companheiro íntimo m.

crook, cajado m.; *(coll.)* ladrão m.

crooked, adj. torto; desonesto.

croon, vb. cantar, cantarolar.

crooner, n. cantor de música popular.

crop, 1. n. colheita, safra f. **2.** vb. cortar. **c. up,** surgir.

crop rotation, n. rotação de culturas f.

croquet, n. croqué m.

croquette, n. croquete m.

cross, 1. adj. mal-humorado. **2.** n. cruz f. **3.** vb. atravessar, cruzar. **c. out,** riscar; **c. oneself,** persignar-se.

crossbreed, 1. n. mestiço -ça. **2.** vb. cruzar.

cross-examine, vb. interrogar; reexaminar.

cross-eyed, adj. zarolho, vesgo.

crossing, n. travessia f.; cruzamento m.

crossroads, n. encruzilhada f.

cross section, n. corte transversal m.

cross street, n. transversal f.

crossword puzzle, n. palavras cruzadas f.pl.

crotch, n. entreperna f.

crouch, vb. acocorar-se.

croup, n. crupe m.

crow, n. corvo m.

crowbar, n. pé-de-cabra m.

crowd, 1. n. multidão f. **2.** vb. comprimir, empurrar.

crowded, adj. cheio (de gente).

crown, 1. n. coroa f. **2.** vb. coroar.

crucial, adj. crucial.

crucible, n. cadinho, crisol m.

crucifix, n. crucifixo m.

crucifixion, n. crucificação, crucifixão f.

crucify, vb. crucificar.

crude, adj. cru; grosseiro, rude; (oil) bruto.

crudeness, crudity, n. crueza f.; grosseria f.

cruel, adj. cruel.

cruelty, n. crueldade f.

cruise, 1. n. cruzeiro m., viagem marítima f. **2.** vb. cruzar; viajar; rodar.

cruiser, n. cruzeiro m.

crumb, n. migalha f.

crumble, vb. esmigalhar; desmoronar.

crummy, adj. *(coll.)* vagabundo.

crumple, vb. amarrotar, enrugar.

crunch, vb. roer ruidosamente; ranger.

crusade, 1. n. cruzada f. **2.** vb. travar uma cruzada.

crusader, n. cruzado m.

crush, 1. n. aperto, esmagamento m.; *(sl.)* paixonite f. **2.** vb. esmagar; triturar.

crust, n. crosta f.

crustacean, n. crustáceo m.

crutch, n. muleta f.

crux, n. xis m.

cry, 1. n. grito m. **2.** vb. gritar; (weep) chorar.

crybaby, n. choramingas m.f.

crypt, n. cripta f.

cryptic, adj. críptico, secreto.

crystal, n. cristal m.

cub, n. filhote m.; (scout) lobinho m.; (reporter) foca m.

Cuban, adj., n. cubano -na.

cube, n. cubo m.

cubic, adj. cúbico.

cubicle, n. cubículo m.

cuckold, 1. n. corno, chifrudo m. **2.** vb. cornear, botar os chifres em.

cuckoo, 1. adj. louco, maluco **2.** n. cuco m.

cucumber, n. pepino m.

cuddle, vb. acariciar, afagar; aninhar.

cudgel, n. cacete, bordão m.

cue, n. taco de bilhar m.; *(theat.)* deixa f.

cuff, n. punho (de camisa). **c. links,** abotoaduras f.pl.

cuisine, n. culinária, cozinha f.

culinary, adj. culinário.

culminate, vb. culminar.

culpable, adj. culpável.

culprit, n. culpado, réu m.

cult, n. culto nm, . seita f.

cultivate, vb. cultivar.

cultivation, n. cultivo m.; cultivação f.

cultural, adj. cultural.

culture, n. cultura f.

cultured, adj. culto.

cumbersome, *adj.* pesado, incômodo.

cumin, *n.* cominho *m.*

cumulative, *adj.* cumulativo.

cunning, 1. *adj.* astucioso. **2.** *n.* astúcia *f.*

cup, *n.* xícara, *(P.)* chávena *f.*; cálice *m.*; (trophy) taça, copa *f.*

cupboard, *n.* armário, guarda-louça *m.*

cupcake, *n.* bolinho *m.*

Cupid, *n.* Cupido *m.*

curator, *n.* administrador -ra; zelador -ra.

curb, 1. *n.* meio-fio *m.* **2.** *vb.* refrear.

curd, *n.* coalhada *f.*

curdle, *vb.* coalhar, coagular.

cure, 1. *n.* cura *f.*; remédio *m.* **2.** *vb.* curar, sarar.

curfew, *n.* toque de recolher *m.*; hora de recolher *f.*

curio, *n.* raridade *f.*

curiosity, *n.* curiosidade *f.*

curious, *adj.* curioso.

curl, 1. *n.* anel, cacho *m.* **2.** *vb.* cachear, anelar, frisar.

curler, *n.* rolo *m.*

curly, *adj.* crespo, ondulado.

currency, *n.* moeda *f.*; curso *m.*

current, *adj., n.* corrente *f.* **c. events,** atualidades *f.*

curriculum, *n.* currículo *m.*

curry, *n.* caril *m.*

curse, 1. *n.* praga, maldição *f.* **2.** *vb.* amaldiçoar; xingar.

cursory, *adj.* rápido, superficial.

curt, *adj.* curto, abrupto.

curtail, *vb.* encurtar, reduzir.

curtain, *n.* cortina *f.*; pano de boca *m.*

curtsy, *n.* mesura, cortesia *f.*

curve, 1. *n.* curva *f.* **2.** *vb.* curvar(-se).

cushion, *n.* almofada *f.*, coxim *m.*

cusp, *n.* cúspide *f.*

cuspidor, *n.* cuspideira *f.*

custard, *n.* creme, flã *m.*

custodian, *n.* guardião *m.*; zelador *m.*

custody, *n.* custódia *f.*

custom, *n.* costume *m.*

customary, *adj.* costumeiro, usual.

customer, *n.* freguês -guesa, cliente *m.f.*

customs, customhouse, *n.* alfândega *f.*

cut, 1. *n.* corte *m.*; ferida *f.*; gravura *f.* **2.** *vb.* cortar.

cute, *adj.* engraçadinho; bonitinho.

cutlass, *n.* cutelo *m.*

cutlet, *n.* costeleta *f.*

cutter, *n.* cortador -ra; cúter *m.*

cutthroat, *n.* assassino -na.

cutting, *n.* corte *m.*; muda *f.*

cybernetics, *n.* cibernética *f.*

cycle, *n.* ciclo *m.*; bicicleta *f.*; motocicleta *f.*

cyclical, *adj.* cíclico.

cycling, *n.* ciclismo *m.*

cyclist, *n.* ciclista *m.f.*

cyclone, *n.* ciclone *m.*

cyclotron, *n.* cíclotron *m.*

cylinder, *n.* cilindro *m.*

cymbal, *n.* prato *m.*

cynical, *adj.* cínico.

cynicism, *n.* cinismo *m.*

cypress, *n.* cipreste *m.*

Cyprus, *n.* Chipre *m.*

cyst, *n.* quisto, cisto *m.*

Czech, *adj., n.* tcheco -ca.

Czechoslovak, *adj., n.* tcheco-slovaco -ca.

Czechoslovakia, *n.* Tchecoslováquia *f.*

D

dab, *n.* tico *m.*; toque ligeiro *m.*

dabble in, *vb.* ocupar-se superficialmente de.

dad, *n.* papai *m.*

daffy, *adj.* amalucado.

dagger, *n.* adaga *f.*

daily, *adj., n.* diário, cotidiano *m.*

daintiness, *n.* delicadeza *f.*; requinte *m.*

dainty, *adj.* delicado; requintado.

dairy, *n.* leiteria *f.*

daisy, *n.* margarida *f.*

dally, *vb.* perder tempo; namoriscar.

dam, 1. *n.* represa, barragem *f.* **2.** *vb.* represar.

damage, 1. *n.* dano, prejuízo *m.* **2.** *vb.* danificar, prejudicar.

dame, n. senhora, dama f.; dona f.

damn, 1. vb. danar, condenar. **2.** interj. droga!, (vulg.) merda!

damned, adj. danado, maldito.

damp, adj. úmido, molhado.

dampen, vb. molhar; arrefecer.

dampness, n. umidade f.

damsel, n. donzela f.

dance, 1. n. dança f.; (ball) baile m. **2.** vb. dançar.

dancer, n. dançarino -na, bailarino -na.

dandelion, n. dente-de-leão m.

dandruff, n. caspa f.

dandy, n. dândi, almofadinha m.

danger, n. perigo m.

dangerous, adj. perigoso.

dangle, vb. suspender; pendurar.

Danish, adj., n. dinamarquês -quesa.

dare, 1. n. desafio m. **2.** vb. desafiar; atrever-se.

daredevil, n. atrevido, (sl.) topa-tudo m.

daring, 1. adj. ousado. **2.** n. ousadia f.

dark, 1. adj. escuro; moreno. **2.** n. escuridão f., escuro m.

darken, vb. escurecer(-se).

darkness, n. escuridão f.

darkroom, n. câmara escura f.

darling, adj., n. querido, amado m.

darn, vb. cerzir.

darned, adj. danado.

dart, 1. n. dardo m. **2.** vb. correr, disparar.

dash, 1. n. arremetida f.; pitada f.; (punc.) travessão m. **2.** vb. correr.

dashboard, n. painel m.

dastardly, adj. covarde.

data, n.pl. dados m.pl. **d. processing,** processamento de dados m.

date, 1. n. data f.; encontro marcado, (sl.) programa m.; datil m. **2.** vb. datar; sair com.

daub, vb. besuntar.

daughter, n. filha f.

daughter-in-law, n. nora f.

daunt, vb. intimidar.

dauntless, adj. intrépido.

dawdle, vb. folgar, perder tempo.

dawn, 1. n. alvorada f. **2.** vb. amanhecer.

day, n. dia m. **d. after tomorrow,** depois de amanhã; **d. before yesterday,** anteontem; **all d.,** o dia todo, todo o dia; **by d.,** de dia; **every d.,** todo dia, todos os dias; **good d.,** bom dia; **the next d.,** no dia seguinte.

daybreak, n. aurora f.

day-care center, n. creche f.

daydream, n. devaneio m., fantasia f.

daylight, n. luz do dia f. **d. saving time,** hora de verão f.

daze, vb. aturdir, atordoar.

dazzle, vb. deslumbrar.

dazzling, adj. deslumbrante.

deacon, n. diácono m.

dead, adj. morto, defunto.

deaden, vb. amortecer.

dead end, n. beco sem saída m.

deadline, n. prazo final m.

deadlock, n. impasse m.

deadly, adj. mortal, mortífero.

deaf, adj. surdo.

deafen, vb. ensurdecer.

deafening, adj. ensurdecedor.

deaf-mute, n. surdo-mudo m.

deafness, n. surdez f.

deal, 1. n. negócio, trato m. **a good/great d.,** muito. **2.** vb. tratar, negociar; dar.

dealer, n. comerciante m.f.; revendedor m.; (cards) banqueiro m.

deal, n. decano m.

dear, adj. caro, querido; caro.

death, n. morte f. **d. certificate,** atestado de óbito m.; **d. penalty,** pena de morte f.

debacle, n. desastre m.

debase, vb. degradar, aviltar.

debatable, adj. discutível.

debate, 1. n. debate m. **2.** vb. debater.

debauch, vb. corromper.

debilitate, vb. debilitar, enfraquecer.

debit, n. débito m.

debonair, adj. cortês; afável.

debris, n. escombros m.pl.

debt, n. dívida f.

debtor, n. devedor -ra.

debunk, vb. desmascarar, desmentir.

debut, 1. n. estréia f., debute m. 2. vb. estrear, debutar.

debutante, n. debutante f.

decade, n. década f., decênio m.

decadence, n. decadência f.

decadent, adj. decadente.

decaffeinated, adj. descafeinado.

decal, n. decalque m., decalcomania f.

decapitate, vb. degolar, decapitar.

decay, 1. n. podridão f.; (teeth) cárie f.; decadência f. 2. vb. apodrecer; (teeth) cariar; decair.

deceased, adj. finado, falecido, morto.

deceit, n. engano m., fraude f.

deceitful, adj. enganoso, mentiroso.

deceive, vb. enganar, iludir, lograr.

December, n. dezembro m.

decency, n. decência f.

decent, adj. decente.

decentralize, vb. descentralizar.

deception, n. engano, logro m.

deceptive, adj. enganoso, ilusório.

decide, vb. decidir, resolver.

decimal, adj., n. decimal.

decimate, vb. dizimar.

decipher, vb. decifrar.

decision, n. decisão f.

decisive, adj. decisivo.

deck, n. (ship) convés, tombadilho m.; (cards) baralho m.

declaration, n. declaração f.

declare, vb. declarar.

declension, n. declinação f.

decline, 1. n. declínio m., decadência f. 2. vb. decair; recusar.

décolletage, n. decote m.

décolleté, adj. decotado.

decompose, vb. decompor.

decongestant, n. descongestionante m.

décor, n. decoração f.

decorate, vb. decorar; (mil.) condecorar.

decoration, n. decoração f.; (mil.) condecoração f.

decorum, n. decoro m.

decoy, n. engodo, chamariz m.

decrease, 1. n. diminuição f. 2. vb. diminuir.

decree, 1. n. decreto m. 2. vb. decretar.

decrepit, adj. decrépito, caduco.

decry, vb. censurar.

dedicate, vb. dedicar.

dedication, n. dedicação f.; (book) dedicatória f.

deduce, vb. deduzir.

deduct, vb. deduzir.

deduction, n. dedução f.; redução f.

deed, n. ação f.; façanha f.; (title) escritura f.

deem, vb. julgar, achar.

deep, adj. fundo, profundo.

deepen, vb. aprofundar.

deer, vb. cervo m.

deface, vb. desfigurar, mutilar.

defamation, n. difamação f.

defame, vb. difamar.

default, 1. n. falta f.; revelia f. 2. vb. faltar; não pagar.

defeat, 1. n. derrota f.; 2. vb. derrotar.

defecate, vb. defecar, (vulg.) cagar.

defect, n. defeito m.

defective, adj. defeituoso, defectivo.

defend, vb. defender.

defendant, n. réu, acusado m.

defender, n. defensor -ra.

defense, n. defesa f.

defenseless, adj. indefeso.

defensive, 1. adj. defensivo. 2. n. defensiva f.

defer, vb. adiar, diferir.

deference, n. deferência f., respeito m.

deferment, n. adiamento, diferimento m.

defiance, n. desafio m., provocação f.

defiant, adj. desafiante.

deficiency, n. deficiência f.

deficient, adj. deficiente.

deficit, n. déficit m.

defile, vb. sujar, macular.

define, vb. definir.

definite, adj. definido, definitivo.

definition, n. definição f.

definitive, adj. definitivo.

deflect, *vb.* desviar.
deflower, *vb.* deflorar.
deform, *vb.* deformar.
deformity, *n.* deformidade *f.*
defraud, *vb.* defraudar.
defray, *vb.* custear.
defrost, *vb.* degelar, descongelar.
deft, *adj.* hábil, destro.
defunct, *adj.* defunto.
defy, *vb.* desafiar.
degenerate, 1. *adj.* degenerado. 2. *vb.* degenerar.
degrade, *vb.* degradar, aviltar.
degree, *n.* grau *m.*; título *m.* **to a certain d.**, até certo ponto.
dehydrate, *vb.* desidratar(-se).
deify, *vb.* deificar, endeusar.
deign, *vb.* condescender. **d. to**, dignar-se a.
deity, *n.* deidade, divindade *f.*
dejected, *adj.* abatido.
dejection, *n.* depressão *f.*
delay, 1. *n.* demora *f.*, atraso *m.* 2. *vb.* atrasar, demorar; (postponement) adiamento *m.*
delegate, 1. *n.* delegado *m.*, representante *m.f.* 2. *vb.* delegar.
delegation, *n.* delegação *f.*
delete, *vb.* suprimir, apagar.
deletion, *n.* supressão *f.*
deliberate, 1. *adj.* deliberado. 2. *vb.* deliberar.
delicacy, *n.* delicadeza *f.*; gulodice *f.*
delicate, *adj.* delicado; frágil.
delicious, *adj.* delicioso, gostoso.
delight, 1. *n.* delícia *f.*, deleite *m.* 2. *vb.* deleitar(-se).
delightful, *adj.* delicioso, agradável.
delimit, *vb.* delimitar.
delineate, *vb.* delinear.
delinquency, *n.* delinqüência *f.*
delinquent, *adj.*, *n.* delinqüente *m.f.*
delirious, *adj.* delirante.
delirium, *n.* delírio *m.*
deliver, *vb.* entregar; (free) libertar; (speech) pronunciar.
delivery, *n.* entrega *f.*; (birth) parto *m.*; libertação *f.*; pronunciamento *m.*
delta, *n.* delta *m.*
delude, *vb.* iludir, enganar.
deluge, *n.* dilúvio *m.*

delusion, *n.* ilusão *f.*, engano *m.*
de luxe, *adj.* de luxo.
delve, *vb.* aprofundar, penetrar.
demagogue, *n.* demagogo *m.*
demagoguery, *n.* demagogia *f.*
demand, 1. *n.* demanda *f.*; (com.) procura *f.* 2. *vb.* demandar, exigir.
demanding, *adj.* exigente.
demarcate, *vb.* demarcar.
demean, *vb.* degradar.
demeanor, *n.* conduta *f.*; porte *m.*
demented, *adj.* demente.
demigod, *n.* semideus *m.*
demise, *n.* morte *f.*
demitasse, *n.* xícrinha *f.*; cafezinho *m.*
democracy, *n.* democracia *f.*
democrat, *n.* democrata *m.f.*
democratic, *adj.* democrático.
demolish, *vb.* demolir.
demon, *n.* demônio *m.*
demonstrate, *vb.* demonstrar.
demonstration, *n.* demonstração *f.*; (polit.) manifestação, passeata *f.*
demonstrative, *adj.* demonstrativo; efusivo.
demonstrator, *n.* manifestante *m.f.*
demoralize, *vb.* desmoralizar.
demote, *vb.* rebaixar.
demur, *vb.* objetar; hesitar.
demure, *adj.* recatado.
den, *n.* toca *f.*, covil *m.*
denial, *n.* negação, recusa *f.*
denigrate, *vb.* denegrir.
denim, *n.* zuarte, brim *m.*
Denmark, *n.* Dinamarca *f.*
denomination, *n.* denominação *f.*; (eccles.) seita *f.*
denominator, *n.* denominador *m.*
denote, *vb.* denotar.
dénouement, *n.* desfecho, desenlace *m.*
denounce, *n.* denunciar.
dense, *adj.* denso; estúpido.
density, *n.* densidade *f.*
dent, 1. *n.* mossa *f.* 2. *vb.* morsegar.
dental, *adj.* dental, dentário. **d. floss**, fio dental *m.*
dentist, *n.* dentista *m.f.*
dentistry, *n.* odontologia *f.*
denture, *n.* dentadura *f.*

denunciation, *n.* denúncia *f.*

deny, *vb.* negar; recusar; repudiar.

deodorant, *n.* desodorante *m.*

depart, *n.* partir, sair.

department, *n.* departamento *m.* **d. store,** loja *f.*, magazine *m.*

departure, *n.* partida *f.*; divergência *f.*

depend, *vb.* depender. **d. on,** depender de.

dependable, *adj.* digno de confiança, seguro.

dependence, *n.* dependência *f.*

dependent, *adj., n.* dependente *m.f.*

depict, *vb.* pintar, representar.

depiction, *n.* pintura, representação *f.*

deplete, *vb.* esgotar.

deplore, *adj.* deplorar.

deploy, *vb.* dispor, distribuir.

deport, *vb.* deportar.

deportment, *n.* comportamento *m.*

deposit, **1.** *n.* depósito *m.* **2.** *vb.* depositar.

deposition, *n.* depoimento, testemunho *m.*

depositor, *n.* depositante *m.f.*

depot, *n.* depósito, armazém *m.*; (railroad) estação *f.*

deprave, *vb.* depravar.

depravity, *n.* depravação *f.*

deprecate, *vb.* desaprovar, censurar.

depreciate, *vb.* depreciar(-se).

depredation, *n.* depredação *f.*

depress, *vb.* deprimir.

depressed, *adj.* demprimido.

depression, *n.* depressão *f.*

deprivation, *n.* privação *f.*

deprive, *vb.* privar.

depth, *n.* profundidade, profundeza *f.*

deputy, *n.* deputado *m.*

derail, *vb.* descarrilar.

derange, *vb.* desarranjar; enlouquecer.

derelict, **1.** *adj.* derrelito; negligente. **2.** *n.* pessoa abandonada *f.*; desabrigado *m.*

deride, *vb.* escarnecer, zombar de.

derision, *n.* escárnio *m.*, zombaria *f.*

derivation, *n.* derivação *f.*

derivative, *adj., n.* derivativo *m.*

derive, *vb.* derivar(-se).

derogatory, *adj.* pejorativo.

derrick, *n.* guindaste *m.*; torre de perfuração *f.*

descend, *vb.* descer; (family) descender.

descendant, *n.* descendente *m.f.*

descent, *n.* descenso *m.*, descida *f.*

describe, *vb.* descrever.

description, *n.* descrição *f.*

descriptive, *adj.* descritivo.

desecrate, *vb.* profanar.

desert, **1.** *n.* deserto *m.* **2.** *vb.* desertar, abandonar.

deserter, *n.* desertor *m.*

desertion, *n.* deserção *f.*

deserve, *vb.* merecer.

design, **1.** *n.* plano, projeto *m.*; desenho *m.*; desígnio *m.* **2.** *vb.* planejar; projetar; desenhar.

designate, *vb.* designar, indicar.

designation, *n.* designação *f.*

designer, *n.* projetista, desenhista *m.f.*; (dress) costureiro *m.*

desirable, *adj.* desejável.

desire, **1.** *n.* desejo *m.* **2.** *vb.* desejar.

desist, *vb.* desistir; parar.

desk, *n.* mesa de trabalho *f.*; carteira, escrivaninha *f.*

desolate, **1.** *adj.* despovoado; devastado; desolado. **2.** *vb.* assolar; desolar.

desolation, *n.* desolação, ruína *f.*

despair, **1.** *n.* desespero *m.* **2.** *vb.* desesperar.

desperado, *n.* criminoso *m.*

desperate, *adj.* desesperado.

desperation, *n.* desespero *m.*

despicable, *adj.* desprezível.

despise, *vb.* desprezar, desdenhar.

despite, *prep.* apesar de.

despoil, *vb.* despojar.

despondent, *adj.* desanimado, deprimido.

despot, *n.* déspota *m.f.*

dessert, *n.* sobremesa *f.*

destination, *n.* destino *m.*

destine, *vb.* destinar.

destiny, *n.* destino *m.*

destitute, adj. destituído; necessitado.

destroy, vb. destruir.

destroyer, n. (naut.) contratorpedeiro, destróier m.

destruction, n. destruição f.

destructive, adj. destrutivo.

detach, vb. separar, desprender.

detachment, n. (mil.) destacamento m.

detail, 1. n. detalhe, pormenor m. **2.** vb. detalhar, pormenorizar.

detain, vb. deter.

detect, vb. descobrir, detectar.

detective, n. detetive m. **d. novel,** romance policial m.

detector, n. detector m.

detention, n. detenção f.

deter, vb. impedir; dissuadir.

detergent, adj., n. detergente m.

deteriorate, vb. deteriorar-se.

determination, n. determinação f.

determine, vb. determinar.

deterrent, n. dissuasão f., estorvo m.

detest, vb. detestar.

detonate, vb. detonar; explodir.

detour, n. desvio m.

detract, vb. diminuir, tirar.

detriment, n. detrimento m., prejuízo m.

detrimental, adj. prejudicial.

devalue, vb. desvalorizar.

devastate, vb. devastar, assolar.

devastation, n. devastação f., estrago m.

develop, vb. desenvolver(-se). (phot.) revelar.

development, n. desenvolvimento m.; (phot.) revelação f.

deviate, vb. desviar-se.

deviation, n. desvio m., divergência f.

device, n. dispositivo m.

devil, n. diabo, demônio m.

devilish, adj. diabólico.

devious, adj. desonesto.

devise, vb. inventar, tramar.

devoid, adj. destituído.

devote, vb. devotar, dedicar.

devotee, n. devoto m.; adepto n.

devotion, n. devoção f.

devour, vb. devorar.

devout, adj. devoto.

dew, n. orvalho, sereno m.

dexterity, n. destreza f.

diabetes, n. diabetes f.

diabolic, adj. diabólico.

diagnose, vb. diagnosticar.

diagnosis, n. diagnose f., diagnóstico m.

diagnostic, adj. diagnóstico.

diagonal, adj. diagonal.

diagram, n. diagrama m.

dial, 1. n. mostrador; quadrante m.; (knob) dial m.; (phone) disco m. **2.** vb. (radio) sintonizar; (phone) discar.

dialect, n. dialeto m.

dialectical, adj. dialético.

dialogue, n. diálogo m.

diameter, n. diâmetro m.

diametrically, adv. diametralmente.

diamond, n. diamante, brilhante m.; (pl.) (cards) ouros n.pl.

diaper, n. fralda f., cueiro m.

diaphragm, n. diafragma m.

diarrhea, n. diarréia f.

diary, n. diário m.

diatribe, n. diatribe f.

dice, n. dados m.pl.

dichotomy, n. dicotomia f.

dictate, 1. n. mandado m.; ditame f. **2.** vb. ditar.

dictation, n. ditado m.

dictator, n. ditador m.

dictatorial, adj. ditatorial.

dictatorship, n. ditadura f.

diction, n. dicção f.

dictionary, n. dicionário m.

didactic, adj. didático.

die, 1. n. (game) dado m.; molde m. **2.** vb. morrer.

diet, n. dieta f.; regime m. **go on a d.,** fazer regime.

dietary, adj. dietético.

differ, vb. diferir.

difference, n. diferença f.

different, adj. diferente.

differentiate, vb. diferenciar, diferençar.

difficult, adj. difícil.

difficulty, n. dificuldade f.

diffident, adj. tímido.

diffuse, 1. adj. difuso. **2.** vb. difundir.

diffusion, n. difusão f.

dig, vb. cavar, escavar.

digest, 1. *n.* digesto *m.* **2.** *vb.* digerir; condensar.

digestion, *n.* digestão *f.*

digit, *n.* algarismo *m.* ; dedo *m.*

digital, *adj.* digital.

dignified, *adj.* nobre; grave; majestoso.

dignify, *vb.* dignificar, honrar.

dignitary, *n.* dignitário *m.*

dignity, *n.* dignidade *f.*

digress, *vb.* divagar.

digression, *n.* digressão *f.*

dike, *n.* dique *m.*

dilapidated, *adj.* dilapidado.

dilate, *vb.* dilatar(-se).

dilemma, *n.* dilema *m.*

diligence, *n.* diligência *f.*

diligent, *adj.* diligente.

dilute, *vb.* diluir.

dim, 1. *adj.* escuro; baço; obscuro; indistinto. **2.** *vb.* obscurecer; apagar.

dimension, *n.* dimensão *f.*

diminish, *vb.* diminuir.

diminutive, *adj.* diminutivo.

dimple, *n.* covinha *f.*

din, *n.* barulho *m.* , gritaria *f.*

dine, *vb.* jantar.

diner, *n.* comensal *m.f.* ; carro-restaurante *m.*

dingy, *adj.* sombrio; encardido.

dining room, *n.* sala de jantar *f.*

dinner, *n.* jantar *m.*

dinosaur, *n.* dinossauro *m.*

diocese, *n.* diocese *f.*

dip, 1. *n.* depressão *f.*; mergulho *m.* **2.** *vb.* descer subitamente; mergulhar; molhar.

diphtheria, *n.* difteria *f.*

diphthong, *n.* ditongo *m.*

diploma, *n.* diploma *m.*

diplomacy, *n.* diplomacia *f.*

diplomat, *n.* diplomata *m.f.*

diplomatic, *adj.* diplomático.

dire, *adj.* horroroso, medonho.

direct, 1. *adj.* direto. **2.** *vb.* dirigir.

direction, *n.* direção *f.* , rumo *m.*

directive, *n.* diretiva *f.*

director, *n.* diretor -ra.

directory, *n.* diretório, catálogo *m.* , lista *f.*

dirge, *n.* endecha *f.*

dirigible, *n.* dirigível *m.*

dirt, *n.* sujeira *f.* ; terra *f.*

dirty, *adj.* sujo. **d. trick,** sujeira *f.*

disability, *n.* incapacidade *f.*; invalidez *f.*

disable, *vb.* incapacitar.

disabuse, *vb.* desenganar.

disadvantage, *n.* desvantagem *f.*

disagree, *vb.* discordar (de); fazer mal a.

disagreeable, *adj.* desagradável.

disagreement, *n.* desacordo *m.* , discordância *f.*; desavença *f.*

disappear, *vb.* desaparecer, sumir.

disappearance, *n.* desaparecimento *m.*

disappoint, *vb.* decepcionar, desapontar.

disappointment, *n.* decepção *f.* , desapontamento *m.*

disapproval, *n.* desaprovação *f.*

disapprove, *vb.* desaprovar.

disarm, *vb.* desarmar.

disarmament, *n.* desarmamento *m.*

disarray, *n.* desarranjo *m.* , desordem *f.*

disassemble, *vb.* desmontar.

disassociate, *vb.* desassociar. **d. oneself from,** desassociar-se de.

disaster, *n.* desastre *m.*

disastrous, *adj.* desastroso.

disavow, *vb.* repudiar.

disavowal, *n.* repúdio *m.*

disband, *vb.* dispersar(-se).

disbelief, *n.* descrença, incredulidade *f.*

disbelieve, *vb.* descrer, desacreditar.

disburse, *vb.* desembolsar.

discard, *vb.* descartar, jogar fora.

discern, *vb.* discernir; perceber.

discerning, *adj.* perspicaz.

discharge, 1. *n.* (duty) desempenho *m.*; (gun) descarga *f.*; *(mil.)* baixa *f.*; (hospital) alta *f.* **2.** *vb.* desempenhar; (gun) disparar; (employee) demitir; *(mil.)* dar baixa a; (hospital) dar alta a.

disciple, *n.* discípulo *m.*

discipline, 1. *n.* disciplina *f.* **2.** *vb.* disciplinar.

disclaim, *vb.* repudiar; rejeitar.

disclose, vb. revelar, descobrir.

disclosure, n. revelação f.

discolor, vb. descorar, descolorir(-se).

discomfit, vb. derrotar; frustrar.

discomfort, 1. n. desconforto m.; mal-estar m. 2. vb. desconfortar; incomodar.

disconcert, vb. desconcertar.

disconnect, vb. desligar.

disconnected, adj. desligado; desconexo.

discontent, n. descontentamento m.

discontented, adj. descontente.

discontinue, vb. descontinuar.

discord, n. discórdia f.; desacordo m.

discordant, adj. dissonante.

discothèque, n. discoteca f.

discount, n. desconto, abatimento m.

discourage, vb. desanimar.

discouragement, n. desânimo, desalento.

discourse, 1. n. discurso m. 2. vb. discursar, discorrer.

discourteous, adj. descortês.

discourtesy, n. descortesia f.

discover, vb. descobrir.

discoverer, n. descobridor -ra.

discovery, n. descobrimento m.; descoberta f.

discredit, 1. n. descrédito m. 2. vb. desacreditar.

discreet, adj. discreto.

discrepancy, n. discrepância f.

discretion, n. discrição f.

discriminate, vb. discriminar. d. against, discriminar.

discrimination, n. discriminação f.; discernimento m.

discuss, vb. discutir.

discussion, n. discussão f.

disdain, 1. n. desdém n. 2. n. desdenhar.

disease, n. doença f.

disembark, vb. desembarcar.

disembody, vb. desincorporar, desencarnar.

disenchantment, n. desencanto m.

disencumber, vb. desembaraçar.

disengage, vb. desligar(-se), desprender(-se).

disentangle, vb. desenredar.

disfavor, 1. n. desfavor m. 2. vb. desfavorecer.

disfigure, vb. desfigurar.

disgorge, vb. vomitar.

disgrace, 1. n. vergonha f.; desonra f. 2. vb. desonrar.

disgraceful, adj. vergonhoso.

disguise, 1. n. disfarce m. 2. vb. disfarçar.

disgust, 1. n. repugnância f. 2. vb. repugnar.

disgusting, adj. repugnante.

dish, n. prato m.; (pl.) louça f.

disharmony, n. desarmonia f.

dishearten, vb. desanimar.

disheveled, adj. despenteado, desgrenhado.

dishonest, adj. desonesto.

dishonesty, n. desonestidade f.

dishonor, 1. n. desonra f. 2. vb. desonrar.

dishonorable, adj. desonroso.

dishwasher, n. máquina de lavar louça f.

disillusion, 1. n. desilusão f., desengano m. 2. vb. desiludir, desenganar.

disinfect, vb. desinfetar.

disinfectant, n. desinfetante m.

disinherit, vb. deserdar.

disintegrate, vb. desintegrar(-se).

disinterested, adj. desinteressado, imparcial.

disjointed, adj. desconexo.

disk, n. disco m. floppy d., disquete m.; hard d., disco rígido, winchester m.

diskette, n. disquete m.

dislike, 1. n. aversão f. 2. vb. não gostar de.

dislocate, vb. deslocar.

dislodge, vb. desalojar.

dismal, adj. lúgubre; horrível.

dismantle, vb. desmantelar, desmontar.

dismay, 1. n. consternação f. 2. vb. consternar.

dismember, n. desmembrar; mutilar.

dismiss, vb. despedir; demitir; rejeitar.

dismissal, n. despedida f.; demissão f.; rejeição f.

dismount, vb. desmontar.

disobedient, adj. desobediente.

disobey, vb. desobedecer.

disorder, 1. n. desordem f. **2.** vb. desordenar.

disorderly, adj. desordenado; desordeiro.

disorganize, vb. desorganizar.

disoriented, adj. desorientado, desnorteado.

disown, vb. repudiar.

disparage, vb. desacreditar.

disparate, adj. díspar.

disparity, n. disparidade f.

dispassionate, adj. desinteressado, imparcial.

dispatch, 1. n. despacho m.; comunicado m.; rapidez f. **2.** vb. despachar; matar.

dispel, vb. dispersar, dissipar.

dispensary, n. dispensário m.

dispensation, n. dispensação f.; dispensa f.

dispense, vb. dispensar, distribuir. **d. with,** prescindir de.

dispersal, dispersion, n. dispersão f.

disperse, vb. dispersar(-se).

displace, vb. deslocar.

display, 1. n. exposição f.; demonstração f. **2.** vb. exibir, mostrar, expor.

display window, n. vitrine f.

displease, vb. desagradar.

displeasure, n. desagrado m.

disposable, adj. descartável; disponível.

disposal, n. disposição f., dispor m.

dispose, vb. dispor. **d. of,** descartar, desfazer-se de.

disposition, n. disposição f.; temperamento m.; tendência f.; decisão f.

dispossess, vb. desapossar.

disproportionate, adj. desproporcionado.

disprove, vb. confutar.

dispute, 1. n. disputa f. **2.** vb. disputar.

disqualify, vb. desqualificar.

disregard, 1. n. desatenção, desconsideração f. **2.** vb. desatender, desconsiderar.

disrepair, n. desconserto, abandono m.

disreputable, adj. infame, desacreditado.

disrepute, n. má fama f., descrédito m.

disrespect, 1. n. desrespeito m. **2.** vb. desrespeitar.

disrespectful, adj. desrespeitoso.

disrobe, vb. despir-se.

disrupt, vb. quebrar; interromper.

dissatisfaction, n. insatisfação f.

dissatisfied, adj. descontente.

dissect, vb. dissecar.

dissemble, vb. dissimular.

disseminate, vb. disseminar, difundir.

dissent, 1. n. dissenção f. **2.** vb. dissentir.

dissenter, n. dissidente m.f.

dissertation, n. dissertação f.; tese f.

disservice, n. desserviço m.

dissident, n. dissidente m.f.

dissimilar, adj. dessemelhante.

dissipate, vb. dissipar.

dissolute, adj. dissoluto, devasso.

dissolve, vb. dissolver(-se); derreter(-se).

dissonant, adj. dissonante.

dissuade, vb. dissuadir.

distance, 1. n. distância f. **2.** vb. distanciar.

distant, adj. distante.

distaste, n. aversão f.

distasteful, adj. desagradável.

distill, vb. destilar.

distillery, n. destilaria f.

distinct, adj. distinto.

distinction, n. distinção f.

distinctive, adj. distintivo.

distinguish, vb. distinguir.

distinguished, adj. distinto, eminente.

distort, vb. distorcer; deformar; deturpar.

distortion, n. distorção f.; deformação f.; deturpação f.

distract, vb. distrair, desviar.

distraction, n. distração f.; perturbação f.; passatempo m.

distraught, adj. perturbado, louco.

distress, 1. n. dor f.; aflição f. **2.** vb. atormentar; afligir.

distribute, vb. distribuir, repartir.

distribution, *n.* distribuição *f.*
distributor, *n.* *(mech.)* distribuidor *m.*
district, *n.* distrito *m.*; bairro *m.*
district attorney, *n.* promotor público *m.*
distrust, 1. *n.* desconfiança *f.* **2.** *vb.* desconfiar de.
distrustful, *adj.* desconfiado.
disturb, *vb.* perturbar; interromper.
disturbance, *n.* distúrbio *m.*
ditch, *n.* vala *f.*, fosso *m.*
ditto, *n.* idem *m.*, o mesmo.
divan, *n.* divã, sofá *m.*
dive, 1. *n.* mergulho *m.*; *(coll.)* baiúca *f.* **2.** *vb.* mergulhar.
diver, *n.* mergulhador -ra; escafandrista *m.f.*
diverge, *vb.* divergir.
divergent, *adj.* divergente.
diverse, *adj.* diverso.
diversify, *vb.* diversificar.
diversion, *n.* desvio *m.*; diversão *f.*
diversity, *n.* diversidade *f.*
divert, *vb.* desviar; divertir.
divest, *vb.* despojar, desapossar.
divide, *vb.* dividir, rachar.
dividend, *n.* dividendo *m.*
divider, *n.* divisor *m.*
divine, 1. *adj.* divino. **2.** *vb.* adivinhar.
diving board, *n.* trampolim *m.*
divinity, *n.* divindade *f.*
division, *n.* divisão *f.*
divorce, 1. *n.* divórcio *m.* **2.** *vb.* divorciar-se de.
divorcé -cée, *n.* divorciado -da.
divulge, *vb.* divulgar.
dizziness, *n.* tontura, vertigem *f.*
dizzy, *adj.* tonto, vertiginoso.
do, *vb.* fazer.
docile, *adj.* dócil.
dock, 1. *n.* cais *m.*, doca *f.* **dry d.,** dique (seco) *m.* **2.** *vb.* atracar.
doctor, *n.* médico -ca; doutor -ra.
doctoral, *adj.* doutoral.
doctorate, *n.* doutorado, doutoramento *m.*
doctrinaire, *adj.* dogmático, doutrinário.
doctrine, *n.* doutrina *f.*

document, 1. *n.* documento *m.* **2.** *vb.* documentar.
documentary, *adj.*, *n.* documentário *m.*
documentation, *n.* documentação *f.*
dodge, 1. *n.* evasão *f.* **2.** *vb.* evadir, esquivar.
doe, *n.* corça *f.*
dog, *n.* cachorro -ra, cão *m.*
dogma, *n.* dogma *m.*
dogmatic, *adj.* dogmático.
dole, *vb.* **d. out,** distribuir.
doleful, *adj.* triste.
doll, *n.* boneco -ca.
dollar, *n.* dólar *m.*
dolphin, *n.* delfim, golfinho *m.*
dolt, *n.* imbecil *m.f.*
domain, *n.* domínio *m.*
dome, *n.* cúpula *f.*
domestic, *adj.*, *n.* doméstico *m.*
domesticate, *vb.* domesticar, domar.
domicile, *n.* domicílio *m.*
dominance, *n.* dominância *f.*
dominant, *adj.* dominante.
dominate, *vb.* dominar.
domination, *n.* dominação *f.*
domineering, *adj.* mandão.
Dominican, *adj.*, *n.* dominicano *m.*
Dominican Republic, *n.* República Dominicana *f.*
dominion, *n.* domínio *m.*; controle *m.*
domino, -noes, *n.* dominó *m.*
donate, *vb.* doar.
donation, *n.* doação *f.*
done, *adj.* feito; terminado; pronto.
donkey, *n.* asno, burro *m.*
donor, *n.* doador -ra.
doom, 1. *n.* destino adverso *m.*; ruína *f.* **2.** *vb.* condenar; perder.
door, *n.* porta *f.*
doorbell, *n.* campainha, sineta *f.*
doorman, *n.* porteiro *m.*
doormat, *n.* capacho *m.*
doorway, *n.* portal *m.*, entrada *f.*
dope, 1. *n.* entorpecente *m.*, droga *f.*; *(coll.)* idiota *m.f.*; *(sl.)* informações *f.pl.* **2.** *vb.* dopar.
dormant, *adj.* dormente.

dormitory, n. dormitório m.

dosage, n. dosagem f.

dose, n. dose f.

dossier, n. dossiê m.; pasta f.

dot, 1. n. ponto m.; pingo m. **on the d.,** em ponto. **2.** vb. pontilhar. **dotted line,** linha pontilhada f.

double, 1. adj. duplo. **2.** n. dobro. **3.** vb. dobrar, duplicar. **4.** adv. em dobro.

double bed, n. cama de casal f.

double-cross, vb. trair.

doubt, 1. n. dúvida f. **2.** vb. duvidar (de).

doubtful, adj. duvidoso.

doubtless, 1. adj. indubitável. **2.** adv. sem dúvida.

dough, n. massa f.; (sl.) dinheiro m., grana f.

doughnut, n. sonho m.

douse, vb. mergulhar; empapar; (coll.) apagar.

dove, n. pombo -ba.

down, 1. adj. doente; por baixo; enguiçado. **2.** n. penugem f.; queda f. **ups and downs,** altos e baixos. **3.** vb. (coll.) devorar, engolir; derrubar. **4.** adv. para baixo; abaixo. **5.** prep. por, ao longo de. **d. the river,** rio abaixo; **d. the street,** rua abaixo.

downcast, adj. cabisbaixo, deprimido.

downfall, n. queda, ruína f.

downhearted, adj. descoroçoado, desanimado.

downhill, adv. ladeira abaixo.

downpour, n. aguaceiro m.

downright, adj. total, completo.

downstairs, adv. embaixo, no andar de baixo.

downstream, adv. rio abaixo, a jusante.

downtown, n. centro, comércio m., cidade f.

downward, 1. adj. descendente. **2.** adv. para baixo.

doze, 1. n. cochilo m. **2.** vb. cochilar.

dozen, n. dúzia f.

drab, adj. desbotado; monótono.

draft, 1. corrente de ar f.; rascunho m.; (com.) letra f.; (mil.) recrutamento m. **2.** vb.

esboçar; (write) redigir; (mil.) recrutar.

draft beer, n. chope m.

draftee, n. recruta m.

drafting table, n. prancheta f.

draftsman, n. desenhista, projetista m.f.

drag, adv. arrastar; (river, etc.) dragar.

dragon, n. dragão m.

dragonfly, n. libélula f.

drain, 1. escoadouro, (cano de) esgoto m. **2.** vb. drenar(-se); esgotar.

drainage, n. escoamento m., drenagem f.

drain pipe, n. cano de esgoto m.

drama, n. drama m.

dramatic, adj. dramático.

dramatist, n. dramaturgo, teatrólogo m.

dramatize, vb. dramatizar.

drape, n. cortina f.

drastic, adj. drástico.

draw, 1. n. (lottery) sorteio m.; (sport.) empate m. **2.** vb. tirar; atrair; sortear; (curtains) correr; (picture) desenhar; (sport.) empatar. **d. up,** redigir.

drawback, n. desvantagem f.

drawbridge, n. ponte levadiça f.

drawer, n. gaveta f.; desenhista m.f.; (pl.) cuecas f.pl.

drawing, n. desenho m.; (lottery) sorteio m.

drawing board, n. prancheta f.

drawl, 1. n. fala arrastada f. **2.** vb. falar arrastadamente.

dread, 1. n. pavor, medo m. **2.** vb. temer.

dreadful, adj. horroroso, medonho.

dream, 1. n. sonho m. **2.** vb. sonhar. **d. of,** sonhar com.

dreamer, n. sonhador -ra.

dreary, adj. monótono e sombrio.

dredge, 1. n. draga f. **2.** vb. dragar.

dregs, n.pl. borra f., fezes f.pl.; (human) ralé f.

drench, vb. encharcar.

dress, 1. n. vestido m.; (attire) traje m. **2.** vb. vestir(-se); (wound) pensar.

dresser, n. (furniture) cômoda f.

dressing, n. (wound) penso m.; (salad) tempero, molho m.; recheio m.

dressing-down, n. descompostura f.

dressing gown, n. penhoar, roupão m.

dressing room, n. camarim m.

dressing table, n. penteadeira f., toucador m.

dressmaker, n. costureira, modista f.

dribble, vb. babar-se; pingar; (sport.) driblar.

drier, n. secador de roupa m. **hair d.,** secador de cabelo m.

drift, n. tendência f.; (current) direção f.; (snow) neve amontoada f. 2. vb. ir à deriva; vaguear.

drifter, n. vagabundo m.

drill, 1. n. exercício, treino m.; (mech.) trado m., broca f. 2. vb. treinar; (holes) perfurar.

drink, 1. n. bebida f.; (sip) gole m.; (alcoholic) drinque m. 2. vb. beber, tomar.

drip, 1. n. pingo m., gota f. 2. vb. pingar, gotejar.

drive, 1. n. passeio m., volta f. (de carro); avenida f.; garra f.; (mil.) ataque m. 2. vb. (car) dirigir; (cattle) tocar; obrigar; impulsionar; (nail) cravar.

drivel, 1. n. baba f. 2. vb. babar-se.

driver, n. motorista m.f.; chofer m. **d.'s license,** carteira de motorista f.

driveway, n. entrada f.

drizzle, 1. n. chuvisco m. 2. vb. chuviscar.

drone, 1. n. (bee) zangão m.; zumbido m. 2. vb. zumbir.

drool, 1. n. baba f. 2. vb. babar-se.

droop, vb. curvar-se, murchar.

drop, 1. n. pingo m., gota f.; queda f. 2. vb. deixar cair; cair. **d. in,** dar um pulo.

dropper, n. conta-gotas m.

drought, n. seca f.

drove, n. manada f.

drown, vb. afogar(-se).

drowsiness, n. sonolência f.

drowsy, adj. sonolento.

drudgery, n. trabalho penoso m.

drug, 1. n. droga f. 2. vb. narcotizar.

drug addict, n. toxicômano -na, viciado -da.

druggist, n. farmacêutico m.

drugstore, n. farmácia, drogaria f.

drum, n. tambor m.

drummer, n. tambor m.

drumstick, n. baqueta f.; coxa (de galinha, etc.) f.

drunk, adj., n. bêbedo -da, -bado -da. **get d.,** embebedar-se.

drunkard, n. bêbedo -da, -bado -da.

drunkenness, n. embriaguez f.

dry, 1. adj. seco, árido. 2. vb. secar.

dry-clean, vb. lavar a seco.

dry-cleaning, n. lavagem a seco f.

dryness, n. secura f.

dual, adj. dual.

dub, vb. chamar; (movie) dublar; (tape) copiar.

dubious, adj. duvidoso.

duchess, n. duquesa f.

duck, 1. n. pato m. 2. vb. abaixar-se; esquivar.

duct, n. canal m.

dude, n. almofadinha m.; (sl.) cara m.

due, adj. devido; pagável.

dues, n.pl. quota, cota f.

duel, 1. n. duelo m. 2. vb. duelar.

duet, n. dueto m.

duke, n. duque m.

dull, 1. adj. embotado; apagado; estúpido; monótono. 2. vb. embotar.

dullness, n. embotamento m.; estupidez f.; monotonia f.

dumb, adj. mudo; bobo, burro.

dumbfound, vb. pasmar.

dummy, n. manequim m.f.; boneco de ventríloquo m.; burro -ra.

dump, 1. n. monte de lixo, depejo m.; espelunca f.; (pl.) (coll.) fossa f. 2. vb. despejar, descarregar (lixo).

dune, n. duna f.

dung, n. esterco m.

dungeon, n. masmorra f., calabouço m.

dunk, vb. molhar.

dupe, 1. n. trouxa f. 2. vb. ludibriar.

duplicate, 1. adj. duplicado. 2. n. duplicata f. 3. vb. duplicar.

duplicity, n. duplicidade f.

durable, adj. durável, duradouro.

duration, n. duração f.

duress, n. compulsão, coação f.

during, prep. durante.

dusk, n. anoitecer, crepúsculo m.

dusky, adj. escuro; moreno.

dust, 1. n. poeira f. 2. vb. espanar.

duster, n. espanador m.

dusty, adj. poeirento; empoeirado.

Dutch, adj., n. holandês -sa.

Dutchman -woman, n. holandês -desa.

dutiful, adj. zeloso; respeitoso.

duty, n. dever m.; tarifa, taxa f. **on d.,** de plantão.

dwarf, n. anão -nã.

dwell, vb. morar, habitar. **d. on,** insistir em (assunto).

dwelling, n. moradia, morada, habitação f.

dwindle, vb. minguar.

dye, 1. n. tintura, tinta f., corante m. 2. vb. tingir, corar.

dying, adj. moribundo.

dynamic, adj. dinâmico.

dynamite, 1. n. dinamite f. 2. vb. dinamitar.

dynasty, n. dinastia f.

dysentery, n. disenteria f.

E

each, 1. adj. cada. 2. pron. cada um -ma. **e. other,** um ao outro.

eager, adj. ansioso, ávido.

eagerness, n. ânsia, avidez f.

eagle, n. águia, f.

ear, n. ouvido m.; (outer) orelha f.; (corn) espiga f.

eardrum, n. tímpano m.

early, adv. cedo.

earn, vb. ganhar.

earnest, adj. sério.

earnings, n. ordenado, salário m.; lucro m.

earphone, n. fone de ouvido m.

earring, n. brinco m.

earth, n. terra f.

earthquake, n. terremoto m.

earthworm, n. minhoca f.

ease, 1. n. repouso m.; facilidade f. 2. vb. aliviar; facilitar.

easel, n. cavalete m.

east, 1. adj. oriental, do leste. 2. n. leste, este, oriente m.

Easter, n. Páscoa f.

eastern, adj. oriental, do leste.

easy, adj. fácil.

eat, vb. comer.

eave, n. beiral m.

ebb, 1. n. baixa-mar, vazante f. 2. vb. vazar; decair.

eccentric, adj. excêntrico.

ecclesiastic, adj. eclesiástico.

echelon, n. escalão m.

echo, 1. n. eco m. 2. vb. ecoar.

eclipse, 1. n. eclipse m. 2. vb. eclipsar.

ecology, n. ecologia f.

economic, adj. econômico.

economical, adj. econômico.

economics, n. economia f.

economist, n. economista m.f.

economize, vb. economizar.

economy, n. economia f.

ecstasy, n. êxtase m.

Ecuador, n. Equador m.

Ecuadorian, adj., n. equatoriano m.

edge, n. beira, orla, borda f.

edible, adj. comestível.

edict, n. edito m.

edifice, n. edifício, prédio m.

edit, vb. redigir.

editing, n. redação f.

edition, n. edição f.

editor, n. redator, diretor m.

editorial, adj., n. editorial m.

educate, vb. educar, ensinar, instruir.

education, n. instrução f., ensino m.; educação f.

educational, adj. educacional, educativo.

educator, n. educador, pedagogo m.

eel, n. enguia f.

efface, vb. apagar.

effect, 1. n. efeito m. **in e.,** vigente, em vigor. 2. vb. efetuar.

effective, *adj.* efetivo, eficaz; em vigor.

effectiveness, *n.* efetividade, eficácia *f.*

effectuate, *vb.* efetuar.

effeminate, *adj.* efeminado.

efficacy, *n.* eficácia *f.*

efficiency, *n.* eficiência, eficácia *f.*

efficient, *adj.* eficiente, eficaz.

effigy, *n.* efígie *f.*

effort, *n.* esforço *m.*

effrontery, *n.* impudência *f.*

effusive, *adj.* efusivo, expansivo.

egg, 1. *n.* ovo *m.* **e. shell,** casca de ovo *f.* **e. white,** clara *f.;* **e. yolk,** gema *f.* **2.** *vb.* **e. on,** incitar.

eggplant, *n.* berinjela, brinjela *f.*

egis, *n.* égide *f.*

ego, *n.* ego *m.*

egocentric, *adj.* egocêntrico.

egotism, *n.* egotismo *m.*

egregious, *adj.* flagrante.

Egypt, *n.* Egito *m.*

Egyptian, *adj., n.* egípcio *m.*

eight, *adj.* oito.

eighteen, *adj.* dezoito.

eighteenth, *adj., n.* décimo-oitavo *m.*

eighth, *adj., n.* oitavo *m.*

eight hundred, *adj.* oitocentos.

eightieth, *adj., n.* octogésimo *m.*

eighty, *adj.* oitenta.

either, 1. *adj., pron.* qualquer dos dois. **2.** *adv.* também, tampouco. **3.** *conj.* **e. . . .or,** ou . . .ou.

ejaculate, *vb.* ejacular; exclamar.

eject, *vb.* ejetar, expulsar.

ejection, *n.* ejeção, expulsão *f.*

eke, *vb.* **e. out,** cavar (a vida).

elaborate, 1. *adj.* intrincado; minucioso; primoroso; pretensioso. **2.** *vb.* elaborar.

elapse, *vb.* passar.

elastic, *adj.* elástico.

elate, *vb.* animar, exaltar.

elbow, 1. *n.* cotovelo *m.* **2.** *vb.* acotovelar.

elder, 1. *adj.* mais velho. **2.** *n.* ancião *m.*

elderly, *adj.* idoso.

eldest, *adj.* o mais velho.

elect, 1. *adj.,n.* eleito. **2.** *vb.* eleger.

election, *n.* eleição *f.*

elective, *adj.* eletivo, facultativo.

elector, *n.* eleitor *n.*

electoral, *adj.* eleitoral.

electorate, *n.* eleitorado *m.*

electric, electrical, *adj.* elétrico.

electrician, *n.* eletricista *m.f.*

electricity, *n.* eletricidade, energia *f.*

electrify, *vb.* eletrificar, eletrizar.

electrocute, *vb.* eletrocutar.

electronic, *n.* eletrônico.

electronics, *n.* eletrônica *f.*

elegance, *n.* elegância *f.*

elegant, *adj.* elegante, chique.

element, *n.* elemento *m.*

elemental, *adj.* elementar.

elementary, *adj.* elementar. **e. school,** escola primária *f.,* primeiro grau *m.*

elephant, *n.* elefante *m.*

elevate, *vb.* elevar.

elevation, *n.* elevação *f.*

elevator, *n.* elevador *m.*

eleven, *adj.* onze.

eleventh, *adj., n.* décimo-primeiro, undécimo.

elf, *n.* elfo, duende *m.*

elicit, *vb.* tirar; provocar.

elide, *vb.* elidir.

eligible, *adj.* elegível.

eliminate, *vb.* eliminar.

elite, *n.* elite *f.*

elk, *n.* alce *m.*

elliptical, *adj.* elíptico.

elm, *n.* olmo *m.*

elocution, *n.* elocução *f.*

elongate, *vb.* alongar.

elope, *vb.* fugir para casar.

eloquence, *n.* eloqüência *f.*

eloquent, *adj.* eloqüente.

else, 1. *adj.* mais; outro. **no one e.,** mais ninguém; **nothing e.,** mais nada.**2.** *adv.* senão.

elsewhere, *adv.* em outra parte, alhures.

elucidate, *vb.* elucidar.

elude, *vb.* eludir.

elusive, *adj.* evasivo.

emaciated, *adj.* emaciado, mirrado.

emanate, *vb.* emanar.

emancipate, vb. emancipar, libertar.

emasculate, vb. emascular.

embalm, vb. embalsamar.

embankment, n. dique m.

embargo, n. embargo m.

embark, vb. embarcar.

embarkation, n. embarque n.

embarrass, vb. embaraçar; envergonhar.

embarrassing, adj. embaraçoso.

embarrassment, n. embaraço n.; vergonha f.

embassy, n. embaixada f.

embed, vb. embutir, encravar.

embellish, vb. embelezar, enfeitar.

ember, n. brasa f.

embezzle, vb. desfalcar.

embezzlement, n. desfalque m.

embitter, vb. amargar.

emblem, n. emblema m.

embody, vb. incorporar, encarnar.

embrace, 1. n. abraço m. 2. vb. abraçar.

embroider, vb. bordar.

embroidery, n. bordado m.

embroil, vb. embrulhar.

embryo, n. embrião m.

embryonic, adj. embrionário.

emerald, n. esmeralda f.

emerge, vb. emergir.

emergence, n. emergência f.

emergency, n. emergência f.

emery, n. esmeril m.

emigrant, adj., n. emigrante m.f.

emigrate, vb. emigrar.

émigré, n. emigrado m.

eminence, n. eminência f.

eminent, adj. eminente.

emissary, n. emissário m.

emission, n. emissão f.

emit, vb. emitir.

emolument, n. emolumento m.

emotion, n. emoção f.

emotional, adj. emocional; emocionante.

empathy, n. empatia f.

emperor, n. imperador m.

emphasis, n. ênfase f.

emphasize, vb. enfatizar.

emphatic, adj. enfático.

empire, n. império m.

empirical, adj. empírico.

employ, 1. n. emprego m. 2. vb. empregar.

employee, n. empregado m.

employer, n. empregador, patrão m.

employment, n. emprego, trabalho m.

emporium, n. empório m.

empower, vb. autorizar; empossar.

empress, n. imperatriz f.

emptiness, n. vazio, vácuo m.

empty, 1. adj. vazio. 2. vb. esvaziar.

emulate, vb. emular.

emulsion, n. emulsão f.

enable, vb. capacitar; permitir.

enact, vb. promulgar, decretar.

enactment, n. lei f., estatuto m.

enamel, 1. n. esmalte m. 2. vb. esmaltar.

enamored, adj. enamorado.

encampment, n. acampamento m.

enchant, vb. encantar.

enchantment, n. encanto m.

encircle, vb. cercar, rodear.

enclave, n. encrave m.

enclose, vb. encerrar; anexar.

enclosed, (letter) anexo, em anexo.

enclosure, n. cercado m.; (letter) anexo m.

encompass, vb. abranger, encerrar.

encore, n., interj. bis m.

encounter, 1. n. encontro m. 2. vb. encontrar.

encourage, vb. encorajar, animar.

encouragement, n. encorajamento m.

encroach, vb. transgredir; usurpar.

encumber, vb. estorvar, embaraçar.

encumbrance, n. estorvo, empecilho m.

encyclopedia, n. enciclopédia f.

end, 1. n. fim m.; ponta f.; propósito m. 2. vb. terminar, acabar.

endanger, vb. pôr em perigo.

endear, vb. acarinhar, fazer amar.

endearment, n. carinho m.

endeavor, 1. *n.* esforço *m.* **2.** *vb.* esforçar-se; procurar.

ending, *n.* conclusão *f.*, término *m.*

endless, *adj.* sem fim.

endorse, *vb.* endossar.

endorsement, *n.* endosso *m.*

endow, *vb.* dotar.

endowment, *n.* dotação *f.*; dote *m.*; fundação *f.*

endurance, *n.* resistência *f.*

endure, *vb.* resistir; suportar.

enema, *n.* enema *m.*, lavagem *f.*

enemy, *n.* inimigo *m.*

energetic, *adj.* enérgico.

energy, *n.* energia *f.*

enervate, *vb.* enervar.

enfold, *vb.* envolver.

enforce, *vb.* executar, fazer cumprir.

enforcement, *n.* execução *f.*, cumprimento *m.*

engage, *vb.* empregar; ocupar; comprometer; travar; engrenar. **e. in,** ocupar-se em/com; **get engaged,** noivar.

engagement, *n.* compromisso *m.*, obrigação *f.*; noivado *m.*

engender, *vb.* engendrar.

engine, *n.* motor *m.*; máquina *f.*; locomotiva *f.*

engineer, *n.* engenheiro -ra; maquinista *m.f.*

engineering, *n.* engenharia *f.*

England, *n.* Inglaterra *f.*

English, *adj., n.* inglês -sa.

Englishman -woman, *n.* inglês -glesa.

engrave, *vb.* gravar.

engraver, *n.* gravador *m.*

engraving, *n.* gravação *f.*; gravura *f.*

engross, *vb.* absorver.

enhance, *vb.* aumentar, realçar.

enhancement, *n.* aumento, realce *m.*

enigma, *n.* enigma *m.*

enigmatic, *adj.* enigmático.

enjoy, *vb.* gozar (de), *(sl.)* curtir. **e. oneself,** divertir-se.

enjoyment, *n.* gozo, prazer *m.*; *(sl.)* curtição *f.*

enlarge, *vb.* aumentar, ampliar.

enlargement, *n.* aumento *m.*, ampliação *f.*

enlighten, *vb.* iluminar; informar.

enlightenment, *n.* esclarecimento *m.*, cultura *f.*; *(cap.)* iluminismo *m.*

enlist, *vb.* alistar(-se), recrutar (-se).

enliven, *vb.* animar.

enmesh, *vb.* enredar.

enormous, *adj.* enorme.

enough, 1. *adj., adv.* bastante **2.** *interj.* basta!, chega! **be e.,** bastar, chegar.

enrage, *vb.* enfurecer.

enrich, *vb.* enriquecer.

enrichment, *n.* enriquecimento *m.*

enroll, *vb.* matricular(-se), registrar(-se).

enrollment, *n.* matrícula *f.*, registro *m.*

enslave, *vb.* escravizar.

ensue, *vb.* seguir-se, decorrer.

entail, *vb.* trazer, acarretar.

entangle, *vb.* enredar.

enter, *vb.* entrar (em).

enterprise, *n.* empresa *f.*, empreendimento *m.*

enterprising, *adj.* empreendedor.

entertain, *n.* divertir, entreter; receber.

entertainer, *n.* artista *m.f.*

entertainment, *n.* divertimento *m.*, entretenimento *m.*

enthrall, *vb.* escravizar; encantar.

enthusiasm, *n.* entusiasmo *m.*

enthusiastic, *adj.* entusiasmado, entusiástico.

entice, *vb.* atrair, seduzir.

enticement, *n.* atração *f.*; engodo *m.*

entire, *adj.* inteiro, todo.

entirety, *n.* totalidade *f.*

entitle, *vb.* autorizar; (book) intitular. **be entitled to,** ter direito a.

entity, *n.* entidade *f.*

entomology, *n.* entomologia *f.*

entourage, *n.* séquito *m.*, comitiva *f.*

entrails, *n.pl.* entranhas *f.pl.*

entrance, 1. *n.* entrada *f.* **2.** *vb.* enlevar.

entreat, *vb.* rogar, suplicar.

entreaty, n. rogo m.; súplica f.

entrée, n. prato principal m.

entrepreneur, n. empresário -ria.

entrust, vb. confiar.

entry, n. entrada f.; inscrição f.; verbete m.

enumerate, vb. enumerar.

enumeration, n. enumeração f.

enunciate, vb. enunciar.

envelop, vb. envolver.

envelope, n. envelope m.

envious, adj. invejoso.

environment, n. ambiente, meio ambiente m.

environmental, adj. ambiental.

environmentalist, n. ecologista m.f.

environs, n.pl. arredores m.pl.

envision, vb. imaginar.

envoy, n. enviado m.

envy, 1. n. inveja f. **2.** vb. invejar.

enzyme, n. enzima f.

eon, n. eternidade f.

epaulet, n. dragona f.

épée, n. florete m.

ephemeral, adj. efêmero.

epic, 1. adj. épico. **2.** n. epopéia f.; épica f.

epidemic, 1. adj. epidêmico. **2.** n. epidemia f.

epigram, n. epigrama f.

epigraph, n. epígrafe f.

epilepsy, n. epilepsia f.

epilogue, n. epílogo m.

Epiphany, n. Epifania f.

episcopal, adj. episcopal.

Episcopalian. adj. n. episcopal.

episode, n. episódio m.

epistle, n. epístola f.

epitaph, n. epitáfio m.

epithet, n. epíteto m.

epitome, n. epítome m.

epoch, n. época f.

equal, 1. adj., n. igual. **2.** vb. igualar.

equality, n. igualdade f.

equalize, vb. igualar.

equalizer, n. (elec.) equalizador m.

equanimity, n. equanimidade f.

equate, vb. igualar, equacionar.

equation, n. equação f.

equator, n. equador m.

equestrian, 1. adj. equestre. **2.** n. cavaleiro m.

equilibrium, n. equilíbrio m.

equine, adj. n. eqüino m.

equip, vb. equipar.

equipment, n. equipamento m., equipagem f.

equitable, adj. eqüitativo.

equity, n. eqüidade f.

equivalent, adj., n. equivalente m.

equivocal, adj. equívoco.

era, n. era, época f.

eradicate, vb. desarraigar, erradicar.

erase, vb. apagar.

eraser, n. apagador m.; (rubber) borracha f.

erect, 1. adj. ereto. **2.** vb. erigir.

erection, n. ereção f.

ermine, n. arminho m.

erode, vb. erodir, causar erosão.

erosion, n. erosão f.

erotic, adj. erótico.

err, vb. errar; enganar-se.

errand, n. recado m.; mandado m.

errant, adj. errante.

erratic, adj. errático.

erroneous, adj. errôneo.

error, n. erro m.

erudite, adj. erudito.

erudition, n. erudição f.

erupt, vb. fazer erupção, explodir.

eruption, n. erupção, explosão f.

escalator, n. escada rolante f.

escapade, n. aventura, travessura f.

escape, 1. n. fuga f.; evasão f. **2.** vb. escapar, fugir.

escape valve, n. válvula de escape f.

eschew, vb. evitar.

escort, 1. n. escolta f. **2.** vb. escoltar.

escutcheon, n. escudo m.

Eskimo, adj., n. esquimó m.

esoteric, adj. esotérico.

especially, adv. especialmente.

espionage, n. espionagem f.

espouse, vb. casar com; advogar.

essay, n. ensaio m.

essence, n. essência f.

essential, adj. essencial.

establish, vb. estabelecer.

establishment, n. estabelecimento m.

estate, n. propriedade f.; bens m.pl.; estamento m.

esteem, 1. n. estima f. **2.** vb. estimar, respeitar.

esthetics, n. estética f.

estimate, 1. n. estimativa f. **2.** vb. estimar, calcular.

estimation, n. estimação f.; estimativa f.; opinião f.

estrange, vb. alhear, alienar.

estuary, n. estuário m.

etch, vb. gravar.

etching, n. gravura f.

eternal, adj. eterno.

eternity, n. eternidade f.

ether, n. éter m.

ethereal, adj. etéreo.

ethic(s), n. ética f.

ethical, adj. ético.

Ethiopia, n. Etiópia f.

ethnic, adj. étnico.

etiquette, n. etiqueta f.

etymology, n. etimologia f.

Eucharist, n. Eucaristia f.

eulogy, n. elogio m.

eunuch, n. eunuco m.

euphemism, n. eufemismo m.

euphoria, n. euforia f.

eureka, interj. heureca!

Europe, n. Europa f.

European, adj., n. europeu -péia.

evacuate, vb. evacuar.

evade, vb. evadir.

evaluate, vb. avaliar.

evaluation, n. avaliação f.

evangelical, adj. evangélico.

evangelist, n. evangelista m.f.

evaporate, vb. evaporar(-se).

evasion, n. evasão f.; evasiva f.

evasive, adj. evasivo.

eve, n. véspera f.

even, 1. adj. liso, plano; igual; equilibrado; quite; (number) par. **2.** adv. mesmo, até. **not e.,** nem mesmo. **3.** vb. igualar; nivelar.

evening, n. anoitecer m.; noite f. **good e.,** boa noite.

evenness, n. uniformidade f.

event, n. evento, acontecimento m. **in any e.,** de qualquer maneira; **in the e. of,** em caso de. **in the e. that,** caso.

eventful, adj. notável.

eventual, adj. conseqüente, final.

eventually, adv. finalmente, com o tempo.

ever, adv. sempre; em qualquer momento; nunca; já. **e. since,** desde que.

everlasting, adj. eterno.

every, adj. cada, todo.

everybody, everyone, pron. todos, todo mundo.

everyday, adj. diário; comum.

everything, pron. tudo.

everywhere, n. em/por toda a parte.

evict, vb. evencer.

eviction, n. evicção f.

evidence, n. evidência f.; prova f.

evident, adj. evidente.

evidently, adv. evidentemente; pelo jeito.

evil, 1. adj. mau, ruim, maligno. **2.** n. mal m.

evoke, vb. evocar, invocar.

evolution, n. evolução f.

evolve, vb. desenvolver; evoluir.

ewe, n. ovelha f.

exacerbate, vb. exacerbar.

exact, 1. adj. exato. **2.** vb. exigir; cobrar.

exaggerate, vb. exagerar.

exaggeration, n. exagero m.

exalt, vb. exaltar; enaltecer.

exam, examination, n. exame m.; interrogatório m.

examine, vb. examinar.

example, n. exemplo m. **for e.,** por exemplo.

exasperate, vb. exasperar.

excavate, vb. escavar.

excavation, n. escavação f.

exceed, vb. exceder.

exceedingly, adv. extremamente.

excel, vb. sobressair.

excellence, n. excelência f.

excellency, n. excelência f.

excellent, adj. excelente.

except, 1. vb. excetuar. **2.** prep. exceto.

exception, n. exceção f.

exceptional, adj. excepcional.

excerpt, 1. n. excerto, trecho m. **2.** vb. extratar.

excess, 1. adj. excessivo. **2.** n. excesso m.

excessive, *adj.* excessivo.

exchange, 1. *n.* troca *f.*; (money) câmbio *m.* **e. rate,** taxa de câmbio *f.* **in e. for,** em troca de; **stock e.,** bolsa *f.*; **telephone e.,** central telefônica *f.* **2.** *vb.* trocar.

excise, 1. *n.* imposto *m.* **2.** *vb.* extirpar.

excite, *vb.* excitar; emocionar; provocar.

excitement, *n.* excitação *f.*; alvoroço *m.*

exciting, *adj.* excitante; emocionante.

exclaim, *vb.* exclamar.

exclamation, *n.* exclamação *f.* **e. point,** ponto de exclamação *m.*

exclude, *vb.* excluir.

exclusion, *n.* exclusão *f.*

exclusive, *adj.* exclusivo. **e. of,** exclusive.

excommunicate, *vb.* excomungar.

excommunication, *n.* excomunhão *f.*

excrement, *n.* excremento *m.*

excrete, *vb.* excretar.

excruciating, *adj.* excruciante.

exculpate, *vb.* exculpar.

excursion, *n.* excursão *f.*

excuse, 1. *n.* desculpa *f.* **2.** *vb.* desculpar.

execute, *vb.* executar.

execution, *n.* execução *f.*

executioner, *n.* verdugo, carrasco *m.*

executor, *n.* testamenteiro *m.*

exemplary, *adj.* exemplar.

exempt, 1. *adj.* isento. **2.** *vb.* isentar.

exemption, *n.* isenção *f.*

exercise, 1. *n.* exercício *m.* **2.** *vb.* exercer; exercitar; fazer exercício.

exert, *vb.* exercer. **e. oneself,** esforçar-se.

exertion, *n.* esforço *m.*

exhale, *vb.* exalar.

exhaust, 1. (car) escape, escapamento *m.* **2.** *vb.* esgotar.

exhausted, *adj.* exausto, esgotado.

exhausting, exhaustive, *adj.* exaustivo.

exhaustion, *n.* exaustão *f.*

exhaust pipe, *n.* cano de descarga/escape *m.*

exhibit, 1. *n.* exibição, exposição *f.* **2.** *vb.* exibir.

exhibition, *n.* exibição, exposição *f.*

exhilarate, *vb.* alegrar, animar.

exhort, *vb.* exortar.

exhume, *vb.* exumar, desenterrar.

exigency, *n.* exigência *f.*

exile, 1. *n.* exílio *m.*; (person) exilado *m.* **2.** *vb.* exilar.

exist, *vb.* existir.

existence, *n.* existência *f.*

existent, *adj.* existente.

existentialism, *n.* existencialismo *m.*

exit, 1. *n.* saída *f.* **2.** *vb.* sair.

exodus, *n.* êxodo *m.*

exonerate, *vb.* absolver, perdoar.

exorbitant, *adj.* exorbitante.

exorcise, *vb.* exorcismar.

exorcism, *n.* exorcismo *m.*

exotic, *adj.* exótico.

expand, *vb.* expandir(-se), estender(-se).

expanse, *n.* expansão, extensão *f.*

expansion, *n.* expansão, extensão *f.*

expatriate, 1. *n.* exilado *m.* **2.** *vb.* expatriar; exilar-se.

expect, *vb.* esperar; contar com.

expectation, *n.* expectativa *f.*

expectorate, *vb.* expectorar.

expedience, expediency, *n.* conveniência *f.*

expedient, 1. *adj.* conveniente. **2.** *n.* expediente *m.*

expedite, *vb.* acelerar, apressar.

expel, *vb.* expulsar.

expend, *vb.* despender, gastar.

expenditure, *n.* despesa *f.*, gasto *m.*

expense, *n.* gasto *m.*, despesa *f.*

expensive, *adj.* caro, custoso.

experience, 1. *n.* experiência *f.* **2.** *vb.* experimentar, conhecer.

experienced, *adj.* experiente, experimentado.

experiment, 1. *n.* experiência *f.*, experimento *m.* **2.** *vb.* experimentar.

experimental, *adj.* experimental.

expert, *adj., n.* experto, perito *m.*

expertise, *n.* perícia *f.*

expiate, *vb.* expiar, remir.

expiration, *n.* expiração *f.*; vencimento *m.*

expire, *vb.* expirar; vencer.

explain, *vb.* explicar.

explanation, *n.* explicação *f.*

explanatory, *adj.* explicativo.

expletive, *adj., n.* expletivo *m.*

explicit, *adj.* explícito.

explode, *vb.* explodir.

exploit, 1. *n.* façanha *f.* **2.** *vb.* explorar.

exploitation, *n.* exploração *f.*

exploratory, *adj.* exploratório.

explore, *vb.* explorar.

explorer, *n.* explorador, descobridor *m.*

explosion, *n.* explosão *f.*

explosive, *adj., n.* explosivo.

exponent, *n.* expoente *m.*

export, 1. *n.* exportação *f.*; artigo exportado *m.* **2.** *vb.* exportar.

exporter, *n.* exportador *m.*

expose, *vb.* exibir; expor.

exposition, *n.* exposição, exibição *f.*

expository, *adj.* expositivo; descritivo.

expostulate, *vb.* suplicar.

exposure, *n.* exposição *f.*; revelação *f.*; contato *m.*

expound, *vb.* expor, explicar.

express, 1. *n.* (train) expresso *m.* **2.** *vb.* expressar, exprimir.

expression, *n.* expressão *f.*

expropriate, *vb.* expropriar, desapropriar.

expulsion, *n.* expulsão *f.*

expunge, *vb.* expungir, apagar.

expurgate, *vb.* expurgar.

exquisite, *adj.* fino, elegante.

extemporaneous, *adj.* extemporâneo.

extend, *vb.* estender.

extension, *n.* extensão *f.*; prorrogação *f.*

extensive, *adj.* extenso.

extent, *n.* extensão *f.* **to a certain e.,** até certo ponto; **to the e. that,** na medida em que.

extenuate, *vb.* atenuar.

exterior, *adj., n.* exterior *m.*

exterminate, *vb.* exterminar.

extermination, *n.* extermínio *m.*

extinct, *adj.* extinto.

extinction, *n.* extinção *f.*

extinguish, *n.* extinguir, apagar.

extinguisher, *n.* extintor *m.*

extirpate, *vb.* extirpar.

extol, *vb.* louvar, elogiar.

extort, *vb.* extorquir.

extortion, *n.* extorsão *f.*

extra, 1. *adj.* extra, extraordinário. **2.** *n.* (actor) extra *m.*

extract, 1. *n.* extrato *m.* **2.** *vb.* extrair.

extraction, *n.* extração *f.*; descendência *f.*

extradite, *vb.* extraditar.

extradition, *n.* extradição *f.*

extraneous, *adj.* estranho, alheio.

extraordinary, *adj.* extraordinário.

extravagance, *n.* extravagância *f.*

extravagant, *adj.* extravagante.

extreme, *adj., n.* extremo *m.*

extremity, *n.* extremidade *f.*

extricate, *vb.* tirar, livrar.

extrovert, *n.* extrovertido *m.*

exuberant, *adj.* exuberante.

exude, *vb.* exsudar.

exult, *vb.* exultar.

eye, 1. *n.* olho *m.* **2.** olhar.

eyeball, *n.* globo ocular *m.*

eyebrow, *n.* sobrancelha *f.*

eyeglasses, *n.pl.* óculos *m.pl.*

eyelash, *n.* cílio *m.*; pestana *f.*

eyelid, *n.* pálpebra *f.*

eye shadow, *n.* sombra *f.*

eyesight, *n.* vista *f.*

eyewitness, *n.* testemunha ocular *f.*

F

fable, *n.* fábula *f.*

fabric, *n.* tecido *m.*; fazenda *f.*

fabricate, *vb.* fabricar; inventar.

fabrication, *n.* fabricação *f.*; mentira *f.*

fabulous, *adj.* fabuloso.

façade, *n.* fachada *f.*

face, 1. *n.* rosto *m.*; cara *f.*; aparência *f.*; prestígio *m.* **make**

faces, fazer caretas, 2. *vb.* enfrentar; dar para.
face lift, *n.* plástica *f.*
facet, *n.* faceta *f.*
facetious, *adj.* brincalhão.
facial, 1. *adj.* facial. 2. *n.* massagem facial *f.*
facile, *adj.* fácil; fluente.
facilitate, *vb.* facilitar.
facility, *n.* facilidade; *(pl.)* facilidades *f.pl.*
facsimile, *n.* fac-símile *m.*
fact, *n.* fato *m.* **in f.,** de fato.
faction, *n.* facção *f.*
factor, *n.* fator *m.*
factory, *n.* fábrica *f.*
factual, *adj.* factual, real.
faculty, *n.* faculdade *f.* ; corpo docente *m.*
fad, *n.* moda, *(sl.)* onda *f.*
fade, *vb.* desbotar; (flowers) murchar; desaparecer.
fag, 1. *n.* *(sl.)* homosexual *m.*, *(sl.)* bicha *f.* 2. *vb.* cansar.
fail, 1. *n.* falta *f.* **without f.,** sem falta. 2. *vb.* falhar, fracassar; *(com.)* falir; (school) ser reprovado, levar pau; **not f. to,** não deixar de.
failure, *n.* fracasso *m.* ; *(com.)* falência *f.* ; (school) reprovação *f.*
faint, 1. *adj.* desmaiado; covarde; fraco. 2. *n.* desmaio *m.* 3. *vb.* desmaiar.
fair, 1. *adj.* justo; lindo; (hair) louro; (weather) bom. 2. *n.* feira *f.*
fairly, *adv.* imparcialmente; razoavelmente; claramente.
fairness, *n.* justiça *f.*
fairy, *n.* fada *f.*, duende *m.* **f. tale,** conto de fadas.
faith, *n.* fé *f.* ; confiança *f.*
faithful, *adj.* fiel.
faithfulness, *n.* fidelidade *f.*
fake, 1. *adj.* falso; *(sl.)* frio. 2. *n.* fraude, imitação *f.* 3. *vb.* falsificar; fingir.
faker, *n.* falsificador -ra, impostor -ra.
falcon, *n.* falcão, gavião *m.*
fall, 1. *n.* queda *f.* ; (price) baixa *f.* ; (water) cataratas *f.pl.* ; (season) outono *m.* 2. *vb.* cair; baixar; cair. **f. due,** vencer; **f. for,** apaixonar-se por; *(sl.)* cair em.

fallacious, *adj.* falaz.
fallacy, *n.* falácia *f.*
fallible, *adj.* falível.
fallout, *n.* precipitação radioativa *f.*
fallow, *adj.* sem cultivo.
false, *adj.* falso; postiço. **f. teeth,** dentadura postiça.
falsehood, *n.* falsidade, mentira *f.*
falseness, *n.* falsidade *f.*
falsify, *n.* falsificar.
falter, *vb.* vacilar; balbuciar.
fame, *n.* fama *f.*
famed, *adj.* famoso, afamado.
familiar, *adj.* familiar. **be f. with,** estar familiarizado com.
familiarity, *n.* familiaridade *f.*
familiarize, *vb.* familiarizar. **f. oneself with,** familiarizar-se com.
family, *n.* família *f.*
family name, *n.* sobrenome, nome de família *m.*
famine, *n.* fome *f.*
famished, *adj.* esfaimado, esfomeado.
famous, *adj.* famoso, célebre.
fan, 1. *n.* leque *m.* ; ventilador *m.* ; *(sport.)* torcedor -ra, fanático -ca; fã *m.f.* 2. *vb.* abanar.
fanatic, *adj.,* *n.* fanático.
fanatical, *adj.* fanático.
fanaticism, *n.* fanatismo *m.*
fanciful, *adj.* fantasioso.
fancy, 1. *adj.* chique, elegante. 2. *n.* fantasia *f.*, capricho *m.* 3. *vb.* imaginar; gostar de.
fanfare, *n.* fanfarra *f.*
fang, *n.* colmilho *m.*
fantastic, *adj.* fantástico.
fantasy, *n.* fantasia *f.*
far, 1. *adj.* longínquo. 2. *adv.* longe. **f. from,** longe de; **as f. as,** até; **as f. as I am concerned,** no que me diz respeito; **as f. as I know,** que eu saiba; **how f.,** a que distância; até onde; **so f.,** até agora.
farce, *n.* farsa *f.*
farcical, *adj.* ridículo.
fare, 1. *n.* passagem *f.* ; comida *f.* 2. *vb.* passar (bem, mal).
Far East, *n.* Extremo Oriente *m.*
farewell, 1. *n.* despedida *f.* **bid**

f. to, despedir-se de. **2.** *interj.* adeus!

farfetched, *adj.* forçado, exagerado.

farm, 1. *n.* sítio *m.*; fazenda *f.* **2.** *vb.* lavrar; cultivar.

farmer, *n.* lavrador -ra, fazendeiro -ra, agricultor -ra.

farmhouse, *n.* casa de sítio ou fazenda *f.*; casa-grande *f.*

farming, *n.* agricultura *f.*; lavoura *f.*

fascinate, *vb.* fascinar.

fascinating, *adj.* fascinante.

fascination, *n.* fascínio *m.*, fascinação *f.*

fascism, *n.* fascismo *m.*

fascist, *adj./n.* fascista *m.f.*

fashion, 1. *n.* moda *f.*; maneira *f.* **be in f.,** estar na moda. **2.** *vb.* amoldar.

fashionable, *adj.* elegante, na moda.

fast, 1. *adj.* rápido; (clock) adiantado; firme. **2.** *n.* jejum *m.* **3.** *vb.* jejuar. **4.** *adv.* rapidamente, depressa.

fasten, *vb.* prender; trancar; pregar.

fastener, *m.* prendedor, fecho *m.*

fastidious, *adj.* melindroso.

fat, 1. *adj.* gordo. **2.** *n.* gordura *f.*

fatal, *adj.* fatal.

fatality, *n.* fatalidade *f.*; morte *f.*

fate, *n.* fado, destino *m.*, sina *f.*

fateful, *adj.* fatal; profético.

father, *n.* pai *m.*; (eccles.) padre *m.*

fatherhood, *n.* paternidade *f.*

father-in-law, *n.* sogro *m.*

fatherland, *n.* pátria *f.*

fathom, 1. *n.* braça *f.* **2.** *vb.* sondar; penetrar em.

fatigue, 1. *n.* fadiga *f.*, cansaço *m.* **2.** *vb.* fatigar.

fatten, *vb.* engordar.

fatuous, *adj.* fátuo.

faucet, *n.* torneira *f.*; bica *f.*

fault, *n.* culpa *f.*; defeito *m.* **at f.,** culpável; **find f. with,** criticar.

faulty, *adj.* defeituoso.

favor, 1. *n.* favor *m.* **be in f. of,** ser a favor de. **2.** *vb.* favorecer.

favorable, *adj.* favorável.

favorite, *adj.* favorito.

fawn, 1. *n.* corça nova *f.* **2.** *vb.* bajular.

faze, *vb.* desconcertar.

fear, 1. *n.* medo *m.* **2.** *vb.* ter medo de.

fearful, *adj.* medroso.

fearless, *adj.* intrépido.

feasible, *adj.* factível.

feast, 1. *n.* banquete. **2.** *vb.* comer e beber; regalar-se.

feat, *n.* façanha, proeza *f.*

feather, *n.* pena, pluma *f.*

feature, 1. *n.* feição *f.*, traço *m.*; (movies) filme principal *m.* **2.** *vb.* apresentar como atração principal.

February, *n.* fevereiro *m.*

feces, *n.pl.* fezes *f.pl.*; excremento *m.*

fecund, *adj.* fecundo.

federal, *adj.* federal.

federation, *n.* federação *f.*

federative, *adj.* federativo.

fee, *n.* honorários *m.pl.*, pagamento *m.*

feeble, *adj.* fraco.

feebleminded, *adj.* débil mental.

feed, 1. *n.* alimentação *f.*; forragem *f.* **2.** *vb.* alimentar; comer. **be fed up,** estar farto.

feedback, *n.* feedback *m.*, retroalimentação *f.*

feel, 1. *n.* sensação *f.* **2.** *vb.* sentir. **f. like,** estar com vontade de, (sl.) estar a fim de.

feeling, *n.* sensação *f.*; sentimento *m.*; impressão *f.*

feign, *vb.* fingir.

felicitous, *adj.* feliz.

feline, *adj.*, *n.* felino *m.*

fell, *vb.* derrubar.

fellow, *n.* sujeito, (sl.) cara *m.*; companheiro *m.*

fellowship, *n.* camaradagem *f.*; bolsa de estudos *f.*

felon, *n.* réu, criminoso *m.*

felony, *n.* delito grave *m.*

felt, *n.* feltro *m.*

female, 1. *adj.* feminino; fêmea. **2.** *n.* fêmea *f.*

feminine, *adj.* feminino.

femininity, *n.* feminilidade *f.*

feminism, *n.* feminismo *m.*

feminist, *adj., n.* feminista *m.f.*
fence, 1. cerca *f.* **2.** *vb.* cercar; *(sport.)* esgrimir.
fencing, *n. (sport.)* esgrima *f.*
fender, *n.* pára-lama *m.*
ferment, 1. *n.* fermento *m.*; tumulto *m.* **2.** *vb.* fermentar.
fern, *n.* samambaia *f.*
ferocious, *adj.* feroz.
ferocity, *n.* ferocidade *f.*
ferris wheel, *n.* roda gigante *f.*
ferry, ferryboat, *n.* barca *f.*; ferryboat *m.*
fertile, *adj.* fértil.
fertility, *n.* fertilidade *f.*
fertilize, *vb.* fertilizar.
fertilizer, *n.* fertilizante, adubo *m.*
fervent, *adj.* fervente, fervoroso.
fervid, *adj.* férvido.
fervor, *n.* fervor *m.*
fester, *vb.* ulcerar-se.
festival, *n.* festival *m.*, festa *f.*
festive, *adj.* festivo.
festivity, *n.* festividade *f.*
festoon, 1. *n.* festão *m.* **2.** *vb.* afestoar.
fetal, *adj.* fetal.
fetch, *vb.* ir buscar, trazer.
fete, 1. *n.* festa *f.* **2.** *vb.* festejar.
fetid, *adj.* fétido.
fetish, *n.* fetiche *m.*
fetter, 1. *n.* grilhão, ferro *m.* **2.** *vb.* agrilhoar.
fetus, *n.* feto *m.*
feud, *n.* rixa *f.*
feudal, *adj.* feudal.
fever, *n.* febre *f.*
feverish, *adj.* febril.
few, *adj.* poucos. **a f.,** alguns; **quite a f.,** muitos.
fiancé -cée, *n.* noivo -va.
fiasco, *n.* fiasco *m.*
fiat, *n.* ordem *f.*, decreto *m.*
fib, 1. *n.* lorota *f.* **2.** *vb.* contar lorotas.
fiber, *n.* fibra *f.*
fiberglass, *n.* fibra de vidro *f.*
fibrous, *adj.* fibroso.
fickle, *adj.* volúvel.
fiction, *n.* ficção *f.*
fictional, *adj.* ficcional.
fictitious, *adj.* fictício.
fiddle, 1. rabeca *f.*; violino *m.* **2.** *vb.* **f. with,** mexer com.
fidelity, *n.* fidelidade *f.*

fidget, *vb.* mexer-se nervosamente.
field, *n.* campo *m.* **f. trip,** excursão *f.*; **f. work,** trabalho de campo *m.*
fiend, *n.* demônio *m.*
fiendish, *adj.* diabólico.
fierce, *adj.* fero, feroz.
fiery, *adj.* ardente.
fiesta, *n.* festa *f.*
fife, *n.* pífaro, pífano *m.*
fifteen, *n.* quinze.
fifteenth, *adj.* décimo quinto.
fifth, *adj., n.* quinto *m.*.
fifty, *n. adj.* cinqüenta.
fig, *n.* figo *m.* **f. tree,** figueira *f.*
fight, 1. *n.* briga, luta *f.* **2.** *vb.* brigar, lutar.
fighter, *n.* lutador *m.*; *(sport.)* pugilista *m.*; (plane) caça *m.*
figment, *n.* invenção *f.*
figurative, *adj.* figurado, metafórico.
figure, 1. *n.* figura *f.*; cifra *f.* **f. of speech,** tropo *m.*, figura *f.* **2.** *vb.* figurar; calcular.
figurehead, *n.* testa-de-ferro *m.*
filament, *n.* filamento *m.*
file, 1. *n.* arquivo *m.*; (tool) lima *f.*; (row) fila *f.* **f. cabinet,** fichário *m.* **2.** *vb.* arquivar; limar.
filet, *n.* filé *m.*
filigree, *n.* filigrana *f.*
fill, *vb.* encher; *(dent.)* obturar; (prescription) aviar. **f. in/out,** preencher.
filling, *n.* recheio; *(dent.)* obturação *f.*
film, 1. *n.* filme *m.*; película *f.*; camada *f.* **2.** *vb.* filmar.
filter, 1. *n.* filtro *m.* coador *m.* **2.** *vb.* filtrar; coar.
filth, *n.* sujeira *f.*
filthy, *adj.* sujo; obsceno.
fin, *n.* barbatana *f.*
final, 1. *adj.* final, último. **2.** *n.* *(sport.)* final *f.*; exame final *m.*
finale, *n.* final *m.*
finalist, *n.* finalista *m.f.*
finally, *adv.* finalmente, afinal.
finance, 1. *n.* finanças *f.pl.* **2.** *vb.* financiar.
financial, *adj.* financeiro.
financier, *n.* financeiro -ra, -cista *m.f.*

financing, n. financiamento m.

find, 1. n. achado m. **2.** vb. achar, encontrar. **f. out,** descobrir.

fine, 1. adj. fino; bom. **2.** n. multa f. **3.** vb. multar. **4.** adv. muito bem. **5.** interj. muito bem, ótimo.

fine arts, n. belas artes f.pl.

fineness, n. fineza f.

finery, n. adornos m.pl.

finesse, n. finura f.

finger, n. dedo m. **f. tip,** ponta do dedo f.

fingernail, n. unha f.

fingerprint, n. impressão digital f.

finicky, adj. melindroso.

finish, 1. n. fim, final m. **2.** vb. acabar, terminar.

finite, adj. finito.

Finland, n. Finlândia, f.

Finnish, adj., n. finlandês m.

fir, n. abeto m.

fire, 1. n. fogo m.; incêndio m. **f. alarm,** alarme de incêndio m.; **f. engine,** carro de bombeiro m.; **f. escape,** escada de incêndio f.; **f. extinguisher,** extintor de incêndio m. **2.** vb. disparar, atirar; (coll.) demitir.

firearm, n. arma de fogo f.

firecracker, n. bombinha f., triquetraque m.

firefly, n. vaga-lume, pirilampo m.

fireman, n. bombeiro m.

fireplace, n. lareira f.

fireproof, adj. incombustível, à prova de fogo.

firewood, n. lenha f.

fireworks, n.pl. fogos de artifício m.pl.

firm, 1. adj. firme. **2.** n. firma, empresa f.

firmness, n. firmeza f.

first, adj. primeiro. **f. floor,** andar térreo m.; **at f.,** no princípio.

first aid, n. primeiros socorros m.pl.

first-class, adj. de primeira classe.

fiscal, adj. fiscal. **f. year,** exercício m.

fish, 1. n. peixe m. **2.** vb. pescar.

fish bowl, n. aquário m.

fisherman, n. pescador m.

fishhook, n. anzol m.

fishing, n. pesca f.

fish market, n. peixaria f.

fishmonger, n. peixeiro -ra.

fishy, adj. (coll.) suspeito.

fission, n. fissão f.

fissure, n. fissura f.

fist, n. punho m.

fit, 1. adj. apto; forte; conveniente. **2.** n. corte, talhe m.; (med.) acesso m., convulsão f.; ataque m. **3.** vb. caber; encaixar-se; (clothes) ficar bem, assentar.

fitful, adj. espasmódico; caprichoso.

fitness, n. aptidão f.; conveniência f.

fitting, adj. conveniente, apropriado.

five, adj. cinco.

five hundred, adj. quinhentos.

fix, 1. n. apuro m., (coll.) encrenca f. **2.** vb. fixar; preparar; (repair) consertar.

fixed, adj. fixo.

fixture, n. fixação f.; acessório m.

fizzle, vb. fracassar, (sl.) pifar.

flabby, adj. flácido, frouxo.

flaccid, adj. flácido.

flag, 1. n. bandeira f. **2.** vb. enfraquecer.

flagellate, vb. flagelar.

flagpole, n. mastro, pau m.

flagrant, adj. flagrante, notório.

flail, vb. malhar.

flair, n. jeito, talento m.

flake, n. floco m.; lâmina f.

flamboyant, adj. vistoso, espalhafatoso.

flame, 1. n. chama f. **2.** vb. chamejar, flamejar.

flame-thrower, n. lança-chamas m.

flamingo, n. flamingo, flamengo m.

flammable, adj. inflamável.

flank, 1. n. ilharga f.; flanco m. **2.** vb. flanquear.

flannel, n. flanela f.

flap, 1. n. aba, orelha f.; (coll.) rififi m. **2.** vb. (wings) bater, (flag) flutuar.

flare, 1. n. brilho m.; labareda

f.; sinalizador *m.* **2.** *vb.* brilhar; enfurecer-se.

flash, 1. *n.* clarão, lampejo *m.*; raio *m.*; *(phot.)* flash *m.*; instante *m.* **2.** *vb.* faiscar; relampaguear.

flashback, *n.* retrospecto, flashback *m.*

flash bulb, *n. (photog.)* flash *m.*

flashlight, *n.* lanterna (elétrica) *f.*

flashy, *adj.* espalhafatoso, vistoso.

flask, *n.* frasco *m.*

flat, 1. *adj.* plano, liso, chato; categórico; fixo; (tire) furado; *(mus.)* abemolado. **2.** *n.* apartamento *m.*; *(mus.)* bemol *m.*

flatness, *n.* planura, lisura *f.*

flatten, *vb.* aplanar, achatar.

flatter, *vb.* bajular, lisonjear.

flatterer, *n.* bajulador -ra.

flattery, *n.* bajulação, lisonja *f.*

flaunt, *vb.* ostentar.

flavor, 1. *n.* sabor, gosto *m.* **2.** *vb.* temperar.

flaw, *n.* defeito *m.*; jaça *f.*

flawed, *adj.* defeituoso.

flawless, *adj.* impecável.

flax, *n.* linho *m.*

flay, *vb.* esfolar; *(fig.)* descompor.

flea, *n.* pulga *f.*

fleck, *n.* pinta, mancha *f.*

fledgling, *n.* ave recém-emplumada *f.*; *(fig.)* novato *m.*

flee, *vb.* fugir.

fleece, 1. *n.* velo *m.* **2.** *vb.* tosquiar; *(fig.)* despojar.

fleet, 1. *adj.* veloz. **2.** *n.* frota, esquadra *f.*

fleeting, *adj.* fugaz.

flesh, *n.* carne *f.* **in the f.,** em carne e osso.

flex, *vb.* flectir, dobrar.

flexible, *adj.* flexível.

flick, 1. *n.* piparote *m.*; movimento rápido. **2.** *vb.* movimentar rapidamente.

flicker, 1. *n.* bruxuleio *m.* **2.** *vb.* bruxulear.

flier, *n.* aviador *m.*; volante *m.*

flight, *n.* vôo *m.*; fuga *f.*; (stairs) lanço *m.* **f. attendant,** aeromoça, *(P.)* hospedeira (de bordo) *f.*; comissário -ria de bordo.

flighty, *adj.* volúvel, frívolo.

flimsy, *adj.* frágil; frívolo.

flinch, *vb.* encolher-se, recuar.

fling, 1. *n.* lanço *m.*; tentativa *f.*; farra *f.* **2.** *vb.* lançar.

flint, *n.* pederneira *f.*

flip, 1. *adj. (coll.)* petulante. **2.** *n.* virada *f.*; salto mortal. **3.** *vb.* virar; dar um salto mortal; *(sl.)* ter um ataque.

flippant, *adj.* petulante, impertinente.

flirt, 1. *n.* namorador -deira; coquete *f.* **2.** *vb.* flertar; *(sl.)* paquerar.

flirtation, *n.* flerte, namorico *m.*

flirtatious, *adj.* namorador.

float, *vb.* flutuar.

flock, 1. *m.* rebanho *m.*, manada *f.* **2.** *vb.* congregar-se; afluir (a).

flog, *vb.* açoitar.

flood, 1. *n.* dilúvio *m.*; inundação, enchente *f.* **2.** *vb.* inundar.

floor, 1. *n.* chão, soalho *m.*; (story) andar *m.* **2.** *vb.* derrubar.

flop, 1. *n.* fracasso *m.* **2.** *vb.* cair; fracassar.

floppy, *adj.* flexível, folgado.

floral, *adj.* floral.

florid, *adj.* floreado.

florist, *n.* florista *m./f.*

floss, *n.* borra de seda *f.*; fio *m.*

flotation, *n.* flutuação *f.*

flounce, 1. *n.* babado *m.* **2.** *vb.* estrebuchar.

flounder, 1. *n.* linguado *m.* **2.** *vb.* debater-se, estrebuchar.

flour, *n.* farinha (de trigo) *m.*

flourish, 1. *n.* floreado *m.* **2.** *vb.* florescer, prosperar.

flout, *vb.* burlar.

flow, 1. *n.* fluxo *m.* **2.** *vb.* fluir.

flower, 1. *n.* flor *f.* **2.** *vb.* florescer. **f. bed,** canteiro *m.*

flowerpot, *n.* vaso de flores *m.*

flowery, *adj.* florido, floreado.

flu, *n.* gripe, influenza *f.*

fluctuate, *vb.* flutuar.

flue, *n.* fumeiro *m.*

fluency, *n.* fluência *f.*

fluent, *adj.* fluente, corrente.

fluff, *n.* felpa, fiapo *m.*

fluffy, *adj.* fofo, felpudo.

fluid, *adj., n.* fluido *m.*

fluidity, *n.* fluidez *f.*

flunk, *vb.* ser reprovado, *(sl.)* levar bomba.

flunky, *n.* lacaio *m.*

fluorescent, *adj.* fluorescente.

flurry, *n.* agitação *f.;* (wind) lufada *f.*

flush, 1. *adj.* próspero. **2.** *n.* (toilet) descarga *f.;* (cards) flush *m.* **3.** *vb.* corar, ruborizar; dar a descarga.

fluster, 1. *n.* confusão *f.* **2.** *vb.* perturbar, afobar.

flute, *n.* flauta *f.*

flutter, 1. *n.* alvoroço *m.;* adejo *m.* **2.** *vb.* agitar-se; adejar.

flux, *n.* fluxo *m.*

fly, 1. *n.* mosca *f.;* (pants) braguilha *f.* **2.** *vb.* voar.

flying saucer, *n.* disco voador *m.*

foam, 1. *n.* espuma *f.* **2.** *vb.* espumar.

focal, *adj.* focal.

focus, 1. *n.* foco *m.;* focalização *f.* **2.** *vb.* focalizar, enfocar.

fodder, *n.* forragem *f.*

foe, *n.* inimigo *m.*

fog, *n.* nevoeiro *m.,* névoa, cerração *f.*

foggy, *adj.* nebuloso, brumoso.

foible, *n.* fraqueza *f.*

foil, 1. lâmina, folha de metal. **aluminum f.,** papel de alumínio *m.;* **tin f.,** papel de estanho *m.* **2.** *vb.* frustrar.

foist, *vb.* impingir.

fold, 1. *n.* dobra, prega *f.;* (sheep) aprisco *m.* **2.** *vb.* dobrar, preguear.

folder, *n.* pasta *f.*

folding, *adj.* dobradiço.

foliage, *n.* folhagem *f.*

folk, 1. *adj.* folclórico, popular. **2.** *n.* povo *m.;* *(pl.)* gente *f.;* pais *m.pl.*

folklore, *n.* folclore *m.*

follow, *vb.* seguir; acompanhar; seguir-se.

follower, *n.* partidário *m.*

following, 1. *adj.* seguinte. **2.** *n.* comitiva *f.;* seguidores *m.*

folly, *n.* loucura *f.*

foment, *vb.* fomentar.

fond, *adj.* apaixonado. **be f. of,** gostar de.

fondle, *vb.* acariciar, afagar.

fondness, *f.* afeição *f.,* apego *m.*

font, *n.* pia batismal *f.;* (printing) fonte *f.*

food, 1. *adj.* alimentício **2.** *n.* comida *f.;* alimento *m.*

foodstuffs, *n.* comestíveis, víveres *m.*

fool, 1. *n.* tolo *m.* **2.** *vb.* enganar. **f. around,** brincar; **f. with,** mexer com.

foolhardy, *adj.* temerário.

foolish, *adj.* tolo; ridículo.

foolishness, *n.* tolice, bobagem *f.*

foot, *n.* pé *m.*

football, *n.* futebol americano *m.*

foothold, *n.* ponto de apoio *m.,* entrada *f.*

footing, *n.* pé *m.,* base *f.*

footlights, *n.pl.* ribalta *f.*

footnote, *n.* nota ao pé da página *f.*

footprint, *n.* pegada *f.*

footstep, *n.* passo *m.*

footwear, *n.* calçados *m.pl.*

for, 1. prep. para; por. **as f.,** quanto a; **what f.,** para quê. **2.** *conj.* pois.

forage, 1. *n.* forragem *f.* **2.** *vb.* forragear.

foray, *n.* incursão *f.*

forbearance, *n.* abstenção *f.;* paciência *f.*

forbid, *vb.* proibir, interditar.

force, 1. *n.* força *f.* **by f., a** pulso. **2.** *vb.* forçar, obrigar.

forceful, *adj.* forte, enérgico.

forcible, *adj.* forçoso.

ford, 1. *n.* vau *m.* **2.** *vb.* vadear.

fore, 1. *adj.* dianteiro. **2.** *n.* frente, dianteira *f.;* *(naut)* proa *f.*

forearm, *n.* antebraço *f.*

forebear, *n.* antepassado *m.*

forebode, *vb.* pressagiar.

foreboding, *n.* presságio *m.*

forecast, 1. *n.* previsão *f.;* prognóstico *m.* **2.** *vb.* prognosticar.

forefather, *n.* antepassado *m.*

forefinger, *n.* dedo indicador *m.*

forefront, *n.* vanguarda *f.*

foregoing, *adj.* precedente.

foregone, *adj.* previsto, predeterminado.

foreground, *n.* primeiro plano *m.*

forehead, *n.* testa, fronte *f.*

foreign, *adj.* estrangeiro. **f. affairs,** relações exteriores; **f. exchange credits,** *n.* divisas *f.pl.*

foreigner, *n.* estrangeiro -ra.

foreman, *n.* capataz *m.*

foremost, *adj.* primeiro.

forensic, *adj.* forense.

forerunner, *n.* precursor -ra.

foresee, *vb.* prever.

foreseeable, *adj.* previsível.

foreshadow, *vb.* prefigurar.

foresight, *n.* previdência, previsão *f.*

forest, *n.* floresta *f.*, bosque *m.*; selva *f.* **f. ranger,** guarda-florestal *m.*

forestall, *vb.* antecipar, impedir.

forestry, *n.* silvicultura *f.*

foretell, *vb.* predizer.

foretoken, *vb.* pressagiar.

forever, *adv.* para sempre.

forewarn, *vb.* prevenir.

foreword, *n.* prefácio *m.*

forfeit, 1. *n.* multa *f.*; prenda *f.* **2.** *vb.* perder.

forge, 1. *n.* forja *f.*; frágua *f.* **2.** *vb.* forjar; falsificar; avançar com dificuldade.

forger, *n.* forjador -ra; falsificador -ra.

forgery, *n.* falsificação *f.*

forget, *vb.* esquecer; esquecer-se de.

forgetful, *adj.* esquecido.

forgive, *vb.* perdoar.

forgiveness, *n.* perdão *m.*

forgo, *vb.* renunciar.

fork, 1. *n.* garfo *m.*; bifurcação *f.* **2.** *vb.* bifurcar-se.

forlorn, *adj.* abandonado, triste.

form, 1. *n.* forma *f.*; (document) formulário *m.* **2.** *vb.* formar.

formal, *adj.* formal; cerimonioso. **f. attire,** traje a rigor *m.*

formality, *n.* formalidade *f.*

format, *n.* formato *m.*

formation, *n.* formação *f.*

former, *adj.* anterior; antigo. **the f.,** aquele.

formerly, *adv.* antigamente.

formidable, *adj.* formidável, tremendo.

formula, *n.* fórmula *f.*

formulate, *vb.* formular.

fornicate, *vb.* fornicar.

forsake, *vb.* abandonar.

forswear, *vb.* abjurar.

fort, *n.* forte *m.*, fortaleza *f.*

forte, *n.* forte *m.*

forth, *adv.* adiante, em/para diante. **and so f.,** e assim por diante; **back and f.,** de um lado para outro; **go f.,** sair.

forthcoming, *adj.* futuro.

forthright, *adj.* franco.

forthwith, *adv.* em seguida.

fortieth, *adj.* quadragésimo.

fortification, *n.* fortificação *f.*

fortify, *vb.* fortificar.

fortitude, *n.* fortitude *f.*

fortnight, *n.* quinzena *f.*

fortress, *n.* fortaleza *f.*

fortuitous, *adj.* fortuito.

fortunate, *adj.* afortunado; feliz.

fortune, *n.* fortuna *f.*; sorte *f.*

fortuneteller, *n.* cartomante *m.f.*; adivinho -nha.

forty, *adj.* quarenta.

forum, *n.* foro, fórum *m.*

forward, 1. *adj.* dianteiro; atrevido. **2.** *vb.* enviar. **3.** *adv.* adiante.

fossil, *n.* fóssil *m.*

foster, 1. *adj.* adotivo, de criação. **2.** *vb.* promover.

foul, 1. *adj.* sujo; fétido; abominável. **2.** *vb.* sujar.

foul-mouthed, *adj.* desbocado.

foul play, *n.* jogo sujo *m.*; crime *m.*

found, *vb.* fundar; (melt) fundir.

foundation, *n.* fundação *f.*

founder, *n.* fundador -ra **2.** *vb.* afundar-se, ir a pique.

foundry, *n.* fundição *f.*

fountain, *n.* fonte *f.*

four, *adj.* quatro. **on all fours,** de gatinhas.

four hundred, *adj.* quatrocentos.

fourteen, *adj.* quatorze, catorze.

fourteenth, *adj.* décimo quarto.

fourth, *adj.,* *n.* quarto *m.*

fowl, *n.* ave *f.*

fox, *n.* raposa *f.*; (*sl.*) gata *f.*

foxhole, *n.* trincheira *f.*

fox trot, *n.* foxtrote *m.*

foxy, *adj.* astucioso.

foyer, *n.* vestíbulo *m.*

fracas, *n.* rixa *f.*; tumulto *m.*

fraction, *n.* fração *f.*

fracture, 1. *n.* fratura *f.* **2.** *vb.* fraturar.

fragile, *adj.* frágil.

fragment, *n.* fragmento *m.*

fragmentary, *adj.* fragmentário.

fragrance, *n.* fragrância *f.*

fragrant, *adj.* fragrante.

frail, *adj.* fraco, frágil.

frailty, *n.* fraqueza, fragilidade *f.*

frame, 1. *n.* moldura *f.*; armação *f.*; corpo *m.* **2.** *vb.* emoldurar; formar; *(sl.)* acusar falsamente.

frame-up, *n.* acusação falsa *f.*

framework, *n.* armação, estrutura *f.*

franc, *n.* franco *m.*

France, *n.* França *f.*

franchise, *n.* franquia *f.*

frank, 1. *adj.* franco. **2.** *n.* franquia postal *f.* **3.** *vb.* (letter) franquear.

frankfurter, *n.* salsicha *f.*

frankness, *n.* franqueza *f.*

frantic, *adj.* frenético, agitado.

fraternal, *adj.* fraternal.

fraternity, *n.* fraternidade *f.*

fraud, *n.* fraude *f.*

fraudulent, *adj.* fraudulento.

fraught, *adj.* carregado.

fray, 1. *n.* rixa *f.*; carga *f.* **2.** *vb.* desgastar.

freak, *n.* monstruosidade *f.*, aborto *m.*

freckle, *n.* sarda *f.*

freckled, *n.* sardento.

free, 1. *adj.* livre; de graça. **2.** *vb.* libertar; livrar.

freedom, *n.* liberdade *f.*

freeway, *n.* auto-estrada *f.*

free will, *n.* livre arbítrio *m.*

freeze, *vb.* congelar, gelar.

freezer, *n.* congelador *m.*; frigorífico *m.*

freight, *n.* frete *m.*; carga *f.*

freighter, *n.* (naut.) cargueiro *m.*

French, *adj.*, *n.* francês -cesa.

French fries, *n.pl.* batatas fritas *f.pl.*

Frenchman -woman, *n.* francês -cesa.

frenzied, *adj.* frenético.

frenzy, *n.* frenesi *m.*

frequency, *n.* freqüência *f.*

frequent, 1. *adj.* freqüente. **2.** *vb.* freqüentar.

fresh, *adj.* fresco; (water) doce; *(coll.)* atrevido.

freshen, *vb.* refrescar.

freshness, *n.* frescura *f.*

fret, *vb.* afligir-se.

fretful, *adj.* irritável.

Freudian, *adj.*, *n.* freudiano *m.*

friar, *n.* frade, (before name) frei *m.*

friction, *n.* fricção *f.*

Friday, *n.* sexta-feira *f.*

fried, *adj.* frito.

friend, *n.* amigo *m.*

friendliness, *n.* amizade, amabilidade *f.*

friendly, *adj.* amistoso, amigável, amigo.

friendship, *n.* amizade *f.*

frigate, *n.* fragata *f.*

fright, *n.* susto, medo *m.*

frighten, *vb.* assustar, apavorar.

frightful, *adj.* medonho.

frigid, *adj.* frígido, frio.

frill, *n.* babado *m.*

fringe, *n.* franja, fímbria *f.*

frisky, *adj.* brincalhão.

frivolous, *adj.* frívolo.

frock, *n.* túnica *f.*; batina *f.* **f. coat,** sobrecasaca *f.*

frog, *n.* rã *f.*

frogman, *n.* homem-rã *m.*

frolic, 1. *n.* brincadeira *f.* **2.** *vb.* brincar.

from, *prep.* de; desde.

frond, *n.* fronde *f.*

front, 1. *adj.* de frente *f.*; frente *f.*; (building) fachada *f.* **in f. of,** em frente de

frontal, *adj.* frontal.

frontier, 1. *adj.* fronteiriço. **2.** *n.* fronteira *f.*

frost, *n.* geada *f.*

frosty, *adj.* gelado.

froth, *n.* espuma *f.*

frown, 1. *n.* carranca *f.* **2.** *vb.* fechar a cara.

frugal, *adj.* frugal.

fruit, *n.* fruta *f.*; fruto *m.* **f. tree,** fruteira *f.*

fruitful, *adj.* produtivo.

fruition, *n.* fruição *f.*

fruitless, *adj.* inútil, vão.

frustrate, *vb.* frustrar.
frustration, *n.* frustração *f.*
fry, *vb.* fritar, frigir.
frying pan, *n.* frigideira *f.*
fuel, *n.* combustível *m.*
fugitive, *adj.,* *n.* fugitivo *m.*
fugue, *n.* fuga *f.*
fulcrum, *n.* fulcro *m.*
fulfill, *vb.* cumprir; preencher.
fulfillment, *n.* cumprimento *m.*; realização *f.*
full, *adj.* cheio; pleno; completo.
full moon, *n.* lua cheia *f.*, plenilúnio *m.*
fullness, *n.* plenitude *f.*
full-time, *adj.* de tempo integral.
fumble, *vb.* fazer/manusear/remexer sem jeito.
fume, **1.** *n.* gás, vapor *m.* **2.** *vb.* fumegar; enfurecer-se.
fumigate, *vb.* fumigar, defumar.
fun, *n.* diversão, brincadeira *f.* **have f.,** divertir-se; **make f. of,** zombar de.
function, **1.** *n.* função *f.* **2.** *vb.* funcionar.
functional, *adj.* funcional.
fund, *n.* fundo *m.*
fundamental, *adj.* fundamental.
funeral, **1.** *adj.* fúnebre. **2.** *n.* funeral, enterro *m.*
fungus, *n.* fungo *m.*
funnel, *n.* funil *m.*
funny, *adj.* engraçado; curioso. **be f.,** ter graça.
fur, *n.* pele *f.*
furious, *adj.* furioso.
furlough, *n.* licença *f.*
furnace, *n.* forno *m.*
furnish, *vb.* fornecer; mobiliar.
furniture, *n.* móveis *m.pl.*; mobília *f.*
furor, *n.* furor *m.*
furrow, **1.** *n.* sulco, rego *m.* **2.** *vb.* sulcar.
furry, *adj.* peludo.
further, **1.** *adj.* mais; adicional. **2.** *adv.* mais; mais longe; além disso. **3,** *vb.* promover.
furthermore, *adv.* além disso, ademais.
furtive, *adj.* furtivo.
fury, *n.* fúria *f.*, furor *m.*
fuse, **1.** *n.* fusível *m.* **2.** *vb.* fundir.
fuselage, *n.* fuselagem *f.*

fusion, *n.* fusão *f.*
fuss, **1.** *n.* alvoroço *m.*; rixa *f.* **2.** *vb.* preocupar-se com ninharias; importunar.
fussy, *adj.* melindroso.
futile, *adj.* fútil.
future, *adj.,* *n.* futuro *m.*
fuzz, *n.* felpa, penugem *f.*
fuzzy, *adj.* felpudo; impreciso.

G

gab, **1.** *n.* tagarelice *f.* **2.** *vb.* tagarelar.
gabby, *adj.* tagarela.
gable, *n.* empena *f.*
gadget, *n.* dispositivo. *m.*
gag, **1.** *n.* mordaça *f.*; piada *f.* **2.** *vb.* amordaçar; engasgar.
gaiety, *n.* alegria *f.*
gain, **1.** *n.* ganho *m.*; aumento *m.* **2.** *vb.* ganhar; aumentar.
gait, *n.* marcha, modo de andar.
gala, *n.* gala *f.*
galaxy, *n.* galáxia *f.*
gale, *n.* ventania *f.*, vendaval *m.*
Galicia, *n.* Galiza *f.*
Galician, *adj.,* *n.* galego -ga.
gall, *n.* bílis, fel *m.*; amargura *f.*; atrevimento *m.* **g. bladder,** vesícula biliar *f.*
gallant, *adj.* intrépido; galante.
gallantry, *n.* intrepidez; galantaria *f.*
galleon, *n.* galeão *m.*
gallery, *n.* galeria *f.*
galley, *n.* galé *f.*; *(naut.)* galera *f.*; cozinha *f.*
gallon, *n.* galão *m.*
gallop, **1.** *n.* galope *m.* **2.** *vb.* galopar.
gallows, *n.* forca *f.*
galore, *adv.* em abundância, *(sl.)* pra burro.
galosh, *n.* galocha *f.*
galvanize, *vb.* galvanizar.
gamble, **1.** *n.* jogo *m.*; risco *m.* **2.** *vb.* jogar; apostar; arriscar.
gambler, *n.* jogador -ra.
gambling, *n.* jogo *m.*
game, *n.* jogo *m.*; brincadeira *f.*; (match) partida *f.*; caça *f.*
gamut, *n.* gama, escala *f.*
gander, *n.* ganso *m.*; espiada *f.*
gang, *n.* bando *m.*; turma *f.*

gangster, n. pistoleiro m.
gap, n. brecha f.; lacuna f.; desfiladeiro m.
gape, vb. bocejar; ficar boquiaberto.
garage, n. garagem f.; oficina f.
garb, n. vestimenta f.
garbage, n. lixo m.
garble, vb. deturpar, mutilar.
garden, 1. n. jardim m. **2.** vb. jardinar.
gardener, n. jardineiro -ra.
gardening, n. jardinagem f.
gargle, 1. n. gargarejo m. **2.** vb. gargarejar.
gargoyle, n. gárgula f.
garland, n. grinalda f.
garlic, n. alho m.
garment, n. peça de roupa f.
garner, vb. acumular.
garnish, 1. n. adorno m. **2.** vb. adornar.
garret, n. sótão m., mansarda f.
garrulous, adj. gárrulo.
garter, n. liga f.
gas, n. gás m.; (coll.) gasolina f. **g. station,** posto de gasolina m.
gash, n. cutilada f.
gasoline, n. gasolina f.
gasp, 1. n. arfada f., suspiro m. **2.** vb. arfar.
gastronomy, n. gastronomia f.
gate, n. portão m.
gather, vb. reunir; recolher; deduzir; reunir-se.
gathering, n. reunião f.
gaucho, n. gaúcho m.
gaudy, adj. espalhafatoso, mirabolante.
gauge, l, n. gabarito m.; medidor m. **2.** vb. medir; avaliar.
gaunt, adj. mirrado, macilento.
gauntlet, n. manopla f.; luva f.
gauze, n. gaze f.
gavel, n. martelo de juiz m.
gawk, vb. olhar de modo apalermado.
gay, adj. **1.** adj. alegre; (sl.) homossexual. **2.** n. homossexual, guei m.
gaze, 1. n. olhar m. **2.** vb. olhar, fitar.
gazebo, n. mirante, belvedere m.
gazette, n. gazeta f.

gear, n. engrenagem f.; marcha f.
gee, interj. puxa!, caramba!
gelatin, n. gelatina f.
gem, n. jóia f.
Gemini, n. Gêmeos m.pl.
gender, n. gênero m.
gene, n. gene m.
genealogy, n. genealogia f.
general, 1. adj. geral. **in g.,** em geral. **2.** n. (mil.) general m.
generalization, n. generalização f.
generalize, vb. generalizar.
generate, vb. gerar.
generation, n. geração f.
generator, n. gerador m.
generic, adj. genérico.
generosity, n. generosidade f.
generous, adj. generoso.
genesis, n. gênese f.; (cap.) Gênese m.
genetic, adj. genético.
genetics, n. genética f.
genie, n. gênio m.
genital, 1. adj. genital. **2.** n.pl. genitália f.
genius, n. gênio m.
genocide, n. genocídio m.
genre, n. gênero m.
genteel, adj. gentil, cortês.
gentile, n. não judeu m.; gentio m.
gentle, adj. suave; manso; gentil.
gentleman, n. cavalheiro, senhor m.
gentleness, n. suavidade f.; mansidão f.
genuine, adj. genuíno.
genus, n. gênero m.
geographical, adj. geográfico.
geography, n. geografia f.
geological, adj. geológico.
geology, n. geologia f.
geometry, n. geometria f.
geranium, n. gerânio m.
germ, n. germe m.
German, adj., n. alemão -mã.
Germany, n. Alemanha f.
germinate, vb. germinar.
gestation, n. gestação f.
gesture, 1. n. gesto m. **2.** vb. gesticular.
get, vb. conseguir; receber; ganhar; (become) ficar. **g. away,** escapar; **g. off,** saltar; **g. on,**

subir; **g. there,** chegar; **g. together,** reunir(-se); **g. up,** levantar-se; **go and g.,** buscar.

getaway, n. fuga f.

get-together, n. reunião f.

Ghana, n. Gana m.

ghastly, adj. horrível; cadavérico.

ghetto, n. gueto m.

ghost, n. fantasma m.

giant, adj., n. gigante m.

gibberish, n. algaravia f.

gibe, 1. n. escárnio m. **2.** vb. escarnecer.

giddy, adj. vertiginoso.

gift, n. presente m.; dádiva f.; (talent) dom m.

gigantic, adj. gigantesco.

giggle, 1. n. risadinha f. **2.** vb. dar risadinhas.

gigolo, n. gigolô m.

gild, vb. dourar.

gill, n. guelra, brânquia f.

gimmick, n. truque, macete m.

gin, n. gim m.

ginger, n. gengibre m.

giraffe, n. girafa f.

gird, vb. cingir.

girdle, n. cinta f.

girl, n. menina f.; moça, (P.) rapariga f.

girlfriend, n. namorada f.

gist, n. essência f., âmago m.

give, vb. dar. **g. back,** devolver; **g. up,** renunciar; dar-se por vencido; **g. rise to,** dar lugar a.

glacial, adj. glacial.

glacier, n. glaciar m.

glad, adj. alegre, contente.

gladly, adv. de bom grado, com prazer.

glamor, n. encanto, glamour m.

glamorous, adj. glamoroso.

glance, 1. n. olhada f. **2.** vb. dar uma olhada.

gland, n. glândula f.

glare, 1. n. brilho m.; reflexo m. **2.** vb. deslumbrar; fuzilar com os olhos.

glaring, adj. evidente, gritante.

glass, n. vidro m.; (drinking) copo m.; (pl.) (eyeglasses) óculos m.pl.

glaze, vb. vidrar.

gleam, 1. n. brilho, fulgor m. **2.** vb. fulgurar.

glee, n. alegria f.

glide, vb. deslizar.

glider, n. planador m.

glimmer, 1. n. vislumbre m. **2.** vb. bruxulear.

glimpse, 1. n. vislumbre m. **2.** vb. vislumbrar.

glisten, 1. n. brilho m. **2.** vb. brilhar.

glitter, 1. n. resplendor, brilho m. **2.** vb. resplandecer.

gloat, vb. regozijar-se; banhar-se em água de rosas.

global, adj. global.

globe, n. globo m.

gloom, n. escuridão f.; tristeza f.

gloomy, adj. escuro; triste.

glorify, vb. glorificar.

glorious, adj. glorioso.

glory, n. glória, fama f.

gloss, 1. n. lustre, brilho m. **2.** vb. **g. over,** disfarçar, atenuar.

glossary, n. glossário m.

glossy, adj. lustroso.

glove, n. luva f.

glow, 1. n. fulgor m. **2.** vb. reluzir, arder.

glue, 1. n. cola f.; grude m. **2.** vb. colar, grudar.

glum, adj. mal-humorado.

glut, 1. n. excesso m., superabundância f. **2.** vb. fartar.

glutton, n. glutão, comilão n.

gluttonous, adj. guloso.

gnash, vb. ranger.

gnat, n. borrachudo m.

gnaw, vb. roer.

go, vb. ir, andar; funcionar. **g. away,** ir(-se) embora; **g. back,** voltar, regressar; **g. by,** guiar-se por; **g. down,** descer; **g. in,** entrar; **g. on,** seguir; **g. out,** sair; **g. over,** examinar, revisar; **g. up,** subir; **g. without,** passar sem.

goad, 1. n. aguilhada f.; estímulo m. **2.** vb. aguilhoar; estimular.

goal, n. meta f., objetivo m.; (sport.) gol m.

goalie, n. (sport.) goleiro.

goat, n. bode m., cabra f.

goatee, n. cavanhaque m.

God, n. Deus. m.

god, -dess, n. deus, deusa.

godchild, n. afilhado -da.

godfather, n. padrinho m.

godmother, *n.* madrinha *f.*
godsend, *n.* achado *m.*
going, *n.* ida *f.*
gold, *n.* ouro *m.*
golden, *adj.* áureo, dourado; de ouro.
goldsmith, *n.* ourives *m.f.*
golf, *n.* golfe *m.*
gong, *n.* gongo *m.*
gonorrhea, *n.* gonorréia *f.*
good, 1. *adj.* bom. **a g. deal,** muito; **be no g.,** não prestar; **do no g.,** não adiantar. **2.** *n.* bem *m.;* (*pl.*) bens *m.pl.,* mercadorias *f.pl.*
good-bye, 1. *n.* adeus *m.* **2.** *interj.* adeus!, até logo!, tchau! **say g. to,** despedir-se de.
goodies, *n.pl.* guloseimas *f.,* quitutes *m.*
good-looking, *adj.* bonito.
goodness, *n.* bondade *f.*
good will, *n.* boa vontade *f.*
goof, 1. *n.* erro *m.,* mancada *f.* **2.** *vb.* errar, dar uma mancada.
goofy, *adj.* boboca, pateta.
goon, *n.* jagunço, cabra *m.*
goose, *n.* ganso *m.*
gore, 1. *n.* sangue *m.* **2.** *vb.* escornar, ferir com os chifres.
gorge, 1. *n.* garganta *f.;* desfiladeiro *m.* **2.** *vb.* empanturrar.
gorgeous, *adj.* divino, bacana.
gorilla, *n.* gorila *m.*
gory, *adj.* sangrento.
gosh, *interj.* nossa!, puxa!
gospel, *n.* evangelho *m.*
gossip, 1. *n.* fofoca *f.,* mexerico *m.;* (person) fofoqueiro *m.* **2.** *vb.* fofocar.
Gothic, *adj.* gótico.
gouge, 1. *n.* goiva *f.* **2.** *vb.* goivar; (*coll.*) tapear.
gourd, *n.* cabaça *f.*
gourmand, *n.* glutão *m.*
gourmet, *n.* gastrônomo *m.*
govern, *vb.* governar.
governess, *n.* governanta *f.*
government, *n.* governo *m.*
governmental, *adj.* governamental.
governor, *n.* governador -ra.
gown, *n.* vestido *m.;* (dressing) roupão *m.*
grab, *vb.* agarrar, arrebatar.

grace, *n.* graça *f.;* gentileza. **good graces,** boas graças.
graceful, *adj.* gracioso.
gracious, *adj.* cortês; misericordioso.
gradation, *n.* gradação *f.*
grade, 1. *n.* grau *m.;* nível *m.;* declive *m.;* série *f.;* nota *f.;* categoria *f.* **g. crossing,** passagem de nível *f.* **2.** *vb.* graduar; nivelar; dar nota a.
gradual, *adj.* gradual.
graduate, 1. *n.* formado *m.* **2.** *vb.* formar-se.
graduate study, *n.* curso de pós-graduação *m.*
graduation, *n.* formatura, colação de grau *f.*
graft, 1. *n.* enxerto *m.;* suborno *m.* **2.** *vb.* enxertar.
grail, *n.* graal *m.*
grain, *n.* grão *m.;* cereal *m.*
grainfield, *n.* seara *f.*
gram, *n.* grama *m.f.*
grammar, *n.* gramática *f.* **g. school,** escola primária *f.,* primeiro grau *m.*
grammarian, *n.* gramático *m.*
grammatical, *adj.* gramatical.
granary, *n.* celeiro *m.*
grand, *adj.* grande; ilustre; mor; ótimo.
granddaughter, *n.* neta *f.*
grandeur, *n.* grandeza *f.*
grandfather, *n.* avô *m.*
grandiloquent, *adj.* grandiloqüente.
grandiose, *adj.* grandioso.
grandmother, *n.* avó *f.*
grandparents, *n.pl.* avós *m.pl.*
grandson, *n.* neto *m.*
grandstand, *n.* arquibancada *f.*
grange, *n.* granja *f.*
granite, *n.* granito *m.*
grant, 1. *n.* concessão *f.;* subvenção *f.;* bolsa de estudos *f.* **2.** *vb.* conceder, outorgar. **take for granted,** dar por certo, não dar valor a.
granular, *adj.* granular.
granulate, *vb.* granular.
grape, *n.* uva *f.*
grapefruit, *n.* toranja *f.,* grapefruit *m.*
grapevine, *n.* videira, parreira *f.*
graph, *n.* gráfico, diagrama *m.*
graphic, *adj.* gráfico.

grapple, vb. agarrar; lutar.

grasp, 1. n. ato de agarrar; aperto de mão m.; poder m.; compreensão f.; **2.** vb. agarrar; compreender.

grass, n. erva f.; grama f.; (sl.) maconha f.

grasshopper, n. gafanhoto m.

grassland, m. pasto m.

grassy, adj. ervoso.

grate, 1. n. grades f.pl.; **2.** vb. ralar.

grateful, adj. grato, agradecido.

gratification, n. gratificação, satisfação f.

gratify, vb. satisfazer, agradar.

grating, 1. n. gradeamento m. **2.** adj. irritante.

gratitude, n. gratidão f.

gratuitous, adj. gratuito.

gratuity, n. gorjeta f.

grave, 1. adj. grave. **2.** n. cova f.

gravel, n. cascalho m.

gravestone, n. lousa, campa f.

graveyard, n. cemitério m.

gravitate, vb. gravitar.

gravity, n. gravidade f.

gravy, n. molho m.

gray, adj. cinza, cinzento; encanecido. **g. matter,** massa cinzenta f.

gray-headed, adj. encanecido.

graze, vb. roçar; (cattle) pastar.

grease, n. gordura f., sebo m.; graxa f. **2.** vb. untar; engraxar.

greasy, adj. gorduroso, seboso.

great, adj. grande; ilustre; ótimo.

Great Britain, n. Grã-Bretanha f.

great-grandchild, n. bisneto -ta.

great-grandfather, n. bisavô m.

great-grandmother, n. bisavó f.

greatly, adv. muito.

greatness, n. grandeza f.

Greece, n. Grécia f.

greed, n. cobiça, avareza f.; gula f.

greedy, adj. cobiçoso, avaro; guloso.

Greek, adj. n. grego -ga.

green, adj. verde. **greens,** verduras f.pl.

greenery, n. verdura, folhagem f.

Greenland, n. Groenlândia f.

greet, vb. cumprimentar, saudar; acolher.

greeting, n. cumprimento m., saudação f.; acolhida f.

gregarious, adj. gregário.

grenade, n. granada f.

grid, n. grade f.

grief, n. dor f., pesar m.

grievance, n. agravo m.; queixa f.

grill, 1. n. grelha f. **2.** vb. grelhar; crivar de perguntas.

grim, adj. sombrio; horrendo.

grimace, 1. n. careta f. **2.** vb. fazer caretas.

grime, n. sujeira f.

grimy, adj. sujo, imundo.

grin, 1. n. sorriso m. **2.** vb. sorrir.

grind, vb. moer; amolar.

grip, 1. n. ato de segurar; aperto de mão m.; mala f. **2.** vb. segurar.

gripe, 1. n. queixa, (coll.) bronca f. **2.** vb. reclamar.

grisly, adj. horrendo, medonho.

gristle, n. cartilagem f.

grit, n. areia f.; coragem f.

grizzled, grizzly, adj. grisalho.

groan, 1. n. gemido m. **2.** vb. gemer.

grocer, n. merceeiro -ra.

grocery, n. armazém m., mercearia f.

groggy, adj. grogue.

groin, n. virilha f.

groom, n. noivo m.

groove, n. estria, ranhura f.

grope, vb. tatear.

gross, 1. adj. grosso; crasso; bruto; grosseiro. **g. national product,** produto nacional bruto m. **2.** n. grossa f.

grossness, n. grosseria f.

grotesque, adj. grotesco.

grotto, n. gruta f.

grouch, n. ranheta m.f.

grouchy, adj. rabugento.

ground, n. chão, solo m.; terra f.; campo m.; terreno m.; (pl.) motivos m.pl. **g. floor,** andar térreo m.

groundless, adj. infundado.

groundwork, n. base f., fundamento m.

group, 1. *n.* grupo *m.*; roda *f.* **2.** *vb.* agrupar.

groupie, *n. (sl.)* macaca de auditório *f.*

grove, *n.* arvoredo *m.*

grovel, *n.* rastejar.

grow, *vb.* crescer; aumentar; cultivar.

grower, *n.* agricultor -ra.

growl, 1. *n.* rosnado *m.* **2.** *vb.* rosnar.

grownup, *n.* adulto -ta.

growth, *n.* crescimento *m.*

grub, *n. (sl.)* bóia *f.*

grubby, *adj.* encardido, sujo.

grudge, *n.* rancor *m.* **bear a g.,** guardar rancor.

gruel, 1. *n.* mingau *m.* **2.** *vb.* estafar; castigar.

gruesome, *adj.* horrível, medonho.

gruff, *adj.* brusco.

grumble, *vb.* chiar.

grumpy, *adj.* rabugento.

grunt, 1. *n.* grunhido *m.* **2.** *vb.* grunhir.

guarantee, 1. *n.* garantia *f.* **2.** *vb.* garantir.

guarantor, *n.* fiador -ra.

guard, 1. *n.* guarda *f.*; (person) guarda *m.* **2.** *vb.* guardar, vigiar.

guarded, *adj.* cauteloso.

guardian, *n.* protetor -ra; tutor -ra.

guardianship, *n.* proteção *f.*; tutela *f.*

Guatemalan, *adj., n.* guatemalteco -ca.

guava, *n.* goiaba *f.*

guerrilla, n. guerrilheiro -ra.

guess, 1. *n.* conjetura *f.*; palpite *m.* **2.** *vb.* adivinhar; (coll.) achar.

guesswork, *n.* conjetura *f.*

guest, *n.* hóspede *m.f.*; convidado -da.

guffaw, 1. *n.* gargalhada *f.* **2.** *vb.* gargalhar.

guidance, *n.* direção, guia *f.*

guide, 1. *n.* guia, cicerone *m.f.*; (book) guia *m.* **2.** *vb.* guiar.

guidebook, *n.* guia *m.*

guided missile, *n.* míssil teleguiado *m.*

guild, *n.* grêmio *m.*

guile, *n.* astúcia *f.*

guillotine, 1. *n.* guilhotina *f.* **2.** *vb.* guilhotinar.

guilt, *n.* culpa *f.*

guilty, *adj.* culpado; culpável.

guinea pig, *n.* cobaia *f.*

guise, *n.* guisa *f.*

guitar, *n.* violão *m.*; (electric) guitarra *f.*

guitarist, *n.* guitarrista *m.f.*

gulch, *n.* ravina *f.*

gulf, *n.* golfo *m.*; abismo *m.*

gull, *n.* gaivota *f.*

gullet, *n.* goela *f.*

gullible, *n.* crédulo.

gully, *n.* barranco *m.*

gulp, 1. *n.* gole *m.* **2.** *vb.* engolir às pressas.

gum, *n.* goma *f.*; chiclete *m.*; (pl.) gengivas *f.pl.*

gummy, *adj.* gomoso.

gun, *n.* revólver *m.*; (rifle) espingarda *f.*; (cannon) canhão *m.*

gunboat, *n.* canhoneira *f.*

gunfire, *n.* tiroteio *m.*

gunman, *n.* pistoleiro *m.*

gunner, *n.* artilheiro *m.*

gunpowder, *n.* pólvora *f.*

gunshot, *n.* tiro *m.*; balaço *m.*

gurgle, 1. *n.* gorgolejo *m.* **2.** *vb.* gorgolejar.

gush, 1. *n.* jorro *m.*, golfada *f.* **2.** *vb.* jorrar, golfar; ser efusivo.

gust, 1. *n.* rajada *f.* **2.** *vb.* soprar, ventar.

gusto, *n.* gosto, prazer *m.*

gusty, *adj.* ventoso.

gut, *n.* tripa *f.*; barriga *f.*; (pl.) coragem *f.*

gutter, *n.* sarjeta *f.*; canaleta *f.*

guttural, *adj.* gutural.

guy, *n.(sl.)* cara *m.*

Guyana, *n.* Guiana *f.*

guzzle, *vb.* entornar.

gym, *n.* ginásio *m.*

gymnasium, *n.* ginásio *m.*

gymnast, *n.* ginasta *m.f.*

gymnastic, *adj.* ginástico.

gymnastics, *n.* ginástica *f.*

gynecology, *n.* ginecologia *f.*

gyp, 1. *n.* trapaça *f.* **2.** *vb.* trapacear.

gypsum, *n.* gesso *f.*

gypsy, *adj., n.* cigano -na.

gyrate, *vb.* girar.

H

haberdashery, n. casa de artigos masculinos m.

habit, n. hábito, costume m. **be in the h. of,** costumar.

habitable, adj. habitável.

habitat, n. habitat m.

habitation, f. habitação, moradia f.

habitual, adj. habitual.

habituate, vb. habituar.

habitué, n. habituado -da.

hacienda, n. fazenda f.

hack, 1. adj. vulgar; mercenário 2. n. talho m.; carro de aluguel, táxi m.; escritor mercenário m. 3. vb. talhar, cortar.

hacker, n. (comput.) hacker m.f.

hackneyed, adj. gasto, trivial.

hacksaw, n. serra para cortar metal f.

hag, n. bruxa f.

haggard, adj. macilento.

haggle, vb. pechinchar.

hail, 1. n. saraiva f., granizo m.; saudação f. 2. vb. saraivar; saudar, chamar.

Hail Mary, n. ave-maria f.

hailstone, n. granizo m.

hair, n. cabelo m.; (body) pêlo m.

haircut, n. corte de cabelo m.

hairdo, n. penteado m.

hairdresser, n. cabeleireiro -ra.

hairpin, n. grampo de cabelo m.

hair-raising, adj. horripilante.

hair spray, n. fixante de cabelo m.

hairy, adj. cabeludo; peludo.

Haitian, adj., n. haitiano -na.

hale, adj. são.

half, 1. adj., adv. meio. 2. n. metade f.

half-hearted, adj. sem entusiasmo.

half-mast, n. **at h.,** a meio pau.

halfway, adv. a meio caminho.

half-wit, n. idiota m.f.

hall, n. corredor m.; salão m.; (entrance) vestíbulo m.

halleluiah, interj. aleluia.

hallmark, n. marca de autenticidade ou qualidade f.

hallow, vb. consagrar.

hallucination, n. alucinação f.

hallway, n. corredor m.

halo, n. halo m.; auréola f.

halt, 1. adj. manco. 2. n. alto m.; parada f. 3. vb. parar. 4. interj. alto!

halter, n. cabresto m.

halve, vb. partir ao meio.

ham, n. presunto m.; (actor) canastrão m.

hamburger, n. hambúrguer m.

hamlet, n. aldeia f., povoado m.

hammer, 1. n. martelo m. 2. vb. martelar.

hammock, n. rede (de dormir) f.

hamper, 1. n. canastra, cesta f. 2. vb. embaraçar; impedir.

hamstring, 1. n. tendão do jarrete. 2. vb. incapacitar.

hand, 1. n. mão f.; (clock) ponteiro m.; ajuda f.; caligrafia f. **on the one/other hand,** por um/outro lado; **shake hands,** dar um aperto de mão. 2. adj. de mão. 3. vb. passar, entregar.

handbag, n. bolsa f., maleta f.

handball, n. handebol m.

handbook, n. manual m.

handcuffs, n.pl. algemas f.pl.

handful, n. punhado m.

handicap, n. handicap m., vantagem f.; desvantagem f.; deficiência física f.

handicraft, n. artesanato m.

handiwork, n. trabalho m.; obra f.

handkerchief, n. lenço m.

handle, 1. n. cabo m., alça f., asa f.; maçaneta f. 2. vb. manusear; tratar.

handlebar, n. guidom m.

handmade, adj. feito à mão.

handshake, n. aperto de mãos m.

handsome, adj. bonito; liberal.

handwriting, n. caligrafia f.

handy, adj. hábil, jeitoso; à mão.

hang, vb. pendurar; enforcar; estar pendurado; ser enforcado.

hangar, n. hangar m.

hanger, n. cabide m.; gancho m.

hanging, 1. adj. pendente, suspenso. 2. n. enforcamento m.

hangman, *n.* carrasco, verdugo *m.*

hangnail, *n.* raigota *f.*

hangover, *n. (sl.)* ressaca *f.*

hangup, *n. (sl.)* grilo *m.*

hanker, *vb.* anelar.

hankering, *n.* anelo *m.*

haphazard, *adj.* casual, acidental.

happen, *vb.* acontecer, passarse.

happening, *n.* acontecimento *m.*

happiness, *n.* felicidade *f.*; alegria *f.*

happy, *adj.* feliz; contente, alegre.

happy-go-lucky, *adj.* despreocupado.

harangue, 1. *n.* arenga *f.* **2.** *vb.* arengar.

harass, *vb.* atormentar.

harbinger, *n.* precursor -ra.

harbor, 1. *n.* porto *m.* **2.** *vb.* abrigar; alimentar.

hard, 1. *adj.* duro; difícil. **2.** *adv.* muito.

harden, *vb.* endurecer.

hard-headed, *adj.* teimoso.

hard-hearted, *adj.* insensível; cruel.

hardly, *adv.* apenas, mal.

hardness, *n.* dureza *f.*

hardship, *n.* miséria *f.*, sofrimento *m.*

hardware, *n.* ferragens *f.pl.*; *(comput.)* hardware.

hardwood, *n.* madeira dura/de lei *f.*

hardy, *adj.* forte, robusto.

hare, *n.* lebre *f.*

harebrained, *adj.* leviano, estouvado.

harelip, *n.* lábio leporino *m.*

harem, *n.* harém *m.*

hark, *vb.* escutar. **h. back to,** voltar a.

Harlequin, *n.* Arlequim *m.*

harlot, *n.* meretriz *f.*

harm, 1. *n.* dano, mal *f.* **2.** *vb.* fazer mal a; prejudicar.

harmful, *adj.* prejudicial, nocivo.

harmless, *adj.* inofensivo.

harmonica, *n.* harmônica, gaita *f.*

harmonious, *adj.* harmonioso.

harmonize, *vb.* harmonizar.

harmony, *n.* harmonia *f.*

harness, 1. *n.* arreios *m.pl.* **2.** *vb.* arrear; atrelar.

harp, *n.* harpa *f.*

harpoon, 1. *n.* arpão *m.* **2.** *vb.* arpoar.

harpsichord, *n.* cravo *m.*

harry, *vb.* assolar; arrasar.

harsh, *adj.* áspero, severo.

harshness, *n.* severidade *f.*

harvest, 1. *n.* colheita, safra *f.* **2.** *vb.* colher.

hash, *n.* picadinho *m.*

hashish, *n.* haxixe *m.*

hassle, *n. (sl.)* bagunça *f.*; *(sl.)* sufoco *m.*

haste, *n.* pressa *f.*

hasten, *vb.* apressar; apressar-se.

hasty, *adj.* apressado, precipitado.

hat, *n.* chapéu *m.*

hatbox, *n.* chapeleira *f.*

hatch, 1. *n.* escotilha *f.*, alçapão *m.* **2.** *vb.* incubar; tramar; chocar.

hatchet, *n.* machadinha *f.*

hate, 1. *n.* ódio *m.* **2.** *vb.* odiar, detestar.

hateful, *adj.* odioso.

hatred, *n.* ódio *m.*

haughty, *adj.* arrogante, altivo.

haul, 1. *n.* puxão *m.*; frete *m.* lucro; distância *f.* **2.** *vb.* puxar.

haunch, *n.* anca *f.*

haunt, 1. *n.* lugar freqüentado. **2.** *vb.* fazer ponto em; assombrar.

haunted, *adj.* mal-assombrado.

have, *vb.* ter; (auxiliary) ter, haver. have **(something) done,** mandar fazer; **have to,** ter que/ de.

haven, *n.* porto *m.*; asilo *m.*

havoc, *n.* estrago *m.*, ruína *f.*

Hawaii, *n.* Havaí *m.*

hawk, 1. *n.* falcão, gavião *m.* **2.** *vb.* mascatear.

hay, *n.* feno *m.*

hay fever, *n.* febre de feno, polenose *f.*

hayloft, *n.* palheiro *m.*

haystack, *n.* meda de feno *f.*

haywire, *adj.* enguiçado; louco.

hazard, 1. *n.* sorte *f.*; perigo *m.* **2.** *vb.* arriscar, aventurar.

hazardous, *adj.* perigoso, arriscado.

haze, *n.* neblina, cerração, bruma *f.*

hazel, *n.* avelã *f.*

hazy, *adj.* brumoso; vago.

he, *pron.* ele.

head, 1. cabeça *f.*; (chief) chefe *m.f.* **heads or tails,** cara ou coroa. **2.** *vb.* dirigir, encabeçar. **h. for,** rumar para.

headache, *n.* dor de cabeça *f.*

headboard, *n.* cabeceira *f.*

headfirst, *adv.* de cabeça.

heading, *n.* cabeçalho *m.*

headlight, *n.* farol dianteiro *m.*

headline, *n.* manchete *f.*, título, cabeçalho *m.*

headlong, 1. *adj.* precipitado. **2.** *adv.* precipitadamente.

head-on, *adv.* de frente.

headquarters, *n.* sede *f.*; (milit.) quartel-general *m.*

headstone, *n.* lousa, campa *f.*

headstrong, *adj.* teimoso.

headwaters, *n.pl.* cabeceiras *f.pl.*

headway, *n.* avanço, progresso *m.*

heady, *adj.* impetuoso; estonteante.

heal, *vb.* curar(-se), sarar.

health, *n.* saúde *f.*

healthful, *adj.* salutar, saudável, salubre.

healthy, *adj.* são, sadio.

heap, 1. *n.* monte *m.*, pilha *f.* **2.** *vb.* empilhar.

hear, *vb.* ouvir. **h. from,** ter notícias de. **h. about/of,** ouvir dizer de.

hearing, *n.* audição *f.*; (interview) audiência *f.*

hearsay, *n.* boato, rumor *m.*

hearse, *n.* carro fúnebre *m.*

heart, *n.* coração *m.*; (pl.) (cards) copas *f.pl.* **by h.,** de cor; **take to h.,** tomar a peito.

heartache, *n.* tristeza *f.*, sofrimento *m.*

heart attack, *m.* colapso cardíaco, enfarte *m.*

heartbreak, *n.* sofrimento, pesar *m.*

heartbroken, *adj.* inconsolável.

heartburn, *n.* azia *f.*

hearten, *vb.* encorajar.

heartfelt, *adj.* sentido, sincero.

hearth, *n.* lareira *f.*

heartless, *adj.* insensível.

heartsick, *adj.* triste.

heart-to-heart, *adj.* franco.

hearty, *adj.* cordial; vigoroso.

heat, 1. *n.* calor *m.*; aquecimento *m.* **2.** *vb.* esquentar, aquecer.

heated, *adj.* acalorado.

heater, *n.* aquecedor *m.*

heath, *n.* charneca *f.*

heathen, *adj.*, *m.* gentio -a, pagão -gã.

heather, *n.* urze *f.*

heating, *n.* aquecimento *m.*

heatstroke, *n.* insolação *f.*

heat wave, *n.* onda de calor *f.*

heave, *vb.* levantar; lançar; arfar; vomitar.

heaven, *n.* céu *m.*

heavenly, *adj.* celestial, divino.

h:avy, *adj.* pesado.

Hebrew, 1. *adj.* hebreu -bréia, hebraico. **2.** *n.* hebreu -bréia; (language) hebreu *m.*

heckle, *vb.* atormentar (um orador).

hectic, *adj.* febril, caótico.

hedge, *n.* sebe *f.*

hedonism, *n.* hedonismo *m.*

heed, 1. *n.* atenção *f.* **2.** *vb.* prestar atenção a.

heedless, *adj.* desatento, incauto.

heel, *n.* calcanhar *m.*; (shoe) salto *m.*; (sl.) patife *m.*

hefty, *adj.* pesado.

heifer, *n.* bezerra, novilha *f.*

height, *n.* altura, altitude *f.*

heighten, *vb.* elevar; exaltar.

heinous, *adj.* hediondo.

heir, heiress, *n.* herdeiro -ra.

helicopter, *n.* helicóptero *m.*

helium, *n.* hélio *m.*

helix, *n.* hélice *f.*

hell, *n.* inferno *m.*

hellish, *adj.* infernal.

hello, *interj.* olá!, oi!; (phone) alô!, pronto!

helm, *n.* leme, timão *m.*

helmet, *n.* elmo, capacete *m.*

helmsman, *n.* timoneiro *m.*

help, 1. *n.* ajuda *f.* **2.** *vb.* ajudar. **h. oneself,** servir-se; **h. to,** ajudar a. **3.** *interj.* socorro!

helper, *n.* ajudante *m.f.*

helpful, *adj.* útil; prestativo.
helpless, *adj.* indefeso; incapaz.
hem, 1. *n.* bainha. 2. *vb.* embainhar.
hemisphere, *n.* hemisfério *m.*
hemlock, *n.* cicuta *f.*
hemophilia, *n.* hemofilia *f.*
hemorrhage, *n.* hemorragia *f.*
hemorrhoids, *n.pl.* hemorróidas, -des *f.pl.*
hemp, *n.* cânhamo *m.*
hen, *n.* galinha *f.*
hence, *adv.* daqui; daqui a; por isso.
henceforth, *adv.* daqui em diante.
henchman, *n.* capanga *m.*
henequen, *n.* henequém *m.*
henhouse, *n.* galinheiro *m.*
hepatitis, *n.* hepatite *f.*
her, 1. *poss. adj.* (o, a, os, as) dela; (o) seu, (a) sua, etc. 2. *obj. pron.* ela; a; lhe.
herald, *n.* arauto *m.*, precursor -ra.
heraldry, *n.* heráldica *f.*
herb, *n.* erva *f.*
herd, 1. *n.* manada *f.*, rebanho *m.* 2. *vb.* arrebanhar; guardar.
here, *adv.* aqui, cá.
hereafter, *adv.* daqui em diante.
hereby, *adv.* pelo presente.
hereditary, *adj.* hereditário.
heredity, *n.* hereditariedade *f.*
herein, *adv.* aqui contido, incluso.
heresy, *n.* heresia *f.*
heretic, *n.* herege *m.f.*, herético -ca.
heretofore, *adv.* até agora.
hereunder, *adv.* abaixo.
herewith, *adv.* em anexo.
heritage, *n.* herança *f.*
hermetic, *adj.* hermético.
hermit, *n.* eremita *m.f.*
hernia, *n.* hérnia *f.*
hero, *n.* herói *m.*
heroic, *adj.* heróico.
heroin, *n.* heroína *f.*
heroine, *n.* heroína *f.*
heron, *n.* garça *f.*
herring, *n.* arenque *m.*
hers, *poss. pron.* (o, a, os, as) dela; (o) seu, (a) sua, etc.
herself, *pron.* si mesma/própria. **by h.,** sozinha; **she h.,** ela mesma/própria.

hesitance, *n.* hesitação *f.*
hesitant, *adj.* hesitante, indeciso.
hesitate, *vb.* hesitar, vacilar.
heterogeneous, *adj.* heterogêneo.
heterosexual, *adj., n.* heterossexual *m.f.*
hew, *vb.* cortar, rachar.
hex, 1. *n.* feitiço *m.* 2. *vb.* enfeitiçar.
hey, *interj.* eh!, ó!
heyday, *n.* auge *m.*
hi, *interj.* oi!, olá!
hiatus, *n.* hiato *m.*
hibernate, *vb.* hibernar.
hibiscus, *n.* hibisco *m.*
hiccup, 1. *n.* soluço *m.* 2. *vb.* soluçar.
hickory, *n.* nogueira amarga *f.*
hidden, *adj.* escondido, oculto.
hide, 1. *n.* couro *m.*, pele *f.* 2. *vb.* esconder(-se).
hide-and-seek, *n.* esconde-esconde *m.*, manja *f.*
hideous, *adj.* horrível.
hide-out, hiding place, *n.* esconderijo *m.*
hierarchical, *adj.* hierárquico.
hierarchy, *n.* hierarquia *f.*
hieroglyphic, *adj., n.* hieroglífico *m.*
high, *adj.* alto, elevado; (price) caro.
highbrow, *adj., n.* erudito *m.*
high fidelity, *n.* alta fidelidade *f.*
highland, *n.* planalto *m.*
highlight, 1. *n.* ponto importante. 2. *vb.* realçar.
highly, *adv.* altamente, sumamente.
high school, *n.* escola secundária *f.*, colégio, curso de segundo grau *m.*
highway, *n.* estrada de rodagem *f.*
hijack, *vb.* seqüestrar.
hijacker, *n.* seqüestrador *m.*
hijacking, *n.* seqüestro *m.*
hike, 1. *n.* caminhada *f.* 2. *vb.* levantar; caminhar.
hilarious, *adj.* hilário, hilariante.
hill, *n.* colina *f.*, morro *m.*; ladeira *f.*

hillbilly, *n.* caipira *m.f.*; matuto *m.*

hilt, *n.* punho *m.* **to the h.**, completamente.

him, *pron.* ele; o; lhe.

himself, *pron.* se; si mesmo/próprio. **by h.**, sozinho; **he h.**, ele mesmo/próprio.

hinder, *vb.* atrapalhar; impedir.

Hindi, *n.* hindi *m.*

hindrance, *n.* obstáculo, impedimento *m.*

Hindu, *adj., n.* hindu *m.f.*

hinge, **1.** *n.* dobradiça, charneira *f.* **2.** *vb.* **h. on**, depender de.

hint, **1.** *n.* insinuação *f.*; palpite *m.*; indireta *f.* **2.** *vb.* insinuar.

hinterland, *n.* interior, sertão *m.*

hippopotamus, *n.* hipopótamo *m.*

hips, *n.pl.* quadris *m.*, cadeiras *f.pl.*

hire, *vb.* contratar; alugar

his, *poss. adj., pron.* (o, a, os, as) dele; (o) seu, (a) sua, etc.

Hispanic, *adj.* hispânico.

hiss, **1.** *n.* silvo *m.*; vaia *f.* **2.** *vb.* silvar; vaiar.

historian, *n.* historiador *m.*

historic, **-al**, *adj.* histórico.

history, *n.* história *f.*

hit, **1.** *n.* golpe *m.*, pancada *f.*; *(coll.)* sucesso *m.* **2.** *vb.* bater.

hitch, **1.** *n.* obstáculo *m.*, encrenca *f.* **2.** *vb.* enganchar; atrelar; pedir/pegar (carona).

hitherto, *adv.* até agora.

hive, *n.* cortiço *m.*, colmeia *f.*

hives, *n.pl.* urticária *f.*

hoard, **1.** *n.* tesouro *m.* **2.** *vb.* acumular; monopolizar.

hoarse, *adj.* rouco.

hoax, **1.** *n.* embuste, logro *m.* **2.** *vb.* enganar.

hobble, *vb.* mancar, cambalear.

hobby, *n.* passatempo, hobby *m.*

hobnob, *vb.* conviver, ter intimidade.

hobo, *n.* vagabundo *m.*

hock, *vb.* empenhar.

hockey, *n.* hóquei *m.*

hodgepodge, *n.* mixórdia *f.*, saco de gatos *m.*

hoe, *n.* enxada *f.*

hog, *n.* porco *m.*

hogwash, *n.* tolice, bobagem *f.*

hoist, *vb.* levantar.

hold, **1.** *n.* domínio *m.*; (ship) porão *m.* **get a h. of**, segurar; conseguir. **2.** *vb.* segurar; prender. **h. on!**, espera aí!; **h. up**, agüentar; atrasar; assaltar.

holdings, *n.* posses *f.pl.*; acervo *m.*

hold-up, *n.* obstáculo *m.*; demora *f.*; assalto *m.*

hole, *n.* buraco, furo.

holiday, *n.* feriado *m.*; dia santo *m.*

holiness, *n.* santidade *f.*

Holland, *n.* Holanda *f.*

holler, **1.** *n.* grito *m.* **2.** *vb.* gritar.

hollow, **1.** *adj.* oco. **2.** *n.* cavidade *f.* **3.** *vb.* escavar.

holly, *n.* azevinho *m.*

holocaust, *n.* holocausto *m.*

hologram, *n.* holograma *m.*

holster, *n.* coldre *m.*

holy, *adj.* santo. **h. day**, dia santo *m.*; **H. Ghost** or **Spirit**, Espírito Santo *m.*; **H. Land**, Terra Santa *f.*; **H. See**, Santa Sé *f.*; **h. water**, água benta *f.*; **H. Week**, Semana Santa *f.*

homage, *n.* homenagem *f.*

home, *n.* casa *f.*; lar *m.* **at h.**, em casa.

homeland, *n.* pátria *f.*

homeless, *adj.* desabrigado, sem lar.

homely, *adj.* feio.

homemade, *adj.* caseiro.

homemaker, *n.* dona de casa *f.*

home office, *n.* sede, matriz *f.*

homesick, *adj.* saudoso.

homesickness, *n.* saudade, nostalgia *f.*

homeward, *adv.* para casa.

homework, *n.* dever (escolar) *m.*

homicide, *n.* homicídio *m.*

homogeneous, *adj.* homogêneo.

homogenize, *vb.* homogeneizar.

homosexual, *adj., n.* homossexual *m.f.*

homosexuality, *n.* homossexualismo *m.*

Honduran, *adj., n.* hondurenho *m.*

hone, *vb.* afiar, amolar.

honest, *adj.* honesto.

honesty, *n.* honestidade *f.*

honey, *n.* mel *m.*

honeycomb, *n.* favo (de mel) *m.*

honeydew melon, *n.* melão *m.*

honeymoon, *n.* lua-de-mel *f.*

honeysuckle, *n.* madressilva *f.*

honk, **1.** *n.* grasnada *f.*; (horn) buzinada *f.* **2.** *vb.* grasnar; (horn) buzinar.

honor, **1.** *n.* honra *f.* **2.** *vb.* honrar.

honorable, *adj.* honrado; ilustre.

honorarium, *n.* honorários *m.pl.*

honorary, *adj.* honorário.

hood, *n.* capuz *m.*, carapuça *f.*; (car) capô *m.*; (sl.) capanga *m.*

hoodlum, *n.* capanga, jagunço *m.*

hoodwink, *vb.* ludibriar.

hoof, *n.* casco *m.*

hook, **1.** *n.* gancho *m.* **2.** *vb.* enganchar.

hooker, *n. (sl.)* mulher-da-vida *f.*

hooky, *n.* **play h.**, matar aula.

hoop, *n.* arco, aro *m.*

hoot, **1.** *n.* pio (de coruja); vaia. *m.* **2.** *vb.* piar; vaiar.

hop, **1.** *n.* pulo *m.* **2.** *vb.* pular.

hope, **1.** *n.* esperança *f.* **2.** *vb.* esperar.

hopeful, *adj.* esperançoso.

hopefully, *adv. (coll.)* tomara (que).

hopeless, *adj.* desesperado; perdido.

hopscotch, *n.* amarelinha *f.*

horde, *n.* horda *f.*

horizon, *n.* horizonte *m.*

horizontal, *adj.* horizontal.

hormone, *n.* hormônio *m.*

horn, *n.* chifre, corno *m.*; trompa *f.*; (car) buzina *f.*

hornet, *n.* vespão *m.*

horoscope, *n.* horóscopo *m.*

horrendous, *adj.* horrendo.

horrible, *adj.* horrível.

horrid, *adj.* hórrido.

horrify, *vb.* horrorizar.

horror, *n.* horror *m.*

horse, *n.* cavalo *m.* **ride a h.**, montar a cavalo.

horseback, *adv.* a cavalo.

horseman, *n.* cavaleiro *m.*

horsemanship, *n.* equitação *f.*; manejo *m.*

horseplay, *n.* brincadeira barulhenta *f.*

horsepower, *n.* cavalo-vapor, cavalo *m.*

horseradish, *n.* rábano picante *m.*

horseshoe, *n.* ferradura *f.*

horticulture, *n.* horticultura *f.*

hose, *n.* mangueira *f.*; (stockings) meias *f.pl.*

hospice, *n.* hospício *m.*; abrigo *f.*

hospitable, *adj.* hospitaleiro.

hospital, *n.* hospital *m.*

hospitality, *n.* hospitalidade *f.*

hospitalize, *vb.* hospitalizar.

host, *n.* anfitrião, dono de casa *m.*; (army) hoste *f.*; (eccles.) hóstia *f.*

hostage, *n.* refém *m.f.*

hostel, *n.* hospedaria *f.*

hostess, *n.* anfitrioa, dona da casa *f.*

hostile, *adj.* hostil.

hostility, *n.* hostilidade *f.*

hot, *adj.* quente; apimentado. **be h.**, estar com calor; (weather) fazer calor, estar quente.

hotbed, *n.* viveiro, ninho *m.*

hot dog, *n.* cachorro-quente *m.*

hotel, *n.* hotel *m.*

hotheaded, *n.* irritadiço, exaltado.

hothouse, *n.* estufa *f.*

hot-water bottle, *n.* saco de água quente *m.*

hound, **1.** *n.* sabujo *m.* **2.** *vb.* acossar; atormentar.

hour, *n.* hora *f.*

hourglass, *n.* ampulheta *f.*

hourly, **1.** *adj.* por hora. **2.** *adv.* a cada hora; por hora.

house, **1.** *n.* casa *f.*; (theat.) platéia *f.* **House of Deputies**, Câmara dos Deputados. **2.** *vb.* alojar, hospedar.

housefly, *n.* mosca *f.*

household, *n.* família *f.*; casa *f.*

housekeeper, *n.* empregada *f.*; governanta *f.*

housemaid, *n.* empregada doméstica *f.*

housewife, *n.* dona de casa *f.*

housework, n. serviço doméstico m.

housing, n. habitação, moradia f.

hovel, n. choupana f.

hover, vb. pairar, flutuar.

how, 1. adv. como. **2.** conj. como; que. **h. about,** que tal; **h. are you?,** como vai?; **h. come,** por quê, porque; **h. far,** a que distância; até que ponto; **h. much,** quanto; **h. many,** quantos; **h. pretty (etc.)!,** que bonito (etc.)!

however, 1. adv. como, quão. **2.** conj. como; por mais que; porém.

howl, 1. n. uivo m. **2.** vb. uivar.

hub, n. (wheel) cubo m.; (fig.) eixo m.

hubbub, n. fuzuê m.

hubcap, n. calota f.

huddle, 1. n. agrupamento m. confusão f. **2.** vb. agrupar-se.

hue, n. cor, nuança f.

huff, 1. n. amuo m. **2.** vb. soprar.

hug, 1. n. abraço m. **2.** vb. abraçar.

huge, adj. imenso.

huh, interj. hein?

hulk, n. casco de navio m.

hull, 1. n. (fruit) casca f.; (naut.) casco m. **2.** vb. descascar.

hullabaloo, n. barulho, bafafá m.

hum, 1. n. zumbido. m. **2.** vb. zumbir; cantarolar.

human, 1. adj. humano. **2.** n. ser humano m.

humane, adj. humano, humanitário.

humanitarian, adj. humanitário.

humanity, n. humanidade f.

humankind, n. gênero humano m.

humble, 1. adj. humilde. **2.** vb. humilhar.

humbug, n. fraude f.; impostor m.

humdrum, 1. adj. ramerraneiro. **2.** n. ramerrão m.

humid, adj. úmido.

humidify, vb. umedecer.

humidity, n. umidade f.

humiliate, vb. humilhar.

humility, n. humildade f.

hummingbird, n. beija-flor m.

humor, 1. n. humor m.; humorismo m. **2.** vb. fazer a vontade de.

humorist, n. humorista m.f.

humorous, adj. cômico, humorístico.

hump, n. corcunda; protuberância f.

humpback, hunchback, n. corcunda m.f.

humpbacked, hunchbacked, adj. corcovado.

humus, n. humo m.

hunch, n. palpite m.

hundred, adj. cem, cento.

hundredth, adj., n. centésimo m.

Hungarian, adj., n. húngaro -ra.

Hungary, n. Hungria f.

hunger, 1. n. fome f. **2.** vb. sentir fome. **h. strike,** greve de fome f.

hungry, adj. faminto. **be h.,** estar com fome.

hunk, n. naco m.; (sl.) bonitão m.

hunt, 1. n. caça f.; busca f. **2.** vb. caçar; procurar.

hunter -tress, n. caçador -ra.

hunting, n. caça, caçada f.

hurdle, 1. n. barreira f.; obstáculo m. **2.** vb. pular; vencer.

hurl, vb. arremessar.

hurricane, n. furacão m.

hurried, adj. apressado.

hurry, 1. n. pressa f. **be in a h.,** estar com pressa. **2.** vb. apressar-se.

hurt, 1. n. ferida, dor f.; prejuízo m. **2.** vb. ferir; prejudicar; doer.

hurtful, adj. prejudicial.

hurtle, vb. precipitar-se.

husband, n. marido, esposo m.

hush, 1. n. calada f. **2.** vb. calar.

husk, 1. casca f. **2.** vb. descascar.

husky, adj. robusto.

hustle, 1. n. atividade, energia f. **2.** vb.(sl.) mandar brasa.

hustler, n. (coll.) pé-de-boi m.; (coll.) virador -ra m.; (sl.) mulher-da-vida f.

hut, *n.* choupana, cabana *f.*
hyacinth, *n.* jacinto *m.*
hybrid, *adj.* híbrido.
hydrangea, *n.* hortênsia *f.*
hydrant, *n.* hidrante *f.*
hydrate, *vb.* hidratar.
hydraulic, *adj.* hidráulico.
hydroelectric, *adj.* hidrelétrico.
hydrogen, *n.* hidrogênio *m.*
hydroplane, *n.* hidravião, hidroplano *m.*
hyena, *n.* hiena *f.*
hygiene, *n.* higiene *f.*
hygienic, *adj.* higiênico.
hymen, *n.* hímen *m.*
hymn, *n.* hino *m.*
hyperbole, *n.* hipérbole *f.*
hypertension, *n.* hipertensão *f.*
hypertensive, *adj.,* *n.* hipertenso *m.*
hyphen, *n.* hífen, traço-deunião *m.*
hyphenate, *vb.* hifenizar.
hypnosis, *n.* hipnose *f.*
hypnotic, *adj.* hipnótico.
hypnotism, *n.* hipnotismo *m.*
hypnotize, *vb.* hipnotizar.
hypochondriac, *n.* hipocondríaco -ca.
hypocrisy, *n.* hipocrisia *f.*
hypocrite, *n.* hipócrita *m.f.*
hypocritical, *adj.* hipócrita.
hypodermic, *adj.* hipodérmico.
hypodermic syringe, *n.* seringa *f.*
hypothesis, *n.* hipótese *f.*
hypothetical, *adj.* hipotético.
hysteria, *n.* histeria *f.*
hysterical, *adj.* histérico.

I

I, *pron.* eu.
Iberian, *adj.,* *n.* ibérico -ca.
ice, *n.* gelo *m.* **i. cube,** pedra de gelo *f.*
iceberg, *n.* iceberg *m.*
icebox, *n.* geladeira *f.*
ice cream, *n.* sorvete *m.*
iced, *adj.* gelado.
Iceland, *n.* Islândia *f.*
icicle, *n.* sincelo *m.*
icon, *n.* ícone *m.*
iconoclast, *n.* iconoclasta *m.f.*
icy, *adj.* gelado.
idea, *n.* idéia *f.*

ideal, *adj.* ideal.
idealism, *n.* idealismo *m.*
idealist, *n.* idealista *m.f.*
idealize, *vb.* idealizar.
identical, *adj.* idêntico.
identification, *n.* identificação *f.*; carteira de identidade *f.*
identify, *vb.* identificar.
identity, *n.* identidade *f.*
ideological, *adj.* ideológico.
ideology, *n.* ideologia *f.*
idiocy, *n.* estupidez *f.*
idiom, *n.* expressão idiomática *f.*, idiotismo *m.*
idiomatic, *adj.* idiomático.
idiosyncrasy, *n.* idiossincrasia *f.*
idiot, *n.* idiota *m.f.*
idiotic, *adj.* idiota.
idle, 1. *adj.* ocioso; desempregado; fútil.
idleness, *n.* ociosidade *f.*
idle talk, *n.* conversa fiada *f.*
idol, *n.* ídolo *m.*
idolize, *vb.* idolatrar.
if, *conj.* se; caso. **i. only,** quem me dera; **even i.,** mesmo que.
igneous, *adj.* ígneo.
ignite, *vb.* acender; pegar fogo.
ignition, *n.* ignição *f.*
ignoble, *adj.* ignóbil.
ignominious, *adj.* ignominioso.
ignoramus, *n.* ignorante *m.f.*
ignorance, *n.* ignorância *f.*
ignorant, *adj.* ignorante.
ignore, *vb.* não fazer caso de, ignorar; negligenciar.
ilk, *n.* laia *f.*, jaez *m.*
ill, 1. *adj.* doente, mau. **2.** *n.* mal *m.* **3.** *adv.* mal.
illegal, *adj.* ilegal, ilícito.
illegible, *adj.* ilegível.
illegitimate, *adj.* ilegítimo.
ill-fated, *adj.* malfadado.
illicit, *adj.* ilícito.
illiteracy, *n.* analfabetismo *m.*
illiterate, *adj.* analfabeto, iletrado.
ill-mannered, *adj.* maleducado.
illness, *n.* doença *f.*
illogical, *adj.* ilógico.
illuminate, *vb.* iluminar.
illusion, *n.* ilusão *f.*
illusory, *adj.* ilusório.
illustrate, *vb.* ilustrar.
illustration, *n.* ilustração *f.*

illustrator, *n.* ilustrador -ra.

illustrious, *adj.* ilustre.

ill will, *n.* má vontade *f.*

image, *n.* imagem *f.*

imagery, *n.* imaginação *f.* ; imagens *f.pl.*

imaginary, *adj.* imaginário.

imagination, *n.* imaginação *f.*

imaginative, *adj.* imaginativo.

imagine, *vb.* imaginar.

imbalance, *n.* desequilíbrio *m.*

imbecile, *n.* imbecil *m.f.*

imbibe, *vb.* beber.

imbroglio, *n.* embrulho *m.* , embrulhada *f.*

imbue, *vb.* imbuir.

imitate, *vb.* imitar.

imitation, *n.* imitação *f.*

imitator, *n.* imitador -ra.

immaculate, *adj.* imaculado.

immaterial, *adj.* imaterial; irrelevante.

immature, *adj.* imaturo.

immediate, *adj.* imediato.

immediately, *adv.* imediatamente, logo, em, seguida.

immense, *adj.* imenso.

immerse, *vb.* imergir, submergir.

immigrant, *adj., n.* imigrante *m.f.*

immigrate, *vb.* imigrar.

imminent, *adj.* iminente.

immobile, *adj.* imóvel.

immoral, *adj.* imoral.

immorality, *n.* imoralidade *f.*

immortal, *adj.* imortal.

immortality, *n.* imortalidade *f.*

immortalize, *vb.* imortalizar.

immune, *adj.* imune, imunizado.

immunity, *n.* imunidade *f.*

immunize, *vb.* imunizar.

impact, *n.* impacto *m.*

impair, *vb.* prejudicar.

impart, *vb.* emprestar, conferir; comunicar.

impartial, *adj.* imparcial.

impasse, *n.* impasse *m.*

impassioned, *adj.* apaixonado, ardente.

impassive, *adj.* insensível.

impatient, *adj.* impaciente.

impeach, *vb.* impugnar; *(polit.)* acusar de malversação *f.*

impeachment, *n.* impugnação *f.* ; *(polit.)* impedimento *m.*

impeccable, *adj.* impecável.

impede, *vb.* impedir.

impediment, *n.* impedimento *m.*

impel, *n.* impelir.

impending, *adj.* iminente.

impenetrable, *adj.* impenetrável.

imperative, *adj.* imperativo.

imperceptible, *adj.* imperceptível.

imperfect, *adj.* imperfeito.

imperfection, *n.* imperfeição *f.*

imperial, *adj.* imperial.

imperil, *vb.* pôr em perigo.

impersonal, *adj.* impessoal.

impersonate, *vb.* personificar; imitar.

impertinent, *adj.* impertinente.

impervious, *adj.* impérvio, impenetrável.

impetuous, *adj.* impetuoso.

impetus, *n.* ímpeto, impulso *m.*

impinge, *vb.* invadir, infringir.

implacable, *adj.* implacável.

implant, *vb.* implantar; inculcar.

implement, **1.** *n.* implemento *m.* **2.** *vb.* implementar.

implicate, *vb.* implicar, envolver, comprometer.

implication, *n.* implicação *f.*

implicit, *adj.* implícito.

implore, *vb.* implorar.

imply, *vb.* implicar (em); insinuar.

impolite, *adj.* descortês.

import, **1.** *n.* importação *f.* ; importância *f.* **2.** *vb.* importar.

importance, *n.* importância *f.*

important, *adj.* importante.

importation, *n.* importação *f.*

importune, *vb.* importunar.

impose, *vb.* impor. **i. on**, abusar de.

imposing, *adj.* imponente.

imposition, *n.* imposição *f.*

impossible, *adj.* impossível.

impostor, *n.* impostor -ra.

impotent, *adj.* impotente.

impound, *vb.* apreender, seqüestrar.

impoverish, *vb.* empobrecer.

impregnate, *vb.* impregnar, emprenhar.

impress, *vb.* impressionar.

impression, *n.* impressão *f.*

impressive, *adj.* impressionante.

imprison, *vb.* encarcerar.

imprisonment, *n.* prisão *f.*; encarceramento *m.*

improbable, *adj.* improvável.

impromptu, *adj.* extemporâneo.

improper, *adj.* impróprio.

improve, *vb.* melhorar; aperfeiçoar.

improvement, *n.* melhoramento *m.*, melhora, melhoria *f.*

improvise, *vb.* improvisar.

impudent, *adj.* impudente.

impugn, *vb.* impugnar.

impulse, *n.* impulso *m.*

impulsive, *adj.* impulsivo.

impunity, *n.* impunidade *f.*

impurity, *n.* impureza *f.*

impute, *vb.* imputar.

in, 1. *adv.* dentro, para dentro; em casa. **2.** *prep.* em, dentro de.

inadvertent, *adj.* inadvertido.

inalienable, *adj.* inalienável.

inane, *adj.* inane.

inasmuch as, *conj.* visto que.

inaugurate, *vb.* inaugurar; empossar.

inauguration, *n.* inauguração *f.*; posse *f.*

Inca, *n.* inca *m.f.*

Incan, *adj.* inca, incaico.

incandescent, *adj.* incandescente.

incantation, *n.* encantamento, sortilégio *m.*

incapacitate, *vb.* incapacitar.

incarcerate, *vb.* encarcerar.

incarnate, 1. *adj.* encarnado. **2.** *vb.* encarnar.

incarnation, *n.* encarnação *f.*

incendiary, *adj.* incendiário.

incense, 1. *n.* incenso *m.* **2.** *vb.* enfurecer.

incentive, *n.* incentivo *m.*

inception, *n.* início *m.*

incessant, *adj.* incessante.

incest, *n.* incesto *m.*

inch, *n.* polegada *f.*

incidence, *n.* incidência *f.*

incident, *n.* incidente *m.*

incidental, *adj.* incidental.

incinerate, *vb.* incinerar.

incipient, *adj.* incipiente.

incision, *n.* incisão *f.*

incisive, *adj.* incisivo, penetrante.

incite, *vb.* incitar, instigar.

inclination, *n.* inclinação *f.*

incline, 1. *n.* declive *m.* **2.** *vb.* inclinar-se.

include, *vb.* incluir.

inclusion, *n.* inclusão *f.*

inclusive, *adj.* inclusivo.

incognito, *adj., n., adv.* incógnito.

income, *n.* renda *f.* **i. tax,** imposto de renda *m.*

incongruity, *n.* incongruência *f.*

incongruous, *adj.* incôngruo.

inconvenience, *n.* inconveniência *f.*, incômodo *m.*

inconvenient, *adj.* inconveniente, incômodo.

incorporate, *vb.* incorporar (-se).

increase, 1. *n.* aumento *m.* **2.** *vb.* aumentar; crescer.

incredible, *adj.* incrível.

incredulous, *adj.* incrédulo.

increment, *n.* incremento *m.*

incriminate, *vb.* incriminar.

incubator, *n.* incubadora, chocadeira *f.*

inculcate, *vb.* inculcar.

incumbent, 1. *adj.* obrigatório. **2.** *n.* titular *m.f.*

incur, *vb.* incorrer em.

indebted, *adj.* endividado.

indeed, *adv.* de fato; mesmo.

indefinite, *adj.* indefinido.

indelible, *adj.* indelével.

indemnify, *vb.* indenizar.

indemnity, *n.* indenidade, indenização *f.*

indent, *vb.* abrir parágrafo.

indentation, *n.* entrada *f.*, parágrafo *m.*

independence, *n.* independência *f.*

independent, *adj.* independente.

index, 1. *n.* índice *m.* **i, card,** ficha *f.*; **i. finger,** dedo indicador *m.* **2.** *vb.* indexar.

Indian, *adj., n.* (Amerindian) índio -dia; (India) indiano -na.

indicate, *vb.* indicar.

indication, *n.* indicação *f.*

indicative, *adj.* indicativo.

indicator, *n.* indicador *m.*

indict, *vb.* indiciar.

indictment, *n.* indiciação *f.*

Indies, *n.pl.* Indias *f.pl.*

indifferent, *adj.* indiferente.

indigenous, *adj.* indígena.

indigent, *adj.* indigente.

indigestion, *n.* indigestão *f.*

indignant, *adj.* indignado.

indignation, *n.* indignação *f.*

indignity, *n.* indignidade *f.*

indigo, *n.* índigo, anil *m.*

indiscreet, *adj.* indiscreto.

indiscriminate, *adj.* indiscriminado.

indispensable, *adj.* indispensável.

indisposed, *adj.* indisposto.

individual, 1. *adj.* individual. 2. *m.* indivíduo *m.*

indivisible, *adj.* indivisível.

indoctrinate, *vb.* doutrinar.

indolent, *adj.* indolente.

Indonesian, *adj., n.* indonésio *m.*

indoor, *adj.* interior. **indoors**, *adv.* em casa, portas adentro.

induce, *vb.* induzir.

induct, *vb.* empossar; iniciar.

induction, *n.* indução *f.*; posse, iniciação *f.*

indulge, *vb.* favorecer; satisfazer. **i. in**, entregar-se a.

indulgence, *n.* indulgência *f.*

indulgent, *adj.* indulgente.

industrial, *adj.* industrial.

industrialist, *n.* industrial *m.f.*

industrialize, *vb.* industrializar.

industrious, *adj.* industrioso.

industry, *n.* indústria *f.*

inebriate, *vb.* embriagar, inebriar.

inept, *adj.* inepto.

inequity, *n.* injustiça *f.*

inert, *adj.* inerte.

inertia, *n.* inércia *f.*

inevitable, *adj.* inevitável.

inexpensive, *adj.* barato.

inexperienced, *adj.* inexperiente.

infallible, *adj.* infalível.

infamous, *adj.* infame.

infamy, *n.* infâmia *f.*

infancy, *n.* infância *f.*

infant, *n.* bebê *m.*, criança *f.*

infantile, *adj.* infantil.

infantry, *n.* infantaria *f.*

infatuated, *adj.* apaixonado.

infect, *vb.* infeccionar.

infection, *n.* infecção *f.*

infectious, *adj.* infeccioso.

infer, *vb.* inferir, deduzir.

inference, *n.* inferência *f.*

inferior, *adj.* inferior.

inferiority, *n.* inferioridade *f.*

infernal, *adj.* infernal.

inferno, *n.* inferno *m.*

infest, *vb.* infestar.

infidel, *n.* infiel *m.f.*, pagão -gã.

infidelity, *n.* infidelidade *f.*

infiltrate, *vb.* infiltrar.

infinite, *adj.* infinito.

infinitesimal, *adj.* infinitésimo.

infinitive, *n.* infinitivo.

infinity, *n.* infinidade *f.*

infirm, *adj.* enfermo, inválido.

infirmity, *n.* enfermidade *f.*

inflame, *vb.* inflamar.

inflammable, *adj.* inflamável.

inflammation, *n.* inflamação *f.*

inflate, *vb.* inflar.

inflation, *n.* inflação *f.*

inflict, *vb.* infligir.

influence, *n.* influência *f.*

influential, *adj.* influente.

influenza, *n.* influenza, gripe *f.*

influx, *n.* influxo *m.*

inform, *vb.* informar.

informal, *adj.* informal.

informant, *n.* informante *m.f.*

information, *n.* informação *f.*

informative, *adj.* informativo.

infraction, *n.* infração *f.*

infrared, *adj.* infravermelho.

infringe, *vb.* infringir, violar.

infuriate, *vb.* enfurecer.

infusion, *n.* infusão *f.*

ingenious, *adj.* engenhoso.

ingenuity, *n.* engenho *m.*

ingenuous, *adj.* ingênuo.

ingest, *vb.* ingerir.

ingot, *n.* lingote *m.*

ingrained, *adj.* arraigado.

ingrate, *adj.* ingrato.

ingratiate, *vb.* insinuar-se.

ingredient, *n.* ingrediente *m.*

inhabit, *vb.* habitar.

inhabitant, *n.* habitante *m.f.*

inhale, *vb.* inalar; aspirar.

inherent, *adj.* inerente.

inherit, *vb.* herdar.

inheritance, *n.* herança *f.*

inhibit, *vb.* inibir.

inhibition, *n.* inibição *f.*

inhuman, *adj.* inumano.

inimical, *adj.* inimigo, hostil.

iniquity, *n.* iniqüidade *f.*

initial, *adj., n.* inicial *f.*

initiate, *vb.* iniciar.

initiation, *n.* iniciação *f.*

initiative, *n.* iniciativa *f.*

inject, *vb.* injetar.

injection, *n.* injeção *f.*

injunction, *n.* injunção *f.*, mandado *m.*

injure, *vb.* ferir, machucar; prejudicar.

injurious, *adj.* prejudicial.

injury, *n.* ferimento *m.*; prejuízo *m.*

ink, *n.* tinta *f.*

inkling, *n.* vaga noção, suspeita *f.*

inkwell, *n.* tinteiro *m.*

inland, 1. *adj.* interior. **2.** *adv.* para o interior.

inlet, *n.* enseada, angra *f.*

inmate, *n.* morador *m.*; preso *m.*

inn, *n.* estalagem, pousada *f.*

innate, *adj.* inato.

inner, *adj.* interno. **i. tube,** câmara de ar *f.*

innocence, *n.* inocência *f.*

innocent, *adj.* inocente.

innocuous, *adj.* inócuo.

innovate, *vb.* inovar.

innuendo, *n.* insinuação *f.*

innumerable, *adj.* inúmero.

inoculate, *vb.* inocular.

input, *n.* entrada *f.*, input *m.*

inquest, *n.* inquérito *m.*, investigação *f.*

inquire, *vb.* perguntar; inquirir.

inquiry, *n.* inquirição *f.*; pergunta *f.*

inquisition, *n.* inquisição *f.*; inquérito *m.*

inquisitive, *adj.* curioso.

inroad, *n.* incursão *f.*

insane, *adj.* louco, insano. **i. asylum,** hospício *m.*

insanity, *n.* loucura, insanidade *f.*

inscribe, *vb.* inscrever.

inscription, *n.* inscrição *f.*

insect, *n.* inseto *m.*

insecticide, *n.* inseticida *m.*

insemination, *n.* inseminação *f.*

insert, *vb.* inserir; intercalar.

insertion, *n.* inserção *f.*

inside, 1. *adj.*, interior; confidencial. **2.** *n.* interior *m.* **3.**

adv. dentro; por dentro. **às avessas. 4.** *prep.* dentro de.

insidious, *adj.* insidioso.

insight, *n.* perspicácia *f.*; compreensão *f.*

insignia, *n.pl.* insígnias *f.pl.*

insignificant, *adj.* insignificante.

insinuate, *vb.* insinuar.

insipid, *adj.* insípido.

insist, *vb.* insistir, fazer questão. **i. on,** insistir em.

insistence, *n.* insistência *f.*

insistent, *adj.* insistente.

insolent, *adj.* insolente.

insomnia, *n.* insônia *f.*

inspect, *vb.* inspeccionar; vistoriar.

inspection, *n.* inspeção *f.*; vistoria *f.*

inspector, *n.* inspetor *m.*

inspiration, *n.* inspiração *f.*

inspire, *vb.* inspirar.

instability, *n.* instabilidade *f.*

install, *vb.* instalar; empossar.

installment, *n.* prestação *f.*; episódio *m.* **i. plan,** crediário *m.*

instance, *n.* ocasião *f.*; exemplo *m.* **for i.,** por exemplo.

instant, *adj., n.* instante *m.*

instantaneous, *adj.* instantâneo.

instant coffee, *n.* café solúvel *m.*

instead, *adv.* em vez disso. **i. of,** em vez de.

instigate, *vb.* instigar.

instill, *vb.* incutir, infundir.

instinct, *n.* instinto *m.*

instinctive, *adj.* instintivo.

institute, 1. *n.* instituto *m.* **2.** *vb.* instituir.

institution, *n.* instituição *f.*

institutional, *adj.* institucional.

instruct, *vb.* instruir.

instruction, *n.* instrução *f.*

instructor, *n.* instrutor -ra.

instrument, *n.* instrumento *m.*

instrumental, *adj.* instrumental.

insulate, *vb.* insular; isolar.

insulation, *n.* insulação *f.*; isolação *f.*

insulator, *n.* isolador *m.*

insulin, *n.* insulina *f.*

insult, 1. *n.* insulto *m.* **2.** *vb.* insultar.

insuperable, *adj.* insuperável.
insurance, *n.* seguro *m.* **i. policy,** apólice de seguros.*f.*
insure, *vb.* segurar.
insurgent, *adj., n.* insurgente *m.f.*
insurrection, *n.* insurreição *f.*
intact, *adj.* intato.
integral, *adj.* integral.
integrate, *vb.* integrar.
integrity, *n.* integridade *f.*
intellect, *n.* intelecto *m.*
intellectual, *adj., n.* intelectual *m.f.*
intelligence, *n.* inteligência *f.*
intelligent, *adj.* inteligente.
intelligible, *adj.* inteligível.
intend, *vb.* pretender; destinar.
intense, *adj.* intenso.
intensify, *vb.* intensificar.
intensity, *n.* intensidade *f.*
intensive, *adj.* intensivo.
intent, 1. *adj.* absorto; decidido. **2.** *n.* intento *m.* ; efeito *m.*
intention, *n.* intenção *f.*
intentional, *adj.* intencional.
inter, *vb.* enterrar, sepultar.
inter-, *pref.* inter-.
intercede, *vb.* interceder.
intercept, *vb.* interceptar.
interchange, 1. *n.* intercâmbio *m.* **2.** *vb.* intercambiar.
interchangeable, *adj.* intercambiável.
intercom, *n.* interfone *m.*
intercourse, *n.* intercâmbio *m.* ; comunicação *f.* ; relações sexuais *f.pl.*
interdict, *vb.* interditar, proibir.
interest, 1. *n.* interesse *m.* ; *(com.)* juros *m.pl.* **2.** *vb.* interessar.
interesting, *adj.* interessante.
interface, *n.* interface *f.*
interfere, *vb.* interferir.
interference, *n.* interferência *f.*
interim, 1. *adj.* interino. **2.** *n.* ínterim *m.*
interior, *adj., n.* interior *m.*
interject, *vb.* interpor.
interjection, *n.* interjeição, exclamação *f.*
interlocutor, *n.* interlocutor *m.*
interlude, *n.* interlúdio *m.*
intermediary, *adj., n.* intermediário *m.*

intermediate, *adj.* intermédio, intermediário.
interment, *n.* enterro *m.*
intermission, *n.* intervalo *m.*
intermittent, *adj.* intermitente.
intern, 1. *n.* interno *m.* **2.** *vb.* internar.
internal, *adj.* interno.
international, *adj.* internacional.
internship, *n.* estágio *m.*
interpret, *vb.* interpretar.
interpretation, *n.* interpretação *f.*
interpreter, *n.* intérprete *m.f.*
interrogate, *vb.* interrogar.
interrogation, *n.* interrogação *f.* ; interrogatório *m.* ; pergunta *f.*
interrogative, *adj.* interrogativo.
interrupt, *vb.* interromper.
interruption, *n.* interrupção *f.*
intersect, *vb.* cruzar, cortar.
intersection, *n.* interseção *f.* ; cruzamento *m.*
intersperse, *vb.* entremear.
intertwine, *vb.* entrelaçar(-se).
interval, *n.* intervalo *m.*
intervene, *vb.* intervir.
intervention, *n.* intervenção *f.*
interview, 1. *n.* entrevista *f.* **2.** *vb.* entrevistar.
intestine, *n.* intestino *m.*
intimacy, *n.* intimidade *f.*
intimate, 1. *adj.* íntimo. **2.** *n.* amigo íntimo *m.* **3.** *vb.* intimar.
intimidate, *vb.* intimidar.
into, *prep.* em, para dentro de.
intonation, *n.* entoação *f.*
intone, *vb.* entoar.
intoxicate, *vb.* embriagar.
intoxication, *n.* embriaguez *f.*
intractable, *adj.* intratável.
intransitive, *adj.* intransitivo.
intravenous, *adj.* intravenoso.
intrepid, *adj.* intrépido.
intricacy, *n.* complexidade *f.*
intricate, *adj.* intrincado, complexo.
intrigue, 1. *n.* intriga *f.* **2.** *vb.* intrigar; fascinar.
intrinsic, *adj.* intrínseco.
introduce, *vb.* introduzir; (person) apresentar.

introduction, *n.* introdução *f.*; apresentação *f.*
introductory, *adj.* introdutório.
introspection, *n.* introspecção *f.*
introvert, *adj., n.* introvertido *m.*
intrude, *vb.* impor-se, ser intruso.
intruder, *n.* intruso *m.*
intuition, *n.* intuição *f.*
inundate, *vb.* inundar.
invade, *vb.* invadir.
invader, *n.* invasor *m.*
invalid, *adj., n.* inválido *m.*
invariable, *adj.* invariável.
invasion, *n.* invasão *f.*
invective, 1. *adj.* invectivo. **2.** *n.* invectiva *f.*
inveigle, *vb.* engodar.
invent, *vb.* inventar.
invention, *n.* invenção *f.*
inventor, *n.* inventor *m.*
inventory, *n.* inventário *m.*
inverse, *adj.* inverso.
inversion, *n.* inversão *f.*
invert, *vb.* inverter.
invertebrate, *adj., n.* invertebrado *m.*
invest, *vb.* investir, aplicar.
investigate, *vb.* investigar.
investigation, *n.* investigação *f.*
investigator, *m.* investigador -ra.
investment, *n.* investimento *m.*
investor, *n.* inversionista *m.f.*
inveterate, *adj.* inveterado.
invidious, *adj.* odioso, ofensivo.
invigorate, *vb.* avigorar, revigorar.
invincible, *adj.* invencível.
invisible, *adj.* invisível.
invitation, *n.* convite *m.*
invite, *vb.* convidar.
invocation, *n.* invocação *f.*
invoice, *n.* fatura *f.*
invoke, *vb.* invocar.
involve, *vb.* envolver; implicar.
involvement, *n.* envolvimento *m.*
inward, 1. *adj.* interno; íntimo. **2.** *adv.* para dentro.
iodine, *n.* iodo *m.*
ion, *n.* íon *m.*
I.O.U., *n.* promissória *f.*, vale *m.*
I.Q., *n.* Q.I. *m.*
Iran, *n.* Irã *m.*

Iranian, *adj., n.* iraniano -na.
Iraq, *n.* Iraque *m.*
Iraqui, *adj., m.* iraquiano -na.
irascible, *adj.* irascível.
irate, *adj.* furioso.
ire, *n.* ira, cólera *f.*
Ireland, *n.* Irlanda *f.*
iridescent, *adj.* iridescente.
iris, *n.* íris *m.f.*
Irish, *adj., n.* irlandês *m.*
Irishman, *n.* irlandês *m.*
irk, *vb.* aborrecer.
iron, 1. *n.* ferro *m.*; ferro de engomar *m.*; (*pl.*) grilhões *m.pl.* **2.** *vb.* passar (roupa).
ironclad, *adj.* couraçado.
ironic, *adj.* irônico.
irony, *n.* ironia *f.*
irrational, *adj.* irracional.
irregular, *adj.* irregular.
irrelevant, *adj.* irrelevante.
irreparable, *adj.* irreparável.
irresistible, *adj.* irresistível.
irrespective (of), *adj.* independente (de).
irresponsible, *adj.* irresponsável.
irreverent, *adj.* irreverente.
irreversible, *adj.* irreversível.
irrigate, *vb.* irrigar, regar.
irrigation, *n.* irrigação *f.*
irritable, *adj.* irritável.
irritate, *vb.* irritar.
Islam, *n.* islame, islã *m.*
Islamic, *adj.* islamítico, islâmico.
island, *n.* ilha *f.*
islander, *n.* ilhéu -lhoa.
isolate, *vb.* isolar.
isolation, *n.* isolamento *m.*, isolação *f.*
Israeli, *adj., n.* israelense *m.f.*
Israelite, *adj., n.* israelita *m.f.*
issuance, *n.* emissão *f.*; publicação *f.*
issue, 1. *n.* emissão *f.*; (magazine) número *m.*; prole *f.*; questão *f.* **2.** *vb.* emitir; sair; publicar.
isthmus, *n.* istmo *m.*
it, *pron.* ele, ela; o, a; lhe.
Italian, *adj., n.* italiano -na.
italic, *adj., n.* itálico, grifo *m.*
italicize, *vb.* grifar.
Italy, *n.* Itália *f.*
itch, 1. *n.* sarna *f.*; coceira *f.*,

comichão f. **2.** vb. sentir comichão.

itchy, adj. sarnento.

item, n. item m.

itemize, vb. relacionar; discriminar.

itinerary n. itinerário m.

its, poss. adj. dele, dela; seu, sua.

itself, reflex. pron. se; si; si mesmo/próprio.

ivory, n. marfim m. **i. tower**, torre de marfim f.

ivy, n. hera f.

J

jab, 1. n. murro m.; espetadela f. **2.** vb. esmurrar; espetar.

jabber, 1. n. tagarelice f. **2.** vb. tagarelar.

jacaranda, n. jacarandá m.

jack, n. (tool) macaco m.; (cards) valete m.; (elec.) tomada f.

jackal, n. chacal m.

jackass, n. asno, burro m.

jacket, n. jaqueta, japona f.; paletó m.

jack fruit, n. jaca f.

jack-in-the-box, n. caixa de surpresa f.

jackknife, n. canivete m.

jack of all trades, n. pau para toda obra m.

jackpot, n. sorte grande f.

jade, 1. n. jade m. **2.** vb. cansar, gastar.

jagged, adj. dentado, pontudo.

jaguar, n. jaguar m., onça-pintada f.

jail, 1. n. cadeia f., cárcere m. **2.** vb. encarcerar.

jailer, n. carcereiro -ra.

jalopy, n. calhambeque m.

jam, 1. n. aperto m.; geléia f. **2.** vb. apertar.

jamb, n. jamba f.

janitor, n. porteiro, zelador m.

January, n. janeiro m.

Japan, n. Japão m.

Japanese, adj., n. japonês -nesa.

jar, 1. n. jarro, frasco m. **2.** vb. sacudir.

jargon, n. jargão m.

jasmine, n. jasmim m.

jaundice, n. icterícia f.

jaunt, n. passeio m.

javelin, n. dardo m., lança f.

jaw, n. maxila, mandíbula f.

jay, n. gaio m.

jazz, n. jazz m.

jealous, adj. ciumento. **be j.**, ter/estar com ciúmes.

jealousy, n. ciúme m.

jeans, n.pl. jeans, calça Lee/Levi.

jeep, n. jipe m.

jeer, 1. n. zombaria, mofa f. **2.** vb. zombar, mofar.

jelly, n. geléia f.

jellyfish, n. medusa, água-viva f.

jeopardize, vb. arriscar.

jeopardy, n. risco, perigo m.

jerk, 1. n. sacudidela f.; (coll.) tolo m. **2.** vb. sacudir; charquear.

jerky, n. charque m., carne seca f.

jersey, n. jérsei m.

jest, 1. n. brincadeira f. **2.** vb. brincar.

jester, n. bobo, palhaço m.

Jesuit, 1. adj. jesuítico. **2.** n. jesuíta m.

Jesus, n. Jesus. **J. Christ**, Jesus Cristo.

jet, n. jato; jorro. **j. plane**, (avião a) jato.

jet-black, adj. azeviche.

jettison, vb. alijar ao mar; jogar fora.

jetty, n. cais m.

Jew, n. judeu -dia.

jewel, n. jóia f.

jeweler, n. joalheiro -ra.

jewelry, n. jóias f.pl. **j. store**, joalheria f.

Jewish, adj. judeu -dia.

jiffy, n. (coll.) instante m.

jig, n. jiga f.

jiggle, 1. n. bamboleio m. **2.** vb. bambolear.

jigsaw puzzle, n. quebra-cabeça m.

jilt, vb. dar o fora em.

jimmy, n. gazua f.

jingle, 1. n. tinido m. **2.** vb. tinir, tilintar.

jinx, 1. n. pé-frio, caipora m. **2.** vb. dar azar.

jittery, adj. nervoso.

job, n. emprego, trabalho, serviço m.

jockey, n. jóquei m.

jocular, jocose, adj. jocoso.

jog, 1. n. empurrãozinho m. **2.** vb. empurrar; (sport.) fazer cooper.

join, vb. juntar, unir; encontrar com; associar-se a.

joint, 1. adj. conjunto. **2.** n. junta; juntura; (coll.) baiúca f.; (sl.) (marijuana) baseado.

joke, 1. n. piada f.; brincadeira f. **2.** vb. contar piadas; fazer brincadeiras.

joker, n. piadista m.f.; gozador m.

jolly, adj. alegre, jovial.

jolt, n. sacudidela f.; choque m. **2.** vb. sacudir.

Jordan, n. Jordânia f.; (river) Jordão m.

jostle, vb. empurrar.

jot down, vb. anotar.

journal, n. diário, jornal m.; revista f.

journalism, n. jornalismo m.

journalist, n. jornalista m.f.

journey, 1. n. viagem f. **2.** vb. viajar.

jovial, adj. jovial.

jowl, n. queixada f.

joy, n. alegria f.

joyful, adj. alegre.

jubilant, adj. jubiloso.

jubilee, n. jubileu m.

Judaic, adj. judaico.

Judaism, n. judaísmo m.

judge, 1. n. juiz m. **2.** vb. julgar.

judgment, n. juízo m.; julgamento m. **value j.,** juízo de valor.

judicial, adj. judicial.

judiciary, adj. judiciário.

judicious, adj. judicioso.

jug, n. jarro, pote, cântaro m.

juggle, vb. fazer malabarismo; escamotear.

juggler, n. malabarista m.f.

juggling, n. jogos malabares m.pl., malabarismo m.

juice, n. suco, (P.) sumo m.

juicy, adj. suculento.

July, n. julho m.

jumble, 1. n. mixórdia f. **2.** vb. embaralhar.

jump, 1. n. pulo, salto m. **2.** vb. pular, saltar.

jumpy, adj. nervoso.

junction, n. junção f.; entroncamento m.

juncture, n. junção f.; conjuntura f.

June, n. junho m.

jungle, n. selva, floresta tropical f.

junior, adj. mais novo; júnior m.

juniper, n. zimbro m.

junk, n. lixo m.; porcaria f.; (naut.) junco m.

junta, n. junta f.

juridical, adj. jurídico.

jurisdiction, n. jurisdição f.

jurisprudence, n. jurisprudência f.

jurist, n. jurista m.f.

juror, n. jurado m.

jury, n. júri m.

just, 1. adj. justo; exato. **2.** adv. exatamente; (only) só. **j. now,** agora mesmo; **to have j.,** acabar de.

justice, n. justiça f.; (judge) juiz m.

justification, n. justificação, justificativa f.

justify, vb. justificar.

jut, vb. sobressair, ressaltar.

juvenile, adj. juvenil.

juxtapose, vb. justapor.

K

kale, n. couve f.

kaleidoscope, n. caleidoscópio m.

kangaroo, n. canguru m.

kapok, n. paina f.

karate, n. caratê m.

keel, 1. n. quilha f. **2.** vb. **k. over,** emborcar.

keen, adj. agudo; penetrante.

keep, vb. manter; guardar; conservar; ficar com. **k. on,** ficar; **k. up with,** acompanhar.

keeper, n. guarda, zelador m.

keepsake, n. lembrança f.

keg, n. barril pequeno m.

kennel, n. canil m.

Kenya, n. Quênia m.

kept woman, n. mulher teúda e manteúda f.

kerchief, *n.* lenço *m.*

kernel, *n.* grão *m.*; âmago *m.*

kerosene, *n.* querosene *m.*

ketchup, *n.* ketchup *m.*

kettle, *n.* caldeira *f.*; chaleira *f.*

kettledrum, *n.* tímpano *m.*

key, 1. *adj.* chave. **2.** *n.* chave *f.*; *(mus.)* clave; (piano) tecla *f.*

keyboard, *n.* teclado *m.*

key ring, *n.* chaveiro *m.*

khaki, *n.* cáqui *m.*

kick, 1. *n.* chute, pontapé *m.* **2.** *vb.* chutar, dar pontapé; *(coll.)* chiar.

kid, 1. *n.* cabrito *m.*; criança *f.* **2.** *vb.* enganar; brincar.

kid gloves, *n.pl.* luvas de pelica *f.pl.*

kidnap, *vb.* seqüestrar.

kidnaper, *n.* seqüestrador -ra.

kidnaping, *n.* seqüestro *m.*

kidney, *n.* rim *m.*

kill, *vb.* matar, assassinar.

killer, *n.* assassino -na.

killing, *n.* assassínio, assassinato *m.*

kill-joy, *n.* desmancha-prazeres *m.f.*

kiln, *n.* forno *m.*

kilo, *n.* quilo *m.*

kilogram, *n.* quilograma *m.*

kilohertz, *n.* quilohertz *m.*

kilometer, *n.* quilômetro *m.*

kilowatt, *n.* quilowatt *n.*

kilt, *n.* saiote *m.*

kin, *n.* parentesco *m.*; parentes *m.pl.*

kind, 1. *adj.* bondoso, amável. **2.** *n.* espécie *f.*, tipo *m.* **k. of,** meio.

kindergarten, *n.* jardim-de-infância *m.*

kindle, *vb.* acender.

kindling, *n.* graveto *m.*

kindly, *adj.* bondoso.

kindness, *n.* bondade *f.*

kindred, 1. *adj.* aparentado; afim. **2.** *n.* parentesco *m.*

kinetic, *adj.* cinético.

kinfolk, *n.pl.* parentes *m.pl.*

king, *n.* rei *m.*

kingdom, *n.* reino *m.*

king-size, *adj.* tamanho-família.

kink, *n.* enroscamento *m.*

kinky, *adj.* enroscado; encarapinhado; *(sl.)* esquisito.

kinship, *n.* parentesco *m.*

kiosk, *n.* quiosque *m.*

kiss, 1. *n.* beijo *m.* **2.** *vb.* beijar.

kit, *n.* utensílios *m.pl.*; estojo *m.*

kitchen, *n.* cozinha *f.*

kite, *n.* papagaio *m.*, pipa, pandorga *f.*

kitten, *n.* gatinho *m.*

Kleenex, *n.* lenço de papel *m.*

knack, *n.* jeito *m.*, bossa *f.*

knapsack, *n.* mochila *f.*

knave, *n.* velhaco *m.*

knead, *vb.* amassar.

knee, *n.* joelho *m.*

kneecap, *n.* rótula *f.*

kneel, *n.* ajoelhar-se.

knickknack, *n.* bugiganga *f.*

knife, 1. *n.* faca *f.* **2.** *vb.* esfaquear.

knight, *n.* cavaleiro *m.*; (chess) cavalo *m.*

knit, 1. *adj.* de malha **2.** *vb.* tricotar, fazer malha.

knitting, *n.* tricô *m.*

knob, *n.* maçaneta *f.*, botão *m.*

knock, 1. *n.* pancada *f.*, golpe *m.* **2.** *vb.* bater, golpear.

knocker, *n.* aldrava, aldraba *f.*

knockout, *n.* (*sport.*) nocaute *m.*; *(sl.)* mulher boa.

knot, 1. *n.* nó *m.* **2.** *vb.* amarrar, dar nó em.

knotty, *adj.* nodoso.

know, *vb.* saber; (acquaintance) conhecer. **as far as I k.,** que eu saiba.

know-how, *n.* know-how.

know-it-all, *n.* sabe-tudo *m.*

knowledge, *n.* conhecimento, saber *m.*

knuckle, 1. *n.* nó dos dedos *m.* **2.** *vb.* **k. down,** meter os peitos; **k. under,** dar o braço a torcer.

Koran, *n.* Alcorão *m.*

Korea, *n.* Coréia *f.*

Korean, *adj.*, *n.* coreano -na.

L

label, 1. *n.* rótulo *m.* **2.** *vb.* rotular.

labor, 1. *n.* trabalho, labor *m.*;

classe operária *f.* **2.** *vb.* trabalhar.

laboratory, *n.* laboratório *m.*

laborer, *n.* trabalhador, jornaleiro *m.*

labor union, *n.* sindicato *m.*

labyrinth, *n.* labirinto *m.*

lace, 1. *n.* renda *f.*; (shoe) cordão *m.* **2.** *vb.* amarrar.

laceration, *n.* laceração *f.*

lack, 1. *n.* falta. **2.** *vb.* ter falta de. **be lacking,** faltar; **she lacks confidence,** falta-lhe a confiança.

lackadaisical, *adj.* indiferente, apático.

lackey, *n.* lacaio *m.*

lackluster, *adj.* sem brilho.

lacquer, 1. *n.* laca *f.*, verniz *m.* **2.** *vb.* laquear, envernizar.

lacuna, *n.* lacuna *f.*

lad, *n.* rapaz, moço *m.*

ladder, *n.* escada (de mão) *f.*

lade, *vb.* carregar, embarcar.

ladle, *n.* colherão *m.*, concha *f.*

lady, *n.* senhora, dama *f.*

ladybug, *n.* joaninha *f.*

lag, 1. *n.* atraso *m.* **2.** *vb.* atrasar.

lagoon, *n.* laguna, lagoa *f.*

laid-back, *adj.* *(sl.)* descontraído.

lair, *n.* toca *f.*, covil *m.*

laity, *n.* laicidade *f.*

lake, *n.* lago *m.*, lagoa *f.*

lamb, *n.* cordeiro *m.* **l. chop,** costeleta de carneiro *f.*

lambaste, *vb.* surrar.

lame, *adj.* coxo, manco, capenga.

lament, 1. *n.* lamento. **2.** *vb.* lamentar.

laminate, 1. *adj.* laminado. **2.** *vb.* laminar.

lamp, *n.* lâmpada *f.* **l. shade,** abajur.

lampoon, 1. *n.* pasquim *m.* **2.** *vb.* pasquinar.

lamppost, *n.* lampião *m.*

lance, 1. *n.* lança *f.* **2.** *vb.* lancetar.

land, 1. *n.* terra. **native l.,** pátria, terra natal. **2.** *vb.* (plane) aterrissar, pousar; (ship) desembarcar.

landing, *n.* (plane) aterrissagem

f., pouso *m.*; (ship) desembarque *m.*; (stairs) patamar *m.*

landing gear, *n.* trem de aterrissagem *m.*

landlady, *n.* senhoria *f.*

landlord, *n.* senhorio; locador *m.*

landmark, *n.* marco; *(fig.)* ponto decisivo.

landowner, *n.* proprietário -ria de terras, fazendeiro -ra.

landscape, *n.* paisagem *f.*

landslide, *n.* desmoronamento (de terra), desabamento *m.*

lane, *n.* pista, faixa; via; alameda *f.*

language, *n.* língua *f.*, idioma *m.*; linguagem *f.*

languid, *adj.* lânguido.

languish, *vb.* languescer.

languor, *n.* languidez *f.*, langor *m.*

lanky, *adj.* magro, esguio.

lantern, *n.* lanterna *f.*, farol *m.*

lap, 1. *n.* colo *m.* **2.** *vb.* dobrar; lamber.

lapel, *n.* lapela *f.*

lapse, 1. *n.* lapso. **2.** *vb.* cair; caducar.

larceny, *n.* furto, roubo *m.*

lard, *n.* lardo *m.*, gordura *f.*

large, *adj.* grande.

largely, *adv.* em grande parte.

largeness, *n.* grandeza *f.*

large-scale, *adj.* em grande escala.

lariat, *n.* laço *m.*

lark, *n.* *(ornith.)* cotovia *f.*

larva, *n.* larva *f.*

larynx, *n.* laringe *m.f.*

lascivious, *adj.* lascivo.

laser, *n.* *(E.)* laser *m.*

lash, 1. *n.* chicote, látego *m.* **2.** *vb.* açoitar, chicotear.

lass, *n.* moça *f.*, *(P.)* rapariga *f.*

lasso, 1. *n.* laço *m.* **2.** *vb.* laçar.

last, 1. *adj.* último, final; passado. **2.** *adv.* por último, final. **at l.,** afinal. **3.** *vb.* durar.

lasting, *adj.* duradouro.

last name, *n.* sobrenome, nome de família *n.*

latch, *n.* trinco *m.*

late, 1. *adj.* tardio; (dead) falecido. **2.** *adv.* tarde.

lately, *adv.* ultimamente.

latent, *adj.* latente.

lateral, *adj.* lateral.

latex, *n.* látex *m.*

lath, *n.* ripa *f.*

lathe, *n.* torno *m.*

lather, 1. *n.* espuma de sabão *f.* **2.** *vb.* ensaboar.

Latin, 1. *adj.* latino. **2.** *n.* latim *m.*

Latin America, *n.* América Latina *f.*

Latin American, *adj., n.* latino-americano *m.*

latitude, *n.* latitude *f.*

latrine, *n.* latrina *f.*

latter, *adj.* último. **the l.,** este, -ta.

lattice, *n.* latada, treliça *f.*

laud, *vb.* louvar, elogiar.

laudable, *adj.* louvável.

laudatory, *adj.* laudatório.

laugh, 1. *n.* riso *m.*, risada *f.* **2.** *vb.* rir. **l. at,** rir-se de.

laughable, *adj.* risível.

laughing, *adj.* risonho.

laughingstock, *n.* joguete *m.*

laughter, *n.* riso *m.*, risada *f.*

launch, 1. *n.* lançamento *m.*; *(naut.)* lancha *f.* **2.** *vb.* lançar.

launching, *n.* lançamento *m.* **l. pad,** plataforma de lançamento *f.*

launder, *vb.* lavar (roupa).

laundress, *n.* lavadeira, lavandeira *f.*

laundry, *n.* lavanderia *f.*

laureate, *adj., n.* laureado *m.*

laurel, *n.* louro *m.* **rest on one's laurels,** dormir sobre os louros.

lava, *n.* lava *f.*

lavatory, *n.* lavatório *m.*

lavender, *n.* alfazema, lavanda *f.*

lavish, 1. *adj.* pródigo. **2.** *vb.* prodigalizar.

law, *n.* lei *f.*; (field) direito *m.*

lawful, *adj.* legal, lícito.

lawless, *adj.* sem lei, ilegal.

lawn, *n.* gramado *m.* **l. mower,** cortador/aparador de grama *m.*

lawsuit, *n.* processo, litígio *m.*

lawyer, *n.* advogado -da.

lax, *adj.* frouxo, lasso.

laxative, *n.* laxativo, purgante *m.*

laxity, *n.* frouxidão *f.*

lay, 1. *adj.* leigo, laico. **2.** *n.* configuração *f.* **3.** *vb.* pôr, colocar.

layer, *n.* camada *f.*; (paint) mão, demão *f.*

layman, *n.* leigo *m.*

layout, *n.* leiaute *m.*

laziness, *n.* preguiça *f.*

lazy, *adj.* preguiçoso.

lead, *n.* chumbo *m.*

lead, 1. *n.* dianteira *f.* **2.** *vb.* conduzir; dirigir; liderar.

leaden, *adj.* plúmbeo.

leader, *n.* líder, diretor *m.*; chefe *m.f.*

leadership, *n.* liderança *f.*

leaf, *n.* folha *f.*

leaflet, *n.* folheto *m.*

league, *n.* liga *f.*; (measure) légua *f.*

leak, 1. *n.* vazamento *m.*; goteira *f.* **2.** *vb.* vazar.

lean, 1. *adj.* magro; enxuto. **2.** *vb.* encostar(-se), apoiar(-se).

leap, 1. *n.* pulo, salto. **2.** *vb.* pular, saltar.

leap year, *n.* ano bissexto *m.*

learn, *vb.* aprender; saber. **l. how,** aprender a.

learned, *adj.* erudito, sábio.

learning, *n.* saber *m.*, erudição *f.*

lease, 1. *n.* arrendamento *m.* **2.** *vb.* alugar, arrendar.

leash, *n.* correia, corrente *f.*

least, *adj.* menor, mínimo. **at l.,** pelo menos.

leather, *n.* couro *m.*

leave, 1. *n.* licença *f.* **2.** *vb.* deixar; sair (de); legar.

leaven, *n.* levedura *f.* **2.** *vb.* levedar, fermentar.

Lebanese, *adj., n.* libanês *m.*

Lebanon, *n.* Líbano *m.*

lecherous, *adj.* luxurioso.

lechery, *n.* luxúria *f.*

lecture, 1. *n.* conferência *f.*; descompostura *f.* **2.** *vb.* fazer uma conferência; descompor.

lecturer, *n.* conferencista *m.f.*

ledge, *n.* saliência, aba *f.*

ledger, *n.* livro de razão, razão *m.*

lee, *n.* abrigo *m. (naut.)* sotavento *m.*

leech, *n.* sanguessuga *f.*

leek, *n.* alho-porro *m.*

leer, *n., vb.* olhar de soslaio *m.*

leery, *adj.* desconfiado.

leeward, *adj.* de sotavento.

leeway, *n.* liberdade de ação *f.*

left, 1. *n.* lado esquerdo *m.*; (*polit.*) esquerda *f.* **2.** *adj.* esquerdo. **3.** *adv.* à esquerda.

left-handed, *adj.* canhoto.

leftist, *adj.* n. esquerdista *m.f.*

leftovers, *n.pl.* restos *m.pl.*; sobras *f.pl.*

leg, *n.* perna *f.*

legacy, *n.* legado *m.*, herança *f.*

legal, *adj.* legal.

legalize, *vb.* legalizar.

legation, *n.* legação *f.*

legend, *n.* lenda *f.*

legendary, *adj.* lendário, legendário.

legging, *n.* perneira, polaina *f.*

legible, *adj.* legível.

legion, *n.* legião *f.*

legislate, *vb.* legislar.

legislation, *n.* legislação *f.*

legislative, *adj.* legislativo.

legislator, *n.* legislador -ra.

legislature, *n.* legislatura *f.*

legitimacy, *n.* legitimidade *f.*

legitimate, *adj.* legítimo.

legitmize, legitimate, *vb.* legitimar.

legume, *n.* legume *m.*

leisure, *n.* lazer *m.*

leisurely, *adj.* lento, ocioso.

lemon, *n.* limão *m.* **l. tree,** limoeiro *m.*

lemonade, *n.* limonada *f.*

lend, *vb.* emprestar. **l. it/oneself to,** prestar-se a.

length, *n.* comprimento *m.*; duração *f.*

lengthen, *vb.* alongar, encompridar.

lengthwise, *adv.* longitudinalmente.

lengthy, *adj.* longo.

lenient, *adj.* indulgente.

lens, *n.* lente *f.*

Lent, *n.* Quaresma *f.*

Lenten, *adj.* quaresmal.

lentil, *n.* lentilha *f.*

Leo, *n.* Leão *m.*

leopard, *n.* leopardo *m.*

leper, *n.* leproso *m.*

leprosy, *n.* lepra *f.*

lesbian, *adj.,* f. lésbica *f.*

lesion, *n.* lesão *f.*

less, *adj. adv.* menos.

lessee, *n.* locatário, arrendatário *m.*

lessen, *vb.* diminuir.

lesser, *adj.* menor.

lesson, *n.* lição *f.*

lessor, *n.* locador, arrendador *m.*

lest, *conj.* para que não.

let, *vb.* deixar, permitir; alugar. **l. down,** desapontar; **l. go or loose,** soltar; **l. on,** dar a entender; **l. up,** cessar.

letdown, *n.* decepção *f.*

lethal, *adj.* letal.

lethargic, *adj.* letárgico.

lethargy, *n.* letargia *f.*, letargo *m.*

letter, *n.* carta *f.*; (alphabet) letra *f.* **l. of credit,** carta de crédito *f.*

letterhead, *n.* timbre *m.*; papel timbrado *m.*

lettuce, *n.* alface *f.*

letup, *n.* cessação *f.*

leukemia, *n.* leucemia *f.*

level, 1. *adj.* plano, nivelado. **2.** *n.* nível, plano *m.*

lever, *n.* alavanca *f.*; manivela *f.*

levitation, *n.* levitação *f.*

levity, *n.* frivolidade *f.*

levy, 1. *n.* arrecadação *f.* **2.** *vb.* impor.

lewd, *adj.* lascivo.

lexicon, *n.* léxico.

liability, *n.* obrigação *f.*; risco *m.*

liable, *adj.* responsável; sujeito; (*coll.*) provável.

liaison, *n.* ligação *f.*; amigação *f.*

liar, *n.* mentiroso *m.*

libel, 1. *n.* calúnia *f.* **2.** *vb.* caluniar.

liberal, *adj.,* n. liberal *m.f.*

liberalism, *n.* liberalismo *f.*

liberalize, *vb.* liberalizar.

liberate, *vb.* liberar, libertar.

liberation, *n.* liberação *f.*

liberator, *n.* liberador *m.*

libertine, *adj.,* n. libertino *m.*

liberty, *n.* liberdade *f.*

libido, *n.* libido *f.*

Libra, *n.* Libra *f.*

librarian, *n.* bibliotecário -ria.

library, *n.* biblioteca *f.*

library science, *n.* biblioteconomia *f.*

license, *n.* licença, permissão *f.* **driver's l.,** carteira de motorista *f.*

license plate, *n.* placa, chapa *f.*

licentious, *adj.* licencioso.

licit, *adj.* lícito.

lick, *vb.* lamber.

licorice, *n.* alcaçuz *m.*

lid, *n.* tampa *f.*

lie, 1. *n.* mentira *f.* **2.** *vb.* mentir. **l. down,** deitar(-se).

lieu, **in l. of,** em lugar de.

lieutenant, *n.* tenente *m.*

life, *n.* vida *f.*

lifeboat, *n.* barco salva-vidas *m.*

lifeguard, *n.* salva-vidas, banhista *m.f.*

life insurance, *n.* seguro de vida *m.*

lifeless, *adj.* sem vida.

lifelong, *adj.* vitalício.

life preserver, *n.* salva-vidas *m.*

lifestyle, *n.* trem de vida *m.*

lift, 1. *n.* carona *f.* **2.** *vb.* levantar, elevar.

ligament, *n.* ligamento *m.*

light, 1. *adj.* leve, ligeiro; (color) claro. **2.** *n.* luz *f.*, lume *m.* **3.** *vb.* iluminar; acender; pousar.

light bulb, *n.* lâmpada elétrica *f.*

lighten, *vb.* aliviar; iluminar; esclarecer.

lighter, *n.* isqueiro *m.*

light-headed, *adj.* tonto.

lighthouse, *n.* farol *m.*

lighting, *n.* iluminação *f.*

lightness, *n.* ligeireza, leveza *f.*

lightning, *n.* raio, relâmpago *m.*

lightning rod, *n.* pára-raios *m.*

light-year, *n.* ano-luz *m.*

like, 1. *adj.* semelhante, igual. **2.** *m.* gosto. **3.** *adv., conj.* como. **4.** *vb.* gostar de; querer.

likeable, *adj.* simpático.

likelihood, *n.* probabilidade *f.*

likely, *adj.* provável.

liken, *vb.* comparar.

likeness, *n.* semelhança *f.*; imagem *f.*

likewise, *adv.* igualmente.

lilac, *n.* lilás *m.*

lilt, *n.* ritmo alegre *m.*; cadência *f.*

lily, *n.* lírio *m.*

limb, *n.* ramo, galho; (body) membro *m.*

limber, 1. *adj.* flexível, ágil. **2.** *vb.* tornar-se flexível.

lime, *n.* cal *f.*; (fruit) lima *f.*, limão-doce *m.*

limelight, *n.* ribalta *f.*; berlinda *f.*

limestone, *n.* calcário *m.*

limit, 1. *n.* limite *m.* **be the l.,** ser o cúmulo. **2.** *vb.* limitar.

limitation, *n.* limitação *f.*

limousine, *n.* limusine *f.*

limp, 1. *adj.* frouxo, mole. **2.** *n.* manqueira *f.* **3.** *vb.* coxear, mancar, claudicar.

limpid, *adj.* límpido *m.*

line, 1. *n.* linha *f.*; fila *f.* **2.** *vb.* forrar. **l. up,** alinhar(-se); pôr (-se) em fila.

lineage, *n.* linhagem *f.*

linear, lineal, *adj.* linear.

linen, *n.* linho *m.*; roupabranca (para cama, etc.) *f.*

liner, *n.* vapor *m.*

linger, *vb.* atrasar, demorar-se.

lingerie, *n.* roupa de baixo feminina *f.*

linguistic, *adj.* lingüístico.

linguistics, *n.* lingüística *f.*

liniment, *n.* linimento *m.*

lining, *n.* forro *m.*

link, 1. *n.* elo *m.* **2.** *vb.* ligar.

linkage, *n.* ligação *f.*

linoleum, *n.* linóleo *m.*

lint, *n.* cotão, fiapo *m.*

lion, *n.* leão *m.*

lioness, *n.* leoa *f.*

lip, *n.* lábio, beiço *m.*

lip gloss, *n.* brilho *m.*

lipstick, *n.* batom *m.*

liqueur, *n.* licor *m.*

liquid, *adj.* líquido *m.*

liquidate, *vb.* liqüidar.

liquidation, *n.* liqüidação *f.*

liquor, *n.* bebida alcoólica *f.*

Lisbon, *n.* Lisboa.

lisp, 1. *n.* ceceio, chiado *m.* **2.** *vb.* cecear, chiar.

list, 1. *n.* lista. **2.** *vb.* registrar.

listen (to), *vb.* escutar.

listener, *n.* ouvinte *m.f.*

listless, *adj.* apático.

litany, *n.* litania, ladainha *f.*

liter, *n.* litro *m.*

literacy, *n.* alfabetização *f.*

literal, *adj.* literal; ao pé da letra.

literary, *adj.* literário.

literate, *adj.* alfabetizado.

literature, *n.* literatura *f.*

litigation, *n.* litígio *m.*

litmus, *n.* tornassol *m.*

litter, 1. *n.* liteira *f.*; maca *f.*; (brood) ninhada *f.* **2.** *vb.* sujar.

little, 1. *adj.* pequeno; (quantity) pouco. **2.** *n.* pouco. **a l.,** um pouco (de). **3.** *adv.* pouco. **l. by l.,** pouco a pouco, aos poucos.

liturgy, *n.* liturgia *f.*

live, 1. *adj.* vivo; ao vivo. **2.** *vb.* viver; (reside) morar.

livelihood, *n.* subsistência *f.*, ganha-pão *m.*

liveliness, *n.* vivacidade *f.*

lively, *adj.* vivo; animado; rápido.

liver, *n.* fígado *m.*

livery, *n.* libré *f.*

livestock, *n.* criação *f.*, gado *m.*

livid, *adj.* lívido.

living, 1. *adj.* vivo. **2.** *n.* vida, subsistência *f.* **earn a l.,** ganhar a vida.

living room, *n.* sala de estar *f.*, living *m.*

lizard, *n.* lagarto *m.*

llama, *n.* lhama *m.*

load, 1. *n.* carga *f.* **2.** *vb.* carregar.

loaf, 1. *n.* pão *m.* **2.** *vb.* vagabundear.

loafer, *n.* vagabundo *m.*

loam, *n.* marga, marna *f.*

loan, 1. *n.* empréstimo *m.* **2.** *vb.* emprestar.

loath, *adj.* relutante.

loathe, *vb.* detestar, odiar.

loathsome, *adj.* repugnante.

lobby, *n.* vestíbulo, saguão *m.*; (polit.) lobby *m.*

lobbyist, *n.* lobista *m.f.*

lobe, *n.* lobo, lóbulo *m.*

lobster, *n.* lagosta *f.*

local, *adj.* local.

locale, *n.* local *m.*, localidade *f.*

locality, *n.* localidade *f.*

locate, *vb.* localizar.

location, *n.* localização, *f.*

lock, 1. *n.* fechadura *f.*; (canal) eclusa *f.*; (hair) trança, *f.* **2.** *vb.* fechar à chave, trancar.

locker, *n.* armário *m.*

locket, *n.* medalhão *m.*

lockjaw, *n.* trismo *m.*

locksmith, *n.* serralheiro *m.*

locomotive, *n.* locomotiva *f.*

locust, *n.* locusta *f.*, gafanhoto *m.*

lode, *n.* filão, veio *m.*

lodge, 1. *n.* pousada *f.*; (Masonic) loja *f.* **2.** *vb.* hospedar (-se); lavrar (queixa).

lodger, *n.* inquilino -na; hóspede *m.f.*

lodging, *n.* alojamento *m.*; (pl.) quartos *m.pl.*

loft, *n.* sótão *m.*

lofty, *adj.* alto, elevado.

log, 1. *n.* tronco de árvore *m.*; (naut.) livro de bordo *m.* **2.** *vb.* derrubar árvores.

logger, *n.* lenhador -ra.

logic, *n.* lógica *f.*

logical, *adj.* lógico.

logistics, *n.* logística *f.*

loin, *n.* lombo *m.*

loincloth, *n.* tanga *f.*

loiter, *vb.* vaguear, flanar.

lollipop, *n.* pirulito *m.*

London, *n.* Londres.

lone, *adj.* solitário, só.

loneliness, *n.* solidão *f.*

lonely, lonesome, *adj.* solitário, sozinho.

long, 1. *adj.* comprido; longo. **l. ago,** há muito tempo; **l. live!,** viva!; **a l. time,** muito tempo. **2.** *adv.* muito tempo, longamente. **as l. as,** enquanto; desde que. **before l.,** dentro em breve; **how l.?,** quanto tempo?; **no longer,** já não; **so l.,** até logo. **3.** *vb.* **l. for,** ansiar por.

longevity, *n.* longevidade *f.*

longing, *n.* anelo *m.*; saudade *f.*

longitude, *n.* longitude *f.*

longshoreman, *n.* estivador *m.*

long-term, *adj.* a longo prazo.

look, 1. *n.* olhar *m.*; olhada *f.*; aparência *f.* **take a l.,** dar uma olhada. **2.** *vb.* olhar (para); (seem) parecer. **l. after,** cuidar de; **l. at,** olhar para; **l. for,** procurar; **l. forward to,** aguardar ansiosamente; **l. like,** parecer-se com; **look out!,** cuidado!; **l. up,** procurar; visitar; **l. up to,** respeitar.

loom, 1. *n.* tear *m.* **2.** *vb.* assomar, avultar.

loop, *n.* laço *m.*; volta *f.*

loophole, *n.* saída, escapatória *f.*

loose, *adj.* solto; frouxo.

loosen, *vb.* soltar; afrouxar.

loot, 1. *n.* despojo, espólio *m.*; *(sl.)* bagulho. **2.** *vb.* pilhar, saquear.

looting, *n.* pilhagem *f.*, saque *m.*

lopsided, *adj.* torto; desequilibrado.

loquacious, *ãdj.* loquaz.

lord, *n.* senhor *m.*; (title) lorde *m.*

lose, *vb.* perder.

loser, *n.* perdedor -ra; vencido -da.

loss, *n.* perda *f.*; derrota *f.*; prejuízo *m.*

lost, *adj.* perdido.

lot, *n.* sorte *f.*; (construction) lote *m.*; **a l. (of), lots (of),** muito, muitos.

lotion, *n.* loção *f.*

lottery, *n.* loteria *f.*

loud, 1. *adj.* alto, barulhento; (color) berrante. **2.** *adv.* alto.

loudspeaker, *n.* alto-falante *m.*

lounge, 1. *n.* espreguiçadeira *f.*; salão *m.* **2.** *vb.* refestelar-se.

louse, *n.* (entom.) piolho *m.*; *(coll.)* safado *m.*

lousy, *adj.* piolhento; *(sl.)* fuleiro.

louver, *n.* veneziana *f.*

love, 1. *n.* amor *m.* **fall in l.,** apaixonar-se; **in l.,** apaixonado. **make l.,** fazer amor. **2.** *vb.* amar, querer.

loveliness, *n.* beleza *f.*

lovely, *adj.* belo, lindo.

lover, *n.* amante *m.f.*; *(sl.)* caso *m.*

low, 1. *adj.* baixo; vil. **2.** *vb.* mugir.

lower, *vb.* abaixar, baixar; diminuir.

lowland, *n.* terra baixa, baixada *f.*

lowly, *adj.* humilde.

low-necked, *adj.* decotado.

lowness, *n.* baixeza *f.*

low tide, *n.* maré baixa, vazante *f.*

loyal, *adj.* leal.

loyalty, *n.* lealdade *f.*

lozenge, *n.* pastilha *f.*

lubricant, *n.* lubrificante *m.*

lubricate, *vb.* lubrificar.

lucid, *adj.* lúcido.

luck, *n.* sorte *f.* fortuna *f.* **bad l.,** azar *m.*; **good l.,** boa sorte.

lucky, *adj.* afortunado, sortudo. **be l.,** ter sorte.

lucrative, *adj.* lucrativo.

ludicrous, *adj.* ridículo.

luggage, *n.* bagagem *f.*

lukewarm, *adj.* morno.

lull, 1. *n.* calmaria *f.* **2.** *vb.* acalentar; acalmar.

lullaby, *n.* canção de ninar *f.*, acalanto *m.*

lumber, *n.* madeira (serrada).

lumberjack, *n.* lenhador *m.*

luminary, *n.* luminar *m.*

luminous, *adj.* luminoso.

lump, *n.* caroço *m.*, protuberância *f.*; (sugar) torrão *m.*

lunacy, *n.* loucura *f.*

lunar, *adj.* lunar.

lunatic, *adj., n.* lunático *m.*

lunch, 1. *n.* almoço *m.* **2.** *vb.* almoçar.

luncheon, *n.* almoço *m.*

luncheonette, *n.* lanchonete *f.*

lung, *n.* pulmão *m.*

lunge, 1. *n.* estocada *f.* **2.** *vb.* dar uma estocada.

lure, 1. *n.* engodo *m.*, isca *f.* **2.** *vb.* aliciar.

lurid, *adj.* chocante.

lurk, *vb.* esconder-se; rondar.

luscious, *adj.* gostoso, suculento.

lush, 1. *adj.* luxuriante. **2.** *n.* *(sl.)* bêbado.

lust, 1. *n.* luxúria *f.* **2.** *vb.* desejar sexualmente.

luster, *n.* lustre, brilho *m.*

lustful, *adj.* luxurioso.

lusty, *adj.* vigoroso, robusto.

lute, *n.* alaúde *m.*

Lutheran, *adj., n.* luterano -na.

luxuriant, *adj.* luxuriante, frondoso.

luxurious, *adj.* luxuoso.

luxury, *n.* luxo *m.*

lye, *n.* lixívia, barrela *f.*

lying, *adj.* mentiroso.

lymph, *n.* linfa *f.*

lynch, *vb.* linchar.

lynx, *n.* lince *m.f.*

lyre, *n.* lira *f.*

lyric, 1. *adj.* lírico. **2.** *n.* poema lírico *m.*; (song) letra *f.*

lyricism, *n.* lirismo *m.*

M

ma'am, *n.* senhora *f.*

macabre, *adj.* macabro.

Macao, *n.* Macau *m.*

macaroni, *n.* macarrão *m.*

macaw, *n.* arara *f.*, macau *m.*

machete, *n.* machete, facão *m.*

machination, *n.* maquinação *f.*

machine, *n.* máquina *f.*

machine gun, 1. *n.* metralhadora *f.* **2.** *vb.* metralhar.

machinery, *n.* maquinaria, -nária *f.*

machinist, *n.* maquinista *m.f.*, mecânico -ca.

macho, *n.* macho, machista *m.*

mackerel, *n.* cavala *f.*

mad, *adj.* louco; furioso.

madam, *n.* senhora *f.*; (brothel) cafetina *f.*

madden, *vb.* enlouquecer; enfurecer.

made, *adj.* feito.

madman -woman, *n.* louco -ca.

madness, *n.* loucura *f.*

Madrid, *n.* Madri.

madrigal, *n.* madrigal *m.*

maelstrom, *n.* redemoinho *m.*

magazine, *n.* revista *f.*

maggot, *n.* gusano *m.*

magic, 1. *adj.* mágico. **2.** *n.* magia, mágica *f.*

magical, *adj.* mágico.

magician, *n.* mago, mágico *m.*

magistrate, *n.* magistrado *m.*

magnanimous, *adj.* magnânimo.

magnate, *n.* magnata, -te *m.*

magnesium, *n.* magnésio *m.*

magnet, *n.* ímã, magneto *m.*

magnetic, *adj.* magnético.

magnificence, *n.* magnificência *f.*

magnificent, *adj.* magnífico.

magnify, *vb.* magnificar.

magnifying glass, *n.* lente de aumento *m.*, lupa *f.*

magnitude, *n.* magnitude *f.*

magnolia, *n.* magnólia *f.*

magpie, *n.* pega *f.*

mahogany, *n.* mogno *m.*

maid, *n.* solteira *f.*; (domestic) empregada *f.*

maiden, *n.* solteira, donzela *f.* **m. name,** nome de solteira *m.*

mail, 1. *n.* correio *m.*, correspondência *f.* **2.** *vb.* enviar pelo correio.

mailbox, *n.* caixa de correio *f.*

mailman, *n.* carteiro *n.*

maim, *vb.* mutilar.

main, *adj.* principal.

mainland, *n.* continente *m.*

maintain, *vb.* manter.

maintenance, *n.* manutenção *f.*; conservação *f.*

maize, *n.* milho *m.*

majestic, *adj.* majestoso.

majesty, *n.* majestade *f.*

major, 1. *adj.* maior; principal. **2.** *n.* (mil.) major *m.*; (study) especialização *f.*

majority, *n.* maioria *f.*; (age) maioridade *f.*

make, 1. *n.* feitura *f.*; (brand) marca *f.* **2.** *vb.* fazer; fabricar; (earn) ganhar.

make-believe, *adj.* fingido.

maker, *n.* fabricante *m.f.*

makeshift, *n.* provisório.

makeup, *n.* composição *f.*; (cosmetics) maquiagem *f.*; exame de segunda época *m.*

malady, *n.* doença *f.*

malaria, *n.* malária *f.*, impaludismo *m.*

male, 1. *adj.* macho; masculino. **2.** *n.* macho *m.*

malefactor, *n.* malfeitor *m.*

malevolent, *adj.* malevolente, malévolo.

malice, *n.* malícia, má vontade *f.*

malicious, *adj.* malicioso, maligno.

malign, 1. *adj.* maligno. **2.** *vb.* caluniar.

malignant, *adj.* maligno.

malinger, *vb.* fingir-se doente.

mall, *n.* alameda *f.*; (shopping) galeria *f.*

mallet, *n.* macete, malho *m.*

malnutrition, *n.* desnutrição *f.*

malt, *n.* malte *m.*

mama, *n.* mamãe *f.*

mammal, *n.* mamífero *n.*

mammoth, 1. *adj.* gigantesco. **2.** *n.* mamute *m.*

man, *n.* homem *m.*

manage, *vb.* manejar; dirigir, administrar; arranjar-se. **m. to,** conseguir.

management, *n.* gerência, administração *f.*

manager, *n.* gerente *m.f.*

mandate, *n.* mandato *m.*

mandatory, *adj.* obrigatório.

mandolin, *n.* bandolim *m.*

mane, *n.* juba *f.*; crina *f.*

maneuver, 1. *n.* manobra *f.* **2.** *vb.* manobrar.

manganese, *n.* manganês *m.*

mange, *n.* sarna *f.*

manger, *n.* manjedoura *f.*

mangle, *vb.* mutilar.

mango, *n.* manga *f.*

mangrove, *n.* mangue *m.*

mangy, *adj.* sarnento.

manhandle, *vb.* maltratar.

manhood, *n.* masculinidade, virilidade *f.*

mania, *n.* mania *f.*

maniac, *adj., n.* maníaco.

manicure, *n.* **get a m.,** fazer as unhas.

manicurist, *n.* manicuro -ra.

manifest, 1. *adj., n.* manifesto *m.* **2.** *vb.* manifestar.

manifestation, *n.* manifestação *f.*

manifesto, *n.* manifesto *m.*

manifold, 1. *adj.* múltiplo. **2.** *n.* (car) cano de distribuição *m.*

manioc, *n.* mandioca *f.*

manipulate, *vb.* manipular.

mankind, *n.* gênero humano *m.*, humanidade *f.*

manliness, *n.* masculinidade, virilidade *f.*

manly, *adj.* másculo.

mannequin, *n.* manequim *m.f.*

manner, *n.* maneira *f.*; modo *m.*; (*pl.*) maneiras *f.pl.*, educação *f.*

mannerism, *n.* maneirismo *m.*; gesto *m.*

manor, *n.* solar *m.*, casa senhorial *f.*

manpower, *n.* mão-de-obra *f.*

mansion, *n.* mansão *f.*, casarão *m.*

mantel, *n.* consolo de lareira *m.*

mantle, *n.* manto *m.*

manual, 1. *adj.* manual, braçal. **2.** *n.* manual *m.*

manufacture, 1. *n.* fabricação *f.* **2.** *vb.* fabricar.

manufacturer, *n.* fabricante *m.f.*

manure, *n.* adubo, esterco *m.*

manuscript, *n.* manuscrito, original *m.*

many, *adj., pron.* muitos; muito.

map, *n.* mapa *m.*

maple, *n.* bordo *m.*

mar, *vb.* estragar.

marathon, *n.* maratona *f.*

maraud, *n.* saquear.

marble, *n.* mármore *m.*; bola de gude *m.*; (*pl.*) jogo de gude *m.*

march, 1. *n.* marcha *f.* **2.** *vb.* marchar.

mare, *n.* égua *f.*

margarine, *n.* margarina *f.*

margin, *n.* margem *f.*

marginal, *adj., n.* marginal *m.f.*

marijuana, *n.* maconha *f.*

marina, *n.* marina *f.*

marine, 1. *adj.* marinho, marítimo. **2.** *n.* fuzileiro naval *m.*

mariner, *n.* marinheiro *m.*

marionette, *n.* marionete *f.*

marital, *adj.* conjugal. **m. status,** estado civil *m.*

maritime, *adj.* marítimo.

mark, 1. *n.* marca *f.*; (German money) marco *m.* **2.** *vb.* marcar.

market, *n.* mercado *m.*; feira *f.* **stock m.,** bolsa de valores *f.*

marketing, *n.* marketing *m.*, mercadologia *f.*

marksman -woman, *n.* atirador -ra.

marksmanship, *n.* pontaria *f.*

marmalade, *n.* geléia de laranjas *f.*

maroon, *adj.* granadino.

marquis, *n.* marquês *m.*

marriage, *n.* matrimônio *m.*; casamento *m.*

married, *adj.* casado. **get m.,** casar(-se).

marrow, *n.* medula óssea *f.*, tutano *m.*

marry, *vb.* casar; casar(-se) com.

Mars, *n.* Marte *m.*

marsh, n. pântano, brejo m.

marshal, 1. n. (mil.) marechal; xerife m. **2.** vb. dispor, ordenar.

marshmallow, n. malvavisco m., altéia f.

marshy, adj. pantanoso.

mart, n. mercado m.

martial, adj. marcial.

Martian, adj., n. marciano m.

martyr, 1. n. mártir m.f. **2.** vb. martirizar.

martyrdom, n. martírio m.

marvel, 1. n. maravilha f. **2.** vb. maravilhar-se.

marvelous, adj. maravilhoso.

Marxism, n. marxismo m.

Marxist, adj., n. marxista m.f.

mascara, n. rímel m.

mascot, n. mascote f.

masculine, adj. masculino.

masculinity, n. masculinidade f.

mash, vb. esmagar. **mashed potatoes,** purê de batatas m.

mask, 1. n. máscara f. **2.** vb. mascarar.

masochism, n. masoquismo m.

mason, n. pedreiro m.; (cap.) maçom, mação m.

masonry, n. alvenaria f.

masquerade, 1. n. mascarada f. **2.** vb. mascarar-se, disfarçar-se.

mass, n. massa f.; (eccles.) missa f. **m. production,** produção em série f.

massacre, 1. n. massacre m. **2.** vb. massacrar.

massage, 1. n. massagem f. **2.** vb. massagear.

massive, adj. maciço, sólido.

mast, n. mastro m.

master, 1. adj., n. mestre m.; senhor m. **2.** vb. dominar.

masterpiece, n. obra-prima f.

master's degree, n. mestrado m.

mastery, n. mestria f.; domínio m.

masturbate, vb. masturbar-se.

mat, 1. n. esteira f.; capacho m. **2.** vb. emaranhar(-se).

match, 1. n. igual m.f.; fósforo m.; jogo m., partida f.; casamento m. **2.** vb. igualar; combinar (com).

matchmaker, n. casamenteiro -ra.

mate, 1. n. companheiro m.; cônjuge m.f.; (chess) mate m. **2.** vb. casar.

material, 1. adj. material; importante. **2.** n. material m.; tecido m. **raw m.,** matéria prima f.

materialism, n. materialismo m.

materialize, vb. materializar.

maternal, adj. maternal, materno.

maternity, n. maternidade f.

mathematical, adj. matemático.

mathematics, n. matemática f.

matinee, n. matinê f.

matriarch, n. matriarca f.

matrimony, n. matrimônio m.

matrix, n. matriz f.

matron, n. matrona f.

matter, 1. n. matéria f.; assunto m. **what's the m.?,** o que é que há? **2.** vb. importar. **it doesn't m.,** não tem importância; não faz mal.

mattress, n. colchão m.

mature, 1. adj. maduro. **2.** vb. madurar, amadurecer; (com.) vencer.

maturity, n. maturidade f.; (com.) vencimento m.

maudlin, adj. piegas.

maul, vb. malhar, marretar.

mausoleum, n. mausoléu m.

maxim, n. máxima f.

maximize, vb. maximizar.

maximum, adj., n. máximo m.

may, vb. poder.

May, n. maio m.

maybe, adv. talvez.

mayonnaise, n. maionese f.

mayor, n. prefeito m.

maze, n. labirinto m.

me, pron. me; mim. **with m.,** comigo.

meadow, n. prado m., campina f.

meager, adj. magro; pobre.

meal, n. refeição f.; farinha de milho f.

mean, 1. adj. vil; médio; miserável. **2.** n. média f.; (pl.) meios m.pl. **by means of,** por meio de; **by no means,** de jeito nenhum. **3.** *vb.* pretender; significar, querer dizer.

meaning, *n.* intenção *f.*; significado *m.* **double m.,** duplo sentido.

meaningful, *adj.* significativo.

meanness, *n.* maldade *f.*

meantime, *m.* **in the m.,** nesse ínterim.

meanwhile, *adv.* enquanto isso.

measles, *n.* sarampo *m.*

measly, *adj.* miserável.

measure, 1. *n.* medida *f.*; *(mus.)* compasso *m.* **2.** *vb.* medir.

measurement, *n.* medição *f.*; medida *f.*

meat, *n.* carne *f.*

meatball, *n.* almôndega *f.*

mechanic, *n.* mecânico *m.*

mechanical, *adj.* mecânico.

mechanics, *n.* mecânica *f.*

mechanism, *n.* mecanismo *m.*

mechanize, *vb.* mecanizar.

medal, *n.* medalha *f.*; condecoração *f.*

medallion, *n.* medalhão *m.*

meddle, *vb.* intrometer-se.

meddler, *n.* intrometido -da.

meddlesome, *adj.* intrometido.

media, *n.* meios *m.pl.*; mídia *f.*

mediate, *vb.* mediar.

mediation, *n.* mediação *f.*

mediator, *n.* mediador -ra.

medical, *adj.* médico.

medication, *n.* medicação *f.*; medicamento *m.*

medicine, *n.* (field) medicina *f.*; medicamento, remédio *m.*

medieval, *adj.* medieval.

mediocre, *adj.* medíocre.

meditate, *vb.* meditar.

meditation, *n.* meditação *f.*

Mediterranean, *adj., n.* Mediterrâneo.

medium, 1. *adj.* médio; mediano. **2.** *n.* meio *m.*; (spiritualist) médium *m.f.*

medley, *n.* potpourri *m.*

meek, *adj.* manso; humilde.

meekness, *n.* humildade *f.*

meet, 1. *adj.* apropriado. **2.** *n.* competição *f.* **3.** *vb.* encontrar; reunir-se; conhecer.

meeting, *n.* encontro *m.*; reunião *f.*

megahertz, *n.* megahertz *m.*

megaphone, *n.* megafone *m.*

melancholy, 1. *adj.* melancólico. **2.** *n.* melancolia *f.*

mellow, *adj.* maduro; suave; brando.

melodic, *adj.* melódico.

melodrama, *n.* melodrama *m.*

melody, *n.* melodia *f.*

melon, *n.* melão *m.*

melt, *vb.* derreter(-se), fundir (-se).

member, *n.* sócio -cia; membro *m.*

membership, *n.* associação *f.*

membrane, *n.* membrana *f.*

memento, *n.* lembrança *f.*

memoir, *n.* memória *f.*

memorable, *adj.* memorável.

memorandum, *n.* memorando, lembrete *m.*

memorial, 1. *adj.* comemorativo. **2.** *n.* memorial *m.*

memorize, *vb.* memorizar, decorar.

memory, *n.* memória *f.*; lembrança *f.*

menace, 1. *n.* ameaça *f.* **2.** *vb.* ameaçar.

mend, *vb.* consertar, remendar.

menial, 1. *adj.* servil. **2.** *n.* criado *m.*

menopause, *n.* menopausa *f.*

menstrual, *adj.* menstrual.

menstruate, *vb.* menstruar.

menstruation, *n.* menstruação *f.*; mênstruo *m.*

mental, *adj.* mental.

mentality, *n.* mentalidade *f.*

menthol, *n.* mentol *m.*

mention, 1. *n.* menção *f.* **2.** *vb.* mencionar.

mentor, *n.* mentor -ra.

menu, *n.* cardápio, menu *m.*

meow, 1. *n.* miau, miado *m.* **2.** *vb.* miar.

mercantile, *adj.* mercantil.

mercenary, *adj., n.* mercenário *m.*

merchandise, *n.* mercadoria, mercancia *f.*

merchant, 1. *adj.* mercante **2.** *n.* comerciante *m.f.* **m. marine,** marinha mercante *f.*

merciful, *adj.* misericordioso.

merciless, *adj.* cruel, desapiedado.

mercury, n. mercúrio m. ; *(cap.)* Mercúrio m.

mercy, n. misericórdia f.

mere, adj. mero, simples.

merge, vb. unir(-se), combinar (-se).

merger, n. fusão, união f.

meridian, n. meridiano m.

meringue, n. merengue, suspiro m.

merit, 1. n. mérito m. **2.** vb. merecer.

meritorious, adj. meritório.

mermaid, n. sereia f.

merriment, n. alegria f. ; brincadeira f.

merry, adj. alegre, festivo.

merry-go-round, n. carrossel m.

merrymaker, n. brincalhão -lhona, folgazão m.

mesh, 1. n. malha f. **2.** vb. engrenar(-se); enredar(-se).

mess, 1. n. confusão, *(sl.)* bagunça f. ; *(mil.)* gororoba f. **2.** vb. **m. up,** desarrumar, *(sl.)* bagunçar.

message, n. mensagem f. , recado m.

messenger, n. mensageiro -ra.

Messiah, n. Messias m.

messy, adj.*(sl.)* bagunçado.

mestizo, n. caboclo -cla.

metabolism, n. metabolismo m.

metal, n. metal m.

metallic, adj. metálico.

metallurgy, n. metalurgia f.

metamorphosis, n. metamorfose f.

metaphor, n. metáfora f.

metaphysics, n. metafísica f.

meteor, n. meteoro m.

meter, n. medidor m. ; (measure) metro m.

method, n. método m.

methodical, adj. metódico.

Methodist, adj., n. metodista m.f.

methodology, n. metodologia f.

meticulous, adj. meticuloso.

metric, adj. métrico.

metropolis, n. metrópole f.

metropolitan, adj. metropolitano.

Mexican, adj., n. mexicano -na.

mezzanine, n. sobreloja f. , mezanino m.

mica, n. mica f.

microbe, n. micróbio m.

microcosm, n. microcosmo m.

microfiche, n. microficha f.

microfilm, 1. n. microfilme m. **2.** vb. microfilmar.

microform, n. microforma f.

microphone, n. microfone m.

microscope, n. microscópio m.

microscopic, adj. microscópico.

microwave, n. microonda f. **m.** oven, forno de microondas m.

mid, adj. meio.

middle, 1. adj. médio; intermediário. **2.** n. meio m. ; (month, year) meados m.pl. **in the m. of,** em meio de.

middle-aged, adj. de meia-idade.

Middle Ages, n. Idade Média f.

middle-class, adj. de classe média.

middle class, n. classe média, burguesia f.

Middle East, n. Oriente Médio m.

middleman, n. intermediário m.

midget, n. anão -nã.

midnight, n. meia-noite f.

midst, n. meio m.

midwife, n. parteira f.

mien, n. semblante m. ; aspecto m.

might, n. poder m. , força f.

mighty, adj. poderoso.

migraine, n. enxaqueca f.

migrant, n. migrador -ra, migrante m.f.

migrate, vb. migrar.

migratory, adj. migratório.

mild, adj. brando, suave, moderado.

mildew, 1. n. mofo, míldio m. **2.** vb. mofar.

mildness, n. brandura, suavidade f.

mile, n. milha f.

milestone, n. marco miliário m.

milieu, n. meio, ambiente m.

militant, adj. militante.

military, 1. adj. militar. **m. man,** militar m. **2.** n. exército m.

militia, n. milícia f.

milk, 1. n. leite m. **2.** vb. ordenhar.

milkman, n. leiteiro m.

milkshake, n. milkshake m.

milky, *adj.* leitoso, lácteo. **M. Way,** *n.* Via Láctea *f.*

mill, 1. *n.* moinho *m.*, moenda *f.*; usina *f.* **2.** *vb.* moer.

millenium, *n.* milênio *m.*

miller, *n.* moleiro *m.*

millet *n.* painço *m.*

milligram, *n.* miligrama *m.*

millimeter, *n.* milímetro *m.*

million, *n.* milhão *m.*

millionaire, *n.* milionário -ria.

millionth, *adj., n.* milionésimo *m.*

millstone, *n.* mó *f.*

mime, *n.* mimo *m.*

mimeograph, 1. *n.* mimeógrafo *m.* **2.** *vb.* mimeografar.

mimic, 1. *n.* mimo, mímico *n.* **2.** *vb.* imitar; arremedar.

mimicry, *n.* imitação *f.*; arremedo *m.*

mince, 1. *n.* picadinho *m.* **2.** *vb.* picar, esmiuçar; (words) falar com rodeios.

mind, 1. *n.* mente *f.*, espírito *m.*; opinião *f.* **have/bear in m.,** ter em mente. **2.** *vb.* obedecer; atender; importar-se com; incomodar-se com. **never m.,** deixa para lá.

mine, 1. *n.* mina *f.* **2.** *vb.* minar. **3.** *pron.* (o) meu, (a) minha.

miner, *n.* mineiro -ra.

mineral, 1. *adj.* mineral. **m. water,** água mineral *f.* **2.** *n.* minério, mineral *m.*

mine sweeper, *n.* caça-minas *m.*

mingle, *vb.* misturar(-se).

miniature, *n.* miniatura *f.*

minimal, *adj.* mínimo.

minimum, *adj., n.* mínimo *m.* **m. wage,** salário mínimo *m.*

mining, *n.* mineração *f.*

minister, 1. *n.* ministro -tra; pastor -ra *m.* **2.** *vb.* ministrar.

ministry, *n.* ministério *f.*

mink, *n.* visom *m.*

minor, *adj.* menor *m.f.*

minority, *f.* maioria *f.*; (age) menoridade *f.*

minstrel, *n.* trovador *m.*, jogral *m.*

mint, 1. *n.* menta *f.*; casa da moeda *f.* **2.** *vb.* cunhar.

minus, *prep.* menos.

minute, 1. *adj.* miúdo,

diminuto; minucioso. **2.** *m.* minuto *m.*

miracle, *n.* milagre *m.*

miraculous, *adj.* milagroso.

mirage, *n.* miragem *f.*

mire, 1. *n.* lamaçal, atoleiro *m.* **2.** *vb.* atolar(-se).

mirror, *n.* espelho *m.*

mirth, *n.* alegria *f.*

misanthrope, *n.* misantropo *m.*

misbehave, *vb.* comportar-se mal.

misbehavior, *n.* mau comportamento *m.*

miscarriage, *n.* aborto *m.*

miscegenation, *n.* miscigenação *f.*

miscellaneous, *adj.* miscelâneo.

miscellany, *n.* miscelânea *f.*

mischief, *n.* travessura, *(coll.)* arte *f.*

mischievous, *adj.* travesso, traquinas.

misconduct, *n.* má conduta *f.*

misdeed, *n.* falta *f.*, delito *m.*,

misdemeanor, *n.* contravenção *f.*

miser, *n.* avarento, *(coll.)* pão-duro *m.*

miserable, *adj.* miserável, infeliz.

miserly, *adj.* avarento.

misery, *n.* miséria *f.*

misfit, *n.* desajustado -da.

misfortune, *n.* desgraça *f.*, infortúnio *m.*

misgiving, *n.* dúvida, apreensão *f.*

mishap, *n.* acidente, contratempo *m.*

mishmash, *n.* mixórdia *f.*

misinformation, *n.* informação incorreta *f.*

misinterpret, *vb.* interpretar mal.

mislead, *vb.* desencaminhar, despistar.

misnomer, *n.* termo impróprio *m.*

misplace, *vb.* guardar em lugar errado, perder.

misrepresent, *vb.* falsificar, deturpar.

miss, 1. *n.* senhorita *f.*; falta *f.* **2.** *vb.* errar; falhar; perder; dar pela falta de; sentir saudades de. **be missing,** faltar.

missile, n. míssil m.

mission, n. missão f.

missionary, n. missionário -ria.

mist, n. névoa, garoa f.

mistake, 1. n. erro, engano. make a m., enganar-se. 2. vb. confundir.

mistaken, adj. errado; enganado.

mister, n. senhor m.

mistreat, vb. maltratar.

mistress, n. senhora f., patroa f.; amante f.

mistrust, 1. n. desconfiança f. 2. vb. desconfiar de.

misty, adj. nevoento.

misunderstand, vb. entender mal.

misunderstanding, n. desentendimento m., desavença f.

misuse, vb. abusar, maltratar.

mite, n. ácaro m.

miter, n. mitra f.

mitigate, vb. mitigar.

mitten, n. mitene f.

mix, 1. n. mistura f. 2. vb. misturar; associar-se. m. up, confundir.

mixture, n. mistura f.

mix-up, n. confusão f.

moan, 1. n. gemido m. 2. vb. gemer.

moat, n. fosso m.

mob, n. multidão, turba f.; quadrilha f.

mobile, 1. adj. móvel. 2. n. móbile m.

mobility, n. mobilidade f.

mobilize, vb. mobilizar(-se).

moccasin, n. mocassim m.

mock, vb. zombar de; arremedar.

mockery, n. zombaria f.; arremedo m.

modality, n. modalidade f.

mode, n. modo m.

model, 1. n. modelo m. 2. vb. modelar.

moderate, 1. adj. moderado. 2. vb. moderar.

moderation, n. moderação f.

moderator, n. presidente m.f.

modern, adj. moderno.

modernize, vb. modernizar (-se).

modest, adj. modesto; recatado.

modesty, n. modéstia f.; recato m.

modify, vb. modificar.

modulate, vb. modular.

module, n. módulo m.

Mohammedan, adj., n. maometano -na.

moist, adj. úmido.

moisten, vb. umedecer.

moisture, n. umidade f.

molar, n. molar m.

molasses, n. melaço m.

mold, 1. n. molde m., fôrma f.; moldura f.; mofo m. 2. vb. moldar; mofar.

molding, n. moldura f.

moldy, adj. mofento.

mole, n. sinal m.; (animal) toupeira f.

molecule, n. molécula f.

molest, vb. molestar.

mollusk, n. molusco m.

moment, n. momento m.

momentary, adj. momentâneo.

momentous, adj. momentoso, importante.

momentum, n. momento m.

monarch, n. monarca m.

monarchy, n. monarquia f.

monastery, n. mosteiro, convento m.

Monday, n. segunda-feira f.

monetary, adj. monetário.

money, n. dinheiro m. m. order, vale postal m.

mongrel, 1. adj. mestiço. 2. n. vira-lata m.

monitor, n. monitor m.

monk, n. monge, frade m.

monkey, n. macaco m.

monocle, n. monóculo m.

monoculture, n. monocultura f.

monogram, n. monograma m.

monograph, n. monografia f.

monolithic, adj. monolítico.

monologue, n. monólogo m.

monopolize, vb. monopolizar.

monopoly, n. monopólio m.

monorail, n. monotrilho m.

monotone, n. monotonia f.

monotonous, adj. monótono.

monseigneur, n. monsenhor f.

monsoon, n. monção f.

monster, n. monstro m.

monstrosity, n. monstruosidade f.

monstrous, adj. monstruoso.

Montevideo, n. Montevidéu.

month, n. mês m.

monthly, adj. mensal.

monument, n. monumento m.

monumental, adj. monumental.

moo, 1. n. mugido m. **2.** vb. mugir.

mooch, vb. (coll.) filar.

mood, n. humor m.; (gram.) modo m.

moody, adj. de lua.

moon, n. lua f.

moon landing, n. alunissagem f.

moonlight, 1. n. luar m. **2.** vb. (coll.) ser um cabide de empregos.

moor, 1. n. charneca f. **2.** vb. amarrar.

Moor, n. mouro m.

Moorish, adj. mouro, mourisco.

moose, n. alce m.

mop, 1. n. esfregão m. **2.** vb. esfregar.

mope, vb. andar triste.

moral, 1. adj. moral. **2.** n. moral f.; (pl.) moral f.

morale, n. moral m.

morality, n. moralidade f.

moralize, vb. moralizar.

morass, n. lamaçal m.

moratorium, n. moratória f.

moray, n. moréia f.

morbid, adj. mórbido.

mordant, adj. mordaz, mordente.

more, adj., adv. mais. **m. and m.,** cada vez mais.

moreover, adv. além disso.

morgue, n. morgue f.

moribund, adj. moribundo.

Mormon, adj., n. mórmon m.f.

morning, 1. adj. matinal, matututino. **2.** n. manhã f.

Moroccan, adj., n. marroquino -na.

Morocco, n. Marrocos.

moron, n. débil mental m.f.

morose, adj. mal-humorado, triste.

morphine, n. morfina f.

morsel, n. bocado m.

mortal, adj., n. mortal m.

mortality, n. mortalidade f.

mortar, n. argamassa f.; (mil.) morteiro m.

mortgage, 1. n. hipoteca f. **2.** vb. hipotecar.

mortify, vb. mortificar.

mortuary, n. funerária f.

mosaic, adj., n. mosaico m.

Moscow, n. Moscou.

Moslem, adj., n. muçulmano -na.

mosque, n. mesquita f.

mosquito, n. mosquito m.

moss, n. musgo m.

most, 1. adj. mais. **2.** adv. mais; sumamente. **3.** n. a maior parte de; a maioria dos.

motel, n. motel m.

moth, n. traça f.; mariposa f.

mothball, n. bola de naftalina f.

mother, n. mãe f.

motherhood, n. maternidade f.

mother-in-law, n. sogra f.

mother-of-pearl, n. madrepérola f.

motif, n. motivo m.

motion, 1. n. moção f. **2.** vb. acenar.

motion picture, n. filme m.

motivate, vb. motivar.

motive, n. motivo, móvel m.

motor, n. motor m.

motorboat, n. barco a motor m.

motorcycle, n. motocicleta f.

motorist, n. motorista m.f.

mottled, adj. mosqueado.

motto, n. lema, mote m.

mound, n. montículo, monte m.

mount, 1. n. monte m., montanha f.; (horse) montaria f. **2.** vb. subir, montar; aumentar.

mountain, n. montanha f., morro m. **m. range,** serra, cordilheira f.

mountaineer, n. montanhês -nhesa; alpinista m.f.

mountainous, adj. montanhoso.

mountaintop, n. cume m.

mourn, n. lamentar, chorar; estar de luto.

mourning, n. lamento m.; luto m.

mouse, n. camundongo, rato m.

mousetrap, n. ratoeira f.

mouth, n. boca f.; (river) foz, desembocadura f.

mouthful, n. bocado m.

movable, adj. móvel, amovível.

move, 1. n. movimento m.; mudança f. **2.** vb. mover(-se), movimentar(-se); (residence) mudar(-se); (emotionally) comover.

movement, n. movimento m.

movie, n. filme m.; (pl.) cinema m.

moving, adj. movente, movediço; comovente.

mow, vb. ceifar; (grass) cortar.

Mozambique, n. Moçambique m.

Mozambican, adj., n. moçambicano -na.

Mr., n. Senhor (Sr.) m.

Mrs., n. Senhora (Sra.) f.

much, adj., adv. muito. **as m. as,** tanto quanto/como; **how m.,** quanto; **so m.,** tanto; **too m.,** demais.

mucus, n. muco m., mucosidade f.

mud, n. lama f.

muddle, 1. n. confusão f. **2.** vb. confundir(-se).

muddy, 1. adj. lamacento. **2.** vb. enlamear.

mudhole, n. atoleiro m.

muffin, n. bolinho doce m.

muffle, n. abafar.

muffler, n. cachecol, cachenê m.; (car) silenciador m.

mug, 1. n. caneco m., -ca f.; (sl.) cara f. **2.** vb. (sl.) assaltar (alguém).

muggy, adj. mormacento.

mulatto, n. mulato -ta.

mulberry, n. amora f.

mule, n. mu m., mula f.

mull, vb. **m. over,** ruminar.

multicolored, adj. multicolor, multicor.

multinational, adj., n. multinacional f.

multiple, adj., n. múltiplo m. **m. choice,** múltipla escolha f.

multiplication, n. multiplicação f.

multiplicity, n. multiplicidade f.

multiply, vb. multiplicar.

multitude, n. multidão f.

mumble, vb. murmurar, resmungar.

mummy, n. múmia f.

mumps, n. caxumba f.

munch, vb. mastigar.

mundane, adj. mundano.

municipal, adj. municipal.

municipality, n. cidade f.

munition, n. munição f.

mural, adj., n. mural m.

murder, 1. n. assassínio m. **2.** vb. assassinar, matar.

murderer, n. assassino -na.

murky, adj. escuro; sombrio.

murmur, 1. n. murmúrio m. **2.** vb. murmurar.

muscle, n. músculo m.

muse, 1. n. musa f. **2.** vb. meditar; refletir.

museum, n. museu m.

mush, n. papa f., mingau m.

mushroom, n. cogumelo, champinhon m.

music, n. música f.

musical, adj. musical.

musician, n. músico m.

musk, n. almíscar m.

musket, n. mosquete m.

must, 1. n. obrigação f.; mofo m. **2.** vb. dever, precisar.

mustache, n. bigode m.

mustard, n. mostarda f.

musty, adj. mofento.

mutant, n. mutante m.f.

mutation, n. mutação f.

mute, 1. adj. mudo. **2.** n. mudo m.; (mus.) surdina f. **3.** vb. abafar.

mutilate, vb. mutilar.

mutiny, 1. n. motim m. **2.** vb. amotinar-se.

mutt, n. vira-lata m.

mutter, vb. resmungar.

mutton, n. carne de carneiro f.

mutual, adj. mútuo.

muzzle, 1. n. focinho m.; mordaça f.; (rifle) boca f. **2.** vb. amordaçar.

my, adj. meu, minha.

myopia, n. miopia f.

myriad, n. miríade f.

myself, pron. me; eu mesmo. **I m.,** eu mesmo, eu próprio.

mysterious, adj. misterioso.

mystery, n. mistério m. **m. novel,** romance policial m.

mystic, adj., n. místico m.

mystify, vb. mistificar.

myth, n. mito m.

mythical, adj. mítico.

mythological, adj. mitológico.

mythology, n. mitologia f.

N

nab, *vb.* pegar, agarrar.

nag, 1. *n.* rocim, matungo *m.* **2.** *vb.* importunar.

nail. 1. *n.* prego *m.*; (finger) unha *f.* **2.** *vb.* pregar.

nail polish, *n.* esmalte *m.*

naive, *adj.* ingênuo.

naked, *adj.* nu, nua.

nakedness, *n.* nudez *f.*

name, 1. *n.* nome *m.* **2.** *vb.* nomear; mencionar.

namely, *adv.* a saber, isto é.

namesake, *n.* xará *m.f.*

nap, 1. *n.* cochilo *m.* **2.** *vb.* cochilar.

nape, *n.* nuca *f.*, cangote *m.*

napkin, *n.* guardanapo *m.*

narcotic, 1. *adj.* narcótico. **2.** *n.* narcótico *m.*; (pl.) entorpecentes *n.pl.*

narrate, *vb.* narrar.

narration, *n.* narração *f.*

narrative, 1. *adj.* narrativo. **2.** *n.* narrativa *f.*

narrator, *n.* narrador -ra.

narrow, 1. *adj.* estreito, apertado. **2.** *vb.* estreitar(-se).

narrow-minded, *adj.* intolerante, bitolado.

nasal, *adj.* nasal.

nasty, *adj.* asqueroso; ruim; desagradável.

nation, *n.* nação *f.*

national, *adj.* nacional.

nationalism, *n.* nacionalismo *m.*

nationality, *n.* nacionalidade *f.*

nationalize, *vb.* nacionalizar, encampar.

native, 1. *adj.* nativo. **2.** *n.* nativo -va, natural *m.f.*; indígena *m.f.*

nativity, *n.* natividade *f.* **n. scene,** presépio *m.*

natural, *adj.* natural. **n. resources,** recursos naturais *m.pl.*

naturalize, *vb.* naturalizar.

nature, *n.* natureza *f.*

naught, *n.* nada.

naughty, *adj.* levado, travesso.

nausea, *n.* náusea *f.*, enjôo *m.*

nauseate, *vb.* nausear, enjoar.

nauseating, *adj.* nojento.

nauseous, *adj.* nauseabundo.

nautical, *adj.* náutico, marítimo.

naval, *adj.* naval.

navel, *n.* umbigo *m.*

navigate, *vb.* navegar.

navigation, *n.* navegação *f.*

navigator, *n.* navegador -ra, navegante *m.f.*

navy, *n.* marinha *f.*

Nazi, *adj., n.* nazista *m.f.*

Nazism, *n.* nazismo *m.*

near, 1. *adj.* próximo, vizinho. **2.** *adv.* perto. **3.** *prep.* perto de.

nearby, 1. *adj.* próximo, vizinho. **2.** *adv.* perto.

nearly, *adv.* quase.

nearsighted, *adj.* míope.

neat, *adj.* limpo; arrumado.

neatness, *n.* limpeza *f.*, asseio *m.*

nebulous, *adj.* nebuloso.

necessary, *adj.* necessário.

necessity, *n.* necessidade *f.*

neck, *n.* pescoço *m.*; (shirt) gola *f.*; (bottle) gargalo *m.*

necklace, *n.* colar *m.*

neckline, *n.* decote *m.*

necktie, *n.* gravata *f.*

need, 1. *n.* necessidade *f.*; pobreza *f.* **2.** *vb.* precisar (de).

needle, *n.* agulha *f.*

needless, *adj.* desnecessário, escusado.

needy, *adj.* necessitado.

negate, *vb.* negar.

negative, 1. *adj.* negativo. **2.** *n.* negativa *f.*; (phot.) negativo *m.*

neglect, 1. *n.* negligência *f.*; descuido *m.* **2.** *vb.* negligenciar, descuidar.

negligée, *n.* négligé; roupão *m.*

negligent, *adj.* negligente.

negligible, *adj.* insignificante.

negotiate, *vb.* negociar.

negotiation, *n.* negociação *f.*

Negro, *adj., n.* negro -gra, preto -ta.

neigh, 1. *n.* relincho, rincho *m.* **2.** *vb.* relinchar, rinchar.

neighbor, *n.* vizinho -nha; próximo *m.*

neighborhood, *n.* vizinhança *f.*, bairro *m.*

neighboring, *adj.* vizinho.

neither, 1. *adj., pron.* nenhum. **2.** *adv.* também não, tampouco. **3.** *prep.* nem; tampouco. **n.** . ..nor, nem. . .nem.

neon, *n.* neônio, néon *m.*

nephew, *n.* sobrinho *m.*

nerve, *n.* nervo *m.*; (*coll.*) coragem *f.*, atrevimento *m.*

nervous, *adj.* nervoso.

nest, *n.* ninho *m.*

nestle, *vb.* aninhar(-se).

net, 1. *adj.* líquido. **2.** *n.* rede *f.* **3.** *vb.* enredar; ganhar.

Netherlands, *n.* Holanda *f.*

nettle, 1. *n.* urtiga *f.* **2.** *vb.* irritar.

network, *n.* rede *f.*

neurology, *n.* neurologia *f.*

neurotic, *adj.*, *n.* neurótico *m.*

neuter, *adj.* neutro.

neutral, 1. *adj.* neutro. **2.** *n.* (car) ponto morto *m.*

neutrality, *n.* neutralidade *f.*

neutron, *n.* nêutron *m.*

never, *adv.* nunca, jamais.

nevertheless, *adv.* porém, no entanto.

new, *adj.* novo.

new-, newly-, *pref.* recém-.

newness, *n.* novidade *f.*

news, *n.* notícia(s) *f.(pl.)*; (TV, radio) noticiário, jornal *m.*

newsboy, *n.* jornaleiro *m.*

newscast, *n.* noticiário, jornal *m.*

newsletter, *n.* boletim *m.*

newspaper, *n.* jornal *m.*

newsreel, *n.* jornal cinematográfico *m.*, atualidades *f.pl.*

newsstand, *n.* banca de jornal *f.*

New Testament, *n.* Novo Testamento *m.*

New World, *n.* Novo Mundo *m.*

New Year, *n.* ano novo *m.*; dia de ano novo *m.*

New York, *n.* Nova Iorque.

next, 1. *adj.* próximo, seguinte; ao lado. **2.** *adv.* logo depois, a seguir. **n. door,** (n)a casa ao lado; **n. to,** ao lado de.

nibble, *vb.* beliscar.

Nicaraguan, *adj.*, *n.* nicaraguano -na, nicaragüense *m.f.*

nice, *adj.* agradável; simpático; excelente.

nickname, *n.* apelido *m.*, alcunha *f.*

niece, *n.* sobrinha *f.*

night, 1. *adj.* noturno. **2.** *n.* noite *f.* **g. night,** boa noite; **last n.,** ontem à noite.

night club, *n.* boate *f.*

nightfall, *n.* anoitecer *m.*

nightgown, *n.* camisola de dormir *f.*

nightingale, *n.* rouxinol *m.*

nightmare, *n.* pesadelo *m.*

nimble, *adj.* ágil.

nine, *adj.* nove.

nine hundred, *adj.* novecentos.

nineteen, *adj.* dezenove.

nineteenth, *adj.*, *n.* décimo nono *m.*

ninetieth, *adj.*, *n.* nonagésimo *m.*

ninety, *adj.* noventa.

ninth, *adj.*, *n.* nono *m.*

nipple, *n.* mamilo, bico do seio *m.*; bico de mamadeira *m.*

nitrogen, *n.* nitrogênio *m.*

nitwit, *n.* bobalhão -lhona.

no, 1. *adj.* nenhum. **n. one,** ninguém. **2.** *adv.* não.

nobility, *n.* nobreza *f.*

noble, *adj.*, *n.* nobre *m.*

nobleman -woman, *n.* nobre *m.f.*, fidalgo -ga.

nobody, 1. *n.* joão-ninguém *m.* **2.** *pron.* ninguém.

nocturnal, *adj.* noturno.

nod, 1. *n.* aceno com a cabeça *m.* **2.** *vb* acenar com a cabeça; cabecear.

node, *n.* nó, nodo *m.*

noise, *n.* barulho, ruído *m.*

noiseless, *adj.* silencioso.

noisy, *adj.* barulhento.

nomad, *n.* nômade *m.f.*

nominal, *adj.* nominal.

nominate, *vb.* indicar; nomear.

nomination, *n.* indicação *f.*; nomeação *f.*

nominee, *n.* candidato -ta.

non-, *pref.* não-.

nonchalant, *adj.* indiferente.

noncommital, *adj.* evasivo.

nonconformist, *n.* não-conformista, inconformista *m.f.*

nondescript, *adj.* indefinido.

none, *pron.* nenhum.

nonentity, *n.* nulidade *f.*

nonexistent, *adj.* inexistente.

nonpartisan, *adj.*, *n.* independente *m.f.*

nonsense, *n.* bobagem, besteira *f.*

nonstop, *adj.* sem escala, direto.

noodle, *n.* talharim *m.*

nook, *n.* recanto *m.*

noon, *n.* meio-dia *m.*

no one, *pron.* ninguém.

noose, *n.* laço, nó corredio *m.*

nor, *conj.* nem. **neither. . .n.,** nem. . nem.

norm, *n.* norma *f.*

normal, *adj.* normal.

north, *adj., n.* norte *m.*

North America, *n.* América do Norte *f.*

North American, *adj., n.* norte-americano -na.

northeast, *adj., n.* nordeste *m.*

northeastern, *adj.* nordestino.

northeasterner, *n.* nordestino -na.

northern, *adj.* do norte, setentrional.

northerner, *n.* nortista *m.f.*

North Pole, *n.* pólo Norte *m.*

northwest, *adj., n.* noroeste *m.*

northwestern, *adj.* noroeste.

Norway, *n.* Noruega *f.*

Norwegian, *adj., n.* norueguês -guesa.

nose, *n.* nariz *m.* **n. cone,** ogiva *f.*

nosebleed, *n.* hemorragia nasal *f.*

nostalgia, *n.* nostalgia, saudade *f.*

nostalgic, *adj.* nostálgico, saudoso.

nostril, *n.* narina *f.*

nosy, *adj.* abelhudo.

not, *adv.* não. **n. at all,** de modo algum.

notable, *adj.* notável.

notary, *n.* notário, tabelião *m.*

notation, *n.* notação *f.*

notch, *n.* entalhe, corte *m.*

note, 1. *n.* nota *f.*, apontamento *m.*; recado *m.* **2.** *vb.* notar.

notebook, *n.* caderno *m.*

noted, *adj.* conhecido, famoso.

noteworthy, *adj.* notável.

nothing, *pron.* nada.

notice, 1. *n.* aviso *m.*; notícia *f.* **2.** *vb.* notar, reparar.

noticeable, *adj.* perceptível; notável.

notification, *n.* notificação *f.*

notify, *vb.* notificar, informar.

notion, *n.* noção *f.*

notoriety, *n.* notoriedade *f.*; má fama *f.*

notorious, *adj.* notório; de má fama.

notwithstanding, *prep.* apesar de.

noun, *n.* substantivo *m.*

nourish, *vb.* nutrir, alimentar.

nourishment, *n.* nutrição, alimentação *f.*

novel, 1. *adj.* novo, original. **2.** *n.* romance *m.*, novela *f.*

novelist, *n.* romancista, novelista *m.f.*

novelty, *n.* novidade *f.*

November, *n.* novembro *m.*

novice, *n.* novato -ta, neófito *m.*

now, *adv.* agora. **n. and then,** de vez em quando; **by n.,** já; **from p. on,** de agora em diante; **just n.,** há pouco; **right n.,** agora mesmo.

nowadays, *adv.* hoje em dia, atualmente.

nowhere, *adv.* em parte alguma.

nozzle, *n.* esguicho *m.*

nuance, *n.* nuança *f.*, matiz *m.*

nuclear, *adj.* nuclear.

nucleus, *n.* núcleo *m.*

nude, *adj.* nu, nua.

nudge, 1. *n.* cutucada *f.* **2.** *vb.* cutucar.

nudist, *n.* nudista *m.f.*

nudity, *n.* nudez *f.*

nugget, *n.* pepita *f.*

nuisance, *n.* aborrecimento *m.*; *(coll.)* chato -ta.

null, *adj.* nulo.

nullify, *vb.* anular.

numb, *adj.* entorpecido.

number, 1. *n.* número *m.*; cifra *f.* **2.** *vb.* numerar, contar.

numeral, *n.* numeral, número *m.*

numerical, *adj.* numérico.

numerous, *adj.* numeroso.

nun, *n.* freira, monja *f.*

nuptial, 1. *adj.* nupcial. **2.** *(pl.)* núpcias *f.pl.*

nurse, 1. *n.* enfermeira *f.*; *(child's)* babá *f.* **2.** *vb.* criar; cuidar; amamentar.

nursemaid, *n.* babá, ama-seca *f.*

nursery, *n.* quarto de criança

m. ; berçário *m.* ; escola maternal *f.* ; sementeira *f.*

nursing, *n.* enfermagem *f.*

nurture, *vb.* nutrir; criar.

nut, *n.* noz, castanha *f.* ; *(mech.)* porca *f.* ; *(sl.)* louco -ca.

nutrient, *n.* nutriente, nutrimento *m.*

nutrition, *n.* nutrição *f.*

nutritional, *adj.* nutritivo.

nutritious, *adj.* nutritivo.

nylon, *n.* náilon *m.*

nymph, *n.* ninfa *f.*

O

oaf, *n.* imbecil *m.f.*

oak, *n.* carvalho *m.*

oar, *n.* remo *m.*

oasis, *n.* oásis *m.*

oat, *n.* aveia *f.*

oath, *n.* juramento *m.* ; (curse) praga *f.*

oatmeal, *n.* farinha/mingau de aveia *f./m.*

obedience, *n.* obediência *f.*

obedient, *adj.* obediente.

obese, *adj.* obeso.

obey *vb.* obedecer.

obituary, *n.* necrologia *f.* , obituário *m.*

object, 1. *n.* objeto *m.* ; objetivo *m.* **2.** *vb.* objetar; opor-se.

objection, *n.* objeção *f.*

objective, 1. *adj.* objetivo. **2.** *n.* objetivo *m.* ; *(phot.)* objetiva *f.*

obligate, *vb.* obrigar.

obligation, *n.* obrigação *f.*

obligatory, *adj.* obrigatório.

oblige, *vb.* obrigar; fazer favor a.

oblique, *adj.* oblíquo.

obliterate, *vb.* obliterar, apagar.

oblivion, *n.* esquecimento, olvido *m.*

obnoxious, *adj.* antipático, *(coll.)* chato.

oboe, *n.* oboé *m.*

obscene, *adj.* obsceno.

obscenity, *n.* obscenidade *f.*

obscure, 1. *adj.* obscuro. **2.** *vb.* obscurecer.

obsequious, *adj.* servil.

observance, *n.* observância *f.* ; cerimônia *f.*

observant, *adj.* atento, observador.

observation, *n.* observação *f.*

observatory, *n.* observatório *m.*

observe, *vb.* observar; celebrar; notar.

observer, *n.* observador -ra.

obsession, *n.* obsessão *f.*

obsolete, *adj.* obsoleto.

obstacle, *n.* obstáculo *m.*

obstetrics, *n.* obstetrícia, obstétrica *f.*

obstinate, *adj.* obstinado, teimoso.

obstruct, *vb.* obstruir.

obstruction, *n.* obstrução *f.* , obstáculo *m.*

obtain, *vb.* obter, conseguir.

obvious, *adj.* óbvio.

occasion, 1. *n.* ocasião, oportunidade *f.* **2.** *vb.* ocasionar.

occasional, *adj.* ocasional; pouco freqüente.

occasionally, *adv.* de vez em quando, às vezes.

occidental, *adj.* ocidental.

occult, *adj.* oculto.

occupant, *n.* ocupante *m.f.*

occupation, *n.* ocupação *f.* ; profissão *f.*

occupy, *vb.* ocupar.

occur, *vb.* ocorrer.

occurrence, *n.* ocorrência *f.*

ocean, *n.* oceano *m.* **o. liner,** transatlântico *m.*

oceanic, *adj.* oceânico.

o'clock, hora(s). **it's one o.,** é uma hora; **it's two o.,** são duas horas; **at. . .o., à/às. . .** (horas).

octane, *n.* octana *f.*

octave, *n.* oitava *f.*

October, *n.* outubro *m.*

octopus, *n.* polvo, octópode *n.*

oculist, *n.* oculista *m.f.*

odd, *adj.* esquisito; • avulso; (number) ímpar; e tantos.

oddity, *n.* esquisitice.

odds, *n.pl.* probabilidade(s) *f.(pl.)* ; disparidade *f.* **o. and ends,** restos *m.pl.* , coisas avulsas *f.* ; **be at o. with,** estar de ponta com.

ode, *n.* ode *f.*

odious, *adj.* odioso.

odor, *n.* cheiro, aroma *m.*

of, *prep.* de.

off, 1. *adv.* fora, à distância,

longe. **2.** *prep.* de, fora de; perto de. **3.** *adj.* desligado; cancelado; errado; ruim; de folga; em marcha.

off-color, *adj.* obsceno, apimentado.

offend, *vb.* ofender.

offense, *n.* ofensa *f.*; crime *m.* **take o.,** ofender-se.

offensive, 1. *adj.* ofensivo. **2.** *n.* ofensiva *f.*

offer, 1. *n.* oferta *f.*, oferecimento *m.*; proposta *f.* **2.** *vb.* oferecer; propor. **o. to,** oferecer-se a.

offering, *n.* oferenda, oferta *f.*

office, *n.* escritório, gabinete *m.*; (doctor) consultório *m.*; (government) repartição *f.*; (position) cargo. *m.* **be in o.,** estar no poder; **take o.,** tomar posse.

office boy, *n.* contínuo, bói *m.*

office hours, *n.pl.* expediente *m.*; horas de consulta *f.*

officer, *n.* diretor -ra; *(mil.)* oficial *m.*; policial *m.*

official, 1. *adj.* oficial. **2.** *n.* funcionário (público) *m.*

officiate, *vb.* oficiar.

officious, *adj.* intrometido, metediço.

offing, *n.* **in the o.,** iminente, na bica.

offprint, *n.* separata *f.*

offspring, *n.* prole *f.*, filhos *m.pl.*

off-the-record, *adj.* confidencial.

often, *adv.* muitas vezes, frequentemente.

ogle, *vb.* comer com os olhos.

ogre, *n.* ogro *m.*

oil, 1. *n.* óleo, azeite *m.*; petróleo *m.* **o. painting,** quadro a óleo *m.*; **o. well,** poço de petróleo *m.* **2.** *vb.* lubrificar.

oily, *adj.* oleoso.

ointment, *n.* ungüento *m.*

okay, O.K., 1. *adj.* certo, O.K. **2.** *n.* aprovação *f.* **3.** *vb.* aprovar. **4.** *adv., interj.* está bem, certo.

okra, *n.* quiabo *m.*

old, *adj.* velho, idoso, antigo. **o. man/woman,** velho -lha; **be ... years old,** ter ... anos; **how**

o. is. . .?, quantos anos tem . . .?

old age, *n.* velhice *f.*

old-fashioned, *adj.* antiquado; fora da moda.

old maid, *n.* solteirona, titia *f.*

oldster, *n.* velho -lha, *(sl.)* coroa *m./f.*

Old Testament, *n.* Velho Testamento *m.*

oligarchy, *n.* oligarquia *f.*

olive, *n.* azeitona, oliva *f.* **o. tree,** oliveira *f.*

olive oil, *n.* azeite de oliva, óleo *m.*

Olympic, 1. *adj.* olímpico. **2.** *n.pl.* jogos olímpicos *m.*, olimpíadas *f.pl.*

omelet, -lette, *n.* omelete *f.*

omen, *n.* agouro, presságio *m.*

ominous, *adj.* ominoso, agourento.

omission, *n.* omissão *f.*

omit, *vb.* omitir.

omnipotent, *adj.* onipotente.

omniscient, *adj.* onisciente.

on, 1. *adv.* adiante, em/por diante. **and so o.,** e assim por diante. **2.** *prep.* em, sobre, em cima de.

once, 1. *adv.* uma vez. **o. and for all,** de uma vez por todas; **o. in a while,** de vez em quando; **o. upon a time,** era uma vez; **at at o.,** de repente. **2.** *conj.* assim que; quando.

one, *adj., pron.* um, uma. **o. another,** um ao outro; no um; ninguém; **that o.,** aquele -la; esse -sa; **this o.,** este -sta.

oneself, *pron.* se; si mesmo/próprio. **with o.,** consigo.

one-way, *adj.* (street) de mão única; (ticket) de ida.

onion, *n.* cebola *f.*

only, 1. *adj.* único; só. **2.** *adv.* só, somente, apenas.

onus, *n.* ônus *m.*

onward, *adv.* para diante, para a frente.

ooze, *vb.* exsudar.

opal, *n.* opala *f.*

opaque, *adj.* opaco.

open, 1. *adj.* aberto; franco. **in the o. (air),** ao ar livre. **2.** *vb.* abrir.

opener, *n.* abridor *m.*

opening, *n.* abertura *f.*; (job) vaga *f.*; estréia *f.*; clareira *f.*

opera, *n.* ópera *f.*

operate, *vb.* operar; funcionar. **o. on,** operar.

operation, *n.* operação *f.*; funcionamento *m.* **have an o.,** operar-se.

operator, *n.* (telephone) telefonista *m.f.*

ophthalmologist, *n.* oftalmologista *m.f.*

opinion, *n.* opinião *f.*

opinionated, *adj.* opinioso, dogmático.

opium, *n.* ópio *m.*

opponent, *n.* oponente *m.f.*, adversário -ria.

opportune, *adj.* oportuno.

opportunist, *n.* oportunista *m.f.*

opportunity, *n.* oportunidade *f.*

oppose, *vb.* opor-se a.

opposite, 1. *adj.* contrário, oposto *m.* **2.** *prep.* defronte de, em frente de.

opposition, *n.* oposição *f.*

oppress, *vb.* oprimir.

oppression, *n.* opressão *f.*

oppressive, *adj.* opressivo.

opt, *vb.* optar.

optic -cal, *adj.* óptico, ótico.

optician, *n.* óptico -ca, ótico -ca.

optics, *n.* óptica, ótica *f.*

optimal, optimum, *adj.* ótimo.

optimism, *n.* otimismo *m.*

optimistic, *adj.* otimista.

optimum, *n.* ótimo *m.*

option, *n.* opção *f.*

optional, *adj.* optativo, opcional.

optometrist, *n.* optometrista *m.f.*

opulent, *adj.* opulento.

opus, *n.* (*L.*) opus *m.*, obra *f.*

or, *conj.* ou.

oracle, *n.* oráculo *m.*

oral, *adj.* oral.

orange, 1. *adj.* alaranjado. **2.** *n.* laranja *f.* **o. tree,** laranjeira *f.*

oration, *n.* oração *f.*

orator, *n.* orador -ra.

oratory, *n.* oratória *f.*

orbit, *n.* órbita *f.*

orchard, *n.* pomar *m.*

orchestra, *n.* orquestra *f.*

orchid, *n.* orquídea *f.*

ordain, *vb.* ordenar.

ordeal, *n.* prova *f.*

order, 1. *n.* ordem *f.*; pedido *m.*, encomenda *f.* **in o. that,** para que; **in o. to,** para; **out of o.,** enguiçado. **2.** *vb.* mandar; (goods) encomendar; (restaurant) pedir.

orderly, *adj.* ordenado.

ordinal, *adj.* ordinal.

ordinance, *n.* ordenança *f.*; postura *f.*

ordinary, *adj.* ordinário; comum.

ore, *n.* minério *m.*

oregano, *n.* orégão *m.*

organ, *n.* órgão *m.*

organic, *adj.* orgânico.

organization, *n.* organização *f.*

organize, *vb.* organizar.

orgasm, *n.* orgasmo *m.*

orgy, *n.* orgia *f.*

orient, 1. *n.* oriente *m.* **2.** *vb.* orientar.

oriental, *adj.* oriental.

orientation, *n.* orientação *f.*

orifice, *n.* orifício *m.*

origin, *n.* origem *f.*

original, *adj.* original.

originate, *vb.* originar(-se).

ornament, 1. *n.* ornamento *m.* **2.** *vb.* ornamentar.

ornamental, *adj.* ornamental.

ornate, *adj.* adornado; pomposo.

ornery, *adj.* genioso.

ornithology, *n.* ornitologia *f.*

orphan, *n.* órfão, órfã.

orphanage, *n.* orfanato *m.*

orthodontist, *n.* ortodontista *m.f.*

orthodox, *adj.* ortodoxo.

orthography, *n.* ortografia *f.*

orthopedic, *adj.* ortopédico.

oscillate, *vb.* oscilar.

osmosis, *n.* osmose *f.*

ostensible, *adj.* ostensivo.

ostentation, *n.* ostentação *f.*

ostentatious, *adj.* ostentoso.

ostracism, *n.* ostracismo *m.*

ostrich, *n.* avestruz *m.f.*

other, *adj., pron.* outro.

otherwise, *adv.* de outra maneira.

otter, *n.* lontra *f.*

ought, *vb.* dever.

ounce, *n.* onça *f.*

our, ours, *adj., pron.* nosso.

ourselves, *reflex. pron.* nós mesmos/próprios; nos.

oust, *vb.* expulsar.

out, 1. *adv.* fora. **o. and o.,** completo; **o. of,** fora de; por; **o. of print,** esgotado; **o. of the way,** fora do caminho; **be o. of,** estar sem; **way o.,** saída *f.* **2.** *prep.* por.

outbreak, *n.* erupção *f.*; eclosão *f.*

outburst, *n.* explosão *f.*

outcast, *n.* pária *m.*

outcome, *n.* resultado, desfecho *m.*

outcry, *n.* clamor *m.*

outdo, *vb.* exceder; ultrapassar.

outdoor, 1. *adj.* ao ar livre. **2.** *adv. pl.* fora de casa; ao ar livre.

outer, *adj.* exterior, externo. **o. space,** espaço cósmico *m.*

outfit, 1. *n.* equipamento *m.*; roupa *f.* **2.** *vb.* equipar; vestir.

outgoing, *adj.* expansivo.

outgrow, *vb.* **she outgrew her clothes,** a roupa ficou pequena para ela.

outgrowth, *n.* conseqüência *f.*

outing, *n.* passeio *m.*, excursão *f.*

outlandish, *adj.* esquisito, extravagante.

outlaw, 1. *n.* bandido *m.* **2.** *vb.* proscrever.

outlet, *n.* saída *f.*; escape *m.*; tomada *f.*

outline, 1. *n.* contorno *m.*, silhueta *f.*; esboço *m.* **2.** *vb.* esboçar.

outlook, *n.* perspectiva *f.*; ponto-de-vista *m.*

out-of-date, *adj.* antiquado.

outpost, *n.* posto avançado *m.*

outpouring, *n.* efusão *f.*

output, *n.* produção *f.*; saída *f.*, output *m.*

outrage, 1. *n.* ultraje *m.*; atrocidade *f.* **2.** *vb.* ultrajar.

outrageous, *adj.* atroz.

outright, *adj.* completo; aberto.

outset, *n.* início *m.*

outside, 1. *adj.* externo, exterior. **2.** *n.* exterior *m.* **3.** *adv.* fora, por fora. **2.** *prep.* fora de.

outsider, *n.* forasteiro *m.*

outskirts, *n.pl.* arredores *m.pl.*

outsmart, *vb.* passar a perna em.

outspoken, *adj.* franco. **be o.,** não ter papas na língua.

outstanding, *adj.* eminente, importante; a pagar/receber.

outward, *adv.* para fora; por fora.

oval, *adj., n.* oval *m.*

ovary, *n.* ovário *m.*

ovation, *n.* ovação *f.*, aplausos *m.pl.*

oven, *n.* forno *m.*

over, 1. *adv.* de novo; lá; completamente; demais; terminado. **o. and o.,** repetidamente; **o. here,** aqui; **o. there,** lá, ali; **all o.,** por toda a parte; por todo . . .; acabado. **2.** *prep.* sobre, em cima de; além de; mais de.

overall, *adj.* total, global.

overalls, *n.pl.* macacão *m.*

overbearing, *adj.* arrogante.

overboard, *adv.* ao mar. **go o.,** passar as raias.

overcast, *adj.* nublado.

overcoat, *n.* sobretudo *m.*

overcome, *vb.* superar, vencer.

overdue, *adj.* atrasado.

overflow, *vb.* transbordar.

overhaul, *vb.* vistoriar; retificar.

overlap, *vb.* sobrepor(-se) a.

overload, *vb.* sobrecarregar.

overlook, *vb.* dar para; passar por alto; fazer vista grossa a.

overnight, *adv.* **stay o.,** passar a noite, pernoitar.

overpopulation, *n.* superpopulação *f.*

overpower, *vb.* subjugar.

overrule, *vb.* invalidar, indeferir.

overseas, 1. *adj.* ultramarino, estrangeiro. **2.** *adv.* além-mar, no estrangeiro.

oversee, *vb.* supervisar, supervisionar.

oversight, *n.* descuido *m.*, inadvertência *f.*

overt, *adj.* aberto.

overtake, *vb.* ultrapassar, alcançar.

overthrow, *vb.* derrubar, derrocar.

overtime, *n.* horas extras/extraordinárias *f.pl.*

overture, *n.* abertura *f.*

overturn, *vb.* virar; capotar.

overweight, *adj.* com um excesso de peso; pesado demais.

overwhelm, *vb.* esmagar.

overwork, 1. *n.* trabalho excessivo *m.* **2.** *vb.* trabalhar em demasia.

overwrought, *adj.* lavrado em excesso; nervoso.

owe, *vb.* dever. **owing to,** devido a.

owl, *n.* coruja *f.*

own, 1. *adj.* próprio. **2.** *vb.* possuir.

owner, *n.* dono -na, proprietário- ria.

ox, *n.* boi *m.*

oxygen, *n.* oxigênio *m.*

oyster, *n.* ostra *f.*

ozone, *n.* ozônio *m.*

P

pace, 1. *n.* passo *m.* **2.** *vb.* andar de uma lado para o outro.

pacemaker, *n.* *(med.)* marcapasso *m.*

pacific, *adj.* pacífico. **P. Ocean,** oceano Pacífico *m.*

pacifier, *n.* pacificador -ra; (baby) chupeta *f.*

pacifist, *n.* pacifista *m.f.*

pacify, *vb.* pacificar.

pack, l, *n.* pacote, embrulho *m.*; fardo *m.*; (cigarettes) maço *m.*, carteira *f.*; mochila *f.*; (dog) matilha *f.*; (crooks) quadrilha *f.*; (cards) baralho *m.* **2.** *vb.* empacotar; embalar; fazer as malas.

package, *n.* embrulho, pacote *m.*; embalagem *f.*

packet, *n.* pacote *m.*; (boat) paquete *m.*

pact, *n.* pacto *m.*

pad, l, *n.* almofada *f.*, coxim *m.* **p. of paper,** bloco de papel *m.* **2.** *vb.* acolchoar, almofadar; rechear; *(coll.)* encher lingüiça.

padding, *n.* acolchoamento, estofamento *m.*; recheio *m.*; *(coll.)* lingüiça *f.*

paddle, 1. *n.* pau (para espancar uma pessoa) *f.*; (oar) remo *m.*; (wheel) pá *f.* **2.** *vb.* espancar; remar.

paddywagon, *n.* camburão, tinteiro *m.*

padlock, *n.* cadeado *m.*

pagan, *adj., n.* pagão -gã.

page, 1. *n.* página *f.*; (boy) pajem *m.* **2.** *vb.* procurar (uma pessoa) num lugar público chamando em voz alta.

pageant, *n.* espetáculo *m.*, representação tradicional *f.*

pagoda, *n.* pagode *m.*

paid-up, *adj.* quite.

pail, *n.* balde *m.*

pain, l, *n.* dor *f.* **be in p.,** estar com dor; **take pains,** caprichar. **2.** *vb.* doer; causar dor a; magoar.

painful, *adj.* doloroso; árduo.

painkiller, *n.* analgésico *m.*

paint, 1. *n.* tinta *f.* **fresh p.,** tinta fresca *f.* **2.** *vb.* pintar.

paintbrush, *n.* pincel *m.*, broxa *f.*

painter, *n.* pintor -ra.

painting, *n.* pintura *f.*; (picture) quadro *m.*

pair, *n.* par *m.*, dupla *f.*; casal *m.*

pajamas, *n. pl.* pijama *m.*

Pakistan, *n.* Paquistão *m.*

pal, *n.* amigo, camarada *m.*

palace, *n.* palácio *m.*

palatable, *adj.* gostoso; agradável.

palate, *n.* paladar *m.*; céu da boca *m.*

palatial, *adj.* suntuoso.

palaver, *vb.* palavrear, tagarelar.

pale, 1. *adj.* pálido. **2.** *vb.* empalidecer.

paleness, *n.* palidez *f.*

Palestine, *n.* Palestina *f.*

Palestinian, *adj., n.* palestino -na.

palette, *n.* paleta *f.*

pall, 1. *n.* pano mortuário *m.*; manto *m.*, nuvem *f.* **2.** *vb.* perder o sabor.

pallbearer, *n.* homem que ajuda a carregar um féretro *m.*

pallid, *adj.* pálido.

palm, 1. *n.* (hand) palma *f.*;

(measure) palmo *m.*; (tree) palmeira *f.* **2.** *vb.* escamotear. **p. off**, impingir.

palm heart, *n.* palmito *m.*

palmistry, *n.* quiromancia *f.*

palm oil, *n.* azeite de dendê *m.*

palpable, *adj.* palpável.

palpitate, *vb.* palpitar.

paltry, *adj.* miserável; insignificante.

pamper, *vb.* mimar.

pamphlet, *n.* panfleto *m.*

pan, *n.* panela *f.*

panacea, *n.* panacéia *f.*

Panama, *n.* Panamá *m.*

Panamanian, *adj., n.* panamenho -nha.

Pan-American,   *adj.* pan-americano.

pancake, *n.* panqueca *f.*

pander, 1. *n.* alcoviteiro *m.* **2.** *vb.* alcovitar.

pane, *n.* vidraça *f.*

panel, *n.* painel *m.* **p. discussion,** mesa-redonda *f.*

pang, *n.* dor *f.*

panic, 1. *n.* pânico *m.* **2.** *vb.* ser tomado de pânico.

panorama, *n.* panorama *m.*

pant, *vb.* ofegar, arfar.

panther, *n.* pantera *f.*

panties, *n.pl.* calcinha(s) *f.(pl.)*

pantomime, *n.* pantomima *f.*

pantry, *n.* despensa *f.*; copa *f.*

pants, *n.pl.* calça(s) *f.(pl.)*

pantyhose, *n.pl.* collant *m.*

papal, *adj.* papal.

papaya, *n.* mamão *m.*

paper, *n.* papel *m.*; (news) jornal *m.*; trabalho escrito *m.*

paperback, *n.* livro brochado *m.*; brochura *f.*

paperboy, *n.* jornaleiro *m.*

paper clip, *n.* clipe *m.*

paper cutter, *n.* guilhotina *f.*

paper money, *n.* papel-moeda *m.*

paperweight, *n.* pesa-papéis *m.*

papyrus, *n.* papiro *m.*

par, *n.* paridade *f.*; **par** *m.*

parable, *n.* parábola *f.*

parachute, *n.* pára-quedas *m.*

parachutist, *n.* pára-quedista *m.f.*

parade, 1. *n.* parada *f.*; desfile *m.* **2.** *vb.* desfilar.

paradise, *n.* paraíso *m.*

paradox, *n.* paradoxo *m.*

paradoxical, *n.* paradoxal.

paragon, *n.* modelo *m.*

paragraph, *n.* parágrafo *m.*

Paraguay, *n.* Paraguai *m.*

Paraguayan, *adj., n.* paraguaio -ia.

parakeet, *n.* periquito *m.*

parallel, 1. *adj.* *n.* paralelo *m.* **2.** *vb.* correr paralelo com.

paralysis, *n.* paralisia *f.*

paralyze, *vb.* paralisar.

paramedic, *n.* socorrista *m.f.*

parameter, *n.* parâmetro *m.*

paramount,   *adj.* supremo, sumo.

paranoid, *adj.* paranóico.

paraphernalia, *n.pl.* parafernália *f.*

paraphrase, 1. *n.* paráfrase *f.* **2.** *vb.* parafrasear.

paraplegic, *adj., n.* paraplégico *m.*

parapsychology,   *n.* parapsicologia *f.*

parasite, *n.* parasito *m.*

parasol, *n.* sombrinha *f.*, pára-sol *m.*

parcel, *n.* (package) embrulho *m.*, encomenda *f.*; (piece) parcela *f.* **p. post,** (F.) colis postaux.

parch, *vb.* queimar, ressequir.

parchment, *n.* pergaminho *m.*

pardon, 1. *n.* perdão *m.*; (jur.) indulto *m.* **2.** *vb.* perdoar. **p. me,** desculpe.

pare, *vb.* aparar; descascar.

parentage, *n.* ascendência *f.*; filiação *f.*

parenthesis, *n.* parêntese, parêntesis *m.*

parents, *n.pl.* pais *m.pl.*

par excellence, *expr.* por excelência.

pariah, *n.* pária *m.*

parish, *n.* paróquia *f.*

parishioner, *n.* paroquiano *m.*

parity, *n.* paridade *f.*

park, 1. *n.* parque *m.* **2.** *vb.* estacionar.

parking, *n.* estacionamento *m.* **p. lot,** estacionamento *m.*

parking meter, *n.* parquímetro *m.*

parking place, *n.* vaga *f.*

parliament, *n.* parlamento *m.*

parliamentary, *adj.* parlamentar.

parlor, *n.* sala *f.*; salão *m.*

parochial, *adj.* paroquial, provinciano.

parody, 1. *n.* paródia *f.* **2.** *vb.* parodiar.

parole, *n.* liberdade condicional *f.*

paroxysm, *n.* paroxismo *m.*

parrot, *n.* papagaio *m.*

parsimony, *n.* parcimônia *f.*

parsley, *n.* salsa *f.*

parson, *n.* padre *m.*; pastor protestante *m.*

part, 1. *adj.* parcial. **2.** *n.* parte *f.*; *(mech.)* peça *f.*; *(theat.)* papel *m.* **on the p. of,** da parte de; **take p. in,** tomar parte em. **3.** *vb.* dividir; partir; separar-se. **p. with,** desfazer-se de.

partake, *vb.* **p. of,** participar de.

partial, *adj.* parcial.

participant, *n.* participante *m.f.*

participate, *vb.* participar. **p. in,** participar de.

participation, *n.* participação *f.*

participle, *n.* particípio *m.*

particle, *n.* partícula *f.*

particular, 1. *adj.* particular; específico; exigente; escrupuloso. **2.** *m.* particular *m.* **in p.,** em particular.

parting, *n.* despedida *f.*

partisan, *n.* partidário -ia.

partition, 1. *n.* tabique *m.* **2.** *vb.* dividir.

partner, *n.* sócio -cia; parceiro -ra.

partnership, *n.* sociedade *f.*; parceria *f.*

partridge, *n.* perdiz *f.*, perdigão *m.*

party, *n.* festa, reunião *f.*; grupo *m.*; *(polit.)* partido *m.*; *(jur.)* parte *f.*

pass, 1. *n.* (permit) passe *m.*; (mountain) desfiladeiro *m.*; (exam) aprovação *f.* **2.** *vb.* passar. **p. away,** falecer; **p. out,** desmaiar.

passable, *adj.* transitável; sofrível.

passage, *n.* passagem *f.*; travessia *f.*; corredor *m.*; trecho *m.*

passé, *adj.* antiquado.

passenger, *n.* passageiro -ra.

passerby, *n.* transeunte *m.f.*

passion, *n.* paixão *f.*

passionate, *adj.* apaixonado.

passive, *adj.* passivo.

passport, *n.* passaporte *m.*

past, 1. *adj.*, *n.* passado *m.* **2.** *prep.* depois de, além de.

paste, *n.* pasta *f.*; (glue) grude *m.*, cola *f.*

pasteboard, *n.* papelão *m.*, cartolina *f.*

pastel, *adj.*, *n.* pastel *m.*

pasteurize, *n.* pasteurizar.

pastime, *n.* passatempo *m.*

pastor, *n.* pastor *m.*

pastoral, *adj.* pastoral.

pastry, *n.* pastelaria *f.*

pasture, *n.* pasto *m.*, pastagem *f.*

pat, 1. *n.* palmadinha *f.* **2.** *vb.* dar palmadinhas em.

patch, 1. *n.* remendo *m.* **2.** *vb.* remendar.

patent, 1. *adj.*, *n.* patente *f.* **2.** *vb.* patentear.

paternal, *adj.* paterno, paternal.

paternity, *n.* paternidade *f.*

path, *n.* picada, trilha, vereda *f.*

pathetic, *adj.* patético.

pathology, *n.* patologia *f.*

patience, *n.* paciência *f.*

patient, *adj.*, *n.* paciente *m.f.*

patio, *n.* pátio *m.*

patriarch, *n.* patriarca *m.*

patriot, *n.* patriota *m.f.*

patriotic, *adj.* patriótico.

patriotism, *n.* patriotismo *m.*

patrol, 1. *n.* patrulha *f.* **2.** *vb.* patrulhar.

patron, *n.* patrono -na. **p. saint,** (santo) padroeiro *m.*

patronize, *vb.* ser freguês de; tratar com condescendência.

pattern, *n.* padrão, modelo *m.*; molde *m.*

paunch, *n.* pança *f.*

pauper, *n.* pobre *m.f.*

pause, 1. *n.* pausa *f.* **2.** *vb.* fazer pausa, pausar.

pave, *vb.* pavimentar; calçar, asfaltar.

pavement, *n.* pavimento *m.*; asfalto *m.*

pavilion, *n.* pavilhão *m.*

paving stone, *n.* paralelepípedo *m.*

paw, *n.* pata *f.*

pawn, *n.* **1.** penhor *m.*; (chess) peão *m.* **2.** *vb.* empenhar, penhorar.

pawnbroker, *n.* penhorista *m.f.*

pawnshop, *n.* casa de penhores *f.*

pay, 1. *n.* (wages) salário; (salary) ordenado *m.* **2.** *vb.* pagar. **p. attention,** prestar atenção; **p. a visit,** fazer uma visita; **p. for,** pagar.

payment, *n.* pagamento *m.*, paga *f.*

payroll, *n.* folha de pagamento *f.*

pea, *n.* ervilha *f.*

peace, *n.* paz *f.* **make p. with,** fazer as pazes com.

peaceable, *adj.* pacífico.

peaceful, *adj.* pacífico, tranqüilo.

peach, *n.* pêssego *m.*

peacock, *n.* pavão *m.*

peak, *n.* pico, cume *m.*; máximo *m.*

peal, 1. *n.* repique *m.* **2.** *vb.* repicar, soar.

peanut, *n.* amendoim *m.*

pear, *n.* pêra *f.*

pearl, *n.* pérola *f.*

peasant, *n.* camponês -nesa.

pebble, *n.* seixo, calhau *m.*

peck, 1. *n.* bicada *f.*; beijinho *m.*; quantidade *f.* **2.** *vb.* bicar.

peculiar, *adj.* peculiar; esquisito.

pedagogue, *n.* pedagogo *m.*

pedagogy, *n.* pedagogia *f.*

pedal, 1. *n.* pedal *m.* **2.** *vb.* pedalar.

pedantic, *adj.* pedante.

peddle, *vb.* vender, mascatear.

peddler, *n.* mascate *m.*

pedestal, *n.* pedestal *m.*

pedestrian, *n.* pedestre *m.f.*

pediatrician, *n.* pediatra *m.f.*

pedigree, *n.* genealogia *f.*; raça *f.*

peek, 1. *n.* espiada *f.* **2.** *vb.* espiar.

peel, 1. *n.* casca *f.* **2.** *vb.* descascar, pelar.

peep, 1. *n.* olhada *f.*; (chirp) pio *m.* **2.** *vb.* dar uma olhada; (chirp) piar.

peer, 1. *n.* par, igual *m.* **2.** *vb.* fitar.

peeve, *vb.* chatear, aborrecer.

peevish, *adj.* mal-humorado.

peg, *n.* prego de madeira, pino *m.*

pelican, *n.* pelicano *m.*

pellet, *n.* bolinha *f.*; grão de chumbo *m.*

pelt, 1. *n.* pele *f.* **2.** *vb.* apedrejar; (rain) cair com força.

pelvis, *n.* pelve, pélvis *f.*

pen, *n.* caneta *f.*; (enclosure) curral *m.*

penal, *adj.* penal.

penalty, *n.* pena *f.*; (sport.) pênalti *m.*

penance, *n.* penitência *f.*

penchant, *n.* pendor *m.*, queda *f.*

pencil, *n.* lápis *m.*

pending, *adj.* pendente.

penetrate, *vb.* penetrar.

penguin, *n.* pingüim *m.*

penicillin, *n.* penicilina *f.*

peninsula, *n.* península *f.*

penis, *n.* pênis *m.*

penitent, *adj.* penitente.

penitentiary, *n.* penitenciária *f.*

penknife, *n.* canivete *m.*

penmanship, *n.* caligrafia *f.*

pennant, *n.* flâmula *f.*, galhardete *m.*

penniless, *adj.* sem tostão, (sl.) duro.

penny, *n.* centavo *m.*

pension, *n.* pensão *f.*; aposentadoria *f.*

pensive, *adj.* pensativo.

pentagon, *n.* pentágono *m.*

penthouse, *n.* cobertura *f.*

pent-up, *adj.* reprimido.

penury, *n.* penúria *f.*

peon, *n.* peão *m.*

people, *n.* povo *m.*; gente *f.*, pessoas *f.pl.*, pessoal *m.*

pep, *n.* energia *f.*

pepper, *n.* pimenta *f.* **black p.,** pimenta-do-reino *f.*; **red p.,** pimenta malagueta *f.*; pimentão *m.*

peppermint, *n.* hortelã-pimenta *f.*

per, *prep.* por.

perceive, *vb.* perceber.

percent, *adv.* por cento.

percentage, *n.* percentagem, porcentagem *f.*

perceptible, *adj.* perceptível.

perception, *n.* percepção *f.*

perceptive, *adj.* perceptivo.

perch, 1. *n.* poleiro *m.* ; (fish) perca *f.* **2.** *vb.* pousar.

percolate, *vb.* filtrar(-se).

percussion, *n.* percussão *f.*

perdition, *n.* perdição *f.*

peremptory, *adj.* peremptório.

perennial, *adj.* perene.

perfect, 1. *adj.* perfeito. **2.** *vb.* aperfeiçoar.

perfection, *n.* perfeição *f.*

perforate, *vb.* perfurar.

perform, *vb.* fazer; executar; (theat.) representar.

performance, *n.* desempenho *m.*, performance *f.* ; (theat.) representação *f.*

performer, *n.* artista *m.f.*

perfume, *n.* perfume *m.*

perfunctory, *adj.* perfunctório.

perhaps, *adv.* talvez.

peril, *n.* perigo *m.*

perilous, *adj.* perigoso.

perimeter, *n.* perímetro *m.*

period, *n.* período *m.* , época *f.* ; (punct.) ponto (final) *m.*

periodic, *adj.* periódico.

periodical, *n.* periódico *m.*

peripheral, *adj.* periférico *m.*

periphery, *n.* periferia *f.*

periscope, *n.* periscópio *m.*

perish, *vb.* perecer.

perishable, *adj.* deteriorável.

perjury, *n.* perjúrio *m.*

permanence, *n.* permanência *f.*

permanent, *adj.* permanente.

permeable, *adj.* permeável.

permeate, *vb.* permear.

permissible, *adj.* permissível.

permission, *n.* permissão *f.*

permissive, *adj.* permissivo.

permit, 1. *n.* permissão *f.* ; guia *f.* **2.** *vb.* permitir.

pernicious, *adj.* pernicioso.

perpetrate, *vb.* perpetrar.

perpetual, *adj.* perpétuo.

perpetuate, *vb.* perpetuar.

perpetuity, *n.* perpetuidade *f.*

perplex, *vb.* confundir, deixar perplexo.

perplexed, *adj.* perplexo.

persecute, *vb.* perseguir.

persecution, *n.* perseguição *f.*

perseverance, *n.* perseverança *f.*

persevere, *vb.* perseverar.

persimmon, *n.* caqui *m.*

persist, *vb.* persistir, insistir.

persistent, *adj.* persistente, insistente.

person, *n.* pessoa *f.*

personage, *n.* personagem *m.f.*

personal, *adj.* pessoal.

personality, *n.* personalidade *f.*

personify, *vb.* personificar.

personnel, *n.* pessoal *m.*

perspective, *n.* perspectiva *f.*

perspiration, *n.* suor *m.*

perspire, *vb.* suar, transpirar.

persuade, *vb.* persuadir.

persuasion, *n.* persuasão *f.*

pertain, *vb.* pertencer; dizer respeito.

pertinent, *adj.* pertinente.

perturb, *vb.* perturbar.

peruse, *vb.* ler.

Peruvian, *adj.* n. peruano -na.

pervade, *vb.* permear, penetrar.

perverse, *adj.* perverso.

perversion, *n.* perversão *f.*

perversity, *n.* perversidade *f.*

pervert, 1. *n.* pervertido *m.* **2.** *vb.* perverter.

pessimism, *n.* pessimismo *m.*

pessimistic, *adj.* pessimista.

pest, *n.* peste *f.* ; inseto *m.* ; (coll.) chato -ta.

pester, *vb.* incomodar, (coll.) encher.

pet, 1. *n.* animal de estimação *m.* ; protegido -da **2.** *vb.* afagar.

petal, *n.* pétala *f.*

petition, 1. *n.* petição *f.* **2.** *vb.* pedir; peticionar.

petrify, *vb.* petrificar(-se).

petroleum, *n.* petróleo *m.*

petticoat, *n.* anágua *f.*

petty, *adj.* pequeno; mesquinho; insignificante.

petulant, *adj.* irascível; petulante.

pew, *n.* banco (de igreja) *m.*

pewter, *n.* peltre *m.*

phallic, *adj.* fálico.

phantom, *n.* fantasma *m.*

Pharaoh, *n.* faraó *m.*

Pharisee, *n.* fariseu *m.*

pharmacist, *n.* farmacêutico *m.*

pharmacy, *n.* farmácia *f.*

pharynx, *n.* faringe *f.*

phase, *n.* fase *f.*

pheasant, *n.* faisão *m.*

phenomenal, *adj.* fenomenal.

phenomenon, *n.* fenômeno *m.*

philanthropy, *n.* filantropia *f.*

philharmonic, 1. *adj.* filarmônico. **2.** *n.* filarmônica *f.*

Philippines, *n.pl.* Filipinas *n.f.*

philology, *n.* filologia *f.*

philosopher, *n.* filósofo -fa.

philosophical, *adj.* filosófico.

philosophy, *n.* filosofia *f.*

phlegm, *n.* escarro *m.*

phobia, *n.* fobia *f.*

phoenix, *n.* fênix *m.*

phone, 1. *n.* telefone *m.* **2.** *vb.*
telefonar, ligar.

phonetic, *adj.* fonético.

phonetics, *n.* fonética *f.*

phony, *adj.* falso, *(sl.)* frio,
fajuto.

phonograph, *n.* fonógrafo *m.*,
vitrola *f.*

phonology, *n.* fonologia *f.*

phosphorus, *n.* fósforo *m.*

photo, *n.* foto *f.*

photocopy, 1. *n.* fotocópia *f.* **2.**
vb. fotocopiar.

photogenic, *adj.* fotogênico.

photograph, *n.* fotografia *f.*

photographer, *n.* fotógrafo -fa.

photography, *n.* fotografia *f.*

phrase, 1. *n.* frase *f.*; expressão
f. **2.** *vb.* frasear.

phraseology, *n.* fraseologia *f.*;
fraseado *m.*

phrasing, *n.* fraseado *m.*

physical, *adj.* físico.

physical therapy, *n.* fisioterapia
f.

physician, *n.* médico -ca.

physicist, *n.* físico -ca.

physics, *n.* física *f.*

physiology, *n.* fisiologia *f.*

physique, *n.* físico *m.*

pianist, *n.* pianista *m.f.*

piano, *n.* piano *m.*

picaresque, *adj.* picaresco.

picayune, *adj.* insignificante.

piccolo, *n.* flautim *m.*

pick, 1. *n.* escolha *f.*; (guitar)
palheta *f.*; (tool) picareta *f.* **2.**
vb. colher; escolher; (guitar)
dedilhar; (teeth) palitar; bater
(carteiras). **p. up,** pegar, apanhar.

picket, *n.* estaca *f.*; piquete *m.*

pickle, *n.* picles *m.pl.*

pickpocket, *n.* batedor de carteiras *m.*

pickup, *n.* camioneta *f.*, pickup *m.*

picnic, *n.* piquenique *m.*

picture, 1. *n.* quadro *m.*; fotografia *f.*, retrato *m.*; filme *m.*
2. *vb.* imaginar.

picturesque, *adj.* pitoresco.

pie, *n.* torta *f.*, pastelão *m.*

piece, *n.* pedaço *m.*; peça *f.*

pier, *n.* cais, molhe *m.*

pierce, *vb.* perfurar, furar.

piety, *n.* piedade *f.*

pig, *n.* porco *m.*

pigeon, *n.* pombo *m.*

pigment, *n.*, pigmento *m.*

pigpen, *n.* chiqueiro *m.*

pile, 1. *n.* pilha *f.* **2.** *vb.* empilhar.

pile driver, *n.* bate-estacas *m.*

pilfer, *vb.* furtar, surripiar.

pilgrim, *n.* peregrino -na,
romeiro -ra.

pilgrimage, *n.* peregrinação *f.*

pill, *n.* pílula *f.*

pillage, *vb.* pilhar, saquear.

pillar, *n.* pilar *m.*

pillow, *n.* travesseiro *m.* **p.
case,** fronha *f.*

pilot, 1. *n.* piloto **2.** *vb.* pilotar.

pimiento, *n.* pimentão-doce *m.*

pimp, *n.* alcoviteiro, cafetão *m.*

pimple, *n.* espinha *f.*

pin, 1. *n.* alfinete *m.*; broche
m.; *(mech.)* pino *m.*; grampo
m. **2.** *vb.* prender.

pinch, 1. *n.* beliscão *m.*; (dab)
pitada *f.* **2.** *vb.* beliscar.

pine, *n.* pinho *m.*; (tree) pinheiro *m.* **p. cone,** pinha *f.*

pineapple, *n.* abacaxi *m.*, *(P.)*
ananás *m.*

ping-pong, *n.* pingue-pongue *m.*

pink, *adj.* cor-de-rosa.

pinnacle, *n.* pináculo, píncaro
m.

pint, *n.* quartilho *m.*

pioneer, *n.* pioneiro -ra.

pious, *adj.* pio, devoto.

pipe, *n.* cano, tubo *m.*; (smoking) cachimbo *m.*; *(mus.)*
flauta *f.*

piper, *n.* flautista *m.f.*

piracy, *n.* pirataria *f.*

pirate, *n.* pirata *m.*

Pisces, *n.* Peixes *m.pl.*

pistol, *n.* pistola *f.*

piston, *n.* pistão *m.*; êmbolo *m.*

pit, *n.* cova *f.*; mina *f.*; caroço *m.*

pitch, 1. *n.* piche *m.*; (slope) declive *m.*; tom *m.*; (ball) lançamento *m.* 2. *vb.* lançar. **p. in,** dar uma mãozinha.

pitcher, *vb.* cântaro, jarro *m.*

pitchfork, *n.* forcado *m.*

pitfall, *n.* armadilha *f.*; perigo *m.*

pith, *n.* medula *f.*

pitiful, *adj.* lamentável, lastimável.

pittance, *n.* ninharia, miséria *f.*

pity, 1. *n.* pena *f.*, dó *m.*; compaixão *f.* **it's a p.,** é pena; **what a p.!,** que pena! 2. *vb.* ter pena de.

pivot, *n.* pino, eixo, pivô *m.*

placard, *n.* cartaz *m.*

placate, *vb.* aplacar.

place, 1. *n.* lugar, local *m.* **take p.,** acontecer. 2. *vb.* colocar.

placement, *n.* colocação *f.*

placid, *adj.* plácido.

plagiarism, *n.* plágio *m.*

plagiarize, *vb.* plagiar.

plague, 1. *n.* peste, praga *f.* 2. *vb.* empestar; atormentar.

plain, 1. *adj.* simples; claro. **in p. clothes,** à paisana. 2. *n.* planície *f.*

plaintiff, *n.* queixoso -sa, querelante *m.f.*

plaintive, *adj.* lamentoso, plangente.

plan, 1. *n.* plano *m.*; projeto *m.* 2. *vb.* planejar; fazer planos.

plane, 1. *n.* plano *m.*; (tool) plaina *f.*; avião *m.* 2. *vb.* aplainar.

planet, *n.* planeta *m.*

planetarium, *n.* planetário *m.*

plank, *n.* prancha, tábua *f.*

planner, *n.* planejador -ra, projetista *m.f.*

plant, 1. *n.* planta *f.*; fábrica *f.* 2. *vb.* plantar.

plantation, *n.* fazenda *f.*; plantação *f.* **sugar p.,** engenho *m.*

planter, *n.* plantador -ra; fazendeiro -ra.

plaque, *n.* placa *f.*

plasma, *n.* plasma *m.*

plaster, *n.* reboco *m.*; gesso *m.*; (*med.*) plastro *m.*

plastic, *adj., n.* plástico *m.* **p. surgery,** (cirurgia) plástica *f.*

plate, *n.* prato *m.*; chapa *f.*; lâmina *f.*

plateau, *n.* planalto *m.*

platform, *n.* plataforma *f.*

platinum, *n.* platina *f.*

platitude, *n.* lugar-comum *m.*

Platonic, *adj.* platônico.

platoon, *n.* pelotão *m.*

platter, *n.* travessa *f.*

plaudit, *n.* aplauso *m.*

plausible, *adj.* plausível.

play, 1. *n.* brincadeira *f.*; jogo *m.*; (*theat.*) peça *f.* 2. *vb.* brincar; (game) jogar; (instrument) tocar; (*theat.*) representar, fazer o papel de.

player, *n.* jogador -ra; (*mus.*) músico *m.*; (*theat.*) ator *m.*, atriz *f.*

playful, *adj.* brincalhão.

playground, *n.* playground.

playmate, *n.* companheiro -ra de brinquedo.

playpen, *n.* cercadinho *m.*

playwright, *n.* teatrólogo -ga, dramaturgo *m.*

plaza, *n.* praça *f.*

plea, *n.* apelo *m.*, súplica *f.*; (*jur.*) declaração *f.*

plead, *vb.* suplicar; (*jur.*) declarar-se.

pleasant, *adj.* agradável; alegre.

please, 1. *vb.* agradar. **pleased to meet you,** muito prazer (em conhecê-lo -la). 2. *adv.* por favor. **p. . . . ,** faça o favor de.

pleasure, *n.* prazer *m.*, satisfação *f.*

pleat, 1. *n.* prega *f.* 2. *vb.* preguear.

plebiscite, *n.* plebiscito *m.*

pledge, 1. *n.* promessa *f.*, voto *m.*; sinal *m.* 2. *vb.* prometer; empenhar.

plentiful, *adj.* abundante.

plenty, *n.* abundância, fartura *f.* **p. of,** bastante.

plethora, *n.* pletora *f.*

pliable, *adj.* flexível.

pliers, *n.pl.* alicate *m.*

plight, *n.* apuro *m.*; sorte *f.*

plod, vb. caminhar com passos pesados.

plot, 1. n. lote m.; plano m.; conspiração, trama f.; (lit.) enredo m. **2.** vb. planejar; conspirar.

plow, 1. n. arado m., charrua f. **2.** vb. arar.

pluck, 1. n. coragem f. **2.** vb. colher; arrancar; depenar; (mus.) dedilhar.

plug, 1. n. tampão m.; bucha f.; (elec.) tomada f.; (sl.) anúncio m. **2.** vb. tapar; (elec.) ligar; (sl.) anunciar; (sl.) balear.

plum, n. ameixa f.

plumage, n. plumagem f.

plumb, 1. n. chumbo, prumo m. **2.** vb. sondar.

plumber, n. encanador m.

plumbing, n. encanamento m.

plume, n. pluma f.

plumed, adj. emplumado.

plummet, vb. precipitar-se.

plump, adj. rechonchudo.

plunder, 1. n. saque m. **2.** vb. saquear.

plunge, 1. n. mergulho m. **2.** vb. mergulhar.

pluperfect, adj., n. mais-que-perfeito m.

plural, adj., n. plural m.

pluralism, n. pluralismo m.

plurality, n. pluralidade f.

plus, prep. mais.

plush, adj. luxuoso.

plutonium, n. plutônio m.

ply, 1. n. camada f.; fio m. **2.** vb. (trade) exercer.

plywood, n. madeira compensada f.

pneumonia, n. pneumonia f.

poach, vb. caçar ilicitamente; (egg) escalfar.

pocket, 1. n. bolso m. **2.** vb. embolsar.

pocketbook, n. carteira f.

pocketknife, n. canivete m.

pod, n. vagem f.

podium, n. pódio m.; plataforma f.

poem, n. poema m.

poet, n. poeta m.

poetess, n. poetisa f.

poetic, adj. poético.

poetry, n. poesia f.

poignant, adj. comovente.

point, 1. n. (sharp) ponta f.; (place, issue) ponto m. **make a p. of,** fazer questão de. **2.** vb. apontar. **p. out,** assinalar.

pointed, adj. pontudo.

point of view, n. ponto-de-vista m.

pointless, adj. inútil.

poise, n. equilíbrio m.; serenidade f.

poison, 1. adj. venenoso. **2.** n. veneno m. **3.** vb. envenenar.

poisonous, adj. venenoso.

poke, 1. n. empurrão m.; cutucada f. **2.** vb. empurrar; cutucar.

poker, n. pôquer m.

Poland, n. Polônia f.

polar, adj. polar.

pole, n. vara f.; poste m.; (geog.) pólo m.

Pole, n. polonês -nesa.

polemic, 1. adj. polêmico. **2.** n. polêmica f.

police, n. polícia f.

policeman, n. policial, guarda m.

policy, n. política f.; (insurance) apólice f.

polio, n. poliomielite f., pólio m.

polish, 1. n. polimento m.; lustre m. **shoe p.,** graxa f. **2.** vb. polir; engraxar.

Polish, adj., n. polonês -nesa.

polite, adj. polido, cortês.

politeness, n. polidez, cortesia f.

political, adj. político.

politician, n. político -ca.

politics, n. política f.

polka, n. polca f. **p. dot,** bolinha f.

poll, n. enquete f.; levantamento m.; (pl.) urnas f.pl.

pollen, n. pólen m.

polliwog, n. girino m.

pollute, vb. poluir.

pollution, n. poluição f.

polyglot, n. poliglota m.f.

polygon, n. polígono m.

pomade, n. pomada f.

pome, n. pomo m.

pomegranate, n. romã f.

pomp, n. pompa f.

pompous, adj. pomposo.

poncho, n. poncho m.

pond, n. lago pequeno m.

ponder, vb. ponderar.

pontiff, n. pontífice m.

pontoon, n. pontão m.

pony, n. pônei m.

pool, n. poça f.; lago pequeno m.; (game) sinuca f.; (group) pool m. **swimming p.,** piscina f.

poor, 1. adj. pobre; (quality) ruim. **p. thing!,** coitado -da! **2.** n.pl. os pobres.

pop, 1. n. estouro m.; estalo m. **2.** vb. estourar; pipocar.

popcorn, n. pipoca f.

pope, n. papa m.

poppy, n. papoula f.

populace, n. povo m., ralé f.

popular, adj. popular.

popularity, n. popularidade f.

popularize, vb. popularizar.

populate, vb. povoar.

population, n. população f.

porcelain, n. porcelana f.

porch, n. varanda f.

porcupine, n. porco-espinho m.

pore, n. poro m.

pork, n. carne de porco f. **p. chop,** costeleta de porco m.

pornography, n. pornografia f.

porous, adj. poroso.

porpoise, n. toninha f.; boto m.

porridge, n. papa f., mingau m.

port, n. porto m.; (naut.) bombordo m.; vinho do Porto m.

portable, adj. portátil.

portal, n. portal m.

portend, vb. prenunciar.

portent, n. portento, presságio m.

porter, n. carregador m.

portfolio, n. pasta f.

porthole, n. vigia f.

portion, n. porção f.

portly, adj. corpulento.

portrait, n. retrato m.

portray, vb. retratar.

portrayal, n. caracterização f., retrato m.

Portugal, n. Portugal m.

Portuguese, adj., n. português -sa.

pose, 1. n. pose f. **2.** vb. posar. **p. as,** fazer-se passar por.

position, n. posição f.; (job) posto m.; (opening) vaga f.

positive, adj. positivo; (certain) certo.

possess, vb. possuir.

possession, n. possessão f.; posse f.

possessive, adj. possessivo.

possibility, n. possibilidade f.

possible, adj. possível.

possum, n. gambá m.f.

post, 1. n. (pole) poste m.; (place, job) posto m.; correio m. **2.** vb. pregar, afixar; (station, mail) postar.

postage, n. porte m.; postagem f. **p. stamp,** selo m.

postal, adj. postal.

postbox, n. caixa postal f.

postcard, n. cartão postal, postal m.

poster, n. cartaz, pôster m.

posterior, 1. adj. posterior. **2.** n. traseiro m.

posterity, n. posteridade f.

posthumous, adj. póstumo.

postman, n. carteiro m.

postmark, 1. n. carimbo do correio m. **2.** vb. carimbar.

post office, n. correio m.

post-office box, n. caixa postal f.

postpone, vb. pospor, adiar.

postponement, n. adiamento m.

postscript, n. pós-escrito m.

posture, n. postura f.

pot, n. pote m.; (cooking) panela f.; (cards) bolo m.; (sl.) (marijuana) maconha f.

potable, adj. potável.

potato, n. batata f.

potbelly, n. pança f.

potent, adj. potente.

potential, adj., n. potencial m.

potion, n. poção f.

potter, n. oleiro m.

pottery, n. olaria, cerâmica f.

pouch, n. bolsa f. **mail p.,** malote m.

poultry, n. aves domésticas f.pl.

pounce on, vb. lançar-se sobre.

pound, 1. n. libra f. **p. sterling,** libra esterlina f. **2.** vb. bater (em) com força.

pour, vb. derramar, verter; servir; fluir; chover muito.

pout, vb. fazer beiço, amuar.

poverty, n. pobreza f.

powder, *n.* pó *m.* ; (gun) pólvora *f.*

powdered, *adj.* em pó.

power, 1. *adj.* mecânico, elétrico. **2.** *n.* poder *m.* ; potência *f.* ; (electric) energia *f.* **in p.,** no poder.

powerful, *adj.* poderoso.

power of attorney, *n.* procuração *f.*

power plant, *n.* usina elétrica *f.*

practical, *adj.* prático. **p. joke,** peça. partida *f.*

practice, 1. *n.* prática *f.* ; costume *m.* **2.** *vb.* praticar; treinar; ensaiar; (profession) exercer.

practiced, *adj.* experiente.

practitioner, *n.* praticante *m.f.* ; facultativo *m.*

pragmatic, *adj.* pragmático.

pragmatism, *n.* pragmatismo *m.*

Prague, *n.* Praga.

prairie, *n.* campina *f.*

praise, 1. *n.* elogio, louvor *m.* , louvação *f.* **2.** *vb.* elogiar, louvar.

praiseworthy, *adj.* louvável.

prance, *vb.* cabriolar; empertigar-se.

prank, *n.* peça, partida *f.*

prawn, *n.* pitu *m.*

pray, *vb.* rezar; rogar.

prayer, *n.* oração, reza, prece *f.*

pre-, *pref.* pré-.

preach, *vb.* pregar.

preacher, *n.* pregador -ra.

preamble, *n.* preâmbulo *m.*

precarious, *adj.* precário.

precaution, *n.* precaução *f.*

precede, *vb.* preceder.

precedence, *n.* precedência *f.*

precedent, *n.* precedente *m.*

preceding, *adj.* precedente.

precept, *n.* preceito *m.*

precinct, *n.* recinto *m.* ; distrito policial *m.*

precious, *adj.* precioso.

precipice, *n.* precipício *m.*

precipitate, 1. *adj.* precipitado. **2.** *vb.* precipitar.

precipitous, *adj.* íngreme; precipitado.

precise, *adj.* preciso.

precision, *n.* precisão *f.*

preclude, *vb.* impedir; evitar.

precocious, *adj.* precoce.

precursor, *n.* precursor -ra.

predatory, *adj.* predatório; de rapina.

predecessor, *n.* predecessor -ra, antecessor -ra.

predicament, *n.* dificuldade *f.* , apuro *m.*

predicate, 1. *n.* predicado *m.* **2.** *vb.* afirmar.

predict, *vb.* predizer, prever.

prediction, *n.* profecia *f.* ; prognóstico *m.*

predispose, *vb.* predispor.

predominance, *n.* predominância *f.* , predomínio *m.*

predominant, *adj.* predominante.

predominate, *vb.* predominar.

preeminent, *adj.* preeminente.

pre-fab, *adj.* pré-fabricado.

preface, 1. *n.* prefácio *m.* **2.** *vb.* prefaciar.

prefer, *vb.* preferir.

preferable, *adj.* preferível.

preference, *n.* preferência *f.*

prefix, *n.* prefixo *m.*

pregnancy, *n.* gravidez *f.*

pregnant, *adj.* grávida, prenhe.

prejudice, 1. *n.* preconceito *m.* **2.** *vb.* prejudicar.

prejudicial, *adj.* prejudicial.

preliminary, *adj.* preliminar.

prelude, *n.* prelúdio *m.*

premature, *adj.* prematuro.

premeditate, *vb.* premeditar.

premier, *n.* primeiro-ministro *m.*

premiere, 1. *n.* estréia *f.* **2.** *vb.* estrear.

premise, *n.* premissa *f.*

premium, *n.* prêmio *m.*

premonition, *n.* pressentimento *m.*

preoccupation, *n.* preocupação *f.*

preoccupy, *vb.* preocupar.

preparation, *n.* preparação *f.* , preparativo *m.*

preparatory, *adj.* preparatório.

prepare, *vb.* preparar(-se).

preponderance, *n.* preponderância *f.*

preposition, *n.* preposição *f.*

preposterous, *adj.* absurdo.

prerogative, *n.* prerrogativa *f.*

Presbyterian, *adj., n.* presbiteriano -na.

prescribe, *vb.* prescrever; *(med.)* receitar.

prescription, *n.* prescrição *f.*; *(med.)* receita *f.*

presence, *n.* presença *f.*

present, 1. *adj.* presente, atual. **2.** *n.* (now, gift) presente *m.* **at p.,** atualmente; **for the p.,** por enquanto. **3.** *vb.* apresentar.

presentation, *n.* apresentação *f.*

present-day, *adj.* atual.

presently, *adv.* agora; daqui a pouco.

preservation, *n.* preservação, conservação *f.*

preservative, *adj., n.* preservativo *m.*

preserve, 1. *n.* compota, conserva *f.*; (game) coutada *f.* **2.** *vb.* preservar, conservar; fazer conservas.

preside, *vb.* presidir.

presidency, *n.* presidência *f.*

president, *n.* presidente *m.f.*

presidential, *adj.* presidencial.

press, 1. *(mech.)* prensa *f.*; (printing) prelo *m.*; (newspapers) imprensa *f.* **2.** *vb.* apertar; pressionar; (iron) passar a ferro; urgir.

press conference, *n.* entrevista coletiva *f.*

pressing, *adj.* urgente.

pressure, 1. *n.* pressão *f.* **p. cooker,** panela de pressão *f.* **2.** *vb.* pressionar.

prestige, *n.* prestígio *m.*

prestigious, *adj.* prestigioso.

presume, *vb.* supor; presumir.

presumption, *n.* suposição *f.*; presunção *f.*

presumptuous, *adj.* presunçoso.

presuppose, *vb.* pressupor.

pretend, *vb.* fingir(-se), fazer de conta. **p. to,** ter aspirações a.

pretender, *n.* pretendente *m.f.*

pretense, *n.* fingimento *m.*; pretensão *f.*

pretension, *n.* pretensão *f.*; presunção *f.*

pretentious, *adj.* pretensioso, presunçoso.

preterite, *adj.* pretérito.

pretext, *n.* pretexto *m.*

pretty, *adj.* bonito, lindo.

prevail, *vb.* prevalecer.

prevailing, prevalent, *adj.* predominante.

prevaricate, *vb.* mentir.

prevent, *vb.* impedir, evitar; prevenir.

prevention, *n.* prevenção *f.*

preventive, preventative, *adj.* preventivo.

preview, *n.* pré-estréia *f.*

previous, *adj.* prévio.

prey, 1. *n.* presa *f.* **2.** *vb.* **p. on,** apresar; vitimar; afligir.

price, *n.* preço *m.*

priceless, *adj.* sem preço, inestimável.

prick, 1. *n.* alfinetada *f.*; picada *f.* **2.** *vb.* alfinetar; picar.

pride, *n.* orgulho *m.*

priest, *n.* sacerdote, padre *m.*

priestess, *n.* sacerdotisa *f.*

priesthood, *n.* sacerdócio *m.*

priestly, *adj.* sacerdotal.

prim, *adj.* meticuloso; afetado; reservado.

primary, *adj.* primário; principal.

primate, *n. (zool.)* primata *m.*; *(eccles.)* primaz *m.*

prime, 1. *adj.* primeiro; principal. **p. time,** horário nobre *m.* **2.** *n.* flor *f.*

prime minister, *n.* primeiro-ministro *m.*

primer, *n.* cartilha *f.*

primitive, *adj.* primitivo.

prince, *n.* príncipe *m.*

princess, *n.* princesa *f.*

principal, 1. *adj.* principal. **2.** *n.* diretor *m.*; *(com.)* principal *m.*

principle, *n.* princípio *m.*

print, 1. *n.* tipo *m.*, letra *f.*; (picture) estampa *f.*; impresso *m.*; (pattern) estampado *m.*; *(phot.)* cópia *f.* **2.** *vb.* imprimir; publicar; escrever em letra de imprensa.

printed matter, *n.* impressos *m.pl.*

printer, *n.* impressor *m.*; (machine) impressora *f.*

printing, *n.* impressão, tiragem *f.* **p. press,** prelo *m.*

print shop, *n.* tipografia, gráfica *f.*

prior, *adj.* prévio.

priority, *n.* prioridade *f.*

prism, *n.* prisma *m.*

prison, *n.* prisão *f.*

prisoner, *n.* preso -sa, prisioneiro -ra.

privacy, *n.* privacidade *f.*; indevassabilidade *f.*

private, 1. *adj.* privado, privativo; particular; indevassável. **2.** *n.* soldado raso *m.*

privilege, *n.* privilégio *m.*

privileged, *adj.* privilegiado.

privy, *n.* privada *f.*

prize, 1. *n.* prêmio *m.* **2.** *vb.* prezar, apreciar.

probability, *n.* probabilidade *f.*

probable, *adj.* provável.

probate, 1. *n.* validação (de testamento) *f.* **2.** *vb.* validar (testamento).

probation, *n.* provação *f.*; sursis *m.*, suspensão condicional da pena *f.*

probe, 1. *n.* sonda *f.*; tenta *f.* **2.** *vb.* sondar, investigar.

problem, *n.* problema *m.*

problematic, *adj.* problemático.

procedure, *n.* procedimento *m.*

proceed, *vb.* prosseguir; proceder.

proceedings, *n.pl.* reunião *f.*; atas *f.pl.*

proceeds, *n.pl.* produto, lucro, rendimento *m.*

process, 1. *n.* processo *m.* **2.** *vb.* processar.

procession, *n.* procissão *f.*

proclaim, *vb.* proclamar.

proclamation, *n.* proclamação *f.*

procrastinate, *vb.* procrastinar.

procreate, *vb.* procriar.

procure, *vb.* obter; alcovitar.

prod, 1. *n.* aguilhada *f.*; espeto *m.*; cutucada *f.* **2.** *vb.* aguilhoar; cutucar; incitar.

prodigal, *adj., n.* pródigo *m.*

prodigy, *n.* prodígio *m.*

produce, 1. *n.* produtos agrícolas *m.pl.* **2.** *vb.* produzir.

producer, *n.* produtor -ra.

product, *n.* produto *m.*

production, *n.* produção *f.*

productive, *adj.* produtivo.

productivity, *n.* produtividade *f.*

profane, 1. *adj.* profano *f.* **2.** *vb.* profanar.

profanity, *n.* profanidade *f.*

profess, *vb.* professar.

profession, *n.* profissão *f.*

professional, *adj., n.* profissional *m.f.*

professor, *n.* professor -ra; catedrático *m.*

proficiency, *n.* proficiência *f.*

proficient, *adj.* proficiente.

profile, 1. *n.* perfil *m.* **2.** *vb.* perfilar.

profit, 1. *n.* proveito *m.*; vantagem *f.*; lucro *m.* **2.** *vb.* aproveitar a. **p. by,** aproveitar-se de; lucrar com.

profitable, *adj.* proveitoso; vantajoso; lucrativo.

profiteer, 1. *n.* explorador -ra. **2.** *vb.* explorar.

profligate, *adj.* pródigo; libertino.

profound, *adj.* profundo.

progeny, *n.* progênie *f.*

prognosis, *n.* prognóstico *m.*

program, 1. *n.* programa *m.* **2.** *vb.* programar.

progress, 1. *n.* progresso *m.* **2.** *vb.* progredir.

progressive, *adj.* progressivo.

prohibit, *vb.* proibir.

prohibition, *n.* proibição *f.*

project, 1. *n.* projeto *m.* **2.** *vb.* projetar.

projectile, *n.* projétil, projetil *m.*

projection, *n.* projeção *f.*

projector, *n.* projetor *m.*

proletarian, *adj., n.* proletário -ria.

proletariat, *n.* proletariado *m.*

proliferate, *vb.* proliferar.

prolific, *adj.* prolífico.

prologue, *n.* prólogo *m.*

prolong, *vb.* prolongar.

promenade, 1. *n.* passeio *m.* **2.** *vb.* passear.

prominent, *adj.* proeminente.

promiscuous, *adj.* promíscuo.

promise, 1. *n.* promessa *f.* **2.** *vb.* prometer.

Promised Land, *n.* Terra da Promissão *f.*

promote, *vb.* promover.

promotion, *n.* promoção *f.*

prompt, 1. *adj.* pronto; rápido. **2.** *vb.* estimular; apontar.

promulgate, *vb.* promulgar.

prone, *adj.* de bruços; propenso.

prong, *n.* dente *m.*; ponta *f.*

pronoun, *n.* pronome *m.*

pronounce, *vb.* pronunciar.

pronouncement, *n.* pronunciamento *m.*

pronunciation, *n.* pronúncia *f.*

proof, *n.* prova *f.*

proofread, *vb.* corrigir (provas).

prop, 1. *n.* apoio *m.*, escora *f.* **2.** *vb.* apoiar, escorar.

propaganda, *n.* propaganda *f.*

propagate, *vb.* propagar(-se).

propel, *vb.* propulsar, propelir.

propeller, *n.* hélice *f.*

propensity, *n.* tendência, propensão *f.*

proper, *adj.* próprio. apropriado; correto.

property, *n.* propriedade *f.*

prophecy, *n.* profecia *f.*

prophesy, *vb.* profetizar.

prophet, *n.* profeta *m.*

prophetic, *adj.* profético.

propitious, *adj.* propício.

proponent, *n.* proponente *m.f.*

proportion, *n.* proporção *f.*

proportional, proportionate, *adj.* proporcional, proporcionado.

proposal, *n.* proposta *f.*

propose, *vb.* propor. **p. to,** propor-se; propor casamento a.

proposition, *n.* proposição, proposta *f.*

proprietor, *n.* proprietário -ria, dono -na.

propriety, *n.* correção *f.*, decoro *m.*

prorate, *vb.* ratear.

prosaic, *adj.* prosaico.

proscribe, *vb.* proscrever.

prose, *n.* prosa *f.*

prosecute, *vb.* processar.

prosecution, *n.* processamento *m.*, acusação *f.*

prospect, *n.* perspectiva *f.*; esperança *f.*

prosper, *vb.* prosperar.

prosperity, *n.* prosperidade *f.*

prosperous, *adj.* próspero.

prostitute, 1. *n.* prostituta *f.* **2.** *vb.* prostituir.

prostitution, *n.* prostituição *f.*

prostrate, 1. *adj.* prostrado. **2.** *vb.* prostrar.

protagonist, *n.* protagonista *m.f.*

protect, *vb.* proteger.

protection, *n.* proteção *f.*; amparo *m.*

protector, *n.* protetor -ra.

protégé, *n.* protegido -da.

protein, *n.* proteína *f.*.

protest, 1. *n.* protesto *m.* **2.** *vb.* protestar.

protestant, *adj., n.* protestante *m.f.*

protocol, *n.* protocolo *m.*

protract, *vb.* prolongar.

protrude, *vb.* projetar-se.

protuberance, *n.* protuberância *f.*

proud, *adj.* orgulhoso; arrogante.

prove, *vb.* provar, comprovar.

proverb, *n.* provérbio, ditado *m.*

proverbial, *adj.* proverbial.

provide, *vb.* fornecer, proporcionar.

provided that, *conj.* contanto que.

providence, *n.* providência *f.*

province, *n.* província *f.*

provincial, *adj.* provinciano.

provision, *n.* provisão *f.*; abastecimento *m.*; *(pl.)* providências; (supplies) mantimentos *m.pl.*

provisional, *adj.* provisório.

provocative, *adj.* provocante.

provoke, *vb.* provocar.

prowess, *n.* heroísmo *m.*; destreza *f.*

prowl, *vb.* rondar.

proximity, *n.* proximidade *f.*

proxy, *n.* procuração *f.*; delegado *m.*

prudence, *n.* prudência *f.*

prudent, *adj.* prudente.

prudish, *adj.* pudico, puritano.

prune, 1. *n.* ameixa seca *f.* **2.** *vb.* podar.

pry, *vb.* abrir/mover com alavanca; intrometer-se.

psalm, *n.* salmo *m.*

pseudonym, *n.* pseudônimo *m.*

psyche, *n.* psique *f.*

psychiatrist, *n.* psiquiatra *m.f.*

psychiatry, *n.* psiquiatria *f.*

psychic, 1. *n.* médium *m.f.* **2.** *adj.* psíquico.

psychoanalysis, *n.* psicanálise *f.*

psychological, *adj.* psicológico.

psychology, *n.* psicologia *f.*

psychotic, *adj., n.* psicótico *m.*

puberty, *n.* puberdade *f.*

pubic, *adj.* púbico.

public, *adj., n.* público *m.*

publication, *n.* publicação *f.*

publicity, *n.* publicidade *f.*

publicize, *vb.* divulgar, anunciar.

publish, *vb.* publicar, editar.

publisher, *n.* editor *m.*; (company) editora *f.*

pudding, *n.* pudim *m.*

puddle, *n.* poça *f.*, charco *m.*

Puerto Rican, *adj., n.* porto-riquenho -nha.

Puerto Rico, *n.* Porto Rico *m.*

puff, 1. *n.* baforada *f.*; sopro *m.*, lufada *f.* **2.** *vb.* soprar; arfar. **p. up,** inchar; envaidecer-se.

pull, 1. *n.* puxão, tirão *m.*; (*coll.*) pistolão *m.* **2.** *vb.* puxar, tirar; arrancar. **p. for,** torcer por; **p. through,** sarar.

pulley, *n.* polia, roldana *f.*

pulp, *n.* polpa *f.*; massa *f.*

pulpit, *n.* púlpito *m.*

pulsate, *vb.* pulsar.

pulse, *vb.* pulso *m.*

pump, 1. *n.* bomba *f.* **2.** *vb.* bombear.

pumpkin, *n.* abóbora *f.*

pun, *n.* trocadilho *m.*

punch, 1. *n.* (hole) punção *f.*; furador *m.*; (sock) soco *m.*; (drink) ponche *m.* **2.** *vb.* (hole) furar; (sock) esmurrar.

punch bowl, *n.* poncheira *f.*

punctual, *adj.* pontual.

punctuate, *vb.* pontuar.

punctuation, *n.* pontuação *f.*

puncture, 1. *n.* punctura *f.*; furo *m.* **2.** *vb.* furar.

pungent, *adj.* pungente, picante.

punish, *vb.* castigar.

punishment, *n.* castigo *m.*

punitive, *adj.* punitivo.

puny, *adj.* fraco, débil.

pup, *n.* filhote *m.*

pupil, *n.* aluno -na; (eye) pupila *f.*

puppet, *n.* títere, fantoche *m.*; boneco -ca.

puppeteer, *n.* titereiro -ra, titeriteiro -ra.

puppy, *n.* filhote *m.*

purchase, 1. *n.* compra *f.* **2.** *vb.* comprar.

pure, *adj.* puro.

purée, *n.* purê *m.*

purge, 1. *n.* purga *f.*; (*polit.*) depuração *f.* **2.** *vb.* purgar; depurar.

purify, *vb.* purificar.

puritanical, *adj.* puritano.

purity, *n.* pureza *f.*

purloin, *vb.* furtar, roubar.

purple, *adj.* roxo; purpúreo.

purport, 1. *n.* significado *m.* **2.** *vb.* significar.

purpose, *n.* propósito *m.* **on p.,** de propósito.

purr, 1. *n.* ronrom *m.* **2.** *vb.* ronronar.

purse, *n.* bolsa *f.*

pursue, *vb.* perseguir.

pursuit, *n.* perseguição, caça *f.*

pus, *n.* pus *m.*

push, 1. *n.* empurrão *m.*; impulso *m.* **2.** *vb.* empurrar.

put, *vb.* pôr, botar; colocar. **p. away,** guardar; **p. in,** meter; **p. off,** adiar; **p. on,** vestir; **p. out,** apagar; incomodar; **p. up with,** agüentar.

putty, *n.* betume *m.*, massa *f.*

puzzle, 1. *n.* enigma *m.*; quebra-cabeça *m.* **2.** *vb.* deixar perplexo.

pyramid, *n.* pirâmide *f.*

Q

quack, 1. *n.* grasnada *f.*; medicastro *m.* **2.** *vb.* grasnar.

quadrant, *n.* quadrante *m.*

quadraphonic, *adj.* quadrafônico.

quadrille, *n.* quadrilha *f.*

quadruple, *vb.* quadruplicar.

quagmire, *n.* atoleiro *m.*

quail, *n.* codorna, codorniz *f.*

quaint, *adj.* curioso; arcaico.

quake, 1. *n.* terremoto *m.* **2.** *vb.* tremer.

qualification, *n.* qualificação *f.*; requisito *m.*

qualified, *adj.* qualificado, capacitado.

qualify, n. qualificar(-se).
qualitative, adj. qualitativo.
quality, n. qualidade f.
qualm, n. apreensão f., escrúpulo m.
quandary, n. incerteza f.
quantitative, adj. quantitativo.
quantity, n. quantidade f.
quarantine, n. quarentena f.
quarrel, 1. n. disputa f. **2.** vb. disputar.
quarry, n. pedreira, canteira f.; presa f.
quart, n. quarta f.
quarter, n. quarto m.; trimestre m.; bairro m.; (pl.) alojamentos m.pl.
quarterly, adj. trimestral.
quartet, n. quarteto m.
quartz, n. quartzo m.
quash, vb. anular, suprimir.
quatrain, n. quadra f.
quaver, vb. tremer.
quay, n. cais m.
queasy, adj. enjoado, nauseabundo.
queen, n. rainha f.
queer, adj. esquisito.
quell, vb. subjugar, sufocar.
quench, vb. saciar, matar.
query, 1. n. pergunta f. **2.** vb. perguntar; questionar.
quest, n. busca, demanda f.
question. 1. n. pergunta f.; questão f.; **q. mark,** ponto de interrogação m. **2.** vb. perguntar; questionar.
questionnaire, n. questionário m.
queue, 1. n. fila f.; (P.) bicha f. **2.** vb. fazer fila.
quibble, vb. disputar sobre ninharias.
quick, adj. rápido; vivo.
quicken, vb. acelerar, apressar.
quicksand, n. areia movediça f.
quiet, 1. adj. quieto; silencioso, calado. **3.** n. calma f.; silêncio m. **3.** vb. acalmar; silenciar. **keep q.,** calar-se.
quill, n. pena f.
quilt, n. colcha f.
quince, n. marmelo m.
quinine, n. quinina f.
quintessence, n. quinta-essência, quintessência f.
quintet, n. quinteto m.

quip, 1. n. gracejo m. **2.** vb. gracejar.
quirk, n. capricho, acidente m.
quit, vb. parar de; demitir-se.
quite, adv. muito, bastante.
quiver, 1. n. aljava f., carcás m. **2.** vb. tremer.
quixotic, adj. quixotesco.
quiz, 1. n. teste m., prova f. **2.** vb. examinar, testar.
quorum, n. quórum m.
quota, n. quota, cota f.
quotation, n. citação f.; (com.) cotação f. **q. marks,** aspas f.
quote, vb. citar; (com.) cotar.
quotient, n. quociente m.

R

rabbi, n. rabino m.
rabbit, n. coelho m.
rabble, n. turba f.; ralé f.
rabid, adj. raivoso, rábido.
rabies, n. raiva, hidrofobia f.
race, 1. n. raça f.; corrida f. **2.** vb. correr.
race track, n. pista de corrida f.; (horse) hipódromo m.
racial, adj. racial.
racism, n. racismo m.
rack, 1. n. prateleira f.; cabide m. **2.** vb. atormentar.
racket, n. (noise) barulho m.; (tennis) raqueta f.; (fraud) marmelada f.
radar, n. radar m.
radiance, n. brilho m.
radiant, adj. radiante, brilhante.
radiate, vb. radiar, irradiar.
radiation, n. radiação f.
radiator, n. radiador m.
radical, adj., n., radical m.f.
radio, n. rádio m.; (station) rádio f.
radioactive, adj. radioativo.
radio amateur, n. radioamador m.
radio announcer, n. locutor de rádio m.
radiography, n. radiografia f.
radio listener, n. radiouvinte m.f.
radiology, n. radiologia f.
radio station, n. estação de rádio, emissora f.

radish, *n.* rabanete *m.*

radium, *n.* rádio *m.*

radius, *n.* raio *m.*; *(anat.)* rádio *m.*

raffle, 1. *n.* rifa *f.* **2.** *vb.* rifar.

raft, *n.* jangada, balsa *f.*

rafter, *n.* caibro *m.*

rag, *n.* trapo *m.*

ragamuffin, *n.* maltrapilho *m.*

rage, 1. *n.* raiva *f.* **2.** *vb.* enfurecer-se.

ragged, *adj.* esfarrapado; desigual.

raid, 1. *n.* reide *m.*; batida policial *f.* **2.** *vb.* invadir, atacar.

rail, 1. *n.* barra *f.*; *(railroad)* trilho *m.* **by r.,** por via férrea. **2.** *vb.* **r. at/against,** denunciar.

railroad, *n.* estrada de ferro *f.*

rain, 1. *n.* chuva *f.* **2.** *vb.* chover.

rainbow, *n.* arco-íris *m.*

raincoat, *n.* impermeável *m.*

rainfall, *n.* precipitação *f.*

rainy, *adj.* chuvoso.

raise, 1. *n.* aumento *m.* **2.** *vb.* levantar; aumentar.

raisin, *n.* passa *f.*

rake, 1. *n.* ancinho *m.*; libertino *m.* **2.** *vb.* limpar com ancinho.

rally, 1. *n.* comício *m.*; *(car)* rali *m.* **2.** *vb.* reunir-se.

ram, *n.* carneiro *m.*

ramble, *vb.* divagar.

rambunctious, *adj.* desordeiro.

ramification, *n.* ramificação *f.*

ramp, *n.* rampa *f.*

rampage, *n.* acesso de violência *m.*

rampant, *adj.* desenfreado, solto.

rampart, *n.* baluarte *m.*

ramshackle, *adj.* decrépito.

ranch, *n.* fazenda *f.*

rancher, *n.* fazendeiro -ra.

rancid, *adj.* rançoso.

rancor, *n.* rancor *m.*

random, *adj.* fortuito; randômico. **at r.,** ao acaso.

range, *n.* extensão *f.*, alcance *m.*; fogão *m.*; cordilheira *f.*; pastagem *f.* **at close r.,** à queima-roupa. *vb.* percorrer; estender-se.

rank, 1. *adj.* rançoso. **2.** *n.* fileira *f.*; classe social *f.*; posto *m.* **3.** *vb.* classificar; ocupar.

ransack, *vb.* saquear.

ransom, 1. *n.* resgate *m.* **2.** *vb.* resgatar.

rant, *vb.* arengar; falar extravagantemente.

rap, 1. *n.* golpe brusco *m.* **2.** *vb.* bater.

rape, 1. *n.* violentação *f.*, estupro *m.* **2.** *vb.* violentar, estuprar.

rapid, 1. *adj.* rápido. **2.** *n.pl.* rápido *m.*, cachoeira *f.*

rapport, *n.* afinidade *f.*

rapprochement, *n.* reconciliação *f.*

rapture, *n.* êxtase *m.*

rare, *adj.* raro; *(meat)* mal passado.

rarity, *n.* raridade *f.*

rascal, *n.* patife *m.*, pilantra *m.f.*

rash, 1. *adj.* precipitado. **2.** *n.* erupção *f.*

raspberry, *n.* framboesa *f.*

rat, *n.* rato *m.*

rate, 1. *n.* velocidade *f.*; taxa *f.*; preço *m.*; tarifa *f.*; razão *f.* **at any r.,** de qualquer forma; **at the r. of,** à razão de. **2.** *vb.* avaliar; ser classificado.

rather, *adv.* antes, preferivelmente; ao contrário; bastante. **r. than,** em vez de; **I would/had r.,** preferiria.

ratify, *vb.* ratificar.

rating, *n.* avaliação *f.*; classificação *f.*

ratio, *n.* razão, proporção *f.*

ration, 1. *n.* ração *f.* **2.** *vb.* racionar.

rational, *adj.* racional.

rationale, *n.* razão fundamental *f.*

rationalize, *vb.* racionalizar.

rationing, *n.* racionamento *m.*

rattle, *n.* chocalho *m.*; barulho *m.* **2.** *vb.* chocalhar; desconcertar.

rattlesnake, *n.* cascavel *f.*

raucous, *adj.* rouco; barulhento.

ravage, 1. *n.* ruína *f.* **2.** *vb.* destruir, arruinar.

rave, *vb.* delirar; elogiar extravagantemente.

raven, *n.* corvo *m.*

ravine, *n.* ravina *f.*

ravish, vb. estuprar; enlevar.

raw, adj. cru -a; inexperiente; obsceno. **r. material,** matéria-prima f.

ray, n. raio m.; (zool.) arraia f.

rayon, n. raiom m.

raze, vb. arrasar, demolir.

razor, n. navalha de barbear, gilete f.; barbeador elétrico m. **r. blade,** lâmina de barbear, gilete f.

razz, n. zombar (de).

re-, pref. re-.

reach, 1. n. alcance m. 2. vb. alcançar; estender(-se).

react, vb. reagir.

reaction, n. reação f.

reactionary, adj., n. reacionário, retrógrado m.

reactor, n. reator m.

read, vb. ler.

reader, n. leitor m.; livro de leitura m.

readily, adv. facilmente.

reading, n. leitura f.

ready, 1. adj. pronto. 2. vb. aprontar.

real, adj. real, verdadeiro.

real-estate, 1. adj. imobiliário. 2. n. bens imóveis m.pl.

realism, n. realismo m.

realistic, adj. realístico, realista.

reality, n. realidade f.

realize, vb. perceber, dar-se conta de; (accomplish) realizar; lucrar.

really, adv. realmente; de fato; mesmo.

realm, n. reino m.; campo m.

realtor, n. corretor de imóveis m.

ream, n. resma f.

reap, vb. ceifar, colher.

rear, 1. adj. posterior, traseiro. 2. n. retaguarda f.; parte traseira f. 3. vb. criar; levantar-se.

rear-view mirror, n. espelho retrovisor m.

reason, 1. n. razão f., motivo m. 2. vb. raciocinar.

reasonable, adj. razoável.

reassure, vb. acalmar, tranqüilizar.

rebate, n. abatimento m.; reembolso m.

rebel, 1. n. rebelde m.f. 2. vb. rebelar-se.

rebellion, n. rebelião f.; rebeldia f.

rebellious, adj. rebelde.

rebirth, n. renascimento m.

rebound, 1. n. ricochete m. 2. vb. ricochetear.

rebuff, 1. n. repulsa f. 2. vb. repulsar, rejeitar.

rebuke, 1. n. repreensão f. 2. vb. repreender.

rebuttal, n. refutação, réplica f.

recalcitrant, adj. recalcitrante.

recall vb. lembrar; fazer voltar.

recapitulate, vb. recapitular.

recede, vb. retroceder.

receipt, n. recibo m.; (receiving) recebimento m.; (pl.) rendimentos m.pl.

receive, vb. receber.

receiver, n. receptor m.

recent, adj. recente.

receptacle, n. receptáculo m.

reception, n. recepção f.; acolhida f.; (receiving) recebimento m.

receptionist, n. recepcionista m.f.

recess, n. recesso m.; recreio m.

recession, n. recessão f.

recipe, n. receita f.

recipient, n. receptor.

reciprocal, adj. recíproco.

recital, n. recital m.

recite, vb. recitar; declamar.

reckless, adj. imprudente.

reckon, vb. contar; calcular.

reclaim, vb. reformar; recuperar.

recline, vb. reclinar(-se), recostar(-se).

recluse, n. recluso m.

recognition, n. reconhecimento m.

recognize, vb. reconhecer.

recoil, 1. n. recuo m.; (rifle) coice m. 2. vb. recuar.

recollect, vb. recordar-se de.

recollection, n. memória f.; lembrança. f.

recommend, vb. recomendar.

recommendation, n. recomendação f.

recompense, 1. n. recompensa f. 2. vb. recompensar.

reconcile, vb. reconciliar.

recondite, *adj.* recôndito.

reconnaissance, *n.* reconhecimento *m.*

reconnoiter, *vb.* reconhecer.

record, 1. *n.* registro *m.*; menção *f.*; (sports) recorde *m.*; (phonograph) disco *m.*; *(pl.)* arquivos *m.pl.* 2. *vb.* registrar; mencionar; gravar.

record player, *n.* toca-discos *n.*, vitrola *f.*

recount, *vb.* relatar, contar.

recourse, *n.* recurso *m.*, apelação *f.*

recover, *vb.* recuperar; recuperar-se.

recovery, *n.* recuperação, convalescença *f.*

recreation, *n.* recreio *m.*, recreação *f.*

recrimination, *n.* recriminação *f.*

recruit, 1. *n.* recruta *m.f.* 2. *vb.* recrutar.

recruitment, *n.* recrutamento *m.*

rectangle, *n.* retângulo *m.*

rectify, *vb.* retificar.

rector, *n.* reitor *m.*

rectum, *n.* reto *m.*

recuperate, *vb.* recuperar-se.

recur, *vb.* repetir-se.

red, *adj.* vermelho.

Red Cross, *n.* Cruz Vermelha *f.*

redeem, *vb.* redimir; resgatar.

redeemer, *n.* redentor *m.*

redemption, *n.* redenção *f.*

red-handed, *adj.* em flagrante.

redhead, *n.* ruivo *m.*

redheaded, *adj.* ruivo.

red-light district, *n.* zona (de meretrício) *f.*

red pepper, *n.* pimenta malagueta *f.*; pimentão *m.*

redress, 1. *n.* reparação *f.* 2. *vb.* reparar, desagravar.

red tape, *n.* burocracia *f.*; papelada *f.*

reduce, *vb.* reduzir; emagrecer.

reduction, *n.* redução *f.*

redundant, *adj.* redundante.

reed, *n.* junco *m.*; *(mus.)* palheta *f.*

reef, *n.* recife, arrecife *m.*

reek, *vb.* tresandar.

reel, 1. *n.* bobina *f.*, carretel *m.*;

(film) rolo *m.*; (fishing) molinete *m.* 2. *vb.* enrolar; cambalear.

refer to, *vb.* referir-se a.

referee, *n.* árbitro, juiz *m.*

reference, *n.* referência *f.*; recomendação *f.* **r. book**, livro de consulta/referência *m.*

referendum, *n.* referendo, referendum *m.*

refill, 1. carga *f.* 2. *vb.* reabastecer.

refine, *vb.* refinar; aperfeiçoar.

refinement, *n.* refinamento *m.*; requinte *m.*; cultura *f.*

refinery, *n.* refinaria *f.*

reflect, *n.* refletir; reflexionar.

reflection, *n.* reflexo *m.*, reflexão *f.*

reflector, *n.* refletor *m.*

reflex, *n.* reflexo *m.*

reform, 1. *n.* reforma *f.* 2. *vb.* reformar(-se).

reformation, *n.* reformação *f.*; *(cap.)* Reforma *f.*

reformatory, *n.* reformatório *m.*

reformer, reformist, *n.* reformista *m.f.*

refrain, 1. *n.* refrão *m.*; estribilho *m.* 2. *vb.* abster-se.

refresh, *vb.* refrescar.

refreshment, *n.* refresco *m.*; *(pl.)* comes e bebes *m.pl.*

refrigerate, *vb.* refrigerar.

refrigerator, *n.* geladeira *f.*, refrigerador *m.*

refuge, *n.* refúgio *m.* **take r.**, refugiar-se.

refugee, *n.* refugiado *m.*

refund, 1. *n.* reembolso *m.* 2. *vb.* reembolsar.

refusal, *n.* recusa *f.*

refuse, 1. *n.* lixo *m.* 2. *vb.* recusar; negar-se (a).

refute, *vb.* refutar.

regain, *vb.* recobrar.

regal, *adj.* real, régio.

regard, 1. *n.* respeito *m.*; *(pl.)* lembranças *f.pl.* **with r. to**, a respeito de. 2. *vb.* considerar; respeitar.

regarding, *prep.* a respeito de.

regardless, 1. *adj.* desatento. 2. *adv.* de qualquer maneira. **r. of**, sem fazer caso de; apesar de.

regent, *n.* regente *m.*

regime, *n.* regime *m.*

regiment, 1. *n.* regimento *m.* **2.** *vb.* regimentar.

region, *n.* região *f.*

regional, *adj.* regional.

register, 1. *n.* registro *m.* **2.** *vb.* registrar(-se); matricular(-se).

registration, *n.* registro *m.* ; matrícula *f.*

registry, *n.* registro *m.* ; cartório *m.*

regret, 1. *n.* pesar *m.* ; remorso *m.* **2.** *vb.* lamentar; arrepender-se.

regular, *adj.* regular, normal.

regulate, *vb.* regular, regularizar.

regulation, *n.* regulamento *m.*

regurgitate, *n.* regurgitar.

rehabilitate, *vb.* reabilitar.

rehearsal, *n.* ensaio *m.*

rehearse, *vb.* ensaiar.

reign, 1. *n.* reinado *m.* **2.** *vb.* reinar.

reimburse, *vb.* reembolsar.

rein, 1. *n.* rédea *f.* **2.** *vb.* refrear.

reincarnation, *n.* reencarnação *f.*

reindeer, *n.* rena *f.*

reinforce, *vb.* reforçar.

reinforcement, *n.* reforço *m.*

reiterate, *vb.* reiterar.

reject, *vb.* rejeitar.

rejoice, *vb.* regozijar-se.

rejuvenate, *vb.* rejuvenescer.

relapse, 1. *n.* recaída *f.* **2.** *vb.* recair.

relate, *vb.* relatar, contar. **r. to,** relacionar-se (com); dar-se (bem) com.

relation, *n.* relação *f.* ; parentesco *m.* ; parente *m.f.* **in/with r. to,** com respeito a.

relationship, *n.* relação *f.* ; relacionamento *m.* ; parentesco *m.*

relative, 1. *adj.* relativo. **2.** *n.* parente *m.f.*

relativity, *n.* relatividade *f.*

relax, *vb.* descansar, descontrair-se; relaxar.

relaxation, *n.* descanso *m.* , descontração *f.*

relay, 1. *n.* revezamento *m.* ; retransmissão *f.* **2.** *vb.* retransmitir.

release, 1. *n.* libertação *f.* **2.** *vb.* soltar.

relegate, *vb.* relegar.

relent, *vb.* ceder.

relevant, *adj.* relevante.

reliability, *n.* confiança *f.* ; fidedignidade *f.*

reliable, *adj.* digno de confiança; fidedigno.

relic, *n.* relíquia *f.*

relief, *n.* alívio *m.* ; *(arch.)* relevo *m.*

relieve, *vb.* aliviar; revezar.

religion, *n.* religião *f.*

religious, *adj.* religioso.

relinquish, *vb.* renunciar.

relish, 1. *n.* sabor *m.* ; gosto *m.* tempero *m.* **2.** *vb.* gostar de.

reluctant, *adj.* relutante, hesitante.

rely, *vb.* **r. on,** confiar em; contar com; depender de.

remain, 1. *n.pl.* restos *m.pl.* **2.** *vb.* ficar; restar.

remainder, *n.* resto, restante *m.*

remark, 1. *n.* observação *f.* **2.** *vb.* observar.

remarkable, *adj.* notável.

remedial, *adj.* corretivo, curativo.

remedy, 1. *n.* remédio *m.* **2.** *vb.* remediar.

remember, *vb.* lembrar, lembrar-se de.

remembrance, *n.* lembrança *f.*

remind, *vb.* lembrar.

reminder, *n.* lembrança *f.* ; lembrete *m.*

reminisce, *vb.* relembrar.

remiss, *adj.* remisso, negligente.

remit, *vb.* remeter.

remittance, *n.* remessa *f.*

remnant, *n.* resto *m.* ; retalho *m.*

remorse, *n.* remorso *m.*

remote, *n.* remoto. **r. control,** controle remoto *m.*

removal, *n.* remoção *f.* ; afastamento *m.*

remove, *vb.* remover, tirar; afastar.

remunerate, *vb.* remunerar.

renaissance, *n.* renascimento *m* ; *(cap.)* Renascimento *m.* , Renascença *f.*

rend, *vb.* rasgar.

render, *vb.* entregar; tornar.

rendezvous, *n.* encontro *m.*

rendition, *n.* interpretação *f.*

renegade, *n.* renegado *m.*

renege, *vb.* roer a corda.

renew, *vb.* renovar; prorrogar.

renewal, *n.* renovação *f.*; prorrogação *f.*

renounce, *vb.* renunciar (a).

renovate, *vb.* renovar.

renown, *n.* renome *m.*

rent, 1. *n.* aluguel *m.* for r., aluga-se. **2.** *vb.* alugar.

rental, *n.* aluguel *m.*

renter, *n.* locatário *m.*

renunciation, *n.* renúncia *f.*

repair, 1. *n.* conserto *m.* **2.** *vb.* consertar.

reparation, *n.* reparação *f.*, reparo *m.*

repeal, 1. *n.* revogação *f.* **2.** *vb.* revogar, rescindir.

repeat, *vb.* repetir.

repel, *vb.* repelir.

repellent, *n.* repelente *m.*

repent, *vb.* arrepender-se.

repentance, *n.* arrependimento *m.*

repercussion, *n.* repercussão *f.*

repertoire, *n.* repertório *m.*

repetition, *n.* repetição *f.*

replace, *vb.* restituir; substituir.

replacement, *n.* restituição *f.*; substituição *f.*; substituto *m.*

replenish, *vb.* reabastecer.

replete, *adj.* repleto.

replica, *n.* réplica *f.*

reply, 1. *n.* resposta *f.* **2.** *vb.* responder.

report, 1. *n.* relatório *m.*; boato *m.*; notícia *f.*; reportagem *f.* r. card, boletim *m.* **2.** *vb.* informar; noticiar; denunciar; apresentar-se.

reporter, *n.* repórter *m.f.*

repose, 1. *n.* repouso *m.* **2.** *vb.* repousar.

repository, *n.* repositório *m.*

reprehend, *vb.* repreender.

represent, *vb.* representar.

representation, *n.* representação *f.*

representative, 1. *adj.* representativo. **2.** *n.* representante *m.f.*

repress, *vb.* reprimir, recalcar; oprimir.

repression, *n.* repressão *f.*, recalque *m.*

reprieve, *n.* comutação *f.*; indulto *m.*

reprimand, 1. *n.* reprimenda *f.* **2.** *vb.* repreender.

reprisal, *n.* represália *f.*

reproach, 1. *n.* reproche *m.* **2.** *vb.* reprochar.

reproduce, *vb.* reproduzir(-se).

reproduction, *n.* reprodução *f.*

reproof, *n.* censura *f.*

reptile, *n.* réptil *m.*

republic, *n.* república *f.*

republican, *adj.* *n.* republicano.

repudiate, *vb.* repudiar.

repugnant, *adj.* repugnante.

repulsive, *adj.* repulsivo.

reputable, *adj.* respeitável.

reputation, *n.* reputação *f.*

repute, 1. *n.* reputação *f.* **2.** *vb.* reputar.

request, *n.* pedido *m.* **2.** *vb.* pedir.

require, *vb.* requerer, exigir.

requirement, *n.* requisito *m.*, exigência *f.*

requisite, 1. *adj.* necessário. **2.** *n.* requisito *m.*

requisition, *n.* requisição *f.*

rerun, *n.* reprise *f.*

reschedule, *vb.* (debt) reescalonar.

rescind, *vb.* rescindir.

rescue, 1. *n.* salvamento *m.*, libertação *f.* **2.** *vb.* salvar, libertar.

research, 1. *n.* pesquisa, investigação *f.* **2.** *vb.* pesquisar, investigar.

researcher, *n.* pesquisador, investigador *m.*

resemblance, *n.* semelhança *f.*

resemble, *vb.* parecer-se com.

resent, *vb.* ressentir-se de.

resentful, *adj.* ressentido.

resentment, *m.* ressentimento *m.*

reservation, *n.* reserva *f.*

reserve, 1. *n.* reserva *f.* **2.** *vb.* reservar.

reservoir, *n.* reservatório *m.*

reside, *vb.* residir, morar.

residence, *n.* residência *f.*

resident, *n.* residente, habitante *m.f.*

residential, *adj.* residencial.

residue, *n.* resíduo *m.*

resign, *vb.* renunciar (a); demitir-se. **r. oneself,** resignar-se.
resignation, *n.* renúncia *f.*; resignação *f.*
resilient, *adj.* resiliente.
resin, *n.* resina *f.*
resist, *vb.* resistir (a).
resistance, *n.* resistência *f.*
resistant, *adj.* resistente.
resolute, *adj.* resoluto.
resolution, *n.* resolução *f.*
resolve, *vb.* resolver.
resonant, *adj.* ressonante.
resort, 1. *n.* recurso *m.*; estação de águas *f.*, lugar de vernaneio *m.* **2.** *vb.* **r. to,** recorrer a.
resound, *vb.* ressoar.
resource, *n.* recurso *m.*
respect, 1. *n.* respeito *m.* **w. r. to,** a respeito de. **2.** *vb.* respeitar.
respectable, *adj.* respeitável.
respectful, *adj.* respeitoso.
respective, *adj.* respectivo.
respiration, *n.* respiração *f.*
respite, *n.* pausa, trégua *f.*
respond, *vb.* responder.
response, *n.* resposta *f.*
responsibility, *n.* responsabilidade *f.*
responsible, *adj.* responsável.
responsive, *adj.* responsivo; receptivo.
rest, 1. *n.* descanso; *(mus.)* pausa *f.* **the r.,** o resto; os demais. **2.** *vb.* descansar; apoiar.
restaurant, *n.* restaurante *m.*
restitution, *n.* restituição *f.*
restless, *adj.* inquieto.
restoration, *n.* restauração *f.*; restituição *f.*
restore, *vb.* restaurar; restituir.
restrain, *vb.* restringir; refrear.
restraint, *n.* restrição *f.*; moderação *f.*
restrict, *vb.* restringir.
restriction, *n.* restrição *f.*
restroom, *n.* banheiro *m.*
result, 1. *n.* resultado *m.* **2.** *vb.* resultar.
resume, *vb.* recomeçar, prosseguir.
résumé, *n.* resumo *m.*
resurgence, *n.* ressurgimento *m.*
resurrect, *vb.* ressuscitar.

resurrection, *n.* ressurreição *f.*
resuscitate, *vb.* ressuscitar.
retail, *adv.* a varejo.
retailer, *n.* varejista *m.f.*
retain, *vb.* reter.
retaliate, *vb.* vingar-se; revidar.
retard, *vb.* retardar.
retarded, *adj.* retardado.
retention, *n.* retenção *f.*
reticence, *n.* reticência *f.*
reticent, *adj.* reticencioso.
retina, *n.* retina *f.*
retire, *vb.* retirar; deitar; (job) aposentar-se.
retirement, *n.* aposentadoria *f.*
retort, 1. *n.* réplica *f.* **2.** *vb.* retorquir.
retract, *vb.* retratar, desdizer.
retread, 1. *n.* pneu recauchutado *m.* **2.** *vb.* recauchutar.
retreat, 1. *n.* retirada *f.*; retiro *m.* **2.** *vb.* retirar-se.
retribution, *n.* retribuição *f.*
retrieve, *vb.* recuperar.
retroactive, *adj.* retroativo.
retrospect, *n.* **in r.,** retrospectivamente.
return, 1. *n.* volta *f.* **by r. mail,** à volta do correio. **2.** *vb.* voltar; devolver.
reunion, *n.* reunião *f.*
reveal, *vb.* revelar.
revel, 1. *n.* farra *f.* **2.** *vb.* farrear.
revelation, *n.* revelação *f.*; *(cap.)* Apocalipse *m.*
revelry, *n.* folguedo *m.*
revenge, *n.* vingança *f.* **get r.,** vingar-se.
revenue, *n.* rendimento *m.*
reverberate, *vb.* reverberar.
revere, *vb.* reverenciar.
reverence, *n.* reverência *f.*
reverend, *n.* reverendo *m.*
reverent, *adj.* reverente.
reverie, *n.* devaneio *m.*
reverse, 1. *adj.* inverso. **r. gear,** marcha à ré *f.* **2.** *n.* reverso; revés *m.* **3.** *vb.* inverter; revogar.
revert, *vb.* reverter.
review, 1. *n.* revisão, recapitulação *f.*; revista *f.* (book) resenha *f.* **2.** *vb.* rever, revisar; repassar; resenhar.
revise, *vb.* revisar.
revised, *adj.* revisto.

revision, *n.* revisão *f.*; edição revista *f.*

revival, *n.* renovação *f.*; revivescimento *m.*

revive, *vb.* ressuscitar; reviver.

revoke, *vb.* revocar, revogar.

revolt, 1. *n.* revolta *f.* **2.** *vb.* revoltar-se.

revolution, *n.* revolução *f.*

revolutionary, *adj., n.* revolucionário *m.*

revolutionize, *vb.* revolucionar.

revolve, *vb.* revolver, girar.

revolver, *n.* revólver *m.*

revolving, *adj.* giratório.

reward, 1. *n.* recompensa *f.* **2.** *vb.* recompensar.

rhapsody, *n.* rapsódia *f.*

rhea, *n.* ema *f.*, nhandu *m.*

rhetorical, *adj.* retórico.

rheumatism, *n.* reumatismo *m.*

rhinoceros, *n.* rinoceronte *m.*

rhubarb, *n.* ruibarbo *m.*

rhyme, 1. *n.* rima *f.*; verso *m.* **2.** *vb.* rimar.

rhythm, *n.* ritmo *m.*

rib, *n.* costela *f.*

ribbon, *n.* fita *f.*

rice, *n.* arroz *m.*

rich, *adj.* rico. **get r.,** enriquecer.

riches, *n.pl.* riquezas *f.pl.*

richness, *n.* riqueza *f.*

rickets, *n.* raquitismo *m.*

ricochet, 1. *n.* ricochete *m.* **2.** *vb.* richochetear.

rid, *vb.* v. **oneself of, get r. of,** livrar-se de; **be r. of,** estar livre de.

riddle, *n.* adivinha *f.*, enigma, quebra-cabeça *m.*

ride, 1. *n.* passeio (de carro, a cavalo, etc.); condução, carona *f.*; divertimento (em parque de diversões) *m.* **go for a r.,** dar um passeio. **2.** *vb.* andar, montar, ir.

rider, *n.* cavaleiro *m.*; passageiro *m.*

ridge, *n.* crista *f.*; (roof) cumeeira *f.*

ridicule, 1. *n.* escárnio *m.* **2.** *vb.* ridicularizar.

ridiculous, *adj.* ridículo, absurdo.

rife, *adj.* abundante. **r. with,** cheio de.

riffraff, *n.* ralé *f.*

rifle, **1.** *n.* espingarda *f.*, fuzil *m.* **2.** *vb.* pilhar.

rift, *n.* fenda *f.*; desavença *f.*

rig, 1. *n.* aparelho *m.*; carruagem *f.* **2.** *vb.* aparelhar; manipular.

right, 1. *adj.* reto; direito; correto, certo. **be r.,** ter razão **2.** *n.* direito *m.*; razão *f.*; lado direito *m.*, direita *f.* **to the r.,** à direita. **3.** *vb.* corrigir; endireitar. **4.** *adv.* certo; mesmo; à direita. **r. here,** aqui mesmo; **r. now,** agora mesmo; **all r.,** tudo bem; (está) certo.

righteous, *adj.* justo.

rightful, *adj.* legítimo.

rightist, *adj., n.* direitista *m.f.*

rightness, *n.* justiça, retidão *f.*

rigid, *adj.* rígido, rijo.

rigor, *n.* rigor *m.*

rigorous, *adj.* rigoroso.

rile, *vb.* irritar.

rim, *n.* borda *f.*; aba *f.*

rind, *n.* casca *f.*

ring, 1. *n.* anel *m.*; argola *f.*; toque *m.*; marca *f.*; roda *f.*; picadeiro *m.*; ringue *m.* **2.** *vb.* tocar; rodear.

rink, *n.* rinque *m.*

rinse, *vb.* enxaguar.

riot, *n.* desordem *f.*, motim *m.*

rip, 1. *n.* rasgo, rasgão *m.* **2.** *vb.* rasgar(-se), descoser(-se). **r. off,** roubar; tapear.

ripe, *adj.* maduro.

ripen, *vb.* amadurecer(-se).

ripoff, *n.* roubo *m.*; trapaça *f.*

ripple, 1. *n.* ondulação *f.*; encrespamento *m.* **2.** *vb.* ondular (-se); encrespar(-se).

rise, 1. *n.* subida *f.*; aumento *m.* **2.** *vb.* levantar-se; aumentar; rebelar-se; (sun) nascer.

risk, 1. *n.* risco, perigo *m.* **run a r.,** correr um risco, arriscar-se. **2.** *vb.* arriscar.

risky, *adj.* arriscado.

risqué, *adj.* picante.

rite, *n.* rito *m.*

ritual, 1. *adj.* ritual. **2.** *n.* rito *m.*

ritzy, *adj.* luxuoso, chique.

rival, 1. *n.* rival *m.f.* **2.** *vb.* rivalizar.

rivalry, *n.* rivalidade *f.*

river, *n.* rio *m.*

rivet, 1. *n.* rebite *m.* **2.** *vb.* rebitar; fixar.

roach, *n.* barata *f.*

road, *n.* estrada *f.*, caminho *m.*

roam, *vb.* vagar, errar.

roan, *adj., n.* ruão *m.*

roar, 1. *n.* rugido, bramido *m.* **2.** *vb.* rugir, bramar.

roast, 1. *adj., n.* assado *m.* **2.** *vb.* assar; torrar.

roast beef, *n.* rosbife *m.*

rob, *vb.* roubar.

robber, *n.* ladrão, gatuno *m.*

robbery, *n.* roubo, furto *m.*

robe, *n.* roupão *m.*; toga *f.*

robin, *n.* tordo *m.*

robot, *n.* robô *m.*

robust, *adj.* robusto.

rock, 1. *n.* pedra *f.*; rocha *f.*; (mus.) roque *m.* **2.** *vb.* balançar; embalar.

rocket, *n.* foguete *m.*

rocking chair, *n.* cadeira de balanço *f.*

rocky, *adj.* rochoso, pedregoso.

rod, *n.* vara *f.*; haste *f.*; barra *f.*

rodent, *n.* roedor *m.*

rogue, *n.* maroto *m.*

roguish, *adj.* maroto.

role, *n.* papel *m.* **play a r.,** fazer/desempenhar um papel.

roll, 1. *n.* rolo *m.*; rol *m.*, lista *f.*; jogo *m.*; pãozinho *m.* **call the r.,** fazer a chamada. **2.** *vb.* rolar, rodar. **r. up,** enrolar.

roller, *n.* rolo *m.* **r. coaster,** montanha russa *f.*

Roman, *adj., n.* romano *m.*

romance, 1. *adj.* românico, neolatino. **2.** *n.* romance *m.*

Romania, *n.* Romênia *f.*

Romanian, *adj., n.* romeno *m.*

romantic, *adj.* romântico.

romanticism, *n.* romantismo *m.*

Rome, *n.* Roma *f.*

romp, 1. *n.* travessura *f.* **2.** *vb.* brincar.

roof, *n.* telhado *m.*

rook, **1.** *n.* (chess) torre *f.* **2.** *vb.* trapacear.

room, *n.* **1.** compartimento *m.*; sala *f.*; lugar *m.* **2.** *vb.* hospedar-se.

roommate, *n.* companheiro de quarto *m.*

roomy, *adj.* espaçoso.

roost, *n.* poleiro *m.*

rooster, *n.* galo *m.*

root, 1. *n.* raiz *f.* **take r.,** arraigar-se. **2.** *vb.* **r. for,** torcer por/para.

rooter, *n.* torcedor *m.*

rope, *n.* corda *f.*

rosary, *n.* rosário *m.*

rose, *n.* rosa *f.* **r. bush,** roseira *f.*

roster, *n.* rol *m.*, lista *f.*

rostrum, *n.* tribuna *f.*

rosy, *adj.* cor-de-rosa.

rot, 1. *n.* podridão *f.* **2.** *vb.* apodrecer.

rotary, *adj.* giratório, rotativo.

rotate, *vb.* rodar, girar.

rotation, *n.* rotação *f.*; **crop r.,** rotação de culturas *f.*

rotten, *adj.* podre.

rotund, *adj.* rotundo.

rouge, *n.* ruge *m.*

rough, *adj.* áspero; duro; bruto; rude; aproximado.

roughneck, *n.* desordeiro *m.*

roulette, *n.* roleta *f.*

round, 1. *adj.* redondo. **r. trip,** viagem de ida e volta *f.* **2.** *n.* roda *f.*; (drinks) rodada *f.*; round *m.* **3.** *vb.* arredondar; dobrar.

roundness, *n.* redondeza *f.*

roundup, *n.* rodeio *m.*

rouse, *vb.* despertar.

rout, 1. *n.* derrota completa *f.* **2.** *vb.* derrotar decisivamente.

route, *n.* rota *f.*; roteiro, itinerário *m.*

routine, 1. *adj.* rotineiro *m.* **2.** *n.* rotina *f.*

rove, *vb.* vagar.

rover, *n.* vagabundo *m.*

row, 1. *n.* fila, fileira *f.*; rixa *f.* **2.** *vb.* remar.

rowboat, *n.* barco de remos *m.*

rowdy, *adj.* desordeiro *m.*

royal, *adj.* real, régio.

royalty, *n.* realeza *f.*; (pl.) royalty *m.*

rub, *vb.* esfregar. **r. against,** roçar; **r. out,** apagar.

rubber, *n.* borracha *f.* **r. band,** elástico *m.*; **r. plant/tree,** seringueira *f.*; **r. plantation,** seringal *m.*; **r. worker,** seringueiro *m.*

rubbish, *n.* lixo, refugo *m.*

rubble, *n.* entulho, pedregulho *m.*

rubric, *n.* rubrica *f.*

ruby, *n.* rubi *m.*

ruckus, *n.* tumulto *m.*

rudder, *n.* leme, timão *m.*

rude, *adj.* rude; grosseiro; descortês.

rudimentary, *adj.* rudimentar.

rue, *vb.* arrepender-se de, lamentar.

ruffian, *n.* rufião, brigão *m.*

ruffle, 1. *n.* babado *m.* **2.** *vb.* franzir; irritar.

rug, *n.* tapete *m.*

rugged, *adj.* áspero, duro; rude.

ruin, 1. *n.* ruína *f.* **2.** *vb.* arruinar, estragar.

rule, 1. *n.* regra *f.*; domínio *m.*; reinado *m.* **as a r.,** via de regra. **2.** *vb.* governar, mandar; decretar.

ruler, *n.* governante *m.f.*; régua *f.*

ruling, 1. *adj.* governante, dirigente. **2.** *n.* decisão *f.*

rum, *n.* rum *m.*

rumble, *vb.* retumbar.

ruminate, *vb.* ruminar.

rummage, 1. *n.* mercadorias usadas *f.pl.* **2.** *vb.* remexer, revolver.

rumor, *n.* boato, rumor *m.*

rump, *n.* rabo *m.*; alcatra *f.*

rumple, *vb.* amarrotar.

rumpus, *n.* confusão *f.*

run, *vb.* correr; funcionar, andar; dirigir; candidatar-se. **r. across,** deparar com; **r. away,** fugir; **r. down,** atropelar; falar mal de; **r. into,** encontrar-se com; chocar com; **r. out,** esgotar-se; **r. over,** atropelar.

runner, *n.* corredor *m.*; mensageiro *m.*

runway, *n.* pista *f.*; *(theat.)* passarela *f.*

rupture, 1. *n.* ruptura *f.* **2.** *vb.* romper.

rural, *adj.* rural.

ruse, *n.* ardil *m.*

rush, 1. *n.* pressa *f.*, rush *m.*; junco *m.* **2.** *vb.* apressar(-se).

rush hour, *n.* hora do rush/pique *f.*

Russian, *adj., n.* russo -sa.

rust, 1. *n.* ferrugem *f.* **2.** *vb.* enferrujar(-se).

rustic, *adj., n.* rústico *m.*

rustle, 1. *n.* sussurro *m.*, farfalhada *f.* **2.** *vb.* sussurrar, farfalhar; roubar (gado).

rusty, *adj.* ferrugento.

rut, *n.* carril, sulco *m.*; rotina *f.*

ruthless, *adj.* cruel, desapiedado.

rye, *n.* centeio *m.*

S

sabbatical, *n.* licença-prêmio *f.*

saber, *n.* sabre *m.*

sabotage, 1. *n.* sabotagem *f.* **2.** *vb.* sabotar.

saboteur, *n.* sabotador -ra.

sac, *n.* saco *m.*, bolsa *f.*

saccharin, *n.* sacarina *f.*

sack, 1. *n.* saco *m.*, saca; (pillage) saque *m.* *f.* **2.** *vb.* saquear.

sacrament, *n.* sacramento *m.*

sacred, *adj.* sagrado, sacro.

sacrifice, 1. *n.* sacrifício *m.* **2.** *vb.* sacrificar(-se).

sacrificial, *adj.* sacrificial.

sacrilege, *n.* sacrilégio *m.*

sacristan, *n.* sacristão *m.*

sacrosanct, *adj.* sacrossanto.

sad, *adj.* triste.

sadden, *vb.* entristecer.

saddle, 1. *n.* sela *f.*, selim *m.* **2.** *vb.* selar. **s. with,** carregar de.

saddlebag, *n.* alforje *m.*

sadistic, *adj.* sádico.

sadness, *n.* tristeza *f.*

safe, 1. *adj.* seguro; salvo. **2.** *n.* cofre *m.*

safeguard, 1. *n.* salvaguarda *f.* **2.** *vb.* salvaguardar.

safety, *n.* segurança *f.*

safety belt, *n.* cinto de segurança *m.*

safety pin, *n.* alfinete de segurança *m.*

saffron, *n.* açafrão *m.*

sag, *vb.* pender, bambear.

saga, *n.* saga *f.*

sagacity, *n.* sagacidade *f.*

sage, 1. *n.* sábio. **2.** *n.* sábio *m.*; *(bot.)* salva *f.*

sail, 1. *n.* vela *f.*; passeio em

barco à vela. **2.** *vb.* navegar; zarpar.

sailboat, *n.* barco à vela *m.*

sailing, *n.* navegação *f.*

sailor, *n.* marinheiro *m.*

saint, *n.* santo -ta.

sainthood, *n.* santidade *f.*

saintly, *adj.* santo.

sake, *n.* **for the s. of**, por; pelo amor de.

salad, *n.* salada *f.* **s. bowl**, saladeira *f.*; **s. dressing**, molho de salada *m.*

salamander, *n.* salamandra *f.*

salami, *n.* salame *m.*

salary, *n.* ordenado *m.*

sale, *n.* venda *f.*; liqüidação *f.* **for s.**, à venda.

salesclerk -man -lady, *n.* caixeiro -ra, vendedor -ra.

sales tax, *n.* imposto de consumo *m.*

salient, *adj.* saliente; notável.

saline, *adj.* salino.

saliva, *n.* saliva *f.*

sally, **1.** *n.* saída *f.* **2.** *vb.* **s. forth**, sair.

salmon, *n.* salmão *m.*

salon, *n.* salão *m.*

saloon, *n.* botequim *m.*

salt, **1.** *n.* sal *m.* **2.** *vb.* salgar.

saltpeter, *n.* salitre *m.*

salt shaker, *n.* saleiro *m.*

salty, *adj.* salgado.

salutary, *adj.* salutar.

salutation, *n.* saudação *f.*

salute, **1.** *n.* saudação *f.*; *(mil.)* continência *f.* **2.** *vb.* saudar; *(mil.)* bater continência (a).

Salvadoran, *adj.*, *n.* salvadorenho -nha.

salvage, **1.** *n.* salvados *m.pl.*; salvagem *f.* **2.** *vb.* salvar.

salvation, *n.* salvação *f.*

salve, *n.* ungüento *m.*

salvo, *n.* salva *f.*

same, *adj.*, *pron.* mesmo. **all the s.**, mesmo assim; **it's all the s. to me**, tanto faz.

sample, **1.** *n.* amostra *f.* **2.** *vb.* experimentar, provar.

sanatorium, *n.* sanatório *m.*

sanctify, *vb.* santificar.

sanctimonious, *adj.* santarrão -rona.

sanction, **1.** *n.* sanção *f.* **2.** *vb.* sancionar.

sanctity, *n.* santidade *f.*

sanctuary, *n.* santuário *m.*; asilo *m.*

sand, *n.* areia *f.*

sandal, *n.* sandália *f.*

sandpaper, **1.** *n.* lixa *f.* **2.** *vb.* lixar.

sandstone, *n.* arenito *m.*

sandwich, *n.* sanduíche *m.f.*

sandy, *adj.* arenoso.

sane, *n.* são (de espírito), sensato.

sanguinary, *adj.* sanguinário.

sanguine, *adj.* sanguíneo.

sanitarium, *n.* sanatório *m.*

sanitary, *adj.* sanitário, higiênico. **s. napkin**, toalha higiênica *f.*

sanitation, *n.* saneamento *m.*

sanity, *n.* sanidade mental *f.*; juízo *m.*

Santa Claus, *n.* Papai Noel *m.*

sap, **1.** *n.* seiva *f.*; *(coll.)* tolo *m.* **2.** *vb.* minar; esgotar.

sapphire, *n.* safira *f.*

sarcasm, *n.* sarcasmo *m.*

sarcastic, *adj.* sarcástico.

sardine, *n.* sardinha *f.*

sash, *n.* faixa, banda *f.*

sassy, *adj.* insolente.

Satan, *n.* satanás *m.*

satanic, *adj.* satânico.

satchel, *n.* bolsa, maleta *f.*

satellite, *n.* satélite *m.*

satiate, *vb.* saciar, fartar.

satin, *n.* cetim *m.*

satire, *n.* sátira *f.*

satirical, *adj.* satírico.

satisfaction, *n.* satisfação *f.*

satisfactory, *adj.* satisfatório.

satisfied, *adj.* satisfeito.

satisfy, *vb.* satisfazer.

saturate, *vb.* saturar.

Saturday, *n.* sábado *m.*

Saturn, *n.* Saturno *m.*

sauce, *n.* molho *m.*; calda *f.*

saucepan, *n.* caçarola *f.*

saucer, *n.* pires *m.*

saucy, *adj.* insolente.

Saudi Arabia, *n.* Arábia Saudita *f.*

sauerkraut, *n.* chucrute *m.*

sausage, *n.* salsicha -chicha *f.*; lingüiça *f.*

savage, *adj.*, *n.* selvagem *m.f.*

save, **1.** *vb.* salvar; guardar;

poupar, economizar. **2.** *prep.* salvo.

savings, *n.pl.* economias *f.pl.*

savior, *n.* salvador *m.*

savor, 1. *n.* sabor *m.* **2.** *vb.* saborear.

savory, *adj.* saboroso, gostoso.

saw, 1. *n.* serra *f.*; serrote *m.*; ditado *m.* **2.** *vb.* serrar.

sawdust, *n.* serradura, serragem *f.*

sawhorse, *n.* cavalete *m.*

sawmill, *n.* serraria *f.*

saxophone, *n.* saxofone *m.*

say, *vb.* dizer, falar. **that is to s.,** isto é, quer dizer; **you don't s.!,** não diga!; **you said it!,** *(sl.)* falou!

saying, *n.* ditado, dito *m.*

scab, *n.* casca de ferida *f.*

scabbard, *n.* bainha *f.*

scaffold, *n.* andaime *m.*; patíbulo *m.*

scald, *vb.* escaldar.

scale, 1. *n.* escala *f.*; (fish) escama *f.*; *(pl.)* balança *f.* **2.** *vb.* escalar; escamar, descascar. **s. down,** reduzir.

scallop, *n.* vieira *f.*

scalp, *n.* couro cabeludo *m.*

scalpel, *n.* escalpelo *m.*

scalper, *n.* cambista *m.f.*

scaly, *adj.* escamoso.

scamp, *n.* moleque *m.*

scamper, *vb.* correr.

scan, *vb.* correr os olhos sobre, folhear.

scandal, *n.* escândalo *m.*

scandalous, *adj.* escandaloso.

Scandinavia, *n.* Escandinávia *f.*

Scandinavian, *adj.*, *n.* escandinavo -va.

scanner, *n.* transdutor óptico.

scant, *adj.* escasso, pouco.

scanty, *adj.* escasso; (clothes) sumário.

scapegoat, *n.* bode expiatório *m.*

scar, *n.* cicatriz *f.*

scarce, *adj.* escasso; raro. **make oneself s.,** sumir.

scarcely, *adv.*, *conj.* apenas, mal.

scarcity, *n.* escassez, falta *f.*

scare, 1. *n.* susto *m.* **2.** *vb.* assustar.

scarecrow, *n.* espantalho *m.*

scarf, *n.* cachecol, lenço de pescoço *m.*

scarlet, *adj.* escarlate. **s. fever,** escarlatina *f.*

scary, *adj.* assustador.

scathing, *adj.* mordaz, cáustico.

scatter, *vb.* espalhar(-se); dispersar(-se).

scatterbrained, *adj.* desmiolado.

scavenger, *n.* gari *m.*; vasculhador -ra.

scenario, *n.* cenário *m.*

scene, *n.* cena *f.*; escândalo *m.* **behind the scenes,** nos bastidores.

scenery, *n.* cenário *m.*; paisagem *f.*

scenic, *adj.* cênico.

scent, 1. *n.* cheiro, perfume *m.*; (sense) olfato *m.* **2.** *vb.* cheirar; perfumar.

scepter, *n.* cetro *m.*

schedule, 1. *n.* horário *m.*; lista *f.*; programa *m.* **2.** *vb.* marcar.

scheme, 1. *n.* plano, esquema *m.*; ardil *m.* **2.** *vb.* tramar.

schemer, *n.* intrigante *m.f.*

schism, *n.* cisma *m.f.*

schizophrenia, *n.* esquizofrenia *f.*

scholar, *n.* erudito -ta; bolsista *m.f.*

scholarly, *adj.* erudito, estudioso.

scholarship, *n.* erudição *f.*; bolsa de estudos *f.* **s. holder,** bolsista *m.f.*

scholastic, *adj.* escolástico; acadêmico.

school, *n.* escola *f.*; (fish) cardume *m.* **elementary s.,** escola primária *f.*, primeiro grau *m.*; **high s.,** escola secundária *f.*, colégio, segundo grau *m.*

school child, *n.* escolar *m.f.*; colegial *f.*

schooling, *n.* educação, escolaridade *f.*

schoolmaster, *n.* mestre-escola *m.*

schoolmate, *n.* colega *m.f.*

schoolroom, *n.* sala de aula *f.*

school year, *n.* ano letivo *m.*

science, *n.* ciência *f.* **s. fiction,** ficção científica *f.*

scientific, *adj.* científico.

scientist, *n.* cientista *m.f.*

scissors, *n.pl.* tesoura *f.*

scoff, *vb.* zombar, mofar. **s. at,** zombar de.

scold, *vb.* repreender, *(coll.)* dar uma bronca em.

scolding, *n.* repreensão, *(coll.)* bronca *f.*

scoop, 1. *n.* colherão *m.*; colherada *f.*; *(journ.)* furo *m.* **2.** *vb.* cavar; tirar.

scoot, *vb. (sl.)* sair/mover apressadamente.

scooter, *n.* patinete *m.*

scope, *n.* alcance *m.*; campo *m.*, esfera *f.*

scorch, *vb.* chamuscar.

scorching, *adj.* abrasador.

score, 1. *n.* contagem *f.*; número de pontos *m.*; vintena *f.*; *(mus.)* partitura *f.* **2.** *vb.* marcar, fazer pontos.

scoreboard, *n.* placar *m.*

scorn, 1. *n.* desprezo *m.* **2.** *vb.* desprezar.

scornful, *adj.* desdenhoso.

Scorpio, *n.* Escorpião *m.*

scorpion, *n.* escorpião *m.*

scotch, 1. *adj. (cap.)* escocês -cesa. **2.** *n.* escocês *m.*; uísque escocês, scotch *m.*

Scotchman, Scotsman -woman, *n.* escocês -cesa.

Scotch tape, *n.* fita durex *f.*

Scotland, *n.* Escócia *f.*

Scottish, *adj.,* *n.* escocês -cesa.

scoundrel, *n.* patife, salafrário *m.*

scour, *vb.* esfregar, limpar; explorar.

scourge, 1. *n.* flagelo *m.* **2.** *vb.* flagelar.

scout, 1. *n.* batedor *m.*; (boy) escoteiro *m.*; descobridor de talento *m.* **2.** *vb.* explorar, bater.

scouting, *n.* exploração *f.*; (boy) escotismo *m.*

scowl, 1. *n.* carranca *f.* **2.** *vb.* fazer carranca.

scram, *vb. (sl.)* cair fora.

scramble, 1. *n.* desordem *f.* **2.** *vb.* subir/arrastar-se/lutar desordenadamente; embaralhar; mexer.

scrap, 1. *n.* migalha *f.*, pedacinho *m.*; *(coll.)* rixa *f.* **s.**

metal, sucata *f.* **2.** *vb.* jogar fora, abandonar; *(coll.)* brigar.

scrapbook, *n.* álbum de recortes *m.*

scrape, 1. *n.* arranhão *m.*; enrascada *f.* **2.** *vb.* raspar; arranhar.

scratch, 1. *n.* arranhão *m.*; rabisco *m.* **2.** *vb.* arranhar; rabiscar. **s. off/out,** riscar.

scrawl, 1. *n.* rabisco *m.* **2.** *vb.* rabiscar.

scrawny, *adj.* magro, ossudo.

scream, 1. *n.* grito *m.* **2.** *vb.* gritar.

screech, 1. *n.* guincho *m.* **2.** *vb.* guinchar.

screen, 1. *n.* biombo *m.*; tela *f.* **2.** *vb.* selecionar; (movie) passar.

screw, 1. *n.* parafuso *m.* **have a s. loose,** ter um parafuso frouxo. **2.** *vb.* apertar (parafuso).

screwdriver, *n.* chave de parafuso/fenda *f.*

screwy, *adj. (coll.)* maluco.

scribble, 1. *n.* rabisco *m.* **2.** *vb.* rabiscar.

scribe, *n.* escriba *m.*

script, *n.* escrita *f.*; texto, roteiro *m.*

scripture, *n.* escritura *f.*

scroll, *n.* rolo (de pergaminho, de papel) *m.*

scrub, *vb.* esfregar, lavar.

scruple, *n.* escrúpulo *m.*

scrupulous, *adj.* escrupuloso.

scrutinize, *vb.* escrutar, esquadrinhar.

scrutiny, *n.* exame atento, escrutínio *m.*

scuffle, 1. *n.* briga, escaramuça *f.* **2.** *vb.* brigar.

sculpt, *vb.* esculpir.

sculptor, *n.* escultor -ra.

sculpture, *n.* escultura *f.*

scum, *n.* escória *f.*; ralé *f.*

scurry, *vb.* correr, apressar-se.

scurvy, *n.* escorbuto *m.*

scuttlebutt, *n.* boato, mexerico *m.*

scythe, *n.* gadanha, ceifeira *f.*

sea, *n.* mar *m.* **put to s.,** fazer-se ao mar.

seacoast, seaboard, *n.* litoral *m.*, orla marítima *f.*

seafarer, *n.* marinheiro *m.*

seafood, *n.* frutos do mar *m.pl.*

sea gull, *n.* gaivota *f.*

sea horse, *n.* cavalo marinho *m.*

seal, 1. *n.* selo *m.*; foca *f.* **2.** *vb.* selar; fechar, lacrar.

sea level, *n.* nível do mar *m.*

sea lion, *n.* leão marinho *m.*

seam, *n.* costura *f.*

seaman, *n.* marinheiro *m.*

seamstress, *n.* costureira *f.*

séance, *n.* sessão *f.*

seaplane, *n.* hidravião *m.*

seaport, *n.* porto de mar *m.*

sear, *vb.* chamuscar.

search, 1. *n.* busca, procura *f.* **in s. of,** em busca de. **2.** *vb.* revistar; procurar. **s. for,** procurar.

searchlight, *n.* holofote *m.*

seashore, *n.* praia *f.*

seasick, *adj.* enjoado, mareado.

seasickness, *n.* enjôo *m.*

season, 1. *n.* estação *f.*; temporada *f.* **2.** *vb.* temperar; sazonar.

seasonal, *adj.* periódico.

seasoning, *n.* tempero, condimento *m.*

seat, 1. *n.* assento *m.*, cadeira *f.*; lugar *m.*; sede *f.* **take a s.,** sentar-se. **2.** *vb.* sentar. **be seated,** sentar-se.

seat belt, *n.* cinto de segurança *m.*

sea urchin, *n.* ouriço do mar *m.*

seaweed, *n.* alga marinha *f.*

secede, *vb.* separar-se.

secession, *n.* secessão *f.*

secluded, *adj.* retirado, remoto; recluso.

seclusion, *n.* isolamento *m.*; reclusão *f.*

second, 1. *adj.,* *n.* segundo *m.* **2.** *vb.* secundar, apoiar.

secondary, *adj.* secundário.

second-hand, *adj.* de segunda mão.

second-rate, *adj.* de segunda.

secrecy, *n.* mistério, sigilo *m.*

secret, 1. *adj.* secreto. **2.** *n.* segredo *m.*

secretary, *n.* secretário -ria; (government) ministro -tra.

secrete, *vb.* segregar; esconder.

secretion, *n.* secreção *f.*

secretive, *adj.* furtivo, misterioso.

sect, *n.* seita *f.*

sectarian, *adj.,* *n.* sectário *m.*

section, *n.* secção, seção, parte *f.*; (newspaper) caderno *m.*

sectional, *adj.* regional.

sector, *n.* setor *m.*

secular, *adj.* secular.

secure, 1. *adj.* seguro, firme. **2.** *vb.* assegurar; garantir; obter.

security, *n.* segurança *f.*

sedate, *adj.* calmo, sossegado; comedido.

sedative, *adj.,* *n.* sedativo, calmante *m.*

sedentary, *adj.* sedentário.

sediment, *n.* sedimento *m.*

sedition, *n.* sedição *f.*

seduce, *vb.* seduzir.

seducer, *n.* sedutor -ra.

seduction, *n.* sedução *f.*

see, 1. *n.* sé *f.*; bispado *m.* **2.** *vb.* ver; compreender. **s. off,** despedir-se de; **s. to,** encarregar-se de.

seed, 1. *n.* semente *f.* **2.** *vb.* semear.

seedy, *adj.* gasto, esfarrapado.

seek, *vb.* procurar. **s. to,** procurar.

seem, *vb.* parecer.

seeming, *adj.* aparente.

seemly, *adj.* decente, decoroso.

seep, *vb.* filtrar.

seer, *n.* vidente *m.f.*

seesaw, 1. *n.* gangorra *f.* **2.** *vb.* oscilar.

seethe, *vb.* ferver.

segment, *n.* segmento *m.*

segregate, *vb.* segregar.

segregation, *n.* segregação *f.*

seismic, *adj.* sísmico.

seize, *vb.* agarrar; confiscar.

seizure, *n.* apreensão *f.*; acesso *m.*

seldom, *adv.* raramente.

select, 1. *adj.* seleto. **2.** *vb.* selecionar, escolher.

selection, *n.* seleção *f.*; seleta *f.*; (goods) sortimento *m.*

selective, *adj.* seletivo.

self, 1. *n.* a própria pessoa *f.*, eu, ego *m.* **by oneself,** sozinho -nha, por conta própria. **2.** *pron.* mesmo, próprio.

self-, *pref.* auto-.

self-centered, *adj.* egocêntrico.

self-conscious, *adj.* auto-consciente; tímido.

self-defense, *n.* legítima defesa *f.*

self-esteem, *n.* amor-próprio *m.*

selfish, *adj.* egoísta.

selfishness, *n.* egoísmo *m.*

self-righteous, *adj.* santarrão.

self-taught, *adj.* autodidata.

sell, *vb.* vender.

seller, *n.* vendedor -ra.

semantics, *n.* semântica *f.*

semblance, *n.* aparência *f.*

semen, *n.* sêmen *m.*

semester, *n.* semestre *m.*

semi-, *pref.* semi-.

semicolon, *n.* ponto e vírgula *m.*

semimonthly, *adj.* quinzenal.

seminar, *n.* seminário *m.*

seminarian, *n.* seminarista *m.*

seminary, *n.* seminário,

senate, *n.* senado *m.*

senator, *n.* senador -ra.

send, *vb.* mandar, enviar; transmitir. **s. away,** mandar embora; **s. back,** devolver; **s. for,** mandar buscar; **s. off,** enviar; despachar; **s. word,** mandar dizer, mandar recado.

sender, *n.* remetente *m.f.*

send-off, *n.* despedida *f.*, bota-fora *m.*

senile, *adj.* senil.

senility, *n.* senilidade *f.*

senior, 1. *adj.* mais velho; sênior. **2.** *n.* pessoa mais velha; bacharelando *m.*

senior citizen, *n.* velho -lha.

seniority, *n.* antiguidade (de serviço) *f.*

sensation, *n.* sensação *f.*

sensational, *adj.* sensacional.

sense, 1. *n.* sentido, senso *m.*; juízo *m.* **2.** *vb.* sentir.

sense of humor, *n.* senso de humor *m.*

sensible, *adj.* sensato.

sensitive, *adj.* sensível.

sensitivity, *n.* sensibilidade *f.*

sensory, *adj.* sensorial.

sensual, sensuous, *adj.* sensual.

sentence 1. *n.* sentença *f.*; oração, frase *f.* **2.** *vb.* sentenciar.

sentiment, *n.* sentimento *m.*

sentimental, *adj.* sentimental.

sentry, *n.* sentinela *f.*

separate, 1. *adj.* separado. **2.** *vb.* separar(-se).

separation, *n.* separação *f.*

September, *n.* setembro *m.*

septic, *adj.* séptico.

sequel, *n.* seqüela *f.*

sequence, *n.* seqüência *f.*

sequential, *adj.* consecutivo.

sequin, *n.* lantejoula *f.*

seraph, *n.* serafim *m.*

serenade, *n.* serenata, seresta *f.*

serenader, *n.* seresteiro *m.*

serene, *adj.* sereno.

serf, *n.* servo -va.

serfdom, *n.* servidão *f.*

sergeant, *n.* sargento *m.*

serial, 1. *adj.* serial, seriado, em série. **2.** *n.* novela *f.*; drama ou filme em série.

series, *n.* série *f.*

serious, *adj.* sério; grave.

seriousness, *n.* seriedade *f.*

sermon, *n.* sermão *m.*

serpent, *n.* serpente *f.*

serum, *n.* soro, sérum *m.*

servant, *n.* criado -da, empregado -da.

serve, 1. *n.* (*sport.*) saque *m.* **2.** *vb.* servir; cumprir; (*sport.*) sacar.

service, *n.* serviço *m.*; forças armadas *f.pl.* **at your s.,** às suas ordens.

service station, *n.* posto de gasolina *m.*

servile, *adj.* servil.

serving, *n.* porção *f.*

servitude, *n.* servidão *f.*

sesame, *n.* sésamo *m.*

session, *n.* sessão *f.*

set, 1. *adj.* fixo; pronto. **2.** *n.* conjunto, jogo *m.*, coleção *f.*; aparelho *m.* **3.** *vb.* pôr, colocar; fixar; (sun) pôr-se. **s. forth,** expor; partir; **s. off/out,** sair; **s. up,** instalar; estabelecer.

setback, *n.* revés *m.*

settle, *vb.* resolver; arranjar; saldar; assentar; estabelecer-se.

settlement, *n.* povoação, colônia *f.*; resolução *f.*; acordo *m.*

settler, *n.* colono -na.

setup, *n.* organização *f.*

seven, *adj.* sete.

seven hundred, *adj.* setecentos.

seventeen, *adj.* dezessete.

seventeenth, 1. *adj.* décimo sétimo. **2.** *n.* dezessete avos *m.pl.*

seventh, *adj.,* *n.* sétimo *m.*

seventieth, *adj.* septuagésimo *m.*

seventy, *adj.* setenta.

sever, *vb.* cortar; quebrar.

several, *adj.,* *pron.* vários, diversos *m.pl.*

severe, *adj.* severo.

severity, *n.* severidade *f.*

sew, *vb.* costurar, coser.

sewage, *n.* despejos *m.pl.*, águas sujas *f.pl.*

sewer, *n.* esgoto *m.*

sewing, *n.* costura *f.* **s. machine,** máquina de costura *f.*

sex, *n.* sexo *m.* **have s.,** ter relações.

sexton, *n.* sacristão *m.*

sexual, *adj.* sexual. **s. intercourse,** relações sexuais *f.pl.*

sexuality, *n.* sexualidade *f.*

sexy, *adj.* sensual, sexy.

shabby, *adj.* gasto; esfarrapado; maltrapilho.

shack, *n.* barracão *m.*

shackle, 1. *n.* grilhão *m.*; algema *f.* **2.** *vb.* agrilhoar; algemar.

shade, 1. *n.* sombra *f.*; tom *m.*; matiz *m.*; estore *m.* **2.** *vb.* sombrear.

shadow, *n.* sombra *f.*

shady, *adj.* sombroso; *(coll.)* barra-pesada.

shaft, *n.* coluna *f.*; haste *f.*; pau *m.*; eixo *m.*; poço *m.*

shaggy, *adj.* peludo, cabeludo.

shake, 1. *n.* sacudidela *f.*; (hand) aperto *m.*; (head) aceno *m.* **2.** *vb.* sacudir; (hand) apertar; (head) abanar; tremer.

shaky, *adj.* trêmulo.

shale, *n.* piçarra *f.*, xisto *m.*

shallow, *adj.* raso; frívolo.

sham, *n.* impostura *f.*, simulacro *m.*

shaman, *n.* xamã *m.*

shambles, *n.pl.* ruínas *f.pl.*, pandarecos *m.pl.*

shame, 1. *n.* vergonha *f.* **be a s.,** ser uma pena. **2.** *vb.* envergonhar.

shameful, *adj.* vergonhoso.

shameless, *adj.* sem-vergonha, cínico.

shampoo, *n.* xampu *m.*

shank, *n.* canela *f.*; haste *f.*

shanty, *n.* barracão *m.*

shape, 1. *n.* forma *f.*; estado *m.* **2.** *vb.* formar, moldar.

shapely, *adj.* bem feito, bem-apanhado.

share, 1. *n.* porção, parte *f.*; ação *f.* **2.** *vb.* compartilhar; rachar.

sharecropper, *n.* meeiro *m.*

shareholder, *n.* acionista *m.f.*

shark, *n.* tubarão *m.*

sharp, 1. *adj.* agudo, afiado, pontudo; esperto. **2.** *n.* sustenido. **3.** *adv.* (time) em ponto.

sharpen, *vb.* afiar, aguçar, amolar; (pencil) fazer ponta em, apontar.

sharpener, *n.* afiador *m.*; (pencil) apontador *m.*

sharpness, *n.* agudeza *f.*; esperteza *f.*

shatter, *vb.* estilhaçar(-se).

shave, *vb.* fazer a barba (de), barbear(-se).

shaver, *n.* barbeador elétrico *m.*

shaving cream, *n.* creme de barbear *m.*

shawl, *n.* xale *m.*

she, *pron.* ela.

sheaf, *n.* gavela *f.*, feixe *m.*

shear, *vb.* tosquiar; cisalhar.

shears, *n.pl.* tesoura *f.*

sheath, *n.* bainha *f.*

shed, 1. *n.* galpão, telheiro *m.* **2.** *vb.* mudar; perder; (tears) verter.

sheen, *n.* lustro, brilho *m.*

sheep, *n.* carneiro *m.*, ovelha *f.*

sheepfold, *n.* aprisco *m.*

sheepish, *adj.* tímido.

sheer, *adj.* diáfano; puro.

sheet, *n.* lençol *m.*; (paper) folha *f.*; lâmina *f.*

sheik, *n.* xeque *m.*

shelf, *n.* prateleira *f.*, estante *m.*

shell, 1. *n.* concha *f.*; casca *f.*; carapaça *f.*; projétil *m.*; cartucho *m.* **2.** *vb.* descascar; bombardear.

shellac, *n.* goma-laca *f.*; verniz *m.*

shellfish, *n.* marisco, molusco *m.*

shelter, 1. *n.* abrigo *m.* 2. *vb.* abrigar.

shepherd -ess, *n.* pastor -ra.

sherbet, *n.* sorvete de fruta *m.*

sheriff, *n.* xerife *m.*

sherry, *n.* xerez *m.*

shield, 1. *n.* escudo *m.* 2. *vb.* proteger.

shift, 1. *n.* mudança *f.*; (work) turno, rodízio *m.* 2. *vb.* mudar. **s. for oneself**, virar-se.

shiftless, *adj.* preguiçoso.

shifty, *adj.* astucioso.

shilling, *n.* xelim *m.*

shimmer, *vb.* tremeluzir.

shin, *n.* canela (da perna) *f.*

shine, 1. *n.* brilho *m.* 2. *vb.* brilhar; distinguir-se.

shingle, *n.* ripa, telha de madeira *f.*

shining, *adj.* brilhante.

shiny, *adj.* brilhante.

ship, 1. *n.* navio *m.*, nave *f.* 2. *vb.* remeter; embarcar.

shipment, *n.* remessa *f.*

shipowner, *n.* armador -ra.

shipwreck, 1. *n.* naufrágio *m.* 2. *vb.* **be shipwrecked**, naufragar.

shipyard, *n.* estaleiro *m.*

shirk, *vb.* esquivar-se a, furtar-se a.

shirt, *n.* camisa *f.*

shiver, 1. *n.* tremor *m.* 2. *vb.* tremer.

shock, 1. *n.* choque *m.*; susto *m.* 2. *vb.* chocar.

shock absorber, *n.* amortecedor *m.*

shocking. *adj.* chocante.

shoddy, *adj.* ordinário, vagabundo.

shoe, 1. *m.* sapato *m.* **s. polish**, *n.* graxa de sapato *f.*; **s. store**, sapataria *f.* 2. *vb.* calçar; (horse) ferrar.

shoehorn, *n.* calçadeira *f.*

shoelace, *n.* cordão de sapato *m.*

shoemaker, *n.* sapateiro -ra.

shoot, 1. *n.* rebento, broto *m.*; tiro *m.* 2. *vb.* atirar; disparar.

shop, 1. *n.* loja *f.*; (factory) oficina *f.* 2. *vb.* fazer compras.

shopkeeper, *n.* comerciante, lojista *m.f.*

shoplifting, *n.* furto *m.*

shopper. *n.* comprador -ra.

shopping, *n.* **to go s.**, fazer compras.

shore, 1. *n.* praia *f.*, litoral *m.* 2. *vb.* **s. up**, escorar.

short, *adj.* curto; (stature) baixinho; escasso. **in s.**, em resumo.

shortage, *n.* escassez, falta *f.*

short circuit, *n.* curto-circuito *m.*

shortcoming, *n.* deficiência *f.*, defeito *m.*

short cut, *n.* atalho *m.*

shorten, *vb.* encurtar, abreviar.

shortening, *n.* banha, manteiga *f.*

shorthand, *n.* taquigrafia *f.*

shortly, *adv.* daqui a pouco, breve.

shortness, *n.* brevidade *f.*; escassez *f.*

shorts, *n.* short *m.*; (underwear) cuecas *f.*

short story, *n.* conto *m.*

shortwave, *n.* onda curta *f.*

shot, *n.* tiro *m.*; (person) atirador -ra; (ammunition) chumbo *m.*; tentativa *f.*, injeção *f.*; foto *f.*; (liquor) dose *f.*

shotgun, *n.* espingarda *f.*

shoulder, 1. *n.* ombro *m.* 2. *vb.* assumir; arcar com.

shoulder blade, *n.* omoplata *f.*

shout, 1. *n.* grito *m.* 2. *vb.* gritar.

shouting, *n.* gritaria *f.*

shove, 1. *n.* empurrão *m.* 2. *vb.* empurrar.

shovel, *n.* pá *f.*

show, 1. *n.* show, espetáculo *m.*; ostentação *f.* **just for s.**, para inglês ver. 2. *vb.* mostrar; demonstrar; passar. **s. off**, exibir-se, fazer farol; **s. up**, aparecer.

showcase, *n.* vitrine *f.*

showdown, *n.* confrontação *f.*

shower, 1. *n.* aguaceiro *m.*; (banho de) chuveiro *m.* 2. *vb.* chover; tomar banho de chuveiro.

showing, *n.* exibição *f.*; sessão *f.*

show-off, *n.* faroleiro *m.*

showroom, *n.* salão de exibição *f.*

showy, adj. espalhafatoso.

shrapnel, n. metralha f.

shred, 1. n. farrapo, fragmento m., tira f. **2.** vb. rasgar em tiras.

shrew, n. megera f.

shrewd, adj. vivo, esperto.

shrewdness, n. esperteza f.

shriek, 1. n. grito, guincho m. **2.** vb. gritar, guinchar.

shrill, adj. estridente.

shrimp, n. camarão m.; (coll.) tampinha m.

shrine, n. santuário m., capela f.

shrink, 1. n. (sl.) psiquiatra m.f. **2.** vb. encolher.

shrinkage, n. encolhimento m.

shrivel, vb. enrugar-se, murchar.

shroud, n. mortalha f.

shrub, n. arbusto m.

shrug, vb. encolher os ombros, dar de ombros.

shudder, 1. n. estremecimento m. **2.** vb. estremecer.

shuffle, 1. n. arrastamento dos pés m.; embaralhamento m. **2.** vb. arrastar os pés; embaralhar.

shun, vb. esquivar-se a, evitar.

shut, vb. fechar. **s. in,** encerrar; **s. off,** desligar; **s. up,** (coll.) calar a boca.

shutter, n. veneziana f.

shuttle, n. trem ou avião que faz viagens curtas de ida e volta. **space s.,** n. ônibus espacial m.

shy, adj. tímido.

shyness, n. timidez f.

sibling, n. irmão -mã.

sic, vb. (dog) açular.

sick, adj. doente. **s. of,** farto de.

sicken, vb. fazer adoecer; adoecer.

sickening, adj. repugnante, enjoativo.

sickle, n. foice f.

sickly, adj. doentio.

sickness, n. doença, enfermidade f.

side, 1. n. lado m., banda f.; partido m. **2.** vb. **s. with,** tomar o partido de.

sideboard, n. guarda-louças, aparador m.

sideburns, n.pl. costeletas, suíças f.pl.

side-step, vb. esquivar-se a.

sidewalk, n. calçada f.

siege, 1. n. sítio, cerco m. **2.** vb. sitiar, assediar.

sierra, n. serra f.

siesta, n. sesta f.

sieve, n. peneira f., crivo m.

sift, vb. peneirar.

sigh, 1. n. suspiro m. **2.** vb. suspirar.

sight, 1. n. vista, visão f.; espetáculo m.; ponto turístico m.; (gun) mira f. **lose s. of,** perder de vista. **2.** vb. avistar.

sightseeing, n. turismo m.

sign, 1. n. sinal m.; placa, tabuleta f.; letreiro m.; cartaz m.; (zodiac) signo m. **2.** vb. assinar, firmar. **s. up,** alistar-se; inscrever-se.

signal, 1. n. sinal m.; sinaleira f. **2.** vb. fazer sinal.

signatory, n. signatário m.

signature, n. assinatura f.

signboard, n. tabuleta f., letreiro m.

signer, n. signatário m.

significance, n. significado m., significação f.

significant, adj. significativo.

signify, vb. significar; indicar.

silence, 1. n. silêncio m. **2.** vb. silenciar.

silent, adj. silencioso, calado, mudo.

silhouette, n. silhueta f.

silicon, n. silício m.

silk, n. seda f.

silky, adj. sedoso.

sill, n. (window) peitoril m.; (door) soleira f.

silliness, n. tolice f., besteira f.

silly, adj. tolo, besta.

silt, n. sedimento m.

silver, 1. adj. de prata; prateado. **2.** n. prata f.

silverware, n. talheres m.pl.; baixela f.

similar, adj. semelhante, similar.

similarity, n. semelhança, similaridade f.

simile, n. símile m.

simmer, vb. ferver a fogo lento.

simple, *adj.* simples, singelo; tolo.

simpleton, *n.* simplório *m.*

simplicity, *n.* simplicidade *f.*

simplify, *vb.* simplificar.

simulate, *vb.* simular.

simultaneous, *adj.* simultâneo.

sin, **1.** *n.* pecado *m.* **2.** *vb.* pecar.

since, **1.** *adv.* desde então. **2.** *prep.* desde. **3.** *conj.* já que.

sincere, *adj.* sincero.

sincerity, *n.* sinceridade *f.*

sinecure, *n.* sinecura *f.*

sinew, *n.* tendão *m.*; músculo *m.*

sinful, *adj.* pecaminoso.

sing, *vb.* cantar.

singe, *vb.* chamuscar.

singer, *n.* cantor -ra.

singing, *n.* canto *m.*

single, **1.** *adj.* só, único; simples; solteiro; de solteiro. **2.** *vb.* **s. out,** apontar.

single file, *n.* fila indiana *f.*

single-handed, *adj.* sozinho.

singular, *adj.* singular.

sinister, *adj.* sinistro.

sink, **1.** *n.* pia *f.* **2.** *vb.* afundar (-se), ir a pique.

sinner, *n.* pecador -ra.

sinuous, *adj.* sinuoso.

sinus, *n.* seio *m.*

sinusitis, *n.* sinusite *f.*

sip, **1.** *n.* sorvo, gole *m.* **2.** *vb.* sorver, bebericar.

siphon, *n.* sifão *m.*

sir, *n.* senhor *m.*

siren, *n.* sirena, -ne *f.*; (mermaid) sereia *f.*

sirloin, *n.* lombo *m.*

sissy, *n.* maricas *m.*

sister, *n.* irmã *f.*

sister-in-law, *n.* cunhada *f.*

sit, *vb.* sentar(-se); pousar. **s. down,** sentar(-se); **s. up,** aprumar-se na cadeira; (at night) velar; **be sitting,** estar sentado.

site, *n.* lugar, local, sítio *m.*

sitting, *n.* sentada *f.*; sessão *f.*

situate, *vb.* situar.

situation, *n.* situação *f.*

six, *adj.* seis.

six hundred, *adj.* seiscentos.

sixteen, *adj.* dezesseis.

sixteenth, **1.** *adj.* décimo sexto. **2.** *n.* dezesseis avos *m.pl.*

sixth, *adj.*, *n.* sexto *m.*

sixtieth, *adj.* sexagésimo.

sixty, *adj.* sessenta.

sizable, *adj.* considerável.

size, *n.* tamanho *m.*; medida *f.*; número *m.*

sizzle, *vb.* chiar (ao fogo).

skate, **1.** *n.* patim *m.* **2.** *vb.* patinar.

skater, *n.* patinador -ra.

skating, *n.* patinação *f.*

skein, *n.* meada *f.*, novelo *m.*

skeletal, *adj.* esquelético.

skeleton, *n.* esqueleto *m.*

skeptic, *n.* céptico -ca.

skeptical, *adj.* céptico.

skepticism, *n.* cepticismo *m.*

sketch, **1.** *n.* esboço *m.*; desenho *m.* **2.** *vb.* esboçar; desenhar.

sketchy, *adj.* superficial, vago.

skewer, **1.** *n.* espeto *m.* **2.** *vb.* espetar.

ski, **1.** *n.* esqui *m.* **2.** *vb.* esquiar.

skid, **1.** *n.* derrapagem *f.* **2.** *vb.* derrrapar.

skier, *n.* esquiador -ra.

skiing, *n.* esqui *m.*

skill, *n.* habilidade *f.*; arte *f.*

skilled, *adj.* hábil; especializado.

skillful, *adj.* hábil, destro.

skim, *vb.* roçar; (milk) desnatar. **s. over,** folhear, ler por alto.

skim milk, *n.* leite desnatado *m.*

skimp, *n.* economizar.

skimpy, *adj.* parco, insuficiente.

skin, **1.** *n.* pele *f.*; casca *f.* **2.** *vb.* esfolar; descascar.

skindiving, *n.* mergulho *m.*, pesca submarina *f.*

skinny, *adj.* magro.

skip, **1.** *n.* salto *m.* **2.** *vb.* saltar. **s. over,** saltar.

skipper, *n.* capitão *m.*

skirmish, *n.* escaramuça *f.*

skirt, **1.** *n.* saia *f.* **2.** *vb.* contornar.

skit, *n.* pecinha cômica *f.*, esquete *m.*

skittish, *adj.* tímido; arisco; assustadiço.

skull, *n.* caveira *f.*; crânio *m.*

skunk, *n.* jaritataca *f.*, cangambá *m.*

sky, *n.* céu *m.*

skylark, *n.* cotovia *f.*

skylight, *n.* clarabóia *f.*

skyrocket, *n.* foguete *m.*

skyscraper, *n.* arranha-céu *m.*

slab, *n.* laje *f.*; fatia grossa *f.*

slack, **1.** *adj.* frouxo, folgado; descuidado. **2.** *vb.* **s. off**, afrouxar.

slacken, *vb.* afrouxar.

slacks, *n.pl.* calças *f.pl.*

slag, *n.* escória *f.*

slam, **1.** *n.* batida (de porta) *f.*; crítica severa *f.* **2.** *vb.* bater, fechar com força; criticar asperamente.

slander, **1.** calúnia, difamação *f.* **2.** *vb.* caluniar, difamar.

slanderous, *adj.* calunioso, difamatório.

slang, *n.* gíria *f.*

slant, **1.** *n.* inclinação *f.*; opinião *f.* **2.** *vb.* inclinar(-se).

slap, **1.** *n.* bofetada *f.* **2.** *vb.* esbofetear.

slapstick, *n.* (comedy) pastelão *m.*

slash, **1.** *n.* talho *m.* **2.** *vb.* talhar.

slat, *n.* ripa, tabuinha *f.*

slate, *n.* lousa *f.*; (electoral) chapa *f.*

slaughter, **1.** *n.* matança *f.* **2.** *vb.* matar; (animal) abater.

slaughterhouse, *n.* matadouro *m.*

slave, **1.** *n.* escravo -va. **2.** *vb.* trabalhar como escravo.

slaveholder, *n.* senhor de escravos *m.*

slavery, *n.* escravidão, escravatura *f.*

Slavic, *adj.* eslavo.

slay, *vb.* matar.

sleazy, *adj.* tênue; vagabundo; sórdido; vil.

sled, *n.* trenó *m.*

sledge hammer, *n.* malho *m.*, marreta *f.*

sleek, *adj.* liso, macio.

sleep, **1.** *n.* sono *m.* **2.** *vb.* dormir.

sleepiness, *n.* sonolência *f.*

sleeping bag, *n.* saco de dormir *m.*

sleeping car, *n.* carro-dormitório *m.*

sleeping pill, *n.* pílula para dormir *f.*

sleepwalker, *n.* sonâmbulo -la.

sleepwalking, *n.* sonambulismo *m.*

sleepy, *adj.* sonolento. **be s.**, estar com sono.

sleepyhead, *n.* dorminhoco -ca.

sleet, *n.* chuva com neve ou granizo.

sleeve, *n.* manga *f.*

sleigh, *n.* trenó *f.*

slender, *adj.* esguio, magro.

sleuth, *n.* detetive *m.*

slice, **1.** *n.* fatia *f.*; talhada *f.* **2.** *vb.* cortar em fatias.

slick, *adj.* liso e lustroso; (coll.) astucioso.

slide, **1.** *n.* escorregamento *m.*; escorregador *m.*; slide, diapositivo *m.* **2.** *n.* escorregar, deslizar.

slide rule, *n.* régua de cálculo *f.*

slight, **1.** *adj.* leve, ligeiro; pequeno. **2.** *n.* desconsideração *f.* **3.** *vb.* desconsiderar.

slim, *adj.* esguio; escasso; fraco.

slime, *n.* limo, lodo *m.*

slimy, *adj.* viscoso; lodoso.

sling, **1.** *n.* funda *f.*; tipóia *f.* **2.** *vb.* atirar.

slingshot, *n.* bodoque, estilingue *m.*, atiradeira *f.*

slink, *vb.* esgueirar-se.

slip, **1.** *n.* escorregamento *m.*; lapso, cochilo *m.*; (garment) combinação *f.*; (paper) pedaço *m.* **2.** *vb.* escorregar; esgueirar-se; ter um lapso. **s. up**, (sl.) dar uma mancada.

slipper, *n.* chinelo *m.*

slippery, *adj.* escorregadio.

slit, **1.** *n.* corte *m.*; fenda *f.* **2.** *vb.* cortar.

slither, *vb.* serpentear.

sliver, *n.* lasca *f.*; cavaco *m.*

slob, *n.* porcalhão *m.*

slobber, *vb.* babar-se.

slogan, *n.* slogan *m.*

slop, **1.** *n.* água suja *f.* **2.** *vb.* salpicar; derramar.

slope, **1.** *n.* declive *m.* **2.** *vb.* inclinar-se.

sloppy, *adj.* porcalhão; bagunçado.

slot, *n.* ranhura *f.* **s. machine,** caça-níqueis *m.*

sloth, *n.* preguiça *f.*

slouch, 1. *n.* incompetente, preguiçoso *m.* **2.** *vb.* andar/sentar-se encurvado.

slovenly, *adj.* desleixado.

slow, 1. *adj.* lento; (clock) atrasado. **2.** *vb.* **s. down,** retardar; ir mais devagar; atrasar.

slowly, *adv.* devagar, lentamente.

slow motion, *n.* câmara lenta *f.*

slowness, *n.* lentidão *f.*

slug, 1. *n.* lesma *f.*; (coll.) soco *m.*; (sl.) bala *f.* **2.** *vb.* (coll.) dar um soco em.

sluggish, *adj.* preguiçoso, mole.

slum, *n.* favela *f.*

slumber, 1. *n.* sono *m.* **2.** *vb.* dormir.

slump, 1. *n.* queda/baixa súbita *f.*; declínio *m.* **2.** *vb.* cair bruscamente.

slur, 1. *n.* insulto *m.* **2.** *vb.* comer (sílabas, sons); insultar.

slush, *n.* lama *f.*; neve parcialmente derretida *f.*

slut, *n.* prostituta, (sl.) vaca *f.*

sly, *adj.* vivo, astucioso.

slyness, *n.* astúcia *f.*

smack, 1. *n.* palmada *f.* **2.** *vb.* dar palmada. **s. of,** cheirar a.

small, *adj.* pequeno, miúdo.

smallness, *n.* pequenez *f.*

smallpox, *n.* varíola *f.*

smart, 1. *adj.* inteligente; elegante. **2.** *vb.* doer; sentir dor.

smart aleck, *n.* cara-de-pau *m.*, sabichão *m.*

smash, 1. *n.* choque *m.*, batida *f.* **2.** *vb.* quebrar; esmagar.

smattering, *n.* conhecimento superficial *m.*

smear, 1. *n.* mancha (de gordura, etc.); difamação *f.* **2.** *vb.* lambuzar; difamar.

smell, 1. *n.* cheiro *m.*; (sense) olfato *m.* **2.** *vb.* cheirar; sentir. **s. of,** cheirar a.

smelt, *vb.* fundir.

smile, 1. *n.* sorriso *m.* **2.** *vb.* sorrir.

smiling, *adj.* sorridente.

smirk, 1. *n.* sorriso ridículo *m.* **2.** *vb.* sorrir ridiculamente.

smite, *vb.* golpear; afligir.

smith, *n.* ferreiro *m.*

smock, *n.* bata *f.*; guarda-pó *m.*

smoke, 1. *n.* fumaça *f.*; (sl.) cigarro *m.* **2.** *vb.* fumar; (food) defumar. **no smoking,** é proibido fumar.

smoker, *n.* fumante *m.f.*

smokestack, *n.* chaminé *f.*

smolder, *vb.* arder sem chama.

smooth, 1. *adj.* liso; macio; suave. **2.** *vb.* alisar.

smoothness, *n.* lisura *f.*; maciez *f.*; suavidade *f.*

smother, *vb.* sufocar; abafar.

smudge, *n.* borrão *m.*

smug, *adj.* presunçoso.

smuggle, *vb.* contrabandear.

smuggler, *n.* contrabandista *m.f.*

smuggling, *n.* contrabando *m.*

smut, *n.* fuligem *f.*; pornografia *f.*

snack, 1. *n.* lanche *m.* **2.** *n.* lanchar.

snag, *n.* empecilho, (sl.) galho *m.*

snail, *n.* caracol *m.*

snake, *n.* cobra *f.*

snap, 1. *n.* estalo *m.*; (fastener) pressão *f.*; (coll.) sopa *f.* **2.** *vb.* estalar; quebrar; mordiscar; falar asperamente.

snapshot, *n.* instantâneo *m.*

snare, *n.* armadilha *f.*, laço *m.*

snarl, 1. *n.* rosnado *m.* **2.** *vb.* rosnar; emaranhar-se.

snatch, *vb.* arrebatar.

sneak, *vb.* furtar; ir/entrar/sair furtivamente; esgueirar-se.

sneakers, *n.pl.* tênis *m.pl.*

sneaky, *adj.* furtivo.

sneer, 1. *n.* sorriso desdenhoso *m.* **2.** *vb.* sorrir com desdém.

sneeze, 1. *n.* espirro *m.* **2.** *vb.* espirrar.

snicker, 1. *n.* riso semicontido *m.* **2.** *vb.* conter o riso.

snide, *adj.* malicioso.

sniff, *vb.* farejar, cheirar.

snip, *vb.* cortar.

sniper, *n.* atirador de tocaia *m.*

snitch, 1. *n.* (sl.) informante *m.f.*; (sl.) dedo-duro *m.* **2.** *vb.* (sl.) bater com a língua nos dentes.

snob, *n.* esnobe *m.f.*

snobbery, *n.* esnobismo *m.*

snobbish, *adj.* esnobe.

snoop, 1. *n.* bisbilhoteiro -ra. **2.** *vb.* bisbilhotar.

snoopy, *adj.* abelhudo.

snooze, 1. *n.* cochilo *m.* **2.** *vb.* cochilar.

snore, 1. *n.* ronco *m.* **2.** *vb.* roncar.

snort, *vb.* bufar.

snot, *n.* (*coll.*) ranho *m.*

snout, *n.* focinho *m.*

snow, 1. *n.* neve *f.* **2.** *vb.* nevar.

snowball, *n.* bola de neve *f.*

snowfall, *n.* nevada *f.*

snowflake, *n.* floco de neve *m.*

snowstorm, *n.* nevasca *f.*

snowy, *adj.* nevoso.

snub, 1. *n.* afronta *f.* **2.** *vb.* afrontar.

snuff, 1. *n.* rapé *m.* **2.** *vb.* **s. out**, apagar.

snug, *adj.* confortável, aconchegado.

so, 1. *adv.* assim; tão; também. **s. as to**, para; **s. that**, para que; **s. . . .as, s. many**, tantos; **s. much**, tanto; tão. . .quanto/como; **s. . . .that**, tão. . .que; **and s. on**, e assim por diante. **2.** *conj.* assim.

soak, *vb.* embeber; pôr de molho.

so-and-so, *n.* fulano -na.

soap, *n.* sabão *m.*; (bar) sabonete *m.*

soap opera, *n.* novela, telenovela *f.*

soar, *vb.* voar alto.

sob, *vb.* soluçar.

sober, *adj.* sóbrio.

so-called, *adj.* chamado, suposto.

soccer, *n.* futebol *m.*

sociable, *adj.* sociável, social.

social, 1. *adj.* social. **2.** *n.* reunião social *f.*

socialism, *n.* socialismo *m.*

socialist, *adj.*, *n.* socialista *m.f.*

socialite, *n.* grã-fino -na.

social science, *n.* ciência social *f.*

social security, *n.* previdência social *f.*

social work, *n.* assistência social *f.*

societal, *adj.* social.

society, *n.* sociedade *f.*

sociology, *n.* sociologia *f.*

sock, 1. *n.* meia *f.*; soco *m.* **2.** *vb.* dar um soco em.

socket, *n.* encaixe *m.*; (*elec.*) tomada *f.*

sod, *n.* grama *f.*; torrão *m.*

soda, *n.* soda *f.*; (pop) refrigerante *m.*

sodality, *n.* irmandade, confraria *f.*

soda pop, *n.* refrigerante *m.*, gasosa *f.*

sodium, *n.* sódio *m.*

sofa, *n.* sofá *m.*

soft, *adj.* macio; mole; brando; suave; fofo.

soft drink, *n.* refrigerante *m.*

soften, *vb.* amaciar; amolecer; abrandar; suavizar.

softness, *n.* maciez *f.*; moleza *f.*; brandura *f.*; suavidade *f.*

soggy, *adj.* empapado.

soil, 1. *n.* solo *m.*; terra *f.* **2.** *vb.* sujar.

soirée, *n.* sarau *m.*

sojourn, *n.* visita *f.*; estada *f.*

solace, 1. *n.* consolo *m.* **2.** *vb.* consolar.

solar, *adj.* solar.

solder, 1. *n.* solda *f.* **2.** *vb.* soldar.

soldier, *n.* soldado *m.*

sole, 1. *adj.* único. **2.** *n.* (shoe) sola *f.*; (foot) planta *f.*; (*ichth.*) linguado *m.*

solely, *adv.* só, apenas.

solemn, *adj.* solene.

solemnity, *n.* solenidade *f.*

solicit, *vb.* solicitar.

solicitous, *adj.* solícito.

solid, *adj.* sólido.

solidarity, *n.* solidariedade *f.*

solitaire, *n.* (cards) paciência *f.*

solitary, *adj.* solitário.

solitude, *n.* solidão *f.*

solo, *n.* solo *m.*

soloist, *n.* solista *m.f.*

soluble, *adj.* solúvel.

solution, *n.* solução *f.*

solve, *vb.* resolver.

solvent, *adj.* solvente.

sober, *adj.* sombrio.

some, *adj.*, *pron.* algum; alguns; uns; um pouco de.

somebody, someone, *pron.* alguém. **s. else**, outra pessoa.

someday, *adv.* algum dia.

somehow, someway, *adv.* de algum modo.

somersault, *n.* salto mortal *m.*

something, *n.* alguma coisa, algo.

sometime, *adv.* algum dia; alguma vez.

sometimes, *adv.* às vezes, algumas vezes.

somewhat, *adv.* meio, um tanto.

somewhere, *adv.* em alguma parte, em algum lugar.

son, *n.* filho *m.*

song, *n.* canção, música *f.*; canto *m.*

sonic, *adj.* sônico.

son-in-law, *n.* genro *m.*

sonnet, *n.* soneto *m.*

soon, *adv.* logo, breve. **s.** after, logo depois; **sooner or later**, mais dia, menos dia; **as s. as**, logo que; **as s. as possible**, quanto antes.

soot, *n.* fuligem *f.*

soothe, *vb.* acalmar.

soothing, *adj.* calmante.

soothsayer, *n.* adivinho *m.*

sooty, *adj.* fuliginoso.

sophisticated, *adj.* sofisticado.

sophomore, *n.* segundanista *m.f.*

sopping, *adj.* empapado.

soprano, *n.* soprano *m.f.*

sorcerer -ess, *n.* feiticeiro -ra, bruxo -xa.

sorcery, *n.* bruxaria, feitiçaria *f.*

sordid, *adj.* sórdido.

sore, **1.** *adj.* dolorido, doído; *(coll.)* zangado. **be s.**, doer. **2.** *n.* ferida *f.*

soreness, *n.* dor *f.*

sorrel, *adj.* alazão.

sorrow, *n.* dor *f.*, pesar *m.*, tristeza *f.*

sorrowful, *adj.* doloroso, pesaroso.

sorry, *adj.* **be s.**, sentir, lamentar; **feel s. for**, ter pena de.

sort, **1.** *n.* tipo *m.*, espécie *f.* **s. of**, meio, um tanto. **2.** classificar.

sortie, *n.* surtida *f.*

so-so, *adj.*, *adv.* mais ou menos.

soufflé, *n.* suflê *m.*

soul, *n.* alma *f.*

sound, **1.** *adj.* são; razoável;

firme. **2.** *n.* som *m.* **3.** *vb.* soar; parecer; (probe) sondar.

sound barrier, *n.* barreira do som *f.*

sound effects, *n.pl.* efeitos sonoros *m.pl.*

sounding, *n.* sondagem *f.*

sound track, *n.* trilha sonora *f.*

soup, *n.* sopa *f.*, caldo *m.*

sour, *adj.* azedo, ácido.

source, *n.* fonte *f.*

sourness, *n.* azedume *m.*, acidez *f.*

south, *adj.*, *n.* sul *m.*

South America, *n.* América do Sul *f.*

South American, *adj.*, *n.* sul-americano -na.

southeast, *adj.*, *n.* sudeste *m.*

southeastern, *adj.* sudeste.

southern, *adj.* sulista.

Southern Cross, *n.* Cruzeiro do Sul *m.*

southerner, *n.* sulista *m.f.*

South Pole, *n.* pólo sul *m.*

southwest, *adj.*, *n.* sudoeste *m.*

southwestern, *adj.* sudoeste.

souvenir, *n.* lembrança *f.*

sovereign, *adj.*, *n.* soberano *m.*

sovereignty, *n.* soberania *f.*

soviet, **1.** *adj.* soviético. **2.** *n.* soviete *m.*

Soviet Union, *n.* União Soviética *f.*

sow, **1.** *n.* *(zool.)* porca *f.* **2.** *vb.* semear.

soy, *n.* soja *f.*

spa, *n.* balneário *m.*, estação de águas *f.*

space, **1.** *n.* espaço *m.* **2.** *vb.* espaçar.

space ship, *n.* nave espacial *f.*

space shuttle, *n.* ônibus espacial *m.*

spacious, *adj.* espaçoso.

spade, *n.* pá *f.*; (cards) espadas *f.pl.*

spaghetti, *n.* espaguete *m.*

Spain, *n.* Espanha *f.*

span, **1.** *n.* extensão *f.*; período de tempo *m.* **2.** *vb.* estender-se sobre.

Spaniard, *n.* espanhol -la.

Spanish, *adj.*, *n.* espanhol -la.

Spanish America, *n.* América Espanhola *f.*

Spanish American, *adj., n.* hispano-americano -na.

spank, *vb.* dar palmada, espancar.

spanking, *n.* surra, coça *f.*

spar, 1. *n.* verga *f.* **2.** *vb.* lutar, brigar.

spare, 1. *adj.* de sobra; sobressalente. **2.** *vb.* poupar.

spare time, *n.* tempo livre *m.*

spare tire, *n.* pneu sobressalente *m.*

spark, 1. *n.* faísca *f.* **2.** *vb.* faiscar.

sparkle, 1. *n.* centelha *f.* **2.** *vb.* cintilar.

spark plug, *n.* vela *f.*

sparrow, *n.* pardal *m.*

sparse, *adj.* ralo, escasso.

spasm, *n.* espasmo *m.*

spat, *n.* briga doméstica *f.*

spate, *n.* enchente *f.*

spatial, *adj.* espacial.

spatter, *vb.* respingar, salpicar.

spatula, *n.* espátula *f.*

spawn, *vb.* desovar; produzir.

speak, *vb.* falar; conversar. **so to s.,** por assim dizer.

speaker, *n.* orador -ra; alto-falante *m.*, caixa de som *f.*

spear, *n.* lança *f.*

spearmint, *n.* hortelã *f.*

special, *adj.* especial.

special delivery, *n.* entrega rápida *f.*

specialist, *n.* especialista *m.f.*

specialization, *n.* especialização *f.*

specialize, *vb.* especializar-se.

specialty, *n.* especialidade *f.*

species, *n.* espécie *f.*

specific, *adj.* específico.

specification, *n.* especificação *f.*

specify, *vb.* especificar.

specimen, *n.* espécime *m.*

specious, *adj.* especioso.

speck, *n.* ponto *m.*; pinta *f.*

speckled, *adj.* mosqueado.

spectacle, *n.* espetáculo *m.*; *(pl.)* óculos *m.pl.*

spectacular, *adj.* espetacular.

spectator, *n.* espectador -ra.

specter, *n.* espectro *m.*

spectrum, *n.* espectro *m.*

speculate, *vb.* especular.

speech, *n.* fala *f.*; discurso *m.*; língua *f.*

speech therapy, *n.* fonoaudiologia *f.*

speed, 1. *n.* velocidade *f.* **2.** *vb.* correr. **s. up,** acelerar.

speeding, *n.* excesso de velocidade *m.*

speed limit, *n.* velocidade máxima *f.*

speedometer, *n.* velocímetro *m.*

speedy, *adj.* rápido.

spell, 1. *n.* feitiço *m.*; período *m.*; *(med.)* acesso *m.* **2.** *vb.* escrever; soletrar.

spellbound, *adj.* enfeitiçado.

spelling, *n.* grafia *f.*; ortografia *f.*

spend, *vb.* gastar; (time) passar.

spendthrift, *n.* perdulário -ria.

sperm, *n.* esperma *m.*

spew, *vb.* vomitar.

sphere, *n.* esfera *f.*

sphinx, *n.* esfinge *f.*

spice, 1. *n.* especiaria *f.*; condimento *m.* **2.** *vb.* condimentar.

spicy, *adj.* condimentado; apimentado.

spider, *n.* aranha *f.* **s. web,** teia de aranha *f.*

spiel, *n.* conversa (de mascate, etc.) *f.*

spigot, *n.* torneira *f.*

spike, *n.* espigão *m.*

spill, *vb.* entornar, derramar.

spin, 1. *n.* giro *m.*, rotação *f.* **2.** *vb.* girar, rodar; (textile) fiar.

spinach, *n.* espinafre *m.*

spinal, *vb.* vertebral.

spindle, *n.* fuso *m.*

spine, *n.* espinha *f.*; espinho *m.*

spinster, *n.* solteirona *f.*

spiny, *adj.* espinhoso.

spiral, *adj.* n. espiral *f.*

spire, *n.* torre *f.*; agulha *f.*

spirit, *n.* espírito *m.*; fantasma *m.*; ânimo *m.*; disposição *f.*

spiritual, *adj.* espiritual.

spiritualism, *n.* espiritismo *m.*

spiritualist, *adj., n.* espírita *m.f.*

spit, 1. *n.* escarro, cuspo *m.* **2.** *vb.* cuspir.

spite, 1. *n.* rancor *m.*; despeito *m.* **in s. of,** apesar de. **2.** *vb.* irritar.

spiteful, *adj.* rancoroso.

spitoon, *n.* cuspideira *f.*

splash, 1. *n.* chape *m.* **2.** *vb.* chapinhar.

spleen, *n.* baço *m.*

splendid, *adj.* esplêndido.

splendor, *n.* esplendor *m.*

splinter, *n.* lasca *f.*, cavaco *m.*

split, 1. *n.* rachadura *f.*; cisão *f.* **2.** *vb.* rachar; cindir.

splurge, *vb.* ostentar; (money) esbanjar.

spoil, 1. *n.pl.* despojo *m.* **2.** *vb.* estragar(-se); mimar.

spoilsport, *n.* desmancha-prazeres *m.*

spoke, *n.* raio (de roda) *m.*

spokesman -woman -person, *n.* porta-voz *m.f.*

sponge, *n.* esponja *f.*

sponsor, 1. *n.* patrocinador -a. **2.** *vb.* patrocinar.

sponsorship, *n.* patrocínio *m.*

spontaneous, *adj.* espontâneo.

spoof, *n.* paródia *f.*

spook, *n.* fantasma *m.*, assombração *f.*

spool, *n.* carretel *m.*, bobina *f.*

spoon, *n.* colher *f.*

spoonful, *n.* colherada *f.*

sporadic, *adj.* esporádico.

spore, *n.* espório *m.*

sport, *n.* esporte, desporto *m.*

sportsman -woman, *n.* esportista *m.f.*

sportsmanship, *n.* esportiva *f.*

spot, 1. *n.* mancha *f.*; ponto *m.*; lugar *m.* **2.** *vb.* manchar; avistar.

spotless, *adj.* imaculado.

spotlight, *n.* holofote *m.* **be in the s.,** estar na berlinda.

spot remover, *n.* tira-manchas *m.*

spotted, *adj.* manchado; mosqueado.

spouse, *n.* cônjuge *m.f.*

spout, 1. *n.* bico, esguicho *m.* **2.** *vb.* jorrar.

sprain, 1. *n.* torcedura *f.* **2.** *vb.* torcer.

sprawl, *vb.* estatelar-se.

spray, 1. *n.* jato *m.*; spray *m.* **2.** *vb.* borrifar.

spread, 1. *n.* extensão *f.*; divulgação *f.*; (bed) colcha *f.*; manteiga *f.*; (coll.) banquete *m.* **2.** *vb.* espalhar(-se); divulgar(-se); passar.

spree, *n.* bebedeira *f.*; farra *f.*

sprig, *n.* rebento *m.*

spring, 1. *n.* mola *f.*; (season) primavera *f.*; pulo *m.*; manancial *m.* **2.** *vb.* pular; nascer. **s. up,** surgir.

sprinkle, 1. *n.* borrifo *m.*; chuvisco *m.* **2.** *vb.* borrifar. chuviscar.

sprinkler, *n.* regador *m.*; regadeira *f.*

sprint, 1. *n.* corrida *f.* **2.** *vb.* correr (numa corrida).

sprite, *n.* elfo *m.*

sprout, 1. *n.* vergôntea *f.* **2.** *vb.* brotar.

spruce, 1. *n.* abeto *m.* **2.** *vb.* **s. up,** enfeitar.

spry, *adj.* ágil.

spunk, *n.* (coll.) brio *m.*

spur, 1. *n.* espora *f.*; estímulo *m.* **2.** *vb.* esporear; estimular.

spurn, *vb.* rejeitar.

spurt, 1. *n.* jorro *m.*; ímpeto *m.* **2.** *vb.* jorrar.

sputnik, *n.* esputinique *m.*

sputter, *n.* crepitar.

spy, 1. *n.* espião -ã. **2.** *vb.* espiar.

squabble, 1. *n.* disputa *f.* **2.** *vb.* disputar.

squad, *n.* esquadra *f.*

squadron, *n.* esquadrão *m.*

squalid, *adj.* esquálido.

squall, *n.* borrasca *f.*

squander, *vb.* desperdiçar, esbanjar.

square, 1. *adj.* quadrado. **2.** *n.* quadrado *m.*; praça *f.*

square dance, *n.* quadrilha *f.*

square root, *n.* raiz quadrada *f.*

squash, 1. *n.* abóbora *f.* **2.** *vb.* esmagar.

squat, 1. *adj.* atarracado. **2.** *vb.* acocorar-se.

squawk, 1. *n.* grasnada *f.* **2.** *vb.* grasnar; (fig.) chiar.

squeak, 1. *n.* guincho *m.* **2.** *vb.* guinchar, ranger.

squeal, 1. *n.* guincho *m.* **2.** *vb.* guinchar; (sl.) dar com a língua nos dentes.

squeamish, *adj.* melindroso.

squeeze, 1. *n.* aperto *m.* **2.** *vb.* apertar; espremer; abraçar.

squelch, *vb.* esmagar; abafar.

squid, *n.* lula *f.*

squint, vb. ter os olhos meio fechados.

squire, n. escudeiro m.; proprietário rural m.

squirm, vb. retorcer-se.

squirrel, n. esquilo m.

squirt, 1. n. esguicho m.; (coll.) tampinha m. 2. vb. esguichar.

stab, 1. n. facada, punhalada f. 2. apunhalar.

stability, n. estabilidade f.

stabilize, vb. estabilizar.

stable, 1. adj. estável. 2. n. estábulo, cavalariça f.

stack, 1. n. montão m., pilha f. 2. vb. empilhar.

stadium, n. estádio m.

staff, n. cajado, bordão m.; pessoal m. general s., estado maior m.

stag, n. cervo, veado m.

stage, 1. n. palco m.; estrado m.; etapa f. 2. vb. encenar.

stagecoach, n. diligência f.

stagflation, n. estagflação f.

stagger, vb. cambalear; trocar pernas.

stagnant, adj. estagnado.

stagnate, vb. estagnar.

staid, adj. sóbrio.

stain, 1. n. mancha f.; corante m. 2. vb. manchar; tingir.

stained glass, n. vitral m.

stainless, adj. inoxidável.

stair, n. degrau m.

stairs, staircase, n. escada f.

stake, 1. n. estaca f.; aposta f.; interesse m. at s., em jogo, 2. vb. estacar; apostar, arriscar.

stale, adj. rançoso; duro; viciado; velho.

stalemate, n. impasse m.

stalk, 1, n. caule m. 2. vb. caçar.

stall, 1. n. baia f.; barraca f. 2. vb. encrencar; (sl.) fazer cera.

stallion, n. garanhão m.

stalwart, adj. firme.

stamina, n. resistência física f.

stammer, 1. n. gagueira f. 2. vb. gaguejar.

stamp, 1. n. selo m.; (rubber) carimbo m. 2. vb. selar; carimbar; bater com o pé; pisar.

stamp collecting, n. filatelia f.

stampede, 1. n. estouro da boiada m. 2. vb. estourar.

stance, n. posição f.

stand, 1. n. barraca f.; posição f.; plataforma f.; pedestal m.; (pl.) arquibancadas f.pl. 2. vb. colocar; estar/ficar em pé; agüentar. s. by, aguardar; s. for, representar; tolerar; s. out, destacar-se; s. up, levantar-se; s. up to, fazer frente a.

standard, 1. adj. padrão, normal. 2. n. padrão, standard m.; nível m.; critério m.; (banner) estandarte m. s. of living, padrão de vida m.

standardize, vb. padronizar, estandardizar.

standardized, adj. padrão.

stand-in, n. dublê m.f.

standing, 1. adj. fixo; permanente. 2. n. posição f.; reputação f.

stand-off, n. impasse m.

standpoint, n. ponto-de-vista m.

stanza, n. estrofe f.

staple, 1. adj. básico. 2. n. grampo m.; (pl.) gêneros básicos m.pl. 3. vb. grampear.

stapler, n. grampeador m.

star, 1. n. estrela f., astro m. 2. vb. estrelar.

starboard, n. estibordo m.

starch, 1. n. amido m.; (clothes) goma f. 2. vb. engomar.

stardom, n. estrelato m.

stare, 1. n. olhar fixo m. 2. vb. fitar.

starfish, n. estrela do mar f.

stark, 1. adj. severo; completo. 2. adv. completamente.

start, 1. n. começo m.; sobressalto m. 2. vb. começar; ligar; partir; arrancar.

starter, n. (car) (motor de) arranque m.

startle, vb. assustar.

starvation, n. fome f.

starve, vb. matar de fome; morrer de/passar fome.

starving, adj. faminto.

stash, vb. esconder, (sl.) malocar.

state, 1. n. estado m. 2. vb. declarar.

stately, adj. majestoso.

statement, n. declaração f.;

depoimento *m.*; (bank) extrato de conta *m.*

state of siege, *n.* estado de sítio *m.*

statesman -woman, *n.* estadista *m.f.*

static, 1. *adj.* estático. **2.** *n.* estática *f.*

station, 1. *n.* estação *f.*; posto *m.*; posição *f.* **2.** *vb.* postar.

stationary, *adj.* estacionário.

stationery, *n.* papel de carta, papel timbrado *m.*; artigos de escritório *m.pl.* **s. store,** papelaria *f.*

stations of the cross, *n.pl.* passos (da Paixão de Cristo) *m.pl.*

station wagon, *n.* camioneta, -nhonete, perua *f.*

statistic, *n.* dado *m.*

statistics, *n.* estatística *f.*

statue, *n.* estátua *f.*

stature, *n.* estatura *f.*

status, *n.* status *m.*, condição *f.*

statute, *n.* estatuto *m.*

staunch, *adj.* firme; fiel.

stave, 1. *n.* aduela *f.* **2.** *vb.* **s. off,** repelir.

stay, 1. *n.* estada, estadia *f.*; adiamento *m.*; esteio *m.* **2.** *vb.* ficar; hospedar-se; **s. away,** ausentar-se; **s. up,** ficar acordado.

stead, *n.* lugar *m.*

steadfast, *adj.* firme, resoluto.

steady, 1. *adj.* estável; firme; constante. **2.** *vb.* estabilizar; firmar.

steak, *n.* bife *m.*

steal, 1. *n.* roubo, furto *m.* **2.** *vb.* roubar, furtar. **s. away,** escapulir-se.

stealth, *n.* procedimento furtivo *m.* **by s.,** às escondidas.

stealthy, *adj.* furtivo.

steam, *n.* vapor *m.*

steamboat, -ship, *n.* vapor *m.*

steam roller, *n.* rolo compressor *m.*

steed, *n.* corcel *m.*

steel, *n.* aço *m.* **s. mill,** (usina) siderúrgica *f.*; **s. wool,** palha de aço *f.*

steep, *adj.* íngreme; caro.

steeple, *n.* torre de igreja, agulha *f.*

steer, 1. *n.* boi *m.* **2.** *vb.* dirigir.

steering wheel, *n.* volante *m.*, direção *f.*

stem, 1. *n.* caule *m.*; (*gram.*) tema *m.* **2.** *vb.* parar; derivar.

stench, *n.* fedor *m.*

stencil, *n.* estêncil *m.*

stenographer, *n.* estenógrafo -fa.

step, 1. *n.* passo *m.*; medida *f.*; (stair) degrau *m.* **take steps,** tomar providências. **2.** *vb.* dar um passo; pisar. **s. back,** recuar; **s. in,** entrar; **s. on,** pisar; **s. out,** sair; **s. up,** aumentar.

stepbrother -sister, *n.* meio-irmão -ia-irmã.

stepfather, *n.* padrasto *m.*

stepladder, *n.* escada de mão *f.*

stepmother, *n.* madrasta *f.*

stepson -daughter, *n.* enteado -da.

stereo, *n.* estéreo *m.*

stereophonic, *adj.* estereofônico.

stereotype, 1. *n.* estereótipo *m.* **2.** *vb.* esterotipar.

sterile, *adj.* estéril.

sterilize, *vb.* esterilizar.

sterling silver, *n.* prata de lei *f.*

stern, 1. *adj.* severo. **2.** *n.* (*naut.*) popa *f.*

stethoscope, *n.* estetoscópio *m.*

stevedore, *n.* estivador *m.*

stew, 1. *n.* guisado, ensopado *m.* **2.** *vb.* guisar; vexar-se; preocupar-se.

steward, *n.* administrador *m.*; camareiro *m.*

stewardess, *n.* aeromoça, comissária de bordo *f.*

stick, 1. *n.* pau *m.*, vara *f.*; bastão *m.* **2.** *vb.* colar; pegar; pôr; ficar preso; atolar-se. **s. it out,** agüentar; **s. out,** projetar-se; dar na vista; **s. to,** aferrar-se a; **s. together,** manter-se unidos; **s. up,** (*sl.*) assaltar; **s. up for,** defender.

sticker, *n.* espinho *m.*; adesivo *m.*

stickler, *n.* caxias *m.*

stick-up, *n.* (*sl.*) assalto *m.*

sticky, *adj.* pegajoso.

stiff, 1. *adj.* rijo, teso. **2.** *n.* (*sl.*) cadáver *m.*

stiffen, *vb.* enrijecer.

stiffness, n. rigidez f.

stifle, vb. sufocar; abafar.

stigma, n. estigma m.

still, 1. adj. imóvel; quieto; calado. **2.** n. alambique m.; calada f. **3.** vb. acalmar. **4.** adv. ainda.

stillborn, adj. natimorto.

still life, n. natureza morta f.

stillness, n. imobilidade f.; calma f.; silêncio m.

stilted, adj. empolado, afetado.

stilts, n.pl. andas f.pl.

stimulant, adj., n. estimulante m.

stimulate, vb. estimular.

stimulus, n. estímulo m.

sting, 1. n. picada f. **2.** vb. picar, aferroar; arder.

stinger, n. ferrão, aguilhão m.

stinginess, n. sovinice f.

stingy, adj. sovina (coll.) pão-duro.

stink, 1. n. mau cheiro, fedor m. **2.** vb. cheirar mal, feder.

stinking, adj. fedorento.

stipend, n. estipêndio m.

stipulate, vb. estipular.

stir, 1. n. alvoroço m. **2.** vb. mexer(-se). **s up,** agitar; despertar.

stirring, adj. emocionante.

stirrup, n. estribo m.

stitch, 1. n. ponto **2.** vb. coser, costurar.

stock, n. sortimento, estoque m.; raça f.; (fin.) ações f.pl. **in s.,** em estoque; **out of s.,** esgotado.

stockade, n. estacada, paliçada f.

stockbroker, n. corretor -ra da bolsa.

stock exchange, n. bolsa de valores f.

stockholder, n. acionista m.f.

Stockholm, n. Estocolmo.

stocking, n. meia f.

stockpile, 1. n. reserva f. **2.** vb. armazenar.

stockroom, n. almoxarifado m.

stocky, adj. atarracado.

stockyard, n. curral (de gado) m.

stoic, adj., n. estóico m.

stoke, vb. atiçar.

stole, n. estola f.

stolid, adj. impassível.

stomach, 1. n. estômago m. **2.** vb. suportar.

stone, 1. n. pedra f. **2.** vb. apedrejar.

stooge, n. lacaio m.

stool, n. banco, tamborete m.

stoop, vb. abaixar-se.

stop, 1. n. parada f.; escala f. **put a s. to,** pôr fim a. **2.** vb. parar; suspender; deter; impedir; (bleeding) estancar. **s. by,** dar um pulo em; **s. doing** (etc.), deixar de fazer (etc.); **s. over,** fazer escala/parada; **s. up,** entupir; tapar.

stopgap, n. expediente temporário, (sl.) safa-onça m.

stop light, n. sinal m., sinaleira f.

stopover, n. escala f.

stoppage, n. interrupção f.; (work) greve f.

stopper, n. tampão m.

stop sign, n. sinal de parada m.

stop watch, n. cronômetro m.

storage, n. armazenamento m.; guarda-móveis m.

store, 1. n. loja f.; armazém m.; reserva f.; provisão f. **2.** vb. guardar; armazenar.

storekeeper, n. lojista m.f.

storeroom, n. almoxarifado m.

stork, n. cegonha f.

storm, n. tempestade f.

stormy, adj. tempestuoso.

story, n. história, estória f.; conto m.; (floor) andar m.

storyteller, n. contador -ra de história.

stout, adj. robusto.

stove, n. fogão m.

stow, vb. guardar.

stowaway, n. clandestino -na.

straddle, vb. escarranchar.

strafe, vb. bombardear.

straggle, vb. extraviar-se; chegarem aos poucos.

straight, 1. adj. reto; direito; direto; ereto. **2.** vb. diretamente; a fio. **s. ahead,** bem em frente.

straighten, vb. endireitar. **s. out,** arrumar.

straightforward, adj. franco.

strain, 1. n. tensão, pressão f.;

variedade *f.* **2.** *vb.* forçar; irritar; coar.

strainer, *n.* coador *m.*, peneira *f.*

strait, *n.* aperto *m.*; *(geog.)* estreito *m.*

strait jacket, *n.* camisa de força *f.*

strait-laced, *adj.* puritano.

strand, 1. *n.* fio *m.* **2.** *vb.* abandonar; encalhar.

strange, *adj.* esquisito, estranho.

strangeness, *n.* esquisitice, estranheza *f.*

stranger, *n.* estranho -nha.

strangle, *vb.* estrangular.

strap, *n.* correia *f.*; alça *f.*

stratagem, *n.* estratagema *f.*

strategic, *adj.* estratégico.

strategy, *n.* estratégia *f.*

stratify, *vb.* estratificar(-se).

stratosphere, *n.* estratosfera *f.*

stratum, *n.* camada *f.*, estrato *m.*

straw, *n.* palha *f.*; (drinking) canudinho *m.* **the last s.,** o cúmulo.

strawberry, *n.* morango *m.*

stray, 1. *adj.* extraviado. **2.** *vb.* extraviar-se.

streak, 1. *n.* listra, lista *f.*; raio *m.*; temporada *f.* **2.** *vb.* listrar.

stream, *n.* ribeirão *m.*; corrente *f.*

streamer, *n.* flâmula, bandeirola *f.*

streamline, *vb.* dinamizar.

street, *n.* rua *f.*

streetcar, *n.* bonde *m.*

streetcleaner, *n.* (person) gari *m.*

streetwalker, *n.* meretriz *f.*

strength, *n.* força *f.*, vigor *m.*

strengthen, *vb.* fortalecer.

strenuous, *adj.* árduo.

stress, 1. *n.* tensão *f.*; estresse *m.*; ênfase *f.*; *(gram.)* acento, *m.* **2.** *vb.* pressionar; estressar; enfatizar.

stressed, *adj.* estressado; *(gram.)* tônico.

stretch, 1. *n.* extensão *f.*; (time) período *m.* **2.** *vb.* estirar; espreguiçar-se. **s. out,** estirar-se.

stretcher, *n.* maca *f.*

strew, *vb.* espalhar.

strict, *adj.* estrito.

stride, 1. *n.* passo largo *m.* **1.** *vb.* andar a passos largos.

strident, *adj.* estridente.

strife, *n.* conflito *m.*

strike, 1. *n.* golpe *m.*; ataque *m.*; greve *f.*; descoberta *f.* **2.** *vb.* bater (em); atacar; fazer greve; descobrir; (clock) bater; (match) acender.

strikebreaker, *n.* fura-greve *m.f.*

striker, *n.* grevista *m.f.*

striking, *adj.* notável.

string, *n.* barbante *m.*; *(mus.)* corda *f.*; série *f.*

stringent, *adj.* estrito.

strip, 1. *n.* tira *f.*; pista *f.* **2.** *vb.* despir(-se); despojar.

stripe, 1. *n.* listra, lista *f.* **2.** *vb.* listrar.

strive, *vb.* esforçar-se.

stroke, *n.* golpe *m.*; *(med.)* ataque *m.*, apoplexia *f.*; (swimming) braçada *f.*; (brush) pincelada *f.* **2.** *vb.* afagar.

stroll, 1. *n.* passeio *m.*, volta *f.* **2.** *vb.* dar uma volta, passear.

stroller, *n.* carrinho de bebê *m.*

strong, *adj.* forte.

strong-box, *n.* cofre *m.*

stronghold, *n.* fortaleza *f.*

structure, *n.* estrutura *f.*

struggle, 1. *n.* luta *f.* **2.** *vb.* lutar.

strum, *vb.* dedilhar.

strut, *vb.* pavonear-se.

stub, 1. *n.* toco *m.*; talão *m.* **2.** *vb.* (toe) topar.

stubborn, *adj.* teimoso.

stubbornness, *n.* teimosia *f.*

stubby, *adj.* atarracado.

stucco, *n.* estuque *m.*

stuck-up, *adj.* convencido.

stud, *n.* garanhão *m.*; botão de colarinho *m.*

student, *n.* estudante *m.f.*; aluno -na.

studio, *n.* estúdio *m.*; (artist) ateliê *m.*

studious, *adj.* estudioso.

study, 1. *n.* estudo *m.* **2.** *vb.* estudar.

stuff, 1. *n.* coisas *f.pl.* **2.** *vb.* encher; rechear; empanturrar.

stuffing, *n.* recheio *m.*

stuffy, *adj.* abafado; entupido; puritano.

stumble, *vb.* tropeçar.

stump, **1.** *n.* toco *m.* **2.** *vb.* deixar perplexo.

stun, *vb.* estontear.

stunt, **1.** *n.* proeza *f.*; acrobacia *f.* **2.** *vb.* enfezar.

stupefy, *vb.* estupefazer.

stupendous, *adj.* estupendo.

stupid, *adj.* estúpido, burro.

stupidity, *n.* estupidez *f.*

stupor, *n.* estupor *m.*

sturdy, *adj.* forte, duradouro.

stutter, **1.** *n.* gagueira *f.* **2.** *vb.* guguejar.

stutterer, *n.* gago -ga.

sty, *n.* chiqueiro *m.*

style, **1.** *n.* estilo *m.*; maneira *f.*; tipo *m.*; (fashion) moda *f.* **2.** *vb.* denominar; estilizar; (hair) pentear.

stylish, *adj.* na moda, elegante.

stylist, *n.* estilista *m.f.*; modista *m.f.*

stylize, *vb.* estilizar.

suave, *adj.* polido, afável.

sub-, *pref.* sub-.

subdue, *vb.* subjugar.

subdued, *adj.* contido, reprimido.

subject, **1.** *adj.* sujeito (a). **2.** *n.* assunto, tema *m.*; (study) matéria *f.*; (gram.) sujeito *m.*; (citizen) súdito -ta. **3.** *vb.* sujeitar, submeter.

subjective, *adj.* subjetivo.

subjugate, *vb.* subjugar.

subjunctive, *adj.* subjuntivo.

sublime, *adj.* sublime.

subliminal, *adj.* subliminar.

submarine, *adj.*, *n.* submarino *m.*

submerge, *vb.* submergir.

submissive, *adj.* submisso.

submit, *vb.* submeter(-se); entregar(-se).

subordinate, **1.** *adj.*, *n.* subordinado -a. **2.** *vb.* subordinar.

subpoena, **1.** *n.* intimação *f.* **2.** *vb.* intimar.

subscribe, *vb.* subscrever. **s. to**, assinar.

subscriber, *n.* assinante *m.f.*

subscription, *n.* subscrição *f.*; (magazine) assinatura *f.*

subsequent, *adj.* subseqüente.

subservient, *adj.* subserviente.

subside, *vb.* acalmar-se; diminuir.

subsidiary, **1.** *adj.* subsidiário. **2.** *n.* subsidiária *f.*

subsidize, *vb.* subvencionar.

subsidy, *n.* subvenção *f.*

subsist, *vb.* subsistir.

substance, *n.* substância *f.*

substantial, *adj.* substancial.

substantiate, *vb.* substantificar.

substantive, *adj.*, *n.* substantivo *m.*

substitute, **1.** *n.* substituto -ta. **2.** *vb.* substituir.

substitution, *n.* substituição *f.*

subterfuge, *n.* subterfúgio *m.*

subtitle, *n.* subtítulo *m.*; (movie) legenda *f.*

subtle, *adj.* sutil.

subtlety, *n.* sutileza *f.*

subtract, *vb.* subtrair.

suburb, *n.* subúrbio *m.*

suburban, *adj.* suburbano.

subversion, *n.* subversão *f.*

subversive, *adj.*, *m.* subversivo *m.*

subvert, *n.* subverter.

subway, *n.* metrô *m.*

succeed, *vb.* ter/fazer sucesso.

succeeding, *adj.* sucessivo.

success, *n.* sucesso, êxito *m.*

successful, *adj.* bem sucedido; próspero. **be s.**, ter sucesso.

succession, *n.* sucessão *f.*

successive, *adj.* sucessivo.

successor, *n.* sucessor -ra.

succinct, *adj.* sucinto.

succor, **1.** *n.* socorro *m.* **2.** *vb.* socorrer.

succulent, *adj.* suculento.

succumb, *vb.* sucumbir; falecer.

such, **1.** *adj.*, *pron.* tal; tanto, tamanho. **2.** *adv.* tão.

suck, *vb.* chupar.

sucker, *n.* (lollipop) pirulito *m.*; (sl.) trouxa *m.*

suckle, *vb.* amamentar; mamar.

suction, *n.* sucção *f.*

sudden, *adj.* repentino. **all of a s.**, de repente.

suddenly, *adv.* de repente.

suds, *n.pl.* espuma de sabão *f.*

sue, *vb.* processar, acionar.

suede, *n.* camurça *f.*

suet, *n.* sebo *m.*

suffer, *n.* sofrer, padecer.

sufferer, *n.* sofredor -ra.

suffering, *n.* sofrimento *m.*

suffice, *vb.* bastar, ser suficiente.

sufficient, *adj.* suficiente.

suffix, *n.* sufixo *m.*

suffocate, *vb.* sufocar.

suffrage, *n.* sufrágio *m.*

sugar, *n.* açúcar *m.* **s. bowl**, açucareiro *m.*

sugar cane, *n.* cana-de-açúcar *f.*

sugar plantation, *n.* canavial *m.*; engenho *m.*

sugary, *adj.* açucarado.

suggest, *vb.* sugerir.

suggestion, *n.* sugestão *f.*

suicide, *n.* suicídio *m.* ; (person) suicida *m.f.* **commit s.**, suicidar-se.

suit, **1.** *n.* terno, (P.) fato *m.*; (woman's) costume *m.*; (jur.) processo *m.*; (cards) naipe *m.* **2.** *vb.* convir a; (clothes) ficar bem em.

suitable, *adj.* conveniente; apropriado.

suitcase, *n.* mala, valise *f.*

suite, *n.* suíte *f.*

suitor, *n.* pretendente *m.*

sulfur, *n.* súlfur, enxofre *m.*

sulk, *vb.* estar amuado.

sullen, *adj.* soturno.

sully, *vb.* manchar, sujar.

sultan, *n.* sultão *m.*

sultry, *adj.* abafado; apaixonado.

sum, **1.** *n.* soma *f.* **2.** *vb.* somar. **s. up**, resumir.

summarize, *vb.* resumir.

summary, **1.** *adj.* sumário. **2.** *n.* resumo, sumário *m.*

summer, *n.* verão *m.*

summit, *n.* cume *m.* **s. meeting**, reunião de cúpula *f.*

summon, *vb.* convocar, intimar.

summons, *n.* intimação *f.*

sumptuous, *adj.* suntuoso.

sun, **1.** *n.* sol *m.* **s. bath**, banho de sol *m.* **2.** *vb.* tomar o sol.

sunburn, **1.** *n.* queimadura do sol *f.* **2.** *vb.* queimar-se ao sol.

sundae, *n.* sundae *m.*

Sunday, *n.* domingo *m.*

sundial, *n.* relógio de sol *m.*

sundown, *n.* pôr do sol *m.*

sunflower, *n.* girassol *m.*

sunglasses, *n.pl.* óculos escuros *m.pl.*

sunlight, *n.* luz do sol *f.*

sunny, *adj.* ensolarado.

sunrise, *n.* nascer do sol *m.*

sunset, *n.* pôr do sol *m.*

sunshine, *n.* luz do sol *f.*

sunstroke, *n.* insolação *f.*

suntan, *n.* bronzeado *m.* **get a s.**, bronzear-se.

super-, *pref.* super-, sobre-.

superb, *adj.* soberbo, excelente.

superficial, *adj.* superficial.

superfluous, *adj.* supérfluo.

superintendent, *n.* superintendente.

superior, *adj.*, *n.* superior *m.*

superiority, *n.* superioridade *f.*

superlative, *adj.* superlativo.

supermarket, *n.* supermercado *m.*

supernatural, *adj.* sobrenatural.

superpower, *n.* superpotência *f.*

supersede, *vb.* suplantar, substituir.

supersonic, *adj.* supersônico.

superstition, *n.* superstição *f.*

superstitious, *adj.* supersticioso.

supervise, *vb.* supervisar, supervisionar.

supervisor, *n.* supervisor -ra.

supper, *n.* jantar *m.*, janta *f.*

supplant, *vb.* suplantar.

supple, *adj.* flexível; ágil.

supplement, **1.** *n.* suplemento *m.* **2.** *vb.* suplementar.

supplier, *n.* fornecedor -ra.

supply, **1.** *n.* provisão *f.* **s. and demand**, oferta e procura. **2.** *vb.* fornecer, abastecer.

support, **1.** *n.* apoio *m.*; sustento *m.* **2.** *vb.* apoiar; sustentar.

supporter, *n.* partidário -ria.

suppose, *vb.* supor. **be supposed to**, dever.

supposed, *adj.* suposto.

supposition, *n.* suposição *f.*

suppository, *n.* supositório *m.*

suppress, *vb.* suprimir.

supremacy, *n.* supremacia *f.*

supreme, *adj.* supremo.

sure, *adj.* certo; seguro. **be s.**, ter certeza.

sureness, *n.* certeza *f.*; segurança *f.*

surf, 1. *n.* ressaca *f.* **s. board,** prancha (de surfe) *f.* **2.** *vb.* surfar.

surface, *n.* superfície *f.*

surfer, *n.* surfista *m.f.*

surfing, *n.* surfismo *m.*

surge, 1. *vb.* onda *f.* ; (*elec.*) sobretensão *f.* **2.** *vb.* ondular; aumentar.

surgeon, *n.* cirurgião -ã.

surgery, *n.* cirurgia *f.*

surgical, *adj.* cirúrgico.

surly, *adj.* grosseiro.

surmise, 1. *n.* conjetura *f.* **2.** *vb.* conjeturar.

surmount, *vb.* superar.

surname, *n.* sobrenome, nome de família *m.*

surpass, *vb.* exceder.

surplus, 1. *adj.* de sobra. **2.** *n.* excesso *m.* ; superávit *m.*

surprise, 1. *n.* surpresa *f.* **2.** *vb.* surpreender.

surprised, *adj.* surpreso; surpreendido.

surprising, *adj.* surpreendente.

surrealism, *n.* surrealismo *m.*

surrender, 1. *n.* rendição *f.* **2.** *vb.* render-se.

surreptitious, *adj.* sub-reptício.

surrogate, *n.* substituto -ta.

surround, *vb.* cercar, rodear.

surrounding, *adj.* circundante.

surroundings, *n.pl.* arredores *m.pl.*

surveillance, *n.* vigilância *f.*

survey, 1. *n.* estudo *m.* ; levantamento *m.* ; panorama *m.* **2.** *vb.* examinar; fazer levantamento de.

surveyor, *n.* agrimensor -ra.

survival, *n.* sobrevivência *f.*

survive, *vb.* sobreviver.

survivor, *n.* sobrevivente *m.f.*

susceptible, *adj.* suscetível.

suspect, 1. *adj.* suspeito. **2.** *n.* suspeito -ta. **3.** *vb.* suspeitar.

suspend, *vb.* suspender.

suspenders, *n.pl.* suspensórios *m.pl.*

suspense, *n.* suspense *m.*

suspension, *n.* suspensão *f.* **s. bridge,** ponte pênsil *f.*

suspicion, *n.* suspeita *f.* **be under s.,** ser suspeito.

suspicious, *adj.* suspeito; suspeitoso.

sustain, *vb.* sustentar, suster.

suture, *n.* sutura *f.*

svelte, *adj.* esbelto, enxuto.

swagger, 1. *n.* bazófia *f.* **2.** *vb.* pavonear-se.

swallow, 1. *n.* gole *m.* **2.** *vb.* engolir.

swamp, *n.* pântano, brejo *m.*

swampy, *adj.* pantanoso.

swan, *n.* cisne *m.*

swanky, *adj.* elegante.

swap, 1. *n.* troca *f.* **2.** *vb.* trocar.

swarm, 1. *n.* enxame *m.* **2.** *vb.* enxamear.

swarthy, *adj.* moreno, trigueiro.

swashbuckling, *n.* fanfarronice *f.*

swat, 1. *n.* palmada *f.* **2.** *vb.* dar palmada; matar (moscas).

sway, 1. *n.* balanço *m.* **2.** *vb.* balançar.

swear, *vb.* jurar; prestar juramento; prometer; xingar.

sweat, 1. *n.* suor *m.* **2.** *vb.* suar.

sweater, *n.* suéter *m.* ; pulôver *m.*

sweaty, *adj.* suado.

Swede, *n.* sueco -ca.

Sweden, *n.* Suécia *f.*

Swedish, *adj.* sueco.

sweep, 1. *n.* varredura *f.* **2.** *vb.* varrer.

sweeping, *adj.* geral, compreensivo.

sweet, 1. *adj.* doce; meigo; amável. **2.** *m.pl.* doces *m.pl.*

sweeten, *vb.* adoçar.

sweetener, *n.* adoçante *m.*

sweetheart, *n.* querido -da; namorado -da.

sweetness, *n.* doçura *f.*

sweet potato, *n.* batata-doce *f.*

swell, 1. *adj.* (*coll.*) legal. **2.** *n.* marulhada *f.* **3.** *vb.* inchar; aumentar.

swelling, *n.* inchação *f.* , inchaço *m.*

swelter, *vb.* sufocar (de calor).

swerve, *vb.* dar uma guinada.

swift, *adj.* veloz; (*coll.*) inteligente.

swig, *n.* trago *m.* , talagada *f.*

swim, 1. *n.* banho (de mar, etc.). **2.** *vb.* nadar.

swimmer, *n.* nadador -ra.

swimming, *n.* natação *f.* **s. pool,**

piscina *f.*; **s. suit**, roupa de banho *f.*; **s. trunks**, calção de banho *m.*

swindle, 1. *n.* trapaça *f.* **2.** *vb.* trapacear.

swindler, *n.* trapaceiro -ra.

swine, *n.* porco -ca.

swing, 1. *n.* balanço *m.*; oscilação *f.* **2.** *vb.* balançar; oscilar.

swipe, 1. *n.* pancada *f.* **2.** *vb.* surripiar.

swirl, 1. *n.* redemoinho *m.* **2.** *vb.* redemoinhar.

swish, 1. *n.* ruge-ruge *m.* **2.** *vb.* fazer ruge-ruge.

Swiss, *adj.* suíço -ça.

switch, 1. *n.* mudança *f.*; *(elec.)* interruptor *m.*; vara *f.* **2.** *vb.* mudar. **s. off**, desligar; **s. on**, ligar.

Switzerland, *n.* Suíça *f.*

swivel, *vb.* girar. **s. chair**, cadeira giratória *f.*

swoon, 1. *n.* desmaio *m.* **2.** *vb.* desmaiar.

swoop, 1. *n.* mergulho (no ar) *m.*; investida *f.* **2.** *vb.* precipitar-se (sobre); *(police)* batida *f.*

sword, *n.* espada *f.*

spordsman, *n.* espadachim *m.*; esgrimista *m.f.*

sycophant, *n.* bajulador -ra.

syllable, *n.* sílaba *f.*

syllabus, *n.* roteiro *m.*

symbol, *n.* símbolo *m.*

symbolic, *adj.* simbólico.

symbolism, *n.* simbolismo *m.*

symbolize, *vb.* simbolizar.

symmetrical, *adj.* simétrico.

sympathetic, *adj.* compassivo; simpático. **be s. towards**, simpatizar com.

sympathize, *vb.* compadecer-se.

sympathizer, *n.* simpatizante *m.f.*

sympathy, *n.* condolências *f.pl.*, pêsames *m.pl.*; compaixão *f.*

symphony, *n.* sinfonia *f.*

symposium, *n.* simpósio *m.*

symptom, *n.* sintoma *m.*

synagogue, *n.* sinagoga *f.*

synchronize, *vb.* sincronizar.

syncopation, *n.* síncope *f.*

syndicate, *n.* associação *f.*

syndrome, *n.* síndrome *f.*

synonym, *n.* sinônimo *m.*

synopsis, *n.* sinopse *f.*

syntax, *n.* sintaxe *f.*

synthesis, *n.* síntese *f.*

synthesize, *vb.* sintetizar.

synthetic, *adj.* sintético.

syphilis, *n.* sífilis *f.*

Syria, *n.* Síria *f.*

Syrian, *adj.* sírio -ria.

syringe, *n.* seringa *f.*

syrup, *n.* xarope *m.*; mel *m.*

system, *n.* sistema *m.*

systematic, *adj.* sistemático.

systemic, *adj.* sistêmico.

T

tab, *n.* aba, alça *f.*; *(coll.)* nota *f.*

table, 1. *n.* mesa *f.*; *(list)* tábua, tabela; *(geol.)* camada *f.* **2.** adiar.

tableau, *n.* quadro *m.*

tablecloth, *n.* toalha *f.*

tablespoon, *n.* colher de sopa *f.*

tablet, *n.* lápide *f.*; tablete *m.*; *(med.)* comprimido *m.*; *(paper)* bloco *m.*

taboo, *n.* tabu *m.*

tacit, *adj.* tácito.

taciturn, *adj.* taciturno.

tack, *n.* tacha *f.*

tackle, *vb.* *(problem)* atacar.

tacky, *adj.* de mau gosto, *(sl.)* cafona.

tact, *n.* tato *m.*

tactic(s), *n.* tática *f.*

tadpole, *n.* girino *m.*

taffy, *n.* puxa-puxa *m.*

tag, *n.* etiqueta *f.*, rótulo *m.*

tail, *n.* cauda *f.*, rabo *m.*

tailor, *n.* alfaiate *m.*

taint, *vb.* contaminar.

take, *vb.* tomar; levar; ficar com; ocupar; precisar de. **t. after**, sair a; **t. away/off/out**, tirar; **t. care of**, tomar conta de; **t. for**, entender por; **t. long**, demorar muito; **t. off**, *(plane)* decolar; **t. over**, tomar posse de.

take-off, *n.* paródia *f.*; *(plane)* decolagem *f.*

talc, *n.* talco *m.*

tale, *n.* história *f.*, conto *m.*

talent, *n.* talento *m.*

talented, *adj.* talentoso.

talk, 1. *n.* fala *f.*; conferência *f.*; discurso *m.*; boato *m.* 2. *vb.* falar.

talkative, *adj.* falador, tagarela.

tall, *adj.* alto.

tally, 1. *n.* conta *f.* 2. *vb.* marcar; contar.

tambourine, *n.* pandeiro *m.*

tame, 1. *adj.* manso. 2. *vb.* domar.

tamper, *vb.* **t. with,** mexer com.

tampon, *n.* tampão *m.*

tan, 1. *adj.* bronzeado. 2. *vb.* curtir; bronzear(-se).

tang, *n.* sabor picante *m.*

tangent, *adj.*, *n.* tangente *f.*

tangerine, *n.* tangerina *f.*

tangible, *adj.* tangível.

tangle, 1. *n.* enredo *m.* 2. *vb.* enredar(-se).

tank, *n.* tanque *m.*

tanker, *n.* (oil) petroleiro *m.*

tannery, *n.* curtume *m.*

tantamount, *adj.* equivalente.

tap, 1. *n.* pancadinha *f.*; (faucet) bica *f.* 2. *vb.* dar pancadinha (em); aproveitar.

tape, 1. *n.* fita *f.* 2. *vb.* prender com fita; gravar.

tape player, *n.* toca-fitas *m.*

taper, *vb.* afilar-se, diminuir.

tape recorder, *n.* gravador *m.*

tapestry, *n.* tapeçaria *f.*, tapete *m.*

tapir, *n.* anta *f.*

tar, 1. *n.* breu, alcatrão *m.* 2. *vb.* alcatroar.

tarantula, *n.* tarântula *f.*

tardy, *adj.* tardio.

target, *n.* alvo *m.*

tariff, *n.* tarifa *f.*

tarnish, 1. *n.* desdouro *m.* 2. *vb.* deslustrar(-se).

tarp, *n.* encerado *m.*

tart, 1. *adj.* ácido. 2. *n.* torta de fruta *f.*

task, *n.* tarefa *f.*

taste, 1. *n.* sabor *m.*; gosto *m.* 2. *vb.* experimentar, provar. **t. like,** ter sabor de.

tasty, *adj.* gostoso.

tatter, 1. *n.* trapo, farrapo *m.* 2. *vb.* esfarrapar.

tattle, *vb.* mexericar.

tattletale, *n.* leva-e-traz *m.f.*

tattoo, 1. *n.* tatuagem *f.* 2. *vb.* tatuar.

taunt, 1. *n.* escárnio *m.* 2. *vb.* escarnecer.

Taurus, *n.* Touro *m.*

taut, *adj.* teso, esticado.

tavern, *n.* taverna *f.*

tawdry, *adj.* de mau gosto, espalhafatoso.

tax, 1. *n.* imposto *m.*, taxa *f.* 2. *vb.* taxar; sobrecarregar.

taxi, *n.* táxi *m.*

taxpayer, *n.* contribuinte *m.f.*

tea, *n.* chá *m.* **teakettle,** chaleira *f.*; **teapot,** bule *m.*

teach, *vb.* ensinar, lecionar.

teacher, *n.* professor, mestre *m.*

teaching, *n.* ensino *m.*

team, *n.* time *m.*, equipe *f.*

tear, 1. *n.* rasgo *m.*; lágrima *f.* **t. gas,** gás lacrimogêneo *m.* 2. *vb.* rasgar.

tease, *vb.* implicar com.

teaspoon, *n.* colher de chá *f.*

teat, *n.* teta *f.*

technical, *adj.* técnico.

technician, *n.* técnico *m.*

technique, *n.* técnica *f.*

technology, *n.* tecnologia *f.*

tedious, *adj.* tedioso.

tedium, *n.* tédio *m.*

teen age, *n.* adolescência *f.*

teenager, *n.* adolescente *m.f.*

teeter, *vb.* oscilar.

teeter-totter, *n.* gangorra *f.*

telegram, *n.* telegrama *m.*

telegraph, 1. *n.* telégrafo *m.* 2. *vb.* telegrafar.

telepathy, *n.* telepatia *f.*

telephone, 1. *adj.*, telefônico. 2. *n.* telefone *m.* 3. *vb.* telefonar (para), ligar (para).

telephone answering machine, *n.* secretária eletrônica *f.*

telephone book, *n.* lista telefônica *f.*, catálogo telefônico *m.*

telephone booth, *n.* cabine telefônica *f.*, *(sl.)* orelhão *m.*

telephone call, *n.* telefonema *m.*

telephone operator, *n.* telefonista *m.f.*

telescope, *n.* telescópio *m.*

televise, *vb.* televisionar, televisar.

television, *n.* televisão, TV *f.*

tell, *vb.* dizer, contar; distinguir. **t. off,** dizer umas verdades a; **t. on,** denunciar.

temper, 1. n. temperamento m.; gênio m. **2.** vb. temperar.

temperament, n. temperamento m.

temperamental, adj. temperamental.

temperance, n. temperança, sobriedade f.

temperate, adj. temperado.

temperature, n. temperatura f.

tempest, n. tempestade f.

template, n. modelo m.

temple, n. templo m.; (anat.) têmpora f.

temporary, adj. temporário, provisório.

tempt, vb. tentar.

temptation, n. tentação f.

ten, adj. dez.

tenacious, adj. tenaz.

tenant, n. inquilino m.

tend, vb. atender, tomar conta de. **t. to,** (incline) tender a.

tendency, n. tendência f.

tender, 1. adj. tenro. **2.** vb. oferecer.

tenderness, n. ternura f.

tendon, n. tendão m.

tenement, n. cabeça-de-porco f., (sl.) treme-treme m.

tenet, n. princípio, dogma m.

tennis, n. tênis m.

tenor, n. teor m.; (mus.) tenor m.

tense, 1. adj. tenso. **2.** n. (gram.) tempo m.

tension, n. tensão f.; estresse m.

tent, n. tenda, barraca f.

tentacle, n. tentáculo m.

tentative, adj. tentativo, provisório.

tenth, adj., n. décimo m.

tenuous, adj. tênue.

tenure, n. posse f.; estabilidade, vitaliciedade f.

tepid, adj. morno, tépido.

term, 1. n. termo m.; prazo m. **2.** vb. chamar.

terminal, 1. adj. terminal. **2.** n. estação f.; terminal m.f.

terminate, vb. terminar; demitir.

termination, n. término m.

terminology, n. terminologia f.

termite, n. cupim m.

terrace, n. terraço m.

terrain, n. terreno m.

terrible, adj. terrível.

terrific, adj. (coll.) formidável, legal.

terrify, vb. assustar.

territory, n. território m.

terror, n. terror m.

terrorism, n. terrorismo m.

terrorist, n. terrorista m.f.

terrorize, vb. aterrorizar.

terse, adj. conciso.

test, 1. n. exame, teste m.; prova f. **2.** vb. examinar, testar.

testament, n. testamento m.

testicle, n. testículo m.

testify, vb. testemunhar, depor.

testimony, n. testemunho m.

test tube, n. proveta f.

tether, 1. n. amarra, corda f. **2.** vb. amarrar.

text, n. texto m. **textbook,** livro escolar, livro de texto m.

textile, 1. adj. têxtil. **2.** n. tecido m.

texture, n. textura, tessitura f.

Thailand, n. Tailândia f.

than, conj. do que, que; de; senão.

thank, vb. agradecer. **t. God,** graças a Deus; **t. you,** obrigado/a.

thanks, 1. n.pl. agradecimentos m.pl. **t. to,** graças a. **2.** interj. obrigado/a!

thanksgiving, n. ação de graças f.

that, 1. dem. adj. esse, essa. **2.** dem. pron. esse, essa; isso. **t. is to say,** isto é; **t. which,** aquele/ aquela/aquilo que. **3.** rel. pron. que, o qual, a qual, etc. **4.** conj. que. **5.** adv. tão. **t. much,** tanto; **t. many,** tantos.

thaw, 1. n. degelo m., descongelação f. **2.** vb. descongelar (-se).

the, def.art. o, a, os, as.

theater, n. teatro m.

theatrical, adj. teatral.

theft, n. roubo m.

their, poss. adj. deles, delas; seu, sua, seus, suas.

theirs, poss. pron. o(s)/a(s) deles, o(s)/a(s) delas; o seu, a sua, os seus, as suas.

them, pron. eles, elas; os, as; lhes.

theme, *n.* tema *m.*

themselves, *ref.pron.* se; si mesmos/próprios. **by t.,** sozinhos; **they t.,** eles mesmos/próprios.

then, *adv.* então, logo, depois; pois.

thence, *adv.* dali, daí.

theology, *n.* teologia *f.*

theoretical, *adj.* teórico.

theory, *n.* teoria *f.*

therapeutic, *adj.* terapêutico.

therapy, *n.* terapia *f.*

there, *adv.* lá, ali, acolá; aí. **t. is/are,** há, tem.

therefore, *adv., conj.* por isso, portanto.

thermometer, *n.* termômetro *m.*

thermonuclear, *adj.* termonuclear.

thermos, *n.* garrafa térmica *f.*

thermostat, *n.* termostato *m.*

thesaurus, *n.* thesaurus, dicionário analógico *m.*

these, *dem. adj., pron.* estes, estas.

thesis, *n.* tese *f.*

they, *pron.* eles, elas.

thick, *adj.* espesso, grosso; cerrado.

thicken, *vb.* engrossar.

thicket, *n.* moita *f.*

thickness, *n.* espessura, grossura *f.*

thief, *n.* ladrão -dra, gatuno *m.*

thigh, *n.* coxa *f.*

thimble, *n.* dedal *m.*

thin, 1. *adj.* magro, fino; ralo; raro; leve. **2.** *vb.* emagrecer (-se).

thing, *n.* coisa *f.*

think, *vb.* pensar; achar, crer, acreditar.

thinker, *n.* pensador *m.*

third, 1. *adj.* terceiro. **T. World,** Terceiro Mundo *m.* **2.** *n.* terço *m.*

thirst, *n.* sede *f.*

thirsty, *adj.* sedento. **be t.,** estar com sede.

thirteen, *adj.* treze.

thirteenth, *adj., n.* décimo terceiro *m.*

thirtieth, *adj., n.* trigésimo *m.*

thirty, *adj.* trinta.

this, *dem. adj., pron.* este, esta; isto.

thistle, *n.* cardo *m.*

thorax, *n.* tórax *m.*

thorn, *n.* espinho *m.*

thorny, *adj.* espinhoso.

thorough, *adj.* completo; meticuloso.

thoroughbred, *adj., n.* puro-sangue *m.f.*

thoroughfare, *n.* via pública *f.*

those, *dem. adj., pron.* esses, essas; aqueles, aquelas.

though, 1. *adv.* no entanto. **2.** *conj.* embora, ainda que. **as t.,** como se.

thought, *n.* pensamento *m.*

thoughtful, *adj.* pensativo; atencioso.

thousand, 1.*adj.* mil. **2.** *n.* milhar *m.*

thousandth, *adj., n.* milésimo *m.*

thrash, *vb.* bater, surrar; trilhar.

thread, *n.* linha *f.*, fio *m.*; (screw) rosca *f.*

threat, *n.* ameaça *f.*

threaten, *vb.* ameaçar.

three, *adj.* três.

three hundred, *adj.* trezentos.

threshold, *n.* limiar *m.*

thrift, *n.* economia, frugalidade *f.*

thrifty, *adj.* econômico, frugal.

thrill, 1. *n.* emoção, vibração *f.* **2.** *vb.* emocionar(-se), vibrar.

thrive, *vb.* medrar, vingar; prosperar.

throat, *n.* garganta *f.*

throb, 1. *n.* palpitação *f.* **2.** *vb.* bater, palpitar.

throne, *n.* trono *m.*

throng, *n.* multidão *f.*

throttle, *n.* acelerador de mão *m.*

through, *prep.* através de, por; por meio de. **be t.,** ter acabado.

throughout, 1. *prep.* por todo, através de, por. . .afora; durante todo. **2.** *adv.* por/em toda parte.

throw, 1. *n.* lançamento *m.* **2.** *vb.* atirar, jogar, lançar. **t. away/out,** jogar fora; **t. up,** (coll.) vomitar.

thrush, *n.* tordo *m.*

thrust, 1. *n.* empurrão *m.* **2.** *vb.* empurrar.

thug, *n.* capanga, jagunço *m.*

thumb, n. polegar m.

thumbtack, n. percevejo m.

thunder, 1. n. trovão m. **2.** vb. trovejar, trovoar.

thundershower, n. aguaceiro m.

Thursday, n. quinta-feira f.

thus, adv. assim. **t. far,** até aqui.

thwart, vb. frustrar.

tic, n. tique m.

tick, 1. n. (entom.) carrapato m. **2.** vb. tiquetaquear.

ticket, n. bilhete m.; (admission) entrada f.; (travel) passagem f.; (parking) multa f.; (political) chapa f. **t. office,** bilheteria f.; **t. window,** n. guichê m.

tickle, 1. n. cócegas f.pl. **2.** vb. fazer cócegas; agradar.

ticklish, adj. cocegüento; delicado. **feel t.,** sentir cócegas.

tick-tack-toe, n. jogo da velha f.

ticktock, n. tique-taque m.

tidal wave, n. vaga sísmica f.

tidbit, n. petisco m.

tide, n. maré f.

tidy, 1. adj. arrumado. **2.** vb. arrumar.

tie, 1. n. gravata f.; laço m.; (game) empate m. **2.** vb. amarrar; (game) empatar.

tier, n. fila, fileira f.

tiger, n. tigre m.

tight, adj. apertado, justo; seguro; (coll.) pão-duro.

tighten, vb. apertar, estreitar.

tightwad, n. (coll.) pão-duro m.

tilde, n. til m.

tile, n. ladrilho m., telha f.; (decorative) azulejo m.

till, 1. prep. até. **2.** conj. até que. **3.** n. caixa f. **4.** vb. lavrar.

tilt, 1. n. inclinação f. **2.** vb. inclinar.

timber, n. madeira f.; viga f.

time, n. tempo m.; (period) época f.; (instance) vez f.; (of day) hora f. **a long t.,** muito tempo; **at times,** às vezes; **for the t. being,** por enquanto; **from t. to t.,** de vez em quando; **have a good t.,** divertir-se; **in t.,** a tempo; **it's t. to,** está na hora de; **on t.,** na hora; **what t. is it?,** que horas são?

timetable, n. horário m.

time zone, n. fuso horário m.

timid, adj. tímido.

tin, n. estanho m.; folha-de-flandres f. **t. can,** lata f.; **t. foil,** papel de estanho m.

tinge, 1. n. toque m. **2.** vb. tingir; dar um toque a.

tingle, 1. n. tinido m.; comichão f. **2.** vb. tinir; formigar.

tinker, 1. n. n. **t. with,** mexer com.

tinkle, 1. n. tinido m. **2.** vb. tinir, tilintar.

tinsel, n. ouropel m.

tint, 1. n. cor f.; toque m. **2.** vb. tingir.

tiny, adj. pequenino.

tip, 1. n. ponta f., bico m.; (gratuity) gorjeta f.; (sl.) palpite m., dica f. **2.** vb. inclinar(-se); tombar; dar gorjeta a.

tipsy, adj. alegre, grogue.

tiptoe, n. **on t.,** na ponta dos pés.

tirade, n. tirada, arenga f.

tire, 1. n. pneu m. **2.** vb. cansar(-se).

tired, adj. cansado.

tireless, n. incansável.

tiresome, adj. cansativo.

tissue, n. tecido m.; lenço de papel.

tit, vb. teta f.

tithe, n. dízima f.

title, 1. n. título m. **2.** vb. titular.

to, prep. a, para, até. **in order t.,** para; **t. and fro,** de um lado para outro.

toad, n. sapo m.

toady, n. bajulador m.

toast, 1. n. torrada f.; (drink) brinde m. **2.** vb. torrar; brindar.

toaster, n. torradeira f.

tobacco, n. tabaco, fumo m.

today, adv. hoje.

to-do, n. bafafá m.

toe, n. dedo do pé m. **big t.,** dedão (do pé) m.

toenail, n. unha do pé f.

together, adv. junto(s). **t. with,** junto com.

toil, 1. n. labuta f. **2.** vb. labutar.

toilet, n. banheiro, sanitário m.

t. paper, papel higiênico m.

token, 1. *adj.* simbólico, nominal. **2.** *n.* sinal *m.*; ficha *f.*

Tokyo, *n.* Tóquio.

tolerance, *n.* tolerância *f.*

tolerant, *adj.* tolerante.

tolerate, *vb.* tolerar.

toll, 1. *n.* pedágio *m.*; tarifa *f.*; (bell) dobre *m.* **t. call,** ligação interurbana *f.* **2.** *vb.* dobrar.

tomato, *n.* tomate *m.*

tomb, *n.* túmulo *m.*, sepultura *f.*

tombstone, *n.* pedra tumular, lousa *f.*

tomorrow, *adv.* amanhã. **t. morning/night,** amanhã de manhã/noite.

tone, *n.* tom *m.*

tongs, *n.pl.* pinça, tenaz *f.*

tongue, *n.* língua *f.*

tonic, *adj.*, *n.* tônico *m.* **t. water,** água tônica *f.*

tonight, *adv.* hoje à noite.

tonsil, *n.* amígdala, tonsila *f.*

too, *adv.* também; demais. **t. bad!,** que pena!; **t. many,** demais, muitos; **t. much,** demais, muito.

tool, *n.* ferramenta *f.*, instrumento *m.*

toot, 1. *n.* apito *m.*; buzinada *f.* **2.** *vb.* apitar; buzinar; tocar.

tooth, *n.* dente *m.*

toothache, *n.* dor de dente *f.*

toothbrush, *n.* escova de dentes *f.*

toothless, *adj.* desdentado.

toothpaste, *n.* pasta de dentes *f.*, dentifrício *m.*

toothpick, *n.* palito *m.*

top, 1. *n.* cume, alto *m.*; (tree) copa *f.*; (lid) tampa *f.* (toy) pião *m.* **2.** *vb.* cobrir; superar.

topaz, *n.* topázio *m.*

topcoat, *n.* sobretudo *m.*

top hat, *n.* cartola *f.*

topic, *n.* tópico, tema *m.*

topping, *n.* glacê *m.*

topple, *vb.* derrubar; tombar.

topsy-turvy, *adv.* de pernas paro o ar.

torch, *n.* tocha *f.*

torment, 1. *n.* tormento *m.* **2.** *vb.* atormentar.

tornado, *n.* tornado *m.*

torpedo, *n.* torpedo *m.* **t. boat,** torpedeiro *m.*

torrent, *n.* torrente *f.*

torrential, *adj.* torrencial.

torrid, *adj.* tórrido.

torso, *n.* torso, tronco *m.*

tortoise, *n.* cágado *m.*; tartaruga *f.*

tortuous, *adj.* tortuoso.

torture, 1. *n.* tortura *f.* **2.** *vb.* torturar.

toss, *vb.* jogar; mexer; agitar-se.

tot, *n.* criancinha *f.*

total, 1. *adj.*, *n.* total *m.* **2.** *vb.* somar, montar a.

totalitarian, *adj.* totalitário.

totality, *n.* totalidade *f.*

tote, *vb.* levar, carregar.

totem, *n.* totem *m.*

touch, 1. *n.* tato *m.*; toque *m.* **in t. with,** em contato com. **2.** *vb.* tocar; comover.

touchy, *adj.* sensível.

tough, 1. *adj.* duro; difícil. **2.** *n.* durão *m.*

toughen, *vb.* endurecer.

toupee, *n.* peruca *f.*, chinó *m.*

tour, 1. *n.* excursão *f.*, passeio *m.*; turnê *f.* **2.** *vb.* viajar, passear.

tourism, *n.* turismo *m.*

tourist, *n.* turista *m./f.*

tournament, *n.* torneio *m.*

tourniquet, *n.* torniquete *m.*

tout, *vb.* apregoar, elogiar muito.

tow, 1. *n.* reboque *m.* **2.** *vb.* rebocar.

toward, *prep.* para, em direção a; para com.

towel, *n.* toalha *f.*

tower, *n.* torre *f.*

town, *n.* cidade, vila *f.*, povoado *m.* **t. hall,** prefeitura *f.*

toxic, *adj.* tóxico.

toxin, *n.* toxina *f.*

toy, *n.* brinquedo *m.*

trace, 1. *n.* traço *m.*; rasto, vestígio *m.* **2.** *vb.* traçar; decalcar.

track, 1. *n.* rasto *m.*; pista *f.*; trilha *f.*; via *f.*, trilho *m.*; (sport.) atletismo *m.* **2.** *vb.* rastejar, seguir a pista de.

tract, *n.* trato *m.*, extensão *f.*; (anat.) sistema, aparelho *m.*

traction, *n.* tração *f.*

tractor, *n.* trator *m.*

trade, 1. *n.* comércio *m.*; troca

f.; ofício *m.* **2.** *vb.* comerciar; trocar.

trademark, *n.* marca registrada *f.*

trade union, *n.* sindicato *m.*

trade wind, *n.* vento alísio *m.*

tradition, *n.* tradição *f.*

traditional, *adj.* tradicional.

traffic, 1. *n.* tráfego, trânsito *m.*; (trade) tráfico. **t. jam,** engarrafamento *m.* **t. light, signal,** sinal *m.*, sinaleira *f.* **2.** *vb.* traficar.

tragedy, *n.* tragédia *f.*

tragic, *adj.* trágico.

trail, 1. *n.* pista *f.*, rasto *m.*; esteira *f.*; picada *f.* **2.** *vb.* seguir a pista de.

trailer, *n.* reboque *m.*

train, 1. *n.* trem, *(P.)* comboio *m.* **2.** *vb.* treinar.

training, *n.* treinamento, treino *m.*

trait, *n.* traço *m.*, característica *f.*

traitor, *n.* traidor -ra.

traitorous, *adj.* traiçoeiro.

trajectory, *n.* trajetória *f.*

tram, *n.* bonde *m.*; bondinho *m.*

tramp, 1. *n.* vagabundo *m.* **2.** *vb.* andar, pisar.

trample, *vb.* pisar, esmagar.

trance, *n.* transe *m.*

tranquil, *adj.* tranqüilo.

tranquility, *n.* tranqüilidade *f.*

tranquilize, *vb.* tranqüilizar.

tranquilizer, *n.* tranqüilizante *m.*

transact, *vb.* transacionar, negociar.

transaction, *n.* transação *f.*

transcend, *vb.* transcender.

transcendent, *adj.* transcendente.

transcendental, *adj.* transcendental, transcendente.

transcribe, *vb.* transcrever.

transcript, *n.* transcrito, histórico *m.*

transfer, 1. *n.* transferência *f.* **2.** *vb.* transferir; baldear-se.

transform, *vb.* transformar.

transformer, *n.* transformador *m.*

transfuse, *vb.* transfundir.

transfusion, *n.* transfusão *f.*

transgress, *vb.* transgredir.

transgression, *n.* transgressão *f.*

transient, *adj.* transitório.

transistor, *n.* transistor *m.*

transit, 1. *n.* trânsito *m.*, passagem *f.* **2.** *vb.* transitar.

transition, *n.* transição *f.*

transitive, *adj.* transitivo.

transitory, *adj.* transitório.

translate, *vb.* traduzir.

translation, *n.* tradução *f.*

translator, *n.* tradutor *m.*

transmission, *n.* transmissão *f.*

transmit, *vb.* transmitir.

transparence, transparency, *n.* transparência *f.*

transparent, *adj.* transparente.

transpire, *vb.* ocorrer.

transplant, 1. *n.* transplante *m.* **2.** *vb.* transplantar.

transport, 1. *n.* transporte *m.* **2.** *vb.* transportar.

transportation, *n.* transporte *m.*, condução *f.*

transpose, *vb.* transpor.

transvestite, *n.* travesti *m./f.*

trap, 1. *n.* armadilha *f.*, laço *m.* **2.** *vb.* apanhar (em armadilha).

trapeze, *n.* trapézio *m.*

trash, *n.* lixo *m.*

trauma, *n.* trauma *m.*

travel, 1. *n.* viagem *f.* **t. agency,** agência de viagens *f.* **2.** *vb.* viajar.

traveler, *n.* viajante *m./f.* **t.'s check,** traveler's check *m.*

traverse, *vb.* atravessar.

travesty, *n.* paródia *f.*

tray, *n.* bandeja *f.*; tabuleiro *m.*

treacherous, *adj.* traiçoeiro.

treachery, *n.* traição *f.*

tread, 1. *n.* banda de rodagem *f.* **2.** *vb.* pisar; trilhar.

treason, *n.* traição *f.*

treasure, 1. *n.* tesouro *m.* **2.** *vb.* prezar.

treasurer, *n.* tesoureiro -ra.

treasury, *n.* tesouro *m.*, tesouraria *f.*

treat, 1. *n.* prazer *m.*; comida ou bebida paga. **2.** *vb.* tratar; convidar.

treatise, *n.* tratado *m.*

treatment, *n.* tratamento *m.*

treaty, *n.* tratado *m.*

tree, *n.* árvore *f.*

trek, 1. *n.* viagem, jornada *f.* **2.** *vb.* viajar.

trellis, *n.* treliça *f.*

tremble, *vb.* tremer, estremecer.

tremendous, *adj.* tremendo; formidável.

tremor, *n.* tremor *m.*; tremor de terra *m.*

trench, *n.* fosso *m.*; *(mil.)* trincheira *f.*

trenchant, *adj.* incisivo; enérgico; cáustico.

trend, *n.* tendência *f.*

trespass, *vb.* invadir, entrar ilegalmente.

tress, *n.* trança *f.*

trial, *n.* prova *f.*; *(jur.)* julgamento.

triangle, *n.* triângulo *m.*

tribal, *adj.* tribal.

tribe, *n.* tribo *f.*

tribulation, *n.* tribulação *f.*

tribunal, *n.* tribunal *m.*

tributary, *n.* tributário, *m.*

tribute, *n.* tributo *m.*

trick, 1. *n.* ardil *m.*; trapaça *f.*; truque *m.*; trote *m.* **2.** *vb.* lograr; trapacear.

trickery, *n.* engano *m.*, trapaça *f.*

trickle, *vb.* escorrer, pingar.

trickster, *n.* trapaceiro, pícaro *m.*

tricky, *adj.* astucioso; complicado.

tricycle, *n.* triciclo, velocípede *m.*

trifle, 1. *n.* ninharia *f.* **2.** *vb.* t. with, brincar com.

trigger, 1. *n.* gatilho *m.* **2.** *vb.* provocar.

trill, 1. *n.* trilo, gorjeio *m.* **2.** *vb.* trilar, gorjear.

trillion, *n.* trilhão *m.*

trilogy, *n.* trilogia *f.*

trim, 1. *adj.* arrumado; enxuto. **2.** *vb.* aparar; enfeitar.

trinity, *n.* trindade *f.*

trinket, *n.* bugiganga *f.*

trio, *n.* trio *m.*

trip, 1. *n.* viagem *f.*; ida *f.* **2.** *vb.* tropeçar.

tripe, *n.* tripa *f.*

triple, 1. *adj.* triplo *f.* **2.** *vb.* triplicar.

triplet, *n.* trigêmeo -a.

tripod, *n.* tripeça *f.*, tripé *m.*

trite, *adj.* trivial, banal.

triumph, 1. *n.* triunfo *m.* **2.** *vb.* triunfar.

triumphant, *adj.* triunfante.

trivia, *n.* trivialidades *f.*

trivial, *adj.* trivial, insignificante.

Trojan, *adj.*, *n.* troiano *m.*

trolley, *n.* bonde *m.*

trombone, *n.* trombone *m.*

troop, *n.* tropa *f.*

trope, *n.* tropo *m.*

trophy, *n.* troféu *m.*

tropical, *adj.* tropical.

tropics, *n.pl.* trópicos *m.pl.*

trot, 1. *n.* trote *m.* **2.** *vb.* trotar.

troubadour, *n.* trovador *m.*

trouble, 1. *n.* apuro *m.*; desordem *f.*; preocupação *f.* **2.** *vb.* incomodar; preocupar.

troublemaker, *n.* desordeiro, *(sl.)* bagunceiro *m.*

troublesome, *adj.* penoso, incômodo.

trough, *n.* gamela *f.*, cocho *m.*

trounce, *n.* surrar; *(sl.)* dar um banho em.

trousers, *n.pl.* calça(s) *f.(pl.)*

trousseau, *n.* enxoval *m.*

trout, *n.* truta *f.*

trowel, *n.* trolha *f.*

Troy, *n.* Tróia *f.*

truant, *adj.*,*n.* gazeteiro, cábula.

truce, *n.* trégua *f.*

truck, *n.* caminhão *m.* **t. driver,** caminhoneiro *m.*

trudge, *vb.* caminhar com dificuldade.

true, *adj.* verdadeiro, real; certo; fiel.

trumpet, *n.* trombeta *f.*; pistão *m.*

trunk, *n.* baú, malão *m.*; (tree, body) tronco *m.*; (elephant) tromba *f.*; (car) porta-malas *m.*

trust, 1. *n.* confiança *f.*; custódia *f.*; *(com.)* truste *m.* **2.** *vb.* confiar (em).

trustee, *n.* fiduciário *m.*

trustworthy, *adj.* fidedigno, digno de confiança.

trusty, *adj.* leal, de confiança.

truth, *n.* verdade *f.*

truthful, *adj.* verídico.

try, 1. *n.* tentativa *f.*, ensaio *m.* **2.** *vb.* experimentar, provar;

(jur.) julgar. **t. on,** experimentar; **t. to,** tentar, tratar de, procurar.

trying, *adj.* penoso; exasperante.

tryout, *n.* prova *f.*

T-shirt, *n.* camiseta *f.*

tub, *n.* banheira, tina *f.*

tuba, *n.* tuba *f.*

tube, *n.* tubo *m.*; bisnaga *f.*; *(anat.)* trompa *f.*

tuber, *n.* tubérculo *m.*

tuberculosis, *n.* tuberculose *f.*

tuck, 1. *n.* dobra *f.* **2.** *vb.* dobrar; meter.

Tuesday, *n.* terça-feira *f.*

tuft, *n.* tufo *m.*

tug, 1. *n.* puxão *m.* **2.** *vb.* puxar.

tugboat, *n.* rebocador *m.*

tug of war, *n.* cabo-de-guerra *m.*

tuition, *n.* anuidades escolares *f.pl.*

tulip, *n.* tulipa *f.*

tumble, 1. *n.* queda *f.*; tombo *m.* cair, tombar; tropeçar.

tummy, *n.* barriga *f.*

tumor, *n.* tumor *m.*

tumult, *n.* tumulto *m.*

tuna, *n.* atum *m.*

tune, 1. *n.* melodia *f.*; música *f.* **in t.,** afinado; em sintonia. **2.** *vb.* afinar; sintonizar.

tunic, *n.* túnica *f.*

tuning fork, *n.* diapasão *f.*

tunnel, *n.* túnel *m.*

turban, *n.* turbante *m.*

turbine, *n.* turbina *f.*

turbulent, *adj.* turbulento.

tureen, *n.* sopeira *f.*

turf, *n.* grama *f.*; turfe *m.*

Turk, *n.* turco *m.*

turkey, *n.* peru *m.*

Turkey, *n.* Turquia *f.*

Turkish, *adj.,* *n.* turco *m.*

turmoil, *n.* tumulto *m.*

turn, 1. *n.* volta *f.*; giro *m.*; turno *m.*, vez *f.* **2.** *vb.* dobrar, virar; transformar; girar, dar voltas; voltar-se; tornar-se. **t. around,** virar-se; **t. back,** voltar; **t. down,** rejeitar; **t. into,** converter-se em; **t. off,** desligar; (light) apagar; (faucet) fechar; **t. on,** ligar; (light) acender; (faucet) abrir; **t. up,** aparecer.

turncoat, *n.* vira-casaca *m.f.*

turnip, *n.* nabo *m.*

turnover, *n.* rotatividade *f.*; pastel doce *m.*

turnstile, *n.* torniquete *m.*, borboleta *f.*

turntable, *n.* toca-discos *m.*

turpentine, *n.* terebintina *f.*

turpitude, *n.* torpeza *f.*

turquoise, *n.* turquesa *f.*

turret, *n.* torrinha *f.*

turtle, *n.* tartaruga *f.*

turtledove, *n.* rola *f.*

tusk, *n.* colmilho *m.*, presa *f.*

tussle, *n.* briga *f.*

tutelage, *n.* tutela *f.*

tutor, 1. *n.* tutor -ra, monitor -ra. **2.** *vb.* ensinar.

tuxedo, *n.* smoking *m.*

twang, *n.* som fanhoso *m.*

tweezers, *n.pl.* pinça *f.*

twelfth, *adj.,* *n.* décimo segundo *m.*

twelve, *adj.* doze.

twentieth, *adj.,* *n.* vigésimo *m.*

twenty, *adj.* vinte.

twice, *adv.* duas vezes.

twig, *n.* ramo, galhinho *m.*

twilight, *n.* crepúsculo *m.*

twin, *n.* gêmeo -a.

twine, 1. *n.* barbante *m.* **2.** *vb.* trançar, entrelaçar.

twinge, *n.* pontada *f.*

twinkle, 1. *n.* brilho *m.* **2.** *vb.* brilhar, cintilar.

twirl, 1. *n.* giro *m.* **2.** *vb.* fazer girar.

twist, 1. *n.* torcedura *f.* **2.** *vb.* torcer(-se), enroscar(-se); deturpar.

twitch, 1. *n.* tique nervoso *m.* **2.** *vb.* contorcer-se.

two, *adj.* dois, duas.

twofold, 1. *adj.* duplo. **2.** *adv.* duplamente.

two hundred, *adj.* duzentos.

twosome, *n.* dupla *f.*

tycoon, *n.* magnata *m.*

type, 1. *n.* tipo *m.* **2.** *vb.* datilografar, bater à máquina.

typewrite, *vb.* datilografar.

typewriter, *n.* máquina de escrever *f.*

typhoon, *n.* tufão *m.*

typical, *adj.* típico.

typing, *n.* datilografia *f.*

typist, *n.* datilógrafo -fa.

tyranny, *n.* tirania *f.*
tyrant, *n.* tirano *m.*

U

udder, *n.* úbere *m.*
u.f.o., *n.* ovni, ufo *m.*
ugliness, *n.* feiúra, fealdade *f.*
ugly, *adj.* feio.
Ukraine, *n.* Ucrânia *f.*
ulcer, *n.* úlcera *f.*
ulterior, *adj.* ulterior; oculto.
ultimate, *adj.* último, final;
definitivo.
ultimatum, *n.* ultimato *m.*
ultra-, *pref.* ultra-.
ultraviolet, *adj.* ultravioleta.
umbilical, *adj.* umbilical.
umbrella, *n.* guarda-chuva *m.*
umpire, *n.* árbitro *m.*
un-, *pref.* in-, des-, não.
unabashed, *adj.* inabalável;
desavergonhado.
unable, *adj.* incapaz.
unabridged, *adj.* completo, não
abreviado.
unanimous, *adj.* unânime.
unarmed, *adj.* desarmado, indefeso.
unbalanced, *adj.* desequilibrado.
unbeaten, *vb.* invicto.
unbelievable, *adj.* inacreditável.
uncertain, *adj.* incerto.
unchanged, *adj.* inalterado.
uncle, *n.* tio *m.*
unconscious, *adj., n.* inconsciente *m.*
unconstitutional, *adj.* inconsti-
tucional.
uncouth, *adj.* grosseiro.
uncover, *vb.* descobrir.
undamaged, *adj.* ileso.
undecided, *adj.* indeciso.
undefeated, *adj.* invicto.
under, 1. *adv.* embaixo, abaixo,
por baixo. **2.** *prep.* sob, debaixo
de.
undercover, *adj.* secreto.
undercut, *vb.* socavar.
underdeveloped, *adj.* subdesenvolvido.
underdog, *n.* pobre diabo *m.*
underestimate, *vb.* subestimar.
undergo, *vb.* sofrer.

undergraduate study, *n.* curso
de graduação *m.*
underground, *adj. n.* subterrâneo *m.*
underhanded, *adj.* sorrateiro.
underlie, *vb.* subjazer.
underline, *vb.* sublinhar.
underling, *n.* subalterno *m.*
underlying, *adj.* subjacente.
undermine, *vb.* minar, socavar.
underneath, 1. *adv.* embaixo. **2.**
prep. debaixo de.
undernourished, *adj.* subnu-
trido.
underpants, *n.pl.* calcinhas *f.pl.*
underprivileged, *adj.* desprivi-
legiado.
underrate, *vb.* subestimar.
undersea, *adj.* submarino.
undershirt, *n.* camiseta, camisa
de meia *f.*
undersign, *vb.* subscrever.
understand, *vb.* entender, compreender.
understate, *vb.* atenuar.
undertake, *vb.* empreender.
undertaker, *n.* agente funerário
m.
undertaking, *n.* empreendimento *m.*, empresa *f.*
underwear, *n.* roupa branca *f.*
underworld, *n.* submundo *m.*
underwrite, *vb.* subscrever.
undo, *vb.* desfazer.
undress, *vb.* despir.
unearned, *adj.* imerecido.
uneasy, *adj.* inquieto.
unemployed, *adj.* desempregado.
unending, *adj.* interminável.
uneven, *adj.* desigual, irregular;
(number) ímpar.
unexpected, *adj.* inesperado.
unfinished, *adj.* incompleto.
unfit, *adj.* inapto; impróprio.
unfold, *vb.* desdobrar(-se).
unforeseen, *adj.* imprevisto.
unforgettable, *adj.* inesquecível.
unforgivable, *adj.* imperdoável.
unfortunate, *adj.* infeliz, desgraçado.
unfriendly, *adj.* hostil.
unfurnished, *adj.* sem móveis.
ungrammatical, *adj.* anti-
gramatical.
ungrateful, *adj.* ingrato.

unharmed, *adj.* ileso.
uniform, 1. *adj.* uniforme. 2. *n.* farda *f.*; uniforme *m.*
uniformity, *n.* uniformidade *f.*
unify, *vb.* unificar.
unilateral, *adj.* unilateral.
unintentional, *adj.* involuntário.
union, *n.* união *f.*; (labor) sindicato *m.*
unique, *adj.* único, singular.
unisex, *adj.* unissex.
unison, *n.* uníssono *m.*
unit, *n.* unidade *f.*
unite, *vb.* unir(-se).
United Kingdom, *n.* Reino Unido *m.*
United Nations, *n.pl.* Nações Unidas *f.pl.*, ONU *f.*
United States, *n.pl.* Estados Unidos *m.pl.*
unity, *n.* unidade *f.*
universal, *adj.* universal.
universe, *n.* universo *m.*
university, *n.* universidade *f.*
unleash, *vb.* desencadear.
unless, *conj.* a não ser que.
unlike, *adj.* diferente.
unlikely, *adj.* improvável.
unlimited, *adj.* ilimitado.
unload, *vb.* descarregar.
unlock, *vb.* abrir (com chave), destrancar.
unlucky, *adj.* azarado.
unmarried, *adj.* solteiro.
unmask, *vb.* desmascarar.
unmistakable, *adj.* inconfundível.
unnecessary, *adj.* desnecessário.
unnoticed, *adj.* despercebido.
unofficial, *adj.* extra-oficial.
unpack, *vb.* desembrulhar, desfazer (as malas).
unpublished, *adj.* inédito.
unravel, *vb.* desenredar(-se).
unreal, *adj.* irreal.
unreasonable, *adj.* irracional.
unreliable, *adj.* irresponsável; indigno de confiança.
unrest, *n.* inquietação *f.*, distúrbio *m.*
unruly, *adj.* indisciplinado, turbulento.
unstable, *adj.* instável.
unstressed, *adj.* átono.
unsuccessful, *adj.* fracassado.

unsuitable, *adj.* impróprio.
untie, *vb.* desamarrar.
until, 1. *prep.* até. 2. *conj.* até que.
unusual, *adj.* insólito.
unvoiced, *adj.* surdo.
unwilling, *adj.* relutante.
unwillingly, *adv.* a contragosto.
unwitting, *adj.* inadvertido, inconsciente.
unworthy, *adj.* indigno.
up, *adv.* para cima, acima, em cima; de/em pé.
update, *vb.* atualizar.
upgrade, *vb.* melhorar.
upheaval, *n.* sublevação *f.*
uphold, *vb.* sustentar.
upholster, *vb.* estofar.
upon, *prep.* sobre, em cima de.
upper, *adj.* superior; alto.
upper-class, *adj.* aristocrático.
upper crust, *n.* alta roda.
upright, *adj.* direito, reto.
uprising, *n.* sublevação *f.*
uproar, *n.* confusão *f.*
uproot, *vb.* desarraigar.
upset, 1. *n.* transtorno *m.*; derrota *f.*; (sl.) zebra *f.* 2. *vb.* virar, transtornar; aborrecer.
upside, *n.* **u. down**, de cabeça para baixo.
upstairs, *adv.* em cima, no andar de cima.
up-to-date, *adj.* atualizado, em dia; moderno.
upward, *adv.* para cima, acima.
uranium, *n.* urânio *m.*
urban, *adj.* urbano.
urchin, *n.* pivete *m.*; ouriço do mar *m.*
urge, 1. *n.* desejo, impulso *m.* 2. *vb.* incitar, insistir em.
urgency, *n.* urgência *f.*
urgent, *adj.* urgente.
urinal, *n.* urinol *m.*; mictório *m.*
urinate, *vb.* urinar, (vulg.) mijar.
urine, *n.* urina *f.*
urn, *n.* vaso *m.*; urna *f.*
Uruguay, *n.* Uruguai *m.*
Uruguayan, *adj. n.* uruguaio *m.*
us, *obj. pron.* nos; nós, a gente.
with u., conosco, com a gente.
usage, *n.* uso *m.*
use, 1. *n.* uso *m.* **it's no u.**, não

tem jeito; **make u. of,** servir-se
de. **2.** *vb.* usar, utilizar. **u. up,**
gastar, esgotar.
used, *adj.* usado; acostumado.
be u. to, estar acostumado a;
get u. to, acostumar-se a.
useful, *adj.* útil.
usefulness, *n.* utilidade *f.*
useless, *adj.* inútil.
user, *n.* usuário *m.*
usher, 1. *n.* (coll.) vaga-lume *m.*
2. *vb.* **u. in,** introduzir, anunciar.
usual, *adj.* usual, normal. **as u.,**
como de costume.
usurer, *n.* usurário, agiota *m.*
usurp, *vb.* usurpar.
usury, *n.* usura, agiotagem *f.*
utensil, *n.* utensílio *m.*
uterus, *n.* útero *m.*
utility, *n.* utilidade *f.*
utilize, *vb.* utilizar.
utmost, *adj.* máximo, sumo.
utopia, *n.* utopia *f.*
utter, 1. *adj.* total, completo. **2.**
vb. proferir, dizer.
utterance, *n.* expressão *f.*; declaração *f.*

V

vacancy, *n.* vaga *f.*
vacant, *adj.* vago.
vacate, *vb.* vagar, desocupar.
vacation, *n.* férias *f.pl.*
vaccinate, *vb.* vacinar.
vaccine, *n.* vacina *f.*
vacillate, *vb.* vacilar.
vaccum, *n.* vácuo, vazio *m.* **v.
cleaner,** aspirador de pó *m.*
vagabond, *n.* vagabundo *m.*
vagina, *n.* vagina *f.*
vagrant, *n.* vagabundo *m.*
vague, *adj.* vago.
vain, *adj.* vão; vaidoso. **in v.,** em
vão.
valet, *n.* criado *m.*
valiant, *adj.* valente.
valid, *adj.* válido.
validity, *n.* validez, validade *f.*
valise, *n.* valise *f.*
valley, *n.* vale *m.*
valor *m.* valentia *f.*
valuable, *adj.* valioso.
value, 1. *n.* valor *m.* **2.** *vb.* dar
valor a, valorizar.

valve, *n.* válvula *f.*
vampire, *n.* vampiro *m.*
van, *n.* caminhão de mudanças
m.; cômbi *f.*
vandal, *n.* vândalo *m.*
vanguard, *n.* vanguarda *f.*
vanilla, *n.* baunilha *f.*
vanish, *vb.* desaparecer, sumir.
vanity, *n.* vaidade *f.*; toucador
m.
vanquish, *vb.* vencer, conquistar.
vapor, *n.* vapor *m.*
variable, *adj., n.* variável *f.*
variant, *adj., n.* variante *f.*
variation, *n.* variação *f.*
variety, *n.* variedade *f.*
various, *adj.* vários, diversos.
varnish, 1. *n.* verniz *m.* **2.** *vb.*
envernizar.
vary, *vb.* variar.
vase, *n.* vaso *m.*, jarra *f.*
vaseline, *n.* vaselina *f.*
vassal, *n.* vassalo *m.*
vast, *adj.* vasto, imenso.
vat, *n.* tanque, tonel *m.*
Vatican, *n.* Vaticano *m.*
vault, 1. *n.* casa-forte *f.*; (arch.)
abóbada *f.* **2.** *vb.* saltar.
veal, *n.* vitela *f.*
veer, 1. *n.* guinada *f.* **2.** *vb.* guinar.
vegetable, *n.* **1.** *adj.* vegetal. **2.**
n. legume *m.*, verdura *f.*
vegetarian, *adj., n.* vegetariano
m.
vegetation, *n.* vegetação *f.*
vehement, *adj.* veemente.
vehicle, *n.* veículo *m.*, viatura
f.
veil, 1. *n.* véu *m.* **2.** *vb.* velar.
vein, *n.* veia *f.*; (mine) veio,
filão *m.*
velvet, *n.* veludo *m.*
vendor, *n.* vendedor *m.*
venerable, *adj.* venerável, venerando.
venerate, *vb.* venerar.
venereal, *adj.* venéreo.
Venezuelan, *adj., n.* venezuelano *m.*
vengeance, *n.* vingança *f.*
vengeful, *adj.* vingativo.
venom, *n.* veneno *m.*
vent, 1. *n.* abertura *f.*, respiradouro *m.* **2.** *vb.* **dar largas
a;** desabafar.

ventilate, *vb.* ventilar.
ventriloquist, *n.* ventríloquo *m.*
venture, 1. *n.* aventura *f.*, empreendimento *m.* **2.** *vb.* arriscar-se.
veracity, *n.* veracidade *f.*
veranda, *n.* varanda *f.*
verb, *n.* verbo *m.*
verbal, *adj.* verbal.
verbose, *adj.* verboso, loquaz.
verdict, *n.* veredicto *m.*
verge, 1. *n.* beira *f.* **2.** *vb.* **v. on,** beirar.
verify, *vb.* verificar.
verisimilar, *adj.* verossímil.
verisimilitude, *n.* verossimilhança *f.*
veritable, *adj.* verdadeiro.
versatile, *adj.* versátil.
verse, *n.* verso *m.*
version, *n.* versão *f.*
vertebra, *n.* vértebra *f.*
vertical, *adj.* vertical.
very, 1. *adj.* mesmo, próprio. **2.** *adv.* muito, bem.
vessel, *n.* vaso *m.*; embarcação *f.*
vest, *n.* colete *m.*
vestige, *n.* vestígio *m.*
veteran, *adj.*, *n.* veterano *m.*
veterinarian, *n.* veterinário *m.*
veto, 1. *n.* veto *m.* **2.** *vb.* vetar.
vex, *vb.* aborrecer, vexar.
viable, *adj.* viável.
viaduct, *n.* viaduto *m.*
vibrate, *vb.* vibrar.
vibration, *n.* vibração *f.*
vicar, *n.* vigário *m.*
vicarious, *adj.* vicário *m.*
vice, *n.* vício *m.*
vice-, *pref.* vice-.
viceroy, *n.* vice-rei *m.*
vicinity, *n.* vizinhança *f.*
vicious, *adj.* vicioso.
victim, *n.* vítima *f.*
victimize, *vb.* vitimar.
victor, *n.* vencedor *m.*
victorious, *adj.* vitorioso.
victory, *n.* vitória *f.*
video, *n.* vídeo *m.*
videocassette, *n.* videocassete *m.* **v. recorder,** videocassete *m.*
videodisk, *n.* videodisco *m.*
videogame, *n.* videogame, videojogo *m.*
videotape, *n.* videotape, videoteipe *m.*

Vietnam, *n.* Vietnã *m.*
Vietnamese, *adj.*, *n.* vietnamita *m.f.*
view, 1. *n.* vista *f.* **2.** *vb.* ver.
viewpoint, *n.* ponto de vista *m.*
vigil, *n.* vigília *f.*
vigilant, *adj.* vigilante.
vigor, *n.* vigor *m.*
vigorous, *adj.* vigoroso.
vile, *adj.* vil.
villa, *n.* vila *f.*
village, *n.* aldeia *f.*, povoado *m.*
villager, *n.* aldeão, -ã.
villain, *n.* vilão, bandido *m.*
vindicate, *vb.* vindicar.
vindictive, *adj.* vingativo.
vine, *n.* vinha, vide *f.*; cipó *m.*
vinegar, *n.* vinagre *m.*
vineyard, *n.* vinha *f.*, vinhedo *m.*
vintage, *n.* vindima *f.*
vinyl, *n.* vinil *m.*
violate, *vb.* violar.
violation, *n.* violação *f.*
violence, *n.* violência *f.*
violent, *adj.* violento.
violet, *n.* violeta *f.*
violin, *n.* violino *m.*
viper, *n.* víbora *f.*
virgin, *n.* virgem *f.*
virginity, *n.* virgindade *f.*
virile, *adj.* viril.
virtual, *adj.* virtual.
virtue, *n.* virtude *f.*
virtuous, *adj.* virtuoso.
virus, *n.* vírus *m.*
visa, *n.* visto *m.*
vise, *n.* torno, sargento *m.*
visible, *adj.* visível.
vision, *n.* visão *f.*
visit, 1. *n.* visita *f.* **2.** *vb.* visitar.
visitor, *n.* visitante *m.f.*, visita *f.*
visor, *n.* viseira *f.*
visual, *adj.* visual.
vital, *adj.* vital.
vitamin, *n.* vitamina *f.*
vivacious, *adj.* vivaz, animado.
vivid, *adj.* vívido, vivo.
vocabulary, *n.* vocabulário *m.*
vocal, *adj.* vocal.
vocalist, *n.* vocalista *m.f.*
vocation, *n.* vocação *f.*
vogue, *n.* voga, moda *f.*
voice, 1. *n.* voz *f.* **2.** *vb.* expressar.
void, 1. *adj.* vazio; nulo. **2.** *n.*

vazio, vácuo *m*. **3.** *vb*. invalidar.
volatile, *adj*. volátil.
volcanic, *adj*. vulcânico.
volcano, *n*. vulcão *m*.
volition, *n*. volição, vontade *f*.
volleyball, *n*. vôlei, voleibol *m*.
volt, *n*. volt *m*.
volume, *n*. volume *m*.
voluntary, *adj*. voluntário.
volunteer, **1.** *n*. voluntário *m*.
  2. *vb*. oferecer-se.
voluptuous, *adj*. voluptuoso.
vomit, **1.** *n*. vômito *m*. **2.** *vb*.
  vomitar.
voodoo, *n*. vodu *m*.
voracious, *adj*. voraz.
vortex, *n*. vórtice *m*.
vote, **1.** *n*. voto *m*.; votação *f*.
  2. *vb*. votar.
voter, *n*. votante *m.f.*
voting, *n*. votação *f*.
vouch, *vb*. **v. for**, garantir; responder por.
vow, **1.** *n*. voto *m*., promessa *f*.
  2. *vb*. fazer votos, jurar.
vowel, *n*. vogal *f*.
voyage, **1.** *n*. viagem *f*. **2.** *vb*.
  viajar, fazer uma viagem.
voyager, *n*. viajante *m.f.*
vulgar, *adj*. vulgar; grosseiro,
  chulo.
vulgarity, *n*. vulgaridade *f*.;
  grosseria *f*.
vulnerable, *adj*. vulnerável.
vulture, *n*. abutre, urubu *m*.

W

wacky, *adj*. aloucado.
wad, **1.** *n*. bola *f*.; maço *m*.;
  (money) bolada *f*. **2.** *vb*. fazer
  uma bola de.
wade, *vb*. vadear.
wafer, *n*. bolacha *f*.; (eccles.)
  hóstia *f*.
waffle, *n*. waffle *m*.
waft, *vb*. soprar, flutuar.
wag, **1.** *n*. meneio *m*.; gozador *m*.
  2. *vb*. abanar.
wage, **1.** *n*. salário *m*. **2.** fazer
  (guerra) (batalha), travar (batalha).
wage earner, *n*. assalariado *m*.
wager, **1.** *n*. aposta, parada *f*. **2.**
  vb. apostar.
wagon, *n*. carro *m*., carroça *f*.

waif, *n*. criança abandonada *f*.,
  pivete *m*.
wail, **1.** lamentação *f*., gemido
  m. **2.** *vb*. lamentar-se, gemer.
waist, *n*. cintura *f*.
wait, **1.** *n*. espera *f*. **2.** *vb*. esperar, aguardar. **w. for**, esperar;
  w. on, servir.
waiter, *n*. garçom, moço *m*.
waitress, *n*. garçonete *f*.
waive, *vb*. pôr de lado, renunciar.
waiver, *n*. renúncia de um
  direito *f*.; isenção *f*.
wake, **1.** *n*. velório *m*.; (ship)
  esteira *f*. **in the w. of**, na esteira
  de. **2.** *vb*. acordar. **w. up**, acordar.
waken, *vb*. acordar.
Wales, *n*. Gales.
walk, **1.** *n*. passeio *m*., volta *f*.;
  caminhada *f*. **take a w.**, dar um
  passeio. **2.** *vb*. andar, caminhar.
wall, *n*. parede *f*.; muro *m*.
wallet, *n*. carteira *f*.
wallow, *vb*. chafurdar.
wallpaper, *n*. papel de parede
  m.
walnut, *n*. noz *f*. **w. tree**, *n*.
  nogueira *f*.
walrus, *n*. morsa *f*.
waltz, **1.** *n*. valsa *f*. **2.** *vb*. valsar.
wand, *n*. vara, vareta *f*.
wander, *vb*. vaguear, errar.
wanderer, *n*. viandante *m.f.*
wane, *vb*. minguar.
want, **1.** *n*. falta, necessidade *f*.;
  desejo *m*. **2.** *vb*. desejar,
  querer; necessitar.
wanton, *adj*. dissoluto; frívolo;
  flagrante.
war, *n*. guerra *f*.
warble, **1.** *n*. gorjeio *m*. **2.** *vb*.
  gorjear.
ward, **1.** *n*. (pol.) bairro *m*.;
  (hospital) ala *f*.; tutelado *m*. **2.**
  vb. **w. off**, repelir.
warden, *n*. diretor de prisão *m*.
wardrobe, *n*. guarda-roupa *m*.
ware, *n*. mercadorias *f.pl.*
warehouse, *n*. armazém *m*.
warfare, *n*. guerra *f*.
warhead, *n*. ogiva *f*.
warm, **1.** *adj*. quente; (fig.)
  caloroso. **be warm**, estar com
  calor; (weather) fazer calor,

estar quente. **2.** *vb.* esquentar; aquecer.

warmth, *n.* calor *m.*

warn, *vb.* avisar, prevenir.

warning, *n.* aviso *m.*

warp, *vb.* (wood) empenar.

warrant, 1. *n.* autorização *f.*; (*jur.*) mandado *m.* **2.** *vb.* garantir; justificar.

warranty, *n.* garantia *f.*

warrior, *n.* guerreiro *m.*

Warsaw, *n.* Varsóvia *f.*

warship, *n.* navio de guerra *m.*

wart, *n.* verruga *f.*

wary, *adj.* desconfiado.

wash, 1. *n.* lavagem *f.* **2.** *vb.* lavar.

washer, *n.* máquina de lavar *f.*; arruela *f.*

washing, *n.* lavagem *f.* **w. machine,** máquina de lavar *f.*

wasp, *n.* vespa *f.*

waste, 1. *n.* desperdício *m.* **2.** *vb.* desperdiçar, gastar à toa.

wasteland, *n.* deserto *m.*

watch, 1. *n.* vigília *f.*; relógio de pulso *m.* **2.** *vb.* olhar, vigiar.

watchdog, *n.* cão de guarda *m.*

watchful, *adj.* vigilante, alerta.

watchmaker, *n.* relojoeiro *m.*

watchman, *n.* vigia, guarda *m.*

water, 1. *adj.* aquático. **2.** *n.* água *f.* **3.** *vb.* regar, irrigar.

water color, *n.* aquarela *f.*

waterfall, *n.* catarata, queda d'água *f.*

water faucet, *n.* bica, torneira *f.*

water fountain, *n.* bebedouro *m.*

watering can, *n.* regador *m.*

watermelon, *n.* melancia *f.*

waterproof, 1. *adj.* impermeável. **2.** *vb.* impermeabilizar.

water skiing, *n.* esqui aquático *m.*

water table, *n.* lençol d'água *m.*

water tank, *n.* caixa d'água *f.*

water wheel, *n.* nora *f.*; roda d'água *f.*

watt, *n.* watt *m.*

wattle, *n.* pau-a-pique *m.*

wave, 1. *n.* onda *f.*; aceno de mão *m.* **short w.,** onda curta *f.* **2.** acenar; (flag) flutuar.

waver, *vb.* vacilar; tremular.

wavy, *adj.* ondulado.

wax, 1. *n.* cera *f.*; (ear) cerume *m.*; (sealing) lacre *m.* **w. paper,** papel encerado *m.* **2.** *vb.* encerar; tornar-se.

way, 1. *n.* caminho *m.*; jeito *m.*, maneira *f.* **a long w.,** muito longe; **by the w.,** por falar nisso; **in a w.,** até certo ponto; **no w,** de jeito nenhum; **on the w. to,** a caminho de; **that w.,** para lá; **this w.,** para cá; **which w.,** por onde; onde fica. **3.** *adv.* muito.

we, *pron.* nós, a gente.

weak, *adj.* fraco, débil.

weaken, *vb.* enfraquecer(-se).

weakness, *n.* fraqueza, debilidade *f.*

wealth, *n.* riqueza *f.*

wealthy, *adj.* rico, abastado.

wean, *vb.* desmamar.

weapon, *n.* arma *f.*

wear, 1. *n.* uso *m.*; traje *m.*, roupa *f.* **2.** *vb.* usar, vestir. **w. out,** gastar(-se); cansar(-se).

weariness, *n.* cansaço *m.*

weary, *adj.* cansado.

weasel, *n.* doninha *f.*

weather, *n.* tempo *m.* **w. forecast,** previsão do tempo *f.*

weatherman   -woman, *n.* meteorologista *m.f.*

weather vane, *n.* cata-vento *m.*

weave, 1. *n.* tecedura *f.* **2.** *vb.* tecer.

weaver, *n.* tecelão -lã -loa.

web, *n.* teia *f.*

wed, *vb.* casar.

wedding, *n.* casamento *m.* **w. ring,** aliança *f.*, anel de casamento *m.*

wedge, *n.* cunha *f.*

wedlock, *n.* matrimônio *m.*

Wednesday, *n.* quarta-feira *f.*

wee, *adj.* pequenino.

weed, 1. *n.* erva daninha *f.* **2.** *vb.* capinar.

week, *n.* semana *f.*

weekday, *n.* dia útil *m.*

weekend, *n.* fim de semana *m.*

weekly, *adj.* semanal.

weep, *vb.* chorar.

weeping, *n.* choro, pranto *m.*

weigh, *vb.* pesar.

weight, n. peso m.

weird, adj. estranho, esquisito.

welcome, 1. adj. bem-vindo. **you're w.,** de nada, disponha. **2.** n. boas-vindas f.pl., acolhida f. **3.** vb. dar as boas-vindas; acolher. **4.** interj. bem-vindo!

weld, 1. n. solda, soldadura f. **2.** vb. soldar.

welfare, n. bem-estar m.; saúde f.; beneficência f.

well, 1. adj. bom, são. **2.** n. poço m. **3.** adv. bem. **as w.,** também; **as w. as,** assim como. **4.** vb. **w. up,** brotar. **5.** interj. ora!, bem!

well-being, n. bem-estar m.

well-done, adj. bem feito; (meat) bem passado.

well-known, adj. bem conhecido.

well-to-do, adj. abastado.

welsh, vb. passar/dar o calote.

Welsh, adj., n. galês.

welsher, n. caloteiro m.

wend, vb. ir, dirigir-se.

werewolf, n. lobisomem m.

west, 1. adj. ocidental, do oeste. **2.** n. oeste, ocidente m.

western, adj. ocidental. **w. movie,** bangue-bangue m.

West Germany, n. Alemanha Ocidental f.

wet, 1. adj. molhado. **get w.,** molhar-se. **2.** vb. molhar.

whale, n. baleia f.

wharf, n. cais m.

what, 1. adj. que, qual. **2.** interrog. pron. que, o que; como?. **w.** for, para quê. **3.** rel. pron. o que. **4.** interj. quê!, que. . .!

whatever, 1. adj. qualquer. **2.** pron. tudo que/quanto; por mais que. . ., seja o que for.

wheat, n. trigo m.

wheel, n. roda f. **w. chair,** cadeira de rodas f.; **steering w.,** volante m.; direção f.

wheeze, 1. n. chiado m. **2.** vb. chiar, ofegar.

when, adv., conj. quando.

whenever, 1. adv. onde. **2.** conj. quando, sempre que.

where, adv., conj., pron. onde, aonde.

whereabouts, n. paradeiro m.

wherever, 1. adv. onde. **2.** conj. onde quer que; seja onde for.

wherewithal, n. recursos m.pl.

whet, vb. amolar, aguçar.

whether, conj. se.

which, 1. adj. que, qual. **2.** interrog. pron. qual. **3.** rel. pron. que, o/a qual; o qual.

whichever, adj., pron. qualquer, qualquer que.

whiff, 1. n. sopro m.; tragada f. **2.** vb. soprar; fumar.

while, 1. n. pouco, tempo m. **once in a w.,** de vez em quando. **2.** conj. enquanto; ao passo que.

whim, n. capricho m.

whimper, 1. n. lamúria f. **2.** vb. lamuriar.

whimsical, adj. caprichoso.

whine, 1. n. lamúria f.; gemido m. **2.** vb. choramingar; gemer.

whinny, 1. n. rincho. **2.** vb. rinchar.

whip, 1. n. chicote, látego m. **2.** vb. chicotear, açoitar; espancar; (food) bater.

whirl, vb. girar.

whirlpool, n. redemoinho m.

whirlwind, n. redemoinho, turbilhão m.

whiskers, m.pl. barba f.; (cat) bigode m.

whiskey, n. uísque m.

whisper, 1. n. sussurro, cochicho m. **2.** vb. sussurrar, cochichar.

whistle, 1. n. assobio m.; apito m. **2.** vb. assobiar; apitar.

white, 1. adj. branco. **2.** m. branco; (egg) clara f.

White House, n. Casa Branca f.

whiten, vb. branquear.

whittle, vb. aparar, talhar.

who, whom, 1. interrog. pron. quem. **2.** rel. pron. que, o/a qual; quem.

whoever, whomever, rel. pron. quem quer que; seja quem for.

whole, 1. adj. todo, inteiro. **the w.,** todo o. **2.** n. todo m., totalidade f. **on the w.,** em geral.

wholesale, adv. por atacado.

wholesaler, n. atacadista m.f.

wholesome, adj. salutar; sadio.

whore, *n.* prostituta, *(vulg.)* puta *f.*

whose, 1. *interrog. pron.* de quem. **2.** *rel. pron.* de quem, cujo.

why, 1. *n.* porquê. **2.** *adv.* por que. **3.** *conj.* porque.

wick, *n.* pavio *m.*, mecha *f.*

wicked, *adj.* mau, ruim, malvado.

wickedness, *n.* maldade *f.*

wicker, *n.* vime *m.*

wide, 1. *adj.* largo, amplo. **2.** *adv.* **w. open,** escancarado.

widen, *vb.* alargar, ampliar.

widespread, *adj.* estendido, difundido.

widow, *n.* viúva *f.*

widower, *n.* viúvo *m.*

widowhood, *n.* viuvez *f.*

width, *n.* largura *f.*

wield, *vb.* brandir, empunhar.

wiener, *n.* salsicha *f.*

wife, *n.* esposa, mulher *f.*

wig, *n.* peruca *f.*

wiggle, 1. *n.* saracoteio *m.* **2.** *vb.* saracotear.

wild, *adj.* selvagem; bravio; silvestre; feroz.

wilderness, *n.* deserto *m.*

wildlife, *n.* fauna silvestre *f.*

wile, *n.* astúcia *f.*

will, 1. *n.* vontade *f.*; testamento *m.* **2.** *vb.* querer; (bequeath) legar.

willful, *adj.* voluntarioso; propositado.

willing, *adj.* **be w. to,** estar disposto a.

willingly, *adv.* de bom grado.

willow, *n.* salgueiro *m.*

willpower, *n.* força de vontade *f.*

wilt, *vb.* murchar.

wilted, *adj.* murcho.

win, 1. *n.* vitória *f.* **2.** *vb.* ganhar, vencer.

wince, *vb.* recuar, encolher-se.

winch, *n.* guincho *m.*

wind, 1. *n.* vento *m.* **w. instrument,** instrumento de sopro *m.* **2.** *vb.* enrolar, enroscar; (watch) dar corda a.

windfall, *n.* inesperado. **2.** *n.* sorte inesperada *f.*

winding, *adj.* sinuoso, tortuoso.

windmill, *n.* moinho de vento *m.*; cata-vento *m.*

window, *n.* janela *f.*; (ticket, teller's) guichê *m.*

windowpane, *vb.* vidro *m.*. vidraça *f.*

window shade, *n.* estore *m.*

windshield, *n.* pára-brisa *m.* **w. wiper,** limpador de pára-brisa *m.*

windward, *n.* barlavento *m.*

windy, *adj.* ventoso. **be w.,** ventar.

wine, *n.* vinho *m.*

wine cellar, *n.* adega *f.*

wing, *n.* asa *f.*; *(arch.)* ala *f.*; *(theat.)* bastidor *m.*

wingspread, *n.* envergadura *f.*

wink, 1. *n.* piscadela *f.* **2.** *vb.* piscar.

winner, *n.* vencedor *m.*

winnow, *vb.* joeirar.

winter, *n.* inverno *m.*

wipe, *vb.* limpar; esfregar; secar. **w. out,** exterminar.

wire, 1. *n.* arame *m.*; fio *m.*; telegrama *m.* **2.** *vb.* telegrafar.

wisdom, *n.* sabedoria *f.*

wise, *n.* sábio; prudente.

wise guy, *n.* sabichão *m.*; cara-de-pau *m.*

wish, 1. *n.* desejo *m.*, vontade *f.*, voto *m.* **2.** *vb.* desejar, querer.

wisp, *n.* fio, tufo *m.*

wit, *n.* juízo, bom senso *m.*; espírito, chiste *m.*; pessoa espirituosa *f.* **to w.,** a saber.

witch, *n.* bruxa, feiticeira *f.*

witchcraft, *n.* bruxaria, feitiçaria *f.*

with, *prep.* com.

withdraw, *vb.* retirar(-se).

withdrawal, *n.* retirada *f.*

wither, *vb.* murchar, secar.

withhold, *vb.* reter, negar.

within, 1. *adv.* dentro, por dentro. **2.** *prep.* dentro de.

without, 1. *adv.* fora, por fora. **2.** *prep.* sem. **do w.,** passar sem.

withstand, *vb.* agüentar, resistir.

witness, 1. *n.* testemunha *f.*; (testimony) testemunho *m.* **2.** *vb.* presenciar; testemunhar.

witticism, *n.* dito espirituoso *m.*

witty, *adj.* espirituoso, chistoso.

wizard, n. feiticeiro, mago m.

wobble, vb. cambalear.

woe, n. pesar m., dor f.

wolf, n. lobo m.

woman, n. mulher f.

womanhood, n. feminilidade, feminidade f.

womb, n. útero m.

wonder, 1. n. maravilha f.; admiração f. **2.** vb. maravilhar-se, estranhar; perguntar-se. **I w.,** será que, gostaria de saber.

wonderful, adj. maravilhoso; ótimo.

wont, 1. adj. acostumado. **2.** n. costume m.

woo, vb. cortejar.

wood, n. madeira f., pau m.; (fire) lenha f.

woodchuck, n. marmota f.

woodcut, n. xilogravura f.

woodcutter, n. lenhador m.

wooden, adj. de madeira.

woodpecker, n. pica-pau m.

woodwind, n. instrumento de sopro m.

woodwork, n. carpintaria f.; (house) madeiramento m.

wool, n. lã f.

word, 1. n. palavra f.; (pl.) (song) letra f. **2.** vb. exprimir.

wordiness, n. verbosidade f.

wording, n. fraseologia f.

wordy, adj. prolixo.

work, 1. n. trabalho, serviço m.; (art, literature) obra f. **2.** vb. trabalhar; obrar; funcionar. **it won't w.,** não dá.

workbook, n. livro de exercícios m.

workday, n. dia útil m.

worker, n. trabalhador, operário m.

working class, n. classe operária f.

working hours, n.pl. expediente m.

workmanship, n. trabalho, acabamento m.

workout, n. treino, treinamento m.

workshop, n. oficina f.

world, n. mundo m.

worldly, adj. mundano.

worldwide, adj. mundial.

worm, n. verme m., minhoca f., bicho m.

worn, adj. usado; gasto. **w. out,** gasto; esgotado, exausto.

worried, adj. preocupado, aflito.

worry, 1. n. preocupação f. **2.** vb. preocupar; preocupar-se.

worse, adj., adv. pior. **get w.,** piorar.

worsen, vb. piorar.

worship, 1. n. adoração f.; culto m. **2.** vb. adorar.

worshiper, n. devoto m.

worst, n., adj., adv. pior.

worth, n. valor m.

worthless, adj. sem valor.

worthwhile, adj. digno, de valor. **be w.,** valer a pena.

worthy, adj. digno.

wound, 1. n. ferida f., ferimento m. **2.** vb. ferir.

wrap, 1. n. manta f. **2.** vb. embrulhar.

wrapper, wrapping, n. envoltório m., embalagem f.

wrath, n. ira, cólera f.

wrathful, adj. colérico.

wreak, vb. descarregar, desencadear.

wreath, n. grinalda f.

wreck, 1. n. ruína f.; batida f. **2.** vb. destruir.

wrench, n. chave inglesa f. **2.** vb. torcer violentamente.

wrest, vb. arrebatar.

wrestle, vb. lutar corpo a corpo.

wretched, adj. miserável.

wring, vb. torcer.

wrinkle, 1. n. ruga f. **2.** vb. enrugar(-se).

wrist, n. pulso m.

wristwatch, n. relógio de pulso m.

writ, n. escritura f.; (jur.) mandado m.

write, vb. escrever. **w. down,** apontar; **w. off,** cancelar.

writer, n. escritor m.

writhe, vb. contorcer-se.

writing, n. escritura f.; escrita f.

writing desk, n. escrivaninha f.

wrong, 1. adj. errado; injusto. **be w.,** não ter razão. **2.** n. injustiça f., agravo m. **right and w.,** o bem e o mal. **3.** adv. mal, incorretamente. **4.** vb. fazer mal a, ofender.

wry, *adj.* torto, torcido.

X

x-ray, 1. *n.* raios X *m.pl.* , radiografia *f.* **2.** *vb.* radiografar.
xylophone, *n.* xilofone *m.*

Y

yacht, *n.* iate *m.*
yachting, *n.* iatismo *m.*
yak, *n.* iaque *m.*
yam, *n.* inhame *m.*
yank, 1. *n.* puxão *m.* ; (coll.) ianque *m.* **2.** *vb.* puxar.
yankee, *n.* ianque *m.*
yard, *n.* quintal *m.* ; (measure) jarda *f.*
yarn, *n.* fio *m.* ; (coll.) história, lorota *f.*
yawn, 1. *n.* bocejo *m.* **2.** *vb.* bocejar.
year, *n.* ano *m.*
yearbook, *n.* anuário *m.*
yearly, *adj.* anual.
yearn, *vb.* anelar, ansiar.
yearning, *n.* anelo, anseio *m.*
yeast, *n.* lêvedo, fermento *m.*
yell, 1. *n.* grito *m.* **2.** *vb.* gritar.
yellow, *adj.* amarelo; (coll.) covarde. **y. fever,** febre amarela *f.* **yen,** *n.* (currency) iene *m.* ; vontade *f.* , desejo *m.*
yes, *adv.* sim.
yesterday, *adv.* ontem.
yet, 1. *adv.* ainda; já; todavia. **not y.,** ainda não. **2.** *conj.* porém, no entanto.
Yiddish, *n.* iídiche *m.*
yield, 1. *n.* rendimento *m.* **2.** *vb.* produzir; ceder.
yoga, *n.* ioga *f.*
yogurt, *n.* iogurte *m.*
yoke, 1. *n.* jugo *m.* canga *f.* **2.** *vb.* jungir.
yokel, *n.* caipira *m.f.*
yolk, *n.* gema *f.*
yonder, *adv.* lá, acolá.
yore, *n.* antanho *m.*
you, *pron.* você, (pl.) vocês; (formal) o senhor, a senhora, (pl.) os senhores, as senhoras; (fam.) tu, (pl.) vós; dir. obj.

pron. o, a, (pl.) os, as; (fam.) te, (pl.) vos. **with you,** com você, etc., com o senhor, etc.; contigo, (pl.) convosco.
young, 1. *adj.* jovem, novo. **2.** *n.* juventude *f.* , jovens *m.pl.*
youngster, *n.* criança *f.* ; jovem *m.f.*
your, *poss. adj.* seu, sua; teu, tua; vosso.
yours, *poss. pron.* o seu, a sua; o teu, a tua; o vosso.
yourself, -selves, *reflex. pron.* se; si; (fam.) te; si; (pl.) vos; vós. **with y.,** consigo; contigo, (pl.) convosco; **you y.,** você mesmo, vocês mesmos, etc.
youth, *n.* juventude *f.* ; (lad) jovem *m.*
youthful, *adj.* jovem; juvenil.
yoyo, *n.* ioiô *m.*
Yugoslav, *adj.,* *n.* iugoslavo *m.*
Yugoslavia, *n.* Iugoslávia *f.*
Yule, *n.* Natal *m.*

Z

zany, *adj.* bobo; extravagante.
zap, *vb.* atingir com um choque elétrico; desintegrar; matar.
zeal, *n.* zelo *m.*
zealot, *n.* fanático *m.*
zealous, *adj.* zeloso.
zebra, *n.* zebra *f.*
zenith, *n.* zênite *m.*
zero, *n.* zero *m.*
zest, *n.* gosto *m.*
zigzag, 1. *n.* ziguezague *m.* . **2.** *vb.* ziguezaguear.
zinc, *n.* zinco *m.*
zip, 1. *n.* zumbido *m.* ; energia *f.* **2.** *vb.* zumbir; fechar com fecho éclair; mover-se rapidamente.
zip code, *n.* CEP, código postal *m.*
zipper, *n.* fecho éclair, zíper *m.*
zodiac, *n.* zodíaco *m.*
zone, *n.* zona *f.*
zoo, *n.* jardim zoológico, zôo *m.*
zoology, *n.* zoologia *f.*
zoom, 1. *n.* zumbido *m.* ; subida rápida *f.* **2.** *vb.* zumbir; subir rapidamente.
zoom lens, *n.* zum *m.*

Useful Words and Phrases/
Palavras e Expressões Uteis

Good morning/day. **Bom dia.**
Good afternoon. **Boa tarde.**
Good evening/night. **Boa noite.**
Hello! Hi! **Oi!/Olá!**
Welcome! **Bem-vindo/a!**
See you later. **Até logo./Tchau.**
Goodbye. **Adeus.**
How are you? **Como vai?/Tudo bem?**
I'm fine, thank you. **Vou bem, obrigado/a.**
Pleased to meet you. **Muito prazer.**
May I introduce . . . **Quero apresentar . . .**
Thank you very much. **Muito obrigado/a.**
You're welcome. **De nada./Disponha.**
Please. **Por favor.**
No thank you. **Obrigado/a.**
Excuse me. (requesting permission) **Com licença./Dá licença.**
Excuse me. (apologizing) **Desculpe./Perdão.**
Good luck! **Boa sorte!**
To your health! **Saúde!**
Congratulations! **Parabéns!**
Please help me. **Pode me ajudar, por favor?**
I don't know. **Não sei.**
I don't understand. **Não entendo/compreendo.**
Do you understand? **Entende?/Compreende?**
I don't speak Portuguese. **Não falo português.**
Do you speak English? **O senhor/a senhora fala inglês?**
How do you say . . . in Portuguese? **Como se diz . . . em**
   português?
What is this? **O que é isto?**
What do you call this? **Como se chama isto?**
Speak (more) slowly, please. **Fale (mais) devagar, por favor.**
Please repeat. **Repita, por favor.**
I don't like . . . **Não gosto de . . .**
I am lost. **Estou perdido/a.**
What is your name? **Como é o seu nome?**
My name is . . . **(O) meu nome é . . .**
I am an American. **(Eu) sou americano/a.**
Where are you from? **O senhor/a senhora é de onde?**
I am from . . . **(Eu) sou de . . .**
How is the weather? **Como está o tempo?**
What time is it? **Que horas são?**
How much is it? **Quanto custa/é?**
It's too much. **É caro/muito/demais.**
What do you want? **O que quer?**

I want to buy . . . **Quero comprar . . .**
It's not exactly what I want. **Não é bem o que eu quero.**
I am hungry. **Estou com fome.**
I am thirsty. **Estou com sede.**
Where is there a restaurant? **Onde tem um restaurante?**
I have a reservation. **(Eu) tenho uma reserva.**
I would like . . . **Quero . . .**
Please give me . . . **Me dê . . . , por favor.**
Please bring me . . . **Me traga . . . , por favor.**
May I see the menu? **Posso ver o cardápio?**
The bill, please. **A nota/conta, por favor.**
Where is there a hotel? **Onde há um hotel?**
Where is the post office? **Onde fica o correio?**
Is there any mail for me? **Tem correspondência para mim?**
Where can I mail this letter? **Onde é que eu posso mandar esta carta?**
Take me to . . . **Me leve para . . .**
I think I am sick. **Acho que estou doente.**
Please call me a doctor. **Pode me chamar um médico, por favor?**
Please call the police. **Pode chamar a polícia, por favor?**
I want to send a telegram. **Quero passar/mandar um telegrama.**
As soon as possible. **Quanto antes.**
Round trip. **Ida e volta.**
Please help me with my luggage. **Pode me ajudar com a bagagem, por favor?**
Where can I get a taxi (bus)? **Onde posso pegar um táxi (ônibus)?**
What is the fare to . . . ? **Quanto custa ir para . . . ?/Quanto é a passagem para . . . ?**
Please take me to this address. **Me leve a este endereço, por favor.**
Where can I change my money? **Onde posso trocar o meu dinheiro?**
Where is the closest bank? **Onde fica o banco mais próximo?**
Can you accept my check? **Pode aceitar o meu cheque?**
Do you accept traveler's checks? **Aceita "traveler's checks"?**
What is the postage on a letter to . . . ? **Quanto custa mandar uma carta para . . . ?**
Where is the nearest pharmacy? **Onde fica a farmácia mais próxima?**
Where is the men's (ladies') room? **Onde fica fica o banheiro dos homens (das senhoras)?**
Please let me off at . . . **Quero saltar em . . . por favor.**
Help! **Socorro!**
Who is it? **Quem é?**
Just a minute. **Um momento/momentinho.**
Come in! **Pode entrar!/Entre!**